Introduction to Social Psychology

To

Claudia Hammer-Hewstone,
Rebecca and William Hewstone
and
Maggie and Katherine Stroebe

THIRD EDITION

Introduction to
SOCIAL
Psychology

A European Perspective

Edited by **Miles Hewstone**
and **Wolfgang Stroebe**

BLACKWELL
Publishers

Copyright © Blackwell Publishers Ltd, 2001

First edition published 1988
Reprinted 1989 (twice), 1990, 1992, 1993, 1994, 1995
Second edition published 1996
Reprinted 1996, 1997

Third edition published 2001

2 4 6 8 10 9 7 5 3 1

Blackwell Publishers Ltd
108 Cowley Road
Oxford OX4 1JF
UK

Blackwell Publishers Inc.
350 Main Street
Malden, Massachusetts 02148
USA

British Library Cataloguing in Publication Data

A CIP catalogue record for this book is available from the
British Library.

Library of Congress Cataloging-in-Publication Data

Introduction to social psychology: a European perspective / edited by Miles
Hewstone and Wolfgang Stroebe – 3rd ed.
    p. cm.
  Includes bibliographical references and index.
  ISBN 0-631-20437-7 (pb: alk. paper)
    1. Social psychology. 2. Social psychology–Europe. I. Hewstone, Miles.
  II. Stroebe, Wolfgang.

  HM1033 .I59 2001
  302–dc21   00-033702

Commissioning Editor: Martin Davies/Sarah Bird
Desk Editor: Brigitte Lee
Picture Researcher: Leanda Shrimpton

Typeset in 10 on 13pt Galliard
by Graphicraft Limited, Hong Kong
Printed in Great Britain by T. J. International, Padstow, Cornwall

This book is printed on acid-free paper

Brief
Contents

Contents

Part II   Construction of the Social World

6 Emotion   **151**
Klaus R. Scherer

Part III Social Interaction and Personal Relationships

Part IV   Social Groups

15   Intergroup Relations   479
Rupert Brown

Part V   Applications

Contributors

John Archer is at the University of Central Lancashire, Preston.

Hans W. Bierhoff is at the University of Bochum.

Herbert Bless is at the University of Mannheim.

Gerd Bohner is at the University of Kent at Canterbury.

Rupert Brown is at the University of Kent at Canterbury.

Bram Buunk is at the University of Groningen.

Carsten De Dreu is at the University of Amsterdam.

Kevin Durkin is at the University of Western Australia.

Klaus Fiedler is at the University of Heidelberg.

Frank Fincham is at State University of New York, Buffalo.

Carl F. Graumann is at the University of Heidelberg.

Miles Hewstone is at Cardiff University.

Klaus Jonas is at the Chemnitz University of Technology.

Tony Manstead is at the University of Amsterdam.

Amélie Mummendey is at the Friedrich Schiller University, Jena.

Sabine Otten is at the Friedrich Schiller University, Jena.

Gün Semin is at the Free University of Amsterdam.

Klaus Scherer is at the University of Geneva.

Wolfgang Stroebe is at the University of Utrecht.

Henk A. M. Wilke is at the University of Leiden.

Arjaan Wit is at the University of Leiden.

Eddy Van Avermaet is at the University of Leuven.

Evert Van de Vliert is at the University of Groningen.

Paul A. M. Van Lange is at the Free University of Amsterdam.

Nico W. VanYperen is at the University of Groningen.

Preface to
Third Edition

When we set out some 16 years ago on a project to produce a textbook of social psychology *for* European students *by* European teachers, we did not envisage that all these years later we would be sitting down to write the preface to the third edition. We are, of course, delighted to be doing so, and thrilled with the success of the book, as evidenced both by the favourable reviews it has received internationally and the extent of its use by university students throughout Europe, and indeed beyond. The previous editions of this book have now been translated into German, Hungarian, Italian, Spanish and even Japanese.

We have revised this edition extensively, in terms of *who* the authors are, *what* material is covered, and *how* it is presented. Only 10 of the 17 chapters have exactly the same authors as in the last edition, and even these chapters have been extensively revised. We have also made four major changes to the structure, some of these in response to the feedback from instructors and students: (1) In Part II (Construction of the Social World), we have moved from two chapters on each of both attitudes and social cognition to one major chapter on each (chapter 5: 'Social Cognition', and chapter 8: 'Attitudes'). This has allowed the authors to provide a more encompassing view of the field in each case, and now treats these topics as the equals of all the other topics covered. (2) We have also moved the chapter on 'Emotion' (chapter 6) into Part II, so that it forms links with both social cognition and affect, and attitudes as affectively laden constructs. (3) In Part III (Social Interaction and Personal Relationships), we have realigned chapters within the section and replaced the chapter on communication with a new one on cooperation and competition in social interaction (chapter 11). This change reflects, in part, the fact that few courses on social psychology were including communication, and that many courses *were* including strategic analyses of social interaction. (4) Finally, in Part V (Applications), we have moved from one general chapter on applied social psychology to two chapters that report the massive and sustained input of social psychology into the areas of health psychology and organizational psychology, respectively. We feel that this enlarged section is an accurate reflection of the impact, potential and actual, that social psychology has on social and societal problems.

As in previous editions, we have done our best to make the chapters consistent in level and coverage. We have also insisted, again, that whatever is covered is done so in sufficient detail for European students, who are much more likely than, for example, North American students to be spending all or a great proportion of their time at university studying psychology. In terms of presentation, we are delighted that Blackwell has managed to continue its feat of improving what was already judged to be an engaging format. We have stayed with the formula whereby each chapter ends with 'Discussion points', 'Suggestions for further reading' and 'Key studies'. Glossary terms are now listed at the start of each chapter under the heading 'Key concepts'. Each term is highlighted in bold on its first appearance in the text, and definitions are given both in the margin and in the Glossary at the end of the book. Another innovation in presentation is the use of 'learning questions' at the beginning of each main section of a chapter. These questions are what students should be able to answer after studying the relevant section, and they help the reader to focus on the message of each section of the chapter.

This textbook can be supplemented with additional publications. First, the recommended key studies are reprinted in the *Blackwell Social Psychology Reader* (edited by Hewstone, Manstead and Stroebe). Here the papers are also 'broken down' and critically interpreted for student readers. Second, again following instructors' feedback, we have replaced the Study Guide with a test bank of multiple-choice questions, which may be downloaded from the book's website (www.blackwellpublishers.co.uk/hewstone). Students and instructors will also find pithy summaries of the core topics in social psychology in the *Blackwell Encyclopaedia of Social Psychology* (edited by Manstead and Hewstone).

It remains for us to thank a few special people. First and foremost, we would like to thank our authors, for all their hard work, their recognition that good writing for students is a goal worth working for, and their willingness to undertake what we know must at times have seemed very irritating revisions of their work. We are sure that both they and their students will find these labours to have been worthwhile. We would also like to thank Martin Davies and Siobhan Pattinson for motivating us with the right mixture of encouragement, cajoling, pleading and outright bribery. Siobhan, in particular, was bold enough (over a glass or two of the black stuff in a Belfast bar) to promise to give up smoking if we got the manuscript in on time. Ultimately, we used this information to encourage our dilatory authors to show how social psychology could be used to help 'save a life', and thereby managed to deliver before the deadline. Finally, we would also like to thank Geoffrey Stephenson. He worked with us as co-editor on the first two editions and was one of the main originators of the idea for a European textbook.

Editing this textbook has become a full-time job. Since we both have several other full-time jobs already, much of the time used for editing this book was really family time. We therefore dedicate this edition to our families in recognition of their tolerance.

Miles Hewstone, Cardiff
Wolfgang Stroebe, Utrecht

Preface to
Second Edition

This is the second, completely revised and updated, edition of what has become a very successful and widely adopted textbook. It consists of 18 chapters which cover the core of social psychology, each doing so in an accessible and engaging style, while focusing the student's attention on both the ideas (theories) that have had an impact on the field and the studies that have been carried out. As judged by sales and adoptions – both in the UK and on the European continent – the first edition did meet the perceived needs of a European audience of students and instructors, both in terms of **level** and **coverage**.

In terms of level, European undergraduate students typically specialize much earlier in (social) psychology than do their North American counterparts, often taking psychology as a single-honours degree course, sometimes as part of a joint-honours degree, and sometimes as a subsidiary subject. They therefore require a more detailed, advanced textbook than the typical American text, which is too basic. Our students need *pages*, not lines, devoted to core areas of social psychology. In terms of coverage, we believe that students in Europe want to learn about the research conducted both in Europe and elsewhere, and that their understanding and appreciation of the field will be enhanced by examples and illustrations that have been chosen with them (not American undergraduates) in mind.

Although our first edition was successful (it has been translated into German, Hungarian, Italian, Spanish and even Japanese), we appreciate that the field of social psychology is growing at an impressive rate, and changing in the light of new theories, new findings and new applications. We therefore decided to embark on a new edition, which includes the core of the old one, but also makes a number of significant changes in content, contributors and style. In terms of content, we have included four completely new chapters, written by new authors. These reflect areas of growing interest (chapter 2: 'Evolutionary social psychology'), burgeoning parts of the field where we felt a second, more detailed chapter was required (chapter 6: 'Processing social information for judgements and decisions'), neglected topics (chapter 10: 'Emotion'), and popular topics where we wanted to publish a different perspective (chapter 12: 'Affiliation, attraction and close relationships').

We have also made stylistic changes, which we hope will make the book even more useful to students. The layout has been improved, there are more graphical illustrations to accompany the text on key studies, and there are more, but carefully chosen, photographs whose aim is not merely to illustrate points but to make the reader think more deeply about the issues at hand (e.g., how do advertisements try to change our attitudes, when do we act on our stereotypes, and what are the consequences of social influence?). We have also added to the material presented at the end of each chapter. This now includes 'Further reading' to direct students' more detailed study; 'Discussion points', to check on their understanding of the text; 'Glossary terms', which highlight the main concepts around which each chapter can be organized; and 'Key studies', which direct students' attention to original research which we think is particularly instructive. The full text of these original papers is reprinted in the *Blackwell Reader in Social Psychology*, which is published alongside this edition, where the studies are also critically discussed. Further help for instructors who adopt the book is available in the form of an Instructor's Manual, which can be obtained from the publishers.

Miles Hewstone, Cardiff
Wolfgang Stroebe, Utrecht
Geoffrey M. Stephenson, Canterbury

Preface to
First Edition

The idea for this book grew out of many conversations the editors had with colleagues from all over Europe at various meetings of the European Association of Experimental Social Psychology. Members of the European Association teach social psychology in more than a dozen different countries and often use American textbooks. They typically report that texts which have been highly rated in the United States are not well received by European students. Since these students have to take more psychology courses than are required of American undergraduates, they find American texts too basic. They also complain that most American textbooks do not adequately cover work done by European social psychologists and published in European journals. Thus, there seemed to be a need for a social-psychology text that would be somewhat more advanced than American undergraduate textbooks and that would present the best of both American and European research in social psychology. Our 'European perspective' refers to the geographical location of our contributors, the literature they cite, and to a lesser extent to their conception of social psychology. There are undoubtedly more similarities than differences between European and North American social psychology, but the present volume is nonetheless distinctive in the attention it gives to such topics as minority influence and intergroup relations, areas in which Europeans have made their most significant contributions.

When we discussed this issue with our American colleagues, we were surprised to learn that many of them shared these views about the limitations of American social-psychology texts. They argued that in the United States, there was also a need for a more advanced text that could be assigned in honours courses or in the initial stages of graduate training. Some even believed that such a text could be used in regular undergraduate social-psychology classes.

While this idea may seem ambitious, it should be remembered that once upon a time there were textbooks of social psychology that were at the forefront of the field. These books were read not only by students but also by researchers and they were widely quoted in the research literature. Thus, the first generation of textbooks by Asch and Newcomb, and the second generation by Jones and Gerard, Brown, and Secord and Backman offered more than mere reviews. These books helped to shape the field by contributing new theoretical ideas, as well as their unique conceptions of social psychology. They tried to excite the reader with ideas rather than cartoons.

When we decided to produce a textbook in the tradition of those great books, and one that would also offer a representative survey of the field, we soon realized that this had to be an edited volume rather than a book written by the four editors. By making it an edited book, we could for each chapter commission a European social psychologist who was an expert in a given area and could thus be expected to give a 'state of the art' presentation of both European and American work. The danger of uneven writing styles and lack of integration could be avoided by giving explicit and extensive instructions to our authors.

After many discussions about who would be the ideal choice for each of the chapters, we had the gratifying experience of finding that our invitations to collaborate on this text were met with great enthusiasm and that all of our authors tried very hard to incorporate the suggestions made by the editors. We would like to use this opportunity to thank them for the patience with which they worked through several revisions of their initial drafts and for their willingness to accept editorial comments. We hope that they and the readers of this book – whether undergraduates, graduate students or teachers – will enjoy and benefit from the final version. We believe that it conveys a critical knowledge of and enthusiasm for social psychology, whatever its geographical provenance.

Miles Hewstone
Wolfgang Stroebe
Jean-Paul Codol
Geoffrey M. Stephenson

Acknowledgements

The authors and publishers wish to thank the following, who have kindly given permission for the use of copyright material.

Figures 2.1 and 2.2: Singh, D. (1995). Female judgements of male attractiveness and desirability for relationships: Role of waist-to-hip ratio and financial status. *Journal of Personality and Social Psychology*, 69, 1089–1101. Copyright © 1995 by the American Psychological Association. Reprinted with permission.

Figure 2.3: Singh, D. (1993). Adaptive significance of female physical attractiveness: Role of waist-to-hip ratio. *Journal of Personality and Social Psychology*, 65, 293–307. Copyright © 1993 by the American Psychological Association. Reprinted with permission.

Figure 2.4: Nisbett, R. E., & Cohen, D. (1996). *Culture of honor: The psychology of violence in the south*. Boulder, CO: Westview Press.

Figure 3.3: Doyle, A.-B., Beaudet, J., & Aboud, F. (1988). Developmental patterns in the flexibility of children's ethnic attitudes. *Journal of Cross-Cultural Psychology*, 19, 3–18.

Figure 5.4: after Bargh, J. A., Chen, M., & Burrows, L. (1996). Automaticity of social behavior: Direct effects of trait construct and stereotype activation on action. *Journal of Personality and Social Psychology*, 71, 230–44. Copyright © 1996 by the American Psychological Association. Adapted with permission.

Figure 5.5: adapted from Bodenhausen, G. V. (1990). Stereotypes as judgmental heuristics. Evidence of circadian variations in discrimination. *Psychological Science*, 1, 319–22.

Figure 5.6: adapted from Macrae, C. N., Hewstone, M., & Griffith, R. J. (1993). Processing load and memory for stereotype-based information. *European Journal of Social Psychology*, 23, 77–87.

Figure 5.8: after Maass, A., Salvi, D., Arcuri, L., & Semin, G. R. (1989). Language use in intergroup contexts: The linguistic intergroup bias. *Journal of Personality and Social Psychology*, 57, 981–93. Copyright © 1989 by the American Psychological Association. Adapted with permission.

Figure 6.4: Scherer, K. R., & Ceschi, G. (1997). Lost luggage emotion: A field study of emotion-antecedent appraisal. *Motivation and Emotion*, 21, 211–35. Reprinted by permission of Plenum Press, New York.

Figure 7.2: data from Miller, J. G. (1984). Culture and the development of everyday social explanation. *Journal of Personality and Social Psychology*, 46, 961–78. Copyright © 1984 by the American Psychological Association. Adapted with permission.

Figure 7.3: Fiske & Taylor (1991), based on Storms, M. D. (1973). Videotape and the attribution process: Reversing actors' and observers' points of view. *Journal of Personality and Social Psychology*, 27, 165–75.

Figure 7.4: after Hewstone, M., & Ward, C. (1985). Ethnocentrism and causal attribution in Southeast Asia. *Journal of Personality and Social Psychology*, 48, 614–23. Copyright © 1985 by the American Psychological Association. Reprinted with permission.

Figure 7.5: Gilbert, D. T. (1995). Attribution and interpersonal perception. In A. Tesser (Ed.), *Advanced social psychology* (pp. 99–147). New York: McGraw-Hill. Reproduced by permission of McGraw-Hill Companies.

Table 7.1: data from Smith, E. R., & Miller, F. D. (1983). Mediation among attributional inferences and comprehension processes: Initial findings and a general method. *Journal of Personality and Social Psychology*, 44, 492–505. Copyright © 1983 by the American Psychological Association. Reprinted with permission.

Figure 8.2: Heider, F. (1946). Attitudes and cognitive organization. *Journal of Psychology*, 21, 107–12.

Figure 8.3: adapted from Petty, R. E., & Cacioppo, J. T. (1986). *Communication and persuasion: Central and peripheral routes to attitude change*. New York: Springer.

Figure 8.4: adapted from Exp. 1, Petty, R. E., Wells, G. L., & Brock, T. C. (1976). Distraction can enhance or reduce yielding to propaganda: Thought disruption versus effort justification. *Journal of Personality and Social Psychology*, 34, 874–84. Copyright © 1976 by the American Psychological Association. Adapted with permission.

Figure 8.7: adapted from Ajzen, I., & Madden, T. J. (1986). Prediction of goal-directed behavior: Attitudes, intentions and perceived behavioral control. *Journal of Experimental Social Psychology*, 22, 453–74.

Figures 10.2 and 10.6: Tedeschi, J. T., & Felson, R. B. (1994). *Aggression and coercive actions: A social interactionist perspective*. Washington, DC: American Psychological Association. Copyright © 1994 by the American Psychological Association. Reprinted with permission.

Figure 10.3: adapted from Bandura, A. (1973). *Aggression: A social learning analysis*. Englewood Cliffs, NJ: Prentice-Hall.

Figure 10.5: adapted from Mummendey, A., Linneweber, V., & Löschper, G. (1984). Actor or victim of aggression: Divergent perspectives – divergent evaluations. *European Journal of Social Psychology*, 14, 297–311.

Figure 10.7: Crick, N. R., & Dodge, K. A. (1994). A review and reformulation of social information-processing mechanisms in children's adjustment. *Psychological Bulletin*, 115, 74–101. Copyright © 1994 by the American Psychological Association. Reprinted with permission.

Figure 11.3: McClintock, C. G. (1972). Social motivation – a set of propositions. *Behavioral Science*, 17, 438–54.

Figure 11.4: Pruitt, D. G., & Rubin, J. Z. (1986). *Social conflict: Escalation, stalemate, and settlement*. New York: Random House.

Figure 11.5: Kuhlman, D. M., & Marshello, A. (1975). Individual differences in game motivation as moderators of preprogrammed strategic effects in prisoner's dilemma. *Journal of Personality and Social Psychology*, 32, 922–31. Copyright © 1975 by the American Psychological Association. Reprinted with permission.

Figure 11.6: Dawes, R. M., McTavish, J., & Shaklee, H. (1977). Behavior, communication, and assumptions about other people's behavior in a commons dilemma situation. *Journal of Personality and Social Psychology*, 35, 1–11. Copyright © 1977 by the American Psychological Association. Reprinted with permission.

Figure 11.8: Carnevale, P. J. (1986). Mediating disputes and decisions in organizations. In R. J. Lewicki, B. H. Sheppard, & M. H. Bazerman (Eds.), *Research on negotiation in organizations* (Vol. 1, pp. 251–70). Greenwich, CT: JAI Press.

Figure 12.2: based on Molleman, E., Pruyn, J., & Van Knippenberg, A. (1986). Social comparison processes among cancer patients. *British Journal of Social Psychology*, 25, 1–13.

Figure 12.3: based on Cohen, S., & Hoberman, H. M. (1983). Positive events and social supports as buffers of life change stress. *Journal of Applied Social Psychology*, 13 (2), 99–125.

Figure 12.4: based on Festinger, L., Schachter, S., & Back, K. (1950). *Social pressures in informal groups: A study of human factors in housing*. New York: Harper.

Figure 13.4: based on Asch, S. E. (1951). Effects of group pressure on the modification and distortion of judgements. In H. Guetzkow (Ed.), *Groups, leadership and men*. Pittsburgh: Carnegie.

Figure 13.5: based on Allen, V. L., & Levine, J. M. (1971). Social support and conformity: The role of independent assessment of reality. *Journal of Experimental Social Psychology*, 7, 48–58.

Figure 14.3: Based on Latané, B., Williams, K., & Harkins, S. (1979). Many hands make light work: The causes and consequences of social loafing. *Journal of Personality and Social Psychology*, 37, 822–32.

Figure 14.5: based on Stewart, D., & Stasser, G. (1995). Expert role assignment and information sampling during collective recall and decision making. *Journal of Personality and Social Psychology*, 69, 619–28.

Figure 14.7: Based on Leavitt, H. J. (1951). Some effects of certain communication patterns on group performance. *Journal of Abnormal and Social Psychology*, 46, 38–50.

Figure 16.4: Prochaska, J. O., Velicer, W. F., Guidagnoli, E., Rossi, J. S., & DiClemente, C. C. (1991). Patterns of change: Dynamic typology applied to smoking cessation. *Multivariate Behavioral Research*, 26, 83–107.

Figures 16.8 and 16.9: adapted from House, J. S., Landis, K. R., & Umberson, D. (1988). Social relationships and health. *Science*, 241, 540–5.

Figure 17.2: VanYperen, N. W., Buunk, B. P., & Schaufeli, W. B. (1992). Communal orientation and the burnout syndrome among nurses. *Journal of Applied Social Psychology*, 22, 173–89.

Figure 17.4: Van de Vliert, E. (1996). Interventions in conflicts. In M. J. Schabracq, J. A. M. Winnubst, & C. L. Cooper (Eds.), *Handbook of work and health psychology* (pp. 405–25). Chichester: Wiley.

Figure 17.5: Fiedler, F. E. (1968). Personality and situational determinants of leadership effectiveness. In D. Cartwright & A. Zander (Eds.), *Group dynamics* (pp. 362–80). New York: Harper & Row.

Plates 2.1: Kobal Collection; 2.2: © Rex Features, London; 3.1: © PhotoDisc/ Monica Lau; 3.2: from *The Social Development of the Intellect*, Pergamon Press; 3.3: Commission for Racial Equality; 4.1: stills from 1965 film *Obedience* © Stanley Milgram as reproduced in *Obedience to Authority* by Stanley Milgram, courtesy of Tavistock Publications; 5.1: © Rex Features, London; 5.2: © Coloursport/ Mitchell Layton; 6.1: reproduced from P. Ekman (1998). Afterword, In C. Darwin, *The expression of emotions in man and animals* (3rd ed., Ed. P. Ekman). London: HarperCollins; 6.2: reproduced from D. Morris (1977). *Manwatching: A field guide to human behavior*. New York: Harry N. Abrams; 6.3: © The Stock Market; 6.4: reproduced from I. Eibl-Eibesfeldt (1995). *Die Biologie des menschlichen Verhaltens: Grundriss der Humanethologie* [Biology of human behavior: Fundamentals of human ethology] (3rd ed.). Munich: Piper; 6.5: adapted from *Journal of Personality and Social Psychology*, 54, 768–77. Copyright © 1988; 7.1: Photo Kevin Lamarque/Popperfoto/Reuters; 7.2: © PhotoDisc/Jeff Maloney; 7.3: Martin Mayer/Network Photographers; 8.1: © Rex Features, London; 8.2: bus © TRIP/H. Rogers. Car driver © Sally Greenhill; 8.3: Photo © Roger Scruton; 9.1: Brian Rasic/Rex Features, London; 12.1: © PhotoDisc/Scott T. Baxter; 12.2:

© The Stock Market; 12.3: © PhotoDisc/Hisham F. Ibrahim; 13.1: Kobal Collection; 13.2: Hulton Deutsch; 14.1: Jess Stock/Stockshot; 15.1: Photo Renate Kuhn/Agence Vandystadt; 15.2: photo Crispin Rodwell/Popperfoto/ Reuters (p. 482), Popperfoto/Reuters (p. 483); 15.3 and 15.4: *Introduction to Social Psychology* (2nd edn); 16.1: © Health Education Authority; 16.2: Tobacco Education Campaign; 17.1: © PhotoDisc/Ryan McVay; 17.2: © PhotoDisc/ Jacobs Stock Photos; 17.3 Photo © Hannah Gal/Corbis.

Every effort has been made to trace all the copyright holders, but if any have been inadvertently overlooked the publishers will be pleased to make the necessary arrangement at the earliest opportunity.

Introduction PART

I

CONTENTS

Introducing Social Psychology Historically

Carl F. Graumann

1

OUTLINE

To understand the contribution of social psychology, and what is distinct about it, we need to understand something of its historical origins. Social thought before the emergence of social science had developed along two alternative lines of interest: (1) the influence of society on its individual members; (2) the role of individuals as constituents of society. These two emphases are still reflected in modern conceptions of social psychology. Two European schools of thought preceding social psychology are briefly sketched: *Völkerpsychologie* and crowd psychology. Although modern social psychology is primarily an American development, emphasizing both the study of the individual and the importance of the experimental method, European refugees were influential in developing social psychology as we know it today. This chapter describes the substantial contribution of American social psychology to the postwar development and institutionalization of the discipline in Europe, and also highlights some theoretical consequences of this influence. Finally, some research tendencies, which are considered to be of European vintage, are briefly outlined and assessed.

KEY CONCEPTS

- Crowd psychology
- Group mind
- Hedonism
- Individualism
- Individuo-centred approach
- Mental contagion
- Positivism
- Socio-centred approach
- Sociology
- Suggestion
- Utilitarianism
- *Völkerpsychologie*

Introduction

Why should we learn about the history of social psychology?

In ordinary language use, 'introducing' means bringing to acquaintance or knowledge of a person or a thing. Hence, an introduction is the beginning of an extended, sometimes life-long, process of knowledge acquisition, the end of which is indeterminate. We are here concerned with the initial phase(s) of an acquaintance process in which a novice is brought or guided to knowledge of a field of science.

There are several ways of introduction, depending on the novelty and accessibility of the field, which account for the extent and quality of previous knowledge: if the field is historically new, having emerged from a recent discovery or invention, say, in molecular biology, astrophysics or nanotechnology, a careful definition and exemplification of its key problems will be helpful. Yet, telling the story of the crucial discovery is much more likely to arouse curiosity and to initiate the acquaintance process. If, however, the field is already well established, but highly specialized and, in its exclusive terminology, of restricted accessibility, an introduction will have to rely on the novice's knowledge of the broader field or discipline from which a given subdiscipline has developed by specialization.

Then, there are fields of study about which everybody seems to know a lot before ever having studied them. Take 'social psychology'; it does not matter whether it is an old or new discipline. Every layperson 'knows' what 'psychology' is about and also what 'social' means. Consumers of mass media are bound to hear, see and read about the 'social' implications or costs of globalization and about the 'psychological' nature of the latest booms and slumps of the stock market. Unlike astrophysics and haematology, 'psychology' has never been exclusively and unambiguously the name of a scientific discipline.

Used in everyday discourse, psychology refers to the inner, mental (conscious as well as unconscious) dynamics attributed to individuals, groups, types, institutions, peoples. And everyday communication makes non-technical use of words that are also used as technical terms in scientific discourse, such as attitudes, emotion, motivation, frustration. This 'psychologizing' is as common and popular as its conclusions are at variance with, and often in contradiction to, those of psychological science (Graumann, 1996). The use of psychological jargon and of naive or common-sense psychology may become research topics of language and social psychology (Heider, 1958), but otherwise should be kept strictly separate from disciplinary reasoning and discourse.

Since we have all become lay psychologists before we ever came into contact with a scholarly discipline named 'social psychology', being introduced into this discipline adopts a special meaning: in order to learn what social psychology is about, we have to unlearn what we already know about the 'social' and the 'psychological'; at least, we should enclose our previous knowledge within brackets until further validation.

It is in this effort of suspending prior knowledge and beliefs that history becomes a helpful guide into the new field. As a scholarly discipline social psychology has existed for only about one hundred years, but its intellectual roots reach far back into history, to the beginnings of (Western) social as well as psychological thinking. It has been ideas about the relationship between what in modern times came to be called 'individual' and 'society' that generated, at least stood sponsor to, social psychology and other related social sciences.

Hence, a look, however brief, into the history of social thought will help us to better understand the identity of social psychology, in the context of both psychology and the social sciences.

Social Thought before the Advent of Social Science

If the 'individual' in 'society' provides the general framework for social psychology, how was this relationship treated in pre-scientific social thought?

Since antiquity there have been various systems of community in which single (i.e., individual) human beings have formed and entertained associations for their mutual benefit. Problems of linking together in communities (such as the *polis*, the city state in ancient Greece) gave rise to different conceptions of the nature of the human being (which we briefly will call 'individual') in relation to the community ('society'). Two major strands of social thought have, over the centuries, come to be called Platonic and Aristotelian, respectively. Plato had emphasized the primacy of the state over the individual who, in order to become truly social, had to be educated under the responsibility of authorities. For Aristotle, the human being is social by nature, and nature can be trusted to enable individuals to live together and to enter personal relationships from which families, tribes and ultimately the state will naturally develop. How much of this is authentic Plato and Aristotle or subsequent interpretation need not concern us here. The two terms signal two traditions of social thought which, in modern times, have been distinguished as the **socio-centred approach** and the **individuo-centred approach**. The former emphasizes the determining function of social structures (systems, institutions, groups) for individual experience and behaviour; by contrast, in the latter, social systems are said to be explicable in terms of individual processes and functions.

In the history of social thought the conception of the primacy of the social has taken many forms. For Hegel (1770–1831), the German idealistic philosopher, the state is not only the ultimate form of society but the incarnation of the (objective) social mind of which individual minds are active participants. Later social-psychological

Socio-centred approach Any approach to the study of individual and social behaviour emphasizing the conditioning functions of the social/societal structural context.

Individuo-centred approach Any approach to the study of social behaviour and social functions relying exclusively or largely on the study of individual experience and behaviour.

Group mind The concept of the supra-individual nature and independence of the collective mind of a social group.

ideas of a (supra-individual) **group mind** have been derived from Hegel's conception. For contemporaries who consider social psychology too exclusively centred on the individual, the philosophy of a social mind is a significant model (see Farr, 1996; Markova, 1982, 1983; Stephan, Stephan, & Pettigrew, 1991; Stryker, 1995). Hence, a theory of society may be considered the framework within which social-psychological theorizing should originate, as is explicitly stated in the social psychology of G. H. Mead (1934) and in related symbolic interactionism (Manis & Meltzer, 1980).

Individualism   The doctrine that emphasizes the rights, values and interests of the individual from which all rights and values of society have to be derived and justified (ethical and political individualism). The doctrine that all explanations of individual or social phenomena are to be rejected unless they are expressed wholly in terms of individuals (methodological individualism).

While in the long prehistory of social psychology we may find other important theories of the primacy of the social and of society over the individual, we should now turn to a few examples of the opposite stance: the philosophical antecedents of an individuo-centred social science. Since, broadly speaking, psychology, and with it social psychology, is the study of individual experience and behaviour, we should expect major impacts of the varieties of **individualism** on psychology. Unfortunately, the term 'individualism' has too many different meanings to be useful without conceptual clarification (Lukes, 1973a). One such clarification, crucial for the psychologist, is the notion of an 'abstract' individual, according to which basic human psychological features (be they called instincts, needs, desires or wants) 'are assumed as given, independently of a social context' (1973a, p. 73).

Since these features are considered to be invariant, a group is a mere union or product of such individual 'faculties'. As a subdiscipline of psychology, social psychology has from its beginning been defined as the scientific study of the individual in the social context. In its focus on the individual, it is very close to, if not part of, general experimental psychology. Recently, individualism in psychology has been characterized and criticized as a self-centred 'denial of the other' (Sampson, 1993). As old as the duality of socio- vs. individuo-centred approaches in social thought may be, it has become codified by the establishment of two different social psychologies of which one, occasionally dubbed 'psychological social psychology' (Stephan & Stephan, 1990; Stephan et al., 1991) has developed in the context and confines of psychology. The other branch, referred to and accentuated as 'sociological social psychology', has been shaped in sociology. Although this sociological branch of social psychology is not explicitly dealt with in this volume, the coexistence (rather than cooperation) of both social psychologies is a historical fact.[1] Both contribute to our understanding of human experience and behaviour in its social context.

Hedonism (psychological) The doctrine that every activity is motivated by the desire for pleasure and the avoidance of pain.

Utilitarianism   The doctrine that the determining condition of individual and social action is the (expectation of the) usefulness of its consequences (psychological utilitarianism). The doctrine that the aim of all social action should be the greatest happiness of the greatest number (ethical utilitarianism).

Historically, a large portion of individualism came under the names of hedonism and utilitarianism. The basic tenet of **hedonism** is the *pleasure principle*, according to which we act in order to secure and maintain pleasure and to avoid and reduce pain. Since Jeremy Bentham (1748–1832), who theoretically transformed the pleasure principle into a principle of utility, **utilitarianism** – the doctrine that advocates the pursuit of the greatest happiness of the greatest number – has entered social thought to stay there. Over many variations of the doctrine and various combinations of individualism, utilitarianism and liberalism, there is one line of tradition leading directly into the foundation of psychology. For most modern theories of conditioning and of motivation, many of which are traded as social-psychological theories, the underlying ideas of individual satisfaction (e.g., reinforcement, reward, profit; reduction of tension, of dissonance, of uncertainty) are variations of the pleasure or utility principle. But only around the middle of the twentieth century did utility become a psychological construct in theories on decision-making when, for example, Edwards (1954) introduced the theory of subjectively expected utility (SEU). Later (von Winterfeldt & Edwards, 1986), utility had to be conceived of multidimensionally in a Multi-Attribute Utility (MAU) theory. Both versions of utility theory were considered useful in conceptions of the attitude–behaviour relationship of which the most influential are the 'theory of reasoned action' (Ajzen & Fishbein, 1980) and its modification, the 'theory of planned behaviour' (Ajzen, 1991; for both see chapter 8). Utility and satisfaction are also involved in theories of *social exchange* and interdependence (see chapters 11 and 12).

Another 'perennial' topic of social thought that returned (rather than continued to exist) in social psychology, is *power* and its role in social relationships. In social philosophy, power, sometimes in close association with egoism, figured most prominently and with lasting effects from Machiavelli (1513/1946) and Thomas Hobbes' (1651/1968) conceptions of the natural state of humankind as the 'war of all against all' and of human's 'desire of power after power' (Nietzsche, 1968).

In social psychology, social power (and social influence) found its proper frames of reference in field theory and social exchange theory (cf. Ng, 1980; Tedeschi, 1974). In the context of Lewinian field theory (Lewin, 1951), 'power' became the term for the potential (of an individual or group) to influence others while 'control' and 'influence' generally refer to power in action (cf. Cialdini & Trost, 1998). Research areas for which power or, since French and Raven (1959), certain types of power have been studied as resources of influence are aggression (see chapter 10), conformity to group pressure and obedience to authority (see chapter 13) and, most recently, power in language (Ng & Bradac, 1993).

Two other intellectual developments in the nineteenth century have contributed significantly to modern social psychology: sociology and evolutionary theory. As a term and a programme, **sociology** was created by Auguste Comte (1798–1857), who has also been praised and condemned as the father of **positivism**. For Comte (1853), positivism was a system of philosophy that implied a model of evolutionary progress of human knowledge from a theological through a metaphysical to a 'positive' stage of scientific knowledge, in which phenomena are taken to be real and certain, and know-

Sociology The social science dealing with social systems/structures such as social relationships, social institutions, whole societies.

Positivism The doctrine according to which knowledge should be based on natural phenomena and their temporal and spatial relationships as identified and verified by the methods (methodology) of empirical science.

ledge is the description of such phenomena and their spatial and temporal order in terms of constancies and variations. Sociology was meant to be the culminating science, which would compare cultures as to their different stages of social evolution. Conventionally, however, Emile Durkheim (1858–1917) is credited with initiating a continuous tradition of sociology. He held that 'social facts' are independent of and exterior to individual consciousness. Hence the '*collective representations*' of a given society have an existence of their own. Although they may have emerged from the association and interaction of individuals, their properties are different and independent from those of individual representations (Durkheim, 1898). While the relative autonomy of the social from the individual made Durkheim ask for a 'collective psychology' independent of individual psychology, most of the early conceptions of a social psychology around the turn of the twentieth century were fashioned after the model of a psychology of the individual. Only very much later did the French social psychologist Moscovici (1981a) take up and revise Durkheim's theory of collective representations (see Flick, 1998; Moscovici, 1984). It should be added that 'positivism', as frequently as the term is still being used, has acquired a negative critical meaning as the doctrine in which social and psychological phenomena are treated like (or even as) natural 'facts'. In this negative sense, Farr (1996) criticizes the positivism of both experimental social psychology and its historiography.

Finally, towards the end of the long prehistory there is the impact of the *theory of evolution*, one of the most powerful intellectual innovations of the nineteenth century. Psychology has been much influenced by its major protagonist, Charles Darwin (1809–82), as well as by his followers. Darwin's antedated contribution to a social psychology is mainly to be found in *The Descent of Man* (1871) and its sibling volume on *The Expression of the Emotions in Man and Animals* (1872/1965). Man is a social animal that has developed the capacity to adapt physically, socially and mentally to a changing environment, part of which is social, as for example the tribe. Hence, the expression of emotions has its social function in inter- and intra-species communication (cf. Buss, 1995, 1996; Buss & Kenrick, 1998). The British philosopher and (early) sociologist Herbert Spencer (1820–1903) generalized and popularized evolutionary theory, mainly in the social domain. But since he combined evolutionary theory with the doctrine of individualism and a *laissez-faire* attitude (let evolution take its course), some historians of social psychology have argued that Spencer did little to foster a social psychology. Even Darwin's own share in the establishment of social psychology went unnoticed for a long time (cf. Farr, 1980). Meanwhile, however, his direct ancestry is claimed, not only by students of emotion (see chapter 6), but by human ethologists accounting for social behaviour (Hinde, 1974) and by sociobiologists (Wilson, 1975). According to Buss (1995), *evolutionary psychology*, which relates psychological 'mechanisms' to original functions of behaviour, has become a new paradigm for psychology with special applications to social psychology (Buss, 1996; Buss & Kenrick, 1998; see chapters 2, 9 and 12, this volume).

Harbingers of Social Psychology

If Americans are right in speaking of a European background of social psychology, what can 'European' mean but cultural diversity?

So far, when we have spoken of social psychology's past or prehistory it has been to underline that the positions, briefly discussed, were not social psychologies in the modern sense of the word. But some of the doctrines that we referred to have contributed to present theorizing. When in this section we still do not speak of modern social psychology, but only of harbingers, the reasons for this distinction must be seen in the fact that the forerunners to be discussed explored and staked off territory that was later, at least partly, taken by social psychology. Their research programmes (with emphasis on programme rather than research) heralded the coming of a social psychology, although some of their research tasks had been given up or left to other social sciences with the institutionalization of modern social psychology.

We shall consider two major European approaches towards social psychology:

1   The *Völkerpsychologie* of Moritz Lazarus (1824–1903), Herrmann Steinthal (1823–99) and Wilhelm Wundt (1832–1920).
2   The crowd psychology of late-nineteenth-century Italian and French writers such as Gabriel Tarde (1843–1904) and Gustave LeBon (1841–1931).

Both are conceptions of a social psychology that is socio-centred rather than individuo-centred, observational-interpretative rather than experimental. And both are nowadays reconsidered by those who try to broaden social psychology towards a (comparative) socio-cultural discipline, which includes the study of language, morality, customs, material culture, collective trends and social change.

Völkerpsychologie

There is no hope of adequately translating *Völkerpsychologie* into English (see Danziger, 1983). Literally, it is a psychology of peoples; in fact, it is a comparative and historical, social and cultural psychology which, in a European textbook, can be left untranslated. Instead of a series of definitions, an outline will be given of its basic rationale.

As an important variant of the 'European background' of social psychology (Karpf, 1932), *Völkerpsychologie* is the prototype of German social-psychological thought from the eighteenth to the twentieth

Völkerpsychologie (German = psychology of peoples) An early (nineteenth- to twentieth-century) form of a historical and comparative socio-cultural psychology dealing with the cultural products (language, myth, custom, etc.) resulting from social interaction.

century. In this tradition the central assumption was that the primary form of human association is the cultural (and linguistic) community (*Volk*), in which the formation and education (*Bildung*) of the individual personality takes place. For philosophers and scholars like Herder, Hegel and Wilhelm von Humboldt, language was the medium in which the community shapes its individual members; these, in turn, actively contribute to their language, which is to be understood as a social product (Markova, 1983). While today the abstract 'society' is considered to be the social context of experience and behaviour, for these German scholars it was the national and cultural community of the *Volk* whose mind (*Volksgeist*) was taken to be the unifying mental principle.

Both *Volk* and *Volksgeist* became topics of the new discipline when it was institutionalized by and in a professional journal, the *Zeitschrift für Völkerpsychologie und Sprachwissenschaft*, in 1860 by M. Lazarus and H. Steinthal. From the beginning, there was no doubt that the new discipline was closely connected with and also meant to contribute to the political efforts towards a German nation-state (Eckardt, 1971). Many enduring questions in social psychology were raised, but because the framework was national rather than social the questions were different from those of French crowd psychology (see below).

Wilhelm Wundt took up *Völkerpsychologie* as the equivalent and complement to experimental individual psychology (Wundt, 1900–20). For him the *raison d'être* of a *Völkerpsychologie* was mainly methodological, which is still of interest for modern psychologists. Since mental contents or cognitions are expressed, communicated and maybe even shaped by language, an adequate study of mind will have to start from its major objectifications, such as language, myth and custom (the main topics of *Völkerpsychologie*), and account for their historical and cultural variations. That is why the experimental psychology of the decontextualized 'subject' must be complemented by a study of the major manifestations of mind. In this respect, *Völkerpsychologie*, the comparative historical study of the objective products of social interaction, was the forerunner of a cultural social psychology (cf. Fiske, Kitayama, Markus, & Nisbett 1998; Gergen, 1973).

Today it is easy to find fault with *Völkerpsychologie* for its deficiency in empirical methodology and research. But if we try an imaginary inversion of perspective and look at the field of present-day social psychology from Wundt's viewpoint, we also recognize the degree to which the cultural scope of the field has shrunk while it has methodologically improved (see Jaspars, 1983, 1986). In retrospect one gets the impression that perhaps not the whole idea but many of the major topics of *Völkerpsychologie* were handed over to neighbouring disciplines, mainly to anthropology and sociology, only to be rediscovered quite recently by European social psychologists. Jaspars (1986, p. 12) even presumed 'a return to the earliest scientific attempt to study social behaviour as advocated by Lazarus and Steinthal'. At least Wundt's final belief that experimental psychology is only half of what psychology can be is finding more and more supporters.

Crowd psychology

The intellectual and scientific background of **crowd psychology** is complex. There are, on the one hand, the many techniques and conceptions of **suggestion**, such as the tradition (art, technique, doctrine and cult) of hypnotism, i.e., the induction of a sleep-like condition that subjects its target persons, with certain limitations, to the suggestions of the hypnotist. Anton Mesmer (1734–1815), who could put people into a trance, had claimed to control a universal animal force ('magnetism') that would strengthen and enhance life and health. Hypnotic suggestion, as it was called later, was meant to lower a patient's level of consciousness, thus rendering her or his mind more 'primitive'. This technique figured as diagnostic and therapy respectively in the famous controversy between the rivalling French medical schools of Nancy and of the Salpétrière in Paris. But it also became one of the most important models of social influence and was appropriated by early crowd psychologists to account for the alleged irrationality, emotionality and 'primitivism' of crowds (see Barrows, 1981; Paicheler, 1985).

> **Crowd psychology** The study of the mind (cf. **group mind**) and the behaviour of masses and crowds, and of the experience of individuals in such crowds.

> **Suggestion** The technique and/or process by which another person is induced to experience and behave in a given way, i.e., as determined by the suggesting agent, e.g., a hypnotist.

The other medical model, even more 'pathological' in origin and kind, was taken from epidemiology. In parallel with bacteriological contagion, which had recently become a scientific fact through the research of 'microbe hunters' like Louis Pasteur (1822–95) and Robert Koch (1843–1910), **mental contagion** was considered to be possible and to account for the spread of affect and 'anomie' in mob-like or otherwise agitated crowds.[2] Mental contagion, a key term in LeBon's influential crowd psychology (LeBon, 1895), although he did not coin it himself (see Nye, 1975), was later interpreted in terms of 'circular reaction' (Allport, 1924) and 'interstimulation' (Blumer, 1946). It thus theoretically lost its 'infectious disease' character (Milgram & Toch, 1969). The 'medical' distortions of the image of the crowd in nineteenth-century thought have been excellently documented and criticized by Barrows (1981) and McPhail (1991). What Barrows did not anticipate is that, after a long silence, the idea of emotional contagion is having a second chance with contemporary social psychologists (Hatfield, Cacioppo, & Rapson, 1994).

> **Mental contagion** The hypothetical mechanism underlying the spread of affect and of ideas in crowds.

Besides medicine, the second scientific root of crowd psychology was criminology. What was a subconscious and affective state of mind from a medical viewpoint, in the juridical perspective was the *diminished responsibility* of the individual submerged in the crowd or even the 'delinquent crowd' (Sighele, 1891; Tarde, 1901). The basic assumption of this medico-legal approach is again that in the crowd the individual becomes more primitive, more infantile than when alone, and hence less intelligent, less guided by reason and therefore less responsible. While all these ideas had been pronounced in a series of Italian and French publications before 1895, LeBon popularized them in his bestseller without giving credit to the original authors. And it was LeBon to whom later students of crowd mind and behaviour referred as the master of crowd psychology (e.g., Freud, 1953; critically Nye, 1975; Moscovici, 1981a).

If we take both sources, the medical and the criminological, together, this 'Latin' conception of the crowd is one of non-normalcy, associated with either disease or crime, at best allowing for mitigating circumstances. In order to understand why collective behaviour and its mental correlates were regarded as anomalous or 'anomic', it is necessary to look at the social and political context in which such conceptions developed. Political events that became conducive to the development of crowd psychology included the following:

- the succession of revolutions in France (1789, 1830, 1871);
- radical economic and social changes due to rapid industrialization and urbanization;
- the rise and 'revolt of the masses' (Ortega y Gasset, 1932);
- the growing strength of the labour unions and of socialism with strikes and May demonstrations;
- corruption and scandals;
- the military defeat of France by Prussia in 1871;
- the revolutionary Paris Commune and its bloody suppression.

All this taken together became a threat to the established political, social and moral order and mainly to the bourgeoisie (van Ginneken, 1992). As Barrows (1981) convincingly argued, there was a general feeling of *décadence* and decline to be accounted for. The masses were 'discovered' (Moscovici, 1981a) and feared as the causes of the general malaise, and science was required to analyse in detail the causal relationship between mass phenomena and the social evils. A criminological as well as a medical (psychiatric or epidemiological) 'explanation' suited the prevailing *Zeitgeist*. In spite of the controversial notions of the 'mental unit of the crowd' (LeBon, 1895) and of a supra-individual entity-like 'crowd mind', which both carried well into the twentieth century (e.g., McDougall, 1920), it is important to see that a major concern of the Latin crowd psychology was the fate of the 'normal' individual who became somehow 'abnormal' under the social condition of the crowd. Whereas LeBon treated mobs and juries, mass demonstrations and parliaments, criminal as well as religious aggregations, all under the category of 'crowds', today we give crowds, social movements, audiences and institutions different treatments. One important distinction, however, had already been made by Tarde (1901) and Park (1972), namely that between the crowd and the public. While the crowd implies physical contact and spatial limitation, the public, mainly owing to the modern media of communication (although only in the form of the press at that time), transcends spatial contiguity and spreads as 'public opinion'.

Like *Völkerpsychologie*, crowd psychology did not develop within the context of academic psychology after McDougall (1920) had once more invoked a supra-individual 'group mind'. But, unlike *Völkerpsychologie*, some of the major topics of crowd psychology were incorporated into the new social psychology after they had been individualized, and thereby become accessible for experimental analysis. This is the case when, for example, in the studies on aggression, phenomena like collective violence and explanatory constructs like deindividuation are dealt with or when modern theories of social identity and of self-categorization account for crowd effects (Turner, Hogg, Oakes, Reicher, & Wetherell, 1987; see chapters 14 and 15). Also under the topic of social influence we recognize this continuity of what once was understood as the effects of suggestion, contagion and imitation (see Moscovici, 1985; Paicheler, 1985; for historicity of crowd and other social phenomena and concepts, cf. Graumann & Moscovici, 1986a, 1986b, 1987).

Orientations and Differentiation in Modern Social Psychology

In spite of its European roots and the impact of the forced emigration from Nazi-occupied countries, it was a predominantly American social psychology that, after 1945, helped Europeans to develop their discipline. But is this much-needed support internationalization?

Social psychology as we know it today may be dated from around the turn of the twentieth century. Many American textbook authors prefer to fix the dates for its beginning at 1898 for the first experiment in social psychology and at 1908 for its first two textbooks. As a matter of fact, both 'firsts' have been shown to be wrong; but it does not make sense to replace them by other 'firsts'. In the late nineteenth century there was not only *Völkerpsychologie* and crowd psychology. There was also the term 'social psychology', applied to existing studies dealing with the individual in society, or a 'psychology of society' (Graumann, 1989; Lindner, 1871; see Lück, 1987). Yet from the very first programmes of a social psychology we find the two different emphases that we have already introduced above: (1) a psychological social psychology which was to deal with the individual and with intra-individual processes, as does all psychology (e.g., McDougall, 1908; Simmel, 1908); (2) a sociological social psychology which should focus on the role of the social (structural) context for individual processes (e.g., Lindner, 1871; Durkheim, 1974; see Lukes, 1973b; Ross, 1908). Although the much-cited books of 1908 were not the first textbooks in social psychology, they may well represent the two different emphases. McDougall's *Introduction to Social Psychology* was a (theoretical) book on 'the native propensities and capacities of the individual human mind' (1908, p. 18), i.e., an individualistic approach to social psychology by means of an instinct theory; in modern terms, a theory of motivation (see Farr, 1996). Ross, the sociologist, dealt in *Social Psychology* with the 'planes and currents that come into existence among men in consequence of their associ-ations' (1908, p. 1). His topic was the uniformities resulting from social influence due to interaction, partly in the tradition of crowd psychology. In his reflection on the history of social psychology, Pepitone (1981, p. 974) is right when he states that 'collective social psychology of the sort presented by Ross remained for the most part in sociology', whereas for psychology 'the individual was the only reality' and, hence, for a social psychology developing from it.

Social psychology in North America

We have seen that social-psychological individualism had its roots in certain social philosophies. But with the establishment of a (psychological) discipline of social psychology this individualism acquired a methodological note. It may be that the 'emergence of social psychology as a distinctive field of empirical research . . . can be viewed . . . as a generational revolt against the armchair methods of social philosophy' (Cartwright, 1979, p. 83). But it definitely happened that, in the view and work of one of the first modern American social psychologists, F. H. Allport (1924), the individualist conception coincided and coalesced with a methodological orientation, the experimental-behavioural approach. For Allport, the first social psychologist in the behaviourist tradition, social psychology became 'the science which studies the behavior of the individual in so far as his behavior stimulates other individuals, or is itself a reaction to this behavior' (1924, p. 12). Yet while the 'behaviour viewpoint' was only a way of conceiving facts, it is the experimental method that yields them (p. vi). The combination of individualistic approach, 'beha-viour viewpoint' and experimental method was meant to make social psychology a scientifically respectable discipline; this effort, according to Cartwright (1979, p. 84), took social psychology the first three or four decades of its existence.

While the greater part of this process took place in America and may historic-ally be traced back to the model of F. H. Allport's early experiments on social facilitation (see chapter 14), one should note that Allport (1924) himself leaned heavily on the experimental work of several of Wundt's students (see Graumann, 1986). In this connection, Pepitone (1981, p. 975) speaks of 'the German roots of the experimental tradition in social psychology'. 'European roots' would have been even more precise, since there was not only the overly (and erroneously) cited example of Triplett, who in 1898 reported an experiment on the impact of co-acting others on an individual's working speed and quality (later to become known as 'social facilitation'). As Haines and Vaughan (1979) have shown, there were other experiments before 1898 deserving to be called social-psychological, mainly in the context of Binet and Henri's studies of *suggestibility* (Binet & Henri, 1894), a topic that had been taken over from the hypnosis tradition discussed earlier.

Even earlier, in the 1880s, Ringelmann conducted investigations of group pro-ductivity (see chapter 14 and Kravitz & Martin, 1986). Historically, however, it is less interesting to find the truly first experiment (an arbitrary decision) than to observe how social psychologists are still trying to identify their history with the experimental rather than with any other methodology. The development of the 'project of an experimental social psychology' from crowd psychology to the period after the Second World War has been reconstructed critically by Danziger (1992).

In spite of the European roots of experimentalism, it happened mainly in the social and scientific climate of the United States after the First World War that social psychology more than elsewhere became a 'science of the individual' (Allport, 1924, p. 4). The effect of this limitation was that social psychology became largely removed from the study of social issues (Katz, 1978, p. 780). It has, at least in its research practice, isolated its participants from their social context; until in economic and political crises, such as the Great Depression and the Second World War, 'the urgency of social problems overwhelmed the purists in their laboratories' (1978, p. 781), as we shall see below.

The major achievement in the 1930s and 1940s was the study and, mainly, the measurement of attitudes (see Danziger, 1997, ch. 8), a preoccupation which was followed in the 1950s and 1960s by a focus on conceptions of attitude change (Petty & Wegener, 1998a; see chapter 8). For the historian the many techniques of attitude measurement that have been developed since the mid-1920s are less interesting than the growing certainty, reconfirmed by each new technique, that 'attitudes can be measured' (Thurstone, 1928) and, by their measurability, can enhance the scientific status of social psychology. This development was further reinforced by the series of experimental studies of opinion change within the Yale Communication Research Program (e.g., Hovland, Janis, & Kelley, 1953). Today the preference for experimental over field designs and for measurement over observation has been institutionalized in curricula and in criteria for the publication of research papers. In addition, fund-raising and grants depend to no small degree on the level of methodological sophistication. But also, what has been called the 'crisis' of social psychology in the 1970s, in which the social meaningfulness and relevance of its major research work was questioned from many angles, was largely attributed to the sovereignty of methods over problems (see Buss, 1979; Israel & Tajfel, 1972).

Historically, there have been deviations from this methodological mainstream whenever pressing social and political problems demanded the cooperation and commitment of social psychologists. This was the case when, during the 1930s, the *Society for the Psychological Study of Social Issues* was founded. It happened again in the 1940s, when, under the pressure of Nazi and Fascist domination and terror, social psychologists in the free countries not only tried to help win the war, but planned for a better world of democratic societies. One of them was Kurt Lewin (1890–1947), a Jewish refugee from Berlin, a member of the Gestalt group that was to influence social psychology in various direct and indirect ways. Lewin, fully aware of what had happened in Germany and then in Europe, had become a social psychologist when he applied his *field theory* to groups (Lewin, 1948, 1951). Less a theory than a general methodology, this approach focused on the principle of interdependence, emphasizing the primacy of the whole (situation or field) over the parts. This broad methodology permitted Lewin and his students to do experiments with groups (as prototypes of 'fields of forces'), but also to work with groups in everyday community life in order to change their conduct, morale, prejudice, style of leadership, etc. – an approach that became known as *action research*. The list of his associates and students, from his years at the University of Iowa's Child Welfare Research Station (1935–44) to those of his own foundation, the Research Center for Group Dynamics (then at the MIT, now in Ann Arbor), is probably the most impressive and influential ever associated with one individual scholar after Wundt (see Festinger, 1980; Marrow, 1968; Patnoe, 1988).

Although Lewin died in 1947, it was largely Lewinians, such as Cartwright, Deutsch, Festinger, French, Kelley, Schachter and Thibaut, who shaped social psychology in America after the Second World War and, consequently, in Europe. Marx and Hillix (1979, p. 322) even concluded 'that it is hardly hyperbole to describe American social psychology as a Lewinian development'. If one adds those Americans who came to be influenced by the other emigrants, it was no exaggeration to summarize as did Cartwright (1979, p. 85): 'One can hardly imagine what the field would be like today if such people as Lewin, Heider, Köhler, Wertheimer, Katona, Lazarsfeld, and the Brunswiks had not come to the United States when they did'. Of these emigrants, Fritz Heider (1958) has become the second most influential social psychologist. Without a strong and productive group of disciples, which Lewin had always had (before and after his emigration), Heider's impact on the social psychology of interpersonal relations, consistency and attribution was mainly effectuated by a few publications. If we add Sherif's early study of social norms (see chapter 13), which owes the conception of the frame of reference to Gestalt theory (Sherif, 1936), and the Gestalt psychologist Asch's experiments on impression formation (Asch, 1946; see chapter 13), the European heritage in American social psychology is evident. It is important to keep this in mind if in American texts one occasionally reads that social psychology has become 'primarily an American product' (Cartwright, 1979, p. 85) or 'largely a North American phenomenon' (Jones, 1985, p. 47). The truth in such statements is that after the arrival of the emigrants many ideas had to be and indeed were indigenized or 'Americanized' in a process of adaptation to the new social and scientific context (see Ash, 1985; Graumann, 1976, 1989). It is equally true that Hitler had emptied most of central Europe of whoever and whatever there was in social psychology. Into this vacuum poured 'American psychology' in the years after 1945; it was not the emigrants returning.

What actually happened in the decades after the Second World War in America and secondarily in Europe was, besides the ongoing methodological refinement, two theoretical changes: *from the behavioural to the cognitive viewpoint* and *from broader to more narrow theory ranges*. At the start of the twenty-first century, both these trends are still strong. It is less observable social behaviour and interactions that are of interest than their cognitive representation. But also social cognition has noticeably changed its meaning since its early Gestaltist conception. This is revealed by a comparison of its different presentations in the successive editions of the standard *Handbook of Social Psychology*, existing since mid-twentieth century and presently in its fourth edition (Gilbert, Fiske, & Lindzey, 1998), and in the recent *Handbook of Basic Principles* (Higgins & Kruglanski, 1996).

Together with the gradual transformation of the usage of social cognition we witness a proliferation and diminution of social-psychological theories. For the historian of psychology a pattern seems to recur. Just as, in the heyday of behaviourism, the kinds of learning proliferated, it is now the concept of cognition that seems to spawn the many mini-theories which, simultaneously, tend to spread over the whole field of social psychology.

One other social change has been noted in the development of American social psychology in the last 25 years, namely the change from a relatively low status and a marginal position within psychology to a more respected and central position. For Berscheid (1992, p. 531), it is even apparent 'that social psychology has emerged as a central pivot for much of contemporary psychology', an assessment which, if at all, may be true for the many new fields of applied social psychology: community, environment, health, law, organization (see part V, this volume).

Social psychology in Europe

The situation of social psychology in postwar Europe can hardly be understood without the dialectics of the transatlantic interchange. There is, on the one hand, the American 'naturalization'. For psychology as a whole, Koch (1985, p. 25) made a convincing case that whatever the European contribution may have been historically – British post-Darwinian comparative psychology, Russia's Pavlovian conceptions, the Gestalt emigration, the discovery of Piaget, 'even' phenomenology and, of course, the neo-positivists' philosophy of the Vienna circle – it was all eagerly received, digested and transformed into something American, partly blended with the indigenous behaviourism and thoroughly individualistic. The vigour with which this was done had been made possible by an early and massive institutionalization. Koch, as others before him, is convinced that a cultural atmosphere favouring pragmatism and experimentalism in all walks of life facilitated the rise of psychology as a new science 'that seemed to promise prediction and control of human affairs' (Koch, 1985, p. 22). 'Naturalized' and institutionally strengthened psychology in the United States soon outnumbered and outweighed efforts in other countries. Psychology became an export commodity wherever there was demand, and demand was greatest in postwar Europe, although in nationally different degrees and for different reasons. What was later critically called the 'Americanization'[3] of European (e.g., German) psychology (see Cartwright, 1979, p. 85) was originally the much-needed and gratefully received reconstruction and internationalization of social science with American aid.

Only to the degree that ideas, problems and their solutions were received and communicated in an uncritical attitude may the term 'Americanization' be justified. In general, however, this process of adaptation has been part of an over-all 'internationalization' of science, with little mutuality though (cf. Graumann, 1999; van Strien, 1997).

What was the situation of social psychology in Europe before the war? Without proper institutionalization there were only individual scholars with some interest in social psychology. For example, in England there was Bartlett, whose major work on *Remembering* (1932) has only recently gained interest among cognitive social psychologists. In Switzerland there was Piaget, who in his many volumes on child development also contributed to our present conception of socialization (see chapter 3), mainly by his focus on moral development (Piaget, 1932b). In Germany there was Moede, whose early experimental group psychology (Moede, 1920) had already impressed Floyd Allport (1924), and there was Hellpach, the founder of the (short-lived) first Institute for Social Psychology in 1921 and the author of the first systematic German textbook of social psychology (Hellpach, 1933). Yet none of these or other European scholars was founder or mediator of a social-psychological tradition; nor did they form a scientific community of social psychologists. After 1933 Hitler contributed to their separation.

Such was the situation in Europe after 1945. Although there were individuals and teams doing social-psychological research and teaching at various European universities, they were 'unaware of each other's existence, . . . the line of communication ran mainly between each centre and the United States', as the first editorial of the *European Journal of Social Psychology* stated in 1971. It was a first American initiative in the 1950s that, starting from Oslo, brought sociologists and social psychologists from seven European nations together for the purpose of an interdisciplinary cross-cultural study on threat and rejection (Schachter et al., 1954). But it took another effort, again initiated by American psychologists, to lay the foundation for a permanent grouping of European social psychologists.

When, in 1966, the European Association of Experimental Social Psychology (EAESP) was founded, it soon became the nucleus of a scientific community of social psychologists in Europe. From a small group in the mid-1960s it has grown into a large community comprising the vast majority of European social psychologists and an increasing number of international affiliates (about 100 in 1999).

The initial dependence on North American social psychology was gratefully acknowledged. But the lack of mutuality in the transatlantic exchange of ideas was also regretted, mainly by those founders of a European association who had hoped for a social psychology of a characteristically European vintage. Among the first to articulate this uneasiness and to search for the identity of social psychology in Europe were Tajfel and Moscovici who, each in his own way, pleaded for a more social social psychology than the one established and developed in America. Critics of the latter have repeatedly maintained that it is wedded to the 'cultural ethos' of 'self-contained individualism' (Sampson, 1977, p. 769, 1993). In contrast, Tajfel and his students emphasized the *social dimension* of individual and group behaviour, i.e., the degree to which our experience and behaviour are embedded in and shaped by the properties of the culture and society we live in (Tajfel, 1981, 1984). Society, however, 'has its own structure which is not definable in terms of the characteristics of individuals' (Moscovici, 1972, p. 54). Therefore, 'social psychology can and must include in its theoretical and research preoccupations a direct concern with the relationship between human psychological functioning and the large-scale social processes and events which shape this functioning and are shaped by it' (Tajfel, 1981, p. 7).

It may be the diversity of social and cultural backgrounds characteristic of Europe that suggests this greater concern for the social (i.e., cultural) context of both social behaviour and its psychological investigation. The concern for social context is evident, for example, from Tajfel's own studies of stereotypes, prejudice and intergroup behaviour, from Moscovici's work on social influence, minorities and social representations (see also Israel & Tajfel, 1972; Jaspars, 1986) and, last but not least, from the belated but growing concern for language and its role in interpersonal and intergroup communication to which European social psychologists are contributing significantly (see the *Journal of Language and Social Psychology* and the *Handbook*, edited by Giles & Robinson, 1990). However, it also belongs to the picture of diversity that many centres of social-psychological research in Europe have not been affected by the European quest for identity, but are still 'following at a distance and with due delays the successive ebbs and flows of the mainstream of American social psychology' (Tajfel, 1981, p. 6), and are not noticeably different, in their theorizing and research, from any centre in North America. But whether there is an overall change in orientation in Europe's social psychology or whether this is restricted to some of its prominent protagonists, as Jaspars (1986, p. 12) wondered, the least one can say about the 'Europeanization' of social psychology is that it has succeeded in generating a more frequent and lively interaction among psychologists. The most important forum is the EAESP, its meetings and summer schools, the journal and the monographs sponsored by it. Other positive symptoms are European textbooks of social psychology, with contributors from several European countries and from North America; and the annual series *European Review of Social Psychology*, a European counterpart to the successful North American *Advances in Experimental Social Psychology*.

Summary and Conclusions

A history of social psychology prepared for a European textbook is obviously written from a European perspective. Summing up, this means that if we emphasize the European background of contemporary social psychology we, at the same time, have to acknowledge that, in its modern form, social psychology is 'largely a North American phenomenon' (Jones, 1985), and that this is internationally so. The European background is not only to be found in the first-mentioned philosophical problems that have later been taken up by social-psychological science. It is also the 'German roots of the experimental tradition' (Pepitone, 1981) and, last but not least, the impact of such European emigrants as Katona, Lazarsfeld, Heider, Köhler, Wertheimer and, above all, Lewin who, mainly through their influential American disciples, have shaped modern social psychology.

Social psychology as it is presented in this textbook is not (and should not be) basically different from what it is in North America. Nevertheless, it is possible to make distinctions. At least there is a tendency to view social psychology in America as more individualistic, ahistorical, ethnocentric and laboratory-oriented than it is in Europe (Scherer, 1993c), and that, in terms of research topics, there is a preference for intergroup relations, social identity and social influence in Europe (Scherer, 1992a). In a formulaic phrase Scherer (1993c, p. 520) summarized what quite a few historiographers and chroniclers of social psychology hold to be a basic distinction between psychology in America and in Europe, namely: there 'the individual and its functioning', here 'the social and cultural determinants of cognition and behaviour'. Yet with regard to the most recent theoretical developments this common classification needs two updates which are both signs of rapprochement as well as research perspectives.

The first comes from the growing concern for *socio-cultural context* (Fiske et al., 1998). Since the primacy of experimental methodology implies the necessity of decontextualizing social phenomena, an explicit concern for the context may serve as a counterbalance, just as Wundt's *Völkerpsychologie* was meant to complement his experimental psychology. The inclusion of context is not only called for with respect to the phenomena under study, but also to the study itself. The social construction of scientific knowledge from the generation of hypotheses through the choice of experimental procedures, the interpretation of results to the process of scientific communication is finding increasing interest in a social psychology of science (Shadish & Fuller, 1994). Another aspect of the recent 'contextualization' is the incorporation of a feminist perspective (Denmark, 1994).

The second qualification of the alleged distinction between American and European research preferences comes from the recent interest in the social construction of *shared reality*. This topic, originating in European phenomenology and sociology, was until quite recently absent from social-psychological texts. Beginning with studies on socially shared cognitions (Resnick, Levine, & Teasley, 1991) and in pursuance of the nagging question 'What's *social* about social cognition?' (Nye & Brown, 1996), research interest has focused on the cognitive and linguistic means by which communicating individuals constitute (or 'construct') a common reality. It is mainly the conception of reciprocal perspective-taking that enables psychologists to give shared reality a social-psychological meaning (Hardin & Higgins, 1996; Ickes & Gonzalez, 1996; Krauss & Fussell, 1996), and social psychologists a promising research perspective and a bridge to sociology.

1 The disconnectedness of both forms of social psychology was studied in detail by Wilson and Schafer (1978).
2 'Anomie' is Durkheim's term for a state in which dominant social norms are questioned, ignored or repudiated.
3 'Americanization' has two different usages in psychological historiography: (a) It refers to the 'naturalization' or 'indigenization' of originally European ideas in North America; (b) it refers to the import and reception of originally US-American ideas in (postwar) Europe.

1 Name and sketch some of the central issues studied in social thought before the advent of social psychology.
2 What was the programme of *Völkerpsychologie* and what were its methodological implications for modern social psychology?
3 What was the political and social context of nineteenth-century crowd psychology?
4 Discuss the 'European background' and the American character of modern social psychology.
5 Is 'Americanization' only a polemical term for certain trends in social psychology?
6 When did social psychology first emerge as a recognizable discipline?

Berscheid, E. (1992). A glance back at a quarter century of social psychology. *Journal of Personality and Social Psychology*, 63, 525–33. A selective and personal retrospective on the growth of social psychology in the United States between 1965 and 1990 by one of the leading women in social-psychological research.

Danziger, K. (1992). The project of an experimental social psychology: Historical perspectives. *Science in Context*, 5, 309–28. A study of historical changes in the conception and evaluation of experimentation for the acquisition of knowledge about social reality. Problems are discussed of the assimilation of Lewinian conceptions by American social psychology.

Farr, R. M. (1996). *The roots of modern social psychology 1872–1954*. Oxford: Blackwell. A European alternative to the mainly North American histories of social psychology with a special regard to the relationship between social psychology and other social sciences.

Gilbert, D. T., Fiske, S. T., & Lindzey, G. (Eds.). (1998). *The handbook of social psychology* (4th ed., Vol. 1, pp. 3–57). New York: McGraw-Hill. Of historical interest are mainly the chapters by E. E. Jones and S. E. Taylor.

Patnoe, S. (1988). *A narrative history of experimental social psychology – The Lewin tradition*. New York: Springer Verlag. Two generations of American students and students of Kurt Lewin altogether 20 social psychologists, were interviewed and report on their training within the 'Lewinian tradition' and on their contributions to social psychology.

Sapsford, R., Still, A., Wetherell, M., Miell, D., & Stevens, R. (Eds.). (1998). *Theory and social psychology*. London: Sage. As a recent example of 'critical social psychology' this book focuses on the diversity in social psychology and on the role of culture in the conception of the discipline.

KEY STUDY

Cartwright, D. (1979). Contemporary social psychology in social perspective. *Social Psychology Quarterly, 42,* 82–93.

Evolutionary Social Psychology

John Archer

2

OUTLINE

Evolutionary social psychology explains current patterns of human social behaviour in terms of their origins as solutions to recurrent problems encountered in ancestral environments. In this chapter, research applying principles derived from evolutionary biology to human psychology is considered to answer two questions, how cooperative or altruistic behaviour could have arisen through natural selection; and how the principle of sexual selection can explain a variety of psychological differences between men and women.

KEY CONCEPTS

- Adaptation
- Altruistic behaviour
- Coefficient of relatedness (*r*)
- Competition
- Cooperation
- Cuckoldry
- Developmental instability
- Evolutionary psychology
- Fitness
- Fluctuating asymmetry
- Helping behaviour

- Inclusive fitness
- Monogamy
- Natural selection
- Parental investment
- Polyandry
- Polygyny
- Prosocial behaviour
- Reciprocal altruism
- Reproductive strategies
- Sexual selection
- Sociobiology

Introduction

What is evolutionary *social psychology, and how does it differ from the conventional form of social psychology?*

In most undergraduate social science courses, there is an unstated assumption that human nature is of little or no importance, because human behaviour can largely be explained by considering societal roles and culture. Social psychologists usually view the origins of people's dispositions and behaviour in terms of social roles and socialization (chapter 3).

These assumptions have been challenged by the increasing numbers of researchers who view human behaviour from the standpoint of modern Darwinian theory. This involves a different way of looking at familiar problems in social psychology. It has led to novel hypotheses, which have generated a great deal of new research (Barkow, Cosmides, & Tooby, 1992; Crawford & Krebs, 1998; Simpson & Kenrick, 1997), arousing much interest in the public domain (e.g., Pinker, 1997; Wright, 1994).

> **Evolutionary psychology** An approach to psychology based on the principle of natural selection. The emphasis is placed more on psychological mechanisms and flexibility than is the case for sociobiology.
>
> **Sociobiology** The application of Darwin's theory of natural selection to explaining the origins and maintenance of social behaviour.

The roots of **evolutionary psychology** lie in the writings of evolutionary biologists in the 1960s, highlighted by E. O. Wilson (1975) in the book *Sociobiology*, where he set out to explain all animal and human behaviour in terms of evolutionary and other biological principles. These principles have since been applied to many topics and issues in the social sciences. The current distinctive tradition of evolutionary psychology developed from **sociobiology**, but differs from it in several ways. It acknowledges the flexibility of human behaviour, and is particularly concerned with explaining current dispositions and behaviour. These are seen in terms of psychological mechanisms which were designed to cope with the environment of the evolving human species.

Evolutionary social psychology is not simply another area of research within social psychology. It is a different perspective on all of social psychology, one that involves principles derived from evolutionary biology. It is therefore necessary to understand these principles before considering their applications. In this chapter, two major concerns of evolutionary psychology are covered: first, the issue of how helping or cooperative behaviour could arise from the apparently selfish process of natural selection; and second, how the process of sexual selection can be used to understand a variety of differences between the psychological dispositions and behaviour of men and women.

Altruism and Natural Selection

Natural selection and behaviour

How has natural selection shaped social behaviour?

The idea that living things possess features that make them well designed, or adapted, for their environments was appreciated before Darwin's time. It was known, for example, that the features of the heart fitted it for pumping blood around the body. Darwin's principle of **natural selection** explained how **adaptations** – features showing good design – could have come into being without the intervention of a supernatural designer (Dawkins, 1986).

Darwin realized that in any environment some heritable variations will be better able than others to survive and reproduce. They are said to possess greater **fitness** than their alternatives, because they provide a better fit with their environment. Over succeeding generations, these individuals will have had greater reproductive success than alternatives, and this will result in a gradual change in the types of organisms found in the population. The resulting forms will be better designed for life in that environment than the earlier alternatives, and in the long run this process can account for the origin of species.

Darwin was mainly concerned with the evolution of physical features, but modern Darwinians have become interested in the evolution of behaviour (Cronin, 1991). The same principle, that better-adapted forms are selected, applies to any feature which has a heritable basis, whether it be a part of the anatomy or a stable disposition to behave in a particular way. Most birds and mammals have a very stable disposition to form close emotional attachments to their young, which can be understood as an adaptation found in all animals that produce a small number of vulnerable young in dangerous environments. This disposition arose because, without it, offspring survival in such environments would be zero. A more specific adaptation is the tendency of herring gull chicks to peck the red spot on their parents' beak. This is only adaptive because it elicits feeding by the parent. Chicks without this disposition would have obtained little food, and therefore would have been unlikely to survive to produce offspring of their own.

These examples explain the existence of present-day behavioural dispositions in terms of their past contributions to survival and reproduction. Evolutionary psychologists explain present-day human dispositions in a similar manner. Why people are currently attracted to chocolate bars and burgers is explained in terms

Natural selection The process whereby individuals with certain characteristics are more frequently represented in succeeding generations as the result of being better adapted for that environment.

Adaptation The possession of characteristics which enable the organism to survive and reproduce better than those with other characteristics. It is implied that these characteristics are better designed for the particular environment than are alternatives.

Fitness The ability of an organism to leave a greater proportion of its genes in succeeding generations than other individuals (*but see also* **inclusive fitness**).

PLATE 2.1   Marilyn Monroe had an 'optimum' waist-to-hip ratio of 0.70

of sugars and fats being nutritionally important yet uncommon foods in the evolutionary environment. Why men of all ages are attracted to young-looking women with a waist-to-hip ratio of around 0.7 is because these features were cues to both health and fertility in the evolutionary environment. We should note that these explanations are specific to food and to mate preferences and are not part of a general mechanism, such as the social learning of cultural values, of the sort used as explanations in conventional psychology.

When evolutionary biologists first applied the principle of natural selection to social behaviour, a number of questions were raised that were not apparent when considering the evolution of bodily structures. Foremost among these was the following dilemma. How is it that an apparently selfish process, whereby individuals that obtain more resources for themselves produce more offspring, could have resulted in anything other than unselfish competitive behaviour? Yet both people and animals frequently do cooperate with, and help, one another. The answer to this dilemma led to a fundamental change in the way that biologists viewed the evolutionary process.

Altruistic behaviour

Why is altruistic behaviour an apparent dilemma for explanations in terms of natural selection?

The term **altruistic behaviour** is used in biology to refer to one animal increasing another's fitness despite a cost (in terms of fitness) to itself. Behaviour fitting this definition occurs throughout the animal kingdom (table 2.1). We can add to this list the many circumstances under which humans help others. They may give money to a stranger begging in the street, or help someone who has collapsed in a public place, and of course they are always doing favours for relatives, friends and colleagues.

Social psychologists have studied the conditions under which people show altruistic behaviour (also referred to as **helping behaviour**). They have defined it not in terms of fitness but of the willingness to benefit another person when there is a choice to do otherwise (see chapter 9 on **prosocial behaviour**). Research on this topic has considered the impact of personality, social norms, and the costs and benefits of specific forms of helping.

At first sight, it is difficult to reconcile such behaviour with the process of natural selection, which has so far been characterized as involving features that enable the individual to leave more descendants.

Altruistic behaviour In evolutionary terms, this is defined as behaviour which helps another individual's fitness despite a fitness cost for the donor. In social psychology, it refers to behaviour characterized by perspective-taking and empathy, which is undertaken with the intention of benefiting another person where the donor has a choice not to do so.

Helping behaviour In its biological meaning, it is equivalent to altruistic behaviour in the most general sense.

Prosocial behaviour In its biological sense, this is

TABLE 2.1 Some examples of altruistic behaviour in animals

1 A male olive baboon helps another male defeat a rival despite the risk of injury.
2 Soldier castes defend a termite colony with their lives.
3 Mexican jays show cooperative breeding, feeding the young of others.
4 Wild dogs hunt cooperatively and share food with non-hunters.
5 Well-fed vampire bats feed those who have been less successful in finding food.

Sources: McFarland (1993); Wilkinson (1988); Wilson (1975).

One way in which earlier generations of biologists overcame this problem was to suppose that animals acted for the good of their group or species. Acting for the good of the group is a noble ideal to which we as humans often aspire. But the reality is that such behaviour leaves it open for another individual to freeload, to take the benefit of others' unselfish acts without themselves contributing. So it is in the animal world. Computer simulations of the process of natural selection have shown that animals behaving solely for the good of the group would be replaced over succeeding generations by individuals whose behaviour benefited themselves rather than others. It seems, therefore, that helping others should lead to extinction of the helpers. If so, why were the examples in table 2.1 maintained by natural selection, and why do humans help one another?

equivalent to altruistic behaviour. In its social-psychological sense, it is narrower than helping behaviour in that the action is intended to improve the situation of the recipient, and the actor is not obliged to help the person receiving help.

Inclusive fitness and the importance of kin

Why do individuals help those who are related to them?

The starting point of modern Darwinian thinking is the realization that reproduction involves the transfer of copies of genes to the next generation. It is therefore these genes (or packages of them) that are the true units of selection. They are the genetic instructions that produce others like us, and the most obvious way they can do so is for them to be passed to our offspring. In the process of sexual reproduction, one parent's genes are merged with those of the other, so that offspring share on average only half the copies of each parent's genes. This is the same proportion as brothers and sisters share. Once we start considering related individuals in terms of their shared genes,[1] the care of parents for their offspring can be viewed as a special case of a general tendency to help any closely related individual.

Consider a gene that controls a tendency to help close kin, even if this means a degree of self-sacrifice. Copies of this gene would be helped to survive and reproduce by selective altruistic behaviour. They would spread in the population and fare better than genes for indiscriminate altruism (Dawkins, 1979). This simple logic was set out mathematically by Hamilton (1964), who emphasized that altruism would be selectively applied to relatives according to the probability that they contain a copy of the gene for kin-induced altruism, in other words their degree of genetic relatedness. He used the term **coefficient of relatedness** (r), from Wright (1922), to denote the proportion of shared genes above those shared by unrelated individuals. For parents and offspring, r is 0.5, as it is for siblings, whereas for cousins it is 0.125. Therefore, in terms of the likelihood of perpetuating a gene for kin-induced altruism, saving the life of a younger sibling with his/her whole reproductive life ahead has the same value as saving one of your own children of the

Coefficient of relatedness (r)
The proportion of shared genes above those shared by unrelated individuals.

same age. Saving a cousin's life brings less benefit in terms of maintaining shared genes in the population since he or she has only one eighth of the same genes. In addition to these calculations, we have to consider whether helping the relative occurs instead of aiding one's own offspring or in addition to it (Grafen, 1982). In the first case, there may be no addition to overall or **inclusive fitness**: there may be a decline. In the second case, there would be a definite benefit – an increase in inclusive fitness – from helping the relative.

Inclusive fitness This refers to the representation of an individual's genes in succeeding generations when help given to relatives is balanced against reproduction.

Of the examples listed in table 2.1, self-sacrifice in insects is entirely due to the sterile soldier and worker castes aiding the reproducing queen's offspring, who are more closely related to them than their own offspring would have been (as a consequence of the mechanism of sex-determination; Dawkins, 1976, pp. 184–91). Kinship underlies all sorts of alliances between social animals, for example the cooperative hunting of wild dogs. It is of course also responsible for parents aiding the survival of their children, in the form of parental care: this can be viewed as another example of kin-induced altruism.

When applied to humans, inclusive fitness can explain why kinship ties are important in all human societies (Daly, Salmon, & Wilson, 1997), and why people give aid and resources to their close kin (chapter 12). The typical use of strangers for laboratory experiments in social psychology (chapter 4) has bypassed issues of kinship, which is so central to a Darwinian understanding of social behaviour. The following examples of the application of inclusive fitness to human behaviour are drawn from research by evolutionary psychologists.

Perhaps the best-known example concerns the risk of child abuse by step-parents. Since parental behaviour is costly, selection would strongly favour individuals who limit it to their own offspring (Daly & Wilson, 1988, p. 83). We should expect substitute parents to care less for their children than natural parents do, and those who had least choice in adopting the parental role (step-parents) to care least of all. Survey data and crime statistics from the US and Canada indicate a much higher incidence of abuse in homes containing a step-parent (nearly always a stepfather) and a natural parent than in those containing two natural parents (Daly & Wilson, 1985, 1988). The increased risk of abuse severe enough to kill is about 100 times greater for an American child in a home containing a step-parent.

Step-parents form part of an important social issue in industrialized Western countries, the break-up and reconstitution of families following divorce. Emlen (1997) argued that humans are adapted for living with close kin in extended families, who will tend to cooperate, and also will be less sexually attracted than unrelated individuals. The contemporary reconstituted family contains biologically unrelated individuals and, as we have seen, step-parents are more likely to harm their mate's prior offspring. They are also more likely to sexually abuse them. Comparisons show that members of step-families fare less well than members of intact families: for example, there is more frequent marital conflict and a higher divorce rate among step-families. Stepchildren leave home earlier, and there is more conflict between step-siblings than full siblings. Emlen argued that these findings parallel similar ones for reconstituted families among animals, and that a similar principle – inclusive fitness – can account for both.

The practical implications of this analysis may assume alarming proportions, considering the growth in numbers of reconstituted families. Emlen's view is that increased awareness of the potential problems can lead to programmes of measures for anticipating the likely conflict areas and for preventing them.

Daly and Wilson (1988) have also examined cooperative homicide in terms of kinship, using archival and ethnographic evidence. They reasoned that killing someone is an extreme outcome of competition, and that collaborative killing is a high-risk cooperative venture. Therefore, they predicted that co-offenders would be more closely related to one another than either would be to the victim. They found that this was the case in a range of societies. According to court records from thirteenth-century England, where two-thirds of homicides were collaborative, co-offenders were six times more likely to be related than were offender and victim.

Burnstein, Crandall and Kitayama (1994) used more traditional psychological methods to test another hypothesis based on inclusive fitness. They asked respondents to choose between helping a series of hypothetical individuals differing in kinship and in features such as sex, age, health and wealth. In five studies, the choice of whom to help followed kinship, and this was especially the case for life and death scenarios.

Reciprocal altruism

Can altruism towards strangers have evolved by natural selection?

Reciprocal altruism Altruistic behaviour shown by an animal or person when the recipient is likely to behave altruistically to the donor in the future.

Although kinship can explain many forms of altruism, there is a further evolutionary reason for helping unrelated individuals. **Reciprocal altruism** (Trivers, 1971) can be described as 'I'll scratch your back if you scratch mine'. However, as with all evolutionary principles, we are not concerned with intentions but with the conditions under which helping behaviour could have arisen by natural selection, in this case among individuals who do not share genes by common ancestry. Trivers identified a fairly restricted set of conditions under which helping would increase fitness: the recipient must return the favour later, and this must (obviously) entail the ability to recognize individuals, in order to discriminate who is 'owed' a favour. Trivers also concluded that helping would only occur where the costs of helping were relatively low and the benefits high, and where there was a way of identifying and excluding individuals who received help but did not return it. This second point is particularly important, since reciprocal altruism will not be maintained unless most cheats are excluded. Indeed, research has shown that a basic aspect of human reasoning in social situations entails a 'search for cheats' strategy (Cosmides & Tooby, 1992).

The conditions necessary for reciprocal altruism fit many examples of helping in intelligent social mammals, particularly primates and, of course, humans. The principle of reciprocal altruism applies to the first example in table 2.1, a male olive baboon helping another male to defeat a rival, and it also fits shared feeding by vampire bats (Wilkinson, 1988).

Humans lived in relatively small bands for most of evolutionary history. These conditions fit better those identified by Trivers than the situations most researched by social psychologists, where people are called upon to help strangers. Nevertheless, the findings still indicate the operation of Trivers' principles (Thompson, 1980): bystander intervention is more likely among smaller integrated communities, where reciprocity is more likely, than among larger anonymous ones.

A wide-ranging review of research on human relationships has shown that the principle of reciprocity is important for relationships as different as those between marriage partners and between colleagues at work (Buunk & Schaufeli, 1999). The authors argue that the consistency across many different types of relationships strongly suggests an evolutionary origin: we expect reciprocity in personal relationships and we react negatively when it is absent.

Cooperation and competition

Do competition and cooperation occur together?

The principles of inclusive fitness and reciprocal altruism answer the question of how helping behaviour could have arisen through the apparently selfish process of natural selection. Without them, further applications of Darwinian theory to human or animal behaviour would have been fruitless. Beyond the question of altruism lie a number of evolutionary models which use the principle of natural selection as a starting point for working out in precise terms when individuals' fitness interests coincide (when they are likely to cooperate) and when they diverge (when they are likely to compete).

Natural selection obviously contains the seeds of **competition**. Because resources necessary for survival and reproduction are limited, genes from individuals who are best able to obtain these resources will be represented in future generations. **Cooperation** occurs through kin selection, and also for mutual benefit, when animals can together achieve something that they could not achieve alone. Reciprocal altruism is a case of mutual benefit separated in time, and therefore requiring ways of guarding against failure to reciprocate.

Shared parenting is a widespread example of two individuals cooperating for mutual benefit. Parents are unrelated, so that they have no evolutionary reason for cooperating if either one can leave

Competition   In evolutionary biology, the process whereby an animal obtains greater or fewer resources necessary for survival and reproduction than another individual. In terms of interdependence theory, it is behaviour that maximizes relative advantage over others.

Cooperation   In evolutionary biology, when two animals pursue an action which enables them to obtain resources of benefit to both.

the other to raise the offspring. In many species, two parents are needed to rear the young successfully: if either deserts, offspring survival is zero. Both parents are equally related to the offspring and so will have the same fitness interests at stake. This sort of reasoning underlies the evolution of biparental care, which occurs in many species of birds and some primates, including humans (Lazarus, 1990; Maynard Smith, 1977).

Animals may show elements of both cooperation and competition in the same situation, as indeed people do. Parents may need one another to rear their off-spring, but if either has the opportunity to increase fitness by an undetected mating with another partner, they will do so. This is true even for birds that were once thought to remain faithful (Mock & Fujioka, 1990). Infidelity among humans is of course more familiar, and its prevalence is probably higher than is generally believed, accounting for between 10 and 30 per cent of offspring born to stable couples (Bellis & Baker, 1990; Diamond, 1991). Thus cooperation with a long-term sexual partner to share parenting may occur alongside infidelity, which is generally resisted by the other partner. Human relationships are widely recognized as involving both unselfish love and conflict generated by self-interest. Evolutionary principles can provide the ultimate reason for why this should be the case.

Sexual Selection and Sex Differences in Behaviour

Sexual selection

Why do males and females behave differently?

Darwin (1871) realized that selection of, and different access to, sexual partners was a form of natural selection (**sexual selection**), and that it had led to characteristic sex differences: for example, he viewed the larger size of males, and their specialization for fighting, as a consequence of competing directly or indirectly for females. Females choose males with particular characteristics, leading to elaborate visual displays among males of certain species such as the peacock.

Sexual selection A form of natural selection which involves selection of, and access to, sexual partners.

Parental investment The contribution in terms of time and energy to feeding, incubating and protecting developing offspring.

Trivers (1972) explained why sexual selection generally took the form of male competition and female choice (table 2.2), arguing that these were not simply a consequence of the animal's sex but of the imbalance in the parental contribution usually associated with the sexes. Trivers used the term **parental investment** to refer to the time and effort spent in producing food for the egg cells, and feeding, incubating and protecting the developing offspring that successful parenting entails. This is usually much greater in the female than the

TABLE 2.2 A summary of Trivers' parental investment theory of sexual selection

1 Where there is no further parental investment, the greater effort required to produce eggs than sperm leads to male competition and female choice.
2 Where there is further parental investment, there is competition among the sex investing the lesser amount (usually the male) for access to the other.
3 Where both parents are needed to rear the offspring, the sexes are similar.
4 Male competition is associated with a greater variation in reproductive success.
5 Where paternity is uncertain, there are counter-strategies such as mate-guarding.

male: it will therefore cost the female much more time and effort to start again if her reproductive contribution is squandered, for example by mating with a low-fitness male. The male, on the other hand, has only to produce more sperm in order to start again, and this is inexpensive.

Trivers saw that the imbalance would lead to different routes to fitness (or different **reproductive strategies**) for the two sexes. Since females have more to lose by starting again, they will be more selective in choosing a mate, preferring males with signs of a high level of fitness. Males could (in theory) fertilize many eggs and therefore leave many offspring. In practice, this is limited by competition between males, and by female choice, leading to some males leaving many offspring and others leaving none. The resulting wider variation in male than female reproductive success applies to most species, including humans. This is illustrated by the highest recorded numbers of children fathered by a man, which is over a thousand, compared to the record of 69 offspring from one woman (Daly & Wilson, 1988).

> **Reproductive strategies**
> Consistent patterns of sexual and parenting behaviour which typically lead to the production of viable offspring.

Where both parents are necessary for the survival of the young, male parental investment approaches that of the female, and competition between males is reduced. In a minority of bird species, the male provides higher parental investment, in the form of incubating the eggs (Jenni, 1974): this is associated with a mating system called **polyandry**, where one female mates with several males. Females are also larger and more aggressive than the males in such species. This reversal of the usual sex differences indicates that it is parental investment, and not the sex of the individual, that produces the differences in size and behaviour between males and females.

Where fertilization is internal and there is shared parental care, female infidelity introduces the possibility that the male will be caring for young sired by another male, a situation known as **cuckoldry**. The cuckolded male would then be caring for unrelated individuals. This behaviour is selected against if responses that overcome or avoid it are possible. Behaviour such as killing a female's existing offspring prior to mating (e.g., Hrdy, 1979), and males guarding their mates

> **Polyandry** A mating system comprising one female and several males. It can also refer to human marriages.

> **Cuckoldry** When a male cares for his female partner's offspring that are not his own.

TABLE 2.3   Some applications of Trivers' parental investment theory to human behaviour

1   Sex differences in preferred numbers of partners.
2   Different mate selection criteria for men and women.
3   Young males will be more risk-taking than other sex and age categories.
4   Homicide will be much more common between men than between women.
5   Males require reassurance over paternity.
6   Men show pronounced jealousy over signs of sexual infidelity by their long-term partners, leading easily to violence.

so that they have exclusive access to them (Parker, 1974), fulfil this function in many species.

The applications of principles involved in Trivers' explanation of sexual selection to human behaviour are summarized in table 2.3. They are elaborated in the next four sections.

Sex differences in preferred numbers of partners

Are men designed to seek casual sex?

The first feature listed in table 2.3 follows from the minimum parental investment that can be made by the two sexes. A man may contribute only his sperm, whereas a woman's involvement is necessarily much more. Consequently, fertilizing many women is a viable strategy for men (as long as someone else cares for the offspring), whereas once a woman has been fertilized, further matings are superfluous.

Monogamy   A mating system comprising one male and one female. It can apply to human marriages.

In most human societies, there are long-term sexual relationships between a man and a woman (**monogamy**), a situation quite different from the temporary liaisons of our nearest relatives – chimpanzees and bonobos. However, cross-cultural surveys show that many cultures allow men with sufficient resources to have more than one wife, a situation that is known as **polygyny** in the animal world.

Polygyny   A mating system comprising one male and several females. It can also refer to human marriages.

There is a persuasive argument that the existence of institutionalized monogamous relationships hides the different sexual natures of men and women (Ridley, 1994; Symons, 1979). Monogamy is generally the preferred option for women, but men would, if possible, seek greater sexual variety. This is typically prevented by female choice, and the possibility of losing the current partner. Where it is not, this disposition becomes manifest in men's behaviour. Throughout history, whenever powerful men have been able to control or attract many women, they have done so (Betzig, 1992).

The behaviour of male film and rock stars, and some politicians, is a present-day manifestation of this tendency. Women may depart from monogamy when this offers a poor option in terms of the fitness and resources of male partners: if there are great differences between available men, women may prefer polygyny in the form of a higher-status man who already has a partner. Where there are few suitable long-term partners, women may prefer short-term liaisons (Campbell, 1995).

One source of evidence supporting the view that men and women have different sexual natures is the preferred sexual strategies in homosexual liaisons. Symons (1979) argued that this shows how each sex behaves when they are not affected by how the other sex wants them to behave. Men from the pre-HIV/AIDS gay communities of the United States typically had vast numbers of sexual partners, whereas lesbians formed relationships similar to those of heterosexual couples, if anything more stable. Symons concluded that:

> Heterosexual men would be as likely as homosexual men to have sex most often with strangers, to participate in anonymous orgies in public baths, and to stop off in public rest rooms for five minutes of fellatio on the way home from work if women were interested in these activities. But women are not interested. (1979, p. 300)

Many studies using more orthodox social-psychological methods support Symons' reasoning (Buss, 1994). These studies typically ask people anonymously what they would *like* to do if they could and if there were no adverse consequences. Among undergraduates, males – compared to females – desire more sexual partners and want intercourse after knowing a woman for a shorter time (Buss & Schmidt, 1993). Men are four times more likely than women to report that they certainly would like to have intercourse with an anonymous person of the other sex who was as attractive as their current partner, if there were no risks or consequences attached (Symons & Ellis, 1989). Women are two and a half times more likely to say that they definitely would not.

Clark and Hatfield (1989) went beyond asking people what they would *like* to do. Students were approached by a moderately attractive member of the opposite sex, who asked them one of three questions, prefaced by the minimal chat-up line, 'I've been noticing you around campus. I find you to be very attractive'. The questions were: 'Would you go out with me tonight?'; 'Would you come over to my apartment tonight?'; and 'Would you go to bed with me tonight?' Fifty per cent of the men agreed to the date, 69 per cent to go to the apartment, and 75 per cent to have sex. Around the same proportion of women as men agreed to the date, but the responses to the other two questions were markedly different, 6 per cent agreeing to go to the apartment, and none agreeing to have sex. Again, the findings suggest that Symons drew the correct inferences from his study of homosexual behaviour.

Mate selection criteria

Is beauty in the eye of the beholder?

On the contrary, argued Symons (1992, 1995), it is in the adaptations of the beholder. People prefer members of the other sex with cues of high mate value, just as they prefer foods with cues of high nutritional value. Although there will be differences in the selection criteria for men and women as a consequence of women's greater parental investment, both sexes will prefer mates with signs of good health and good reproductive prospects. Hamilton and Zuk (1982) argued that features signalling resistance to infectious agents such as parasites are generally valued when animals select a mate. In an analysis of 29 human societies, Gangestad and Buss (1993) found a high correlation between the prevalence of pathogens in a location and the importance people attached to looks for mate selection. A follow-up examination found that women were more likely to use skin markings, such as scarring or tattooing their stomachs and breasts, to enhance their attractiveness when pathogen severity was high (Singh & Bronstad, 1997).

Studies of the features used to select a mate consistently find that women are concerned with men's potential as a provider and protector of future offspring, as indicated by status and wealth, whereas men place more importance on cues that predict a woman's reproductive health, notably signs of youth and looks (Buss, 1994). These differences, which have been found in many different cultures (Buss, 1989; Symons, 1995), can be viewed as a consequence of women's greater parental investment. However, they do not mean that women are unaffected by men's looks. In response to Henry Kissinger's famous phrase that 'power is the ultimate aphrodisiac', one woman commented that he needed it to be. The past decade has seen the publication of research showing that women do respond preferentially to bodily cues that are related to health and fitness.

Singh (1995) asked young women to rank in attractiveness drawings of male body shapes differing in build and waist-to-hip ratio (WHR; see figure 2.1). Normal-weight figures with a waist-to-hip ratio of 0.9 were preferred over all others (figure 2.2). This particular body shape coincides with that produced by high testosterone and low oestrogen levels, and it is associated with better health than other body builds and WHRs. A second study also provided information about the financial status of the men being portrayed, and found that wealth increased the attractiveness of the figures independently of WHR, although when both of these features were optimal the figure was seen as the most attractive, with either a casual or a long-term relationship in mind. However, even wealth did not compensate for the unattractiveness of the least preferred body shape.

Another line of research involved a more subtle bodily cue, the extent to which the body deviates from perfect bilateral symmetry, measured by comparing a number of features on the left and right sides of the body. This is termed

PLATE 2.2 Power can make a man who is not especially physically attractive, even unattractive, more attractive to women

FA or **fluctuating asymmetry**,[2] and it provides an external marker of **developmental instability**, the extent to which development has been influenced by genetic abnormalities and environmental disruptions such as toxins and parasites. Among a range of animals, bodily symmetry is associated with signs of fitness, such as survival, growth rate and fecundity (Gangestad & Thornhill, 1997a). Symmetry can therefore be viewed as an external marker of 'good genes'.

Studies of humans show that women find symmetry an attractive bodily feature in a man: low FA predicts the numbers of sexual partners a man has had, and in particular those that were in addition to a current relationship (Gangestad & Thornhill, 1997a, b). Symmetry is also associated with muscularity, vigour and social dominance,

Fluctuating asymmetry The degree to which an individual deviates from perfect bilateral symmetry.

Developmental instability The extent to which development has been influenced in a direction other than bilateral symmetry by genetic abnormalities and environmental disruptions such as toxins and parasites.

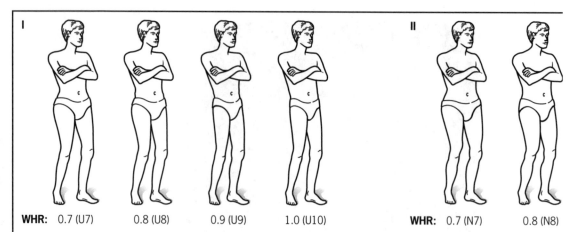

WHR: 0.7 (U7)   0.8 (U8)   0.9 (U9)   1.0 (U10)   WHR: 0.7 (N7)   0.8 (N8)

FIGURE 2.1 Line drawings used by Singh (1995) to represent (a) three body weight categories, (I) under-weight (U), (II) 'normal' weight (N) and (III) overweight (O); and (b) four waist-to-hip ratios (WHRs), for men. The letters and numbers in parentheses identify each drawing in terms of the two categories (Singh, 1995, p. 1091)

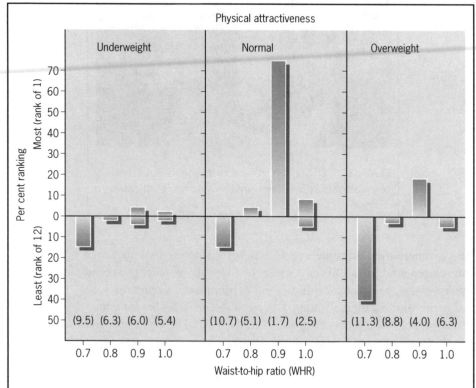

FIGURE 2.2 Histograms showing the percentage frequency of the first rankings (1) and the last rankings (12) in attractiveness for the drawings shown in figure 2.1. The numbers in parentheses are the mean attractiveness rankings for the figures (Singh, 1995, p. 1092)

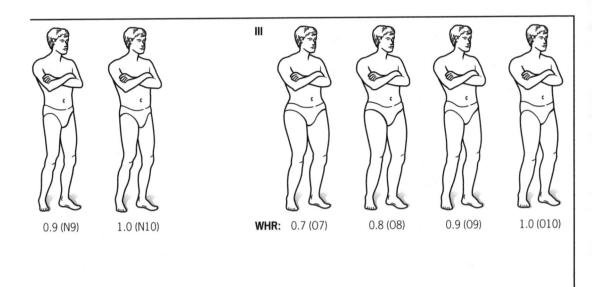

0.9 (N9)   1.0 (N10)   **WHR:** 0.7 (O7)   0.8 (O8)   0.9 (O9)   1.0 (O10)

features which predict earlier sexual involvement among teenagers (Mazur, Halpern, & Udry, 1994). Men's symmetry also predicted greater frequency of orgasms among their partners (Thornhill, Gangestad, & Comer, 1995).

Women's attraction to men's wealth and status and to their bodily features represent characteristics that are valuable for long- and short-term liaisons, respectively. While a Henry Kissinger may be a good potential provider for future children, the symmetrical man with a waist-to-hip ratio of 0.9, but no money or status, is still a good bet as far as his genetic potential is concerned. However, as Singh's study indicated, men who combine both are particularly attractive as short- or long-term mates.

Symons (1995) argued that the cues men find most attractive in women are those associated with women just beginning ovulatory menstrual cycles but not yet pregnant. In preliterate societies, most women marry between 15 to 18 years of age and are thereafter pregnant or lactating for most of the time. In current Western societies the same bodily cues are maintained for longer by the change in reproductive life and the enhancement of attractiveness cues by cosmetics, diet and exercise.

A waist-to-hip ratio (WHR) between 0.67 and 0.80 is a reliable predictor of a woman's reproductive success, in particular her hormonal status, fertility and long-term health. Studies have shown that men of different ages and from different ethnic groups prefer this body shape when presented in the form of line drawings (figure 2.3; see Singh, 1993; Singh & Luis, 1995). Miss America winners and women appearing in *Playboy* also possess the optimal WHR (Singh, 1993), indicating that the laboratory studies generalize to the world outside.

By linking sexually attractive cues to health and reproductive prospects, evolutionary psychologists have challenged the view that arbitrary cultural values

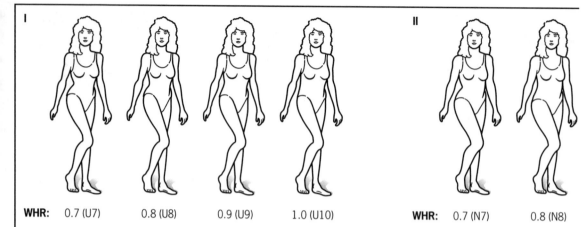

| **WHR:** | 0.7 (U7) | 0.8 (U8) | 0.9 (U9) | 1.0 (U10) | **WHR:** | 0.7 (N7) | 0.8 (N8) |

FIGURE 2.3   Line drawings used by Singh (1995) to represent (a) three body weight categories, (I) under-weight (U), (II) 'normal' weight (N) and (III) overweight (O); and (b) four waist-to-hip ratios (WHRs), for women. The letters and numbers in parentheses identify each drawing in terms of the two categories (Singh, 1993, p. 298)

PLATE 2.3   Ideal waist-to-hip ratios

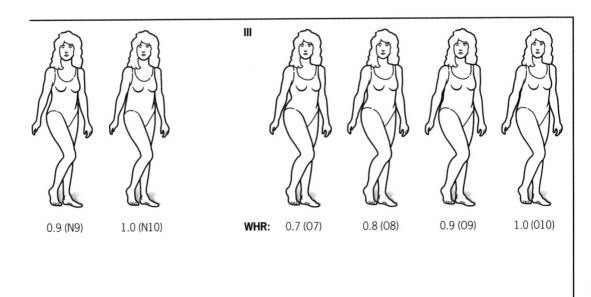

| 0.9 (N9) | 1.0 (N10) | **WHR:** | 0.7 (07) | 0.8 (08) | 0.9 (09) | 1.0 (010) |

mediated by social learning are responsible for what people find attractive in the other sex. They have also provided another important link between social psychology and health (see chapter 16).

Young men: risk, violence and honour

Why do young men tend to engage in risky and violent behaviour?

Throughout the world, young men are drawn to risky pursuits, particularly those that confer status in the eyes of their peers and elders (Gilmore, 1990), and they are the most likely to be violent and to kill one another. The background to these features (table 2.3) is that in animals (as in humans), males show a shorter average life expectancy than females, attributable to the direct and indirect effects of male competition. The greater the disparity in reproductive success between males of a species, the more they will tend to risk their lives in competing with others to obtain access to females or to the resources necessary for successful reproduction (Daly & Wilson, 1988; Trivers, 1972).

Most of us live in societies subject to the rule of law and individual moral restraint. Where these two features are absent, and people have resources that can be readily stolen (such as sheep or cattle), men have a lot to gain by successfully challenging others, and a lot to lose by backing off when challenged. In these societies, a man's reputation for being able to defend himself becomes all important. Studies of the behaviour and attitudes of men who originate from such herding societies

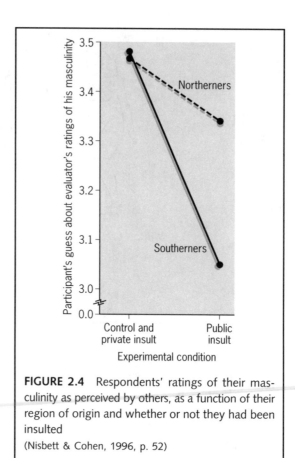

FIGURE 2.4 Respondents' ratings of their masculinity as perceived by others, as a function of their region of origin and whether or not they had been insulted

(Nisbett & Cohen, 1996, p. 52)

show that they retain the legacy of this culture of honour today. Cohen (1996) used historical records to analyse the response of juries in the south of the United States to homicides committed following insults to honour, and Cohen and Nisbett (1994) used survey methods to assess present-day attitudes in the southern states. They also carried out laboratory experiments involving students from the north and south being insulted by a confederate who had bumped into them, and testing their reactions in a variety of ways (Nisbett & Cohen, 1996). Insulted southerners were different in a number of ways from controls who had not been insulted and from insulted northerners: they were more likely not to move out of the way when an imposing-looking man came towards them; they were more likely to provide a violent end to a scenario involving sexual jealousy; and they felt more judged in terms of whether they had behaved in a manly way when another man had observed them being insulted (figure 2.4).

The culture of honour is based on the principle of retaliation for the slightest challenge – to give the message to others that the cost of a future challenge will be unacceptably high. The principle of retaliation or tit-for-tat is one which underlies social behaviour in many circumstances. Computer simulations of the evolution of strategies of aggression show that it cannot be beaten (Wright, 1994, pp. 196–204). It is therefore not surprising that it is found again and again in masculine subcultures where there is no alternative arbiter of disputes. We should note that this explanation is a more general one than that offered by Nisbett and Cohen, which involves historically produced attitudes originating from a particular way of life (herding). Incidentally, the differences in violence they found between people from the north and south of the United States could not be explained by some alternative theories, such as the legacy of slavery, general attitudes to violence, or response to the hotter climate (Nisbett & Cohen, 1996).

Cuckoldry and jealousy

Why do men react so strongly to sexual infidelity?

The last two features in table 2.3 are consequences of uncertainty concerning paternity. The term cuckoldry refers to the case of a man rearing his wife's child by another man. Folklore and codified laws have consistently viewed a wife's adultery more seriously than a husband's, and have linked this with the likelihood of cuckoldry. Why it should matter psychologically to bring up another man's child is only fully explained by inclusive fitness. Studies of relatives' comments about which parent a new baby resembles indicate that they are more likely to comment that the child resembles the father than the mother, findings that have been interpreted in terms of a need to reassure the supposed father about his paternity (Daly & Wilson, 1982; Regalski & Gaulin, 1993).

It has long been recognized that adultery or the threat of it are associated with dangerous emotions, particularly in men. Sexually proprietary motives feature prominently in the motives for wife killings (Wilson & Daly, 1992). Laboratory studies have also shown that the thought of a partner's sexual infidelity causes more distress and physiological arousal among men than women (Buss, Larsen, Westen, & Semmelroth, 1992; Buunk, Angleitner, Oubaid, & Buss, 1996). Women, in contrast, are more upset than men by the thought of a partner forming an emotional bond to someone else. Figure 2.5 illustrates these findings, from three different nations.

Summary and Conclusions

What can evolutionary psychology contribute to social psychology?

Evolutionary psychology provides a coherent view of human nature. It is a way of understanding human social behaviour within a framework of principles

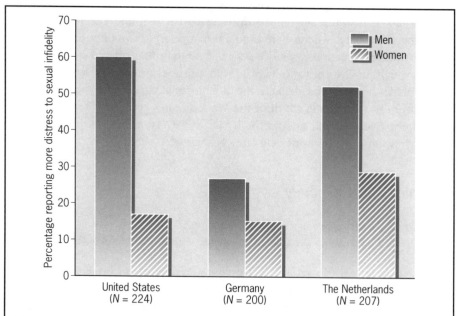

FIGURE 2.5 Percentage of respondents from three countries indicating greater distress when imagining their partner enjoying passionate sexual intercourse with another person than when imagining their partner forming a close emotional bond to another person of the opposite sex
(Buunk et al., 1996, p. 12)

derived from natural selection. These principles lead us to expect the following: that people will not provide aid and help others indiscriminately; that they will not abandon their own children and look after those of strangers; that men and women will not approach sexual relations in the same way, and will not look for the same features when choosing a mate; and that young men typically do not behave with caution. All these activities are within the realms of possibility for human beings as they do not require wings or superhuman intelligence or X-ray eyes. Indeed, sometimes people may behave in these ways. The important point is that most humans in most societies do not, and that the principle of natural selection indicates exactly why they do not. In this way, it provides a view of what we expect human nature to be like.

The evolutionary viewpoint also enables us to deduce circumstances under which human behaviour varies in particular ways. We have encountered some examples, such as variations in the importance of physical attractiveness in populations varying in pathogen severity. Whenever aspects of the environment crucial to fitness are likely to be uncertain or variable from time to time, widespread flexibility of responding evolves, so that behaviour can be better fitted to the circumstances. Adaptive flexibility is a crucial aspect of modern evolutionary psychology.

Conventional social psychology has derived concepts one at a time from research on how people actually behave. In contrast, evolutionary psychology has a clear overriding principle to direct research. This has led to novel findings in areas unexplored before, for example the link between step-parents and child abuse, and between bodily symmetry and attractiveness. In some cases, evolutionary predictions contradict those derived from a non-evolutionary view. For example, the theory that conflicts between parents and offspring should concern resources is at odds with the Freudian view that they are based on sexual jealousies (Daly & Wilson, 1988). The view that sex differences in social behaviour are best explained by the principle of sexual selection contradicts an explanation in terms of historically produced social roles (Archer, 1996).

The evolutionary approach has helped to broaden sources of data used in social-psychological investigations. Laboratory-based research involving undergraduate participants (see chapter 4) has been used in many evolutionarily based studies, but there is always the suspicion that we are dealing with a specialized group of people bounded by their place in history, geography and culture. The need to supplement such studies with cross-cultural data has been recognized, and these studies became an integral part of evolutionary psychology. Daly and Wilson's investigations of evolutionary-based hypotheses about human violence involved evidence derived entirely from historical, anthropological and criminological sources. Their reliance on these data bases provides an interesting addition to the debate about the importance of including historical and cultural dimensions in social psychology, begun by Gergen (1973; see chapter 4).

NOTES

1 Strictly speaking, we should refer to the proportion of genes they share in addition to the many genes shared by unrelated individuals.
2 The term describes the fluctuation of asymmetry that occurs within a population and not within the same individual, although some soft tissue features such as breasts do show variation in asymmetry over time within individuals, thus introducing potential confusion in the terminology.

DISCUSSION POINTS

1 To what extent is evolutionary history apparent in present-day psychological dispositions?
2 What would be the main differences in men's and women's behaviour if sexual jealousy did not exist?
3 How does an evolutionary perspective inform our understanding of the social dynamics of step-families?
4 Why is kinship an important feature in evolutionary psychology but not in conventional psychology?
5 How can evolutionary psychology further our understanding of violent behaviour between young men?

FURTHER READING

Buss, D. M. (1994). *The evolution of desire: Strategies of human mating*. New York: Basic Books. A fascinating summary of research on sex differences associated with mate choice and mate attraction, including much of the author's own research.

Buss, D. M. (1999). *Evolutionary psychology: The new science of the mind*. Needham Heights, MA: Allyn & Bacon. Described as the first comprehensive text in the field, containing up-to-date research presented in a clear and engaging way with many examples from culture and the media. It also contains applications of the research 'to the personal lives of students'!

Daly, M., & Wilson, M. (1988). *Homicide*. New York: Aldine de Gruyter. This book describes the systematic application of Darwinian thinking to research on homicide using criminological, historical and anthropological sources. It is original and provocative, and has dated little since its publication.

Demos Quarterly (1996), Issue 10: *Matters of life or death: The worldview from evolutionary psychology*. A series of essays on the implications of Darwinian thinking for the human sciences, from medicine to economics, including psychology. All written by acknowledged experts in their fields.

Dawkins, R. (1989). *The selfish gene* (2nd ed.). New York: Oxford University Press. This classic book (first published in 1976) explains the basic principles of the then new evolutionary approach to behaviour. It is popular science in which the ideas are not diluted but clarified in a way that pulls the reader into the logic of the arguments.

Dawkins, R. (1986). *The blind watchmaker*. London: Longman. The logic of natural selection and the objections to alternative accounts of human origins are explained in a way that surpasses even *The Selfish Gene* as exemplary popular science writing.

Symons, D. (1979). *The evolution of human sexuality*. New York: Oxford University Press. A well-written book on the applications of sexual selection to human behaviour. It is full of ideas and examples from many sources. Despite the enormous growth of research in this area, the book has dated little.

Wright, R. (1994). *The moral animal: Evolutionary psychology and everyday life*. New York: Pantheon. An excellent, readable and thoughtful introduction to evolutionary social psychology that uses the novel approach of interspersing all the relevant ideas and research with a partial biography of Charles Darwin and how the principles applied to events in his life.

KEY STUDY

Buss, D. M., Larsen, R. J., Westen, D., & Semmelroth, J. (1992). Sex differences in jealousy: Evolution, physiology, and psychology. *Psychological Science*, 3, 251–5.

Developmental Social Psychology 3

Kevin Durkin

OUTLINE

Developmental social psychology investigates the origins and developmental courses of human social behaviour from infancy to old age. This chapter addresses four main themes: the nature of socialization, the development of relationships, the development of language, and the development of social knowledge. The chapter shows that life is social from the outset, and that development is profoundly affected by involvement with other people. It shows also that social behaviour is itself affected by the developmental statuses of the participants: where we are in the lifespan affects how we experience, understand and respond to the social world, and how other people perceive and respond to us.

KEY CONCEPTS

- Attachment
- Decentration
- Extended identity
- Mutuality model
- Secure base

- Socialization
- Socio-cognitive conflict
- Strange Situation
- Zone of proximal development

Introduction

How do we get into the social world in the first place? Do we change as we progress through it? And if we do change – for example, as we get older – how does this affect our social behaviour?

As a student of social psychology, you will be giving a lot of thought to processes of interpersonal and intergroup behaviour, to the ways in which cognitive activity mediates and reflects social actions, to social influences, to attitude formation and change, and to the contexts in which people behave aggressively, or generously, or competitively, or cooperatively, or seductively. Flicking through the pages ahead, you can gauge already that the agenda is lengthy and detailed. The study of social behaviour among humans is multifaceted and rich in challenges to even the most resourceful of investigators. But to each of these mysteries, there is a further complication: the fact that people develop and change over time.

Responding to other people, discerning their properties, evaluating their merits and negotiating understandings with them are not phenomena unique to the adult world. Our developmental histories and prospects affect many aspects of our behaviour; our knowledge, attitudes and expectations change as we move through life. We develop as social beings over a long time, and development ceases only with death. Furthermore, our interpersonal worlds are rarely oriented exclusively to members of one age group. As social beings, much of our time and energies are entangled with people of varied developmental statuses. Consider the people in your own life whom you know as parents, children, instructors, novices, experts, superiors, subordinates and peers. We happen not only to *be*, but also to *live among*, developing social beings.

The ways in which we develop socially, and the consequences of developmental changes for our social activities and understanding, are the province of the new and growing field of developmental social psychology. Developmental social psychology draws upon both of the subdisciplines incorporated in its title, and aims to investigate the developmental courses and the social contexts of human social behaviour (Doise, 1996; Durkin, 1995). Necessarily, it is a field of vast potential, ranging through the origins of social competencies, the development of relationships, the impact of institutions, the emergence of social reasoning, changes through the lifespan, and much more. In this introduction, four main themes of developmental social psychology will be addressed. First, responding to our initial question of how a person gets into social life in the first place, we consider the nature of **socialization**. Second, we consider the development of relationships, and development within relationships. Third, we consider the development of language, the pre-eminent medium of human communication. Finally, we examine aspects of the development of social knowledge. Human social functioning requires the ability to represent, interpret and respond to the social world;

Socialization The process whereby people acquire the rules of behaviour and the systems of beliefs and attitudes that equip a person to function effectively as a member of society.

developmental social psychologists' investigations of these capacities highlight the mutual relevance of the study of change and the study of social context.

The Nature of Socialization

What do social scientists mean when they refer to 'socialization'?
How do concepts of socialization differ?

Socialization is the process whereby people acquire the rules of behaviour and the systems of beliefs and attitudes that equip a person to function effectively as a member of society. In some areas of psychology and the neighbouring social sciences, socialization has often been taken to refer to processes by which an individual is shaped or restrained so as to fit into the society to which he or she belongs. It is seen as something which is 'done to' a malleable target or a potential menace to ensure that he or she behaves acceptably. Recent work in developmental social psychology has called this notion seriously into question.

Discussing some of the conceptual issues, Schaffer (1996) points out that traditional models represent socialization as a largely *unidirectional* process with the impetus for change and regulation coming from outside the individual being socialized (e.g., Watson, 1928). On the other hand, there are theories of socialization that see the child as arriving in society with a range of instincts and desires which she or he is disposed to vent or gratify with little concern initially for the feelings and desires of others (e.g., Freud, 1933).

Both of these theories have intuitive appeal. At the beginning of life, children do not seem fully informed on the values of the surrounding culture, and it falls to others to advise them. We know that people growing up in different communities around the world acquire markedly different sets of values and ways of behaving (Super & Harkness, 1999; Triandis, 1994). Intuitively, it seems possible that people *are* malleable – perhaps infinitely so. However, if you have ever tried to control a two-year-old in range of chocolate mousse and a banana milk shake, you may agree that junior members of the species do appear to have a will of their own, and can resist violently if necessary any cultural practices that stand in the way of their immediate goals. We can beat them down in the end, but intuitively it seems possible that humans *are* initially impulsive, hedonistic and in need of restraint. Note that our intuitions, like our scientific leaders, have just led us to two diametrically opposed conceptions of socialization: human beings are infinitely malleable, and human beings are hard to shape or restrain. You get the point: explaining everyday processes such as socialization proves much more contentious than we might have first thought.

As indicated above, in developing and testing our theories, much depends on what we choose to observe. However, in recent years our observational facilities have improved with the advent of video-recording. This technology enables researchers to look more closely at the beginnings of socialization – the early inter-

Mutuality model   A model of socialization which assumes that caregiver and child have reciprocal effects on each other's behaviour.

actions between infants and their caregivers. In the course of this work, a new perspective on socialization gained ground, a perspective which Schaffer (1996) calls the **mutuality model**. In contrast to both of the unidirectional theories sketched above, the mutuality model represents the child as an active participant in her or his own social development and it stresses the interdependence of parent and child in much of their social transactions. It does not, of course, maintain that there is no conflict in parent–child relations (see Rijt-Plooj & Plooj, 1993), but it does stress that the diverse processes that are entailed in social development are from the outset negotiated through mutual exploration and stimulation. Let us examine the beginnings of these processes.

Children as social beings from birth

Recent advances in infancy research have dispelled the early behaviourists' notion that children are blank slates at birth. There is abundant evidence that neonates bring reflexes, capacities and predispositions into the world, and that they explore and initiate as well as respond to people and things around them (Bremner, 1994). Studies of infants using measures of attentional preference and discrimination have found that from very early in life they are particularly interested in the kinds of sensory experiences that other human beings provide. For example, they prefer parents who move and talk, rather than parents who (at the experimenter's request) sit still and show no acknowledgement of their presence (Gusella, Muir, & Tronick, 1988; Legerstee, 1991). Among visual stimuli, they prefer faces to other symmetrical shapes (Johnson & Morton, 1991). In sum, the infant's perceptual capacities ensure that it attends to other people. And other people, for their part, are usually very interested in the behaviour of infants – especially their own. This fortunate coincidence results in social activities which often involve synchrony and cooperation with parental behaviour rather than opposition and reluctance (Papousek & Papousek, 1989; Schaffer, 1996).

Caregivers set the scene for early interactions by maximizing the physical opportunities for mutual interest: they hold the baby so that they are face-to-face. This simple manipulation takes advantage of both parties' interests. The baby finds a face and voice presented conveniently for attention and familiarization, and the caregiver has extensive scope to search this highly attractive new person for any and all signs of inquisitiveness, enjoyment or distress. More interestingly, a distribution of power is achieved. While the adult has greater scope for mobility and manipulation, the baby has influential resources, too: he or she can affect the intensity and pace of an interaction by withdrawing or averting gaze (Stern, 1985; Trevarthen, 1982). This promotes patterns of reciprocal effects rather than unidirectionality. During the first few weeks, mother–infant dyads evolve a rhythm to their burst–pause engagements, almost as though they were practising one of the distinctive features of human conversational interaction, namely turn-taking. Elsewhere in everyday interactions, parent and infant adjust in response to each other's movements, rather like dancers coordinating their steps (Stern, 1985). By five months or so, infants are beginning to take the initiative, especially when the interaction involves something particularly interesting, such as a new toy (Danis, 1997).

Early interactions, then, exhibit a good deal of mutuality. From the start, the infant is actively involved in her or his own social development. There is controversy among researchers concerning the relative contributions of caregiver and child to the kinds of processes summarized here (see Kochanska, 1997; Schaffer, 1996), but broad agreement that progress is only possible because of some level of *joint* activity. This bidirectional involvement is characteristic of learning about the social world throughout childhood (Durkin, 1995; Valsiner & Lawrence, 1997).

This does not end the story of socialization, but it does cast its beginnings in a new light. The infant is neither an infinitely malleable lump of clay nor a wilful beast in need of restraint. Instead, she or he is a social participant, less skilled and less informed than others, to be sure, but oriented by predispositions and circumstances to engage *with* others in the collective construction of a social world and thus become a member of the surrounding culture (Messer & Collis, 1996).

Socialization and social psychology

The findings just summarized seem interesting enough in their own terms, but why should they bear on the concerns of the social psychologist (who, it might be supposed, deals with people who have already been socialized)? In fact, socialization was once regarded as the central theme of social psychology (Sherif, 1948) and there are at least two reasons why its relevance needs to be reasserted. First, there is the 'preface' reason: this is where it all begins. From the social processes described above develop patterns and skills that are fundamental to all of our face-to-face interactions throughout life.

Second, it is in fact mistaken to imagine that socialization is only a phenomenon of childhood. Adolescence, for example, is a period of great importance in this respect, because this is a time during which adults begin to reduce their contributions to the process and young people become autonomous in organizing their social behaviour (Emler & Reicher, 1995). But each phase of adulthood typically brings new challenges and new external expectations of the developing person: we are socialized into careers, we learn and plan for the demands of new roles (partners, parents, grandparents, citizens, pensioners; see Baltes & Staudinger, 1996; Smith, 1996). Throughout life – whether as a new student at university, a trainee in the workforce, a manager or a retiree – we face recurrently the issues we met first in infancy: how do we find out what is going on, what are the limits, how much of what we do is autonomous and how much is determined in negotiation with others? The questions which preoccupy investigators of socialization, such as whether we conform, innovate, negotiate or obey, turn out to be central to social psychology (see chapter 13). These questions recur in relation to each of the three other major themes of developmental social psychology that will be addressed here, namely the development of relationships, the development of language and the development of social knowledge.

The Development of Relationships

How do our relationships with other people influence our development?
Is there continuity among patterns of relationships from infancy to adulthood?

We have seen that infants are involved with other people from the outset. One of the key themes to emerge from studies of young children's social development concerns the implications of the first relationships (with caregivers) for subsequent relationships (with peers and other people). Numerous studies have demonstrated that what happens at home is associated with what happens at the preschool and school (Hart, Nelson, Robinson, Olsen, & McNeilly-Choque, 1998; Hinde & Tamplin, 1983; Turner, 1993). Relationships have implications for other relationships (Duck, 1998; Fletcher & Fincham, 1991): for example, if a child experiences profoundly stressful relationships with the caregiver, the likelihood increases that he or she will experience difficulties in relating to siblings or to peers outside the home (Hart et al., 1998; Hay, Vespo, & Zahn-Waxler, 1998; Montagner et al., 1984).

Attachment An enduring emotional tie between one person and another one.

Although there are many interesting dimensions to the development of relationships (see also chapter 12), one particular topic has been very influential in the field of social development – the study of **attachment**.

Attachment

An attachment is a specific affectional tie formed between one person and another (Ainsworth & Bell, 1970). The formation of an attachment is reflected in a repertoire of attachment behaviours, which serve essentially to maintain proximity to the attachment figure. Examples of attachment behaviours include preferential attention, touching, clinging, calling for and crying in the absence of the specific individual or smiling in her or his presence. Such behaviours are commonly observed in infants from the second half of the first year (Schaffer, 1996). It should be noted in passing that these phenomena are by no means peculiar to infants, and attachments (as well as most of the above attachment behaviours) occur among individuals throughout life; we will return to this point. For the moment, though, let us concentrate on children's attachments.

The most influential theoretical account of the development of attachment has been that developed by the British psychiatrist John Bowlby (1969, 1988) and extended by the American social developmentalist, Mary Ainsworth (Ainsworth, Blehar, Waters, & Wall, 1978). Drawing heavily on ethological theory and

PLATE 3.1   A secure base

research, Bowlby interpreted attachment as an adaptive system of behaviour that has evolved to maximize the infant's survival prospects. Attachment behaviours, as we have seen, serve to maximize proximity to a potential caregiver and to elicit responses from her or him. They increase the likelihood that a vulnerable or distressed infant can obtain help, and they help ensure that the infant develops a **secure base** – a reliable, specific individual in the social environment whose attention and affection can be depended upon as one begins to explore the wider environment. This theory does not maintain that learning experiences with actual caregivers are irrelevant to the development and consequences of attachment, but it does hold that the capacities and organization of behaviours that promote attachment are built-in by nature rather than emerging as a result of reinforcement contingencies. Importantly, for Bowlby the secure base of a stable attachment is crucial to a child's well-being and developmental prospects.

Secure base   The feeling of security and trust associated with a specific person or place, such as a child's orientation towards his or her primary caregiver.

Types of attachment

Studies of infants and parents in quite diverse social systems around the world confirm that attachment is a normative development, occurring in almost all

Strange Situation A standardized procedure used in attachment research to test infants' reactions to separation from their caregiver and responsiveness to strangers.

children within roughly the same age span (van IJzendoorn, 1990). However, researchers soon noticed that there are individual differences in the nature of infant–caregiver relationships and in children's responses to separation from and reappearance of the caregiver. In order to study these differences systematically, Ainsworth and her colleagues devised a simple experimental procedure, known as the **Strange Situation**, in which the infant is placed (with caregiver) in an observational room. Once the child is settled down, a stranger enters and shortly afterwards she or he initiates interaction with the baby; at some point, the caregiver leaves and the stranger, after attempting to play with the child, also leaves; shortly afterwards, the stranger returns; eventually the caregiver returns and the stranger leaves.

On the basis of observational measures of the child's reactions to each of these various stresses and reunions, Ainsworth and colleagues identified three main types of attachment relationship that seem to be found in sample after sample. These are: (1) *Type A, Anxious/avoidant*: these babies show relatively little distress on the removal of the mother, and appear disinterested in interaction with her during the reunion stages of the procedure; (2) *Type B, Securely attached*: these babies seek actively to maintain proximity and interaction with the mother; they will wander and explore confidently when she is present, may show distress on her departure and they greet her return enthusiastically; (3) *Type C, Anxious/ambivalent*: these children manifest distress on the removal of the mother, yet resist contact and interaction during the reunion episodes; they appear ambivalent about the relationship, seeking proximity at times but also displaying anger.

In most samples, approximately 70 per cent of infants display Type B relationships; about 20 per cent fall into Type A, and 10 per cent into Type C (Ainsworth et al., 1978). Why this should be of interest becomes particularly clear when we go on to examine the correlates of attachment type.

Much research has been conducted into this matter, and interpretation of the findings is somewhat controversial (Lamb & Nash, 1989), but the most common published result is evidence of a social and developmental advantage to Type B, Securely attached, children. Among other things, children identified during their second year as having Type B attachments have been found during their preschool and kindergarten years to score higher on measures of interpersonal competence, self-efficacy, cognitive development, toy play, exploratory skills and eagerness to learn (Meins, 1997; Suess, Grossmann & Sroufe, 1992; Youngblade & Belsky, 1992). Kirsh and Cassidy (1997) found that securely attached preschoolers paid more attention to illustrations of the emotional dimensions of parent–child relationships and remembered them better than did insecurely attached peers. These kinds of findings are consistent with the attachment theorist's premise that the provision of a secure base is fundamental to subsequent development: as noted above, relationships have implications for other relationships.

Relationships, social development and social psychology

The study of relationships has long held a prominent place in the work of social psychologists and is one of the most promising areas for fruitful collaborations between social and developmental psychologists (Erwin, 1993; Hartup, 1991). Even so, surely the study of attachment in particular is a concern for the developmentalist rather than the social psychologist? It appears to be something to do with children and whether they grow up feeling good around people. But there are several reasons why the topic merits more careful attention from social psychologists.

First, attachment is bidirectional. It is important not only for the child but also for the caregiver(s). People report radical changes in many aspects of their lives with parenthood (Ruble, Fleming, Hackel, et al., 1988), and not least among them are the emotional and cognitive adjustments to new dependants. These are not merely domestic matters: they affect directly the parents' orientation towards the larger society, influencing their vocational orientations, economic needs and outlook, residential requirements, expectations of educational, health and welfare systems and so on. Individuals' developmental contexts and expectations influence their social contexts, and vice versa.

A second reason why attachment is important to the social psychologist returns us to an earlier point: that we continue to form attachments throughout life and they are very important to us (Berlin & Cassidy, 1999). Just as for infants, our attachments (to our partners, our family, our close friends) afford a secure base which helps us to face the hazards of the larger environment. For example, young people whose attachments have been poorly established or disrupted due to family problems are at greater risk of falling into homelessness during adolescence (Tavecchio & Thomeer, 1999; see also chapter 16 on the importance of social support to well-being). Among very old people (over 85 years), opportunities for new attachments, such as to great-grandchildren, contribute importantly to the quality of life (Wagner, Schütze, & Lang, 1999).

Interesting studies by Shaver and colleagues indicate that adults' romantic orientations can be categorized in three major patterns that are very similar to Ainsworth's typology of infant–caregiver relationships (Hazan & Shaver, 1987; Shaver, Hazan, & Bradshaw, 1988). Adults, too, exhibit the characteristics of secure, anxious/ambivalent and avoidant attachments. And, just like infants, securely attached lovers seem to have an advantage. They find close personal relationships comfortable and rewarding. They feel they can rely upon their partner but allow him or her space as an independent person. Anxious/ambivalent adults are more uncertain about their relationships, they worry that their partner may not love them enough and may leave, they demand assurances yet are inconsistent in their own displays of affection. Avoidant lovers find close relationships uncomfortable and are reluctant to commit themselves fully to their partner. Feeney, Noller and Patty (1993), in studies of undergraduates' romantic relationships, found that while secure types reported more satisfying and enduring relationships, anxious/ambivalent individuals tended to have shorter relationships, and avoidant individuals were more accepting of casual sex, presumably because they prefer uncommitted relationships.

Third, attachment is relevant not only to interpersonal relations, but also to the study of individuals' orientation to social groups and to society more generally. For example, Smith, Murphy and Coates (1999) found that people experience different psychological reactions to the social groups of which they are members: some are securely attached and feel positive about their group and its implications for their sense of self, while others experience reactions of anxiety and avoidance very similar to those of infants who have Type A or C relationships with their parents. Silverberg, Vazsonyi, Schlegel and Schmidt (1998) found in a study of German adolescents that the quality of the young person's attachment to adults predicted their optimism towards their career futures. Attachment style also appears to be associated with differences in how individuals respond to societal events, including crises. Mikulincer, Florian and Weller (1993) investigated the reactions of young Israeli adults to the Iraqi Scud missile attacks during the Gulf War. While secure types coped with the trauma by seeking support from others, ambivalent people become more emotionally volatile and avoidant people tried to distance themselves psychologically from the events. In general, insecure people suffered greater psychological distress – lacking a secure base, they found it more difficult to deal with perilous events.

It should be stressed that there are alternative explanations of the origins of attachments, and considerable controversy about their consequences (see Birns & Hay, 1988). Nevertheless, this area of research reminds us that human beings are emotional and socially entangled creatures. Our lives are influenced profoundly by relations to others, by feelings, attractions, fears of losses, dependencies and obligations. To study these adequately calls for a developmental social psychology.

The Development of Language

How do social factors contribute to the development of human beings' most distinctive cognitive capacity: language?

Much of the excitement of psycholinguistics since the 1960s has been associated with debates about origins of language and about its implications for our understanding of human nature. Following the work of the American linguist, Noam Chomsky (1965), controversy has raged over the proposition that the grammatical complexities of natural languages are such that only a species endowed with highly specific (innate) knowledge could master a language within the space of a few years. If this hypothesis is correct, then it certainly hammers a very long nail into the conceptual coffins of those who hold that human knowledge is given by experience, and that children are infinitely malleable. From this theoretical perspective, 'where it all begins' is set back very early indeed, in the child's genetic endowment.

Language raises important issues for psychology as a whole. To a large extent these issues are pursued by researchers outside of social psychology, such as psycholinguists. However, if we follow the paths of those who have tried to explain the acquisition of language, we soon find that they lead directly to factors that call for the attention of developmental social psychologists.

Social factors in the acquisition of language

Chomsky's provocative ideas set off an explosion of research into the early stages of language acquisition. Many saw support for the innateness hypothesis in the intricacies and rapidity of normal development; this remains the dominant theoretical standpoint among linguists (see Lightfoot, 1998). Others were equally impressed by the child's early achievements but saw connections between language acquisition and other developments, especially cognitive development; this perspective has greater appeal to many psychologists (Brown, 1973; Cromer, 1991; Sinclair-de-Zwart, 1967).

Social aspects of language development were not widely studied during this era, largely because the idea that interpersonal or environmental factors may be relevant seemed to have been undermined by some of the early discoveries of developmental psycholinguists. For example, children develop forms according to rules rather than simply copying adult models (e.g., they produce overregularizations such as 'comed', 'runned', 'mouses', 'mans' which are not imitations of adult utterances, but do appear to have a systematic basis); children are often impervious to the attempts of caregivers to correct their linguistic 'mistakes' (McNeill, 1970).

However, Brown's (1973) detailed longitudinal study of the language of three American preschoolers showed that one of the most fruitful means of investigating language development is to study it as it occurs spontaneously in its naturalistic contexts. Many other researchers followed suit, and it soon became clear that what the child is producing *is* related to its social experiences: to what other people are saying and doing, to the ways in which they phrase their speech to the learner, to the opportunities and feedback they provide. During the 1980s a new wave of child language research began to dissect the social contexts of language development (Golinkoff, 1983; Snow, 1986).

This research revealed a number of important ways in which language development involves social factors. For example, consistent with other evidence that infants have an interest in the distinctive properties of humans, researchers found that babies show attentional preferences for human voices, and particularly for voices that are high-pitched and varied in intonation (Fernald, 1989; Masataka, 1992). Caregivers modify the complexity of their speech to early language learners, speaking more slowly, in shorter and simpler utterances, using greater emphasis and more repetition than in adult–adult conversations (Moerk, 1992;

Snow, 1999). Caregivers work hard to develop and then exploit a meaningful shared context for language experiences (Akhtar, Dunham, & Dunham, 1991; Saxon, 1997; Tomasello, 1992): they follow or guide the child's attention (for example, to an interesting object) and then supply the appropriate label ('Look – it's a gorilla!', 'Mummy's got a biscuit'). Language acquisition is not a task that the infant embarks on alone, but a highly interactive engagement affected by the social context.

This conclusion is borne out as we follow children further along their developmental path. Linguistic advances are manifest in formal properties (e.g., more complex syntax, greater phonological control, rapidly expanding vocabularies), but also in terms of what young language users become able to do with others. Conversational skills provide a key example. While very early conversations depend greatly on the efforts of the more proficient caregiver for their momentum and structure, during the preschool years children become more active partners, taking the initiative more often and then sustaining the topic for longer (McTear, 1985). During this period, children are also learning the rules of politeness in discourse: they learn that sometimes it is more effective to express a request indirectly ('That's a lovely cake, Daddy') than directly ('Gimme cake'), and that conventional markers such as 'please' and 'thank you' can facilitate everyday negotiations (Baroni & Axia, 1989; Ninio & Snow, 1999).

Some conversational skills are especially demanding, and develop over a long time. For example, taking adequate account of an interlocutor's perspective requires awareness of others' minds, the ability to conceive of a different way of looking at something, understanding of when and how to supply information verbally, detection of possible ambiguities in what is being said, and the ability to monitor both one's own performance in these respects and others' reactions (Robinson & Whittaker, 1986). Not surprisingly, these are not instantaneous achievements. For example, Lloyd, Camaioni and Ercolani (1995), testing English and Italian children, found that fewer than 10 per cent of six-year-olds and only 20 per cent of nine-year-olds were able to detect ambiguities in a task that involved sharing information with a peer.

There are many other ways in which language is integral to social life and development. Language serves as a social marker (Giles & Powesland, 1975), revealing a person's group membership (such as social class, regional affiliation, ethnicity), and children and adolescents become increasingly sensitive to the importance of this information and adjust their behaviour and attitudes towards others accordingly (Durkin, 1995; Ninio & Snow, 1999).

Language and social psychology

Clearly, these issues raise vital matters for developmentalists, but do they bear on the work of social psychologists? At a general level, of course, we encounter the 'preface' point again: all of the aspects of language we have touched upon here are relevant to adult communicative processes (and adults, as stressed earlier, interact with individuals of varied developmental statuses). A full understanding of language use can only be achieved if we incorporate a plausible account of its development.

More specifically, both developmental and social psychologists have become interested in the intersections of language and social cognition: for example, in questions such as how our social purposes are reflected in our language patterns, and how the structures of the language and vocabulary may influence our social perceptions and social behaviour (Semin & Fiedler, 1992; Wigboldus, Semin, & Spears, 2000; see also chapter 5). Social psychologists have drawn attention to speech accommodation processes (Giles & Coupland, 1991), whereby we adjust our speech style according to the language of our interactant – sometimes moving closer (e.g., shifting towards his or her accent) and sometimes moving away (e.g., exaggerating a regional accent, speaking in a language that the other party does not know). This work raises questions about the developmental origins of such processes, and the possibility that social-psychological theories can provide more general explanatory frameworks for phenomena that developmentalists have studied. One example is the kinds of speech modifications adults make when talking to very young children, discussed earlier. Many adults make very similar adjustments when addressing elderly people: they speak to them slowly, simplifying sentence structure, using a higher pitch and emphasizing or repeating key words (Coupland & Coupland, 1995; Kemper, Ferrell, Harden, Finter-Urczyk, & Billington, 1998). While perhaps well-intentioned, this speech accommodation sends an implicit message to the older person that she or he is perceived as less competent, almost child-like. Thus, investigating language uses requires both a social perspective (to account for the influence of interpersonal relations and expectations) and a developmental one (to account for the effects of age of addressee).

Language is crucial to our involvements with others. It is integral to the sharing of cultural understandings, to the expression and regulation of social status, and to the recording and transmission of societies' achievements, beliefs and aspirations. These are inextricably developmental and social processes, and they continue to develop throughout life.

The Development of Social Knowledge

How do we develop an understanding of people and society?
Does interaction with others affect cognitive processes and their development?
How do children develop preferences for and against different groups of people?

As we have seen, if you are going to participate in the social world, you need to be able to orient to others, to form relationships with selected individuals, to learn the local system of communication – but there is more. You need also to find ways of sharing ideas with other people, of learning from what they know, of developing solutions jointly; you need to understand what people are, how they function psychologically and how they organize social relations. These are among the principal tasks of the development of social knowledge, or social cognition. In this section, we consider research into these topics under two main headings: social interaction and understanding, and understanding the social world.

Social interaction and understanding

The great Swiss psychologist, Jean Piaget (1896–1980), acknowledged the relevance of social psychology to his pioneering studies of the development of reasoning in children (e.g., 1973). He maintained, for example, that interactions with peers were a crucial factor in the development of reasoning about social topics (such as moral understanding; Piaget, 1932a). However, in practice much of his work and that of other Piagetians focused on the cognitive achievements of the 'individual' child, who was represented in the theory as a kind of mini-scientist evolving, testing and revising his or her understanding through logically progressive stages of reasoning.

As a reminder, let us review briefly Piaget's standard conservation experiments. The child participant is presented with two identical amounts of some substance. In the best-known version, these are two identical amounts of liquid in identical beakers. Once the child has confirmed that they are the same amount, the contents of one of the original beakers is transferred to a third beaker of a different shape: say, taller and thinner. Then, the child is asked whether the new beaker contains the same amount of liquid as the remaining original beaker. Intriguingly, children aged below about six years usually declare that the contents of the new beaker are different – either more or less than the original. Often, they add explanations like ''cos it's taller' or 'that one's thinner'. In other words, children seem to fail to conserve mentally the volume of the transferred liquid, and instead are seduced by the perceptual transformation that makes it look greater or less than the original. A child who gives this sort of response is usually termed a 'non-conserver'.

Decentration The ability to take account simultaneously of different aspects of a task rather than to centre exclusively on one.

Piaget theorized that the non-conserving child was failing to perform at least two critical mental operations. First, the child fails to reverse the transformation: he or she seems not to consider that if the liquid removed from the first beaker is returned to it, it will fill exactly the same amount of space that it left. Second, the child fails to **decentre**: that is, he or she focuses on one aspect of the transformed liquid (such as its new height) and ignores the compensating changes on other dimensions (such as its new width).

If you run this experiment with a five-year-old you will get a sense of the alluring questions that Piaget's simple but ingenious techniques provoke. Whether or not Piaget's explanation is correct and the extent to which methodological procedures in tasks such as the conservation test might distort our impressions of children's underlying abilities have occasioned much dispute among developmentalists. In the course of this work, the child's involvement with other people was not always a foremost consideration, and the central question was usually: 'How does the mini-scientist tackle this or that logical or mathematical problem?'

Recent developments in developmental social psychology, especially in Europe, have cast these issues in a new, more social, perspective. A group of Genevan psychologists and their collaborators have revived interest in Piaget's (1932a) early argument that cognitive disagreement among peers promoted cognitive development (Doise & Mugny, 1984; Doise & Palmonari, 1984; Perret-Clermont, 1980).

Peer interaction and cognitive development

The starting point of this work was a study in 1975 by Doise, Mugny and Perret-Clermont. Using a conservation of liquid task, these researchers reported the interesting finding that six- to seven-year-olds working together (in twos or threes) performed at a higher level than they had done individually in pre-tests. Furthermore, initially non-conserving children who worked with peers who could conserve subsequently performed at a higher level on post-tests than children who did not participate in the collaborative sessions.

It might be argued that, noteworthy as such an outcome is, the children have merely learned to imitate the behaviour of more competent peers, and have not actually advanced their understanding of the cognitive problem posed to them. However, the children were able to provide explanations of their judgements at a higher level than at the outset, making reference now to matters such as reversibility, compensations for changes in height or width and so on – responses that suggest definite insights had been gained.

Even so, in this study at least one of the participants knew the 'correct' answer, and could pass the explanation on to her or his peers. Still more interesting are other experiments showing that non-conserving children can profit from social interaction with other non-conservers (see, for example, Mugny, Levy, & Doise, 1978; Rijsman, Zoetebier, Ginther, & Doise, 1980). It seems that generating contradictory perspectives – even if each perspective is erroneous – may promote decentring, which we saw above was one of the things that individual children seem not to do in the standard conservation task. Doise and Mugny maintain that social interaction is fundamental to cognitive development because 'a conflict is created which makes the difference explicit' (1984, p. 160).

The benefits of **socio-cognitive conflict** are not restricted to children struggling with conservation problems. Other research using similar experimental paradigms has shown that gains acquired through social interaction can be generalized to other tasks (Perret-Clermont, 1980; Valiant, Glachan, & Emler, 1982). Improved

Socio-cognitive conflict The communication of discrepancies between the perspectives of two or more participants in a task, which promotes opportunities for the participants to become more aware of deficiencies in their individual understanding.

PLATE 3.2   Conservation and social interaction: sharing fruit juice can promote attention and insight
(Doise & Mugny, 1984)

performance as a result of social interaction on more advanced cognitive tasks has also been demonstrated with older children and adolescents (Blaye, Light, Joiner, & Sheldon, 1991; Doise & Hanselmann, 1990; Howe, Tolmie, & Rodgers, 1992). For example, Light, Littleton, Messer and Joiner (1994) found that 11-year-olds, given a complex computer task over a series of sessions, fared better if working in pairs; importantly, the relative advantage to children who had worked jointly (in Sessions 1 and 2, in figure 3.1) was sustained even when they were tested again individually (Session 3).

This work in turn has led to differences of opinion among psychologists as to what is entailed in the social interactive processes. Doise and Mugny (1984) emphasize socio-cognitive conflict (i.e., conflict with others), but other researchers stress the *intra*psychological processes (i.e., conflict within the self) that may be engaged by the tasks (Emler & Valiant, 1982; Howe et al., 1990). Although the debate continues, it has affected the character of cognitive developmental research by bringing social processes to the fore (Azmitia, 1996; Durkin, 1995). In this respect, it illustrates one of the principal ways in which developmental psychology has begun to profit from a closer relationship with social psychology. Let us turn now to another.

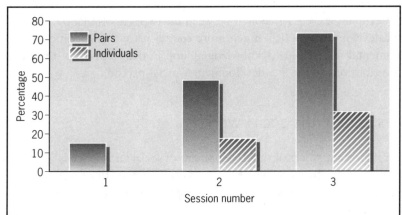

FIGURE 3.1 Percentages of children succeeding on a complex computer task for each condition in each session. Note that in Session 3 all children are working individually so that here 'pairs' denotes those who *previously* worked in pairs
(Light et al., 1994)

Vygotskyan perspectives on social interaction and knowledge

The work of another influential European psychologist, Vygotsky (1896–1934), has also inspired developmentalists to study socio-cultural factors in the genesis of knowledge (Rogoff, 1990; Wertsch & Tulviste, 1992). Vygotsky maintains that through participation in social activity the individual becomes immersed in practices which gradually transform his or her own capabilities. He argues that through doing things with others, children progressively take on the skills and knowledge of their more competent partners until eventually they become capable of autonomous performance.

One of Vygotsky's most stimulating ideas is that of the **zone of proximal development** (ZPD). This concept is concerned essentially with the child's potentialities; it refers to the distance between what the child can do unaided and what he or she can do in collaboration with, or under the guidance of, others. Vygotsky asserts a central function for the social exchanges between learner and partners working within the child's ZPD. Much of Vygotsky's and his followers' research has been focused on how these processes occur, including studies of how children increase their abilities to take advantage of more advanced individuals' expertise and how adults organize their input around the child's current level of functioning (see Lloyd & Fernyhough, 1999).

Zone of proximal development
The distance between what the child can do unaided and what he or she can do in collaboration with, or under the guidance of, others.

You can see that there are some differences and some similarities between Vygotskyan theory and that of the social Genevans. Vygotsky stresses cooperation and guidance among tutors and learners (or 'apprentices'), while Doise and Mugny highlight conflict and resolution. But these may be differences in emphasis rather than mutually exclusive perspectives (Tudge, 1999; Rogoff, 1990). Certainly, there is agreement between the two schools that the social dimensions of development merit a much more central place than traditional cognitive developmental research has acknowledged, and in this respect both make important contributions towards a developmental social psychology.

Understanding the social world

Another important aspect of the development of social knowledge is understanding social phenomena. In recent years there has been a growth of research into how children perceive and think about other people, about social relations and about the social structure.

Developing understanding of other people's attributes, feelings and mental processes

Knowledge of the personal attributes and mental processes of others is a prerequisite to many tasks in social reasoning. The child needs to grasp that other people have unique characteristics, which help us to distinguish among them, and to appreciate that they are thinking, knowing and feeling entities, which helps us to interact with them. This knowledge can only be obtained in social contexts. Family and peer relationships provide the natural starting point for discoveries about other people's characteristics, including their beliefs, intentions and emotions (Dunn, 1988; Meins, 1997).

Although this knowledge is initiated early in life, its development proceeds throughout childhood, adolescence and beyond. Person *descriptions* become more focused on internal, psychological properties with age (Newman, 1991; Yuill, 1992). In tasks using different methodologies, it has been demonstrated that by at least five years of age children can use information about a person's psychological attributes to predict how he or she will behave in another situation (Bennett, 1985–6; Yuill, 1993). Even earlier, children are developing a 'theory of mind' – an understanding that they and other people have mental processes, such as thought, perception and memory (Flavell, 1999; Mitchell, 1997).

These are complex and elusive matters for the young child. After all, we never observe directly other people's mental activities or even their emotions. At most, we witness external correlates or outcomes and from these we make inferences about what underlies a person's behaviour. Although challenging, young children do make progress in this domain and it seems that learning about the psychological world depends crucially upon involvement in social contexts (Dunn, 1999; Newton, Reddy, & Bull, 2000; Symons & Clark, 2000).

An interesting example of the importance of interpersonal processes to the development of emotional understanding is provided by research into the concept of

extended identity (Bennett, Yuill, Banerjee, & Thomson, 1998; Semin & Papadopoulou, 1990). Semin and Papadopoulou asked mothers to estimate their own and their child's embarrassment in the course of everyday mishaps (such as dropping a bottle in a supermarket, spilling soup in a restaurant). The older the child, the greater the degree of embarrassment the mother expected him or her to feel. But the less

> **Extended identity** The awareness that social judgements of us may reflect our associations with other people.

embarrassment the child felt, the more the mother anticipated for herself. It appears that the parent perceives herself and child as a unit, and feels a responsibility for the unit to meet public requirements. In such ways, we learn much about feelings through involvement with those who already have them (see chapter 6). Bennett et al. found that children themselves develop, during middle childhood, a sense of extended responsibility and sense of embarrassment for the (mis-)behaviour of their parents, playmates or younger children in their care (see figure 3.2).

The tasks of understanding other people are highly motivating and decidedly adaptive. It is vital to know who is who in the social environment, and what different individuals are likely to do for – or to – you. Children begin to differentiate among others in infancy, but from the preschool years on they are increasingly able to take into account people's psychological properties, making inferences about intentions, beliefs and emotions and in due course coming to

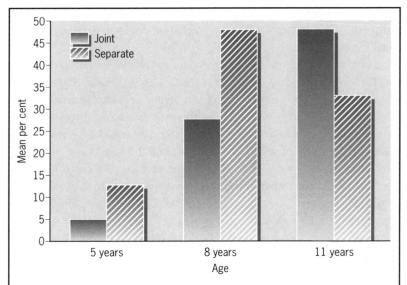

FIGURE 3.2 Children's sense of extended identity as a function of age (Adapted from Bennett et al., 1998)
'Joint' = belief that an audience would judge child and companion jointly for the companion's misbehaviour (e.g., 'They'd think we were a pair of troublemakers').
'Separate' = belief that an audience would judge child and companion independently (e.g., 'They're just thinking that my mum is stupid').

appreciate that these are reciprocal processes: that other people also attempt to interpret our mental states and purposes (Mitchell, 1997).

National and ethnic categorization

If we move to still broader levels of social structure, such as the relations between different societies or different ethnic groups, then much more is entailed than cognitive computation. Tajfel (1981) has long stressed that cognitive and affective factors become inseparable in this domain. People are not only categorized into different groups, but they tend to have strong feelings about their group membership and about other groups (see chapter 15).

Prejudice is one of the core topics of social psychology (Brown, 1995). There are theoretical challenges in explaining why people hold derogatory attitudes towards others based on their membership of a social group, and there are obvious practical reasons why we need to understand the origins and consequences of this hostility.

People do not suddenly become prejudiced in adulthood. While we can certainly study prejudice among adults, to investigate where it comes from, a developmental perspective is indispensable. When, for example, do children begin to classify people according to social categories? When do children first form prejudices? Why do some children become or appear to be very prejudiced, and others do not? The answers to these questions are not as straightforward as might first be expected.

Children are able to identify some aspects of ethnicity – particularly skin colour – during the preschool years. Clark and Clark (1947) found that young Americans responded with above-chance accuracy when asked to identify a 'white' or a 'brown' doll from choices presented by the experimenters; three-year-olds were good at this task, five-year-olds were near perfect. It could be objected that this is little more than a test of colour knowledge, but the Clarks also found that the white and black children tended to identify themselves with the doll of the same ethnicity, and these and other researchers have reported that preschoolers tend to show ethnic preferences in these kinds of tasks (see Brown, 1995; Nesdale, in press, for more extensive discussions).

Children also develop views about the importance of national categorization. An early study by Tajfel and Jahoda (1966) revealed that by around age six or seven years, although children's empirical knowledge of different countries was minimal (e.g., they knew little of matters such as relative size), their affective orientation was well established; they had quite firm views about which countries they liked or disliked. In a series of studies of six- to 12-year-olds conducted in England, the Netherlands, Austria, Scotland, Belgium and Italy, Tajfel and Jahoda and their collaborators asked children to identify their likes and dislikes from a set of photographs of young men, and on a separate occasion to distinguish which of the men they believed were members of their own national group.

They found that the younger children showed a distinct preference for photographs of men they would also categorize as from their own country; the preference was less marked in older children, though still present in some countries.

For Tajfel, the importance of these kinds of findings is that they provide 'evidence of the very high sensitivity of young children to the more primitive aspects of the value systems of their societies' (1981, p. 206). However, there appears to be more to the development of national and ethnic prejudices than the direct absorption of adult prejudices (Aboud, 1988; Brown, 1995). For example, the correlations between children's prejudices and those of their parents have been found in several studies to be rather weak (see Brown, 1995). In a review of several decades' research into children's prejudices, Aboud shows that children's views are not invariably direct replicas of those of their parents or other salient community sources. In fact, at around ages four or five, children's ethnic biases are often *stronger* than those of adults. Aboud argues that this is a function of an early social-cognitive reliance on perceptual features (such as colour of skin, clothing, language) that provide an easy basis for comparing self with others. Once a distinction is made, then it tends to be accompanied with a strong affective orientation – typically, wariness or even dislike of the outgroup. With further social-cognitive development, children build up a greater amount of factual knowledge about other social categories and increasing awareness that intergroup relations are reciprocal (i.e., that if you are a foreigner to me, then perhaps I am a foreigner to you). This may mitigate the simplistic concepts and starker prejudices of the younger child (Doyle, Beaudet, & Aboud, 1988; see figure 3.3).

Aboud's work, then, indicates that there is a strong cognitive developmental component to the development (and eventual demise) of prejudice. On the other hand, this theory does not explain fully why some individuals retain prejudices into adolescence and beyond, despite normal cognitive development. Some studies find that prejudices against outgroups on the basis of nationality or ethnicity do not decline or may even increase during middle childhood (Nesdale, in press), or emerge only among older children (over ten years; see Rutland, 1999), or even increase during the college years (Hoover & Fishbein, 1999): how many racially prejudiced people have you met at university? Children's social-cognitive development is part of the picture, but the intergroup relations, social stratification and ideological structures of the surrounding society appear also to play an important role in the development of prejudice.

In sum, part of the developing person's task is to discover what the social world is like: what are the properties of people, how are things organized, what are the rules, and so on. But these are not just interesting intellectual puzzles for the mini-social psychologist to work on in preparation for adulthood. From the outset, the child is immersed in a social world, is learning through participation, and participation affects the content and processes of learning. Part of the challenge of developmental social psychology is to account for the dynamic tensions arising from the intersection of developmental changes in capacities and the social contexts in which development comes about.

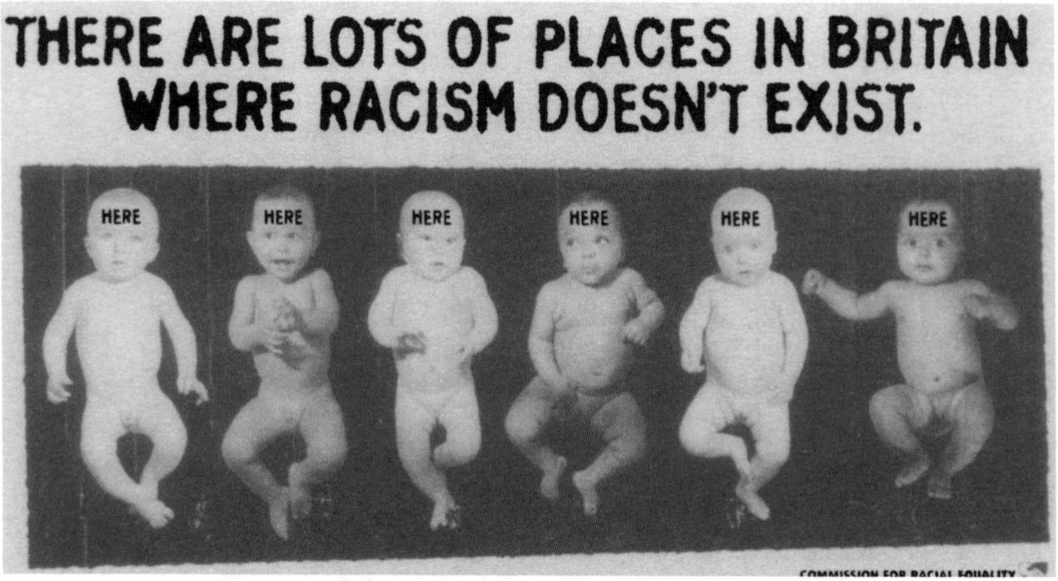

PLATE 3.3   This advertisement, part of an anti-racism campaign run by the Commission for Racial Equality, raises the question: 'when does prejudice develop?'

Social knowledge and social psychology

Why should all this matter to the social psychologist? Once again, is it not reasonable to assume that adults have already dealt with these matters, and by the time they get to the laboratory are fully functioning in mature state? As above, part of the answer rests on the preface argument: a comprehensive account of human social reasoning entails an understanding of its origins and development. For example, some theories of prejudice among adults assume that some stereotypes (such as ethnicity) are deeply ingrained because of their lengthy developmental history, and hence are activated automatically in response to relevant stimuli (such as a person from a particular group), even among individuals who are expressly non-prejudiced (Devine, 1995). In fact, recent work in developmental social psychology has shown that all of the central processes of interest to investigators of adult social cognition, to be discussed in more detail in chapters 5 to 8, have complex developmental origins (Durkin, 1995). It is also the case that biases in social reasoning may reflect strategies that proved useful at earlier stages of development. For example, it was an early observation of Piaget's (1928) – that the first thing to interest a child about a country was its name – which provided the starting point to Tajfel's later studies of the influence of group membership and group identity upon social judgements (see chapter 15).

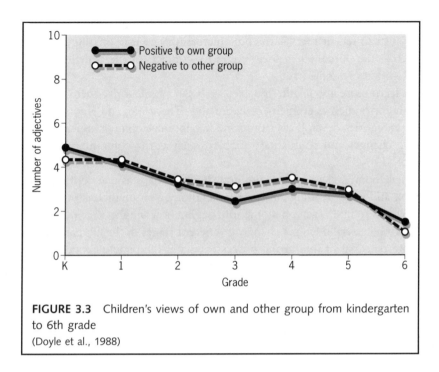

FIGURE 3.3   Children's views of own and other group from kindergarten to 6th grade
(Doyle et al., 1988)

Summary and Conclusions

We develop as social beings over time. As we develop, we interact with, and learn from, other people who are also developing. The study of these processes requires a synthesis of two fields: developmental social psychology.

This chapter has introduced some of the issues investigated by developmental social psychologists. We considered broadly the nature of socialization. We saw that traditional theories of infants as either infinitely malleable or wilful beasts in need of restraint have been displaced by theories that emphasize mutuality and negotiation as the bases for discovering the social world. Research reveals that infants are very active – perceptually, cognitively, emotionally – as they strive to make sense of their environment.

From the first months, forming and maintaining relationships with others is fundamental. This starts in infancy but is not unique to that phase of life: relationships are important throughout. Interestingly, recent research in social psychology has drawn heavily on developmental models of attachments to further our understanding of the origins and consequences of different patterns of relationship.

Becoming a social being involves all the basic psychological processes, including perceptual discrimination, cognition and communication. In all of these, other people are important not simply as things to be learned about, but as agents with whom we collaborate and as sources of different points of view. Developmental psychologists in recent years have come increasingly to take account of social factors, such as the outcomes of socio-cognitive conflicts or the benefits of 'apprenticeship' to a more skilled tutor.

As we learn more about other people, we begin to categorize them. We draw on social categories such as ethnicity or nationality. The values and emotions attached to these categories develop over time and, again, development appears to involve cognitive changes and contextual variables (such as the community's values and prejudices).

The developmental story does not end there. Perhaps as you continue through this book and other readings in social psychology, you might ask yourself: when and how does this social phenomenon begin, how might the individual's responses to that social dilemma change at different stages of the lifespan, how might those interpersonal or intergroup processes vary if the people concerned were in different age bands? These kinds of questions underline the need for a developmental social psychology.

DISCUSSION POINTS

1 Describe the chief differences between unidirectional and mutual models of socialization.
2 Outline some of the perceptual capacities of the human infant, and summarize their consequences for relating to other people.
3 List some of the attachment behaviours of (a) infants, (b) older children and (c) adults. What functions do these behaviours have in common?
4 Do patterns of attachment formed in infancy influence social relationships in adulthood?
5 How does the developmental status of the addressee influence the language of the speaker?
6 What is socio-cognitive conflict and what are its consequences?
7 Why do some young children exhibit stronger ethnic prejudices than their parents?
8 When does social development stop? Consider the implications of your answer for social psychology.

FURTHER READING

Aboud, F. (1988). *Children and prejudice*. Oxford: Blackwell. A review of research into ethnic prejudice in children and a social-cognitive model of developmental changes.

Bennett, M. (Ed.). (1993). *The child as psychologist. An introduction to the development of social cognition*. New York: Harvester Wheatsheaf. A valuable set of essays on developmental social cognition.

Cassidy, J., & Shaver, P. R. (Eds.). (1999). *Handbook of attachment: Theory, research and clinical applications*. New York: Guilford Press. A thorough review and synthesis of the current state of knowledge about attachment and loss in children and adults.

Doise, W., & Mugny, G. (1984). *The social development of the intellect.* Oxford: Pergamon. The standard introduction to the work of the 'social Genevans'.

Durkin, K. (1995). *Developmental social psychology: From infancy to old age.* Oxford: Blackwell. A fuller account of the issues introduced in this chapter and of other key topics in developmental social psychology, including gender, media, aggression, prosocial behaviour, morality and development through adulthood.

Emler, N., & Reicher, S. (1995). *Adolescence and delinquency.* Oxford: Blackwell. A developmental social psychological study of the nature and causes of delinquency.

Ruble, D. N., & Goodnow, J. (1998). Social development from a lifespan perspective. In D. T. Gilbert, S. T. Fiske, & G. Lindzey (Eds.), *The handbook of social psychology* (4th ed., pp. 741–87). New York: McGraw-Hill. An extensive review of the intersection of developmental and social psychology.

Schaffer, H. R. (1996). *Social development.* Oxford: Blackwell. An authoritative account of social development in childhood.

Tajfel, H., Nemeth, C., Jahoda, G., Campbell, J. D., & Johnson, N. B. (1970). The development of children's preference for their own country: A cross-national study. *International Journal of Psychology*, 6, 245–53.

KEY STUDY

Methodology in Social Psychology: Tools to Test Theories

4

Antony S. R. Manstead and Gün R. Semin

OUTLINE

In this chapter we describe the main methods used by social psychologists in gathering empirical information. We distinguish between three basic types of research – descriptive, correlational and experimental – and we note that social-psychological research is typically experimental or quasi-experimental in nature. We draw a distinction between research strategies and data collection techniques. Three research strategies are described: survey research, quasi-experiments and true randomized experiments. Experimentation is singled out for detailed discussion because of its prominence as a research strategy in social psychology. We identify three principal data collection techniques: observational measurement, self-report measurement and implicit measures. Finally, we note that some social psychologists have questioned the utility of conventional methods, and of laboratory experiments in particular.

KEY CONCEPTS

- Confederate
- Confounding
- Construct
- Construct validity
- Control group
- Cover story
- Debriefing
- Demand characteristics
- Dependent variable
- Experiment
- Experimental group
- Experimental scenario
- Experimenter effects
- External validity
- Factorial experiment
- Field experiment
- Hawthorne effect
- Hypothesis
- Implicit measures
- Independent variable
- Interaction effect
- Interaction process analysis (IPA)
- Internal validity
- Likert scale

- Main effect
- Manipulation check
- Mediating variable
- Meta-analysis
- One-shot case study
- Operationalization
- Participant observation
- Post-experimental enquiry
- Post-test only control group design
- Quasi-experiment
- Quota sample
- Reactivity
- Reliability
- Sample survey
- Sampling
- Semantic differential
- Simple random sample
- Social desirability
- Stooge
- Theory
- True randomized experiment
- Unobtrusive measures
- Validity
- Variable

Introduction

How do social psychologists develop their theories?
How do social psychologists go about testing their theories?

Procedures for gathering information in any discipline are known as *methods*. Methods provide a means of translating a researcher's ideas into actions. The researcher's ideas will generally revolve around one or more questions about a phenomenon. An example of such a question in social psychology would be: 'How can a group of capable people make a decision that is stupid and could have been shown to be so at the time the decision was taken?' (cf. Janis, 1982b, and chapter 13 of this book). A researcher interested in this question might have a hunch or a theory to explain this phenomenon. For example, it might be thought that the poor decision arises from the fact that the group has a powerful leader who expresses a preference early in the decision-making process and thereby stifles systematic evaluation of superior options. Assessing the correctness of this hunch would necessitate the collection of information about styles of leadership in groups making poor decisions. Methods are the procedures the researcher would follow in gathering that information, and *methodology* is a term used to refer to all aspects of the implementation of methods.

Although this chapter is concerned above all with the methods used by social psychologists to test the validity of their ideas, it is worth giving some consideration to the issue of where these ideas originate. In the typical case, the researcher begins with a **theory** about the phenomenon under investigation. Where does such a theory come from? One obvious source is observation of real-world events. For

> **Theory** A set of abstract concepts (i.e., constructs), together with propositions about how those constructs are related to one another.

example, Janis' (1982b) theory concerning the poor quality of decision-making that is sometimes apparent in groups, even when the groups consist of competent and experienced persons, was stimulated by reading accounts of how the United States government took the decision to invade Cuba in 1961, a decision that has been called 'the perfect failure' (Janis, 1982b, p. 14). Here is the starting point for Janis' theory of defective decision-making by groups: a puzzling real-world phenomenon, namely the ability of a highly qualified group of individuals to arrive at a remarkably poor decision. Having previously conducted a good deal of research on group dynamics, Janis was acquainted with the way in which strong normative pressures can build up in groups, encouraging their members to maintain friendly relations with each other at the expense of critical thinking. The undermining of critical and independent thinking in social groups that results from strong pressures towards uniformity is what Janis called 'groupthink'. Thus a second important element of theory-building in social psychology is existing theory. The fact that Janis was already conversant with research on group processes and social influence in groups provided him with a conceptual armoury that he could use to explain defective decision-making by groups.

Another version of this process of theory-building begins not with a puzzling real-world phenomenon but with a puzzling set of apparently conflicting findings from previous research. A well-known example in social psychology is Zajonc's (1965) attempt to reconcile conflicting findings in previous studies of the effects on individual task performance of being observed by others (see chapter 14). Zajonc pointed out that some researchers had found that being observed by others had beneficial effects on task performance, whereas other researchers had found that being observed by others resulted in poorer performance. To explain these conflicting findings, Zajonc drew on principles derived from learning theory. Once again, then, the theorist began with a phenomenon that required an explanation, and drew on existing theoretical concepts and processes to make sense of that phenomenon.

In what sense does a theory 'explain' a phenomenon such as the defective decision-making of high-calibre groups, or the conflicting effects of being observed on task performance? Social-psychological theories usually consist of a set of concepts and a set of statements concerning the relationships among these concepts. For example, Janis' (1982b) theory consists of one group of concepts representing the antecedent conditions of groupthink, another set representing the symptoms of groupthink, and a third set representing the process linking antecedent conditions with symptoms. An example of an antecedent condition is a 'cohesive group', that is, a group whose members are psychologically dependent on the group. Because they are dependent on their group membership, reasoned Janis, they will be more likely to conform to what they believe to be the consensus position in the group. An example of a symptom of groupthink is the presence in the group of 'mind guards', the term Janis used to describe group members who take it upon themselves to protect the group from information that would question the correctness or morality of the emerging decision. The mediating process specified by Janis is a 'concurrence-seeking tendency', a powerful preference for agreement with fellow group members. Thus antecedent conditions are linked to symptoms via a mediating process.

Three concepts need to be introduced at this point. **Construct** is the term used to refer to abstract concepts in a theory. For example, in Janis' theory concepts such as group cohesiveness and concurrence-seeking tendency are theoretical *constructs.* **Variable** is a term used to refer to a measurable representation of a construct. To represent the construct of group cohesiveness, for example, we might assess one or more of the following: how long the group has been in existence; the extent to which group members nominate each other as personal friends; how much group members say they value their membership of the group; and how much conflict and dissent is expressed within the group. Here we can see that the construct of cohesiveness has several possible ways of being represented as a variable. In their research, social psychologists work with variables, rather than constructs, because variables can be measured. **Operationalization** refers to the way in which a construct is turned into a measured variable in a particular study. If we choose to measure group cohesiveness in terms of how much group members value their membership of the group, this is a different operationalization of cohesiveness than if we choose to measure how much dissent there is in the group.

> **Construct**   An abstract theoretical concept (such as social influence).

> **Variable**   The term used to refer to the measurable representation of a construct (*see also* **independent variable** and **dependent variable**).

> **Operationalization**   The way in which a theoretical construct is turned into a measurable dependent variable or a manipulable independent variable in a particular study.

How can a theory be used to guide research? Having proposed a theory, one normally derives predictions from it. In the case of Janis' theory, one prediction that can be logically derived from the theory is that groups that are characterized by greater cohesiveness should be more prone to poor-quality decisions than groups that are lower in cohesiveness. Armed with such a prediction (or **hypothesis**), the researcher will then set about trying to accumulate evidence to support the prediction. To the extent that the evidence is consistent with the prediction, confidence in the theory from which the prediction was derived is enhanced. Correspondingly, if the evidence is inconsistent with the prediction, confidence in the underlying theory is weakened. Methods are the means by which researchers put their ideas to the test.

> **Hypothesis**   A proposed explanation for an observed relationship between events.

It is useful at this point to distinguish between three broad types of research: descriptive, correlational and experimental. *Descriptive research* is intended to provide the researcher with an accurate description of the phenomenon in question ('Does *A* occur?'). For example, a researcher may want to know (as did Milgram,

1963) whether the average adult would obey orders from an authority figure to administer painful and potentially lethal electric shocks to a fellow human (see chapter 13). The researcher would begin by observing and recording the proportion of adults that obeys an authority's orders. This simply describes the phenomenon. Social-psychological research rarely stops at this point. The researcher typically wants to know *why* people behave as they do. If one finds, as did Milgram, that 65 per cent of a sample of adults are fully obedient to orders to administer shocks, an obvious question is, 'Why?'

Correlational research takes us part of the way to answering this question. The goal here is to describe the extent to which variations in some behaviour, such as obedience, are related systematically to variations in some other factor ('Is *A* related to *B*?'). For example, do those who obey orders tend to be particular *types* of persons (men rather than women, introverts rather than extroverts, and so on)? In posing such questions, the researcher is looking for relationships, or *correlations*, between the measured variables. Discovering such a relationship is a helpful first step in establishing why a phenomenon occurs, but causal conclusions cannot be unambiguously drawn on the basis of correlational information. To understand why this is so, take the case of a correlational finding from Milgram's (1965) study of obedience. It was found that persons who were more obedient tended also to report experiencing more tension during their participation in the study. How should we interpret this correlation? Is the tension a sign of fear of the consequences of disobedience, which would suggest that obedience is 'caused' by individuals' fears about what might happen to them if they were disobedient? Alternatively, might the tension simply reflect concern about the possible harm befalling the 'victim'? In the first case, the relationship between obedience (*A*) and tension (*B*) is explained as '*B* leads to *A*'; in the second case, the same relationship is interpreted as '*A* leads to *B*'. Yet another possibility is that the relationship between *A* and *B* is caused by some third variable, *C*. In the Milgram case, for example, one possibility is that both the obedience and the tension are caused by aggressiveness, and that the relationship between obedience and tension is therefore not a causal one at all. In the absence of further information, any of these interpretations is plausible. This is why it is almost always impossible to infer causality from correlational research.

Experimental research is explicitly designed to yield causal information. The goal of an **experiment** is to see what happens to a phenomenon, such as obedience, when the researcher deliberately modifies some feature of the environment in which the phenomenon occurs ('If I change variable *B*, will there be resulting changes in variable *A*?'). By controlling the variation in *B*, the researcher can arrive at stronger conclusions about causality if it is found that *A* and *B* are related.

Experiment A method in which the researcher deliberately introduces some change into a setting to examine the consequences of that change.

Instead of simply knowing that more of variable *A* is associated with more of variable *B*, the experimental researcher discovers whether *A* increases when *B* is increased, decreases when *B* is reduced, remains stable when *B* is left unchanged, and so on. Such a pattern of results would suggest that the manipulated variations in *B cause* the observed variations in *A*. We will have a lot more to say about experimental research below.

The descriptive, correlational and experimental research types are very general kinds of research method, and are by no means specific to psychology or social psychology. Which of these approaches is adopted by a researcher in conducting a particular investigation depends to a large extent on the type of question he or she is trying to answer. Although the typical case in social-psychological research is one in which the researcher's goal is to test a specific prediction, there are also cases where the researcher's goal is more exploratory and descriptive. If the research goal is to *describe* some phenomenon (e.g., to establish whether it exists, the conditions under which it is found, and so on), this implies a different type of method to the one suggested by the research goal of *hypothesis-testing*. Note that descriptive research can often be a prelude to hypothesis-testing research. For example, if in the course of descriptive research an investigator notices that a phenomenon often occurs under a particular set of conditions, this observation can form the basis of a theory concerning the relationship between the conditions and the phenomenon, and thereby lead to specific predictions and thus to hypothesis-testing research. The ultimate goal of most social-psychological research is *explanation*, and the steps by which explanations are arrived at are (1) the formulation of theoretical statements about the relationships between constructs; and (2) the conduct of empirical research in which evidence concerning these relationships is gathered. This type of research endeavour is typical of what is often called 'psychological social psychology' (see chapter 1).

Our general goal in the present chapter is to present an overview of research methods as practised by social psychologists whose ultimate object is the explanation of social phenomena by observing relationships between constructs, by proposing theories to account for such relationships, by deriving predictions from these theories, and by collecting evidence to test such predictions. These are the research methods most often employed in social-psychological research. Our principal aim here is to enable the reader to evaluate social-psychological research, as it is presented in subsequent chapters of this book; a secondary aim is to provide some preliminary guidance for the conduct of this type of research.

To facilitate the process of describing and discussing research methods, we will consider separately two facets of research methodology. First, we will describe various *research strategies*; by research strategy we mean the broad orientation one adopts in addressing a question. We will then go on to focus on one research strategy, laboratory experimentation, in particular, in recognition of the prominent role it plays in social psychology, and we will also discuss some of the most important threats to the validity of conclusions drawn from experimental research. Next we shall describe some of the most popular *data collection techniques*; these are the specific procedures the researcher follows in gathering information. The selection of a particular technique will be determined partly by the researcher's objectives and partly by the available resources.

Selection of Research Strategies

What are the principal research strategies available to the social psychologist?
What are the strengths and weaknesses of each strategy?

The strategies available for social-psychological research differ in terms of several attributes. Three that we highlight here are: the *representativeness* of the data that are collected, the *realism* of the setting in which data are collected, and the degree of *control* over the setting in which the data are collected. In this section we provide an overview of what we regard as the major research strategies available to social psychologists and briefly describe the distinctive attributes of each strategy.

Survey research

One strategy for gathering information is to survey public opinion and/or behaviour, either by interview or by questionnaire. This type of research strategy is known as a **sample survey**, and is well known in everyday life in the form of opinion polls (Schwarz, Groves, & Schuman, 1998). This strategy does not directly address questions of causality; rather, the objective is to describe the characteristics of one or more groups of people. Such descriptions can range from the simple (e.g., describing the percentage of persons eligible to vote in a particular constituency who say that they intend to vote for a particular political candidate) to the more complex (e.g., describing the personal and social characteristics associated with illegal use of drugs among school-age children and teenagers). Note that the first type of description is 'pure' description, while the second describes relationships between variables – such as those between drug use, on the one hand, and age, sex, socio-economic status, educational achievement, on the other, and thereby constitutes correlational research.

Sample survey   A research strategy that involves interviewing (or administering a questionnaire to) a sample of respondents who are selected so as to be representative of the population from which they are drawn.

The survey researcher's primary concern is with the extent to which the respondents are representative of a population (such as all adults living in a particular community, region or country). How does the survey researcher tackle the issue of representativeness? One solution to this issue would be to interview or collect completed questionnaires from the entire population in question (as is done in a census). Here the issue of representativeness is circumvented by collecting data from all members of the population: if you are really able to describe the entire population, there can be little doubt that the findings are 'representative' of that population. In most cases, however, interviewing or administering questionnaires to all members of a population is simply not practicable. Then the survey researcher is confronted with the business of choosing which members of that population should receive questionnaires or be interviewed. The process of

Sampling   The process of selecting a subset of members of a population with a view to describing the population from which they are taken.

Simple random sample   A sample in which each member of the population has an equal chance of being selected and in which the selection of every possible combination of the desired number of members is equally likely.

selecting a subset of members of a population with a view to describing the population from which they are taken is known as **sampling**.

Two main types of sampling are used in survey research: probabilistic and non-probabilistic. The most basic form of probabilistic sampling is the **simple random sample**. A simple random sample is one which satisfies two conditions: first, each member of the population has an equal chance of being selected; second, the selection of every possible combination of the desired number of members is equally likely. To explain the second condition, imagine that the population size is 10 (consisting of persons labelled A to J) and the sample size is 2. There are 45 possible combinations of 2 members of the population (A + B, A + C, A + D, and so on, to I + J). In simple random sampling, each of these 45 possible combinations of 2 members has to be equally likely. In practice, this kind of sampling is achieved by allocating numbers to each member of the population, and then using computer-generated random numbers to select a sample of the required size. Thus the first randomly generated number defines the first member of the population to be sampled, and so on, until the sample is full. Even if you do not have access to a computer program that generates random numbers, most statistics textbooks contain tables of random numbers that can be used for this purpose.

Quota sample   A sample that fills certain pre-specified quotas and thereby reflects certain attributes of the population (such as age and sex) that are thought to be important to the issue being researched.

Because it is expensive and time-consuming to do probability sampling, non-probability sampling is more commonly used for research purposes. The most typical form of non-probability sample is the **quota sample**. In a quota sample, the objective is to select a sample that reflects the basic attributes of the population. These attributes might be age and sex. Thus if you know the age and sex composition of the population concerned, you ensure that the age and sex composition of the sample faithfully reflects that of the population. The term 'quota' refers to the number of persons of a given type (e.g., females between the ages of 55 and 60) who have to be interviewed. The major advantage of quota sampling is that the interviewer can approach potential respondents until all quotas are filled, without needing to recruit a specifically identified respondent. In simple random sampling, by contrast, the members of the population who are thrown up by the random number selection process are the ones who have to be interviewed, but some of these persons may be difficult to contact or uncooperative, requiring several repeat calls and visits. Although quota sampling saves time and money for the researcher, there is a necessary loss of accuracy involved, as compared with probability sampling. Detailed discussion of the advantages and disadvantages of the two methods are beyond the scope of this chapter, and readers are referred to Schwarz et al. (1998) for a more specialist treatment.

Experiments and quasi-experiments

The survey researcher is not concerned about the physical and social setting in which the data are collected (e.g., the respondent's home, a shopping mall, or a street corner) and assumes this to be irrelevant. The setting in which data are collected is much more of a concern for other researchers, typically because they want to examine the relationship between certain features of the setting, ranging from social features (e.g., whether it is a public or private one) to physical features (e.g., how rainy it is, or how hot it is) and certain aspects of an individual's or group's behaviour (e.g., how conformist their expressed attitudes are, how positive their social judgements are, or how aggressive their behaviour is). This type of research is much more geared towards causal explanation than is survey research.

To address the issue of causality, social psychologists typically use some variation on the general theme of the experimental method. However, this is a theme with many variations. Two of the most common of these variations are the **quasi-experiment** and the **true randomized experiment**. They differ with respect to two of the attributes of research strategies that we listed earlier, namely the realism of the setting in which the data are collected, and the degree of control that the researcher has over that setting. In the typical case, the quasi-experiment is one conducted in a natural, everyday life setting, over which the researcher has less than complete control. The lack of control over the setting arises from the very fact that it is an everyday life setting. Here the realism of the setting is relatively high, the control relatively low. The true randomized experiment, by contrast, is one in which the researcher has complete control over key features of the setting; however, this degree of control often involves a loss of realism. It is sometimes possible to conduct a true randomized experiment in an everyday setting; this is called a **field experiment**.

To grasp the essential difference between a quasi-experiment and a true experiment, we need to define what we mean by the term 'experiment'. Experiments are studies in which the researcher examines the effects of one class of variables (independent variables) on another class of variables (dependent variables). In a true randomized experiment, the researcher has control over the independent variable and also over who is exposed to this variable. Most importantly, the researcher is able to allocate research participants randomly to different conditions of the experiment. True experiments are often conducted in laboratory settings, where the researcher is able to control many features of the setting. In a quasi-experiment the researcher cannot control who is exposed to the independent variable. In a typical quasi-experiment, pre-existing groups of people are either exposed or not exposed to the independent variable. Quasi-experiments are often conducted in natural, or 'field' contexts, where the researcher has less control over the setting. Examples of each method may help to bring out the points of difference.

As will be clear from chapter 10, an issue much studied by social psychologists interested in aggression is whether exposure to violent film and television material has an impact on the subsequent behaviour of the viewer. This is an issue that can be studied using true randomized experiments or quasi-experiments. An

Quasi-experiment An experiment in which participants are not randomly allocated to the different experimental conditions (typically because of factors beyond the control of the researcher).

True randomized experiment An experiment in which participants are allocated to the different conditions of the experiment on a random basis.

Field experiment A true randomized experiment conducted in a natural setting.

example of a true experiment on this issue is the study reported by Liebert and Baron (1972). Male and female children in each of two age groups were randomly allocated to one of two experimental conditions, one in which they viewed an excerpt from a violent television programme and another in which they viewed an exciting athletics race. Later both groups of children were ostensibly given the opportunity to hurt another child. Those who had seen the violent material were more likely to use this opportunity than were those who had seen the non-violent material. Because children had been allocated to the violent and non-violent conditions randomly, the observed difference can be attributed with confidence to the difference in type of material seen, rather than any difference in the type of children who saw the material.

An example of a quasi-experimental study of the same issue is the study reported by Black and Bevan (1992). They asked people to complete a short questionnaire measure of tendency to engage in aggressive behaviour under one of four conditions: while waiting in line outside a cinema to see a violent movie; while waiting in line to see a non-violent movie; having just seen a violent movie; and having just seen a non-violent movie. The researchers found that those waiting to see the violent film had higher aggression scores than those waiting to see the non-violent film; and also that those who had just seen the violent film scored higher than those waiting to see the violent film, although there was no difference in aggression scores between those who had just seen a non-violent movie and those waiting to see a non-violent movie. While this pattern of findings is consistent with the conclusion that viewing a violent movie increases the tendency to aggress, the fact that participants were not allocated at random to the different conditions of the study means that other explanations cannot be ruled out. For example, it may be that violent movies only increase aggressive tendencies among those who are attracted to view such movies in the first place.

Reflection on the strengths and weaknesses of real experiments and quasi-experiments suggests that they each have an important part to play in social-psychological research. The prime quality of the real experiment is the confidence with which causal inferences can be drawn concerning the observed relationships between independent and dependent variables. Its major drawback is the often artificial nature of the setting in which data are gathered, which raises questions about the degree to which the observed cause–effect relationships are ones that occur outside the context of the experimental setting. A prime quality of the quasi-experiment is that it can be conducted under relatively natural conditions. As far as drawing causal conclusions is concerned, the quasi-experiment is inferior to the real experiment, which means that the real experiment has to be the preferred method if one is interested in testing predictions about cause–effect relationships. One way to combine the best of these approaches is to conduct a true experiment in a natural setting (i.e., a field experiment). Another is to use both true experiments and quasi-experiments to test a given prediction; to the extent that the findings are consistent across methods, confidence in the validity of the underlying theory will be enhanced.

The fact that quasi-experiments can be conducted under natural conditions is not the only reason for using this strategy. Often the only way in which to conduct an experimental study of a social phenomenon is via a quasi-experiment. Ethical and practical considerations frequently make it impossible to allocate people randomly to different experimental conditions. If, like Stroebe, Stroebe and Domittner (1988), you wish to study the effects of bereavement, for example, you obviously cannot randomly allocate research participants to a 'bereaved' and 'non-bereaved' condition. The same problem applies in many other fields of research. All social interventions, such as new teaching methods in schools, new ways of treating those who are suffering from physical or psychological disorders, new public information campaigns, and new management techniques, share the characteristic that people are not randomly assigned to participate or not to participate in these programmes. Either they themselves choose to participate in such a programme (e.g., by volunteering for a new method of psychological treatment) or someone else chooses for them but does so on a non-random basis (e.g., when the board of directors of a corporation decides to introduce a new management system in one factory but not in another). The effects of such interventions can only be studied quasi-experimentally. Thus the choice of research strategy is often a compromise between what is optimal and what is practicable. Fortunately, the sophistication of some quasi-experimental designs is such that it is possible to draw conclusions about causality (Judd & Kenny, 1981a).

The strategies compared

Now that we have examined three main research strategies, we can see how they compare with respect to the three attributes we mentioned at the start of this section. These attributes are shown in the rows of table 4.1. The three research strategies we have just described are shown in the columns of this table. The entries in the table summarize our view of how the strategies measure up with respect

TABLE 4.1 How three research strategies typically measure up with respect to three attributes

	Research strategies		
Attributes	*Survey*	*Experiments*	*Quasi-experiments*
Representativeness of data	High	Low	Low
Realism of setting in which data are collected	Low	Low	High
Control over setting in which data are collected	Low	High	Medium

to each attribute. It should be clear that each strategy has its own particular strength, and that none of them scores highly on all three attributes.

Key Features of the Social-Psychological Experiment

What are the main elements of a social-psychological experiment?

As noted earlier, experimentation has been the dominant research method in social psychology, mainly because it is without equal as a method for testing theories that predict causal relationships between variables. Standard guides to research in social psychology (e.g., Aronson, Ellsworth, Carlsmith, & Gonzales, 1990; Aronson, Wilson, & Brewer, 1998) tend to treat experimentation as the preferred research method. In fact, there are grounds for questioning the extent to which experimental studies provide unambiguous evidence about causation, as we shall see later. However, first we will describe the principal features of the experimental approach to social-psychological research. To assist this process of description, we will use one experiment as an illustrative example. The work in question is the well-known study of obedience conducted by Milgram (1965), already referred to at the beginning of this chapter (also see chapter 13 for a fuller discussion of this study).

The **experimental scenario** is the context in which the study is presented. In a field experiment the scenario would ideally be one that occurs naturally, without contrivance on the experimenter's part. In laboratory settings, however, it is important to devise a scenario for which there is a convincing and well-integrated rationale, because the situation should strike participants as realistic and involving, and the experimental manipulations and the measurement process should not 'leap out' at the participant. There is a sense in which the typical laboratory experiment is like staging a play, with the exception that the participants' lines are unscripted. In the case of Milgram's study, the scenario presented to participants was that of an investigation of the effects of punishment on learning. The participant was allocated, apparently at random, the role of 'teacher', while an accomplice of the experimenter, posing as another participant, took the role of 'learner'. (It is worth noting in passing that an accomplice of the experimenter who performs a prescribed role in an experiment is generally referred to as a **confederate**, or **stooge**.) The learner's ostensible task was to memorize a list of word pairs. The teacher's task was to read out the first word of each pair, to see whether the learner could correctly remember the second word, and to administer a graded series of punishments, in the form of electric shocks of increasing severity, if the learner failed to recall the correct

Experimental scenario The 'package' within which an experiment is presented to participants. In field experiments it is, ideally, something that happens naturally. In laboratory experiments it is important to devise a scenario that strikes the participant as realistic and involving.

Confederate (or **stooge**) An accomplice or assistant of the experimenter who is ostensibly another participant but who in fact plays a prescribed role in the experiment.

word (which he had been instructed to do from time to time). The experimental scenario was set up with a view to convincing the participant that the shocks were genuine (which they were not), and that the learner was indeed a fellow participant who was actually receiving the shocks. Thus what was actually a study of the extent to which participants would obey the experimenter's instruction to deliver steadily increasing electric shocks was presented as a study of the effects of punishment on learning.

The **independent variable** is the variable that is deliberately manipulated by the experimenter. All other aspects of the experimental scenario are held constant, and the independent variable is changed in some respect with a view to assessing the consequences of this manipulation. Each change in the independent variable produces a new 'condition' of the experiment: one change yields two conditions, two changes yield three conditions, and so on. For example, in Milgram's study a key independent variable was the proximity of the 'learner' to the 'teacher'. In one condition, learner and teacher were in separate rooms, and the teacher could not hear or see the learner's reactions to the shocks; in a second condition, the teacher could hear the learner, but still could not see him; in the third condition, the teacher could both see and hear the learner's reactions; in the fourth condition, the teacher had to hold the learner's hand down on a metal plate in order for the shock to be delivered (the Touch-Proximity Condition, see plate 4.1). All other aspects of the experimental setting were held constant, so that variations in the

> **Independent variable** The variable that an experimenter manipulates or modifies in order to examine the effect on one or more dependent variables.

PLATE 4.1 General arrangement for Touch-Proximity Condition and obedient subject in Touch-Proximity Condition in Milgram's (1965) study
(Stills from 1965 film *Obedience* © Stanley Milgram as reproduced in *Obedience to Authority* by Stanley Milgram, courtesy of Tavistock Publications)

teacher–participants' behaviour in these four different conditions should have been attributable only to the change in proximity between teacher and learner.

The adequacy of an experiment often hinges on the effectiveness of manipulations of the independent variable. By *effectiveness* we mean (1) the extent to which changes in the independent variable capture the essential qualities of the construct that is theoretically expected to have a causal influence on behaviour; and (2) the size of the changes that are introduced. For example, in Milgram's study, we should consider how well the four proximity conditions capture the construct of proximity. What is being manipulated, quite clearly, is *physical* proximity (rather than, say, psychological proximity); as long as this is what the experimenter intends to manipulate, all well and good. We should also consider whether the changes between the four conditions are sufficiently large to have an effect. In this particular case, it is difficult to see how the proximity variable could have been manipulated more powerfully, but an investigator who adopts weaker manipulations runs the risk of failing to find the predicted effects simply because the variations across levels of the independent variable are too subtle to have any impact. It has become standard practice in social-psychological experiments to include among the measured variables one or more measures of the effectiveness of the manipulation, and these measures are known as manipulation checks. We will have more to say about these later.

As we have already seen, a key feature of the true experiment is that participants should be randomly allocated to different experimental conditions. Failure to adhere to this stipulation interferes with one's ability to draw causal inferences from the results. For example, in the four conditions of Milgram's study described above, it was found that the number of shocks teacher–participants were prepared to administer steadily declined as the proximity between teacher and learner increased. This appears to show that obedience to the experimenter's instructions diminished as the learner's suffering became more salient to the teacher. Such an inference could *not* be drawn if there were grounds for thinking that the type of participant recruited for the four conditions differed in some systematic way.

Assessing the impact of an independent variable requires the experimenter to measure some feature of the participant's behaviour or internal state. This measured variable is known as the **dependent variable**, so called because systematic changes in this measured variable should *depend upon* the impact of the independent variable. In the Milgram study, the dependent variable was the number of shocks in a 30-step sequence that the teacher was prepared to deliver by throwing switches corresponding to each shock level. A key question to ask of any dependent variable is the extent to which it is a good measure of the underlying theoretical construct. For example, is the willingness to deliver what appear to be increasingly strong shocks to another person a good measure of 'destructive obedience'? In addition to this question of the 'fit' between a theoretical construct and the measured or dependent variable, the most important issue

Dependent variable The variable that is expected to change as a function of changes in the independent variable. Measured changes in the dependent variable are seen as 'dependent on' manipulated changes in the independent variable.

involved in designing dependent variables is what type of measure to use. This is a matter that will be discussed in more detail below.

As well as measuring the main dependent variables, the experimenter usually tries to collect other kinds of measures. One of the most important of these supplementary measures is the **manipulation check**, referred to earlier as an assessment of the effectiveness of the independent variable. A typical manipulation check is designed to measure participants' perceptions of those features of the experimental scenario that are relevant to the manipulation in question. For example, Isen, Daubman and Nowicki (1987) conducted four experimental studies of the impact of positive affect on creative problem solving, to test the prediction that positive affect promotes creativity. In their second experiment they manipulated affect in two different ways (by showing comedy films or giving participants a candy bar) and measured participants' performance on a test of creativity. In addition, they checked the manipulation of participants' affective state by asking them to rate their affective state, after the manipulation but before the creativity test. They found that the film manipulation did have a significant impact on participants' reported affective state, whereas the candy bar gift did not. Interestingly, creative problem solving was enhanced in the comedy film condition (relative to negative and neutral film conditions), but was no better in the candy bar condition than in a no-gift condition. Thus the negative results for the gift condition may have been attributable to the ineffectiveness of the manipulation. A major function of the manipulation check, then, is to aid in interpretation of the findings, especially in the case where the independent variable does not have the predicted effect on the dependent variable.

> **Manipulation check**   A measure of the effectiveness of the independent variable.

It is worth noting that laboratory experiments often involve some measure of deception, in the sense that the participant is misled about some aspect of the research. The extent of this deception can range from simply withholding information about the true purpose of the research to deliberately misleading participants into thinking that the research is concerned with something that differs from its real purpose. The primary reason for using deception is that participants would act differently if they were aware of the true objective of the study. If Milgram's participants knew from the outset of the experiment that it was a study of obedience to authority, we can be reasonably sure that the rate of disobedience would have been higher: like most people, the participants would presumably have wanted to demonstrate (both to themselves and to others) their ability to resist orders to harm a fellow human being. Attitudes to the use of deception in social-psychological research have changed during the past 25 years, such that deliberately misleading participants about the nature of an experiment is now viewed more negatively than it used to be. This change of attitude is based partly on moral grounds (i.e., wherever possible one should avoid deceiving someone else, whether or not this is in the context of an experiment) and partly on practical grounds (if participants are deliberately misled about some aspect of the study on a routine basis, they will enter any future participation in the expectation that they are going to be misled, which may well influence their behaviour). Striking the right balance between the desire to be honest and open and wanting to study people without their behaviour being unduly influenced by their knowledge of the nature and purpose of an experiment is a tricky business. Because experimenters have a vested interest that may lead them to be inclined to use deception when it is not strictly necessary, most universities in Europe, North America and Australasia have an 'ethics committee' that oversees research involving human participants. Furthermore, both the American Psychological Association and the British Psychological Society have published guidelines that should be followed by their members in conducting research using human participants.

A further aspect of the Milgram experiment that warrants some comment is the stress that was experienced by many of his participants. Administering shocks to a fellow human being is not something that the average citizen does coolly or calmly, and many of Milgram's participants were quite agitated. The obvious question that arises is whether it is reasonable to place participants under stress in the cause of social-psychological research. The climate of opinion has changed in relation to this issue, too: experimenters are more sensitive to the need to protect the well-being and self-respect of participants than used to be the case (although it is worth noting that Milgram was keenly aware of the ethical aspects of his research). Certain topics are almost impossible to study without exposing participants to a certain amount of stress. If one conducts an experimental study of the impact of negative mood or negative self-esteem on task performance, for example, certain participants will be exposed to a procedure that is designed to create a negative mood or negative self-esteem. Ethics committees will want to be assured that the research question being addressed justifies the use of such procedures, and also that any negative affect experienced by participants is kept within reasonable bounds.

Debriefing   The practice of explaining to participants the purpose of the experiment in which they have just participated, and answering any questions the participant may have. It is especially important to debrief participants when the experimental procedure involved deception – in which case, the debriefing should also explain why the deception was considered to be necessary.

One of the key ways in which experimenters can address the ethical issues entailed in using deception or exposing participants to stress is by practising **debriefing**. Debriefing takes place at the end of the experimental session and refers to the process of informing the participants as fully as possible about the nature and purpose of the experiment, and the role their particular participation played in the study as a whole. Although debriefing research participants is good practice in any form of research using human participants, it is particularly important wherever the participant has been deceived about the purpose of the experiment and/or about some aspects of the experimental procedure. In Milgram's obedience research, for example, care was taken to assure participants that the 'shocks' they had administered were in fact bogus, and that the learner had not been harmed in any way; the reason for the deception was also carefully explained. Ideally, the debriefing process should leave participants understanding the purpose of the research, satisfied with their role in the experiment, and with as much self-respect as they had before participating in the study.

Experimental Designs

Why is it important to have a control condition in an experiment?
What is an interaction effect?

We have already seen that it is important (1) that experimenters keep all theoretically irrelevant features of the experimental setting constant across conditions, manipulating just the key independent variable; and (2) that participants are allocated randomly to the different conditions of an experiment. Failure to achieve these goals hinders the researcher's ability to draw the inference that observed differences in the dependent variable across conditions result from changes in the independent variable. We shall now examine more closely the question of designing experiments in such a way that alternative inferences are ruled out as far as possible.

Consider first a design for a study that may *appear* to be an experiment but cannot truly be described as an experimental design. This is the so-called **one-shot case study**. Following Cook and Campbell (1979), we shall use the symbol X to stand for a manipulation (i.e., of the independent variable) and the symbol O to stand for observation (i.e., the dependent variable). In these terms the one-shot design looks like this:

To take a concrete example, imagine that an educational researcher wanted to know the effect of a new teaching method on learning. The researcher takes a class of students, introduces the new method (X), and measures the students' comprehension of the taught material (O). What conclusions can be drawn from such a design? Strictly speaking, the answer is none; the point is that there is nothing with which O can be compared, so the researcher cannot infer whether the observed comprehension is good, poor or indifferent.

A simple extension of the one-shot design provides the minimum requirements for a true experimental design, and is known as the **post-test only control group design**. Let R stand for random assignment

One-shot case study A research design in which observations are made on a group after some event has occurred or some manipulation has been introduced. The problem is that there is nothing with which these observations may be compared, so one has no way of knowing whether the event or manipulation had an effect.

Post-test only control group design A minimal design for a true experiment. Participants are randomly allocated to one of two groups. One group is exposed to the independent variable; another (the control group) is not. Both groups are assessed on the dependent variable, and comparison of the two groups on this measure indicates whether or not the independent variable had an effect.

of participants to conditions, and X and O stand for manipulation and observation, as before. This design looks like this:

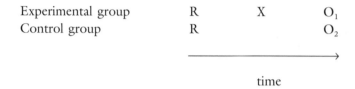

| Experimental group | R | X | O_1 |
| Control group | R | | O_2 |

time

Compared with the one-shot design, there are two important modifications. First, there are two conditions. In one the participants are exposed to the manipulation (this is usually referred to as the experimental condition, and participants in this condition are known as the **experimental group**), and possible effects of the manipulation are measured. In the other no manipulation is introduced (this is usually referred to as the control condition, and participants in this condition are known as the **control group**), but these participants are also observed on the same dependent variable and at the same time-point as the experimental group. Now the observation made in the experimental condition (O_1) *can* be compared with something, namely the observation made in the control condition (O_2). In the example we have been using, the researcher might compare one group of students who have been exposed to the new teaching method with another group who continued to receive the normal method, with respect to their comprehension of the taught material. The second important modification is that in this design participants are randomly allocated to the two conditions, ruling out the possibility that differences between O_1 and O_2 are due to differences between the two groups of participants that were present before X was implemented. It follows that if O_1 and O_2 differ markedly, it is reasonable to infer that this difference is caused by X.

Although the post-test only control group design is one of the more commonly used experimental designs in social psychology, there are several other more sophisticated and complex designs, each representing a more complete attempt to rule out the possibility that observed differences between conditions result from something other than the manipulation of the independent variable (see Cook & Campbell, 1979, for a full discussion). The prime object of experimental design, then, is to enhance the validity of the researcher's inference that differences in the dependent variable result from changes in the independent variable.

A common design in social-psychological experiments is the **factorial experiment**, in which two or more independent variables are manipulated within the same study. The simplest case can be

Experimental group   A group of participants allocated to the 'experimental' condition of the experiment, i.e., the condition in which participants are exposed to that level of the independent variable that is predicted to influence their thoughts, feelings or behaviour.

Control group   A group of participants who are typically not exposed to the independent variable(s) used in experimental research. Measures of the dependent variable derived from these participants are compared with those derived from participants who are exposed to the independent variable (i.e., the experimental group), providing a basis for inferring whether the independent variable determines scores on the dependent variable.

Factorial experiment   An experiment in which two or more independent variables are manipulated within the same design.

represented diagrammatically as follows, where R stands for random assignment of participants to conditions, X stands for a variable with two levels (X_1 and X_2), and Y stands for another variable with two levels (Y_1 and Y_2):

R	X_1Y_1	O_1
R	X_1Y_2	O_2
R	X_2Y_1	O_3
R	X_2Y_2	O_4

$$\longrightarrow$$

time

The essential feature of a factorial design is that it contains all possible combinations of the independent variables. In the design shown above, each independent variable has two levels, resulting in four conditions (2×2). Adding one level to each variable would result in nine conditions (3×3), whereas adding another two-level variable would result in eight conditions ($2 \times 2 \times 2$). The main benefit of a factorial design is that it allows the researcher to examine the separate and combined effects of two or more independent variables. The separate effects of each independent variable are known as **main effects**. If the combined effects of two independent variables differ from the sum of their two main effects, the combination is known as an **interaction effect**.

> **Main effect** A term used to refer to the separate effects of each independent variable in a factorial experiment.

> **Interaction effect** A term used when the combined effects of two (or more) independent variables in a factorial experiment yield a pattern that differs from the sum of the main effects.

To illustrate such an interaction, let us consider a hypothetical set of results from a study of attitude change in which two variables are manipulated: argument quality, i.e., whether a persuasive message that participants are given to read consists of strong arguments or weak arguments; and involvement, i.e., whether participants' involvement with the topic of the message is high or low. Such a design tests one of the basic predictions derived from Petty and Cacioppo's (1986b) elaboration-likelihood model of persuasion (see chapter 8). The prediction is that argument quality will have a stronger influence on attitudes when participants are involved with the message topic than when they are not. Figure 4.1 shows hypothetical data from such a study. It can be seen (panel a) that argument quality does have a main effect on attitudes, such that strong messages are more persuasive than weak ones. Involvement has no main effect on attitudes (see panel b): attitudes do not vary as a function of level of involvement. However, when the combined effects of these two variables are examined (see panel c), it is clear that there is an interaction: the effect of argument quality is much greater when involvement is high than when it is low, just as the theory predicts. Because the predicted effect is an interaction, testing this prediction requires conducting a factorial experiment.

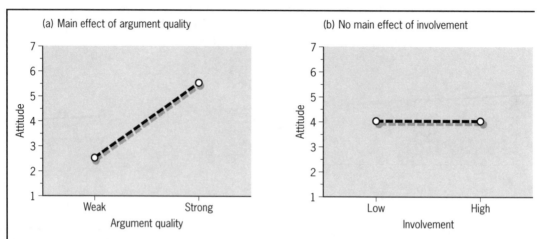

FIGURE 4.1 Hypothetical data illustrating a main effect (panel a), an absence of a main effect (panel b) and an interaction effect (panel c)

Threats to Validity in Experimental Research

What is the difference between internal and external validity?
What is meant by the term 'confounding' in the context of experimental research?

In the context of research, validity refers to the extent to which one is justified in drawing inferences from one's findings. Experimental research attempts to maximize each of three types of validity: internal validity, construct validity and external validity.

Internal validity refers to the validity of the conclusion that an observed relationship between independent and dependent variables reflects a *causal* relationship, and is promoted by the use of a sound experimental design. We have already seen that the use of a control group greatly enhances internal validity, but even if one uses a control group there remain many potential threats to internal validity (Cook & Campbell, 1979, list 13). Among these is the possibility that the groups being compared differ with respect to more than the independent variable of interest.

> **Internal validity** Refers to the validity of the inference that changes in the independent variable result in changes in the dependent variable.

For example, assume for one moment that in the experiment described previously, Milgram had used a different experimenter for each of the four conditions, such that experimenter 1 ran all participants in one condition, experimenter 2 ran all participants in the next condition, and so on. Although it might seem sensible to divide the work of running the conditions among different experimenters, to do so in this way poses a major threat to the internal validity of the

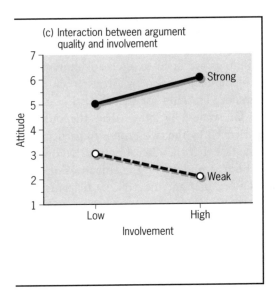

(c) Interaction between argument quality and involvement

experiment. This is because the four conditions would no longer differ *solely* in terms of the physical proximity of the 'victim'; they would also differ in that each would be conducted by a different experimenter. Thus the differing amounts of obedience observed in the four conditions *might* reflect the causal influence of the physical proximity independent variable, *or* the influence of the different experimenters (or, indeed, some combination of these two factors). The problem is that the physical proximity variable would be **confounded** with a second variable, namely experimenter identity. It is impossible to disentangle the effects of confounded variables.

Even when we are confident that the relationship between X and O is a causal one, in the sense that internal validity is high, we need to consider carefully the nature of the constructs involved in this relationship. **Construct validity** refers to the validity of the assumption that independent or dependent variables adequately capture the variables (or 'constructs') they are supposed to represent.

With regard to the construct validity of independent variables, the issue is whether the independent variable really represents a manipulation of the intended theoretical construct. For example, in a well-known experiment Aronson and Mills (1959) found that participants who underwent an embarrassing initiation in order to join what turned out to be a tedious sex discussion group subsequently reported greater liking for that group than did participants who underwent a milder initiation. This was interpreted as evidence in support of a prediction derived from dissonance theory (see chapter 8). According to dissonance theory, the knowledge that one has suffered in order to attain a goal is inconsistent with the

Confounding A variable that incorporates two or more potentially separable components is a confounded variable. When an independent variable is confounded, the researcher's ability to draw unambiguous causal inferences is seriously constrained.

Construct validity The validity of the assumption that independent and dependent variables adequately capture the abstract variables (constructs) they are supposed to represent.

knowledge that the goal turns out to be worthless, thereby generating cognitive dissonance. To reduce this uncomfortable state of dissonance, it is argued, the individual re-evaluates the goal more positively. Gerard and Mathewson (1966) pointed out that Aronson and Mills' findings are open to alternative interpretations which accept that the initiation manipulation used by Aronson and Mills was responsible for the observed differences in liking for the discussion group, but assert that this effect resulted from something other than the differing amounts of dissonance supposedly experienced by the two groups of participants. For example, it could be argued that the fact that the discussion was tedious was actually a relief to those participants who had undergone the embarrassing initiation, who as a consequence found it more pleasant than did participants who had undergone a milder initiation. To rule out this alternative explanation (and others like it), Gerard and Mathewson devised an experimental condition in which participation in the group discussion followed an aversive experience but was not contingent upon that experience. For the alternative explanation, it should make no difference whether or not the discussion is dependent on the aversive experience, whereas for dissonance theory the contingent relationship between 'suffering' and the group discussion is crucial. Gerard and Mathewson showed that increased liking for the discussion group was only positively related to severity of the prior experience when group membership was dependent on that experience.

Even if the researcher has reason to feel satisfied with the construct validity of the independent variable, there remains the question of whether the dependent variables actually assess what they were intended to assess. As we shall see below, devising a measure to capture the essence of a social-psychological construct is by no means straightforward. There are three main types of threat to the construct validity of dependent variables in social-psychological experimentation: social desirability, demand characteristics and experimenter expectancy.

Social desirability is a term used to describe the fact that participants are usually keen to be seen in a positive light, and may therefore be reluctant to provide honest reports of fears, anxieties, feelings of hostility or prejudice, or any other quality which they think would be regarded negatively. Equally, participants may 'censor' some of their behaviours so as to avoid being evaluated negatively. To the extent that a researcher's measures are contaminated by social desirability effects, they will obviously be failing to assess the theoretical construct of interest. The most obvious means of reducing social desirability effects is to make the measurement process as unobtrusive as possible, on the premise that if participants do not know what it is that is being measured, they will be unable to modify their behaviour.

Demand characteristics are cues in the experimental setting which convey to the participant the nature of the experimenter's hypothesis. The point here is that individuals who know that they are being studied will often be curious about what the experimenter is looking at and what types of responses are expected. Participants

Social desirability A term used to describe the fact that participants are usually keen to be seen in a positive light and are therefore reluctant to report on their negative qualities.

Demand characteristics Cues that are perceived as telling participants how they are expected to behave or respond in a research setting, i.e., cues that 'demand' a certain sort of response.

may then attempt to provide the expected responses in order to please the experimenter. When behaviour is enacted with the intention of fulfilling the experimenter's hypotheses, it is said to be a response to the demand characteristics of the experiment. Orne (1962, 1969) has conducted a great deal of research into demand characteristics and has suggested various methods of pinpointing the role they play in any given experimental situation. For example, he advocates the use of in-depth **post-experimental enquiry** in the form of an interview, preferably conducted by someone other than the experimenter, the object of which is to elicit from the participant what he or she believed to be the aim of the experiment, and the extent to which this belief affected behaviour in the experiment. Clearly, researchers should do all they can to minimize the operation of demand characteristics, for example by using **unobtrusive measures**, or by telling participants that the purpose of the experiment cannot be revealed until the end of the study and that in the meantime it is important that they do *not* attempt to guess the hypothesis. A **cover story** which leads participants to believe that the purpose of the study is something other than the real purpose is a widely used means of lessening the impact of demand characteristics. However, an unconvincing cover story can create more problems than it solves, raising doubts in the mind of the participant that otherwise may not have arisen.

Experimenter expectancy refers to the experimenter's own hypothesis or expectations about the outcome of the research. This expectancy can unintentionally influence the experimenter's behaviour towards participants in such a way as to enhance the likelihood that they will confirm his or her hypothesis. Rosenthal (1966) called this type of influence the **experimenter expectancy effect**. The processes mediating experimenter expectancy effects are complex, but non-verbal communication is centrally involved. The extent to which experimenter expectancy can influence a phenomenon may be assessed by using several experimenters and manipulating their expectations about the experimental outcome. An obvious strategy for reducing these effects is to keep experimenters 'blind' to the hypothesis under test, or at least blind to the condition to which a given participant has been allocated; other possibilities include minimizing the interaction between experimenter and participant, and automating the experiment as far as possible. The goal in each case is to reduce the opportunity for the experimenter to communicate his or her expectancies.

Even if the experimenter manages to circumvent all the above threats to internal and construct validity, an important question concerning validity remains: to what extent can the causal relationship between X and O be generalized beyond the particular circumstances of the experiment? **External validity** refers to the generalizability of an

Post-experimental enquiry A technique advocated by Orne for detecting the operation of demand characteristics. The participant is carefully interviewed after participation in an experiment, the object being to assess perceptions of the purpose of the experiment.

Unobtrusive measures (also called non-reactive measures) Measures that the participant is not aware of, and which therefore cannot influence his or her behaviour.

Cover story A false but supposedly plausible explanation of the purpose of an experiment. The intention is to limit the operation of demand characteristics.

Experimenter effects (sometimes referred to as **experimenter expectancy effects**) Effects unintentionally produced by the experimenter in the course of his or her interaction with the participant. These effects result from the experimenter's knowledge of the hypothesis under test, and they increase the likelihood that the participants will behave in such a way as to confirm the hypothesis.

External validity Refers to the generalizability of research findings to settings and populations other than those involved in the research.

observed relationship beyond the specific circumstances in which it was observed by the researcher. One important feature of the experimental circumstances, of course, is the type of person who participates in the experiment. In many cases, participants volunteer their participation, and to establish external validity it is important to consider whether results obtained using volunteers can be generalized to other populations. There is a good deal of research on differences between volunteers and non-volunteers in psychological studies (see Rosenthal & Rosnow, 1975, for a review; and Cowles & Davis, 1987, for an example of a study). The general conclusion is that there *are* systematic personality differences between volunteers and non-volunteers. More importantly, in studies such as one reported by Horowitz (1969), it has been found that the effects of some manipulations used in attitude-change research were actually *opposite* for volunteers and non-volunteers. Such findings are explained in terms of volunteers' supposedly greater sensitivity to and willingness to comply with demand characteristics. The external validity of studies based only on volunteers' behaviour is therefore open to question, and the solution to this problem is to use a 'captive' population, preferably in a field setting. Another frequently voiced criticism of social (and indeed other) psychological experiments is that the participants are often university students. Although university students are undoubtedly not very representative of the general population, being younger, more intelligent and more highly educated than the average citizen, this is usually *not* a threat to the validity of the research. This is because the goal of much social-psychological experimentation is to understand the process(es) underlying a phenomenon (such as attitude change or friendship formation) rather than to describe the general population (a goal for which survey research is much better suited). In any case, there is often little or no reason to suppose that the processes underlying a phenomenon such as attitude change or friendship formation differ in some fundamental way between students and non-students.

Data Collection Techniques

What are the principal data collection techniques used in social-psychological research?
What are the strengths and weaknesses of each of these techniques?

Whichever research strategy is adopted by an investigator, he or she will need to measure one or more variables. In correlational designs, the researcher has to measure each of the variables that are expected to correlate. In experimental designs, the researcher needs to measure the dependent variable. In either case, the investigator is confronted with the task of translating a theoretical construct (for example, aggression or attraction) into a measurable variable (for example, willingness to harm someone, or willingness to help someone). Two important issues arise in connection with this process. Any psychological measure should be both reliable and valid. **Reliability** here refers to the stability of the measure. If you measure an adult's height (assuming you are doing it carefully), the measurement will be highly stable from one day to the next, and will also be independent of who is doing the measuring. These are the hallmarks of a reliable measure: it is not dependent on the time of measurement or on the person taking the measurement. However, a measure can be highly reliable and yet be low in validity. To pursue the height measurement example, let us imagine that what you *really* want to measure is a person's weight. In the absence of a proper weighing scale you decide to measure height

Reliability   A measure is reliable if it yields the same result on more than one occasion or when used by different individuals.

Validity   A measure is valid to the extent that it measures precisely what it is supposed to measure.

instead, because you do have a tape-measure. Of course, height and weight are correlated with each other, so height may be a better measure of weight than simple guesswork. But clearly height is not especially valid as a measure of weight. Thus **validity** in this context refers to the extent to which the measured variable really captures the underlying construct.

The researcher's first goal should be to specify what it is that he or she wants to record in order to represent the construct in a meaningful way. Imagine that a researcher wishes to measure aggressive behaviour. Would willingness to deliver a painful shock to another person, expressed behaviourally, be a *valid* index of the construct of aggression as conceptualized by the investigator, or would it be better to adopt another index, such as the number of verbal insults directed at the person (cf. chapter 10)? Having decided what general form the measured variable should take, the next task of the researcher is to try to ensure that the measure is *reliable*. In social-psychological research, the investigator typically chooses to measure a variable using observational measures, self-report measures or (a more recent development) implicit measures.

Observational measures

If the object of one's research is to collect information about social *behaviour*, an obvious means of doing so is by observation. Many behaviours that are of interest to social psychologists are detectable without the assistance of sophisticated equipment and are enacted in public settings, which makes them suitable for observation. Although observational methods vary in kind, as we shall see, from the relatively informal and unstructured to the highly formal and structured, the object in each case is the same: to abstract from the complex flux of social behaviour those actions that are of potential significance to the research question, and to record each instance of such actions over some period (Weick, 1985).

Sometimes the nature of the research setting or topic dictates that observation is conducted in a relatively informal and unstructured manner, with the researcher posing as a member of the group being observed. A classic example of research employing this method is Festinger, Riecken and Schachter's (1956) study of the consequences of blatant disconfirmation of strongly held beliefs. The

Participant observation   A method of observation in which the researcher studies the target group or community from within, making careful records of what he or she observes.

investigators identified a religious sect which predicted that the northern hemisphere would be destroyed by flood on a certain date. By joining that sect, members of the research team were able to observe what happened when the predicted events failed to materialize. Under such circumstances, observation clearly has to be covert and informal: if other sect members suspected that the researchers were not *bona fide* believers, the opportunity for observation would be removed. This type of observation is known as **participant observation**, for the obvious reason that the observer participates in the activities of the group that is being observed.

More formal methods of observation can be used when it is possible to record actions relevant to the research question without disrupting the occurrence of the behaviour. An example is Carey's (1978) series of studies investigating the hypothesis that when one pedestrian approaches another on the street, a rule of 'civil inattention' applies, whereby each looks at the other up to the point where they are approximately eight feet apart, after which their gaze is averted. This hypothesis was first advanced by Goffman (1963), on the basis of informal observation. Carey's purpose was to verify, using more formal methods, the existence of this rule, and to establish parameters such as the distance between pedestrians when gaze is first averted. He covertly photographed pairs of pedestrians as they approached and passed each other on a street, taking the photographs from upper storeys of buildings overlooking the street. The resulting still photographs were then coded for variables such as distance between the pair, whether their heads and eyelids were level or lowered, and whether gaze direction was towards or away from the approaching person.

The two examples cited above have in common the fact that the targets of the researchers' observations were unaware that they were being observed. Although such failure to inform persons of their involuntary participation in a research project may raise tricky ethical questions, it does overcome a problem peculiar to any research that uses humans as participants, namely the tendency for the measurement process itself to have an impact on participants' behaviour, a phenomenon known as **reactivity**. It is well established that the simple knowledge that one is being observed can influence behaviour enacted in front of observers. The best-known instance of such an effect is a study of worker productivity conducted at the Hawthorne plant of the Western Electric Company (Roethlisberger & Dickson, 1939), where it was found that merely observing workers raised their motivation and thereby increased productivity. Instances of such influence have come to be known as **Hawthorne effects**. Awareness of this problem has led many researchers to develop unobtrusive methods of observing and measuring behaviour. An entertaining and very useful sourcebook of methods of unobtrusive measurement has been compiled by Webb, Campbell, Schwartz, Sechrest and Grove (1981).

Reactivity   A measurement procedure is reactive if it alters the nature of what is being measured (i.e., if the behaviour observed or the verbal response recorded is partly or wholly determined by the participant's awareness that some aspect of his or her behaviour is being measured).

Hawthorne effect   A term used to describe the effect of participants' awareness that they are being observed on their behaviour.

The most formal type of observational method is one in which the researcher uses a predetermined category system for scoring social behaviour. A well-known example of such a system is Bales' (1950) **interaction process analysis (IPA)**, developed to study interaction in small social groups. Here the verbal exchanges between group members are coded in terms of 12 predetermined categories (e.g., 'requests information'). The scores of group members can then be used to determine (among other things) who is the leader of the group (see Bales & Slater, 1955). Observational methods of data collection have two main advantages over the self-report methods we shall consider below: first, they can often be made unobtrusively; second, even where the participant knows that his or her behaviour is being observed, enacting the behaviour is typically quite engrossing, with the result that participants have less opportunity to modify their behaviour than they would when completing a questionnaire. Nevertheless, there are some types of behaviour that are either impossible to observe directly (because they took place in the past) or difficult to observe directly (because they are normally enacted in private). Moreover, social psychologists are often interested in measuring *people's perceptions, cognitions* or *evaluations*, none of which can be directly assessed simply through observation. For these reasons, researchers often make use of self-report measures.

> **Interaction process analysis (IPA)**   A formal observational measurement system devised by Bales for coding the interactions of members of small social groups. It consists of categories and procedures for coding interaction in terms of these categories.

Self-report measures

The essential feature of data collection using self-report measures is that questions about the participant's beliefs, attitudes, behaviour or whatever are put directly to the participant. His or her responses constitute self-report data. Self-report measurement is usually quicker, cheaper and easier to use than observational measurement. The researcher does not have to contrive a laboratory setting or find a natural setting in which to observe a behavioural response; furthermore, there is typically no need to train observers or to use recording equipment, for self-reports are usually recorded by the participant in the form of written responses. Finally, as noted above, some of the variables that are of most significance to social psychologists are not directly observable. For these various reasons, self-report measurement is very common in social-psychological research, and it is not unusual for studies to depend exclusively on self-report data. As we shall see, however, self-report measures are not without problems.

There are two principal methods of collecting self-report data: the questionnaire and the interview. In the *questionnaire* method, participants are handed a set of questions, along with instructions on how to record their answers. In the *interview* method, questions are put to the participant by an interviewer, who then records the participant's responses. Interviewing is particularly useful when there is reason to believe that the questions might be difficult to understand without clarification. A tactful and sensitive interviewer should be able to establish rapport with the respondent and ensure that the latter fully comprehends a question before answering. On the other hand, interviewing is a costly procedure in terms of time and money, and a poorly trained interviewer can easily bias the respondent's answers by hinting at a desired or socially acceptable response. Questionnaires are especially useful for gathering data from large numbers of participants with minimal expense, and the comparative anonymity of the process might be preferable when the questions touch on sensitive issues. On the other hand, many people who are given questionnaires fail to complete and/or return them. Response rates for questionnaires sent by mail to randomly selected names and addresses vary between 10 and 50 per cent. Because there is always the danger that non-respondents differ systematically from respondents in some respect, low response rates are undesirable. In practice, social psychologists often manage to get round this problem by administering their questionnaires to participants who are in some sense 'captive', in that they have already volunteered to participate in the study, and by having them complete the questionnaire in a lecture theatre or laboratory rather than letting them take it home.

Questionnaires are undoubtedly the most widely used form of data collection in social-psychological research. Some idea of the richness and variety of data collected exclusively by means of questionnaires can be gained by considering a study reported by Folkman and Lazarus (1985). These investigators used questionnaire techniques to study how people appraised a stressful event (a university examination), what emotions they experienced as the event approached and passed, and how they coped with the stress induced by the event. It is difficult to envisage how Folkman and Lazarus could have conducted such a study without using questionnaires. It is certainly possible to measure some psychophysiological indices of stress, such as heart rate, before, during and after exposure to a noxious stimulus such as an electric shock; but one cannot assume that the short-term stress induced by shock in a laboratory is comparable with the longer-term stress induced by 'natural' events such as examinations, ill health, divorce or bereavement. Furthermore, the individual's appraisals, emotions and coping strategies could not be assessed satisfactorily without the use of self-report measures.

Devising a good questionnaire or interview schedule is a harder task than one might imagine. As with any psychological measure, the goal is to produce questions that are reliable and valid. Reliability in this context means that the questions would evoke the same response from a given individual if he or she were tested more than once under similar circumstances. Validity means that the questions measure exactly what the researcher intends them to measure. Although there are many potential sources of unreliability in the construction of questionnaires, the most serious threat to question reliability is *ambiguity*: if a question is ambiguous, a given respondent might well interpret it differently on different occasions and therefore give different answers. The most serious threat to question validity is failure on the part of the investigator to have *specific objectives* for each question: the hazier the intent of the researcher in posing a particular question, the greater are the chances that it will fail to elicit information relevant to his or her objectives. Even if a question is unambiguous, however, and has been formulated with a clear goal in mind, there are other sources of unreliability and invalidity which cannot easily be controlled. A simple rule-of-thumb in questionnaire research is never to assume that answers to a single question will reliably or validly measure any construct. If the average of two (or preferably more) items is used to measure that construct, the variable factors (such as question ambiguity, mis-understanding on the part of the participant, the context provided by the imme-diately preceding question) that decrease reliability and validity of responses to any single question should cancel each other out, and the resulting measure will be a purer reflection of the underlying construct.

Because it is difficult to envisage all the potential pitfalls in questionnaire con-struction, there is no substitute for pilot work in which prototypes of the final questionnaire are administered to groups of participants whose answers and com-ments provide a basis for revision. Constructing an entirely fresh questionnaire can therefore be a time-consuming and painstaking process. Fortunately, there are collections of previously developed and pre-tested questionnaires, such as the one edited by Robinson, Shaver and Wrightsman (1991). It is worth checking such a source before setting out to construct an original questionnaire. If no suitable questionnaire already exists, the researcher should consult a text on questionnaire design such as the one by Oppenheim (1992) before devising a fresh questionnaire. It is also advisable to familiarize oneself with recent research on the cognitive pro-cesses that underlie respondents' answers to survey questions (see Schwarz, 1990a).

A particularly important class of self-report measures in social psychology are those that purport to measure attitudes. The measurement of attitudes has a long history in psychology, dating back to 1928 when Thurstone published a paper titled 'Attitudes can be measured'. Since then several methods for measuring attitudes have been developed. Readers looking for a comprehensive review of this topic should consult Himmelfarb (1993). We will limit ourselves here to a brief description of two methods commonly used in present-day social-psychological research. The 'method of summated ratings' was developed by Likert (1932), and is commonly referred to as 'Likert scaling'. To develop a **Likert scale** of, say, attitudes towards the European Union (EU), one would first collect a large pool of state-ments (usually called 'items') that are relevant to the EU. These could be expressions of belief about the EU (e.g., 'The European Union has helped to raise standards of living in member countries'), expres-sions of affect in relation to the EU (e.g., 'The level of farm subsidies within the European Union makes me feel angry'), or state-ments about behaviour (e.g., 'I intend to vote in the next elections for the European Parliament'). These items should between them reflect a set of attitudinal posi-tions that range in evaluation from very pro-EU to very anti-EU. The next step in developing a Likert scale is to ask a set of respondents to express the extent of their agreement or disagreement with each of these items by choosing one of the following options:

Likert scale A technique for measuring attitudes developed by Rensis Likert. The key feature of this method is that respondents are asked to rate the extent of their agreement or disagreement with a set of statements about the attitude object.

1	2	3	4	5
strongly disagree	disagree	undecided	agree	strongly agree

The pattern of agreement and disagreement with the large initial pool of items is used to select items for the final Likert scale. The selection is done by means of item analysis. The most important criterion here is the extent to which the answers to a given item correlate with the total score summed across all items. Items that correlate weakly or not at all with the total score will be discarded, so that one ends up with a smaller set (say, 10–20 items) that measure the same underlying attitude. This smaller set constitutes the final Likert scale. Responses to this final scale are also measured in terms of strength of agreement or disagreement, and a respondent's agreement ratings are summed to obtain a score representing his or her attitude (hence the term 'method of summated ratings').

A second very popular way of measuring attitudes is the **semantic differential**. This method, developed by Osgood, Suci and Tannenbaum (1957), entails asking respondents to rate the attitude object (e.g., the European Union) on a set of bipolar adjective scales, as shown below:

Semantic differential A technique for measuring attitudes (among other things) developed by Charles Osgood and his colleagues. The key feature of this method is that respondents are asked to rate the attitude object on several bipolar adjective scales.

The European Union

good	:____:____:____:____:____:____:____:	bad
harmful	:____:____:____:____:____:____:____:	beneficial
pleasant	:____:____:____:____:____:____:____:	unpleasant
foolish	:____:____:____:____:____:____:____:	wise
right	:____:____:____:____:____:____:____:	wrong

Respondents are asked to rate the attitude object by placing a tick or a cross in one of the seven spaces on each of the rating scales. These ratings are usually scored on a −3 to +3 scale, with ratings on the negative side of each scale being given a minus score. Then the scale scores are summed or averaged to obtain an overall index of attitude.

In deciding which of these two methods to use, the researcher will be guided by considerations such as the need to capture different facets of the underlying attitude and how easy it is to use the measure in question. As our brief descriptions of the two methods should have made clear, a strength of the Likert method is its ability to capture different aspects of attitude, ranging from beliefs to behaviour. It is also possible to assess strength of agreement or disagreement with relatively complex belief statements (e.g., 'The European Union will be strengthened by admitting former Eastern bloc countries'). By contrast, the semantic differential focuses on simple evaluative beliefs (e.g., that the European Union is 'good' or 'bad'), and is suited to measuring affective and behavioural aspects of attitude. The great strength of the semantic differential is the ease and speed with which it can be used.

Self-report measures have several advantages, among the most important being their ability to assess psychological constructs such as attitudes in a relatively economical way. What are their drawbacks? Chief among these is the fact that it is not possible to collect self-report data completely unobtrusively: participants are always aware that they are under investigation, and may modify their responses as a result of this awareness. In particular, there is ample opportunity for the respondent's answers to be influenced by motivational factors, such as social desirability. There is no simple solution to this problem, although there are some steps that can be taken which together should reduce the scale of the problem. First, it is worth emphasizing to participants whenever possible that their responses are anonymous. Second, it is worth stressing the point that there are no right or wrong answers. Third, it is often possible to increase participants' motivation to respond truthfully by treating them as research accomplices rather than 'guinea-pigs'.

Implicit measures

A recent development in social-psychological research methods has been the increasing use of techniques for measuring perceptions, cognitions and evaluations that do not rely on the usual type of self-report measure, thereby avoiding the disadvantages of the latter. These techniques are often referred to as **implicit measures** (Greenwald & Banaji, 1995). The use of such measures has quite a long history in social psychology: a classic paper on the indirect assessment of attitudes was published by Campbell (1950) half a century ago. What is different about the modern use of implicit measures is that they usually take advantage of computer technology. Here computers are used not only for the presentation of experimental materials, but also (and more importantly) for the precise measurement of various aspects of the participants' responses to these materials. An example of an implicit measure is the use of response latencies (i.e., how long it takes a participant to answer a particular question). Such measures can provide fresh insights into cognitive structures and processes. For instance, in the study reported by Gaertner and McLaughlin (1983), the automatic operation of stereotypes was assessed by the speed (response latency) with which participants made judgements about pairs of words. The participants' task was to say 'yes' if there was an association between each pair of words. White participants responded significantly faster to white–positive word-pairs (e.g., white–smart) than black–positive word-pairs (e.g., black–smart), thereby suggesting that they engaged in automatic stereotyping of racial groups.

> **Implicit measures** are measures of constructs such as attitudes and stereotypes that are derived from the way respondents behave (such as how long they take to make a decision or to answer a question) rather than from the content of their answers to explicit questions about these constructs. They are a class of **unobtrusive measure**.

In principle, implicit measures are capable of generating information that is unaffected by the biases that can influence conventional self-report measures. For example, university students are quite likely to be 'on guard' against appearing racist, and therefore to take care to avoid evaluating white–positive word-pairs more positively than black–positive word-pairs. Computer-aided techniques also provide the opportunity to examine the way in which cognitive structures influence processes in an unconscious (automatic) way. One of the major ways of investigating social-cognitive processes entails priming techniques (see Bargh & Chartrand, in press). These involve the temporary activation of a category or a representation which then influences the way people interpret another (often ambiguous) situation, without their being aware that the activated context is influencing their interpretation (see chapter 5; Bargh, 1996; Higgins, Bargh, & Lombardi, 1985). In another study of the automatic operation of stereotypes, Dovidio, Evans and Tyler (1986) presented participants with the primes 'black' and 'white', it being clear that these terms referred to racial groups. This is an example of what Bargh and Chartrand (in press) call *conceptual priming*. It involves the activation of an internal mental representation that is of interest. This is done in such a way that participants are not aware of the influence that this activated mental construct may have upon their response times. In the Dovidio et al. (1986) experiment, participants were then presented with target words that represented either positive or negative traits. The participants' task was to judge whether the target trait could 'ever be true' (i.e., of blacks or of whites, depending on condition) or was 'always false'. The results showed that participants responded significantly faster to positive traits after being exposed to a white prime than after being exposed to a black prime. Furthermore, negative traits were responded to faster when preceded by the black prime than when preceded by the white prime. This is a further illustration of the automatic operation of stereotypes and the way in which priming can be used to reveal such automatic processes. In addition to conceptual priming techniques, Bargh and Chartrand (in press) describe *mindset priming* and *sequential priming*. The common element in all these techniques is that they investigate the 'unintended consequences of an environmental event on subsequent thoughts, feelings and behavior' (p. 7 (MS)).

The major advantage of implicit measures is that they are not reactive. That is, implicit measures are not subject to biases such as social desirability, demand characteristics, etc., since they tap processes that operate outside awareness. However, it is by no means certain that such measures have high validity. How does one know, for example, whether a fast reaction time reflects automatic stereotyping as opposed to individual differences in lexical knowledge? To address questions such as this, one ideally needs to have other measures (e.g., observational) that provide evidence that converges with the evidence provided by implicit measures. In principle, such convergent operations (see below) help to establish the validity of both types of measure. However, the argument that implicit measures tap processes in a way that is less subject to the influence of self-presentational concerns than are other measures (especially self-report) obviously raises some tricky issues with regard to cross-validating one measure by means of another.

Choosing a measure

As we have seen, all three types of measure considered here have certain advantages and disadvantages. Although there are no hard-and-fast rules for choosing one type of measure rather than the other, there are two points that should be borne in mind when judging the appropriateness of a dependent measure. First, the three types of measure – observational, self-report and implicit – can be used in conjunction with each other in many types of research. Second, the three types of measure differ in terms of the type of information they yield. Let us consider each of these points more closely.

Assume that you wish to study interpersonal attraction. Under laboratory or field conditions you introduce two people, previously unknown to each other, and ask them to get to know each other in the course of a 15-minute discussion. If you want to measure how much these two like each other at the end of the session, you could simply depend on self-report measures, such as responses to questions about how much each person liked the other, would be prepared to work with the other, and so on. You could also use observational measures: unobtrusively video-recording the interaction would permit you to measure various aspects of behaviour, both verbal (e.g., the extent to which the two persons discovered mutual interests or shared attitudes) and non-verbal (e.g., the amount of smiling or direct looking at the other person).

Consider the advantages of using each type of measure. First, the observational data provide one type of check on the validity of the self-report and implicit data, and vice versa. Just as questionnaire data can be distorted by respondents' motivations, so too can observers' perceptions be distorted by the nature of the coding system they are using; and although implicit data are by their very nature less liable to distortion, the precise meaning of such data is not always unclear. If all three kinds of data point to the same conclusion, this would enhance confidence in their validity. A second, potentially more important, advantage is that while self-report and implicit measures of attraction can be said to be an *outcome* of the interaction, observational measures may provide an insight into the *processes* mediating that outcome. Researchers would typically be interested not only in establishing whether people liked or disliked each other, but also in finding out *why* they did or did not like each other; examining the behaviours that occurred during the interaction might shed some light on this.

In summary, using more than one type of measure is often helpful to the researcher. If observational, self-report and implicit measures of the same conceptual variable point to the same conclusion, this enhances confidence in that conclusion. Furthermore, self-report and implicit measures often assess the outcome of a process; by using observational measures as well, the researcher may gain insight into the process responsible for that outcome.

Problems with Experimentation

What are the main criticisms that have been levelled at the use of experiments in social psychology?

What is meant by the term 'mediation' in the context of psychological research?

It is widely assumed that the experimental method provides the 'royal road' to causal inference (cf. Aronson et al., 1998). In fact, causal inference from the results of experiments is more problematic than some commentators allow. One problem concerns what Gergen (1978) has called the *cultural embeddedness* of social events, by which he means that 'few stimulus events considered independently have the capacity to elicit predictable social behavior' (p. 509). It follows that, even in the most tightly controlled laboratory experimental demonstration that the manipulation of independent variable X has a causal impact on dependent variable O, the circumstances in which X was manipulated may play a key role in producing the observed effects on O. The inference that 'X causes O' may therefore only be true under particular circumstances.

A related problem, also articulated by Gergen, is that although the experimental method purportedly allows us to trace the causal sequence from antecedent conditions to the behaviour of interest, its capacity to do so depends on the assumption that external events are related in a one-to-one fashion with particular states or processes in the individual. Gergen argues: 'In dealing with human beings in a social setting it is virtually impossible to manipulate any variable in isolation of all the others. Even the most elemental variations in an independent variable have the capacity to elicit a host of intervening reactions' (1978, p. 515). The result is that what one experimenter believes to be a demonstration of the effect of X on O via the mediating process Z, another will prefer to explain in terms of an alternative mediating process. Social psychology abounds with such debates between rival accounts for findings (see Greenwald, 1975; Ostrom, 1977; Tetlock & Levi, 1982; Tetlock & Manstead, 1985), and some have come to the view that experimentation is not a suitable way to settle such between-theory disputes.

The heart of the problem identified by Gergen is that phenomena of interest to social psychologists often entail *chains* of events. If we strip this issue down to its bare essentials, we can ask whether variable X influences variable O *directly*, or whether the relation between X and O is mediated by another variable, Z. By conducting an experiment we may establish that there is a causal relation between X and O; but had we also measured Z, we might have found that the relation between X and Z is also very high, as is the relation between Z and O. Indeed, we might find that once the X–Z and Z–O relationships are statistically taken into account, the originally established relationship between X and O disappears. This is the type of situation in which one can infer that the relationship between X and O is *mediated* by Z (Baron & Kenny, 1986). Indeed, one strategy that helps to overcome the problem of alternative explanations identified by Gergen is to design experiments that include the assessment of possible **mediating variables**.

In analysing such studies it is important to observe the following steps (see Judd & Kenny, 1981b; Kenny, Kashy, & Bolger, 1998). First, establish that there is a clear relationship between the independent variable (X) and the dependent variable (O); second, demonstrate that there is a relationship between X and the proposed mediator (Z); third, show that Z is related to O; and fourth, show that Z accounts fully for the relationship between X and O, such that the effect of X upon O is reduced to non-significance if one controls for Z. A final step is to test for so-called 'reverse mediation'; this entails testing whether X influences Z via O, i.e., reversing the roles of O and Z in the analyses just described. To take a concrete example, imagine that you are conducting research on persuasive communication using as your theoretical model Petty and Cacioppo's (1986b) elaboration likelihood model (see chapter 8). According to this model, the effect of manipulating argument quality (the X variable) on attitude change (the O variable) is mediated by the proportion of positive thoughts an individual has while reading or listening to a persuasive communication (the Z variable). Thus argument quality should influence attitude change; argument quality should also influence the proportion of positive thoughts; the proportion of positive thoughts should be related to attitude change; and the effect of argument quality on attitude change should disappear when controlling for proportion of positive thoughts. Finally, when the roles of the proposed mediator (thoughts) and the dependent variable (attitudes) are reversed, argument quality should *not* affect thoughts via its effect on attitudes.

Yet another inferential problem confronting the experimental researcher in social psychology also arises from the fact that social behaviour is culturally embedded. In every culture there are norms that define the boundaries of appropriate social behaviour in particular settings, with the result that most individuals behave quite similarly in such settings. Such behaviour is best regarded as the product of that culture's conventions or rules, rather than intraindividual psychological processes. Experimental settings are not free from the operation of cultural norms; indeed, there are grounds for thinking that laboratory experiments may promote the occurrence of behaviours that are guided by norms (Semin & Manstead, 1979). Inferential difficulties can arise when behaviour in such settings is interpreted exclusively in terms of hypothetical internal processes. For example, it might be argued that cultural norms prescribe that one does not question the instructions of someone running a scientific experiment, and that when one is asked to deliver an increasingly strong series of shocks to another person, apparently in the interests of scientific

Mediating variable   A variable that mediates the relation between two other variables. Assume that independent variable X and dependent variable O are related. If a third variable Z is related to both X and O, and if the X–O relation disappears when we take the role of Z into account, then Z is said to mediate the relation between X and O.

research, one should do so. That people are willing to do so, even when the shocks are strong enough to produce fatal results, is by no means uninteresting; but whether it reveals something about the psychological processes mediating obedience to authority is another matter. In short, it is important to avoid the temptation to formulate causal laws in terms of psychological processes where there are grounds for thinking that the phenomena being 'explained' have their origins in cultural convention (cf. Brandstädter, 1990; Semin, 1986; Smedslund, 1985).

One final and related problem worth mentioning in this context is that although the ostensible goal of social-psychological experimentation is the accumulation of scientific knowledge, in the form of laws or principles of social behaviour that are valid across time, there is some reason to doubt whether experimentation (or, indeed, any other method) is capable of generating evidence that could be the basis of such laws. To understand why this is the case in social sciences but not in natural sciences, we need to take account of the fact that the relationship between researcher and the object of the research is radically different in the two types of science. The testing of theories in the natural sciences is concerned with the analysis and explanation of the *object world*, a world that does not engage in the construction and interpretation of the meaning of its own activity. This contrasts with the objects of investigation in social sciences: being people, these 'objects' do of course attribute meaning and significance to their actions. Social psychology cannot therefore be neatly distinguished from what it studies; lay persons and social psychologists alike are concerned with understanding and interpreting their social environments. Lay persons are able to acquire social-psychological knowledge and use it to modify their actions in a way that atoms, elements and particles cannot. As Giddens (1982) puts it: 'The fact that the "findings" of the social sciences can be taken up by those to whose behaviour they refer is not a phenomenon that can, or should be marginalised, but it is integral to their very nature. . . . Human beings . . . are not merely inert objects of knowledge, but agents able to – and prone to – incorporate theory and research within their own action' (pp. 14–16). One implication of this is that social-psychological theories should not be regarded as embodying 'laws' that will necessarily hold good across time: if learning about a social-psychological theory leads people to modify the very behaviour that the theory tries to explain, it is clear that the theory has only limited temporal validity. Gergen (1973, 1978) has been the leading advocate of this sobering view, although his arguments have been challenged by Schlenker (1974) and by Semin and Manstead (1983, ch. 5). It is also worth noting that some of the problems of accumulation of knowledge in social psychology can be addressed through the use of **meta-analysis**, a relatively recently developed technique for statistically integrating the results of independent studies of the same phenomenon in order to establish whether findings are reliable across a number of independent investigations (see Cooper, 1990; Hedges & Olkin, 1985).

Meta-analysis A set of techniques for statistically integrating the results of independent studies of a given phenomenon, with a view to establishing whether the findings exhibit a pattern of relationships that is reliable across studies.

What are the implications of these problems for the status of experimentation in social-psychological research? It should be noted that even some of the severest critics of the experimental approach do not advocate the abandonment of experimentation. For example, Gergen acknowledges that experiments will continue to play an important role in the explication of the relationship between biological processes (such as physiological arousal) and social behaviour; that studies such as the Milgram experiment are useful for raising consciousness about the insidious nature of social influence; that experiments can increase the impact of theories by providing vivid demonstrations of conditions under which a theory does make successful predictions; and that experimentation can be useful to evaluate social reforms, such as the effectiveness of measures designed to conserve energy. Thus the debate about the utility of experimentation revolves around the types of inference that can reasonably be made on the basis of experimental evidence, with 'traditionalists' such as Aronson et al. (1998) sticking to the view that experimentation provides a firm basis on which to build knowledge, and critics such as Gergen questioning this assumption.

Summary and Conclusions

Methods are procedures followed by researchers in gathering information that helps them to answer research questions. Methodology is the term used to refer to all aspects of the implementation of these methods. The type of method used by a given researcher will depend to a large extent on the kind of question he or she is addressing. We distinguished between three basic types of research – descriptive, correlational and experimental – and we noted that social-psychological research is typically experimental or quasi-experimental in nature, having the goal of explaining the phenomenon under investigation.

In describing methods in more detail, we drew a distinction between research strategies and data collection techniques. Three research strategies were described: survey research, quasi-experiments and true randomized experiments. Two key ways in which these strategies differ are in terms of (1) the degree to which one is able to generalize to a population, and (2) the degree to which one can draw inferences about causality.

Experimentation was singled out for more detailed discussion because of its prominence as a research strategy in social psychology during the last four decades. The main features of experimentation were identified as: the experimental scenario; the independent variable; the dependent variable; the manipulation check; and debriefing.

A true experimental design is one that enables the researcher to infer that changes in the independent variable produce changes in the dependent variable. Such a design must therefore incorporate more than one condition, allowing the researcher to compare observations made under different conditions. The minimal true experimental design is the post-test only control group design, in which participants are randomly allocated to one of two conditions, only one of which involves being exposed to the manipulation. Several more complex designs are available, and of these the factorial design is very commonly used, mainly because of its ability to test predictions concerning interaction effects.

Drawing strong inferences from social-psychological research depends on three types of validity: internal, construct and external. We identified confounding as a threat to internal validity; social desirability effects, demand characteristics and experimenter effects as threats to construct validity; and volunteer/non-volunteer differences as a threat to external validity.

We identified three principal methods of collecting data in social-psychological research: observational measurement, self-report measurement and implicit measures. Observational measures have the advantage of being less susceptible to social desirability effects, and can be made completely unobtrusive. On the other hand, they cannot directly tap covert cognitive phenomena such as attitudes, causal attributions and stereotypes (see chapters 5–7). Here the researcher has traditionally relied on self-report measures, although there has been an increasing tendency to make use of implicit measures, the goal of which is to reveal phenomena that may either be outside the awareness of the individual or are likely to be misreported in conventional self-report measures due to social desirability concerns. The advantages of using these different types of measure in conjunction should not be overlooked.

Finally, we noted that some social psychologists have questioned the utility of conventional methods, and of laboratory experiments in particular. The cultural embeddedness of social behaviour, the fact that social behaviour is determined by multiple factors, the difficulty of discriminating between normative and psychological causation, and the ability of humans to modify their behaviour in the light of social-psychological theories, were identified as grounds for questioning the assumption that experimentation generates cumulative knowledge of the laws governing social behaviour.

DISCUSSION POINTS

1 Is it possible to capture the complexity of human social behaviour in the form of an experiment?

2 Is it ethical to subject humans to deceptive and/or stressful procedures in the name of science?

3 The best way to understand a phenomenon is to begin by carefully describing it. Discuss.

4 Can self-report measures ever be trusted?

5 What should we do if a self-report measure points to one conclusion, but an implicit measure or an observational measure leads to another?

6 Is human social behaviour governed by 'laws', in the same way that the behaviour of inanimate objects appears to be?

7   Laboratory experiments provide the only proper basis for drawing causal conclusions in social-psychological research. Discuss.

FURTHER READING

Aronson, E., Ellsworth, P. C., Carlsmith, J. M., & Gonzales, M. H. (1990). *Methods of research in social psychology* (2nd ed.). New York: McGraw-Hill. A comprehensive introduction to research methods in social psychology, with an emphasis on experimentation.

Cook, T. D., & Campbell, D. T. (1979). *Quasi-experimentation: Design and analysis issues for field settings.* Chicago, IL: Rand McNally. An authoritative account of how to minimize threats to validity by careful research design.

Gergen, K. J. (1978). Experimentation in social psychology: A reappraisal. *European Journal of Social Psychology*, 8, 507–27. A thought-provoking analysis by one of the leading critics of the use of experimentation in social psychology.

Gilbert, D. T., Fiske, S. T., & Lindzey, G. (Eds.). (1998). *The handbook of social psychology* (4th ed., 2 vols.). New York: McGraw-Hill. The most recent edition of this essential handbook, containing contributions on experimentation (chapter 3), survey methods (chapter 4), measurement (chapter 5) and data analysis (chapter 6).

Greenberg, J., & Folger, R. (1988). *Controversial issues in social research methods.* New York: Springer. This book does a good job of presenting the debates surrounding key issues in research.

Greenwood, J. D. (1989). *Explanation and experiment in social psychological science: Realism and the social constitution of action.* New York: Springer. An interesting, critical treatment of the philosophical background to research methods.

Jones, R. A. (1985). *Research methods in the social and behavioral sciences.* Sunderland, MA: Sinauer. This is an unusual book: it presents the whole gamut of methods used by social scientists in an intelligent, informative and entertaining way. Highly recommended.

KEY STUDY

Gergen, K. J. (1978). Experimentation in social psychology: A reappraisal. *European Journal of Social Psychology*, 8, 507–27.

Construction of the Social World

PART II

CONTENTS

Social Cognition

Klaus Fiedler and Herbert Bless

5

OUTLINE

This chapter deals with social information processing, and reviews a number of approaches in social psychology that have imported concepts and methods from cognitive psychology. However, the cognitive processes involved in perceiving, encoding, thinking, inferring, remembering, judging and communicating social information are distinct from cognitive processes about the physical world. In this chapter, we present the major research topics and theories of social cognition within a framework of the different stages involved in processing information. We review relevant research on a number of fascinating issues, including person perception and person memory, stereotyping, cognitive biases, judgement tendencies and linguistic communication. Other major sections of this chapter are devoted to the application of these modules of social cognition to social hypothesis testing and to adaptive behaviour in a complex world.

KEY CONCEPTS

- Accessibility
- Anchoring and adjustment
- Assimilation
- Availability
- Bottom-up processing
- Category
- Contrast
- Ease of recall
- Evaluative priming
- Exemplar-based representation
- Illusory correlation
- Implicit verb causality
- Judgemental heuristic
- Linguistic categories
- Linguistic intergroup bias

- Memory-based judgement
- Mood congruency
- On-line judgement
- Primacy effect
- Priming effect
- Prototype
- Representativeness
- Salience
- Script
- Simulation heuristic
- Social hypothesis testing
- Standard of comparison
- Stereotype
- Subtyping
- Top-down processing

Introduction

What ideas has social cognition borrowed from cognitive psychology?
How can social cognition be set apart from the behaviourist tradition?
How does prior knowledge interact with a stimulus?

Imagine Harry Olds, a 40-year-old personnel manager. He is interviewing applicants for a vacant position. One female applicant presents herself in the following way: 'I am not really sure whether I have the ability to perform this task right now, but I am very motivated, and I hope I can learn.' How might Harry Olds interpret this statement? On the one hand, he might infer that the applicant is not trained enough for the job and somewhat insecure. On the other hand, he might think the applicant is motivated, honest and does not overstate her abilities. How do you think Harry Olds will interpret the applicant's statement? Will he hire her?

Obviously, Harry Olds' decision depends not only on the applicant's actual statement but also on the way he interprets this statement. To predict social judgement and behaviour we need to understand the cognitive processes that mediate between a given stimulus (e.g., the applicant's statement) and a response (e.g., Harry Olds' hiring decision). Psychologists have not always been interested in the hidden link between external stimuli and overt behavioural responses. Behaviourists (e.g., Skinner, 1938), in particular, have argued that behaviour can be explained better in terms of reinforcement contingencies (reward and punishment) than of mediating cognitive processes. In contrast, Gestalt theorists (e.g., Koffka, 1935; Wertheimer, 1945) have always emphasized that it is not the stimulus *per se* that influences our behaviour but how we see it – in other words, how we mentally construct and represent reality. The cognitive link between stimulus and response allows social behaviour to be far more context-sensitive than rigid biological routines. Excluding this link from social-psychological research would result in a severely impoverished picture of human conduct. To quote from one of the most prominent European social psychologists, Henri Tajfel (1969): '[T]he greatest adaptive advantage of man [*sic*] is his capacity to modify his behaviour as a function of the way in which he perceives and understands a situation' (p. 81).

If social behaviour is not directly determined by the external stimulus situation but is mediated by the internal mental representation of a given situation, we need to understand how individuals construct their subjective reality in order to understand social behaviour and its mediating factors. Social-cognition research addresses precisely this question. Social cognition is concerned with the study of social knowledge and the cognitive processes that are involved when individuals construct their subjective reality. The aim is to investigate how information is encoded, stored and retrieved from memory, how social knowledge is structured

TABLE 5.1   Examples of social-cognition research questions

How is our knowledge about the world stored and retrieved from memory?
How are Harry's stereotypes retained and organized? Which conditions trigger their use?

When different knowledge structures are available, which one is most likely to be applied to a specific situation?
For example, Harry might not only hold a sexist stereotype about female insecurity, but also a positive stereotype about the prestigious university from which the female applicant graduated. Which knowledge structure will guide his interpretation?

How do individuals search for new information?
Which questions will Harry ask? Will he ask more questions pertaining to the applicant's insecurity, or more questions pertaining to motivation and adjustment?

In which way do aspects of the present input information trigger prior knowledge?
For example, does it matter whether the applicant is the only female among many males, or whether there is an equal number of male and female applicants?

How do our knowledge structures change in the light of contradictory information?
Would Harry's expectation of female inferiority change if this applicant is hired and performs superbly?

Which aspects of the situation influence the relative impact of prior knowledge as compared to new stimulus information on the resulting interpretation of reality?
Would Harry's interpretation depend on whether he is distracted by an important phone call while making the interview? What if his own salary depended on the applicant's subsequent performance?

and represented, and what processes are involved when individuals compute judgements and make decisions (see table 5.1 for a summary of research questions, applied to Harry Olds' decision).

By emphasizing the need to investigate cognitive structures and cognitive processes, social cognition has become a melting pot for theoretical developments from some of the most fertile and popular endeavours of social psychology, namely attitude change (see chapter 8), attribution research (see chapter 7) and stereotyping (see chapter 15). It is important to note that by focusing on cognitive structures and processes, researchers have by no means confined cognition to 'cold rationality'. Indeed, proponents of the social-cognition approach have been even more interested in affect and emotion (see Clore, Schwarz, & Conway, 1994), irrational behaviour (Kahneman, Slovic, & Tversky, 1982) and intergroup affairs than in purely intellectual processes of thinking, judging and recalling (see Fiske & Taylor, 1991; Wyer & Srull, 1994).

In concentrating on the representation of information and on mental processes, social cognition has borrowed many concepts and assumptions from cognitive psychology (Anderson, 1976). One basic assumption holds that (social) judgements are only partly determined by the stimuli of a given situation, for example

PLATE 5.1   Study of social cognition helps us to understand how information is processed in social situations such as a job interview

by the applicant's statement. Our judgements will also heavily depend on the *prior knowledge* we bring to that situation. As a consequence, the applicant's statement could result in a variety of different reactions depending on which prior knowledge Harry Olds applies in making his interpretation. His reactions would presumably be very different if his sexist stereotype holds that women in general are insecure and not suitable for the job, or if it holds that women are often highly motivated and adjust quickly to new situations. Depending on which prior knowledge guides the interpretation, Harry will ask different questions, attend to different features of the situation, and later remember different aspects of the interview.

A second basic assumption holds that our thinking is strongly influenced by the limitations of processing capacity. In many situations people do not have the time and the capacity to consider all relevant information. Moreover, even if they had all the necessary processing resources, they are often not motivated to think about a situation in great depth. Individuals' processing capacity and motivation are assumed to determine the degree to which they think about a particular situation. Depth of processing is strongly related to the impact of prior knowledge on cognitive processes. In general, the less processing capacity and motivation there is, the stronger the impact of prior knowledge on new incoming

information (**top-down processing**). Conversely, the more processing resources individuals allocate, the greater the likelihood that
new information will change their existing knowledge (**bottom-up
processing**). As a consequence, the amount or depth of processing
can heavily influence resulting judgements. It comes as no surprise,
therefore, that the concept of depth of processing plays a key role in
social-cognition theorizing.

Top-down processing
Information processing driven
by abstract, superordinate
knowledge structures in
memory (e.g., schema,
expectation) which influence the
perception and interpretation of
new stimuli.

Third, cognitive processes can differ with respect to their automaticity and controllability (Shiffrin & Schneider, 1984). Some processes can be controlled more easily than others. For example, when
required, individuals can actively call to mind some particular content from their memory, such as the applicant's performance in an
assessment centre. However, information may also come to mind automatically. Thus, by assigning a person to a group (the female applicant to the category women), a person's general expectations about that group
may pop up spontaneously, without voluntary control (Devine, 1989; Fiske &
Neuberg, 1990).

Bottom-up processing
Information processing driven
by new stimulus input rather
than abstract knowledge
structures in memory.

The remainder of this chapter is devoted to some of the major developments
in social-cognition research. We shall elaborate how the above assumptions are
linked to the structure of social knowledge and to the sequence of cognitive processes. Before doing so, however, we shall briefly address the question of what is
social about social cognition.

What is Social about Social Cognition?

How does the social world differ from the physical world?
What makes social cognition so prone to constructions and illusions?

The emphasis on *cognitive* processes is but one side of the social-cognition coin;
the other stresses the *social* nature of information processing. Given the above
sketch of research assumptions, one might wonder how social cognition is different from cognition about inanimate objects. First, and perhaps most obviously,
social-cognition research is specific because of the social nature of the stimulus
and its relation to the perceiver. For example, in contrast to judgements about
objects, judgements about other persons are usually more complex and the targets
of social judgements tend to change over time – in particular when the target is
aware of being observed. In addition, there is usually a stronger link to the perceiver's self – again increasing the complexity of the processes (see Fiske & Taylor,
1991).

The social aspect, however, is not confined to the nature of the stimulus as such. Just as a young child could hardly learn her first language from a radio, and just as social interaction in peer groups is a necessary condition in Piaget's (1932b) theory of cognitive development (cf. chapter 3), the most important message guiding the present chapter is that (social) cognition is a genuinely social process.

The importance of the social component of human intelligence can be illustrated by Cosmides' (1989) evolutionary approach to logical reasoning. The persistent failure of even highly intelligent people in logical reasoning tasks is due to the fact that reasoning experiments are often detached from the social context in which the reasoning ability has evolved. In a typical research paradigm modelled after Wason (1966), four cards, which show the symbols 2, A, B, 1, are presented and participants are told that each card has a letter on one side and a number on the other (see figure 5.1, upper part). Their task is to select those cards

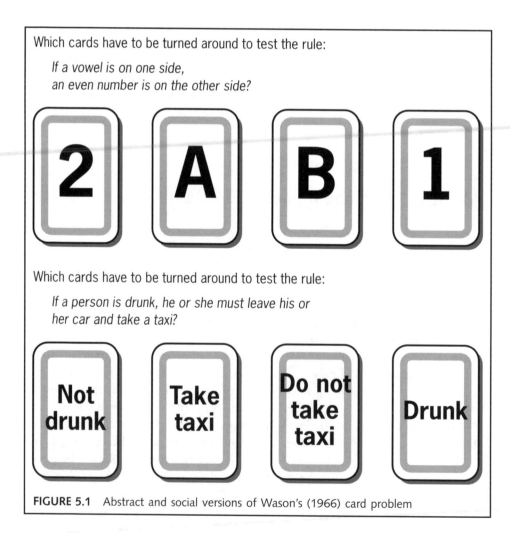

Which cards have to be turned around to test the rule:

If a vowel is on one side,
an even number is on the other side?

2   **A**   **B**   **1**

Which cards have to be turned around to test the rule:

If a person is drunk, he or she must leave his or
her car and take a taxi?

Not drunk   **Take taxi**   **Do not take taxi**   **Drunk**

FIGURE 5.1   Abstract and social versions of Wason's (1966) card problem

that permit a logically sound test of a rule such as, *If a vowel is on one side, an even number is on the other side.* So what choice is appropriate?

What most people do is to select those cards that match the attributes mentioned in the rule: A (vowel) and 2 (even number). However, an appropriate choice would be to look at the cards that affirm the antecedent (i.e., the vowel A) and that negate the consequent (i.e., the odd number 1). Almost everybody understands that card A must be considered. When the A card is turned around, the 2 must show up; if the 1 appears, the rule is falsified. The 2 card is quite irrelevant. The rule does not exclude that even numbers may also come along with consonants. However, the 1 card, which represents the negation of the consequent, affords a crucial but less obvious test. Given the odd number 1, the letter on the front side must not be a vowel; otherwise the rule is falsified.

Two decades of research on this particular task have conveyed a rather pessimistic picture of human reasoning ability. Even when the rule refers to familiar and meaningful contents, the reasoning errors persist. However, Cosmides has reported a series of very influential studies which demonstrate that people have no difficulty solving logically equivalent problems if the rule constitutes a *social contract* that is reminiscent of social exchange principles. Given a rule such as, *If a person is drunk, then the person must not drive but take a taxi*, social intelligence tells us that we have to look for both people who are drunk and those who drive (negation of the consequent), in order to detect 'cheaters' who violate social contracts (Gigerenzer & Hug, 1991).

Another example of how social involvement may trigger logical thinking is evident in Schaller's (1992) work on statistical reasoning. If students are presented with statistical tables indicating that female performance is inferior to male performance, for example, they usually fail to consider the spurious nature of such a correlation. Thus, the apparent relationship between gender and performance may be due to some third variable (e.g., women have to work under less favorable conditions). However, statistical reasoning can improve markedly when respondents are socially or emotionally involved, as when feminist participants are motivated to defend the gender group to which they belong.

There is another, equally important, but less obvious, answer to the question of what is social about social cognition. While the physical environment consists of stimulus attributes – such as colour, size or pitch – which are amenable to direct perception and for which we have developed sensory receptors, the social ecology extends to numerous attributes that cannot be perceived directly or assessed objectively. The attributes of greatest interest, such as *risk, intelligence, honesty, love, danger, gains* and *losses*, refer to distal entities which have to be inferred or construed from more proximal cues, and sometimes have no objective existence at all. Therefore, the concepts used for the causes, goals or consequences of behaviour are often ill defined. For instance, the frequent use in Western cultures of personality traits or dispositional terms such as 'extraversion' or 'independence' does not rely on direct experience with the traits themselves, but on indirect experience with behavioural cues (e.g., talkativeness, voice quality, style of clothing etc.), which are used to construe the 'perception' of such traits. Thus, an apparent correlation between, say, extraversion and leadership may be due to the fact that both traits are construed or inferred from the same behavioural cues (cf. Shweder, 1975). In a similar vein, personnel manager Harry Olds' stereotypical belief that male employees are more rational and logical than female employees may be hard to falsify simply because the 'perception' of masculinity is based on the same cues (e.g., reduced emotional expression, deep voice, dominant communication style) as the 'perception' of rationality.

The Cognitive Stages of Social Information Processing

Which stages of information processing can be distinguished?
How are these stages ordered and interrelated?

What does the available empirical evidence tell us about human information processing in such a fallible environment? As in cognitive psychology, one can organize the sequence of cognitive processes into the different stages as depicted in figure 5.2. First, we have to *perceive* the observed stimulus events, then we need to *encode* and interpret this perception. The encoding state is already heavily influenced by prior *knowledge* stored in memory. The encoded perception will be stored in memory and will potentially affect the assessment of future events. Both the newly encoded input and the old knowledge in memory will then provide

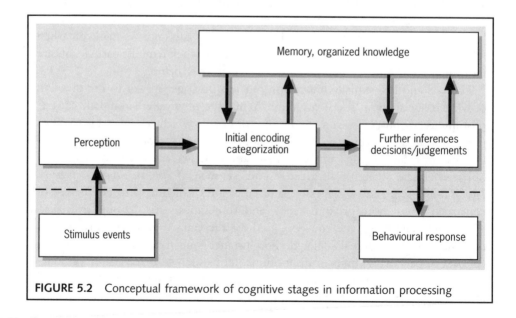

FIGURE 5.2   Conceptual framework of cognitive stages in information processing

the basis for further processing, leading to *inferences* and *judgements*. Sometimes, but not always, the final outcome of this cognitive process is manifested in an overt *behavioural response*.

Although the different processing stages – from perceptual input to behavioural output – are interdependent and characterized by various feedback loops, the sequence has a sound logical basis in that later stages (e.g., categorization) take earlier stages (e.g., perception) for granted, whereas the reverse is not necessary, albeit possible. For instance, we cannot encode a face as belonging to some ethnic group unless we have perceived the face, but we can perceive facial attributes independently of social categorization. Likewise, memory for faces cannot be organized in terms of ethnic similarities unless the faces are encoded in the first place. Finally, inferences presuppose an organized knowledge structure, and retrieval takes inferences and organized knowledge as an input.

Nevertheless, it is important to understand that the bottom-up processing of new information is influenced and restricted from the beginning by the old knowledge that the individual has acquired about the social and physical world. Before we turn to the interesting findings that social-cognition research has generated about the stages of perception, encoding, organization, retrieval and judgement, we should briefly consider the basic units of the generic knowledge that people use to make sense of new stimulus information.

The structure of generic knowledge

How is social and environmental knowledge organized in memory and what knowledge units have to be distinguished? Here is the basic terminology. The term **category** denotes an elementary knowledge structure, corresponding to a singular concept or class of objects. Identifying a perceived target as belonging to a category (e.g., a person as belonging to the category feminist) allows the perceiver to infer more information than is actually given. Such category-based inferences are valid in many cases (because many feminist persons may really share the common attributes of the category). However, categories will sometimes give rise to erroneous inferences about targets that are less typical of the category. For instance, the inference that feminists endorse legislation favouring abortion may not hold for particular women who, although feminist on other issues, reject abortion for ethical reasons. As this example refers to a social group, it may be more convenient to use the term **stereotype** to denote this social category. Although often charged with more sentiment and personal value, stereotypes obey similar rules to all other categories.

Social individuals approach the world with a large number of categories, based on what they have learned previously. Our personnel manager Harry Olds has acquired categories for female and male applicants, feminists and machos, vocational categories, tools and instruments, political positions, hobbies, music and

Category   Grouping of two or more distinguishable objects that are treated in a similar way. Classes of objects in the world.

Stereotype   Shared beliefs about personality traits and behaviours of group members. By stereotyping we overlook individuality.

writers. Being equipped with such world knowledge, his 'perception' will not be restricted to objectively present stimulus information.

How are categories represented in memory? It has been suggested that categories are represented as **prototypes** (Barsalou, 1985). A prototype is defined as the average or central tendency of a category (e.g., the average attitude and appearance of feminist women). Given the central tendency, some specific exemplars may be perceived as rather dissimilar to the prototype, though they are still considered part of the category. For example, although penguins belong to the category of birds, they are rather dissimilar to the prototype of this category (Rosch, 1978). The idea that categories are represented by their average or prototype has been opposed to the assumption that categories are represented by specific exemplars (**exemplar-based** models, e.g., Smith & Zaraté, 1992). In this case, knowledge about feminists is based on memory traces of specific exemplars (i.e., encounters with particular persons of that category).

> **Prototype**   The best exemplar of a given category; an abstract representation of the attributes associated with a category, which is stored in memory and used to organize information.

> **Exemplar-based representation**   Memory representation of a concept (group, category) in terms of concrete exemplars rather than abstracted features.

Most social knowledge is organized hierarchically, from abstract to specific, with abstract knowledge allowing for a greater variety of inferences than specific knowledge. Besides different levels of abstraction, categories may refer to different contents. As described above, stereotypes refer to the attributes that are assigned to a social group. In addition, categories may also refer to the representation about the self (Markus, 1977), about social roles, or about the sequence of events. Knowledge structures that describe standardized sequences of behaviours, events and states are denoted as **scripts** (Abelson, 1981). Scripted episodes include checking in at the airport, going to church, having a drink in a bar or celebrating Christmas. Harry Olds undoubtedly has a well-defined script of a job interview; his evaluation of applicants will strongly depend on whether the applicant behaves in accordance with this script.

> **Script**   Knowledge structure representing routinized action episodes in particular domains.

The impact of stored social knowledge depends not merely on the contents and representation format of individual categories, but even more so on their interconnections. The associative network (see figure 5.3) that connects multiple categories in memory is for the most part organized by semantic similarity. Categories of similar meaning (sharing many features) are functionally closer to each other than dissimilar categories. Thus, when Harry Olds thinks of one category (feminist), related categories (activist, gender roles, lesbian) afford very close associates that invite knowledge-based inferences.

Within such a framework, it becomes obvious that the implications of a particular knowledge structure depend strongly on its relation to other knowledge structures. This aspect is nicely illustrated in Solomon Asch's (1946) classical work. He presented participants with lists of trait adjectives and asked them to form an impression. He found that the impression resulting from a list of seven trait adjectives (e.g., intelligent, skilful, industrious, warm, determined, practical, cautious) could change dramatically when one single trait was replaced. Interestingly,

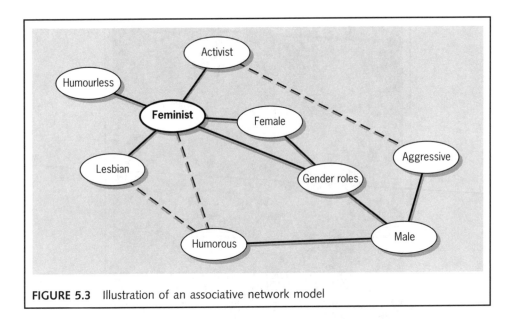

FIGURE 5.3   Illustration of an associative network model

some traits had a particularly strong impact on the implications for other traits. For example, replacing 'warm' with 'cold' had a stronger impact than replacing 'adventurous' with 'not adventurous'. Asch called these traits central traits. He also found that traits presented at the beginning of the list had a more pronounced impact on impressions than traits presented at the end of the list. This **primacy effect** may, however, be limited to judgements that are formed 'on-line' in a given situation. When judgements are formed later, on the basis of what is recalled from memory ('off-line' or 'memory-based' judgements, Hastie & Park, 1986), information at the end of the list is sometimes particularly influential because of its retrieval advantage (Anderson, 1976).

Primacy effect The tendency for information received early to have a stronger influence than later information on one's judgements or memory about persons, objects or issues.

Let us now consider the ways in which stored knowledge structures interact with incoming information across the various stages of cognitive processing.

Perception and attention

Imagine you are at a party with many people in the same room. Several groups are having lively conversations, and you find yourself in one of those groups. In this situation, there is an endless number of stimuli your senses could register. You could attend to what all the different people are saying, the verbal and non-verbal reactions of their partners, the sound of the music, the smell of the different foods, the taste of your wine, and much more.

A basic assumption of the social-cognition approach is that the capacity of human information processing is limited. We cannot process all stimuli that reach

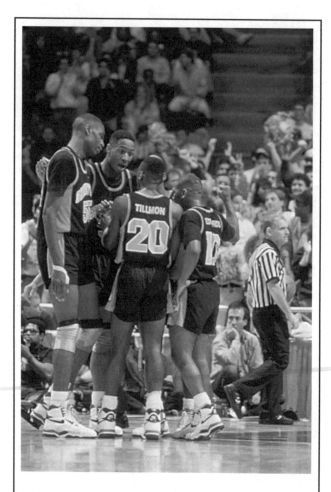

PLATE 5.2   The salience of stimulus characteristics (e.g., ethnic group, height) varies across situation, depending on who or what is present

our sensory system. Suppose you were later asked what the group in the other corner of the party room had discussed. You would probably have no idea. Obviously, the entire conversation would be lost although it had reached your senses. Imagine, however, you had overheard someone in a distant group mentioning your name. Even if you continued to converse in your own group, you would probably direct some of your attention towards that other conversation, and later you would be able to recall parts of it.

This example illustrates how the ability to direct one's attention at specific targets in the environment allows us to deal with the limitations of our cognitive capacity (Broadbent, 1958). This raises the question of what objects or events attract our attention. First, a specific stimulus may be *distinctive* in the context of other stimuli. For example, the short person in a team of tall basketball players or, conversely, the only tall person among rather petite gymnasts will presumably attract attention. Note that it is not the property of the stimulus as such, but its relation to the context that creates **salience**. Second, a stimulus may capture our attention because it is unexpected. Finally, we attend to stimuli that appear particularly relevant to our current goals (for further readings, see Fiske & Taylor, 1991; McArthur, 1981).

Salience The distinctiveness of a stimulus relative to the context (e.g., a male in a group of females; a group of people, one of whom is in the spotlight).

Encoding and interpretation

Once we have perceived a specific stimulus, we need to encode it in memory in order to give it meaning. Encoding comprises various processes that are involved when an external stimulus is transformed into an internal representation. Encoding is accomplished by relating the new stimulus to what we already know. Imagine you are driving down the road and see the letters STOP in white on a red background. You can categorize this stimulus input into a meaningful category, namely stop signs, and your prior information about this category helps you to interpret the meaning of the input. Once a stimulus is classified into some meaningful category, the perception is enriched with stimulus-independent knowledge about that category. This 'going beyond the information given' (Bruner, 1957) is also evident when Harry's sexist categorization of a person as female rather than male lends different meaning to that person's behaviour. For instance, the same careless behaviour (e.g., forgetting to ask for permission) may be interpreted as a sign of autonomy in males, but as a sign of negligence in females.

Thus, we have to realize that perception comes to interact with the **accessibility** of categories comprising the perceiver's world knowledge. The fate of a stimulus event depends on what category happens to be accessible at the time of perception, especially when the stimulus is ambiguous and open to different interpretations.

Accessibility The ease and speed with which information in memory can be found and retrieved.

What factors influence the likelihood that a category is accessible in the perceiver's working memory? First, *frequently* used categories are more likely to be accessible than rarely used categories (for example, Bargh & Pratto, 1986; Higgins, King, & Mavin, 1982; see Bargh, 1997). Second, categories that have been used very *recently* are more likely to be accessible than categories used a long time ago. This recency principle provides the basis for so-called **priming** experiments, in which recently activated categories have been shown to possess enhanced accessibility.

Priming effect The finding that a schema is more likely to be activated if it has recently been presented or used in the past.

A well-known experiment by Higgins, Rholes and Jones (1977) may serve to illustrate the notion of a priming effect. Participants had to form an impression of a target person who was described, in a written personality sketch, as a highly self-confident individual who engages in many risky and dangerous activities. While the topic of description was clearly defined and obviously related to courage and autonomy, the evaluative tone of the description was unclear, allowing for positive as well as negative interpretations. The same behaviours could be interpreted as either self-confident and persistent, or as reckless and aloof.

The priming treatment was hidden in a verbal learning task which preceded the impression formation task as part of a seemingly unrelated experiment. Participants had to memorize (for 8–10 seconds) several words while naming the colours of slides. The words to be memorized differed in valence and applicability to the behaviour descriptions, yielding four experimental conditions. In the *Positive–Applicable* condition, the words pertained to favourable traits that were clearly relevant to the description of the target (i.e., adventurous, self-confident, independent, persistent). In the *Negative–Applicable* condition, the trait terms were similarly relevant but negative in valence (reckless, conceited, aloof, stubborn). In two other conditions, the words used for priming were *Positive–Non-applicable* (obedient, neat, satirical, grateful) or *Negative–Non-applicable* (disrespectful, listless, clumsy, sly).

Priming of positive trait categories prior to reading the stimulus sketch resulted in more favourable impressions of the target person than priming of negative trait categories, and the effect was even more pronounced after an interval of 10 to 14 days. However, this priming effect was entirely confined to the applicable condition where the trait terms were clearly relevant to the specific contents of the behaviour description. Priming of non-applicable categories did not affect the impressions at all.

The consequences of priming are not restricted to evaluative judgements. Priming effects have also been demonstrated on a large variety of judgements, inferences, recall tasks or decisions (see Higgins, 1996). Moreover, recent research has demonstrated that priming may also have a direct effect on social behaviour (Bargh, 1997). For example, when participants were primed with the concept of rudeness, they interrupted the experimenter more often and more quickly than participants who were primed with neutral or polite concepts (Bargh, Chen, & Burrows, 1996; see figure 5.4).

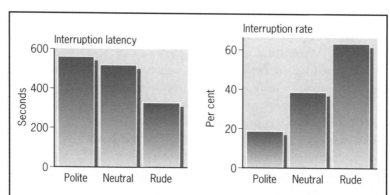

FIGURE 5.4   The influence of priming polite, neutral or rude concepts on the latency and probability of interrupting the experimenter's conversation
(After Bargh et al., 1996)

Theoretically, the influence of category priming can be explained within an associative network model of human memory, in which concepts are represented as nodes and the distance between nodes indicates their dissimilarity (see figure 5.3). The more similar two concepts are in meaning, the smaller is the distance between their nodes. In such a framework, 'priming' can be understood as a process of spreading activation from one node (the prime) to adjacent nodes in the network, and the strength of this effect should dissipate with increasing distance from the origin of the activation. For instance, if the 'reckless' and 'aloof' nodes are primed (in a verbal learning task), the activation should spread to other negatively valenced nodes related to adventurous behaviours. As a consequence, negative concepts should become more accessible and subsequent judgements should be biased accordingly.

Priming has become one of the most important methodological tools in social-cognition research (see Bargh, 1996), which has also identified some important limiting conditions, such as the applicability of the prime, the timing of the priming, and the consciousness of the activation. We shall address these issues in turn.

Let us first consider the applicability condition. It seems plausible that priming in the Higgins et al. (1977) experiment was most apparent in the applicable conditions, because the primed concepts (reckless, aloof) and the activated stimulus behaviours (e.g., skydiving, crossing the Atlantic in a sailboat) pertain to closely related nodes in the network. Judgements of these specific aspects should thus be influenced by the joint activation of specifically applicable category nodes. However, the theory does not strictly exclude an effect of non-applicable primes which only convey a positive or negative evaluation, without being descriptively relevant. The prime words used by Higgins and colleagues are descriptively very homogeneous, revolving around the same behavioural topic. If, however, generally positive or negative primes are used which cover a wider range of descriptive meanings, the priming effect should be broader and less specific. **Evaluative priming** of this kind should activate the diffuse feeling that the target person is unlikeable (or likeable).

> **Evaluative priming** Presenting a positive vs. negative stimulus facilitates the subsequent perception and processing of another stimulus of the same positive vs. negative valence.

Another possible restriction pertains to the timing of category priming. In the Higgins et al. experiment, the trait categories were activated *before* the presentation and encoding of the behaviour description. Several studies suggest that the encoding stage is especially sensitive to priming effects. For instance, Srull and Wyer (1980) manipulated the order in which the priming task, the presentation of stimulus information and the impression judgement task were applied. They obtained an effect only when the priming treatment was administered before the target information, but not when categories were primed after stimulus encoding. However, there is at least some evidence to suggest that under certain conditions an already formed impression may be changed by categories primed *afterwards*. One such demonstration comes from Snyder and Uranowitz (1978), who provided their participants with a written personality sketch about a female target person named Betty K. which resulted in a moderately favourable impression. Later on, the participants in one experimental condition received additional information about Betty's lesbian lifestyle. The activation of this category led to a substantial updating of judgements about Betty; impressions became less favourable and biased towards a lesbian stereotype. In principle, then, post-encoding information can have a retrograde influence on already existing memory representations (Belli, 1989; Tversky & Tuchin, 1989).

Interpreting stimulus observations in terms of primed categories does not require an intentional or conscious process; Bargh and Pietromonaco (1982) have reported a judgement bias towards semantic categories presented so quickly that conscious recognition was impossible. On the contrary, too high a degree of consciousness may undermine or even reverse the effect of priming. If participants get the feeling that blatant priming procedures may influence the outcome of their impression formation, they may attribute their biased impression to the external influence attempt and correct their judgements in the opposite direction. Lombardi, Higgins and Bargh (1987) used the same priming and stimulus materials as in the above study by Higgins et al. (1977) and showed that the judgement bias disappeared in those participants who recalled the concepts primed in the preceding verbal learning tasks. Similarly, Strack, Schwarz, Bless, Kübler and Wänke (1993) found that a priming effect can be eliminated and even reversed when judges are reminded of the priming episode. Thus, awareness is not a precondition of the priming effect and may actually interfere with it.

A large number of studies have investigated the priming of stereotypes, which are then shown to influence the encoding and interpretation of social behaviour (for overviews, see Hamilton & Sherman, 1994; Leyens, Yzerbyt, & Schadron, 1994; see also chapter 15 on intergroup relations). Stereotypes act in ways that are similar to other knowledge structures; they help to encode a specific situation and may serve as 'energy-saving' devices (Macrae, Milne, & Bodenhausen, 1994). By assigning an individual person to a stereotypical category (e.g., lesbian), a good deal of mental effort can be saved. This category can then be used to make inferences and predictions about the person. As long as interest and processing motivation are low, social judgements rely on this energy-saving, category-driven mode (Fiske & Neuberg, 1990). Only in exceptional circumstances will judges engage in more strenuous processing of individuating information that is specific to the particular target. As a rule, stereotypes have a particularly strong impact when individuals' processing motivation and capacity are low. The impact of stereotypes decreases when processing motivation and processing capacity are sufficiently high (Fiske & Neuberg, 1990; Kruglanski, 1989). Examining the role of *processing motivation*, Neuberg and Fiske (1987) found that the stereotype of schizophrenics influenced the behaviour of a person assigned to this category. The influence was reduced, however, if participants expected that they would have to cooperate with the target person on a subsequent task. Presumably, the expected interaction increased participants' willingness to take a closer look at the available data rather than merely relying on their pre-existing stereotype. Consistent findings have been obtained with respect to the impact of *processing capacity*. Stereotypes are more influential when time pressure (Kruglanski & Freund, 1983) or task complexity (Bodenhausen & Lichtenstein, 1987) reduce processing capacity.

Bodenhausen (1990) has reported a neat demonstration of how capacity can influence the impact of stereotypes. His study is based on the assumption that individuals have different circadian rhythms, that is, individuals have their highs and lows of cognitive abilities at different times during the course of the day. Based on a pre-test, Bodenhausen divided participants into 'morning' and 'evening' people. Participants had to judge the guilt of a target person who allegedly had physically attacked another person. The target person was described either as *Robert Garner* or as *Roberto Garcia*, with the latter presumably activating the American students' stereotype about Hispanics. As the description of the incident itself was held constant, different evaluations based on the two different name versions reflect the impact of the stereotype. The experimental sessions were scheduled either early in the morning, in the afternoon, or in the evening. As expected, if judgements were made early in the morning (9 a.m.), evening people reported more stereotypic judgements (i.e., seeing the Hispanic Roberto Garcia as more aggressive than Robert Garner) than morning people (figure 5.5); conversely, morning people made more stereotypic judgements than evening people if the sessions were scheduled later in the day (3 p.m. or 8 p.m.). Presumably, the reduced processing capacity of evening people in the morning session, and of morning people in the evening session, required them to rely on the stereotype to interpret the situation.

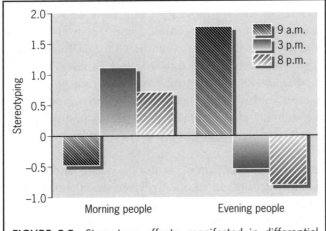

FIGURE 5.5 Stereotype effects, manifested in differential aggression judgements of 'Roberto Garcia' and 'Robert Garner', are most pronounced at non-preferred times of day (After Bodenhausen, 1990)

Organization

Understanding and interpreting a new stimulus in an ongoing situation is but one aspect of the social perceiver's task. Individuals need to organize this information in memory, and this organization provides the basis for behaviour in later situations. For example, if the applicant has interpreted Harry Olds' behaviour as sexist, this interpretation might not only be helpful for her behaviour in the current situation, but also for later encounters with Harry. Given the necessity to store and retrieve information, it is important that individuals store information in such a way that it can be easily retrieved when needed. Similar to filing information in a cabinet, we need an effective organization system that allows us quickly to find stored information when required. The most natural way of organizing social information in memory is by categories, and a most prominent type of category is the individual person. When complex social information refers, in random order, to different persons' behaviours with respect to different topics (e.g., group discussions, parties, etc.), people tend to organize their memories in a person-by-person fashion (Sedikides & Ostrom, 1988). The order in which the information is recalled reveals person clusters rather than topic clusters; that is, behaviours belonging to the same persons are grouped together in memory.

When the clusters of information about individual persons become too large, it is important to organize information in memory in an economic fashion. Imagine getting acquainted with somebody who tells you about her hobbies or interests. Altogether, she talks about 12 different interest categories (e.g., sports, finance) with four different items per category (e.g., tennis, handball, boxing, rowing, stock market, interest rates, share capital, foreign currencies) but in random order. A highly efficient strategy for memorizing a remarkably large amount of information in such an overloaded task is to form a memory code at the categorical level. Rather than trying in vain to memorize all the 48 original items, one can rely on categorical information such as *she is interested in all kinds of sports* or *she is interested in financial topics.* By reducing memory load from 48 specific units to 12 more abstract units, one can use world knowledge to reconstruct the specific contents of the stimulus information. Several studies (e.g., Fiedler, 1986) have shown that people use such higher-order memory codes in highly efficient and economical ways.

The organization of information in memory is greatly affected by the processing goals or task instructions. In an often-cited study, Hamilton, Katz and Leirer (1980) presented their participants with behaviour descriptions related to four topics (sports, intellectual, interpersonal, religious). In one experimental condition, participants were explicitly asked *to memorize* the stimulus behaviours, whereas in another condition they were instructed *to form an impression* of the target person. Although there was no mention of a memory test in the impression formation condition, the recall performance was higher than under the memorization instruction. This advantage of incidental over intentional learning reflects the impact of an *impression formation goal* on the construction of a coherent memory representation, which subsequently can be used for efficient retrieval.

Relating stimulus information to prior knowledge – consistent and inconsistent information

While interviewing the applicants, the personnel manager Harry Olds may encounter information that is both consistent and inconsistent with his stereotype. Which information is Harry more likely to recall two days later? On the one hand, one might assume that he would chiefly recall information that is consistent with his stereotype. On the other hand, one might speculate that unusual exceptions can be recalled very well. The answer to the question, which type of information is memorized better, is less clear than one might expect. Both consistent and inconsistent information may have a memory advantage, though for different reasons and under different circumstances.

One intuitively surprising finding is that inconsistent or unexpected information is often recalled better than information consistent with an expectation (Hastie, 1980). For example, if we learn that a priest robbed an old lady or that an active sportsman is physically handicapped, we are likely to elaborate on such surprising events and are unlikely to forget them. Srull (1981) has shown that an explicit impression-formation instruction serves to reinforce this advantage of inconsistent information. The goal of forming an overall impression highlights the need to integrate and make sense of the inconsistent information, thereby forcing the individual to invest extra cognitive effort in the processing of inconsistent information. In other words, inconsistent observations receive deeper cognitive elaboration. Other findings support this explanation. The enhanced memory for inconsistent information disappears when stimulus behaviours refer to groups rather than individuals (Stern, Marrs, Millar, & Cole, 1984); less cognitive effort is obviously needed to reconcile inconsistencies between members of a group than inconsistencies within the same individual. In the same vein, Bargh and Thein (1985) found that it was possible to eliminate the advantage of inconsistent information by presenting stimuli at a rate fast enough to prevent extra processing.

However, the enhanced salience and memory of surprising and inconsistent information is only one side of the coin. Information that is consistent with prior knowledge may also have a strong impact on memory, albeit for different reasons. While the inconsistency effect is due to the extra attention and cognitive effort devoted to unexpected stimuli, consistent information has the advantage of being derivable from systematic world knowledge (Stangor & McMillan, 1992). Thus, whereas an extraordinary instance of criminal behaviour by a monk is not likely to be forgotten, his normal, benevolent behaviour can be derived from general knowledge about his other attributes (religious, moral, follows rules of conduct). In other words, the inconsistency advantage reflects the bottom-up processing of discrepant stimuli (and disappears when processing capacity is reduced). In

contrast, enhanced memory of consistent information reflects the top-down influence of embedding knowledge structures (and disappears when links to semantic
knowledge are missing).

A study by Macrae, Hewstone and Griffith (1993) nicely demonstrates the
different processes that may lead to the recall of consistent and inconsistent
information. The authors assume that the memory advantage of information inconsistent with expectations is only observed when sufficient processing capacity is
available, while the recall of consistent information is independent of the amount
of processing during encoding. Participants watched a videotaped conversation
between two women talking about their interests, lifestyle and so on. The presented information was either consistent or inconsistent with the targets' profession (doctor and hairdresser). Half of the participants had to remember an 8-digit
number as they were watching the video (high cognitive load), while the remaining half had no additional task (low cognitive load). Later, participants were asked
to recall the conversation. Participants under low cognitive load displayed a preferential recall for stereotype-inconsistent information. However, participants subject to high cognitive load recalled more consistent than inconsistent information
(figure 5.6).

Knowledge-congruent inferences may override the attention-grabbing value of
incongruent information to the extent that appropriate knowledge structures are
activated. This is the case when social stereotypes are involved. Stereotypical expectancies are often maintained in spite of contradicting observations. For instance, our
sexist personnel manager Harry Olds may be exposed to striking evidence of women
outperforming their male colleagues on the job. If memory were only dependent

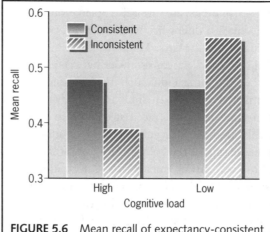

FIGURE 5.6   Mean recall of expectancy-consistent
vs. expectancy-inconsistent information as a function of cognitive load
(After Macrae et al., 1993)

on the recallability of individual items, these inconsistent observations would be well remembered and would change Harry's stereotype before too long. However, since Harry's memory is organized by a network of sexist categories, he will use these categories as retrieval cues. That is, he will probably scan his memory for instances of female naivety, unreliability or hysterical reactions, and these retrieval cues as starting points may override the primary advantage of stereotype-inconsistent observations. The impact of category priming on subsequent judgements of related targets that was described in an earlier section can be considered as a special case of this knowledge-driven consistency effect.

Judgements

The relationship between memory and judgement is commonly interpreted as a causal influence from memory to judgement. In Hovland, Janis and Kelley's (1953) early approach to attitude change, the persuasiveness of a message was conceived of as a function of memory for pro and contra arguments (see chapter 8). This same one-sided assumption has long dominated research on social judgement. The notion that memory triggers judgement, and not the other way around, has guided above all the modern research programme on **judgemental heuristics** (Kahneman et al., 1982). The notion of a heuristic highlights the fact that cognitive information processing is rarely exhaustive or meets the standards of logic, but has to reach a compromise between rationality and economy. A heuristic is a cognitive device which enables the social individual to make judgements by rules-of-thumb that require little effort but yield valid results most of the time. However, the price of economy is systematically biased judgements under certain conditions.

> **Judgemental heuristic** Rules-of-thumb that allow quick and economic judgements, even under high uncertainty.

The so-called **availability** heuristic (Tversky & Kahneman, 1973) makes possible, first of all, judgements of frequency and probability in the absence of valid statistical information. For instance, even if we did not count the number of rainy and sunny days in 1998, we can estimate their respective frequencies from the availability of relevant information in memory. If a brief memory scan yields as many sunny days as rainy days, our numerical estimates will also tend to be equal. However, while this heuristic procedure is often quite accurate, the resulting judgements may be biased when the memory sample is biased. For instance, if memory is biased towards pleasantness and we selectively recall a greater number of sunny days, the frequency estimates will also be biased. Combs and Slovic (1979) demonstrated that judgements of lethal risks are biased towards the frequency with which newspapers report causes of death. Since the media are more likely to report spectacular events such as catastrophes or homicides than heart disease or suicides, the frequency of the former events is overestimated relative to the latter.

> **Availability** Judgemental heuristic for judging the frequency or probability of events on the basis of the ease with which relevant memories come to mind.

Representativeness
Judgemental heuristic used to estimate event probabilities on the basis of crude similarity principles. For instance, a symptom is taken as evidence for a threatening disease even when the objective base-rate of the disease is extremely low.

Other judgement heuristics are also based on the assumption of a causal impact of memory on judgement. According to the **representativeness** heuristic (Kahneman & Tversky, 1972), a person described as interested in model aircraft, chess and computers is more likely to be classified as a physicist than a teacher, simply because the information is more representative of the former than the latter profession. In fact, the base-rate of teachers (i.e., their relative frequency in the population) is so much higher than that of physicists that this judgement is probably wrong. However, the heuristic is guided by resemblance in semantic memory (between concepts like physicist, aircraft and computers) rather than statistical base-rates.

The **anchoring and adjustment** heuristic (Tversky & Kahneman, 1974) implies that quantitative judgements are often biased towards an initial anchor because a memory-based adjustment process is often incomplete. Imagine you are planning a two-week vacation in Florida and you want to calculate the costs in advance. You may start from a low anchor of £350 for airfare and think about additional costs in an upward adjustment process. Alternatively, you may start from the high anchor of £2,500 that your well-off friend spent on a similar trip, and subtract whatever expenditures could be saved. Since the memory search for costs to be added or saved is typically incomplete (Strack & Mussweiler, 1997), the upward adjustment process will usually result in a lower estimate than the downward adjustment process.

Anchoring and adjustment
Judgemental heuristic that leads to characteristic biases: quantitative tendency to be biased towards the starting value or anchor. The subsequent adjustment process is typically incomplete.

While most research has treated judgements as a dependent variable and memory as an independent variable, it is by now clear that a simple monocausal model cannot account for the relationship between memory and judgement. More systematic accounts of the empirical evidence suggest that recall measures are often uncorrelated with judgemental tendencies (Hastie & Park, 1986). This is because many social judgements are already 'pre-formed' and stored in memory, and do not have to be formed on the basis of memorized raw information. For example, a woman who is asked to judge the jealousy of her husband need not scan her memory for relevant experiences but already knows that he is notoriously jealous. Pre-formed judgements of this kind make up a considerable part of social memory. As Hastie and Park (1986) have shown, only **memory-based judgements** that cannot use pre-formed **'on-line' judgements** should bear a substantial correlation with recall of stimulus information. Of course, if you are asked to estimate the number of children on your street and you have never thought about this before, your judgement *has to rely* on available memory.

Memory-based judgement
Typically, an unexpected judgement that has to rely on whatever relevant information can be retrieved from memory.

On-line judgement Judgement formed immediately upon presentation of stimulus information.

Even for memory-based judgements, the best predictor need not be the amount of recallable information. A refined version of the availability heuristic proposed by Schwarz, Bless, Strack, Klumpp, Rittenauer-Schatka and Simons (1991) states that judgements reflect the experienced **ease of recall** rather than the recall output itself. Thus, if participants are asked to think about either six or 12 episodes in which they have shown self-assertive behaviour, they come up with more recalled items in the latter condition. However, subsequent self-ratings of assertiveness exhibit an opposite bias. Since thinking about a few examples is experienced as easier and less strenuous than thinking about many examples, enhanced assertiveness can be inferred from the experienced ease of recalling only six examples. This reformulation of the availability heuristic is related to the **simulation heuristic**, according to which the ease with which possible events or outcomes can be imagined or mentally simulated is crucial to judgements. For example, judgements of the risk of driving after drinking alcohol should depend on one's ability to imagine or 'mentally simulate' being involved in an accident. Our reluctance to create such a mental scenario will typically lead to an underestimation of the actual risk. An overview of cognitive heuristics and the resulting judgement biases is given in table 5.2.

Common to all judgement heuristics considered thus far is the implicit assumption that the influence of biased memory on judgements can be described as an **assimilation** rather than a **contrast** effect. That is, judgements are assumed to be biased towards the output of the heuristic process rather than the other way round. Thus, if pleasant memories are more readily available, the current situation should be judged to be rather pleasant (assimilation). However, it is

Ease of recall   The subjective feeling that information pertaining to some topic can be easily found and retrieved from memory; not to be confused with objective recall success.

Simulation heuristic   Outcomes or events are judged to be likely to the extent that they can be mentally simulated or imagined.

Assimilation   A shift in the frame of reference caused by a context stimulus such that judgements of other stimuli are biased towards the context stimulus (e.g., in the context of humour, other utterances may appear more humorous).

Contrast   A shift in the frame of reference caused by a context stimulus such that judgements of other stimuli tend away from the context

TABLE 5.2   Overview of most popular judgement heuristics

Heuristic	Field of application	Illustration/example
Availability	Judgements of frequency or probability	Recallability of risk episodes determines judgements of risk
Representativeness	Judgements of likelihood that observations belong to a category	Birth order son-daughter-son-daughter more representative of random event than son-son-son-son
Anchoring and adjustment	Quantitative estimates towards starting value	Cost calculations biased
Simulation heuristic	Counterfactual reasoning	More regret experienced when missing train by two minutes than by 20 minutes because it is easier to mentally undo the former event

stimulus (e.g., other people appear rather poor in contrast to an extremely rich person).

Standard of comparison
Position of an anchor or comparison stimulus on a judgement scale.

also possible that our present situation appears less pleasant (contrast) if the very pleasant memories that are activated set a high **standard of comparison** (Strack, Schwarz, & Gschneidinger, 1985).

Consider a study reported by Bless and Schwarz (1998). When the highly respected former German Bundespräsident (representative head of state) Richard von Weizsäcker was introduced to participants as a member of the Christian Democratic Union (CDU), other politicians of the same party received more favourable judgements. However, this assimilation effect was turned into a contrast effect when von Weizsäcker was introduced as the independent head of state. In this case, the availability of von Weizsäcker created a particularly high standard of comparison that led to less favourable judgements of other politicians. As a rule, the activation of a context stimulus (e.g., von Weizsäcker) causes assimilation if the context stimulus is *included* in the category of the judgement target (Weizsäcker as a CDU party member), whereas a contrast effect can be expected if the context stimulus is *excluded* from the target category (Weizsäcker as an independent head of state; see Bless & Schwarz, 1998; Schwarz & Bless, 1992).

Verification and Falsification of Social Hypotheses

Why are stereotypical beliefs so resistant to change?
How can the notion of illusory correlations be explained?
What are the processes by which social hypotheses can verify themselves?

In everyday life, the cognitive operations of perception, encoding, organization and judgement are embedded in goal-directed action or problem-solving. A teacher has to evaluate her students' achievement, a personnel manager (like Harry Olds) has to select among job applicants, and we all have to structure the social world as we learn conceptions of various social groups. All these everyday problems involve **social hypothesis testing**, about the abilities of students, the qualifications of applicants or the attributes of groups. Social hypothesis testing can be understood as the overall process by which old knowledge is updated in the light of new stimulus data. This process is essentially conservative. For a variety of reasons, expectancies and stereotypes that should be discarded will often be conserved. First, expectancies may arise in the absence of any substantial 'objective' evidence supporting them. Second, people often create the kind of reality they expect; such self-fulfilling prophecies (e.g., Snyder, Tanke, & Berscheid, 1977) reduce the rate of disconfirming evidence. Third, people may actively seek confirming evidence. Fourth, when contradictory evidence cannot be denied, it can be set aside from the hypothesis at hand. And fifth,

Social hypothesis testing
Verifying or falsifying propositions through socially motivated processes of attention, information search, logical reasoning and (often selective) memory.

ambivalent information can be disambiguated in line with the guiding hypo-thesis. The following section will address all these possibilities.

Stereotypes and illusory correlations

Social stereotyping amounts to testing hypotheses about subjectively expected cor-relations between group membership and behavioural attributes. Harry's sexist stereotype implies a correlation between gender groups and formal thinking, to the effect that girls are supposed to have weaker logical abilities than boys. As the previous sections have shown, such an expected correlation can affect all stages of information processing (Hamilton, 1981). Harry is inclined to *judge* women and girls more negatively in terms of logical ability because he more readily *retrieves* stereotype-confirming information from memory. Moreover, he can integrate confirming evidence more efficiently within the global memory *organization*. The stereotype may even attune his *attention* and *perception* in such a way that Harry 'perceives' the same logical achievement to be higher in a boy than in a girl.

When a stereotypical expectation overrides the correlation that actu-ally describes a series of stimulus observations, we refer to it as an **illusory correlation** to highlight the illusion inherent in stereotyp-ical thinking. Hamilton and Rose (1980) presented their participants with a series of sentences about members of three vocational groups (accountants, doctors, salesmen), with each sentence describing a per-son by two trait terms. Stimulus traits varied in stereotypicality for the various professions (e.g., accountant – 'perfectionist' vs. accoun-tant – 'helpful'). However, the series were constructed to represent zero correlations, such that each occupational group was described by each trait adjective exactly two times. Nevertheless, participants' frequency judgements were biased towards the stereotypes, with the result that the co-occurrence of typ-ical traits with the occupational groups was overestimated (e.g., accountants were seen as more perfectionist than were salesmen). Since it is impossible actually to remember the group associations of so many stimulus behaviours, judges must often resort to guessing and rely on stereotypical knowledge when they try to reconstruct what they have observed. Fiedler, Hemmeter and Hofmann (1984) demonstrated an illusory correlation in an experiment in which students were erro-neously reported to have proposed more liberal educational attitudes than con-servative clerks. Again, the biased frequency judgements were correlated with a corresponding recall bias, but the illusion was also shown to reflect participants' perception and comprehension of the attitude statements. That is, the identical attitude statements were from the outset interpreted as more liberal when a stud-ent as opposed to a clerk proposed them. Quite independent of any sentiments and affectively charged prejudices, the expectancy-driven nature of human informa-tion processing provides a universal source of stereotyping. To keep within our example, even when girls exhibit formal thinking as often and obviously as boys,

Illusory correlation An overestimation of the strength of a relationship between two, usually distinct, variables (e.g., 'crime' and 'immigrants'); a possible cognitive basis of stereotyping.

the formal qualities of girls may go unnoticed, or may be forgotten, as memory for the original observations declines, while stereotypes survive to determine the reconstruction of memories. As a result of such a 'vicious circle', it may be difficult to change a stereotype even when disconfirming evidence is available. If anything, stereotype change is most likely when disconfirming evidence is unambiguous and clearly pertains to prototypical members of the stereotyped group (Rothbart & Lewis, 1988). That is, the girl who disconfirms the stereotype, showing superb formal thinking, should still be a typical girl in at least some respects (e.g., dress, appearance, hobbies). Otherwise, a **subtyping** process may protect the stereotype from falsification (Johnston & Hewstone, 1992; Kunda & Oleson, 1995, 1997; Weber & Crocker, 1983). That is, the high-performing girl may be classified as belonging to a rather exceptional subtype of girls, who are more like boys.

> **Subtyping** Stereotypes can be maintained by attributing disconfirming observations to a subtype of people who are separated from the stereotyped group.

Self-verification processes

The tendency of hypothetical expectations to become social reality is, however, not solely determined by biases in the hidden cognitive stages of perception, encoding, retrieval and judgement formation. Rather, the manner in which social hypotheses are tested in social interaction may help the hypothesis to come true. In an intriguing series of studies, Snyder and Swann (1978) asked their participants to find out whether their interaction partner was an extravert or an introvert, depending on the experimental conditions. There was a strong tendency for the resulting impression to be biased in the same direction as the question: when the task referred to extraversion, a more extravert impression of the partner emerged than in the reverse condition. Closer analyses revealed that this was due to one-sided information search in verbal interaction. To find out if a partner was an extravert, participants asked questions such as 'What would you do if you wanted to liven things up at a party?' or 'What kind of situation do you seek out if you want to meet new people?' By contrast, to find out if someone was an introvert the typical interview questions were, 'In what situations do you wish you could be more outgoing?' or 'What things do you dislike about loud parties?' Since the discussion partners had good reasons for providing confirming evidence for both sets of questions (because almost everybody sometimes engages in extravert and sometimes in introvert behaviour), the questions evoked confirmatory evidence for the trait the questioner had in mind. Furthermore, observers of the videotaped interaction were biased in the same direction in that they inferred a disposition from the respondents' extravert or introvert answers, disregarding the one-sided questions that evoked those answers.

This intriguing demonstration of how hypotheses become social reality was originally attributed to the impact of a prior belief. However, it is not even necessary that the interviewer actually believes in the hypothesis being tested; even completely arbitrary hypotheses that are formulated by the experimenter, detached from the individual's beliefs or expectations, can be verified through social interaction.

This was demonstrated by Semin and Strack (1980) in a study based on the independent manipulation of both prior expectations and the arbitrary hypothesis to be tested. Again, researchers manipulated the focus of the hypothesis by asking participants to find out if their interview partner was either extravert or introvert. However, within both conditions, different subgroups of participants were given background information about the target person's profession, thus creating an expectancy that the target was an extravert or an introvert; in a control condition, no expectation was induced. As it turned out, the biased information search (e.g., the tendency to ask many extraversion questions) was not determined by the expectation itself but by the arbitrary direction of the question. Thus, even when participants believed that the target was presumably an introvert (because he was introduced as a librarian rather than a salesman), the task of testing the extraversion hypothesis led them to ask predominantly extravert questions.

The verification bias is robust and unrestricted in still another respect. Although the verification effect is facilitated by the fact that social interaction partners tend to provide behavioural confirmation for any question contents (Snyder, 1984), the process is not strictly contingent on behavioural confirmation. Even when the target person does not actually confirm the hypothesis being tested, it is sufficient that the participant perceives or infers confirmation. That is, interviewers may simply assume or imagine that the target would presumably confirm the question; confirmation may thus be implicit or 'conjectural'. Thus, Swann, Giuliano and Wegner (1982) used audiotaped interactions involving a female interviewer mentioning either extravert or introvert topics to interviewees who were instructed to respond spontaneously. Afterwards, the audiotaped conversation was presented to observers who had to rate the respondent for extraversion or introversion. Depending on the experimental condition, the tape included (a) only the interviewer's questions, (b) only the respondent's responses, (c) the questions plus the responses, or (d) nothing but minimal background information about the respondent (no-evidence control condition). Relative to the control condition, the resulting impressions in all other conditions were clearly biased in the direction suggested by the interviewers' questions (extravert vs. introvert). It did not matter whether observers received the responses as behavioural evidence or only the question contents; the effect was substantial in all experimental conditions (see figure 5.7).

In fact, even *disconfirming* evidence will not prevent hypotheses from being verified. For example, Wegner, Wenzlaff, Kerker and Beattie (1981) were concerned with the effects of incriminating innuendo in the mass media, such as the question 'Is Bob Talbert linked to the Mafia?' The audience's impression of the target was swayed in a negative direction, even when the innuendo entailed a denial ('Bob Talbert not linked to the Mafia'). Such an innuendo effect may reflect a constructive memory process of the same type that has often been demonstrated in research on eyewitness testimony (Loftus, 1979). The mental act of thinking about Bob Talbert linked to the Mafia may force the participant to imagine or construe Bob Talbert for a moment in the semantic context of the Mafia and criminality, if only to deny the innuendo. However, this constructive experience

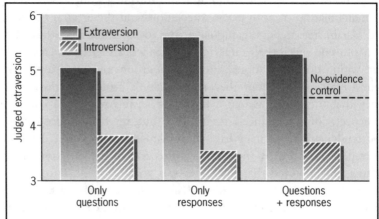

FIGURE 5.7   Mean attribution of extraversion as a function of task condition (test extraversion vs. test introversion) and evidence type (only questions, only responses, questions plus responses)

may be sufficient to leave its trace in memory. Later on, person impressions may confound actually observed information with these sorts of self-generated constructions (Johnson & Raye, 1981), making it difficult to get rid of the innuendo effect.

Cognitive Adaptation in a Social Environment

In which way is the processing of social information sensitive to sample size?
What is the role of language in social stereotyping?
How do cognitive processes change as a function of affective states?

In order to understand social cognition and behaviour, it is important to describe the stimulus environment that impinges on the social individual. In this final section, we shall illustrate the interplay of cognitive processes and environmental influences with reference to three intriguing issues. We first show that judgement biases may reflect the distributions of stimuli in the social world before any cognitive distortions or motivational forces come into play. Then we briefly address the impact of language as a powerful aspect of the human environment. Finally, we shall consider the interplay of cognition and emotional states.

Distribution of stimulus information

The origin of what seems to be a serious cognitive bias can often be found in the stimulus environment. For example, one cognitive illusion that originates in a skewed stimulus distribution is the illusory correlation phenomenon first shown by Hamilton and Gifford (1976) and referred to above. They constructed a series of desirable and undesirable behaviours by two groups, denoted A and B, to avoid any associations to real groups. The series included 18 desirable and 8 undesirable behaviours by group A, and 9 positive and 4 negative behaviours by a smaller group B. The ratio of positive to negative behaviours is therefore the same in both groups (18+/8− = 9+/4−), which means that positivity is uncorrelated with groups. But the stimulus distribution is skewed: observations about group B are less frequent than about group A, rendering B a minority and A a majority. Moreover, negative behaviours are less frequent than positive behaviours, which is also representative of the social world, because negative behaviour deviates from social norms (Skowronski & Carlston, 1989). Therefore, Hamilton and Gifford's stimulus series can be considered an experimental analogue of an actual social environment in which a majority and a minority do not differ in positivity. Nevertheless, a more negative impression is created of the minority B. This is evident in biased group impression ratings, frequency estimates of the relative number of positive vs. negative behaviours in both groups, and in a tendency to associate positive behaviours with the majority rather than the minority in a recall test.

This phenomenon has been replicated in numerous experiments (Mullen & Johnson, 1990) and can be considered a permanent source of minority derogation. One explanation of the illusion is in terms of a cognitive processing bias towards the most infrequent event, negative minority behaviour, which is assumed to be particularly distinctive or salient and which should therefore be memorized better than the rest of the information. However, subsequent research has shown that the illusion is also obtained when a memory advantage of infrequent observations is ruled out (Fiedler, 1991; Klauer & Meiser, in press). Even when all stimulus events have an equal likelihood of being retained in memory, the prevalence of positive over negative behaviours will be more likely detected in the majority than in the minority, simply because the 18+/8− ratio rests on a larger sample of observations than the 9+/4− ratio. Just as any reasonable learning theory predicts that rule learning increases with the number of trials, the 26 (18 + 8) learning trials about the majority convey the prevailing positivity more efficiently than the 13 (9 + 4) minority trials. Thus, what appeared to be a purely cognitive bias turns out to be predetermined by the frequency distribution of stimuli in the environment.

Language and communication

Language is the medium within which social knowledge is acquired and communicated in books, mass media and face-to-face interaction. A considerable part of social knowledge is therefore built into the lexicon and the rules of language. The socially shared word meanings and communication rules provide an important external store of social knowledge, quite independent of the internal representations within the brains of individual persons. At the lexical level, to begin with, the choice of words we use to describe people and their behaviour has rich implications for cognitive inferences and implicit attributions. For instance, the notion of **implicit verb causality** (Brown & Fish, 1983; Fiedler & Semin, 1988) refers to the systematically different causal attributions suggested by *action verbs* (help, hurt, comply with) and *state verbs* (abhor, like, respect). Thus, the same behaviour might be described by the sentence, *The student complies with the teacher* (action verb), or, *The student respects the teacher* (state verb). The former sentence attributes the behaviour to the student's compliance, whereas the latter suggests an attribution to the teacher's respectability. In general, the semantic meaning of action verbs implies subject causation, whereas the meaning of most state verbs implies object causation.

Implicit verb causality The tendency to infer causes within the sentence subject from action verbs and causes within the object from state verbs.

The adjectives we use to characterize the traits and dispositions of persons and groups differ markedly with respect to the variety of behaviours they refer to and the amount of behavioural evidence that is necessary to confirm or disconfirm a trait hypothesis (Rothbart & Park, 1986). An *honest* person is honest most of the time, whereas the opposite trait, *dishonest*, is justified by very few observations of such behaviour. Adjectives also differ in the breadth of their domain: *talkative* refers to a more narrow range of behaviours than *extravert*. The latter term conveys a more global and broadly applicable attribution than the former, although both terms might be used to describe exactly the same behaviour in the same situation. It is no wonder, then, that the words used to describe people and behaviours can greatly affect the formation and change of social stereotypes. Little evidence is needed to verify the stereotype that a group is *dishonest*, but once the stereotype is established it has broad implications, and strong evidence is required to falsify the stereotype and to verify that a person or group is in fact *honest*.

Semin and Fiedler (1988, 1991) have proposed a systematic taxonomy of the verbs and adjectives that make up interpersonal language. At the most specific level, *descriptive action verbs* refer to specific behaviours in specific situations, with little interpretation beyond the observable behaviour (e.g., to shake hands, to kiss, to turn away from). *Interpretative action verbs* (to help, to hurt, to hinder) also refer to singular action episodes, but abstract from the physical and perceptual features by which the action is manifested. At the next level of abstractness, *state verbs* (to admire, to respect, to dislike) refer to more enduring affective or mental states which abstract from a single action episode. At the highest level, *adjectives* (honest, unreliable, brutal) are used to abstract from specific actions, situations as well as object persons.

The choice of **linguistic categories** has important implications for the way in which social behaviour is interpreted and represented cognitively. As one moves up the abstractness scale from descriptive action verbs to adjectives, very different attributions can be suggested for the same behaviour. For instance, a female applicant's verbal behaviour may be characterized as *speaking softly* and *hesitating before speaking* (descriptive and interpretative action verbs), or as *timid* and *not*

Linguistic categories Different types of verbs and adjectives that can take the role of predicates in behaviour descriptions.

self-confident (adjectives). The latter more abstract style appears to reveal a lot about her personality, suggests a stable attribution and a lack of voluntary control (i.e., adjectives rarely allow for an imperative: 'Stop being timid!'). By contrast, a more specific language style implies less stable attributions, a higher degree of context dependence (i.e., she may behave differently in another context), and a higher level of voluntary control. Moreover, specific terms entail clearer references to the empirical world, rendering critical tests and falsification attempts more likely than in the case of abstract traits. Presumably, abstract terms play an essential role in Harry Olds' sexist language.

Maass, Salvi, Arcuri and Semin (1989) have applied the above linguistic category model to the study of intergroup behaviour in natural settings, with Palio teams as participants. Palio is a traditional horse-racing competition between north Italian towns with considerable between-group animosities. Maass and colleagues presented their participants with cartoon-like scenes depicting desirable and undesirable behaviours by members of either their own or the opposing team. Respondents were free to select any of the above language levels to describe the behaviour in question. A **linguistic intergroup bias** was manifested in a systematic tendency to describe negative outgroup behaviour and positive ingroup behaviour in more abstract terms than positive outgroup and negative ingroup behaviour (see figure 5.8). This means that independently of cognitive biases or affective conflicts within individual people, the language used to communicate social knowledge between people and in the media (Maass, Corvino, & Arcuri, 1994) will serve to reinforce and maintain an ingroup-serving bias. Rather than denying the occurrence of positive outgroup and negative

Linguistic intergroup bias The tendency to use more abstract linguistic categories to describe positive ingroup and negative outgroup behaviour than to describe negative ingroup and positive outgroup behaviour.

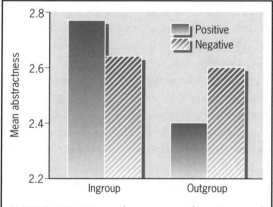

FIGURE 5.8 Mean abstractness of positive and negative sentences referring to ingroups vs. outgroups
(After Maass et al., 1989)

ingroup behaviours, the linguistic intergroup bias operates in a more subtle and refined manner, raising ingroup-serving attributes to a more abstract level.

Cognitive–affective regulation

The interface between cognition and the environment is charged with emotional experience as the stimulus events are relevant to the individual's wishes and personal values. Countless studies have addressed the interplay of affect and cognition over the last two decades, but we are only just beginning to understand this fundamental issue of behaviour regulation.

Mood congruency The tendency to perceive, encode, store and recall information more efficiently that is effectively congruent with one's emotional state. Also refers to the tendency to give more positive (negative) judgements in positive (negative) mood states.

The term 'behaviour regulation' here alludes to the double function of cognitive processes, which have to support emotional reactions, on the one hand, and prevent perpetuating reactions, on the other hand. The former aspect has been widely noted as the principle of **mood congruency** (Bower, 1981; Isen, 1984). There is a basic selective tendency for people in a positive mood state to perceive, encode and retrieve positive material more efficiently than negative information, and a relative processing advantage for negative information in negative mood states. This principle can account for the pessimistic contents in depressive people's thoughts and memories, as well as the ability of elated mood states to facilitate recall of pleasant memories (Bower, 1981) and benevolent social judgements (Forgas & Bower, 1987). Such congruency effects can be derived within the aforementioned associative network model: if we assume that positive mood states are represented in the associative neighbourhood of other pleasant stimuli or events (see figure 5.3), the spreading activation that emanates from the positive-mood node should raise the activation level of other positive memory contents (pertaining to pleasant stimuli) but not influence, or even block, the activation of affectively incongruent nodes (pertaining to unpleasant contents). As a consequence, a positive affective state leads to more positive and optimistic social judgements (Mayer & Salovey, 1988) and to decreasing judgements of risk and danger (Johnson & Tversky, 1983).

The congruency principle alone would lead to a perpetuating effect which might contribute to pathological developments. For instance, a depressive state may result in pessimistic memory contents and pessimistic social judgements, which may manifest themselves in antisocial behaviour. The social environment will react aversively to such antisocial behaviour, causing an even stronger depressive reaction, which may in turn lead to further pessimistic cognitions, and so forth. Analogous to such a vicious circle, Isen, Shalkner, Clark and Karp (1978) have proposed a positive loop to account for the altruistic influence of positive mood states. Good moods may trigger positive memory content and benevolent behaviour towards other people, who will in turn mirror the person's prosocial behaviour and reinforce the positive mood state.

Fortunately for the adaptation of the individual, several regulatory processes counter the free and uncontrolled operation of these self-perpetuating circles. First, a mood-congruent judgement bias may vanish if an external cause for the current mood becomes salient, suggesting an external attribution for the mood effects (Schwarz & Clore, 1988). Second, the associative effects of depressive moods can be counteracted by motivated processes of 'mood-repair'. Depressed people may attempt to improve their situation by actively avoiding unpleasant thoughts or by consciously seeking for more pleasant thought contents.

A third process of mood-contingent regulation refers to the different cognitive styles triggered by emotional states and suggests some of the cognitive strategies that can be used to repair one's negative mood, or to prevent one's elated mood from being perpetuated. There is converging evidence from many studies that negative emotional states elicit more systematic processing and cognitive discipline than positive states (Isen, Means, Patrick, & Nowicki, 1982). In contrast, positive mood states elicit a more creative style (Isen, Daubman, & Nowicki, 1987), which sometimes interferes with exhaustive or accurate processing. People in a positive mood produce less common word associations (Isen, Johnson, Hertz, & Robinson, 1985), seek less information before decisions (Isen et al., 1982), and sometimes make less accurate judgements than people in a bad mood (Sinclair & Mark, 1992). However, good mood may lead to better performance than bad mood in demanding tasks that call for creativity and productive thinking (Ellis & Ashbrook, 1988; Murray, Surjan, Hirt, & Surjan, 1990).

While the empirical evidence for mood-contingent cognitive styles is strong and incontestable, the theoretical explanation is less than clear. It has been suggested that the experience or 'administration' of positive and negative mood occupies a different amount of cognitive resources, or that happy people may simply avoid cognitive effort that could spoil their pleasant state. However, research by Martin, Ward, Achee and Wyer (1993) suggests that mood effects on cognitive styles reflect adaptive strategies rather than absolute capacity constraints. Participants read a series of behaviours to form an impression of a target person. Instructed to stop reading 'when you feel you have enough information', happy people stopped sooner than sad people did. However, when instructed to read behaviours 'until you no longer enjoy' the task, positive mood led people to engage in longer, seemingly more elaborate information processing. This experiment nicely illustrates the flexibility and adaptability of affective-cognitive regulation. The influence of mood states on cognitive processing depends on the task goal. If the task calls for care and scrutiny, performance may profit from negative mood states. If, however, the same task is framed in terms of enjoyment, it is more likely to be supported by positive affective states.

Summary and Conclusions

The social-cognition approach emphasizes both the cognitive mediation of social behaviour and the reverse, the social impact on cognitive processes. Personal involvement, affective states or environmental factors can have a considerable influence on logical thinking, stereotyping, judgements and decisions. We have broken down the scope of social cognition into stages of information processing, such as perception, encoding, organization, inference-making, retrieval and judgement. At all stages, an individual's older knowledge interacts with new input information. Often the prior knowledge or stereotypical expectations override unexpected or inconsistent information. But we have also noted a primary memory advantage of inconsistent or unexpected information. The phenomenon of priming effects is due to the memory activation of semantic categories (e.g., negative traits) which may influence subsequent judgements. However, the activation of a category need not always result in a congruent assimilation effect on judgement (e.g., negative priming causing negative judgements), but may also result in a contrast effect (e.g., more positive judgements after negative priming).

The manner in which social hypotheses are tested in conversation and social interaction may help the hypotheses to come true. This verification bias may be due to constructive memory processes elicited by the question contents, and to the tendency of interaction partners to exhibit the kind of behaviour suggested by the question contents.

Finally, we have to recognize that the outcome of cognitive processes is not solely determined by cognitive and motivational forces within the individual, but is partly predetermined by the environment that impinges on the social individual. In this respect, we have addressed the differential impact of large and small groups (majorities vs. minorities), the subtle implications of the language used to describe interpersonal behaviour, and the affective influences on cognitive processes that arise from the individual's coping with the social environment. All the issues covered in this chapter have obvious implications for judgements and decisions in important natural settings, such as the court-room, marketing, politics, health or intergroup encounters.

DISCUSSION
POINTS

1   What are the genuinely social aspects that distinguish social cognition from cognitive psychology?
2   Try to answer the questions at the beginning of the chapter pertaining to Harry Olds' reactions.
3   Try to think about the irrationality vs. adaptive value of judgemental heuristics under natural conditions.
4   What could be done to correct unjustified social stereotypes at the various stages of cognitive processing that are depicted in figure 5.2?
5   What are the most intriguing examples of self-verification in social life? Under what conditions can hypothesis testing be debiased?
6   How could language analysis be used to analyse political biases in newspapers?
7   Under what conditions are individuals more susceptible to expectancy-consistent or to expectancy-inconsistent information?

Eagly, A. H., & Chaiken, S. (1993). *The psychology of attitudes*. Fort Worth, TX: Harcourt Brace Jovanovich. This volume is currently the most comprehensive reference for students of attitude and persuasion, and it will certainly continue to be so in the next decade.

Fiske, S. T., & Taylor, S. E. (1991). *Social cognition* (2nd ed.). New York: McGraw-Hill. The Fiske–Taylor textbook is incontestably the most frequently cited textbook that is specially devoted to the cognitive approach in social psychology.

Higgins, E. T., & Kruglanski, A. W. (Eds.). (1996). *Social psychology: Handbook of basic principles*. New York: Guilford Press. The chapters in sections II and III provide an excellent overview of the central research topics in social cognition.

Kahneman, D., Slovic, P., & Tversky, A. (Eds.). (1982). *Judgment under uncertainty: Heuristics and biases*. Cambridge: Cambridge University Press. This edited volume contains reprints of the most important original articles on cognitive fallacies and biases.

Leyens, J.-P., Yzerbyt, V., & Schadron, G. (Eds.). (1994). *Stereotypes and social cognition*. London: Sage. With a special focus on person perception and stereotyping, the book offers a coherent overview of the principles of social cognition.

Markus, H. and Zajonc, R. B. (1985). The cognitive perspective in social psychology. In G. Lindzey & E. Aronson (Eds.), *The handbook of social psychology* (3rd ed., Vol. 1, pp. 137–230). New York: Random House. This handbook article is less up-to-date than the volumes of the Wyer–Srull handbook, but it provides a more condensed alternative.

Martin, L. L., & Tesser, A. (Eds.). (1992). *The construction of social judgment*. Hillsdale, NJ: Erlbaum. The book covers a variety of social-cognition research paradigms and offers a more in-depth look at developments in social-cognition theorizing.

Wyer, R. S., & Srull, T. K. (Eds.). (1994). *Handbook of social cognition* (2nd ed., 2 vols.). Hillsdale, NJ: Erlbaum. A comprehensive sourcebook covering even very recent developments in cognitive social psychology, written clearly and interestingly by distinguished scientists.

FURTHER READING

Hamilton, D. L., Katz, L. B., & Leirer, V. O. (1980). Cognitive representation of personality impressions: Organizational processes in the first impression formation. *Journal of Personality and Social Psychology*, 39, 1050–63.

Snyder, M., & Uranowitz, S. W. (1978). Reconstructing the past: Some cognitive consequences of person perception. *Journal of Personality and Social Psychology*, 36, 941–50.

KEY STUDIES

Emotion

Klaus R. Scherer

6

OUTLINE

Much of social psychology deals with emotion and emotional behaviour, explicitly and implicitly, in the context of social cognition and judgement, interpersonal relations and communication, or group behaviour. This chapter defines the phenomenon, reviews classic and current theories, and summarizes relevant research on the elicitation and differentiation of emotional reactions. It focuses on the major components of emotion, including motor expression, psychophysiological symptoms, motivational changes and subjective experience, as well as on their complex interrelationships. In addition, issues such as emotion regulation and control, intercultural similarities and differences, and applied aspects of emotion research are covered.

KEY CONCEPTS

- Activation
- Affect
- Appraisal
- Discrete emotions
- Display rules
- Emotion
- Emotional reaction triad
- Expression
- Facial feedback hypothesis
- Feeling
- Mood
- Proprioceptive feedback
- Social constructivism
- Sympathetic arousal
- Universality

Introduction

Why should social psychologists study emotion?
What is the role of emotion in social interaction?

Imagine strolling through a park on a sunny Sunday afternoon in May. The first flowers are out, the birds are chirping, and you are feeling great – particularly given the fact that a very special person is walking hand-in-hand with you. All of a sudden, you notice a man emerging from behind some bushes along the path. He is holding a knife and there seems to be blood on his hands . . .

Emotion Earlier often used synonymously with feeling or affect. Modern usage assumes emotion to be a hypothetical construct denoting a process of an organism's reaction to significant events. Emotion is generally presumed to have several components: physiological arousal, motor expression, action tendencies and subjective feeling.

Chances are that you would be experiencing what is commonly called an **emotion**. But what seems a straightforward, albeit highly aversive, reaction turns out to be a major problem for social psychologists. For example, what exactly is *the* emotion? The quickening of your heartbeat? Your mouth and eyes opening widely? Your gasp? The sudden urge to run away? Or the feeling that you are in *danger* – something you will call *fear* when interrogated about your state of mind at the time? Or a combination of all of these different aspects? We will have to discuss different views as to how to define the phenomenon. Another issue of debate is the question of why we have emotions. Are they irrational passions that prevent us from being reasonable human beings? What is their function? Do animals have emotions? Are there differences between cultures? How would an Inuit react if a man with blood on his hands appeared from behind a snowdrift? All of these questions are linked to the issue of the social nature of the human species and are thus a proper topic for social-psychological investigation.

But even apart from such fundamental issues, social psychologists stumble across emotion at many points in the study of social cognition and behaviour. If the sight of the man with the knife has frightened you out of your wits, your judgement as to the likelihood of his attacking you and the person next to you may be impaired. You may overreact. The event, if traumatic, may affect your memory of park strolls with a significant other for years to come. You may change your opinion about certain races or nationalities – if the man should happen to be a member of a social group different from your own. Major effects of emotion on social cognition have been demonstrated in the literature: perception, judgement, memory, problem-solving, task performance and many other aspects of individual functioning can all be strongly affected by different emotions (Forgas, 1991; Keltner, Ellsworth, & Edwards, 1993; see chapter 5). Emotion has also been shown to play an important role in attitude change (Breckler, 1993; see also chapter 8).

Emotion also strongly affects social interaction. Your interaction with the man will be very different depending on whether you are frightened or angry. Of particular importance is *emotional signalling*, via expressive behaviour. Process and outcomes of negotiations and social encounters depend heavily on the exchange of such signals, e.g., of threat or appeasement (see below and chapter 11). The reaction of the knifeman towards you will be determined in large part by the emotion signals you are providing.

In general, the phenomenon of aggression is closely tied to emotion, particularly frustration and anger (Averill, 1982; Berkowitz, 1962; Wyer & Srull, 1993; see chapter 10). If your partner has frustrated you just before encountering the man, and if you feel strong enough to deal with the person, you are more likely to attack than flee. Emotions also influence the opposite pole, prosocial behaviour. A number of studies have shown that the likelihood of altruistic behaviour being shown is dependent, in a complex manner, on mood and emotion (Davis, 1994; Isen, 1993; see also chapter 9).

As one might expect, emotions play a major role in the establishment and management of social relationships, such as in friendship and marriage (Berscheid, 1991; Fitness, 1996; Gottman, 1993) as well as in the case of the loss of a partner (Bonanno & Keltner, 1997; Stroebe & Stroebe, 1987; Stroebe, Schut, & Stroebe, 1998). But emotions also play a role in more mundane social encounters. A long-term research programme conducted by Rimé and his collaborators (Rimé, Finkenauer, Luminet, Zech, & Philippot, 1998) has shown that most people tend to share their emotions by talking about their emotional experiences to others (see chapter 12).

One of the areas of social psychology for which emotion is of major relevance is group dynamics (see Ashforth & Humphrey, 1995; Barsade & Gibson, 1998; Heise & O'Brien, 1993) and collective behaviour. LeBon's (1895/1960) early work on mass behaviour relied strongly on the mechanism of *emotional contagion*, which he used to explain the irrational behaviour he claimed was typical of people in large crowds (see chapter 1). To use our park example to illustrate: if you show strong fear responses upon seeing the knifeman, it is likely that you will *infect* your partner, who might have first reacted in a rather cool fashion, with your fright. This interesting phenomenon, after having been neglected for decades, is now finding renewed interest among social psychologists (see Hatfield, Cacioppo, & Rapson, 1994; Levenson & Ruef, 1997). Among the most infectious affect displays are yawning and laughter.

Little wonder that emotion is central to social-psychological analysis. This chapter will summarize some of the major debates and illustrate some of the research efforts in this area.

What is an Emotion?

What is the fundamental tenet of the James–Lange theory of emotion?
How can emotion be defined in a fashion that is useful for social-psychological research?

'What is an emotion?' This was the title of one of the most influential journal articles ever written in psychology. It appeared in 1884 and its author was

	Stage 1	Stage 2	Stage 3	Stage 4	Stage 5
Pre-James	perception of an event	elicitation of an 'emotion = feeling'	'emotion = feeling'	differentiated pattern of physiological arousal and appropriate action tendencies	
Example:	seeing a man with a knife		feeling afraid	heart racing, knees trembling; wanting to run	
James	perception of an event	elicitation of a specific response	differentiated pattern of physiological arousal and appropriate action tendencies	'emotion = feeling'	
Example:	seeing a man with a knife		heart racing, knees trembling; wanting to run	feeling afraid	
Schachter	perception of an event	elicitation of non-specific arousal	general activation of the sympathetic branch of the ANS (autonomic nervous system)	cognitive explanation, based on event and situational cues	'emotion = feeling'
Example:	seeing a man with a knife		heart racing, knees trembling, face flushing		feeling afraid
Modern	perception and appraisal of an event	initiation of changes in all major subsystems of organism	differentiated and adaptive changes in physiology, expression, motivation	reflection of these component changes in a monitoring system	changes in feeling state (one component of the total emotion process)
Example:	seeing a man with a knife and evaluating the potential consequences given one's own resources		heart racing, knees trembling, face flushing; eyes, mouth wide open; wanting to run		feeling afraid (in a manner that reflects the situation and the bodily changes)
Continuous process					

FIGURE 6.1 The sequence of the emotion process as seen by different theorists

William James, one of the founding fathers of modern experimental psychology. In this essay, James defended what he considered a revolutionary thesis concerning the nature of emotion; namely 'that the bodily changes follow directly the *perception* of the exciting fact, and that our feeling of the same changes as they occur *is* the emotion' (James, 1884/1968, p. 19; emphases in the original).

The James–Lange theory

James illustrated his point of view with an example that has become a classic: we meet a bear in the forest, our heart races, our knees tremble and, because we are *perceiving* these physiological changes, we *feel* afraid. A year after the appearance of James' seminal article, the Danish physiologist Carl Lange (1885) proposed a model of emotion which, in spite of many minor differences, suggested the same basic mechanism with respect to the causal sequence as James. Because of this similarity, we traditionally speak of the James–Lange theory of emotion, also referred to as a *peripheral* position (since it focuses on the peripheral, i.e., the autonomous and somatic rather than the central nervous system). According to this view, then, an emotion is elicited by a person's awareness of a specific pattern of bodily changes and the consequent interpretation of the event in terms of emotion.

The James–Lange position is compared to the established view of emotion at the beginning of the twentieth century in the first two rows of figure 6.1 (to which we shall keep returning for comparisons with more recent theories). Since the likelihood of encountering bears has steadily decreased since 1884, our more realistic example of an eliciting situation for the experience of fear in the modern world is used.

Obviously, there is quite a large amount of overlap between the 'pre-James' and 'James' views. Both positions agree on the 'components' of the phenomenon: an event, the perception/evaluation of the event, a wide variety of bodily reactions and action tendencies, and a characteristic feeling state. Both positions use the term *emotion* to refer to the **feeling** state component of the total phenomenon. Furthermore, both positions agree on the existence of a process, a sequence of events and on the differentiation of causes and consequences. The disagreement concerns precisely the status of 'emotion = feeling': is it a cause of characteristic bodily reactions and action tendencies, or rather their consequence? This issue has been at the root of a lively controversy that still persists today. How can modern social psychology settle this classic dispute?

Feeling   Earlier used synonymously with emotion. Modern use is restricted to the component of subjective experience of emotional arousal, often conscious and verbalizable by using emotion words or expressions.

Affect   Often used synonymously with emotion. Some social psychologists restrict the use to the valence aspect, pleasant vs. unpleasant or positive vs. negative, of feelings.

Emotion as a social-psychological construct

We first need to have a working definition of what we mean by emotion or **affect** and/or feeling. Unfortunately, there seem to be as many

Expression Muscular actions in the face, the vocal organs, the hands and the skeletal musculature generally that are linked to internal states of the organism and thus provide indices of such states, thereby serving communicative purposes. As a consequence, expression is often manipulated to produce appropriate signals in social interaction.

Emotional reaction triad See emotion; the three response components: physiological arousal, motor expression and subjective feeling.

definitions of emotions as there are theories of emotion (Kleinginna & Kleinginna, 1981). Like many other psychological terms, both in lay and scientific psychology, emotion is a *hypothetical construct* which is not directly observable as such, but which is inferred from a number of indices and their interaction. There is a growing consensus that the construct *emotion* should not be used as a synonym for *feeling*, as has often been the case in the past (notably in the case of William James). Feeling is now generally considered to be just one of several *components* of the total emotion construct. Other components are neurophysiological response patterns (in the central and autonomous nervous systems) and motor **expression** (in face, voice and gesture). Social psychologists often refer to these three components – feeling, physiology and expression – as the **emotional reaction triad**.

Another component seen as an essential part of the emotion construct is the *action tendency* resulting from the evaluation of the eliciting event – such as wanting to run away or to hide out of fear of attack by a bear or a thug. Some authors have argued that the action tendency component is in fact the most important aspect of an emotion in the sense that it defines its specificity, e.g., *wanting to flee* being specific to fear or *wanting to attack* being specific to anger (Frijda, 1986, 1987; Plutchik, 1980). It is important to note that most emotion psychologists distinguish action tendencies from overt instrumental behaviour. The actual running or hitting are not generally considered to be *components* of emotion but rather *behavioural consequences* of emotion.

It seems reasonable to assume that the emotion construct should also include a *cognitive* component. Clearly, mental processes must be part of the adaptive reactions of the organism to an emotion-eliciting event since the latter always requires some kind of evaluative information processing, no matter how rudimentary, to make sense of what happens. Thus, a bear hunter will evaluate the appearance of James' bear very differently from how a picnicker would. You might react quite differently to the knife-brandishing man if you were a member of the national karate team. The cognitive activity of evaluation often changes rapidly when new information becomes available. For example, we will evaluate the man with the knife very differently once we notice that he has carved a stick for a little boy playing nearby and has inflicted a minor cut on himself.

Appraisal Evaluation of the significance of an object, event or action to a person, including an evaluation of one's coping activities. It can occur at various levels of the central nervous system and need not be conscious.

In consequence, one might argue that cognitive evaluation or **appraisal** is also one of the components of the emotion construct (a point that is indeed argued by several contemporary emotion psychologists and will be described below). This cognitive perspective on emotion fits the strong rise of cognitive approaches in social psychology (see chapter 5).

The number of emotion components enumerated so far – feeling, physiological changes, motor expression, action tendencies and cognitive processing – include most if not all parts of psychological functioning. How can we distinguish emotion from other kinds of psychological processes?

To define the term more precisely, we suggest using *emotion* as a shorthand for a *process* that involves rather massive, interrelated changes in several organismic subsystems occurring in response to an eliciting event of major significance to the individual. Rather than talk about *emotional states*, we should refer to *emotion episodes* to underline the fact that emotion is a dynamic process which has a beginning and an end and is of relatively brief duration. This allows us to differentiate emotion from other psychological constructs such as **mood** (generally considered to be more diffuse, to last much longer and to be not necessarily elicited by a concrete event).

> **Mood** Major differences from emotion are a diffuse origin (rather than a specific eliciting event), a much longer duration and a lower overall intensity.

One way to highlight the special nature of emotion as a *crisis response* (in a positive or negative sense) is to postulate that the various psychological and physiological components interact in a very specific way during the emotion episode. Scherer (1984b, 1993a) has suggested that the subsystems of an organism which normally 'do their own thing' become *synchronized* or *coupled* during the emotion process in order to allow the organism to cope with the emergency situation created by the eliciting event. For example, while you are strolling peacefully through the park with your friend, the vegetative part of your autonomous nervous system is slowly digesting lunch, your respiration and heartbeat are optimally tuned to provide the required oxygen for your strolling and speaking pace, your facial muscles are involved in sending smiles of various sorts, and your thoughts revolve around the conversation and further planning of the afternoon's activities. As soon as you see the man, the knife and the blood, digestion stops, your respiration and heartbeat change dramatically, your facial muscles tense, your eyebrows rise, your mouth opens, the conversation stops, and your thoughts are frantically concerned with making sense of the situation and deciding what to do next. The regional blood supply to your lower body increases, preparing your leg muscles for vigorous running. Thus, all of your bodily and mental systems are being coordinated and synchronized to deal with what might be a major emergency situation, recruiting all resources available to the organism to deal with the emergency – a situation threatening one of your major goals in life: to stay alive and unhurt.

Summary

We have reviewed the classic controversy around the James–Lange theory of emotion, which focuses on the causal sequence of bodily changes and emotion in the sense of a feeling state. Part of the dispute is taken care of by more precise definitions. *Emotion* is currently seen as a superordinate *hypothetical construct*, which includes *feeling* as one of several components (motor expression, physiological changes, action tendencies and cognitive processing). If *emotion* is defined as an *episode* of interrelated, synchronized changes in these components in response to an event of major significance to the organism, the sequence problem becomes an issue concerning the dynamic interrelationships between the components in a particular emotion episode.

Why do we have Emotions?

What are the adaptive functions of emotion?
Why does the feeling component of emotion play a special role?

Obviously, the synchronization of psychological and physiological processes in an attempt to mobilize all the resources of the organism to face a significant event is a rather costly affair. Not only are some of the subsystems involved prevented from carrying out their normal function (for example, we cannot digest or think very well when we are in the grip of a powerful emotion), but there is also a strong mobilization of energy which constitutes a drain on the organism's resources (this is why very prolonged emotional arousal can be considered as *stress*). What is the reason for the existence of such a costly mechanism?

The evolutionary significance of emotions

Hebb and Thompson (1979), in an in-depth analysis of the significance of animal studies for social psychology, have shown humans to be the most emotional of all animals. This is surprising given the established idea of humans as the first truly rational beings. How can we understand this paradox? One answer comes from the father of evolutionary theory, Charles Darwin (see chapter 2). In *The Expression of Emotions in Man and Animals* (1872/1998), he argued that the emotions serve useful functions for the organism, both with respect to the preparation of adaptive behaviour and to the regulation of interaction in socially living species. Focusing on the functionality of emotional expression, Darwin attempted to show for each of the major emotions how the different features of expression, particularly in the face and the body, could be analysed in terms of adaptive behaviour patterns of which they were considered to be the rudiments. For example, raising the eyebrows in order to increase the acuity of vision, pulling up the nose to avoid exposure to unpleasant odours (see Ekman, 1979, for a critical review). Darwin's central idea that we can find precursors of human emotional expressions in animal signalling has been supported by ethological research (van Hooff, 1972; Redican, 1982; Scherer, 1985). As an example, figure 6.2 illustrates the relationships between chimpanzee and human facial expression.

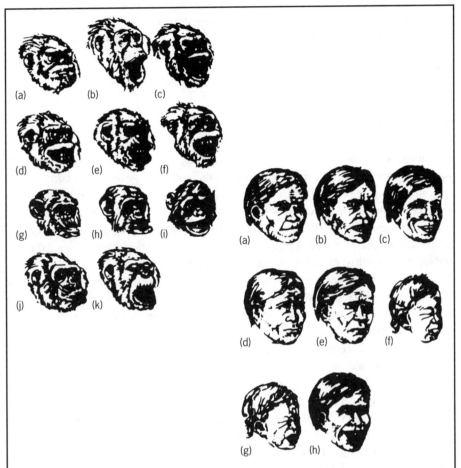

FIGURE 6.2 Continuity of facial expression from chimpanzees to humans (Reproduced from Chevalier-Skolnikoff, 1973)

Emotion as a social signalling system

The expression of an organism's emotion allows others to infer not only the reaction of the expresser to a particular event or action, it also signals a particular action tendency (e.g., aggression in the case of anger) which can strongly determine the subsequent interaction process. Let us assume that the knife-wielding man in the park is an apprentice mugger and you are his first 'case'. Much of the interaction will depend on the emotional signals you are sending. If you are freezing while uttering a fearful scream, the man will see that he has frightened you and, if he can prevent you from running away, that it is safe to demand your wallet. If you shout angrily at him and move forward (since you are a karate champion), he is likely to see that you are angry and might attack him. Obviously, then, the subsequent interaction depends strongly on the emotional signals sent by the interaction partners. The social psychology of human social interaction also demonstrates the importance of emotion signals in the delicate business of dealing with our fellow men/women in establishing relationships, interacting in groups and in many other social domains (see contributions in Feldman & Rimé, 1991).

Emotion affords behavioural flexibility

Emotions are quasi-automatic response mechanisms which we are not totally free to switch on and off at will, but which do not blindly execute simple stimulus–response chains (S–R chains). Whereas in S–R chains a specific response is directly coupled or linked to the eliciting stimulus, emotions *decouple* stimulus and response, i.e., they separate event and reaction by replacing the automatism of instinctive reactions with a preparation for several reaction alternatives. In other words, the organism can choose from several possible responses to a given event. This is a much more flexible mechanism, providing the organism with greater choice in its behavioural reactions. Yet, a certain automatism remains – the emotions do prepare us, whether we want to or not, for particular types of adaptive behaviour (Scherer, 1984b).

Let us take our concrete example. If I were a karate champion and if I were exclusively governed by a stimulus–response mechanism, I would immediately attack the man with the knife. Being endowed with the emotion of anger rather than a simple insult–aggression chain, I will immediately get angry, which, among other things, will prepare my organism for aggressive action by providing the necessary **activation**, optimal blood circulation in the areas of the body likely to be involved, and preparatory muscle tension. However, since anger decouples the stimulus and the response, I do not hit the person right away. While the emotion has prepared a response that could be considered evolutionarily adaptive, I have now gained some *latency time*, which permits me to choose an optimal reaction from a large repertoire of possible behaviours.

Activation   A heightened state of the central and particularly the autonomous nervous system. Some authors use the term to refer specifically to the sympathetic branch of the autonomous nervous system.

For example, I might not want to hit the man if he appeared to be much stronger than I am, or if I discovered, a split-second after first seeing him come out of the bushes, that he has just carved a stick for a child. Thus, the latency time that intervenes between the elicitation of the emotion and the execution of an actual reactive behaviour pattern allows further evaluation of the situation, including an appraisal of the likelihood of success and the seriousness of the consequences of a particular action.

This decoupling of stimulus and response, providing time for further situation and response evaluation as well as behavioural negotiation and social interaction, would seem to be the most important function of emotion. But, as mentioned before, evolution in its wisdom also provides a specific preparation for action that the organism can fall back on, particularly when there is great urgency and when

too much further evaluation and exchange of signals might have negative consequences, as in the case of imminent danger. These built-in provisions for preparation and direction for appropriate action have been described by a number
of psychologists (Frijda, 1986; Plutchik, 1980). Thus, emotion strongly affects
motivation (see also Buck, 1985).

Information processing

Once we can no longer rely on innate S–R mechanisms, we need criteria to
evaluate the massive information that constantly impinges upon us. Cognitive
social psychologists increasingly realize that human information processing
does not work in the same rule-governed, 'cold' information-sifting and sorting
fashion that is typical of computers (see chapter 5). Human information processing, particularly in the social domain, often consists of 'hot cognition' (emotional
reactions helping us to sort the relevant from the irrelevant, the important from
the not so important; see Frijda, 1986; Lazarus, 1991). As already mentioned
by the early philosophers, valence (i.e., pleasure and pain, agreeableness and
disagreeableness) plays a major role in turning cold cognitions into hot ones. Some
of the criteria used to evaluate incoming information are based on innate preferences. For example, newborn infants will react with positive affect to sweet
and with negative affect to bitter tastes (Chiva, 1985; Steiner, 1979). However,
many of the criteria that we employ in stimulus evaluation are acquired or learned
during socialization (see chapter 3), and represented by needs, preferences, goals
and values.

Regulation and control

What is the function of feeling as one of the most prominent components of human
emotions? As already suggested by James, it is probable that individuals constantly
monitor their organismic processes. Rather than limiting the monitoring only to
the physiological changes, we propose that feeling is a reflection of everything
that goes on in the process of synchronization of different organismic subsystems
in an emotional episode (Scherer, 1984a, 1984b, 1993a). Thus, our feeling state
serves to reflect and integrate all the components of the emotional episode such
as our evaluation or appraisal of the situation, the bodily changes occurring in
our nervous system, the action tendency or preparedness for particular behaviours,
and the expressive signals that we are giving off to the social environment. Since
in the process of emotion the state of all these components and their synchronization or desynchronization changes constantly, our feeling, as an integrated
reflection of all of these subprocesses, would allow us a constant monitoring of
what goes on. This is, of course, a fundamental requirement for being able to
regulate or *manipulate* the emotion process (see below).

We can now return to the sequence issue discussed above. If feeling fulfils a monitoring function, reflecting and integrating all other components involved in the emotion construct, it must indeed be, as postulated by James and Lange, a *consequence* rather than a *cause*. However, rather than assuming simple causal chains, such as 'I tremble therefore I feel afraid', we expect to find a complex dynamic network of interrelationships among the different components. In particular, feelings reflect not only bodily changes but also the individual's evaluation of the emotion-eliciting situation. This may be the key to the problem, and it is to this issue that we shall turn next.

Summary

Following the pioneering lead of Darwin, social psychologists and ethologists have highlighted a large number of important functions of the emotion mechanism. In the course of evolution, the development of emotion has allowed a decoupling of instinctive stimulus–response contingencies, providing a latency time during which to choose from a large repertoire of possible responses, but at the same time automatically preparing particular action tendencies to allow adaptive emergency responses. The expression of emotion serves important signalling functions, allowing subtle interpersonal negotiations. Finally, the feeling component of emotion is a powerful mechanism to facilitate regulation and control of emotional behaviour. The regulation of emotion is often used strategically in social interaction.

How are Emotions Elicited and Differentiated?

Much of the work of social psychologists interested in emotion has been concerned with the question of which situations are capable of provoking emotional responses (elicitation), and which out of the many possible emotions is the one that is elicited by a particular type of situation (differentiation).

Philosophical notions

How did philosophers define emotion over the last centuries?

For most philosophers, this question did not constitute a major problem. An insult to our honour would obviously produce anger, an attack by a powerful enemy fear, and so on. This normative approach, adjudicating the appropriateness of particular emotions to eliciting situations and persons, postulates a clear match between the type of eliciting situation and the type of emotion. Lay people also do not quite understand the question: it seems clear to them why someone reacts with a particular emotion in a particular situation, for example being afraid when encountering a bear or a man with a knife. So what is the problem? The problem lies in the fact that information about the situation alone often does not allow us to predict the ensuing emotion. As we have seen, a hunter might be quite happy to see the bear trot out of the forest. A plainclothes police officer might be relieved finally to happen upon the mugger she has been tracking for days in the park. It seems that one of the decisive factors in emotion elicitation and differentiation is the interaction between the type of situation and the significance of the event to the person experiencing the emotion.

This is why all eminent philosophers who dealt with emotion have explicitly or implicitly defined the different kinds of emotions in terms of the significance of the events or actions to the person – or as we might say today, in terms of the person's evaluation of an event with respect to important needs, goals and values. Even James, bent on arguing the revolutionary hypothesis that the type of emotion experienced was determined by the perception of the patterns of bodily changes, had to admit that the nature of these bodily changes in turn was determined by the overwhelming 'idea' of the significance of the elements of a situation for the well-being of the organism (e.g., the probability that the bear will kill us or that we will kill it; James, 1894, p. 518). In modern parlance, this sounds suspiciously close to the notion of the *appraisal* of the event in terms of the organism's important needs, goals and values. Nobody had said it exactly that way since it was not a major issue of the social psychology of emotion. It seemed trivial. Then came non-trivial social psychology and complicated things.

The Schachter–Singer theory of emotion

How is the Schachter–Singer theory different from other peripheral theories?
Why has this non-trivial theory lost its appeal for social psychologists?

At the beginning of the 1960s, the experimental social psychologist Schachter was one of the first to propose a *cognitive* theory of emotion. While accepting several of the fundamental tenets of the James–Lange theory (such as equating emotion with verbally reported feeling and assigning a central role to arousal in the peripheral nervous system), he doubted that there could be as many differentiated patterns of physiological changes to account for the great variety of moods and emotion states for which there are verbal expressions (particularly since physiological psychologists seemed to have trouble demonstrating such differences even between major emotion categories experimentally). Thus, contrary to James, Schachter suggested that the perception of heightened *non-specific* arousal (defined in terms of sympathetic activation, as indexed by sensations like the heart beating faster, limbs trembling, face flushing, etc.) is sufficient to *elicit* emotion = feeling. With respect to the factors responsible for the *differentiation* of the emotions – where James would have answered 'the specific nature of the bodily changes' – Schachter, argued for a 'steering function' of cognitions arising from the immediate situation as interpreted on the basis of past experience.

According to this view, there are two factors that are necessary to elicit and differentiate emotion as feeling: (1) the perception of heightened **sympathetic arousal**, and (2) cognitions concerning the interpretation of the situation in the light of one's past experiences

Sympathetic arousal *See* **activation.**

(see sequence diagram in figure 6.1). Schachter acknowledged that: 'In most emotion inducing situations, of course, the two factors are completely interrelated. Imagine a man walking alone down a dark alley, a figure with a gun suddenly appears. The perception-cognition "figure with a gun" in some fashion initiates a state of physiological arousal; this state of arousal is interpreted in terms of knowledge about dark alleys and guns and the arousal is labelled "fear"' (Schachter & Singer, 1962, p. 380). Note that contrary to James–Lange, Schachter does not presume that it is differentiated physiological patterning that produces a particular feeling – he assumes, for the 'normal case', that non-specific sympathetic arousal and the simultaneous cognitive interpretation of the eliciting event produce the feeling.

But Schachter was not really interested in the normal case; he focused on situations in which the two factors are *not* linked. What happens, he asked, if a person experiences heightened arousal for which there are neither immediate explanations nor appropriate cognitions? Schachter argued that this situation will elicit an 'information search and self-attribution' process (see chapters 5 and 7 in this volume). We can state the presumed mechanism in a somewhat simplified manner: if I detect a heightened level of sympathetic arousal that I cannot attribute to an extraneous factor, I know that I am likely to feel an emotion. I will then carefully scrutinize my physical and social environment and, based on all pertinent cues, decide which emotion is appropriate. It is this emotion, then, that I will be feeling (of course, there is no assumption that any of this is voluntary or conscious).

In a now classic experiment, Schachter and his collaborator Singer tested this notion (Schachter & Singer, 1962). They administered either adrenaline (= epinephrine) or placebo injections to participants who had been told that the experiment was to test the transient effects of a vitamin compound on vision. Within a complex experimental design, they varied the type of information they gave to participants with respect to the effects that the injection would probably produce in them (i.e., feel aroused vs. feel tired). The expectation was that participants who could attribute their arousal to the drug would not look any further – they had enough justification for what they experienced. In contrast, participants who were ignorant of potential side effects or who expected the opposite effects should be looking for other reasons for their arousal in the situation. Such reasons were provided by the experimenters in the form of a confederate who, depending on the condition in the experimental design, would behave in a euphoric or an angry manner. The experimenters expected that if (1) there was *real arousal* (in the adrenaline but not in the placebo group), and if (2) the participants did not have an *obvious explanation* for this arousal (in the ignorant or misinformed rather than the correctly informed groups), they would use the emotion cues provided by the confederate to attribute the respective emotion (euphoria or anger, depending on the condition) to themselves. While the design may be difficult to follow without reading the study, the fundamental idea is simple: the experimenters generated the need for participants to find explanations for a change in physiological state and the corresponding feelings, for which they did not have appropriate expectations. Then, an appropriate explanation was offered in the form of the emotional behaviour of a confederate – 'If he feels in that way about this situation, I must be feeling the same, and that explains my arousal'. Thus, the emotion is believed to be constituted by the felt arousal and the cognitive interpretation of the situation based on the model's behavioural expression.

Schachter and Singer used self-ratings and some observational data to test their hypotheses. They concluded that the data supported their theoretical position, although the evidence was not overwhelming. Apart from the weak results, the methods used in this study have been strongly criticized. Furthermore, attempts at replication have been generally unsuccessful (see Gordon, 1987; Reisenzein, 1983, for a review of these issues).

In spite of these shortcomings, the experiment has had an enormous influence on the social psychology of emotion as it demonstrated the possibility that in a case where we cannot easily account for an abnormal degree of arousal, we will turn to the social environment to find cues that might explain this internal state. It is by now an established finding in social psychology that we use information from the social environment (particularly other people) as a guide to judgement and choice in situations of uncertainty (see chapter 5 in this volume). Schachter and Singer were among the first to point to the possibility that our emotional experience, which had always been thought to be a very private domain and directly linked to the intricate goings-on in the body, is also subject to a multitude of social influences and, under certain conditions, might even be completely open to manipulation.

Unfortunately, rather than treating the Schachter–Singer paradigm as a special case, as the authors had suggested themselves, many subsequent authors, including Schachter himself, used it as the basis for what has become known as the *Schachter–Singer theory of emotion*, the only theory of emotion to be covered in most textbooks of social psychology in the past 30 years. (At this point, please refer back to the diagram in figure 6.1 to recall exactly what the Schachter–Singer emotion *theory* is all about.) Clearly, as a *general theory* of emotion, trying to explain how emotions are *typically* elicited and which factors determine their differentiation, the Schachter–Singer approach seems not only of limited value but actually misleading. While it was a clever idea to induce arousal via adrenaline injection and to manipulate attributions about its effects, it was in no way an operationalization of how emotional arousal is produced under normal circumstances. This issue is addressed by what seems to be the majority view among social psychologists studying emotion elicitation and differentiation today – *appraisal theory*.

Appraisal theory

What is the role of cognition in emotion?
What are the dimensions used in evaluating events that provoke different emotions?

Arnold (1960) was among the first psychologists to propose formally that the significance of an emotion-eliciting event to the experiencing person (which had been implied by all major thinkers on emotion) was established through a process of evaluation or appraisal of the event based on a set of criteria specific to the person. A few years later, Lazarus (1966) made a major contribution in pointing out that there is a *process* of appraisal, with *reappraisals* often changing and correcting first impressions, and thus changing the resulting emotion. Lazarus also introduced the distinction between what he called *primary and secondary appraisal* of an emotion- or stress-eliciting event: while the primary evaluation deals with the pleasantness and unpleasantness of an object or whether an event helps or hinders satisfying a need or attaining a goal (i.e., the 'goal conduciveness' of the event), the secondary appraisal determines to what extent the person will be able to cope with the consequences of an event, given his or her competencies, resources or power. Lazarus calls his model 'transactional' – the significance of the event is determined not only by the nature of the event but also by the needs, goals and resources of the person. These two determinants interact or transact, and it is the result of this transaction that will determine the nature of the emotion (or the amount of stress suffered; Lazarus, 1968, 1991).

One of the major advances due to the development of appraisal theories is the detailed specification of appraisal dimensions or criteria. Appraisal theorists have established lists of such criteria which are assumed to be used in evaluating emotion-antecedent events. Examples of such criteria are the novelty or expectedness of the event, its pleasantness, whether it helps or hinders reaching one's goals, and how well one can cope with the consequences (see Scherer, 1999; Smith & Lazarus, 1993, for details). Let us return to our park example. When you see the man with the knife emerge from the bushes, a very rapid process of cognitive evaluation of the significance of this event for your own personal well-being will ensue, illustrating some of the central appraisal criteria suggested by emotion theorists. What is the intention of that man (causality, agency, responsibility)? Will his actions affect my own plans and goals, such as survival, remaining unharmed, enjoying myself (goal conduciveness)? Will I be able to deal with an attack, i.e., am I stronger, is it promising to call for help (coping potential, power)? The outcome of the event appraisal, using these and other evaluation criteria, will determine your emotional reaction.

Many appraisal theorists have ventured predictions as to when particular types of emotion should occur as the result of particular patterns of appraisal results (Roseman, Antoniou, & Jose, 1996; Scherer, 1984b, 1993b; Smith & Ellsworth, 1985). The second column in figure 6.3 shows some examples of concrete hypotheses about antecedent appraisal profiles for some of the major emotions (see Scherer, Schorr, & Johnstone, 2000, for a comprehensive overview of the current state of appraisal theory).

Much of recent social-psychological research on emotion has been directed at testing some of these predictions or studying the relationships between appraisal results and emotional responses in a more inductive fashion. Generally, particip-ants are asked to *recall* episodes of typical emotions, such as anger, fear or shame, and are then asked to respond to questions about the underlying cognitive appraisal processes (Roseman, Spindel, & Jose, 1990; Smith & Ellsworth, 1985; Scherer, 1997a). In a variant of this procedure, Scherer (1993b) used a com-puter expert system to obtain information on participants' appraisals of import-ant events that had happened to them and to predict (with a success rate of about 70 per cent), on the basis of theoretical assumptions, which emotion terms they would use to describe their experience. An alternative strategy is to systematically construct scenarios or vignettes on the basis of the predicted appraisal profiles and to ask participants to *imagine* experiencing this situation and to indicate their probable emotional reactions (Smith & Lazarus, 1993).

Such studies have generally provided strong support for the theoretical expecta-tions formulated by appraisal theorists (Reisenzein & Hofmann, 1993; Scherer, 1999; see examples in Scherer et al., 2000). Yet another empirical approach con-sists of choosing a particular emotion-inducing event that affects many people at the same time, such as term examinations for students, and then obtaining information about both the differential appraisals of the situation and the type of emotional response. Such studies, in addition to providing evidence for the predicted appraisal–emotion links, have shown the importance of *emotion blends*, the fact that the complex appraisal of a given situation by a particular person is likely to give rise to a mixture of several emotions rather than only one specific emotion (Folkman & Lazarus, 1985; Smith & Ellsworth, 1987). A field study in an international airport confirmed this hunch. Scherer and Ceschi (1997) video-taped and interviewed airline passengers whose luggage was lost. Figure 6.4 shows the special mix of emotions for each of the passengers. The data from this study illustrate not only the fact that emotions seem to be always mixed but also the central tenet of appraisal theory: while the event was the same for all passengers – their luggage being lost – the special mix of emotions produced depended on the specific appraisal of the significance of the event made by each person. Thus, as one might expect, passengers who judged the consequences of the loss as seriously interfering with their plans and evaluated their coping potential as relatively low tended to report more negative emotion blends.

A major methodological problem for testing of these appraisal theories empiric-ally is the difficulty of assessing the nature of the emotion-antecedent cognitive

Verbal label	Appraisal profile	Facial expression	Vocal expression	Physiological symptoms
Happiness/Joy	Event seen as highly conducive to reaching an important goal or satisfying a need		Increases in pitch level, range and variability as well as vocal intensity	Heart beating faster, warm skin temperature
Anger/Rage	Unexpected event, intentionally caused by another person, seen as obstructing goal attainment or need satisfaction; person judges own coping ability as high, considers action as violating norms		Increases in pitch level and intensity level. Increase in high-frequency energy in the spectrum	Heart beating faster, muscles tensing, changes in breathing, hot skin temperature
Sadness/Dejection	Event that permanently prevents need satisfaction, seen as uncontrollable by human agency, subject feels totally powerless with respect to consequences		Decrease in pitch level and range as well as intensity level. Decrease in speech rate.	Lump in throat, crying/sobbing, muscles tensing
Fear/Terror	Suddenly occurring event, potential but not certain consequences threatening fundamental goal of survival or bodily integrity, urgent reaction required, subject uncertain about ability to control the situation		Strong increase in pitch level and range. Increase in high-frequency energy in the spectrum. Increased speech rate	Heart beating faster, muscles tensing, change in breathing, perspiring, cold skin temperature, lump in throat

FIGURE 6.3 Illustrations of differentiated appraisal and response profiles for four major emotions (based partly on theoretical predictions and partly on results of empirical studies using verbal report data)

(See Scherer, 1984b, 1986; Scherer & Wallbott, 1994; facial expressions reproduced from Ekman & Friesen, 1975)

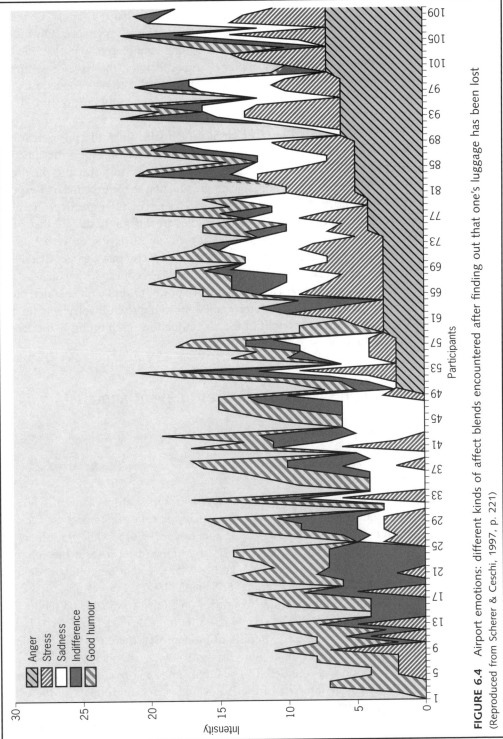

FIGURE 6.4 Airport emotions: different kinds of affect blends encountered after finding out that one's luggage has been lost (Reproduced from Scherer & Ceschi, 1997, p. 221)

appraisal processes independently of the underlying feeling state. Most of the research described above has relied on retrospective verbal self-report as to the nature of the evaluation that has preceded the emotional experience. Obviously, this kind of evidence is very imperfect since one cannot rule out that the respondent will construe the likely appraisal antecedents on the basis of culturally shared ideas (social representations) about which types of events produce particular emotions. The same problem besets the use of vignette or scenario studies (see Parkinson, 1997; Parkinson & Manstead, 1993).

One way to avoid the danger of circularity in this kind of approach is for researchers to manipulate situations in such a way that one can expect the appraisal process to produce certain types of results. Obviously, one may run into the problem that some participants may not evaluate the situation as the experimenter expects them to do, particularly if their needs, goals and resources differ greatly from other participants in the experiment. While such studies are difficult to design, they offer the only chance to solve the methodological problem of relying on verbal recall. One promising approach in this direction is the use of computer games that allow researchers to manipulate the events the player has to deal with (such as the sudden occurrence of goal obstacles, the relative power to deal with enemies, etc.). In addition, aficionados of computer games show high self-involvement in the game, which is the major condition for the induction of emotion in the laboratory (see examples in Scherer et al., 2000).

Cultural and individual differences in event appraisal

What are the potential sources of cultural differences in emotion-antecedent appraisal?

For social psychologists, the emotion-antecedent appraisal mechanism is of particular importance since it may help to explain cultural differences in eliciting situations and emotional experience. As mentioned before, while there may be some innate or universally acquired appraisal criteria, in most cases the appraisal criteria will depend on acquired needs and to a large extent on culturally defined goals and values (see Mesquita, Frijda, & Scherer, 1997). For example, in a large intercultural study conducted in 37 countries on all five continents, Wallbott and Scherer (1995) found that for respondents in individualistic cultures (placing a high value on the rights and interests of individuals), there was relatively little difference between shame and guilt; in both cases, the behaviour that had elicited the emotion was considered to be highly immoral. In collectivistic cultures (giving priority to the interests of the family and of social groups), on the other hand, guilt experiences were provoked more frequently by events that were judged to be much more immoral than those that produced shame. Consistent with these different appraisal tendencies in collectivistic and individualistic cultures, the data showed rather striking differences in the other components of these two emotions. Shame experiences in collectivistic cultures were intense but brief, without major consequences. In contrast, in individualistic cultures, the reaction profiles for shame experiences were very much like those of guilt experiences (involving long-term effects on self-evaluation). Thus, it is to be expected that socio-cultural value systems can strongly affect emotional life. Another potential source of appraisal differences between cultures could be variations in belief structures. In the large 37-country study referred to above, respondents in African countries consistently attributed greater external causality and immorality to emotion-inducing events than respondents in other cultures. One possible explanation for this finding is the widespread belief in sorcery and witchcraft found in many African countries, which implies a belief structure that privileges external attribution and the assignment of moral blame to presumed unnatural agents of harmful events (Scherer, 1997b).

In addition to differences between ethnic or national cultures, we can also expect differences in appraisal processes between members of different cultures even within a particular ethnic group or nation-state. Thus, goals and values often differ between social classes, generations or political affiliations, making it likely that the very same event will provoke different emotions among members of such different groups.

In addition to cultural and group differences, one also finds sizeable *individual differences* in appraisal that determine the type of emotional reaction. Apart from differences in goal hierarchies, differences in the structure of the self-concept may play a major role. For example, Brown and Dutton (1995) showed that participants with low self-esteem have more severe emotional reactions to failure than high self-esteem people. This is particularly true for emotions that directly implicate the self (e.g., shame or humiliation). The authors suggest that this result is due to low self-esteem people overgeneralizing the negative implications of failure. No differences were found for emotions that do not directly involve the self in appraisal (e.g., happiness, unhappiness). There is good evidence that the organization of the self may be affected by cultural value systems (see Markus & Kitayama, 1994). A systematic overview of the potential determinants of individual differences in appraisal is provided by Van Reekum and Scherer (1997).

Summary

We can now return to our starting point: what is the proper sequence of the different emotion components? The last section has pitted appraisal theory against peripheral theories, arguing that it is the prior cognitive evaluation of an event that will elicit the emotion and produce differentiated feeling states. Hopefully, this discussion has shown that (1) many peripheralists may have meant the feeling component when they talked about 'emotion' (in which case, there is no contradiction with an appraisal account), and (quite apart from the difficulties of replicating some of the results relied upon by peripheral theories) that (2) under normal circumstances, the appraisal view seems more realistic than the idea that we have to search for cues in the social environment in order to feel the proper emotion.

Are there Specific Response Patterns for Different Types of Emotions?

What theoretical issues are involved in the debate concerning the existence of emotion-specific response patterns?

Why do discrete emotion theorists postulate a limited number of 'basic' emotions?

While almost all theorists of emotion agree that there is differentiation for the feeling component (which would be difficult to deny given the large number of emotion labels in all languages), this is not the case with respect to the response patterns in the peripheral systems (e.g., expression and physiology). In fact, this issue even cuts across the different theoretical approaches. As we have seen earlier, some peripheral theorists (for example, James) hold that it is highly patterned **proprioceptive feedback** from peripheral systems that determines the differentiation of the emotions. Others (particularly Schachter and Singer) claim that it is *general, non-specific physiological arousal or activation* combined with situational cues that produces differentiation. Cognitive theories of emotion also differ in this respect. While some theories do not address the issue of physiological and expressive differentiation (e.g., Oatley & Johnson-Laird, 1987), others argue that appraisal results will produce specific response profiles, including physiological differentiation (Lazarus, 1991; Scherer, 1986, 1992b; Smith, 1989; Smith & Scott, 1997). This claim is based on the notion that if emotions do have adaptive functions, they should bring about action tendencies that allow the individual to cope with the eliciting event. These action tendencies, in turn, should produce differentiated patterns of responses and expressive signals.

Proprioceptive feedback Proprioception refers to the capacity of internal organs to provide sensory information about changes in the body. Proprioceptive feedback refers to changes in one internal system upon detection of changes in another system.

This is the point at which to introduce another major theoretical tradition – discrete emotion theories. In the 1960s, Tomkins postulated the existence of a limited number of basic or fundamental **discrete emotions**, largely based on Darwin's work, and suggested that innate neural motor programmes are executed when the respective emotion is induced by appropriate stimulation. These neural programmes are expected to produce, in addition to typical facial expressions, differentiated reaction patterns in the voice as well as in

Discrete emotions The theoretical notion that there is a limited number of highly differentiated basic or fundamental emotions that are common to different species and cultures.

physiological response systems (see Tomkins, 1984, for a summary). Tomkins' theoretical approach strongly influenced Ekman and Izard, whose theoretical and empirical work on emotion-specific facial expression has dominated the emotion area for the last 30 years (Ekman, 1972, 1982, 1992; Izard, 1971, 1991). Both researchers defend the theoretical view that there is a small number of well-delimited universal emotions with very specific expressive and physiological response patterns.

So far, all of these considerations are based on theoretical assumptions. We shall deal separately with each of the three major components constituting the so-called response triad of the emotions – motor expression, physiological changes and feeling states.

Motor expression

What are the social functions of facial and vocal emotion expression?
Are the emotional expressions in the face and the voice universal, i.e. similar across cultures?

If emotional expression in face, body and voice is to serve a major function in communicating an individual's emotional reaction and intended action (as outlined in the first section of this chapter), there must be clearly differentiated signals corresponding to different types of emotion. We shall examine the evidence for facial and vocal expression separately.

Facial expression

The expression modality studied most intensively in the century after Darwin's pioneering work has been the face. If one assumes that innate neural motor programmes produce specific response patterns for primary emotions (as discrete emotion theorists do), the facial expressions of emotion should be very similar across cultures. Early work by Ekman (1972) and Izard (1971) showed indeed that participants from widely different cultures were able to identify the emotions facially expressed by American encoders in series of photographs rather accurately (as illustrated by the photos in figure 6.3). Critics were quick to point out, of course, that this procedure may not have been the correct way of investigating the **universality** of facial expression of emotion since the wide distribution of Hollywood films all over the world may have taught people in other cultures to identify American facial expressions reliably. In response to these criticisms, Ekman, Sorensen and Friesen (1969) conducted a study which showed that members of a tribe in a remote area of New Guinea, who had had very little contact with the outside world, identified Western facial expressions

Universality Psychobiological notion assuming that evolved behavioural mechanisms should be found all over the world, independent of culture (although culturally determined modifications are always considered possible).

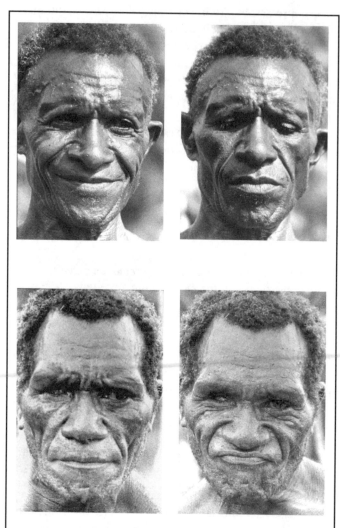

PLATE 6.1 Photographs of facial expressions in members of a tribal society in New Guinea that had little prior contact with the outside world. Guess which expressions correspond to which of the following scenarios: Your friend has come and you are happy / Your child has died / You are angry and about to fight / You see a dead pig that has been lying there a long time. Easy, isn't it?
(Reproduced from Ekman, 1998, p. 380)

quite accurately. They also produced expressions of specified emotions that were similar to those seen in the West when asked to show a face typical of specific emotion-eliciting situations (Ekman, 1972). Plate 6.1 shows some of the expressions videotaped by Ekman in New Guinea.

Since then, there have been quite a number of studies in this area, with respect to both the decoding and encoding of the different primary emotions. The bulk of the evidence indicates that actor-portrayed facial expressions can be decoded rather accurately by judges from different cultures (Ekman, 1982, 1989; Ekman & Rosenberg, 1997). This generally supports the Darwinian notion of facial expressions having evolved from formerly 'serviceable habits' which in principle should be the same for all cultures in the world. Comparative studies (Redican, 1982; van Hooff, 1972) show that there are a number of elements that can be traced back to functional behaviour patterns, and which we find in similar forms in other animals (see figure 6.2) as well as in young babies. However, these studies also show that there are features that are specific to human facial expression and for which it is difficult to find functional explications in a biological sense. Furthermore, while the intercultural studies of facial expression have demonstrated considerable universality, there has also been evidence for cultural specificity. This is true for decoding where cultural influences on emotion perception in the face have been demonstrated (Matsumoto, 1989) as well as for encoding. For example, contradicting the claim of a pan-cultural facial expression for contempt (Ekman & Friesen, 1986), Ricci-Bitti, Brighetti, Garotti and Boggi Cavallo (1989), who compared contempt expression in the United States and Italy, found rather marked differences in the facial patterning of this emotion. What could be the origins of such cultural differences in expression? One possibility is that cultures may differ with respect to the socially desirable amount of control of expression, to be discussed below.

Even apart from the existence of cultural differences, there are some questions with respect to the existence of 'innate motor programmes' expected reliably to produce full-blown, emotion-specific facial expression patterns. There is increasing evidence that actors, when asked to portray typical facial expressions of emotion, use only parts of the fully fledged emotion-specific muscle-movement patterns described by Ekman and Izard. Gosselin, Kirouac and Doré (1995) videotaped actors portraying six different emotions. They showed that observers, as expected, reached a high accuracy score in correctly decoding the posed emotions. However, a detailed analysis of the facial muscle movements used in portrayal showed that in the large majority of cases, only subsets of the theoretically postulated patterns were found. Similarly, Galati, Scherer and Ricci-Bitti (1997) asked both seeing and blind participants without any prior experience in acting to portray some of the major emotions. These lay people also showed only partial patterns (with even fewer movements than professional actors), yet observers were still able to decode the emotion with better than chance accuracy. Carroll and Russell (1997) studied the facial expressions that accompany a basic emotion in four Hollywood films. The expressions judged as surprised, afraid, angry, disgusted or sad rarely showed the full predicted pattern. Rather, the actors tended to use only one or two parts from the full pattern. In fact, this might be expected from good actors. Since the film context already suggests the intended emotion (see Wallbott & Ricci-Bitti, 1993, on the role of context), good actors seem to underplay rather than overplay the respective expression (see Wallbott & Scherer, 1986).

Proponents of the idea that expressions are the results of innate neural motor programmes (such as Ekman, 1972, 1992) could argue that actors' posing represents only an approximation to the automatic triggering of neural motor programmes subserving expression under real-life conditions. Unfortunately, most of the research so far has been conducted on posed expressions and we have precious little hard evidence on what the expressive patterns in natural emotional expression really look like. One exception is the work by the human ethologist Eibl-Eibesfeldt (1995), who has filmed naturally occurring emotional expressions in a wide variety of cultures, often with a hidden camera. While these film documents provide excellent case studies, there is not enough systematic evidence to settle the issue of universal motor programmes. Another possible approach is to study very young infants who are not yet able to control or regulate their emotional expression (which is often the problem in experimental emotion induction in adults). According to discrete emotion theorists, the expression patterns (or the neural motor programmes) are innate and are expected to occur, albeit in rudimentary form, at a very early age (Izard, 1971, 1991). On the whole, however, the issue of whether the rudimentary expression patterns in infants support the assumption of the existence of innate motor programmes remains to be settled.

The idea of innate programmes can also be challenged on theoretical grounds. In recent years, some theorists have suggested a componential approach to explaining expression patterns, assuming that the individual elements in a dynamic expression may be selectively determined by cognitive processing and the resulting action tendencies (Frijda & Tcherkassoff, 1997; Scherer, 1984b, 1992b; Smith & Scott, 1997).

Vocal expression

Can judges recognize an emotion expression on the basis of voice and speech cues alone, i.e., without pertinent verbal information? Many such studies have been conducted (mostly using actor portrayals of vocal emotion expressions) and reviews of the studies in this area (Johnstone & Scherer, 2000) have reached the conclusion that judges performed far beyond what one would expect by chance. In the first large-scale cross-cultural study of vocal expressions, Scherer, Banse and Wallbott (in press) were able to show above-chance recognizability of vocally expressed emotions across language and culture boundaries.

These data tend to support the hypothesis that vocal expression, like facial expression, is at least partly biologically based (Frick, 1985), an assumption that is supported by strong comparative evidence pointing towards the evolutionary continuity of vocal emotion expression. Behavioural biologists, studying vocal animal communication, have pointed to important similarities in the vocal expression and communication of motivational-emotional states in many different species. Thus, angry, hostile, dominant states are generally expressed by harsh, loud vocalizations, whereas states of fear and helplessness give rise to high-pitched, thin-sounding vocalizations. To a large extent, this also seems to be true for the equivalent human vocalizations (Scherer, 1985). However, as for facial expression, there are also differences between species and cultures.

In fact, the cultural influences on the voice are even more pronounced than those on the face, since in the course of the evolution of language the voice has also become the carrier signal for speech. Thus, while the facial muscles do serve other functions related to vision, eating and speaking (see Ekman, 1979), their major function seems to be the facial expression of affective states. In contrast, the voice often does double duty in carrying linguistic (phonological and morphological) and extra-linguistic (related to speaker state) meaning. Since different languages with widely different phonological and syntactical structures are spoken in different cultures, we might expect a certain degree of cultural and/or linguistic diversity of emotion signalling in the voice. However, in spite of such diversity, the underlying emotion may still be recognizable across cultures, as suggested by the results of the cross-cultural studies reported above.

In the study of facial expression, researchers have used fine-grained objective coding schemes to analyse the facial muscle movement configurations that occur for specific emotions (Ekman, 1992). In the vocal domain, researchers have used analogue or digital voice and speech analysis to determine the prototypical acoustical profiles, or signature, for the major emotions. Some results of the work in this research tradition (see Scherer, 1986; Banse & Scherer, 1996) are shown in figure 6.3.

Control and strategic manipulation of expression

The discussion so far may have suggested that automatically and involuntarily produced differentiated patterns of expression in the face and the voice are always available to infer the emotion of the expresser. While this is indeed postulated by many theorists, it is only half of the picture. In this section we need to discuss the ways in which individuals – consciously or unconsciously – monitor and modify these processes. Virtually all theories of emotion have assumed that while we are thrown into emotion or passion, we are not totally helpless: we can control, regulate or modulate the emotion. The feeling component of emotion, which may be the only one absent in the emotional system of the non-human mammals, and even of the higher primates, is precisely what we need as a feedback system for such regulation attempts – often in the service of social norms. Wundt (1900) pointed out very early on that emotional expression is subject to cultural control and that many cultures sanction explicitly or implicitly what expressions can be legitimately shown under particular circumstances. Ekman and Friesen (1969) have called these cultural prescriptions **display rules**, describing different forms of suppressing, de-intensifying, masking or replacing the spontaneous expression. Apart from cultural prescription, controlling one's

Display rules Modern term denoting the old observation that there are socio-cultural norms that govern the type of emotional expressions that are acceptable in specific situations.

PLATE 6.2   A snapshot of manipulated expressions in a society setting, revealing beautiful cues of non-verbal leakage – despite the individual's attempt to show the proper affect (Reproduced from Morris, 1977, p. 107)

emotional expression is of course also of strategic interest, particularly if one wants to deceive one's interaction partners. A number of investigators have, over the years, conducted systematic research into expressive cues to lying and deception (see Anolli & Ciceri, 1997; Ekman & Rosenberg, 1997; DePaulo & Friedman, 1998). Plate 6.2 provides a nice illustration of a tactically manipulated expression.

Regulation of expression is not limited to suppression or inhibition of emotion. In fact, in one of the earliest psychological treatments of emotion, Aristotle, in the *Nicomachean Ethics* (e.g., in McKeon, 1941), beautifully illustrates that one needs to be able to get angry for the right reason, at the right person and in the right manner in order to be taken seriously – an early lesson in 'emotional intelligence' (Salovey & Mayer, 1990). Therefore, emotion expression management has important implications for applied social psychology. A particularly interesting case is provided by negotiation situations where emotion signals are often sent for tactical reasons (e.g., a trade union official's feigned anger at a 'ridiculously low' pay rise offer by the management). Hochschild (1983) has shown that there are also positive 'feeling rules' requiring an intensification of appropriate feelings in the service of particular social interests (e.g., stewardesses creating positive social

PLATE 6.3   One of the major functions of emotional expression is communication – often in the service of social bonding or inter-actional strategy

affect routines towards airline passengers). The argument is that these rules require not only feigning a particular emotion (i.e., by emitting the appropriate signals), but also actually feeling it. This aspect of regulation has become an important topic in the social psychology of organizations – while some of the writers in this tradition highlight the effort and potential alienation involved in this 'emotion work' (Hochschild, 1983), others emphasize the functionality of the tactical use of emotion management (Ashforth & Humphrey, 1995; Rafaeli & Sutton, 1987). Thus, Staw, Sutton and Pelled (1994) review evidence showing how

PLATE 6.4 Examples of the 'eyebrow flash', a positive affect greeting signal found all over the world. These pairs of faces show, from left to right, French woman; Yanomani man; Yanomani woman; !Kung woman; Huli (Papua-New Guinea) man; Balinese man
(Reproduced from Eibl-Eibesfeldt, 1995, p. 643)

positive emotion can help employees to obtain favourable outcomes at work, whereas Morris and Feldman (1996) suggest that frequency of emotional display, attentiveness to display rules, variety of emotions to be displayed and emotional conflict will lead to 'emotional exhaustion' and will lower job satisfaction.

Thus, emotional expression is often used in a strategic, somewhat manipulative sense. The anthropologist/sociologist Erving Goffman (1959, 1971) has brilliantly analysed how emotion displays are used to present oneself in a positive light and in order to get one's way in social interactions. A classic field study demonstrates the way in which the emission of emotion signals may be motivated by social communication. Kraut and Johnston (1979) went to a bowling alley and videotaped bowlers' smiling behaviour. The study showed that the commonly observed joyful or triumphant smiles following a good throw did not appear at the moment the skittles fell – they appeared only when the bowlers turned around to look at their fellow players. Clearly, then, one of the major functions of emotional expression is communication – often in the service of social bonding or interactional strategy (see also chapter 2). The universality of such emotionally expressive messages is nicely illustrated by the 'eyebrow flash', a greeting expression signalling something like 'I am very happily surprised to see you here', that Eibl-Eibesfeldt (1995) has been able to film all over the world (see plate 6.4).

It would be exaggerated, however, to claim that expression does not at all 'ex-press' the state of the expresser and must be exclusively analysed as a strategic message to real or imagined interaction partners ('im-press'), as is claimed from time to time (see Fridlund, 1994, for an extreme example). Rather, emotional expression is multifaceted – expression is determined both by a person's reaction to an event and by the attempt to manipulate this expression for strategic reasons in a social interaction. The extent to which our emotional expression is either 'pushed out' by our inner arousal or is 'pulled' towards particular signals for the benefit

of observers varies tremendously over situations (Scherer, 1994). Clearly, the more we are 'overwhelmed' by an emotion, the more difficulty we have in manipulating the expression. In the park example above, we might want to produce angry and aggressive cues, but if we are really frightened, a faltering voice might give us away.

Summary

On the whole, then, empirical evidence suggests that there are specific expression patterns in the face and the voice for many of the major emotions. This is as one would expect if emotional expression is to provide unambiguous signals in social communication informing others about an organism's emotional reaction and consequent behavioural intention. However, the situation is complicated by the fact that our emotions, and particularly their expression, are continuously monitored and regulated (suppressed, amplified or even feigned) for the purpose of more or less strategically motivated interaction moves.

Physiological changes

Are there differentiated, emotion-specific physiological response patterns for a set of basic emotions?
What would be the functions of such 'physiological response packages'?

Throughout the centuries, the notion of emotion implied the presence of rather sizeable physiological reactivity. As we have seen, one of the central issues that has been hotly debated concerns the *specificity* of this activation or arousal for discrete emotions.

Changes in physiological state do not primarily serve communicative purposes (although blushing, increased respiration rate, general muscle tension, etc. can be quite obvious signs of emotional arousal and can be used as a basis for emotion attribution by observers). A primary function of the physiological changes is the provision of energy and the preparation for specific action. This was the main thesis of Cannon (1929), a physiologist who was one of the main adversaries of James and Lange. Contrary to their *peripheralist* position (see also Schachter, 1970), he took a *centralist* viewpoint, assuming that for each major emotion special mechanisms in the central nervous system produce physiological changes appropriate for adapted action in the different subsystems of the organism.

Unfortunately, empirical studies in this domain suffer from a major methodological difficulty. Due to both ethical and practical problems, it is almost impossible to induce strong, realistic emotions in the laboratory using systematic manipulation. Consequently, emotion-specific differences have rarely been demonstrated empirically, at least for humans. Because of this lack of evidence, some psychologists have argued that the notion of physiological differentiation should be replaced by the assumption of generalized non-specific *arousal* or *activation* (see the discussion of the position of Schachter & Singer, 1962, above).

This corresponds to throwing the baby out with the bath water. It is certainly the case that the methods actually used for emotion induction in laboratory studies (such as imagination and film viewing) are unlikely to produce very powerful emotions, but they may nevertheless help to settle the issue. A review of the pertinent studies to date by Cacioppo, Klein, Berntson and Hatfield (1993) shows that the evidence for complete autonomic differentiation of each of the major emotions (i.e., a specific, typical configuration of physiological symptoms for each emotion) is inconclusive, but that there seem to be consistent patterns of differences between specific pairs of emotions on some physiological parameters. For example, one finds consistent differences between fear and sadness with respect to heart rate across different studies (see figure 6.3). If even weak emotions, as generated in the laboratory, yield discernible physiological response patterns, one might expect that stronger emotions will show more strongly differentiated patterns.

One of the most comprehensive, methodologically controlled and ecologically valid studies in this area has been conducted by Stemmler and his associates (Stemmler, Heldmann, Pauls, & Th. Scherer, in press). These researchers controlled for context effects by using (in a within-subjects design) both real-life laboratory inductions of emotion and an imagery method (asking participants to imagine an emotional situation). For the induction of fear they used highly realistic threats of having to give a speech under severe evaluation conditions and of having to endure a rather invasive blood-drawing procedure. To induce anger, participants were harassed and insulted by the experimenter. In the imagery condition, participants were asked (1) to imagine strong fear or anger situations they experienced in the past, and (2) to imagine reliving the real-life experimental induction they went through before. The control groups experienced the same procedures but were told about the manipulations. A very comprehensive set of physiological variables was measured in all conditions. While the data did show effects of context (imagination vs. real-life induction), the researchers were able to identify specific physiological response profiles for fear and anger. Stemmler et al. argue that the different patterns can be explained by the functional, adaptive requirements in fear and anger situations. Fear is characterized by increases in heart rate, contractility of the heart musculature and respiration rate. In this way, the blood distribution is 'centralized' to ensure blood supply to the heart and brain – effects that constitute a protective circulatory response to severe blood loss (as might be expected from an attack by a predator). In anger, on the other hand, one finds the response profile that prepares the organism for extended muscular exertion, as might be needed in a fight for superiority: rise in diastolic blood pressure and in peripheral resistance.

Summary

While the evidence is still rather preliminary, it seems justified to assume that there is at least some degree of emotion-specific physiological patterning linked to the action tendencies that characterize major emotions such as fear and anger. This seems quite functional if emotions are to prepare (but not to immediately execute) adaptive actions, as postulated at the outset.

Subjective feelings

How can subjective feelings be analysed and described?
Are there cultural differences in the way feelings are labelled with emotion words?

In some ways, this may be the most important component of emotion. We could indeed ask whether we can speak about having an emotion at all if we do not have a conscious experience of it, a specific feeling that we can then label with an appropriate verbal concept. Not surprisingly, throughout the history of the study of emotion, many theorists have tended to *equate* emotion with feeling (see above). It seems more reasonable, however, to view the feeling component as a reflection of the changes occurring in *all* other components (see Scherer, 1993a). This proposal maintains the important role assigned to the conscious experience of what is happening in our body but situates the experience in the *total context* of our particular self with its history, its preferences and its present state being affected by a particular event.

Dimensions of feeling

Throughout the history of philosophy it has been claimed that the major dimension of feeling is linked to pleasure and pain, agreeableness and disagreeableness or, as it is often glossed in modern social psychology, positive or negative *valence*. In fact, quite a few modern social psychologists believe that feeling can be quite conveniently reduced to the valence aspect (positive or negative affect) with respect to persons, objects or events. This position, however, does not acknowledge major advances in our understanding of feeling states that were made during the final part of the nineteenth century. Wundt (1874) proposed a tridimensional system to characterize the specific nature of these complex emotional feeling states by adding *excitement vs. depression* and *tension vs. relaxation* to the classic *pleasantness vs. unpleasantness* dichotomy (see also Plutchik, 1980; Schlosberg, 1954).

Much of the modern work has relied on short-hand descriptors of the felt experience – in particular emotion words and photographs of facial expressions. An almost countless number of studies has shown that participants are able to judge the similarity of verbal emotion concepts or to evaluate the emotion words on rating scales related to the three dimensions mentioned above. The data consistently confirm two of Wundt's dimensions, pleasantness/unpleasantness and excitement/depression (the latter being more often described as high/low activation or active/passive in subsequent research). In addition to finding these two dimensions in virtually all studies, researchers have also been able to locate particular emotion labels (or facial expressions) in clearly identified regions of the two-dimensional space, independently of the language or culture in which these studies have been conducted (Davitz, 1964; Osgood, May, & Miron, 1975; Russell, 1983). Figure 6.5 illustrates these findings, plotting a number of emotion terms in a two-dimensional space defined by positive/negative (the horizontal axis) and active/passive (the vertical axis). The position of the terms in the space is determined by similarity judgements made by judges (see Scherer, 1984a).

The extraordinary degree of replicability of the positioning of emotion terms (and facial expressions) in a two-dimensional space has led to the formulation of a number of *dimensional theories of emotion*. One example is the circumplex model postulated by Russell (1983) and illustrated by the grey circle and the grey labels in capital letters in figure 6.5. The claim is that the major emotions (or rather, feelings) are naturally arranged in the form of a circle or circumplex in a two-dimensional space. However, as figure 6.5 shows, the empirical evidence adduced for this claim may well be an artefact of the judicious choice of labels used for similarity judgements. Once more labels are used, all of the space is filled.

While the individual emotions can be projected into a two- or three-dimensional scheme, this is always a simplification. The enormous number of verbal labels for emotions, particularly subjective feeling, that exist in virtually all the languages in the world, indicate that a much more subtle differentiation of emotional processes is possible. Depending on the criteria used by the individual

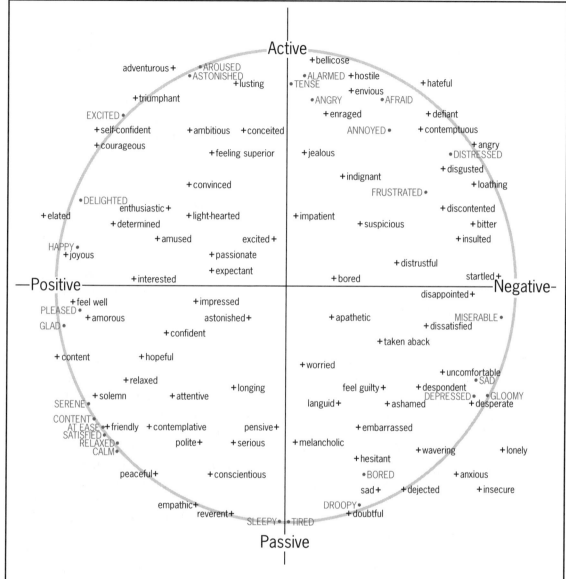

FIGURE 6.5 A two-dimensional representation of emotion terms (vertical dimension: active/passive; horizontal dimension: positive/negative)

(Adapted from Russell, 1980, p. 1167, and Scherer, 1984a, p. 51)

researcher, between 200 and close to 1,000 such terms have been identified for some of the languages studied. The use of such emotion labels may well be our major access to feeling states. If subjective feeling is restricted to the conscious experience of emotion, then it would seem that the verbal expression we use to describe this state is the closest we can come to defining it.

Verbal labelling of feeling states

Not surprisingly, then, words have consistently been one of the major manifestations of the emotions studied. In recent years, anthropologists have relied strongly
on the use of emotion labels to discuss similarities and differences in the emotions experienced in different cultures. Generally, these researchers find informants
in the culture they are studying and elicit from them the terms that are currently
used to describe affective states. They then try to establish the equivalence of
such terms to the emotion vocabulary in Western languages.

For example, Levy (1984) found that Tahitian islanders had very few words for
sadness-related emotions, talking mostly about 'feeling heavy or fatigued' or 'not
feeling a sense of inner push' in such cases, whereas they had a much richer set
of terms for other emotions such as anger. He concluded that cultures may be
more or less prone to perceive and talk about particular types of emotions. Similar
studies conducted in a number of non-Western cultures (see Lutz & White, 1986;
Mesquita et al., 1997), have shown a large cultural diversity of emotion vocabularies and ways of talking about emotional phenomena. This has led some anthropologists to conclude that there is little universality of emotion. Rather, according
to this view, emotions are mainly determined by culture-specific values and modes
of interaction (see Shweder, 1993).

This anthropological evidence, as well as indications of historical
changes in emotion concepts, has served as a basis for the claim that
emotions are socially constructed. Social psychologists proposing
this view, generally referred to as **social constructivism** (Averill, 1980;
Harré, 1986; see also Oatley, 1993), presume that emotions have no
reality other than that which is culturally created, or socially constructed.
This idea is of course partially consistent with the concept of subjective feeling states as reflecting the total context of the emotional
episode – the appraisal of the eliciting event or situation and the nature

Social constructivism Notion
that social and cultural factors
create reality for the individual,
independent of biological
processes, providing a language
for the definition of self and
experience in the world.

of the response. Obviously, the cultural context, the values concerned by the event,
and the role of the individual in the situation will all differentially affect the
particular feeling state likely to result. Cultural differences in value systems, social
structures, interaction habits and many other factors may thus influence emotion
experiences and be reflected in cultural specificities of feeling states. These differences are likely to be most pronounced with respect to the labelling of specific
aspects of the emotional experience, given the effect of cultural evolution on
language.

However, such cultural differences in feeling states and ways of talking about
them do not necessarily invalidate the notion that the basic *emotion mechanism*
is common among cultures. In order to argue that all of emotion is socio-
culturally constructed and that there is little or no universality, one would need
to show strong differences in appraisal processes, expressive behaviours, physiological reaction patterns and action tendencies in different cultures. The evidence

so far points in the opposite direction. The large-scale cross-national studies mentioned earlier (see also Scherer, Wallbott, & Summerfield, 1986; Scherer & Wallbott, 1994) found cultural differences in reported profiles of different feeling states, but these were rather minor in comparison to a massive effect of universal differences between emotions. We may conclude, then, that feeling, as expressed by verbal emotion labels, is more likely to be affected by socio-cultural variation than other components of emotion. This makes sense because the subjective feeling state represents both the cultural and situational context as well as all of the other components of the emotion process.

Summary

The empirical evidence shows rather consistent emotion-specific profiles for facial and vocal expression, and recent data suggest that at least pairs or groups of emotions can be differentiated with respect to specific physiological parameters. Feelings have been exclusively studied through verbal labels. Many studies have shown that a small number of superordinate dimensions is sufficient to summarize these feeling labels. Cross-cultural studies revealed strong cultural differences in emotion terminology, possibly reflecting differences in feeling state.

Given that there is some evidence for emotion-specific response profiles, what is the conclusion with respect to the sequence issue that has haunted us from the outset of the chapter? The last sequence model at the bottom of figure 6.1, labelled 'Modern', suggests how one might envisage the problem. Clearly, the assumed mechanism is much more complex than that envisaged in the earlier models. The basic assumption is that the differentiation produced by the results of an evaluation or appraisal of the eliciting event is in the service of an adaptation to the situation created by the event and concerns several subsystems of the organism. Subjective feeling as one of the components of the emotion process reflects these changes and is thus necessarily a consequence. However, feeling in itself serves as a stimulus which is perceived and appraised by the individual and may thus in turn influence the nature and direction of the total emotion process.

How do the Emotion Components Interact?

Does the free expression of emotion increase or decrease the intensity of feeling? What are the short-term and long-term consequences of emotion control?

It has been pointed out repeatedly that the components of emotion are all highly interconnected. What happens if we try to change one of them deliberately, for example by suppressing our spontaneous facial expression. Will that have an effect on the other components – our physiological reaction, our feeling state? If so, we could think of therapeutic interventions or social engineering, for example making people happier by getting them to smile more often! This fascinating issue will be explored in this section.

Catharsis

One of the major functions of Greek tragedy was supposed to be *catharsis*: the spectators, in the process of observing the strong emotions displayed on the stage, were supposed – via a process of empathy – to drain or cleanse their negative affects and thus achieve a serene state. In subsequent thinking one often finds the idea that strong emotional arousal can be drained by violent motor expression and acting out (see chapter 10). The mechanism of catharsis apparently involves the interaction of three components of emotion – expression, physiology and feeling. By amplifying expression, one is supposedly able to soothe the organism, reduce arousal and, at the same time, change or de-amplify the subjective feeling state.

Proprioceptive feedback

Facial feedback hypothesis
See **proprioceptive feedback**; here specifically the notion that amplification or inhibition of facial expression of emotion will modify the intensity and possibly the nature of subjective feeling.

The mechanism postulated here is quite the opposite. Increased physiological activity or strong expressive behaviour is expected to *amplify* the subjective feeling state. The most recent version of proprioceptive feedback notions, studied extensively in social psychology, has been the so-called **facial feedback hypothesis**. Following Tomkins' (1984) postulate of a central role of the face in emotion regulation, it is assumed that facial expressions of emotion consistent with a particular state will enhance the respective feeling, whereas a de-amplification or incompatible facial expressions would de-emphasize the accompanying feeling state.

Lanzetta, Cartwright-Smith and Kleck (1976) asked different groups of participants either to amplify or suppress their facial expression while receiving electric shocks during an experimental procedure, supposedly to fool observers. As predicted, participants attempting to suppress or inhibit their expressiveness rated the shocks as less painful than those asked to exaggerate expressions. This type of result has been found repeatedly in studies using an amplification–suppression paradigm.

Another paradigm for the study of facial feedback uses an artificial induction of muscular activation patterns. Under the guise of studying psychomotor co-ordination, Strack, Stepper and Martin (1988) asked participants to hold a pen in their mouths in ways that either inhibited (holding with the lips only) or facilitated (holding with teeth only) the muscles typically associated with smiling

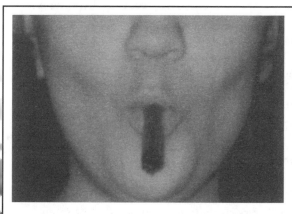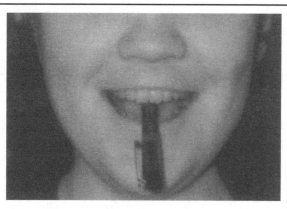

PLATE 6.5   Facial configurations used in the facial feedback experiment by Strack, Stepper and Martin (1988)

(see plate 6.5). In two studies, participants using their 'smiling muscles' to hold the pen reported more intense humour responses to cartoons presented during the experimental procedure (but see Laird, 1974, for a discussion of individual differences in such studies).

A recent study suggests that such feedback effects may be moderated by social-psychological factors such as attention to internal vs. situational cues and self-awareness. Kleinke, Peterson and Rutledge (1998) asked participants to look at photographs of positive or negative facial expressions and to communicate these facial expressions as accurately as they could to a video camera (participants in a control group being asked to maintain neutral facial expressions). Participants verbally reported increased positive moods when they engaged in positive facial expressions and decreased positive moods when they engaged in negative facial expressions. These effects were stronger in a condition where participants saw themselves in a mirror and for participants with high private self-consciousness.

The strength of the facial feedback effects and the nature of the mechanism are still hotly debated (see McIntosh, 1996, for a review of the issues). Nevertheless, the finding that feelings elicited by particular stimuli can be amplified or de-amplified by appropriate or inappropriate muscular innervation in the expression component of emotion seems quite logical within a componential view of emotion. If feeling is a reflection of all the other components, then, by definition, feelings would monitor the states of the other subsystems of the organism and thus be more intense if there is strong rather than weak expression. Unfortunately, the issue is more complicated. If the feeling component really reflects all of the other components of emotion, then it will also reflect voluntary or involuntary efforts to hide or de-amplify emotional expression. One could imagine that being forced to show a friendly smile while experiencing intense anger would actually increase the feeling of anger rather than decrease it.

The effects postulated by a weak version of the facial feedback hypothesis (amplification or de-amplification of feelings elicited by appropriate stimuli) can be accounted for by the notion that the feeling state is a reflection of whatever goes on in other parts of the body as well as in our head (appraisal). This is not the case for the strong version of the hypothesis, which claims there are hard-wired connections between the emotional reaction components and therefore postulate that it is possible to induce a fully fledged emotion artificially by the appropriate manipulation of one of the components (for example, posing a specific facial expression).

In a widely discussed paper, Ekman, Levenson and Friesen (1983) reported evidence that the induction of particular motor expressions may not only amplify feeling state but actually create a specific emotion as indexed by differential physiological responses and verbal feeling reports *without* any other kind of stimulation. These researchers asked actors to produce combinations of facial muscle movements on the basis of detailed coaching as to how and when to move particular parts of the face. At the same time, their physiological responses were measured. After completion of the so-called 'directed facial action task', the actors were asked to rate their feeling state. The combinations of facial action units that the actors were requested to make were those theoretically predicted to be characteristic for fundamental discrete emotions (Ekman, 1989). Although ostensibly the task had nothing to do with emotion and the actors had not been told that this was the purpose of the study, the results did show a clear differentiation of the physiological response patterns for the different facial combinations, largely corresponding to theoretical expectations. Furthermore, there was a tendency for the actors to feel the emotion whose facial signs they had unwittingly produced in their face. The study has been repeatedly criticized with respect to possible experimental artefacts. For example, the actors might have noticed that the facial configuration shaping up in their faces as a result of the instructions formed the expression of a particular emotion, which might suggest other emotion-induction mechanisms such as imagination or compliance with the experimenter's expectations. Also, some configurations might require more effort and thus affect psychophysiological responding (e.g., Boiten, 1996). However, the authors have since replicated the results with both North American and Sumatran participants (Levenson, Ekman, & Friesen, 1990; Levenson, Ekman, Heider, & Friesen, 1992), providing some evidence against the suggestion of artefacts raised by critics.

If findings such as these can be replicated reliably and the detailed patterns of connections between emotional reaction components uncovered, it would seem fruitful to study whether the emotion process can be triggered by activating any one of the contributing components. In particular, feeling state should be readily influenceable by making use of internal feedback mechanisms. Unfortunately, the study of the relationships and interactions between emotion components has barely begun. Such studies would evidently have important implications for application, for example in therapy. There is, however, the danger, as in the Schachter/Singer experiment, that the ecological validity of the phenomenon is lost from sight as it is unlikely that our emotions are frequently elicited by systematic manipulations of our facial muscles or other peripheral body organs.

Consequences of emotional regulation

As has been shown above, emotions are almost never raw or pure – as soon as they are elicited, they are – at least in humans – monitored and regulated, controlled or manipulated. There are different ways in which emotions can be regulated. One possibility is to avoid an emotional response even before it has a chance to develop, by trying actively to control the appraisal of a potentially emotion-inducing event. In a classic experiment, Lazarus, Speisman, Mordkoff and Davison (1962) showed that it was possible to change the participants' physiological responses to a stressful film (e.g., showing a subincision in gory detail) by varying the verbal commentary (stressing the painful experience of the person vs. stressing the social function of the rite). In a similar fashion, we can convince ourselves that what we are seeing is not really very serious and should not affect us, a kind of reappraisal. Alternatively, if the emotion has already been produced, we can try to suppress a particular response such as facial expression. As we have seen above, such masking, often accompanied by specific display rules, is often demanded by social norms. In other cases, individuals may attempt to regulate their emotion to avoid being carried away by a powerful emotional response or because they believe that they can shorten negative emotional experiences by regulation.

What are the differences between these two types of regulation? In part this depends on the context and the relative difficulty of exerting control. In situations in which an event obviously has powerful consequences for us, it may be unrealistic to engage in reappraisal. With respect to controlling our responses, there are major differences between response modalities. Whereas we can always control at least parts of our facial expression (and manage a pained smile, for example), it may be more difficult to regulate more automatic processes such as respiration or muscle trembling (which will affect our voice). Furthermore, there may be differences in the effects of these two types of regulation. Gross (1998) showed a disgusting film to participants while their experiential, behavioural and physiological responses were recorded. Depending on the experimental condition, they were told either to (1) think about the film in such a way that they would feel nothing (reappraisal), (2) behave in such a way that someone watching them would not know they were feeling anything (suppression) or (3) just watch the film (a control condition). In both the reappraisal and suppression conditions, participants showed less expressive behaviour than in the control condition. However, reappraisal decreased disgust experiences (as one might expect from an effort to nip the emotion in the bud), whereas suppression increased sympathetic activation, suggesting an interaction between different emotion components (see chapter 10).

An interesting issue concerns individual or group differences with respect to the proneness to control one's emotions. A widely held stereotype is that women are 'more emotional' than men. In particular, they are expected to show their emotions more readily, i.e., control or mask them less, and to recognize the emotional expressions of others more accurately. In fact, it is often assumed that this emphasis on emotionality is an important part of the female gender role, highlighting socio-affective skills, in contrast to men, who are supposed to control their emotions tightly ('men don't cry') and get on with their job (see Grossman & Wood, 1993). Is there a kernel of truth to this popular stereotype? Kring and Gordon (1998) had undergraduates view emotional films and compared their expressiveness, their skin conductance responses and their subjective feelings. As expected, women were more expressive than men. They also showed different patterns of skin conductance responding. However, there were no differences in verbal reports of experienced emotion. Interestingly, there were important individual differences in the relationship between sex and expressivity depending on the participants' definition of gender role and the level of expressiveness in the family. The second part of the stereotype – women being more accurate in recognizing others' emotional expressions – has received some confirmation: a large-scale meta-analysis of pertinent non-verbal recognition studies suggests that women may be a bit better at this task than men (Hall, 1998).

Summary

The interrelationships between the different emotion components have not yet been studied extensively. Most of the research to date has been directed at the effects of motor expression on feeling state. There is some evidence for *both* catharsis *and* proprioceptive feedback effects. While these two mechanisms may seem contradictory at first sight, a process perspective may help to accommodate both mechanisms in naturally occurring situations: on the one hand, uncontrolled motor expression following the elicitation of an emotion episode is likely to intensify the respective feeling (as predicted by proprioceptive feedback theories). On the other hand, this will lead to a more rapid depletion of the arousal elicited by the respective event (as predicted by catharsis notions). This decrease of arousal may, in turn, reduce the intensity of the feeling more quickly than would be the case if the expression had been partially suppressed. Thus, uncontrolled expression may lead, in the short run, to an amplification of feeling, but in the long run to a more rapid dissipation. Suppressed expression may lead to a short-term decrease in feeling intensity, but may also have the effect that this lower level is maintained for a longer period of time. There is also evidence that trying to regulate or control one component of emotion may have immediate consequences for another component, illustrating the extreme interconnectedness of the components during emotion episodes.

Summary and Conclusions

Emotion is a ubiquitous phenomenon in human social behaviour. As a mechanism selected in the course of evolution it subserves adaptation to significant changes in the physical and social environment by allowing the flexible choice of response alternatives. However, emotions at the same time automatically produce action tendencies that prepare adaptive action. The signalling function of emotional expression is of particular importance for socially living species allowing the negotiation of interactive moves. Finally, the feeling component plays a major role in monitoring and regulating emotional reactivity. Given its key function in adaptation, it is not surprising that emotion involves virtually all organismic subsystems, which are synchronized during the emotion episode to muster all the resources of the organism in an effort at adaptation. The complex interrelationships between the different components of emotion are currently under study. Recent social-psychological work has shown the importance of the individual's appraisal of potentially emotion-eliciting events with respect to major needs, goals and resources available for coping. Because of the strong cultural influences on the definition of goals and values, one can expect important effects of social groups and cultural variability on emotional experience. This is also true for different ways of labelling and regulating particular feeling states in different cultures.

Research on emotion is currently mushrooming in social psychology. Recent theorizing and empirical work have greatly expanded our knowledge of the phenomenon and allowed us to formulate powerful hypotheses. Increasingly, research is directed towards the study of strong, real-life emotions rather than on the laboratory induction of relatively weak and non-specific emotional processes.

It is important to overcome the widening gulf between a psychobiological approach, mostly interested in the emotion-specific externalization of internal states, and a socio-anthropological approach, postulating the primacy of the social and cultural construction of emotional experience. There is much evidence that emotion is the result of both psychobiological mechanisms (which humans largely share with animals) and social and cultural factors that determine the elicitation, the type of response, the regulation and, in particular, the verbal and non-verbal communication of the feeling component. In general, as the discussion in this chapter has shown, one cannot overemphasize the important role of the dynamic interrelationships of the different emotion components, in particular the relationship of the subjective feeling state to the physiological and expression components.

As mentioned at several points in this chapter, scholars from many different disciplines have wrestled with the complexity of emotion phenomena in the course of the last two millennia. Students of human behaviour, particularly social psychologists, increasingly find that emotion plays a central role as a mediating mechanism between motivation, cognition and behaviour – especially in social contexts. As a consequence there has been an explosion of interest in affective phenomena during recent years, and there is hope that it may not take another two millennia to advance our understanding of emotion.

DISCUSSION
POINTS

1   As mentioned repeatedly in this chapter, emotion plays a major role in many social-psychological phenomena. Look at some of the other chapters in this textbook – e.g., those on attitudes, social cognition, group performance – and discuss how various types of emotions might affect the phenomena described.

2   Take an emotion-eliciting event that happened to you and try to remember all the details. Now look again at figure 6.1 and analyse how each of the theoretical positions described there might explain what you experienced. Elaborate the criteria you use to decide which of the explanations to prefer.

3   Think of a very typical emotion-producing event, such as failing an important examination, the death of a close friend or relative, and discuss how various social-psychological processes described in this textbook might account for differences between cultures.

4   Reread the summary of the section on emotion control and regulation suggesting that both catharsis and proprioceptive feedback could be operative – but at different points in time. Design an experiment that could test this idea experimentally.

5   Compile a list of the different theories of emotion mentioned in this chapter. Are the claims made by these theories contradictory, or can the theories be seen as complementing one another, focusing on different aspects or components of the emotion phenomenon?

6   Draw up a list of all the factors that could potentially produce differences between individuals, groups and cultures with respect to their emotional reaction to an identical situation. Discuss the mechanisms that could mediate these effects.

FURTHER
READING

Ekman, P., & Davidson, R. J. (Eds.). (1994). *The nature of emotion: Fundamental questions.* New York and Oxford: Oxford University Press. A novel format. Prominent emotion theorists and researchers provide their view on major questions outlined by the editors.

Frijda, N. H. (1986). *The emotions.* Cambridge and New York: Cambridge University Press. In addition to presenting Frijda's own theory, this book contains a wide-ranging and learned discussion of relevant theory and research.

Izard, C. E. (1991). *The psychology of emotions.* New York: Plenum Press. Based on Izard's theory, the book attempts to integrate many of the major aspects of emotion.

Lazarus, R. S. (1991). *Emotion and adaptation.* New York: Oxford University Press. A highly readable account of Lazarus' theoretical approach, cross-referencing many major approaches and highlighting possible application of emotion research, particularly in the health area.

Lewis, M., & Haviland-Jones, J. M. (Eds.). (2000). *Handbook of emotions* (2nd ed.). New York: Guilford Press. A comprehensive overview of the significant aspects of research on emotion in several disciplines.

Scherer, K. R. (Ed.). (1988). *Facets of emotion: Recent research*. Hillsdale, NJ: Erlbaum. A series of chapters presenting empirical data on different aspects of emotion such as appraisal, response characteristics and communication. The annex contains useful materials for further study.

Scherer, K. R., & Ekman, P. (Ed.). (1984). *Approaches to emotion*. Hillsdale, NJ: Erlbaum. A collection of original chapters presenting some of the important theoretical approaches in the field.

Schachter, S., & Singer, J. E. (1962). Cognitive, social and physiological determinants of emotional states. *Psychological Review*, 69, 379–99.

Ekman, P., & Friesen, W. V. (1971). Constants across cultures in the face and emotion. *Journal of Personality and Social Psychology*, 17, 124–9.

KEY STUDIES

Attribution Theory and Research: From Basic to Applied

Frank Fincham and
Miles Hewstone

OUTLINE

In our everyday lives we frequently seek to explain, or assign causes for, our own or other people's behaviour. Attribution theory deals with this broad class of phenomena. This chapter considers both theories about the way people explain events, and applications of this theory to real-world problems. The analysis of theories looks at when, why and how we make attributions as we do. This involves considering the information people use to make attri-butions and whether they tend systematically to give certain kinds of explanations (e.g., those favouring themselves). The review of applications looks at how attributions are related to feelings and motivation (e.g., when we try harder following a failure), the use of attributions in clinical psychology, and the role of attributions in close relationships, such as marriage.

KEY CONCEPTS

- Actor–observer difference
- Attributional biases
- Attribution theory
- Attributional style
- Augmentation principle
- Causal attribution
- Causal schemata
- Correspondence bias
- Covariation principle

- Discounting principle
- Fundamental attribution error
- Learned helplessness
- Normative model
- Salience
- Self-serving bias
- Self-handicapping
- Social representation

Introduction

A well-known television advertisement for a British newspaper shows a man (a skinhead) running after another man (a businessman). The camera focuses on the businessman's briefcase. Why is the skinhead running after him? This is a typical example of the kind of 'why' questions we ask in every-day life, which is the subject of **attribution theory**. This general area of research deals not only with explanations or causal attributions for other people's behaviour, but also self-attributions. Imagine you have just found out that you failed the statistics exam you took last month. Why? The research we review in this chapter deals with how you answer such 'why' questions. We look at the kind of information you use, and how you process it; for example, do you compare your own outcome with that of other students? We also look at the consequences that follow from your explanation. For example, if you ascribe your failure to a lack of ability, you may experience a loss of self-esteem and not bother to study for the retake. On the other hand, if you attribute the failure to lack of effort, you can take a positive approach and work hard to make sure that you pass next time. In our interactions with others, we are much influenced by our interpretations of their motives, and in setting our own goals we depend to a great extent on realistic assessment of our own abilities (inferred from our perception of the causes of success and failure). You can see that the topic of **causal attribution**, how people attribute effects to causes, is an important one, and it is one that has been of great interest to social psychologists.

Attribution theory The conceptual framework within social psychology dealing with lay, or common-sense, explanations of behaviour.

Causal attribution The inference process by which perceivers attribute an effect to one or more causes.

In this chapter we are concerned with people's causal attributions for social events, including their own and other people's behaviour. In the first half of the chapter we deal, first, with two classic theories about the way people *attribute* behaviour to discrete causes. We then consider some of the most interesting theoretical questions and research which tries to answer four broad questions: What are the main characteristics of attributions? Do people's attributions show any systematic biases? When do we make attributions? And how do we make attributions? In the second half of the chapter we look at applications of attribution theory, focusing on three main topics: motivation, clinical psychology and close relationships.

Theories of Causal Attribution

The naive analysis of action

How does Heider's 'naive scientist' make common-sense explanations?

In a classic book, *The Psychology of Interpersonal Relations*, Fritz Heider (1958) laid out the foundations for attribution theory as part of what he called a 'common-sense psychology'. He argued that it was crucial to know what people believed, because those beliefs would guide behaviour. One of the questions he asked was, 'What do people do when they try to explain events in their social and physical world?' Heider (1958) viewed the layperson as a *naive scientist*, linking observable behaviour to unobservable causes. We shall note here two fundamental insights from this early work, which have had a great impact on subsequent research. First, Heider made an important distinction between 'internal' and 'external' causes. According to Heider, the job of the perceiver is to decide whether a given action is due to something within the person who is performing it (e.g., ability, effort, intention), or to something outside the person (e.g., the difficulty of the task, or luck). Understanding which set of factors should be used to interpret the behaviour of another person will, according to Heider, make the perceiver's world more predictable, and give a sense of control. Second, Heider noted that perceivers tend to ignore, partly or completely, situational factors when explaining behaviour. Heider's work is somewhat discursive, but many of his ideas were clarified and made more amenable to experimental investigation by later theorists (e.g., Kelley, 1967; Jones & Davis, 1965; Weiner, 1979). In this chapter we will focus here on Kelley's scientific model of attribution and, later, on Weiner's more motivational approach.

Covariation and configuration

What is the 'ANOVA' model, and what are its limitations?
How do we make attributions when we only have limited information?

The next theory to emerge was 'correspondent inference theory' (Jones & Davis, 1965). Although important historically, its impact has been limited and we do not discuss it here. Instead, we consider the next addition to attribution theory, Kelley's (1967, 1973) model. Kelley begins with the question of what information is used to arrive at a causal attribution. He outlines two different cases, which depend on the amount of information available to the perceiver. In the first case, the perceiver has information from multiple observations, at different times, in different situations, and can perceive the *covariation* of an observed effect and its possible causes. For example, if you have just failed a statistics examination, how do you explain this? If you know that you failed the same subject last year, that you passed all your other exams, and that several of your friends also failed statistics, you will be more likely to attribute this failure to the particular examination (e.g., its nature or topic) than to yourself. In the second case, the perceiver is faced with a single observation and must take account of the *configuration* of factors that are plausible causes of the observed effect. For example, if you see a car knock down a pedestrian, you cannot normally ask about the number of previous accidents involving either driver or pedestrian. You have to take note of such factors as a wet road surface, whether the driver was drunk, and so on. We deal with both covariation and configuration in turn.

Attributions based on multiple observations: covariation

Covariation principle In Kelley's theory of causal attribution, a perceiver with sufficient time and motivation can make attributions by perceiving the covariation of an observed effect and its possible causes. The effect is attributed to the condition that is present when the effect is present, and absent when the effect is absent.

Where the perceiver has information from multiple sources, Kelley (1967, 1973) suggests that her purpose, like the scientist's, is to separate out which effects are to be attributed to which of several factors. He proposes that a **covariation principle** is used: an effect is attributed to a condition that is present when the effect is present, and absent when the effect is absent. Kelley based his model on a statistical technique, the analysis of variance (ANOVA), which examines changes in a dependent variable (the effect) by varying independent variables (the conditions).

We can demonstrate the ANOVA model by considering an example studied by McArthur (1972): 'Neil falls asleep during Professor Brown's lecture'. This outcome could be caused by something in the person (Neil), the circumstances (e.g., the hot lecture theatre or the fact that last night had been too late), the entity (Professor Brown), or some combination of these factors. The independent variables constitute the three possible ways of examining variations in effects (see figure 7.1): (a) over persons (from which *consensus* information is derived); (b) over time/modalities (from which *consistency* is derived); and (c) over entities (from which *distinctiveness* is derived). The dependent variable is, of course, whether the effect occurs or not. The covariation principle suggests that the effect is seen as caused by the factor with which it covaries.

If we assume that each type of information could be given a high or low value, then we could generate a total of eight different patterns of information. McArthur (1972) did this and produced results apparently consistent with the

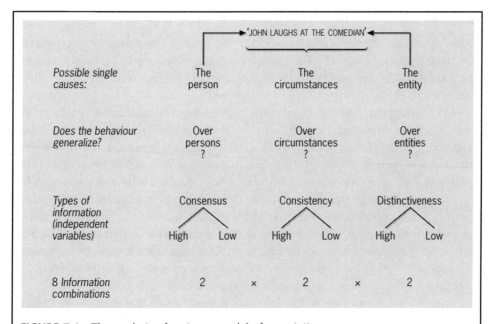

FIGURE 7.1 The analysis of variance model of covariation

Note: An explanation for a simple sentence of this type can be generated by identifying each possible single cause (person/circumstance/entity), asking whether the behaviour generalizes across persons, circumstances and entities, and thus specifying the level of information in each case (from Hewstone, 1989; after Kelley, 1967; McArthur, 1972).

model, confirming that consensus, distinctiveness and consistency did indeed affect the attribution of causality in the way predicted by Kelley and in line with the covariation principle. Subsequent studies were more critical. Attention focused on what patterns of information lead to the three main types of causal attribution: person, entity and circumstances. For person and entity attributions, the model works well. Thus if only Neil fell asleep during Professor Brown's lecture (low consensus), he has done so in the past (high consistency), and he also falls asleep during other lectures (low distinctiveness), then the effect is seen as caused by something in the person (Neil). And if everyone falls asleep in the lecture (high consensus), Neil has done so in the past (high consistency), and he does not fall asleep in other lectures (high distinctiveness), then the effect is seen as caused by something in the entity (Professor Brown). Where the model falls down is in accounting for circumstance attributions; these seem to be maximized whenever consistency is low (Neil has not slept in Professor Brown's lectures in the past), but there does not seem to be one specific pattern of information (as there was for person and entity attributions) that clearly leads to circumstance attributions (Försterling, 1989; Hewstone & Jaspars, 1987).

Critical issues relating to the covariation principle

Although initial studies seemed to support the model, it has since been criticized on three major grounds: (1) The covariation principle is limited as a basis for inferring causality. As statistics books remind us, correlation does not necessarily imply correlation. (2) In the type of experiment used to test the model (e.g., McArthur, 1972), participants are provided with 'pre-packaged' covariation information which, under normal circumstances, they might neither seek out nor use (see Garland, Hardy, & Stephenson, 1975). This limitation is made more serious by the fact that people are not very skilled at assessing covariation between events (Alloy & Tabachnik, 1984). (3) Although participants' attributions may appear *as if* they used the covariation principle, their actual information processing may be completely different from that set out by Kelley. Just because people's attributions seem to fit the ANOVA framework, this does not mean that they are doing anything like that in their heads. Can you? Most of us find it hard enough with a calculator, or even a computer. We will return below to the interesting question of the cognitive processes involved in causal attribution.

Later work on this theory has focused on exactly *how* perceivers make causal attributions, given consensus, consistency and distinctiveness information, sometimes using very complex models (e.g., Cheng, 1997; Van Overvalle, 1998). Hilton and Slugoski (1986) provide an elegant but simple alternative in their 'abnormal conditions focus' (ACF). According to this model, we select as a cause the necessary condition that is *abnormal* when compared with the background of the target event. The ACF model proposes that participants treat consensus, distinctiveness and consistency information as 'contrast cases' that define the abnormal conditions facilitating the production of the event. The abnormal conditions are then treated as the causes of the event. Specifically, Hilton and Slugoski suggested that *low consensus* information ('hardly anyone else does it') identifies the target *person* as abnormal; *high distinctiveness* information ('the target person does it to hardly anything else') identifies the *entity* as abnormal; and *low consistency* information ('the target event has hardly ever happened before') identifies the present *circumstances* as abnormal.

Hilton and Slugoski illustrated the functions of consensus, distinctiveness and consistency using the example case of the man who suffers indigestion after eating parsnips. They showed how the definition of the abnormal condition depends on the nature of the contrast case(s) chosen to compare the target event against. For example, the man's doctor would contrast the man with other patients (thus focusing on 'something about the man' as the abnormal condition), but his wife would contrast the man's reaction to his reactions after eating other vegetables (thus focusing on 'something about the parsnips' as the abnormal condition). Assuming the perspective of a neutral observer, neither doctor nor wife, we would wish to contrast not only the man with other men (consensus information), but also the parsnips with other vegetables he eats (distinctiveness information). We might also wish to contrast the current occasion on which the man eats parsnips with previous occasions on which he has eaten parsnips (consistency information). Imagine if the man always gets indigestion after eating parsnips, hardly anyone else does, the man does not suffer indigestion after eating other vegetables, and in the past he has always suffered indigestion after eating parsnips. Using the dimensions of consensus, distinctiveness and consistency information in this way, the abnormal conditions focus model would predict attributions to both the person (the man) and the entity (the parsnips) because both, respectively, are abnormal conditions in the context of the consensus and distinctiveness information supplied. However, the consistency information indicates that there was nothing abnormal about the circumstances (present occasion) when the man ate parsnips, and this should lead us to see the present occasion as a mere condition and not a cause.

Attributions based on a single observation: configuration

Another drawback of the covariation model is that it requires multiple observations, yielding consensus, consistency and distinctiveness information. Yet we often do not have that information when making attributions in everyday life. Kelley (1972) acknowledged that the ANOVA model was 'idealized' and that there were many occasions on which the perceiver lacks the information, time or motivation to examine multiple observations. In these cases of incomplete data, attributions are made using **causal schemata**. These schemata are ready-made beliefs, preconceptions and even theories, built up from experience, about how certain kinds of causes interact to produce a specific kind of effect. A perceiver can interpret information by comparing it, and integrating it, with a schema (see chapter 5).

Causal schemata Abstract, content-free conceptions of the way certain kinds of causes interact to produce an effect (e.g., multiple necessary cause schema; multiple sufficient cause schema).

One of the simplest causal schemata is the multiple sufficient cause schema (Kelley, 1972). According to this schema, any of several causes (e.g., problems at home, poor school environment or lack of effort) acting individually can produce the same effect (e.g., a child's examination failure). Kelley also put forward a number of attributional principles that accompany the causal schemata. The multiple sufficient cause schema is associated with the **discounting principle**: given that different causes can produce the same effect, the role of a given cause in producing the effect is *discounted* if other plausible causes are present. Consider a child who fails an exam at school. Could

Discounting principle The discounting principle (originally invoked in relation to causal schemata) implies that the role of a given cause in producing an effect is decreased if other plausible causes are present.

it be that he is just not trying (i.e., lack of effort is the cause)? We are likely to discount this cause if we learn that the child's mother has been seriously ill (i.e., this provides a plausible alternative cause). The discounting principle is still incompletely understood (see McClure, 1998), and recent research has attempted to identify conditions under which discounting is, and is not, part of a rational judgement process (Morris & Larrick, 1995).

Augmentation principle The augmentation principle (originally invoked in relation to causal schemata) implies that the role of a given cause is increased if an effect occurs in the presence of an inhibitory cause. This idea has also been used to explain the social influence exerted by minorities.

Kelley (1972) also proposed an **augmentation principle**: the role of a given cause is *augmented* (increased) if an effect occurs in the presence of an inhibitory cause. Thus a student who succeeds in an examination despite suffering from glandular fever should have her performance attributed more to effort and ability than would a healthy student. The augmentation principle applies to both the multiple sufficient cause and to the more complex multiple necessary cause schema (Kelley, 1972). According to the multiple necessary cause schema, several causes must operate together to produce the effect. Kelley hypothesized that this schema would be invoked to account for unusual or extreme effects (Cunningham & Kelley, 1975).

Kelley (1972) proposed that there are many other kinds of causal schema available to the layperson, and they are important for three main reasons: (1) they help the perceiver to make attributions when information is incomplete; (2) they are general conceptions about causes and effects which may apply across content areas; (3) they provide the perceiver with a 'causal shorthand' for carrying out complex inferences quickly and easily (Fiske & Taylor, 1991).

Critical issues relating to causal schemata

Despite the apparent advantages of causal schemata, there are still issues which require theoretical and empirical attention. According to Fiedler (1982), two issues are central: (1) The existence and functioning of causal schemata, while intuitively plausible, have not been successfully demonstrated. Fiedler criticizes some of the research for being artificial, and for having a built-in device for finding a causal schema in any kind of attribution by the perceiver. Thus different responses are seen as evidence of the use of different kinds of schemata. But how do we know that a schema was used at all? All we can say, at present, is that people act *as if* they use schemata. (2) Fiedler also criticized the abstract, content-free conception of schemata. A schema should represent organized knowledge based on cultural experience and not just an abstract relation between cause and effect.

Covariation and configuration: an integration

In spite of the critical issues raised by our discussion, both covariation and configuration notions are central to attribution research. There has been extended discussion of whether attributions are 'data driven' (by covariation) or 'theory driven' (by configuration). In fact, there is an interaction between data and expectations, with preconceptions influencing not only how, but what, data are processed (Alloy & Tabachnik, 1984).

Theories of causal attribution: a summary

Attribution theories converge on the following general themes: mediation between stimulus and response; active and constructive causal interpretation; and the perspective of the naive scientist or layperson. Most importantly, all share a concern with common-sense explanations and answers to the question 'why?'. Based on the rich, descriptive work of Heider (1958), subsequent theories tried ambitiously to formalize the rules people might be using to make causal attributions. In doing so, they answered many questions, and raised a great deal more, about the nature of common-sense explanations, and when and how they are made. We now consider some of these questions.

Fundamental Questions for Attribution Research

The initial enthusiasm for attribution research, stimulated by the testable theories reviewed above, was followed by deeper, more critical research and theorizing on fundamental issues: what exactly are causal attributions; how are they biased; when do they occur; and how do perceivers make them?

The nature of causal attribution

Is the distinction between 'internal' and 'external' attribution valid?

Since Heider's (1958) work, there has been a great emphasis on the distinction between internal and external attributions. Although this distinction is important, two major problems threaten its use and value (Miller, Smith, & Uleman, 1981).

First, what is the relation between internal and external attributions? Heider proposed an inverse relation between personal and situational causality. The more the person is seen as causing the action, the less the environment will be perceived as causal (and *vice versa*). According to this view, measures of personal and situational attribution should be negatively correlated. However, several studies have reported positive or only slightly negative correlations between attributions to the person and attributions to the situation when rated on separate scales (e.g., Taylor & Koivumaki, 1976). People are also more likely to employ combinations of both internal and external attributions under certain conditions, such as when explaining extreme events (Kelley, 1973) or complex interpersonal events such as marital interaction (Fincham, 1985).

Second, can internal and external attributions be distinguished? A central problem is that statements which seem to imply external attributions can be rephrased as statements implying internal attributions (and *vice versa*; Ross, 1977). This problem is particularly evident where researchers have attempted to code attributions from a free-response format. Nisbett and colleagues (1973, Study 2) asked students to write brief paragraphs describing why they had chosen their college degree subject. A statement such as 'I want to make a lot of money' was coded as internal, while 'Chemistry is a high-paying field' was coded as external. An obvious criticism of this method is that the two types of statements contain similar information and in fact imply one another. A number of researchers have also noted that the categories of internal and external causality are very broad, containing a heterogeneous collection of attributions (see Lalljee, 1981). Some researchers have reported that many of their participants failed to understand the distinction, and/or did not find it meaningful (Taylor & Koivumaki, 1976).

This research raises serious questions about the validity of the distinction between internal and external attribution. An improved and multidimensional approach to the structure of perceived causality has been developed over some years by Weiner and colleagues (see Weiner, 1986). This taxonomy of causes specifies their underlying properties in terms of three dimensions. *Locus* refers to the familiar location of a cause internal or external to the person; *stability* refers to the temporal nature of a cause, varying from stable (invariant) to unstable (variant); and *controllability* refers to the degree of volitional influence that can be exerted over a cause. Causes can theoretically be classified within one of eight cells (2 locus levels × 2 stability levels × 2 controllability levels). As will be seen in the second half of the chapter, Weiner has developed this approach into an important theory of motivation and emotion.

The instigation of causal attributions

Do unexpected events trigger spontaneous attributions?

'Spontaneous' causal attribution

Thus far we may have created the impression that people always make attributions, and perhaps exert some effort in doing so. Is this the case? Langer (1978) argued that we know that people are capable of perceiving the world in cause-and-effect terms, but not how often, and under what circumstances, they do so. Her critique raised the question of how much thinking the ordinary attributor does, and she argued that much ostensibly thoughtful action was, in fact, 'mindless'. She proposed that, most of the time, people were not consciously seeking explanations, nor were they actively engaged in monitoring new information. Especially when performing familiar activities, people rely on well-learned and general 'scripts' (e.g., Abelson, 1981). There are also individual differences in the degree of complexity with which people make attributions (see Fletcher, Danilovics, Fernandez, Peterson, & Reeder, 1986).

So, when do people make attributions? To answer this question, Weiner (1985) reviewed all the available evidence for what he called 'spontaneous' causal thinking. He deliberately excluded all studies that had measured attributions obtrusively, and concentrated on studies where normal (verbal) behaviour had been observed and coded. For example, Lau and Russell (1980) content-analysed attributions in the sports pages of newspapers and found, as one would predict, that unexpected outcomes elicited a greater number of attempts at explanation than did expected results. Similarly, Seligman and his colleagues have coded attributions from a variety of sources, including diaries, election speeches and psychotherapy sessions (see Peterson, Maier, & Seligman, 1993). From his review, Weiner concluded that there were two key factors in eliciting attributions: unexpected (vs. expected) events, and non-attainment (vs. attainment) of a goal. Kanazawa (1992) designed an experiment to vary both expectancy (expected vs. unexpected events) and outcome (success vs. failure). For example, participants read about a person who did well (or poorly) at school, and then went on to university and graduated with distinction (or did poorly). Kanazawa found that only expectancy had an independent effect on spontaneous causal thinking. Before concluding, however, that causal attributions are generally spontaneous, we recommend that you read the section on 'process' below.

PLATE 7.1 We are more likely to ask 'why' questions after unexpected outcomes (e.g., unknown Labour candidate Stephen Twigg's surprise election victory over Conservative heavyweight Michael Portillo in the British general election, May, 1997)

Other instigating factors

Researchers have also identified a number of additional triggers of attributional activity, including loss of control (Liu & Steele, 1986), and different emotions such as sadness and anger (Keltner, Ellsworth, & Edwards, 1993). A quite different approach to the instigation of attributions involves looking at the conversational context in which attributions are made (see Hilton, 1990, 1991; Turnbull & Slugoski, 1988). The linguistic philosopher Grice's (1975) work on conversational rules pointed to the fact that in communication we try to avoid redundancy and, for example, only tell people what they do not already know. Lalljee (1981) developed this work and proposed four general principles that might underlie the presentation of a particular explanation: (1) 'Assumptions concerning the knowledge of the other'; (2) 'The relationship between the inter-actors'; (3) 'Topic and activity implications'; and (4) 'Interpersonal consequences'. Thus the same event might receive different explanations (or perhaps no explanation at all), depending on the conversational context. For a detailed treatment of when and where attributions are being made, see Schuster, Rudolph and Försterling (1998).

Errors and biases in the attribution process

Do laypeople's attributions reveal systematic 'errors', 'biases' or 'mistakes'?
How do cognitive and motivational accounts attempt to explain the main attributional biases?

Normative model   Standard, optimally correct way of making an inference or judgement (e.g., Kelley's ANOVA model).

Attributional biases   A bias occurs if the perceiver systematically distorts (e.g., over- or underuses) some otherwise correct procedure, or indeed if the result of the procedure itself is distorted.

As we saw earlier, Kelley's (1967) ANOVA model views the perceiver as a fairly rational person. It has been considered as a **normative model**, which indicates how perceivers *should* make accurate causal attributions. In practice, perceivers do not act like scientists in following such detailed and formal models. Rather, they make attributions quickly, using much less information and showing clear tendencies for certain sorts of explanation. We need, then, to consider more *descriptive* models of *how* perceivers actually make attributions.

A number of studies concluded that, compared with scientists or statisticians, laypeople are biased and make **attributional biases** or 'errors'. There are two major classes of explanation for these apparent defects of lay explanations – motivational (or 'need') and cognitive (or 'informational'). We will consider both, and later discuss whether it is possible to choose between them. But first, are we justified in referring to such tendencies as errors or biases? The term *error* should be reserved for deviations from a normative model (Fiske & Taylor, 1991) or departures from some accepted criterion of validity (Kruglanski & Ajzen, 1983). Such models or criteria are, however, rarely available for attribution research. For this reason, the term *bias* should be used, although we still use the term *error* where the original, if inaccurate, label has stuck. A bias occurs if the social perceiver systematically distorts (e.g. over- or overuses) some otherwise correct procedure (Fiske & Taylor, 1991). A rather different view has been put forward by Funder (1987), who has argued that what have been termed 'errors' are largely a function of the laboratory context and might not result in 'mistakes' in the real world. From different perspectives, researchers have also shown that even well-established attributional biases can be reversed or wiped out by reframing problems or by subtle changes in the information presented (Cheng & Novick, 1992; Försterling, 1995). As we shall see, such biases can help to provide a better descriptive analysis of causal attribution than do complex normative models, and we will look now at some of the best-known biases.

The fundamental attribution error/correspondence bias

Imagine you are watching your favourite football team. The star player receives the ball in front of the goal, with only the goalkeeper to beat . . . then he slips and miscues the ball. No goal. You curse your erstwhile star, and label him 'clumsy', 'unfit' or worse. But you completely overlooked the fact that it has been raining solidly for three days, the ground is sodden, and the game only went ahead after a referee's pitch inspection just before kick-off. Why did you ignore the situation and concentrate on the person? Some of the first modern studies on attribution have already revealed that not all potential causes (i.e., persons, entity, circumstance) are selected (everything else being equal) with the same likelihood. Rather, there is a general preference for making attributions to the person (e.g., to an actor's traits and/or personal dispositions). To illustrate, consider the finding of a number of studies, that perceivers consistently fail to make adequate allowance for the effects of social roles on behaviour. A classic experimental demonstration was provided by Ross, Amabile and Steinmetz (1977). They randomly assigned participants in a quiz game to the roles of questioner and contestant, with the former told to set difficult questions for the latter. Both contestants and 'quiz masters' overlooked the advantages conferred by the role of the questioner (i.e., choosing difficult questions from their areas of expertise) and rated the questioner much more knowledgeable than the contestant. Many other studies show that perceivers seem to overestimate personal or dispositional factors and underestimate situational factors (e.g., Jones & Harris, 1967; Ross, Amabile, & Steinmetz, 1977). This bias came to be called the **fundamental attribution error**. In view of the fact that the bias is far from universal, and criteria for accuracy are lacking, we should prefer a more modest label for this nonetheless important effect – the **correspondence bias** refers to the attribution of behaviour to dispositions, even in cases where we should not (Gilbert, 1995; Jones,

Fundamental attribution error The tendency for perceivers to underestimate the impact of situational factors and to overestimate the role of dispositional factors in controlling behaviour. This bias can be explained in terms of cognitive, cultural and linguistic factors (see **correspondence bias**).

Correspondence bias The tendency to infer an actor's personal characteristics from his or her observed behaviours, even when the inference is unjustified because other possible causes of the behaviour exist (see **fundamental attribution error**).

1990). There are many possible explanations for this effect and we consider just the main ones here (see Gilbert & Malone, 1995).

A general, motivational explanation refers to the fact that dispositional attribution gives us a sense of *control*. Miller, Norman and Wright (1978) argued that the behaviour of another person can be made to seem more probable, and possibly controllable, when we can trace their past behaviour to their underlying, stable dispositions. This control function of attribution helps us to understand a wide variety of counter-intuitive attributional phenomena. For example, people have been found to derogate others who are victims of negative events (and see them as deserving such outcomes), in an attempt to maintain the belief that negative events will not happen to them personally (the 'just-world hypothesis'; see Lerner, 1980).

Cognitive accounts of the correspondence bias emphasize the knowledge base of attributions and social information processing. For example, a general, **salience** explanation argues that the actor's behaviour is typically more distinctive than the situation. From this perspective, one could perhaps increase situational attributions by making it easier for participants to bring situational constructs to mind (as found by Rholes & Pryor, 1982; see also Quattrone, 1982). Another cognitive explanation refers to differential rates of forgetting for situational and dispositional causes. This explanation requires evidence that attributions made some time after the behaviour in question tend to emphasize dispositional causes more, and situational causes less, than attributions made immediately. However, although some studies show just this (Moore, Sherrod, Liu, & Underwood, 1979; Peterson, 1980), others have reported exactly the opposite (e.g., Burger, 1991; Miller & Porter, 1980; cf. Funder, 1982).

Salience The distinctiveness of an entity relative to the context (e.g., a male in a group of females; a group of people, one of whom is in the spotlight).

All the explanations considered so far approach the problem as if dispositional and situational attributions were two sides of a coin (see critique above). An alternative approach suggests that we should think of them as sequential operations. Quattrone (1982) suggested that people first make dispositional inferences, and then change these inferences into (more) situational ones. From this perspective, people always start from dispositional inferences, so that the correspondence bias may be explained in terms of a cognitive heuristic, namely *anchoring* (Tversky & Kahneman, 1974; see chapter 5). We will consider this failure to use available information below, when we look in more detail at process models of attribution.

Whether we choose to emphasize motivational or cognitive factors, it should be noted that the correspondence bias is subject to cultural variation. As we move from more 'individualist' cultures (e.g., Western Europe, North America) to more 'collectivist' cultures (e.g., Asian countries), attributions tend to become less dispositional and more situational. Miller (1984) reported a developmental increase in reference to dispositional factors in an American sample, but an increase in reference to contextual factors in an Indian-Hindu sample (see figure 7.2). Similarly, Morris and Peng (1994) found that Chinese people (whether living in mainland China or in the United States) were less susceptible to the correspondence bias

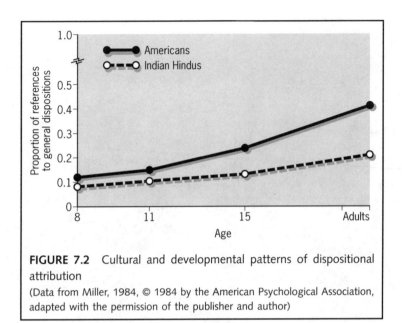

FIGURE 7.2   Cultural and developmental patterns of dispositional attribution

(Data from Miller, 1984, © 1984 by the American Psychological Association, adapted with the permission of the publisher and author)

than Americans (see also Choi, Nisbett, & Norenzayan, 1999). Cultural differences also emerged in a comparison of accounts of the same event given by English-language and Chinese-language newspapers (Morris, Nisbett, & Peng, 1995; Morris & Peng, 1994). Asians (e.g., Koreans) do succumb to the correspondence bias, but they are more sensitive to information indicating situational constraints than are Americans (Choi & Nisbett, 1998; see Fiske, Kitayama, Markus, & Nisbett, 1998).

Thus the correspondence bias seems to involve a variety of motivational and cognitive factors. It also reflects a dispositionalist 'worldview' or a **social representation** (Moscovici, 1981b) that is shared by many individuals, and can vary across and within societies (see, for example, different explanations of poverty and unemployment discussed in Hewstone, 1989). Studying attributions using the framework of social representations may help us to better understand the question of where attributions come from (see Hewstone & Augoustinos, 1998).

Social representation   A collective belief that is shared among many members of a society (e.g., concerning science, religion, individualism) and which involves both the representation and transformation of knowledge.

Despite the evidence that people tend systematically to make more personal attributions, dispositional inferences are not inevitable (Gilbert, 1998). There are circumstances under which people will overattribute another person's behaviour to situational factors: most notably, when behaviour is inconsistent with prior expectations (Kulik, 1983), and when attention is focused on situational factors that could have produced a person's behaviour (e.g., Quattrone, 1982). Less reliance on dispositional information, and more on situational information, can also be found when perceivers are in a negative mood (Forgas, 1998), more highly motivated (Webster, 1993), made suspicious of the actor's motives (Hilton, Fein,

PLATE 7.2   If *you* feel shy in seminars, you are more likely to attribute this to situational factors than you do for other students

& Miller, 1993), or made more interested in learning about the situation (e.g., before entering a new situation themselves; Krull & Erickson, 1995).

Actor–observer differences

Many of our everyday social interactions involve dyads – husband and wife, doctor and patient, teacher and pupil, coach and athlete. Can we assume that both people share explanations for the same outcome, or even that they see the outcome in the same way? In fact, both partners in such dyads often have different explanations, and these can be both a source and a reflection of problems within the relationship (see discussion of attributions and marital distress, below). According to Jones and Nisbett (1972), actors tend to attribute their actions to the situation, whereas observers tend to attribute the same actions to stable personal dispositions. Thus the pupil whose classroom fighting is being punished by the teacher claims he was pushed first by another boy; but the teacher tells the boy off for being 'aggressive'. Watson (1982) has provided a comprehensive review of these **actor–observer differences**. He prefers the terms *self* and *other* rather than actor and observer, because in many studies there is not, in fact, one person acting while another observes. As Watson

Actor–observer difference The claim that actors attribute their actions to situational factors, whereas observers tend to attribute the same actions to stable personal dispositions. The effect is confined to a difference in situational attribution, and appears due to differences in information, perceptual focus and linguistic factors.

shows, there *is* an effect, but it is confined to self–other differences in situational attribution: self-attributions to situations are higher than other-attributions to situations. Thus, for example, we attribute our own shyness in seminars more to the situation than we do for other students.

There are two main explanations for this actor–observer/self–other effect, both of them cognitive. The first is that self–other differences arise from the greater amount of *information* available to the actors or self-raters. We know more about our own past behaviour, and its variability across situations, than we know about the behaviour of others (e.g., Nisbett et al., 1973, Study 2). The second explanation is more interesting, and argues that *focus of attention* explains actor–observer differences. An ingenious experiment by Storms (1973) followed up the most fundamental difference between self and other: the fact that they have, quite literally, different 'points of view'. Storms set up a getting-acquainted conversation involving two strangers, A and B, each watched by one observer, and each filmed by one video camera (see figure 7.3). He hypothesized that it should

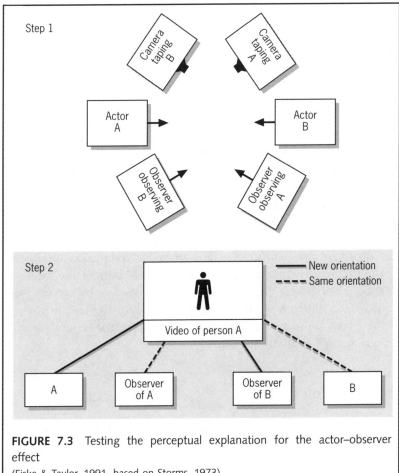

FIGURE 7.3 Testing the perceptual explanation for the actor–observer effect
(Fiske & Taylor, 1991, based on Storms, 1973)

be possible to change the way actors and observers interpret behaviour by changing their visual orientations: actors who come to see themselves should make more dispositional attributions about their own behaviour; and observers who come to see another aspect of the actor's situation should become more situational in attributing the actor's behaviour. Storms compared three orientation conditions: *no video* (control); *same orientation* (video used simply to repeat the participant's original orientation); and *new orientation* (video used to reverse the orientation of actors and observers).

Storms found, as predicted, a reversal of actors' and observers' attributions when participants were shown a new orientation: actors' attributions became *less* situational, and observers' became *more* situational. Unfortunately, Storms' findings have not always been replicated. It seems that the participant in the centre of the visual field (person A to the observer of A, person B to the observer of B) *is* rated as more causally important, but that this weighting does not always have a clear effect on dispositional and situational attributions (Taylor, Crocker, Fiske, Sprinzen, & Winkler, 1979). Nevertheless, Storms' findings underline the general point that methods exist for shifting the perspectives of actors and observers. Salience effects on the weighting of dispositional and situational attributions have also been found in other studies. For example, McArthur and Post (1977) had observers watch a conversation in which one conversant was made salient (e.g., by being illuminated with a bright light), while the other was non-salient (dim light). Observers rated the salient conversant's behaviour as more dispositionally, and less situationally, caused.

Buehler, Griffin and Ross (1995) have extended actor–observer differences to other kinds of judgement, and identified a motivational component of the effect. They examined people's predictions of how long it would take them to complete various tasks and activities. They found evidence of an optimistic bias, whereby people underestimate their own completion times. But this optimistic bias disappears when observers make forecasts concerning the completion times of other people. Indeed, these observers' estimates show a pessimistic bias, whereby observers overestimate the time taken for completion by others. The same pattern emerged from a study on forecasts concerning the future course of romantic relationships. Actors were too optimistic and observers were too pessimistic. Thus differences in perspective are likely to have important and interesting effects on many different types of interpersonal relations (we discuss attributions in close relationships below).

Self-serving biases

Kingdon (1967) interviewed successful and unsuccessful American politicians about five months after elections and asked them to summarize the major factors (causes) that led to their victories or defeats over the years. The politicians attributed their wins to internal factors – their hard work, personal service to constituents, matters of campaign strategy, building a reputation, and publicizing themselves. They attributed their losses to external factors – the party make-up of the district, the familiar name of their opponent, national and state trends, and lack of money. This is an example of a more general **self-serving bias**, whereby people are more likely to attribute their successes to internal dispositions, such as abilities, whereas they attribute failures to situational causes, such as high task difficulty. Taking credit for success and avoiding the blame for failure is something that most of us do at least some of the time.

> **Self-serving bias** People are more likely to attribute their successes to internal causes such as ability, whereas they tend to attribute failures to external causes such as task difficulty. This bias appears due to cognitive and motivational factors, varying across public and private settings.

There are, in fact, two biases at issue here – a *self-enhancing* bias (taking credit for success) and a *self-protecting* bias (denying responsibility for failure). Miller and Ross (1975) claimed support only for the self-enhancing bias, and they argued that it could be explained by cognitive factors. For example, if people intend and expect to succeed, and if behaviour can be seen as due to their efforts (whereas failure occurs *despite* their efforts), then it may be perfectly reasonable to accept more responsibility for success than failure.

Zuckerman's (1979) systematic summary of the literature concluded in more motivational terms, that the need to maintain self-esteem directly affected the attribution of task outcomes. But he argued that the strength of this effect depended on factors including the extent to which self-esteem concerns were aroused in experimental participants. He concluded that there are self-serving effects for both success and failure in most, but not all, experimental paradigms. Weary (1980) discussed self-serving attributions in the context of self-presentation. People may attribute outcomes in ways that avoid embarrassment and/or gain public approval, especially under public vs. private conditions (e.g., Weary et al., 1982).

The evidence so far rests on explanations given after a performance, but it has also been suggested that actors sometimes provide attributions before a performance, revealing a more subtle form of self-serving attribution. This proactive attributional bias has been termed '**self-handicapping**', and it refers to the way in which someone may use extraneous causal factors to obscure the link between performance and evaluation, thereby mitigating the impact of failure. For example, someone who expects to fail on a task may take debilitating drugs or consume large quantities of alcohol in order to provide a self-serving explanation for their imminent failure (see Jones, 1990).

> **Self-handicapping** A subtle form of self-serving bias, whereby someone manipulates causes of their failure before it happens to obscure the link between performance and evaluation.

Group-serving biases

There is now extensive evidence that attribution biases are influenced by group membership. For example, success and especially failure by members of the 'ingroup' and 'outgroup' may receive quite different explanations (see Hewstone, 1990). This bias acts to preserve and protect stereotypes of the ingroup ('we are intelligent') and the outgroup ('they are stupid').

An illustrative study was carried out by Hewstone and Ward (1985) using members of the majority-Malay and minority-Chinese ethnic groups in Malaysia. Participants read stories that were either positive or negative, and involved either an ingroup or an outgroup actor. They then had to choose between internal or external attributions for the behaviour described. As figure 7.4 shows, when members of the majority-Malay group explained behaviour by an ingroup member, they gave more internal attributions for positive than negative behaviour. But the reverse was true when they explained behaviour by an outgroup member. Thus there was clear evidence of 'ethnocentric' or ingroup-favouring attributions. The results for the minority-Chinese respondents, however, showed a different pattern. When explaining the behaviour of an ingroup member, they gave fewer internal attributions for positive than negative behaviour; but they gave more internal attributions for positive than negative behaviour by an outgroup member. This pattern of attributions is outgroup-favouring.

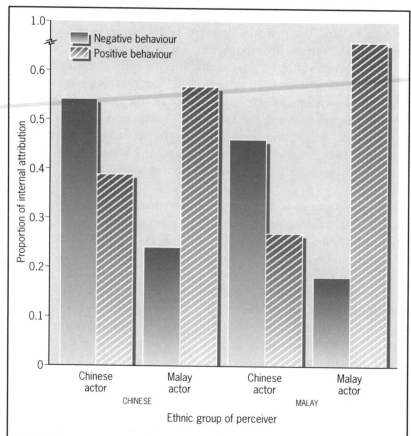

FIGURE 7.4 Proportion of internal attribution as a function of ethnic group of perceiver, ethnic group of actor and outcome (Malaysia)
(After Hewstone & Ward, 1985, © 1985 by the American Psychological Association, reprinted by permission of the publisher and author)

Islam and Hewstone (1993b) extended this research by having group members first give attributions, and then give their affective reactions. The groups used were majority-Muslims and minority-Hindus in Bangladesh. The results showed robust intergroup attributional bias by the majority and only mild bias by the minority. This pattern has also been found in other studies, but not inevitably (it depends on the context of intergroup relations; see chapter 15). Islam and Hewstone also found that causal dimensions were especially predictive of positive affects for outcomes associated with ingroup actors. For example, for Muslims, feelings of happiness and pride were maximized when the cause of a positive outcome by an ingroup member was perceived as internal (something about the person) and global (likely to occur across situations).

This group-serving bias could have a cognitive basis, as argued for the self-serving bias. If members of one group expect the other group to behave in a negative way, and see their expectations confirmed, they are behaving quite logically in giving an internal, stable attribution. However, group-serving biases are not limited to stereotypical (i.e., expected) behaviours and outcomes, so this cognitive account is incomplete. The most obvious motivational basis for inter-group attributions is the desire to view one's own group positively, thus achieving, maintaining or defending one's self-esteem. Intergroup biases in attribution can, therefore, be seen as part of a much wider process – the search for positive social identity (see chapter 15). Group members could use their attributions to achieve or enhance a positive social identity (e.g., by attributing positive ingroup, or negative outgroup, acts to internal causes), or to protect that identity (e.g., by attributing negative ingroup, or positive outgroup, acts to external causes).

Explaining bias: motivation or cognition?

We have noted that there are compelling motivational and cognitive explanations for each of the biases we have considered. Researchers have sometimes tried to distinguish between these accounts, but they have encountered a number of problems. It has been claimed that the cognitive explanations actually contain motivational aspects (Zuckerman, 1979), and that the cognitive research pro-gramme is so flexible that it can generate the predictions of virtually any mot-ivational theory (Tetlock & Levi, 1982). In addition, motivational factors can have an effect on information processing. Thus it appears impossible to choose between the cognitive and motivational perspectives (see Tetlock & Manstead, 1985); both are important.

The process of causal attribution

What are the advantages and disadvantages of a process-oriented approach to attribution?

Having looked at some of the most prominent attributional biases, it does seem that causal attribution may often be a rapid process based on limited information processing. Further understanding of this process, or processes, has been achieved by a social-cognition approach to attribution (see Smith, 1994; and chapter 5, this volume). This has involved borrowing both methodology and theory from cognitive psychology, as we shall now see.

Methodologically, social psychologists interested in how social information is processed have used a variety of sophisticated cognitive measures, all of which are attempts to sidestep a major methodological problem – the fact that we can never tap directly what is going on in the heads of our research participants (Taylor & Fiske, 1981). These measures include visual attention, information search, memory and, especially, response time.

Smith and Miller's (1983) study illustrates some of the benefits of response-time methodology. They distinguished the different types of inference used in attribution research – for example, causal judgements, trait judgements about an actor and judgements of the actor's intent – and measured how long participants took to make each kind of inference. The rationale for using response-time measures is simple. If the question corresponds to a process that occurs spontaneously during the initial comprehension of behaviour, then the answer to the question will be readily available and the participant's response time will be short. In contrast, if the question asks about something not inferred from the comprehension stage, then the participant must retrieve the relevant information and make the inference before responding to the question, leading to a longer response time.

Smith and Miller reported that judgements of intention and trait inferences did not take significantly more time than a 'control' question concerning the actor's gender (see table 7.1). This finding suggested that these judgements may also

TABLE 7.1   Response times to different questions in Smith and Miller's (1983) research

Question	Response time[a]	
	Study 1	Study 2
Gender	2.14	4.24
Intention	2.41	4.56
True trait	2.48	4.37
False trait	3.02	5.09
Person cause	3.42	5.68
Situation cause	3.80	6.05

[a] Response times are in seconds. In Study 1 responses indicate question-answering time, in Study 2 responses indicate time taken to read a sentence and answer a question about it.
Source: Data drawn from Smith and Miller, 1983, © 1983 by the American Psychological Association, reprinted with the permission of the publisher and author.

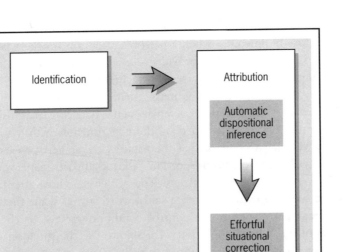

FIGURE 7.5   A three-stage model of attribution
(From Gilbert, 1995)

be made during comprehension, or at least that they could be easily inferred. The slowest responses were to person-cause and situation-cause questions. Smith and Miller concluded that the 'basic' attribution (probably made during the initial process of comprehension) was a judgement of intention or a trait attribution or both, *not* a person or situation cause. The longer response time for person- and situation-cause questions could also be due to the fact that people are not used to thinking about and answering questions in these terms. From these data causal processing does not seem to occur automatically (i.e., without effort, intention, awareness or controllability; Bargh, 1989; Winter, Uleman, & Cunniff, 1985). What occurs during the comprehension phase seems to be a simple trait inference, with no attempt to understand the causal basis of the behaviour.

The kind of theoretical contribution that can be made by a process approach is illustrated by summarizing Gilbert, Pelham and Krull's (1988) 'three-stage model' of attribution (see figure 7.5), which draws on the notion of *automaticity* (see Bargh, 1989). The first stage of the model ('identification') is a necessary pre-requisite for any attribution process: we must first perceive or 'identify' what is happening before we can ask why (Trope, 1986). The next two attributional stages are conceived as sequential, following Quattrone's (1982) proposal, discussed earlier. The first attributional stage (*dispositional inference*) is conceived as a relatively automatic operation, which can be carried out without conscious thought or deliberation, and little or no mental effort (Gilbert, 1998; Uleman, Newman, & Moskowitz, 1996). This is consistent with Smith and Miller's (1983) finding, noted above, that trait inferences are made relatively quickly. The second attributional stage (*situational correction*), in contrast, is conceived as more effortful and should therefore be impaired when a person's attention is otherwise occupied.

Gilbert and colleagues (1988) provided support for the model in a clever study, which included use of a divided-attention technique to use up part of some participants' attentional resources (or make them 'cognitively busy'). Participants watched a series of video clips of a female actor behaving anxiously as she discussed a number of topics assigned by the experimenter with a stranger. Some participants were led to believe that the topics were anxiety-provoking, whereas others were told they were mundane. The task for all participants was to estimate the actor's level of dispositional anxiety. The perceivers whose attentional capacity was reduced had to silently rehearse a set of word strings while they watched the video, whereas perceivers in the control condition merely watched the video. Participants in the control condition were able to use the situational information (that the woman was discussing 'intimate sexual fantasies' vs. 'home gardening') to 'correct' their dispositional attributions. Thus they saw the same fidgety woman as less anxious when discussing sex than gardening. The cognitively busy perceivers were able automatically to generate dispositional inferences about the persons whose behaviour they observed, but unlike the non-busy perceivers, they were unable to correct their inferences to take account of situational information. Thus these data are consistent with the suggestion that dispositional inferences are automatic, but situational correction is effortful.

Let us return for a moment to the example at the beginning of the chapter of the skinhead running after the businessman. Seeing the skinhead chasing the other man would be the *identification* stage in Gilbert's model. We watch the drama unfold in the advertisement, and we immediately infer that the skinhead is aggressive and is going to hit the man and take his case (*dispositional inference* stage). But then the camera shows a crane swinging around on an adjoining building site. It is suddenly clear that the skinhead is trying to push the other man out of the way, to safety (*situational correction*). As the advertisement caption for the newspaper runs, 'get the whole story'.

As these two studies have illustrated, a more process-oriented approach to attribution offers methodological precision and theoretical sophistication. But process analysis also has limitations. First, measures such as response times are best used to rule out alternative models rather than to support a particular model. Second, by definition the attempt to measure cognitive process interferes with normal thinking. Measures such as recall and response times may not be informative about normal, extra-laboratory information use. Third, and consequently, there may be a trade-off between precision of measurement and generalizability of results. Thus we see mini-experiments with cognitive measures as a complement to studies of thinking and behaviour outside the laboratory, as we now see in considering applied research on attribution theory.

Applications of Attribution Theory

It is no exaggeration to say that few applied problems have escaped analysis from the perspective of attribution theory. Some idea of the scope of application is indicated by the following very incomplete list of problems analysed from an attribution perspective: shyness, helping, mortality in old age, smoking, stigma, intergroup conflict, depression, sales performance, HIV infection, spouse and child abuse, pain management, physical illness, anxiety, international relations, sport and consumer satisfaction (see, e.g., Amirkhan, 1998; Graham & Folkes, 1990; Weiner, 1995). Extensive attribution literatures now exist in many applied areas.

A key element in understanding the importance accorded attribution theory therefore lies in the extent to which it lends itself to the analysis of applied problems. Weiner (1990) argues that attribution theory has been so amenable to practical use because many of the pioneers in this area were committed to both theory development and theory utilization and did basic research on issues that lend themselves to application. Before illustrating some applications of attribution theory, it is important to note that the relation between the attribution models described earlier and applied research is often not straightforward. There are three reasons for this circumstance. First, some attribution principles (e.g., the covariation principle) are so pervasive that they are no longer associated with a particular model (e.g., the ANOVA model), and they often remain implicit in analyses of applied problems.

Second, findings obtained in basic attribution research cannot simply be extrapolated to applied settings without further examination. For example, much basic attribution research examines attributions made for hypothetical others, but it has been found that attributions vary as a function of (1) expected interaction with the attribution target (Knight & Vallacher, 1981); (2) the nature of the attributor's relationship (e.g., acquaintance, friend, spouse) to the attribution target (Taylor & Koivumaki, 1976); and (3) the affect experienced towards the attribution target (Regan, Straus, & Fazio, 1974).

Third, applied work has generated ideas that are not found in the writings on attribution theory and has also led to slightly different perspectives on some existing attribution ideas. An example concerns individual differences in attributions; references to constructs such as attributional style (labelled 'explanatory style' by some researchers) are frequently found in applied writings despite their absence from the models described earlier in the chapter. Similarly, the analysis of responsibility attribution, which deals not with who or what caused an event but with accountability for the event, has been considerably expanded in applied work.

In the remainder of this section, we illustrate the application of attribution theory in three broad areas, motivation, clinical psychology and close relationships.

Attributions and motivation

How are the underlying dimensions of perceived causes related to feelings and motivation?

Recall that statistics exam that you have just failed. No doubt you'll experience some general negative affect. But what specific affect will you feel? Who will be the target of that affect? And what implications, if any, will this experience have for your future behaviour? Weiner's (1986, 1995) attributional theory of motivation provides answers to such questions. According to Weiner, the specific answers will depend on what you perceive to be the cause of your exam failure.

Let's say you were distracted by extra-curricular activities and you just did not study for this test. You'd probably feel some guilt. If your course teacher believed that your failure was due to lack of effort, he or she would most likely experience anger and act in a punitive manner towards you. After all, you could have made an effort and cut back on these other activities. But what if you attributed your failure to lack of intellectual ability? In this case, you would probably experience shame. If you view your ability as something that is unlikely to change, you'd also experience hopelessness and expect to fail on future statistics exams. Perhaps you might even withdraw from studying psychology altogether. In this case, your teacher would most likely experience pity/sympathy and be inclined to act in a helpful manner. Contrast these responses to the response you would have if you thought you failed because the marking was unfair or the test was inappropriately difficult. In these circumstances, you would most likely experience anger towards the person who marked/set the test and would not draw any adverse conclusions about your performance on other psychology tests.

This example contains the essential features of Weiner's (1986) extensively researched theory of motivation. Weiner has argued that how we ascribe causes can influence how we feel, but also that some emotions can be elicited without intervening thought processes. He has made an important distinction between two kinds of achievement-related affects: 'outcome-dependent' and 'attribution-linked' affects. Outcome-dependent affects refer to the very general, even 'primitive' emotions (see chapter 6) that are experienced following success and failure outcomes. These emotions include 'happy', following success, and 'frustrated' or 'sad', following failure; they are labelled outcome-dependent because they depend on (non-)attainment of a desired goal, not on causal attributions given for the outcome. Attribution-linked affects, in contrast, are influenced by the specific causal attribution for the outcome. Especially if an outcome is negative, unexpected or especially important, one makes causal attributions in order to make sense of it. In turn, these causal attributions have psychological consequences, including future expectancies and affective reactions, which themselves lead to behaviour. Weiner's model can be summarized in the following way:

PLATE 7.3 Your attributions for exam failure are likely to affect motivation and affect

Event (exam failure) → outcome-dependent affect → causal attribution → psychological consequences (future expectancies, affect) → behaviour

As noted earlier, Weiner developed a three-dimensional scheme of causal dimensions (locus × stability × controllability), and showed what implications this had for achievement motivation. He noted that although both effort and ability are internal causes, achievement evaluation was influenced more by effort than ability (Weiner & Kukla, 1970). This is because they differ in causal stability over time, and expectancies relating to future performance are determined by causal stability rather than causal locus. Effort and ability also differ in terms of controllability, and this latter dimension is the mediator of reward and punishment (Weiner, 1995).

Weiner's scheme was later extended to classify causes in the social as well as the achievement domain and each dimension was found to be associated with specific affects:

locus → pride, self esteem;

stability → hopefulness, hopelessness;

controllability → shame, guilt [when self-directed] and anger, gratitude, pity [when directed towards others].

Although a considerable body of research has provided support for this theory, it is not without problems. An important concern is whether the everyday perception of causes matches the logical analysis offered by Weiner. This issue can be broken down into at least three questions: Do people naturally organize causes using the dimensions postulated? Are the dimensions truly different (orthogonal to each other) or are they correlated, suggesting that fewer than three dimensions are needed? And, can specific causes be mapped onto these dimensions, or is the perception of specific causes idiosyncratic to perceivers and/or situations?

There is strong evidence that people organize causes along various dimensions. However, they may not be limited to Weiner's three dimensions. For example, several studies distinguish an intentional–unintentional dimension. In one of the few studies examining causes outside the achievement domain, Passer, Kelley and Michela (1978) investigated the dimensions underlying causes given for interpersonal conflict. As shown in figure 7.6, they found evidence of a dimension that reflected the attitude towards the attribution target. Weiner, however, has argued that the bulk of the evidence supports his three-dimensional scheme. Although reasonable, this is not an entirely satisfactory argument because of the nature of the available data. It is limited not only by the number of studies conducted, but also by the fact that unless a broad sample of causes is investigated, the dimensions that emerge will be constrained by the causes examined. In other words, the structure uncovered by an investigator will depend, in part, on how stimuli are sampled and the majority of available studies sample stimuli from only one domain, most frequently the achievement domain.

The second question concerning whether causal dimensions are separate (orthogonal) is more easily answered. At the empirical level, causal dimensions are intercorrelated (e.g., Anderson, 1983). However, the magnitude of the correlations shows that for any two dimensions, there is more unshared variability than shared variability. In addition, it makes conceptual sense to keep the dimensions separate, just as it makes sense to keep height and weight separate, even though they are highly correlated.

Turning to the final question, it is clear that there is variability across people and situations in mapping specific causes onto causal dimensions. For example, Krantz and Rude (1984) asked respondents to classify four widely studied causes in the achievement domain (ability, effort, task difficulty, luck) in terms of the three causal dimensions postulated by Weiner. Few respondents classified causes on the dimensions in the expected manner. Just under half, for instance, classified ability as unstable. Individual differences in the perception of supposedly 'stable' causes (e.g., intelligence) have subsequently been investigated and given

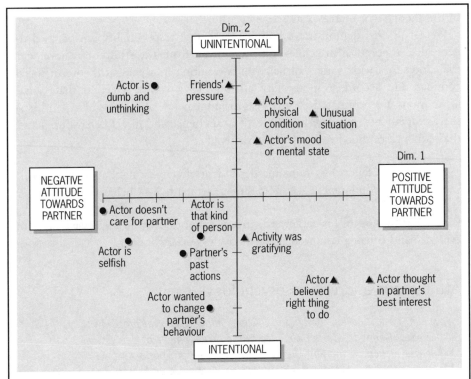

FIGURE 7.6 Two-dimensional solution for 'actor' condition; the types of explanations preferred by actors are indicated by triangles
(From Passer et al., 1978, © 1978 by the American Psychological Association, reprinted with the permission of the publisher and author)

rise to another theory of motivation that divides people into 'incremental' theorists (intelligence/ability can be increased through effort) and 'entity' theorists (intelligence/ability is fixed; see Dweck & Leggett, 1988). Such individual differences mean that psychologists cannot always accurately map causes onto underlying dimensions. This does not invalidate Weiner's typology; it simply reminds us that it is important to evaluate the respondent's perception of a cause.

Other objections could be raised about Weiner's application of attribution theory. For instance, most of the research supporting the theory rests on the use of rather 'artificial' procedures (e.g., ratings of hypothetical scenarios, impoverished stimuli, laboratory-manipulated success and failure) and assesses respondents' statements about how they will behave (their behavioural intentions) rather than their actual behaviour. However, such concerns should not blind us to the fact that the attributional analysis of motivation has led to the documentation of highly robust and easily replicated phenomena. This alone attests to its usefulness. In addition, it has resulted in important advances in attribution theory. Whatever one thinks of Weiner's theory, one cannot help being impressed by its comprehensiveness. We end this section by outlining briefly a recent development of the theory that increases its scope even further.

Weiner (1995) demonstrates how judgement of responsibility can be used to generalize theoretical principles initially derived from the study of achievement evaluation to a wide variety of behaviours resulting in a general theory of social conduct. He accords responsibility attributions a central role, in that causal attributions are postulated to give rise to judgements of responsibility, and it is these judgements that determine affective experience and direct behaviour. Thus, the sequence outlined earlier has been altered to:

Event (exam failure) → outcome-dependent affect → causal attribution → responsibility judgement → affect (anger, sympathy) → behaviour

Weiner's extension of his earlier sequence is supported by an impressive body of evidence and offers a comprehensive theory of social conduct.

Attributions and clinical psychology

How can 'misattribution' be helpful in understanding clinical problems?
What role, if any, do attributions play in the development of depression?
What is achieved by training clients to change their attributions?

Since the inception of experimental social psychology there have been attempts to apply social-psychological principles in clinical psychology (Snyder & Forsyth, 1991). Not surprisingly, therefore, applications of attribution theory to clinical problems emerged soon after the publication of correspondent inference theory and the ANOVA model. Some of the applications, especially early ones, are explicitly related to classic attribution models, but many others simply reflect an attributional perspective and are not related to basic attribution research. Indeed, in some applications it is clear that the authors have never read the most basic statements of attribution theory in the social-psychological literature!

Unlike the application to motivation, the attempts to apply attribution theory in clinical psychology are so diverse that it is difficult to do them justice in a brief summary (for an excellent treatment of this topic, see Försterling, 1988). With this caveat in mind, we begin with an actual case study (published in Johnson, Ross, & Mastria, 1977) and derive from it a simple dichotomy that can be used to organize clinical applications of attribution theory.

Case study

Mr J. came to the attention of psychiatrists when he claimed that he was being sexually aroused and brought to orgasm by a 'warm form'. These experiences were distressing to Mr J. and after disclosing them, he was diagnosed as schizophrenic, institutionalized and administered Thorazine, an antipsychotic drug. Although the psychiatric staff believed Mr J. to be mentally ill, careful observation showed that he was inadvertently stimulating himself through leg movements. The 'delusional behaviour' disappeared when the patient was taught to attribute the cause of his sexual arousal to his leg movements and remained absent through the six-month follow-up period.

The case of Mr J. illustrates that a client's beliefs about the cause of behaviour can be dysfunctional. In this case the absence of an understandable cause for the erotic experience resulted in misattribution ('delusional thinking') that led Mr J. to be seen as insane. Once the misattribution was diagnosed, appropriate treatment could proceed. In Mr J.'s case, 'reattribution training' took place in that a plausible, alternative cause was offered for his experience. According to the discounting principle, this should lessen belief in the first cause, which is in fact what happened.

An important distinction illustrated by this case is that between *diagnosis* (determining the nature of the problem) and *treatment* (intervening to bring about more adaptive functioning). Although there is an interplay between diagnosis and treatment, most clinical applications of attribution theory can be classified according to these two categories. However, there is a huge imbalance in the distribution of studies that fall into the two categories. The vast majority analyse or diagnose problems in attributional terms with far fewer investigating attributional treatments. Each will be examined in turn.

Misattribution

The phenomenon of misattribution, especially of physiological arousal, was the subject of many of the early attempts to understand clinical problems. For example, Storms and Nisbett (1970) demonstrated that insomniacs who attributed the arousal that kept them awake to a neutral source (a pill) reported a reduction in the time it took to fall asleep as compared to participants who could not attribute their arousal to the pill. Although plagued by a host of problems (e.g., difficulty in replicating findings, the absence of attribution measures to support the misattribution interpretation; Fincham 1983), the ideas that prompted research on misattribution are still helpful in understanding clinical problems.

More recent research has focused on multiple attribution dimensions and shown that attributions which do not specifically reflect lack of knowledge about the cause of a problem, as in the case of Mr J., may be maladaptive. Thus, for example, there is considerable evidence that seeing oneself as the cause of a negative event, viewing the cause as stable or unlikely to change, and as global or affecting various areas of one's life, is associated with several failures of adaptation (see Buchanan & Seligman, 1995; Peterson et al., 1993).

Learned helplessness and depression

Learned helplessness A state characterized by learning deficits, negative emotion and passive behaviour when organisms learn that their responses are independent of desired outcomes.

Perhaps the most intensively investigated problem is the phenomenon of **learned helplessness**. Because it has been proposed as a model of depression and has stimulated a great deal of research in its own right, we briefly examine learned helplessness before illustrating applications of attribution theory pertaining to treatment.

Learned helplessness describes the response pattern that often occurs following exposure to non-contingent or uncontrollable outcomes. It is associated with motivational, emotional and cognitive deficits. For example, dogs exposed to uncontrollable shock, compared to animals in a control group, are passive (motivational deficit), unemotional (emotional deficit), and fail to learn (cognitive deficit) when the shock is avoidable. This response pattern is similar to the symptoms of depression and generated considerable interest in learned helplessness. To account for human depression an attributional reformulation of learned helplessness was proposed (Abramson, Seligman, & Teasdale, 1978). It was argued that causal attributions determine responses to non-contingent events. The model proposed is shown below:

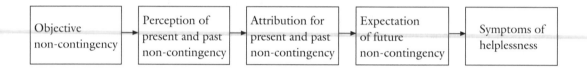

Objective non-contingency → Perception of present and past non-contingency → Attribution for present and past non-contingency → Expectation of future non-contingency → Symptoms of helplessness

(taken from Abramson et al., 1978)

Again, however, it is the underlying dimensions of the attributions that are considered important. Specifically, the internal–external dimension relates to self-esteem deficits; the extent to which the cause is global vs. specific, or affects many areas of life rather than one area of life, is related to the generality of symptoms; and the stable–unstable dimension affects their chronicity. Even though no attempt was made to link these dimensions to Kelley's (1967) criteria of consensus, distinctiveness and consistency, they are similar if not identical. What is different, however, is that unlike the ANOVA model, individual differences in responses on the dimensions have become the focus of attention in the attributional reformulation of learned helplessness. **Attributional style** is conceived as a personality trait that mediates between negative events and depression. A 'depressive attributional style' refers to the tendency to view negative events as caused by factors that are internal, stable and global.

Attributional style The tendency to make a particular kind of causal inference across different situations and across time.

As a model of clinical depression, learned helplessness has been controversial. Although a large meta-analysis has established that there is at least a moderate correlation (about +0.3) between attributional style and depression

(Sweeney, Anderson, & Bailey, 1986), such a correlation does not speak to the role of attributions in *producing* depression (we cannot infer causation from correlation). However, there is some evidence that attributions predict depressive symptoms at a later point in time (e.g., Nolen-Hoeksema, Girgus, & Seligman, 1992) and that attributions predict increases in depressed mood for students who receive bad marks on an exam (e.g., Metalsky, Halberstadt, & Abramson, 1987). Such data provide stronger grounds for believing that attributions lead to depression, but it is still only correlational evidence (albeit longitudinal).

Because it is unethical to induce clinical depression, experimental evidence relating attributions to depression comes from laboratory analogue studies that examine depressed mood. Although these studies often yield results consistent with the reformulated model of learned helplessness, it is difficult to generalize from temporary mood changes induced in the laboratory to clinical depression. This problem is not encountered when therapy outcome research is examined. In one relevant study (Hollon, Shelton, & Loosen, 1991), depressed patients were randomly assigned to receive 12 weeks of treatment comprising cognitive therapy or tricyclic antidepressant drugs or both treatments. All groups experienced relief from depression. Interestingly, there was a correlation between change in attribution and change in depression in both the cognitive-therapy condition (correlation of 0.77) and the combined-treatments condition (correlation of 0.55). Although encouraging, there are at least two problems with these results. First, there was no correlation in the drug-treatment group. Why would this happen? Second, even if attributions bring about relief from depression, it does not logically follow that they caused the depression.

What can we conclude about learned helplessness? First, crucial tests of the attributional reformulation of learned helplessness have not been conducted. Even though examination of expectancies, the most direct determinant of helplessness, is considered crucial to testing the validity of the model (Alloy, 1982), such examination has not occurred. Similarly, examination of the *pattern* of attribution responses postulated (internal, stable, global) has been forgone in favour of examining mean scores across dimensions. But mean scores can be generated by many different patterns of responses (Horneffer & Fincham, 1995). Finally, we know very little about the developmental origins of the attributions associated with learned helplessness (Fincham, Beach, Arias, & Brody, in press), an important omission if we seek to prevent learned helplessness.

Notwithstanding these concerns, several converging lines of evidence suggest that attributions are relevant for understanding depression, or perhaps more likely, a subtype of depression. Even though learned helplessness theory has been revised to offer a more clearly articulated theory of a subtype of depression, 'hopelessness depression' (see Abramson, Metalsky, & Alloy, 1989), attributions remain as an important contributory factor to the development of depression, according to this theory. It seems safe to conclude that attributions constitute a vulnerability factor that can lead to depression in the presence of a stressful life event, but that they are neither necessary nor sufficient causes of depression. Perhaps more important is the fact that this work has led to a focus on attributions that have now been associated with numerous problems. In our judgement, the real contribution to emerge from the reformulated model is not an increased understanding of depression but of numerous other problems where application of the causal dimensions postulated in the model has advanced understanding of the problem. Before turning to the example of close relationships, we briefly consider the impact of attribution theory on treatment.

Attributional retraining

Numerous studies demonstrate convincingly that inducing unstable attributions (e.g., lack of effort) for failure increases performance and persistence on achievement tasks (see Försterling, 1988, for a review of 'attributional retraining'). Although promising, the generalizability of this finding to many therapy contexts is open to question because of the exclusive focus on changing attributions for academic or experimental tasks in non-clinical, child samples. Perhaps the most significant limitation of this literature is the use of clinically naive interventions in analogue studies. For example, in a widely cited study, the 25-session intervention consisted of saying to a child after each experimentally induced failure 'that means you should have tried harder' (Dweck, 1975). The relative efficacy of such interventions is misleading because they are often not compared to more common clinical interventions. For example, Dweck (1975) compared the attribution intervention to one in which children received continual success. Thus, the alternative intervention consisted of 'treating' a problem that involves reaction to failure by avoidance of failure!

In retrospect, the claims for an 'attribution therapy' have been overstated and have detracted attention from the legitimate, but more restricted, role of attributions in therapy. With some exceptions (such as the case of Mr J.), the proper role of reattribution in therapy is as a technique utilized as part of a more broadly based intervention (e.g., as in cognitive therapy; DeRubeis & Hollon, 1995). In particular, clients' attributions for behaviour change require attention if the effect of the change is to be maximized. For example, a depressed client who is induced to establish social contact with others may not change his negative beliefs about himself if he attributes the change to the therapist's skill, luck or the friendliness of other people.

In view of the above arguments, the absence of research on an 'attribution therapy' is less problematic than it might have first appeared to be. Close examination shows that most therapeutic approaches include attention to patient attributions, even though they might not discuss attributions explicitly. In fact, it is hard to conceive of a therapy that does not deal with attributions in some form or another. However, there is still a need for research on attribution as an adjunctive therapy technique that can be used in conjunction with other clinical interventions.

Close relationships

What is the relationship between different types of attributions and marital or relationship satisfaction?
In such relationships, do attributions guide responses to a partner's behaviours?

Research on close relationships has recently emerged as a speciality area and social psychology has taken its place alongside other disciplines in an attempt to understand such relationships (see chapter 12). Attribution theory has been enormously productive in this field. Most attributional research has focused on understanding partnership/marriage, and the findings in this area are among the most robust in the relationship literature (Fincham & Bradbury, 1990).

Stimulated in part by learned helplessness theory, initial attributional research examined the hypothesis that attributions might help us understand relationship satisfaction and the breakdown of relationships. Specifically, interest in attributions rested on the assumptions that attributions:

1   maintain current levels of relationship satisfaction and can initiate changes in relationship satisfaction; and
2   mediate or give rise to the response one partner makes to the other's behaviour.

We examine each of these assumptions in turn.

Attributions and relationship satisfaction

In distressed compared with non-distressed marriages, attributions are hypothesized to accentuate the impact of negative partner behaviour (e.g., 'she was home late because she doesn't care about me') and minimize the impact of positive partner behaviour (e.g., 'he only brought me flowers because he wanted to have sex'). Notice that once again the critical element is the characteristics of the causal attribution (e.g., for negative behaviours the cause is located in the partner, is global or influential in other areas of the marriage, and is stable or likely to be present in the future). In contrast to these *distress-maintaining* attributions, satisfied partners are thought to make *relationship-enhancing* attributions that minimize the impact of negative partner behaviours (e.g., 'she was home late because the traffic was heavier than usual') and accentuate positive partner behaviours (e.g., 'he brought me flowers because he really appreciates me').

Although attributions in close relationships usually focus on responsibility and blame, researchers did not initially investigate these constructs and tended to treat judgements of cause, responsibility and blame as interchangeable. Yet, there is a body of attribution research that clearly documents differences in responses to questions regarding cause, responsibility and blame, and shows that lawful relationships exist between these different judgements (see Fincham & Jaspars, 1980;

Shultz & Schleifer, 1983; Shaver, 1985). Briefly stated, causal judgements deal with who or what caused an event (i.e., they are primarily descriptive) whereas responsibility and blame deal with accountability for the event and with sanctions (i.e., with evaluation) once the cause of the event is known.

Soon after research on attributions in close relationships began, Fincham (1983, 1985) attempted to expand the attributions studied in close relationships. In his research, spouses are asked to rate responsibility criteria such as partner motivation, intent and blameworthiness (these are called 'responsibility' attributions as partners in close relationships do not appear to distinguish responsibility from blame; Fincham & Bradbury, 1992). Just as in the case of causal dimensions, responsibility attributions can be seen as relationship-enhancing (e.g., positive partner behaviour seen as intentional, unselfishly motivated and praiseworthy) or distress-maintaining (e.g., negative partner behaviour seen as intentional, selfishly motivated and blameworthy). The attributional hypothesis can therefore be examined in relation to causal and responsibility attributions, and the nature of the hypothesis is summarized in figure 7.7.

Numerous studies have examined the attributions of distressed and nondistressed spouses, with marital distress being defined by spouses' reports on standard measures of marital satisfaction. Across a variety of attributional stimuli (e.g., couple problems, partner behaviour), attributions have been shown to be related to marital satisfaction (see Bradbury & Fincham, 1990; Fincham, 1998).

An interesting variant of the attribution hypothesis has been less widely examined. This variant states that attributional style or consistency in attribution responses is related to marital distress. Thus interest shifts from mean scores to variability of responses. Such variability can be viewed in two ways: consistency of responding to items assessing the same attribution dimension and consistent use of particular patterns of responses across attributional dimensions (e.g., a partner-stable-global pattern). Baucom, Sayers and Duhe (1989) found some evidence to support the attribution style hypothesis in that (1) less variable or more consistent responses to items assessing the same attribution dimension were associated with marital distress; (2) use of fewer patterns of responding across attribution dimensions was associated with husbands' distress; and (3) reliance on a single pattern of responding across dimensions was related to wives' distress. Although these results are promising, Horneffer and Fincham (1995) were only able to replicate them in part; they found that use of theoretically derived benign and non-benign patterns of responding across attribution dimensions was related to marital distress. It therefore remains to determine whether attribution style, conceptualized in terms of consistency of responses, exhibits as robust an association with marital satisfaction as the attribution mean scores that have typically been investigated.

Although an association exists between attributions and relationship satisfaction, it does not tell us whether attributions initiate changes in marital satisfaction rather than *vice versa*. This issue is a very difficult one to investigate owing to ethical problems in manipulating the variables involved, and to the fact that marital sat-

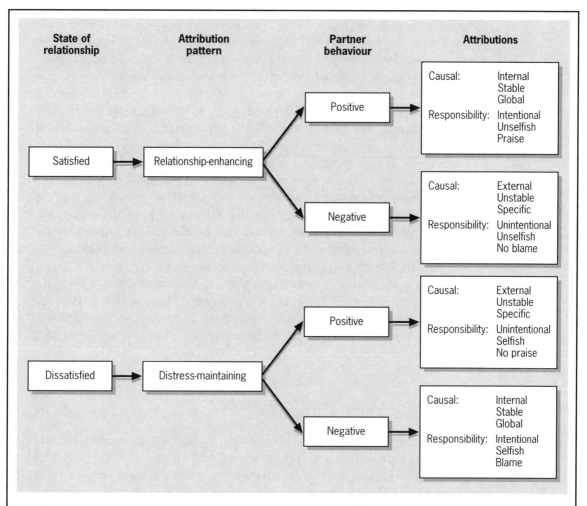

FIGURE 7.7   The attributional hypothesis in close relationships: attributions vary as a function of the state of the relationship and the nature of partner behaviour

isfaction tends to be quite stable over time. Nevertheless, several studies have been conducted in an attempt to address this issue by examining the association between attributions and satisfaction over time.

In an initial study, attributions and satisfaction were assessed at two points in time separated by a 10–12 month interval (Fincham & Bradbury, 1987). Initial causal and responsibility attributions were used to predict later satisfaction after statistically controlling for initial satisfaction. For wives, both types of attributions predicted later satisfaction. However, earlier satisfaction did not predict later attributions, suggesting that attributions influence satisfaction and not *vice versa*. Why significant results were obtained only for wives was unclear, though the small sample (39 couples) may account for this finding.

A second 12-month longitudinal study using a larger sample was therefore conducted (Fincham & Bradbury, 1993). Two important improvements were made in this study. The first addressed the possibility that depression and self-esteem might account for the attribution satisfaction association. Because both depression and self-esteem are related to attributions and to marital satisfaction, it is reasonable to ask whether attributions and satisfaction are related simply because of their association with these variables. Second, the study excluded people with chronic depression or marital distress. This is important because depression and distress tend to be quite stable, which can artificially inflate longitudinal relations between them. It was found that attributions were still related to satisfaction even when depression and self-esteem were statistically controlled. Senchak and Leonard (1993) replicated this finding, in showing that attributions account for unique variance in marital satisfaction independently of both depression and anger. Perhaps more importantly, attributions predicted later satisfaction for both husbands and wives, but satisfaction did not predict later attributions.

In a final study using a sample of newlywed husbands, maladaptive responsibility attributions contributed to declines in reported satisfaction 12 months later, but not *vice versa* (Fincham, Bradbury, Byrne, & Karney, 1997). Thus the longitudinal pattern of findings extends beyond the population of relatively stable and established married couples. The available evidence is therefore consistent with the view that attributions initiate changes in satisfaction.

Attributions and responses to behaviour

What of the second assumption that stimulated interest in attributions and close relationships? Do attributions guide responses to partner behaviour? This question was addressed initially by asking whether attributions correlate with behaviour. Early studies supported such an association for attributions, but did not show that the attribution–behaviour relation occurred independently of marital satisfaction. This is a major shortcoming, because research has shown that behaviour and marital satisfaction are associated. With marital satisfaction statistically controlled, three effects have been shown. First, wives' distress-maintaining responsibility attributions were related to less effective problem-solving behaviours, which were coded from an observed marital interaction (Bradbury & Fincham, 1992, Study 1). Second, husbands' and wives' distress-maintaining causal and responsibility attributions were related to increased rates of negative behaviour during problem-solving (Bradbury & Fincham, 1992, Study 2), and support-giving tasks (Miller & Bradbury, 1995), and to increased rates of specific negative affects such as whining and anger (Fincham & Bradbury, 1992). Third, the attribution–behaviour relationship is independent of depression (Bradbury, Beach, Fincham, & Nelson, 1996).

Finding that spouses' attributions are related to their rates of behaviour is encouraging but does not address whether the attributions guide responses to particular partner behaviours and not others. For example, attributions are thought to be evoked by and guide responses to negative behaviour. Consistent with this view, there was a correlation between wives' maladaptive attributions and the tendency to reciprocate negative husband behaviour, the hallmark of marital distress (Bradbury & Fincham, 1992, Study 2). But again, such relations may simply be due to the documented relation between marital satisfaction and behaviour. Bradbury and Fincham (1992) ruled out this possibility by showing that the correlations remained significant even when satisfaction was partialed out of the relation. Finally, these attribution–behaviour relations are stronger for distressed spouses (e.g., Miller & Bradbury, 1995).

Although impressive, such correlational data can never be as convincing as experimental data for inferring causation. It is therefore worth noting that the data reviewed are consistent with the findings of the one experimental study conducted on this topic (Fincham & Bradbury, 1988). In this study, spouses read an unflattering description of themselves which they thought was either written spontaneously by their partner ('partner locus') or was solicited by the experimenter ('experimenter locus'). In this latter case, they could *discount* the partner's role in producing the negative description and so one might expect that there would be less negative behaviour towards the partner in this condition. Although individually tailored, the descriptions were in fact equally negative across both conditions. Whether the negative description could be attributed to the partner or the experimenter led to different reactions only in the distressed spouses in a five-minute discussion that took place after the descriptions were read (see figure 7.8). The distressed spouses showed considerably more negative behaviour, when the description apparently came from the partner. Thus, both correlational and experimental findings are consistent with the view that attributions influence marital behaviour.

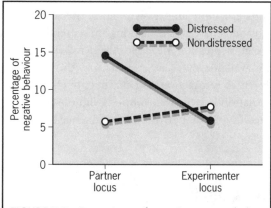

FIGURE 7.8   Percentage of negative spouse behaviour displayed after reading partner's description (Based on Fincham & Bradbury, 1988)

Critical issues

Despite the tremendous progress made in the study of attributions in close relationships, the research is not without problems. One of the most obvious problems concerns the heavy reliance on self-report. Both attributions and marital satisfaction are usually measured using questionnaires and the relation between them could be inflated by common method variance. It is therefore worth noting that an attribution–satisfaction association has been obtained using attributions coded from conversations (e.g., Holtzworth-Munroe & Jacobson, 1988; Stratton, Heard, et al., 1986). Such data rule out the possibility that the association simply reflects method variance as different methods are used to assess attributions (observation) and satisfaction (self-report). In a similar vein, it is often argued that the use of self-report shows little more than that a person's negativity is expressed consistently across questionnaires. However, Karney, Bradbury and colleagues (1994) showed that the attribution–satisfaction association remains significant even when negative affectivity is statistically controlled.

Perhaps more important than the above considerations is the restricted range of issues in close relationships that have been analysed from an attribution perspective. For example, we know relatively little about the role of attributions in different phases of relationships. Yet we might expect attributions to be more salient in phases of the relationship where there is a lot of change (e.g., early in the relationship as partners get to know each other and in the termination phase of the relationship) than when the relationship is relatively stable. Similarly, little is known about attributions that are communicated between partners. What is the relation between such communicated attributions and attributions that remain private? And how do communicated attributions influence the relationship? Although it has not escaped attention, more also needs to be learned about the conditions which instigate attributions in relationships.

Notwithstanding these and other limitations, available data on attributions in close relationships are quite impressive. There is clearly a robust association between attributions and marital satisfaction, and several artifactual explanations for the association (e.g., depression, negative affectivity, self-esteem) have been ruled out. Moreover, the available data are consistent with the view that attributions maintain current levels of satisfaction and can initiate changes in satisfaction. Finally, there is an association between attributions and observed relationship behaviour, and evidence to suggest that attributions influence a person's response to the partner's behaviour.

Summary and Conclusions

We began this chapter by reviewing some classic attribution theories, which address the kinds of information that people use to determine causality, the kinds of causes that they distinguish, and the rules they use for going from information to inferred cause. We then looked in detail at more recent research on the nature of causal attributions, systematic biases that characterize them, what factors instigate them, and what processes underlie them. These issues revealed the breadth and depth of research in this area, but also yielded a more measured view of attribution research. Specifically, it is important to go beyond the distinction between internal and external attributions; far from being scientific, attributions actually reveal many biases; they are triggered by specific factors rather than being either spontaneous or automatic; and they are typically less detailed and more biased than the classic theories imply.

In contrast to the measured view that emerged from the first half of this chapter, the second half started with the observation that the emergence of attribution theory was the most important development in social psychology. The attempt to understand this observation led us to explore some of the main applications of attribution theory. In doing so, we could only sample from a large and diverse literature. Nonetheless, research on motivation, clinical psychology and close relationships demonstrates the continued vitality of attribution research, and the tremendous impact of attribution theory in advancing our understanding of applied problems.

1   To what extent is Kelley's ANOVA model 'idealized', and how has it been improved upon in more recent research?
2   A great deal of attribution research rests on the distinction between internal and external causal attributions. How are they related to one another?
3   Are causal attributions made 'spontaneously', 'automatically', both, or neither?
4   Evaluate the contributions of cognitive and motivational accounts of attributional bias.
5   In what ways do attributions differ in satisfied and distressed relationships?
6   Why has attribution theory been so productive in applied research?
7   How has attribution theory contributed to psychotherapy?

DISCUSSION POINTS

Fletcher, G. J. O., & Fincham, F. D. (Eds.). (1991). *Cognition in close relationships*. Hillsdale, NJ: Erlbaum. A detailed treatment of attributional and other social-cognitive approaches to close relationships by leading scholars in the field.

Gilbert, D. T. (1998). Ordinary personology. In D. T. Gilbert, S. T. Fiske, & G. Lindzey (Eds.), *The handbook of social psychology* (4th ed., Vol. 2, pp. 89–150). Boston, MA: McGraw-Hill. A wide-ranging essay on how ordinary people come to know about each other's temporary states and enduring dispositions.

FURTHER READING

Hewstone, M. (1989). *Causal attribution: From cognitive processes to collective beliefs*. Oxford & Cambridge, MA: Blackwell. A comprehensive analysis of theory and research, including intrapersonal, interpersonal, intergroup and societal attribution, and reviewing both American and European developments.

Jones, E. E. (1990). *Interpersonal perception*. New York: Macmillan. A personal account of attribution theory, written by one of its major figures. Particularly good on the strategic nature of attributions in interpersonal interactions.

Jones, E. E., Kanouse, D. E., Kelley, H. H., Nisbett, R. E., Valins, S., & Weiner, B. (1971). *Attribution: Perceiving the causes of behaviour*. Morristown, NJ: General Learning Press. A now-classic collection of some of the most important early theoretical statements on attribution, including actor–observer differences, and causal schemata.

Weary, G., Stanley, M. A., & Harvey, J. H. (1989). *Attribution*. New York: Springer Verlag. This book is concerned with the application of attribution theory, especially in clinical and other settings outside the laboratory.

Weiner, B. (1986). *An attributional theory of motivation and emotion*. New York: Springer Verlag. A scholarly monograph outlining the development of Weiner's theory and detailing the importance of attribution in predicting both motivational behaviour and affective reactions.

Weiner, B. (1995). *Judgments of responsibility: A foundation for a theory of social conduct*. New York & London: Guilford Press. In presenting a general theory of social motivation, this book provides extensive overviews of several research areas. It also includes experiments that can be completed by the student to illustrate attributional phenomena.

KEY STUDIES

Bradbury, T. N., & Fincham, F. D. (1992). Attributions and behavior in marital interaction. *Journal of Personality and Social Psychology*, 63, 613–28.

Storms, M. D. (1973). Videotape and the attribution process: Reversing actors' and observers' points of view. *Journal of Personality and Social Psychology*, 27, 165–75.

Attitudes

Gerd Bohner

OUTLINE

Attitude is one of the key concepts in social psychology. In this chapter, the concept of attitude will be defined, and issues of attitude structure and function will be addressed. Among the determinants of attitudes, the pro- cessing of persuasive messages and behavi- oural influences will be highlighted. Finally, the consequences of having attitudes for people's information processing and behaviour will be examined.

KEY CONCEPTS

- Aggregation principle
- Attitude
- Attitudinal selectivity
- Balance theory
- Central route to persuasion
- Classical conditioning
- Cognitive dissonance
- Cognitive response approach
- Correspondence principle
- Dual-process models of persuasion
- Elaboration likelihood model
- Expectancy-value models
- Heuristic cue
- Heuristic processing
- Heuristic–systematic model
- Implicit attitudes
- Insufficient justification
- Inter-attitudinal structure
- Intra-attitudinal structure
- Knowledge function
- Mere thought
- Message-learning approach
- MODE model
- Mood-as-information hypothesis
- Need for cognition
- Operant conditioning
- Overjustification effect
- Peripheral route to persuasion
- Persuasion
- Psychological reactance
- Selective exposure
- Self-esteem maintenance function
- Self-monitoring
- Self-perception theory
- Social identity function
- Sufficiency principle
- Systematic processing
- Theory of planned behaviour
- Theory of reasoned action
- Thought-listing technique
- Three-component model of attitude
- Utilitarian function

Introduction

People love and hate, approve and disapprove, like and dislike. They agree or disagree, argue, persuade and sometimes even convince each other. Every day we are the targets of countless influence attempts through personal communication and the mass media, aimed at changing or reinforcing our attitudes. We typically approach things and people we like, and we avoid those we dislike. Throughout the history of social psychology, the concept of attitude has been one of its central topics (Allport, 1935; Eagly & Chaiken, 1998; Petty & Wegener, 1998a).

But why is the study of attitudes important? The first answer is that attitudes are assumed to guide behaviour. If this is true, then we can reduce the risk of HIV/AIDS by changing people's attitudes towards using condoms; establishing more favourable health-related attitudes might contribute to decreasing addictive behaviours; and we could enhance environmental protection if we better understood the conditions leading to favourable environmental attitudes. But the attitude–behaviour relation is just one of many interesting facets of attitude research. In a broad sense, the study of attitudes is important because attitudes are important for our social lives.

At the *individual level*, attitudes influence perception, thinking and behaviour. A person who strongly disapproves of nuclear energy will easily retrieve relevant knowledge from memory and interpret new information in the light of her attitude. She will also act according to her attitude, perhaps by signing a petition to shut down nuclear power plants. At the *interpersonal level*, information about attitudes is routinely requested and disclosed. If we know others' attitudes, the world becomes more predictable. Our own thinking and behaviour may be shaped by this knowledge, and we may try to control others' behaviour by changing their attitudes. At the *intergroup level*, attitudes towards one's own groups and other groups are at the core of intergroup cooperation and conflict (see chapter 15).

In this chapter, we first discuss *basic conceptual issues*. Then we present work on informational and behavioural *determinants of attitudes*. Finally, we address the *effects of attitudes* on information processing and behaviour (for attitude measurement, see chapter 4).

Basic Issues in Attitude Research

How is the concept of attitude defined?
What are attitudes good for, and how are attitudes represented in a person's memory?

Definition of the attitude concept

Most contemporary researchers define **attitude** as a summary evaluation of some object, as the following quotation from a recent handbook chapter exemplifies: 'An attitude is a psychological tendency that is expressed by evaluating a particular entity with some degree of favor or disfavor' (Eagly & Chaiken, 1998, p. 269). The two main elements in this definition of attitude are the mental process of evaluation and the presence of an attitude object.

Attitude A psychological tendency that is expressed by evaluating a particular entity with some degree of favour or disfavour.

To begin with the latter, an *attitude object* can be anything a person discriminates or holds in mind. Attitude objects may be concrete (e.g., anchovy pizza) or abstract (e.g., feminism), may be inanimate things (e.g., personal computers), persons (e.g., Tony Blair) or groups (e.g., British politicians). Some attitudes are referred to in special terms according to the attitude object involved: attitudes towards social groups, especially if negative, are called *prejudices*; attitudes towards oneself are studied under the label of *self-esteem*; and attitudes towards abstract entities (e.g., 'freedom of speech') are frequently termed *values* (Eagly & Chaiken, 1998).

The *tendency to evaluate* is not directly observable and intervenes between certain stimuli (i.e., attitude objects) and certain responses. It is assumed to be grounded in experience, and to have various observable manifestations. Both the experiences that lead to a certain attitude and its manifestations are often divided into three components: *cognition*, *affect* and *behaviour* (Rosenberg & Hovland, 1960; see figure 8.1). The cognitive component consists of *beliefs* about the attitude object; the affective component entails *emotions* and *feelings* elicited by the attitude object; and the behavioural component comprises *actions* directed at the attitude object as well as *behavioural intentions*. Thus, a positive

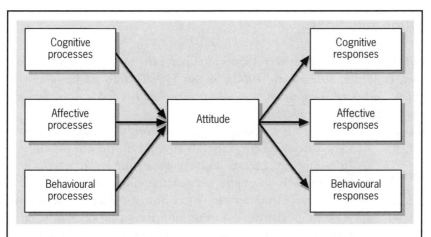

FIGURE 8.1 A three-component model of attitude: attitude is a product of cognitive, affective and behavioural processes, and has cognitive, affective and behavioural manifestations

Three-component model of attitude   This model assumes that attitudes are a combination of three distinguishable modes of experience and reactions to an object: affective, cognitive and behavioural.

attitude towards the Green party may entail (1) the expectation that their participation in government will advance environmental protection (a positive belief); (2) one's admiration for Green politicians (a positive feeling); and (3) the intention to donate money to the party's election campaign (a positive behaviour). The validity of this **three-component model of attitude** was demonstrated by Breckler (1984), who assessed affective, behavioural and cognitive aspects of students' attitude towards snakes. Using confirmatory factor analysis, Breckler found that a three-factor model accounted better than a one-factor solution for the covariation among measures.

To mediate evaluative responses, attitudes need to be represented in memory and to be retrieved when the attitude object is encountered or considered. This retrieval process can be either effortful and *controlled*, or spontaneous and *automatic*: when asked about their evaluation of a particular entity, individuals may actively construct an attitude judgement from relevant information that is accessible in memory (Schwarz & Bohner, in press; Wilson & Hodges, 1992). However, the mere presence of an attitude object may automatically elicit an evaluative response, without any conscious thought or recollection being involved (Bargh, 1997; Bargh, Chaiken, Govender, & Pratto, 1992). Importantly, such automatic attitudes may influence seemingly unrelated judgements or behaviours without the person being aware of their influence.

Implicit attitudes   Evaluative tendencies that may influence judgements or behaviours without the individual being aware of their influence.

For example, people prefer letters of the alphabet that are part of their own name over other letters, without being aware of the name–letter connection (Nuttin, 1985). Greenwald and Banaji (1995) coined the term **implicit attitudes** to describe such influences (see also chapters 4 and 5).

Attitude functions

What purposes do attitudes serve? Drawing upon early taxonomies (M. B. Smith, Bruner, & White, 1956; Katz, 1960), Shavitt (1989) distinguishes a *knowledge function*, a *utilitarian function*, a *social identity function* and a *self-esteem maintenance function* of attitudes.

Knowledge function   An attitude's function of guiding, organizing and simplifying information processing.

Most basic is the **knowledge function**, which all attitudes serve to some extent. As M. B. Smith et al. (1956) noted, attitudes help us in 'sizing up' objects and events in our environment, and an attitude towards an object saves us the effort of figuring out anew each time we encounter the object how we shall behave towards it (p. 41). Empirical work on this information-processing function of attitudes is reviewed below in the section on attitudinal selectivity (see also chapter 5).

Utilitarian function   An attitude's function of maximizing rewards and minimizing punishments in guiding behaviour.

The postulate of a **utilitarian function** is rooted in learning theory. Attitudes can help people to attain positive outcomes and to avoid negative outcomes. Accordingly, we come to like or dislike objects inasmuch as they are associated with rewards or punishments. For example, one's attitude towards pizza should be based on the rewards (pleasant taste, repletion) and punishments (weight gain, high cholesterol level) associated with pizza. It may guide behaviour that maximizes the rewards and reduces the punishments (e.g., eating one's favourite variety, but only once a month).

Theorizing on the **social identity function** comprises the aspects of self-expression and social interaction. Katz (1960) proposed a *value-expressive function*, according to which attitudes facilitate the expression of one's core values and self-concept. M. B. Smith and colleagues (1956) emphasized the social aspects of self-expression in their *social adjustment function*. The holding and expression of

> **Social identity function** An attitude's function of expressing an individual's values and of establishing identification with particular reference groups.

certain attitudes can establish a person's identification with particular reference groups. Thus, an individual may define herself as a member of the social groups of feminists or conservatives by holding 'feminist' or 'conservative' attitudes, respectively.

Finally, there are two ways in which attitudes can fulfil the **function of self-esteem maintenance** (Shavitt, 1989). First, attitudes may set the person apart from negative objects, through a function termed *ego-defence* (Katz, 1960) or *externalization* (M. B. Smith et al., 1956). Inspired by the psychoanalytic concept of defence mechanisms, these authors assumed that negative attitudes, mainly

> **Self-esteem maintenance function** An attitude's function of setting the self apart from negative objects and aligning it with positive objects.

towards minorities or ethnic outgroups, may help to distance the individual from the threat that these groups are assumed to pose. Second, attitudes may help to align the self with liked objects and thus enable the individual to '*bask in reflected glory*', for example by becoming a fan and displaying the insignia of a successful sports team (Cialdini et al., 1976).

Early theorists assumed that evaluations of the same object may entail different functions for different individuals, thus linking attitude functions to personality (M. B. Smith et al., 1956). They also proposed that attempts at changing a person's attitude would be most effective if they addressed the proper functional basis of that attitude (e.g., Katz, Sarnoff, & McClintock, 1956). Until recently, however, these approaches inspired little research, because they lacked precision in operationalizing their constructs (but see, e.g., Petty & Wegener, 1998b). Moreover, an attitude may serve various functions simultaneously, and the impact of a particular function may depend on what aspect of the attitude object is most salient in a given situation (Shavitt, 1989). Contemporary research has supported some claims of an individual-difference approach to attitude functions. Snyder and DeBono (1987) found that attitudes of people high in **self-monitoring** (who tailor their behaviour to fit situational cues and the reactions of others; Snyder, 1974) were more likely to serve a social-adjustive than a value-expressive function, whereas the reverse was true for people low in self-monitoring (whose behaviour mainly reflects their internal states

> **Self-monitoring** A personality trait. Individuals high in self-monitoring tailor their behaviour to fit situational cues and the reactions of others, whereas individuals low in self-monitoring act more in accordance with their internal states and dispositions.

and dispositions). Research that has applied the functional approach to the attitude–behaviour relation is reviewed below.

Attitude structure

What properties of internal structure do attitudes possess? How are attitudes towards different objects interrelated? These questions refer to *intra-attitudinal* and *inter-attitudinal structure*, respectively (Eagly & Chaiken, 1993, 1998).

Intra-attitudinal structure

Intra-attitudinal structure
Comprises aspects of an attitude's representation in memory, such as its polarity, its dimensionality and the degree of consistency among the components of an attitude (see **three-component model of attitude**).

Research on **intra-attitudinal structure** has examined how a person's attitude is represented as a point on an evaluative continuum. It has also addressed the properties of the evaluative continuum itself, and has examined how consistent single components of an attitude (e.g., beliefs and evaluations) are with each other.

Judd and Kulik (1980) proposed that an attitude functions like a *schema* in information processing (see chapter 5). Thus, information 'fitting' a person's attitude schema should be processed more efficiently than information not fitting the schema. In their study, students read belief statements concerning several issues (e.g., 'The Equal Rights Amendment should be supported by all who believe that discrimination is wrong'; 'Majority rule would only complicate the lives of most South Africans'). For each statement, participants indicated *how much they agreed with it* and *how favourable or unfavourable it was*; response times were measured, and free recall for the statements was assessed later. Results showed that more extreme statements, in terms of both subjective agreement and objective favourability, were processed faster and recalled better than less extreme statements. This was true for statements both opposite and congenial to respondents' own positions. Thus, information may fit an attitude schema to the extent that it is located near the poles of a bipolar continuum.

Not all attitudes are likely to be represented as a bipolar continuum, however. Pratkanis (1989) showed that bipolar representations are most common for controversial social issues like abortion, whereas *unipolar structures* are usually found for less disputed topics like music and sports. For these unipolar issues, people mainly possess knowledge congruent with their own position and find it difficult to encode information opposing their attitudes.

Another question of intra-attitudinal structure is how attitudes are derived from more elementary cognitions about the attitude object. Fishbein's (1967a, b) approach to this question features the expectancy-value principle that is central to various motivation theories (see Feather, 1982). He describes an attitude towards an object as the sum of 'expectancy × value'-products:

$$A_o = \sum_{i=1}^{n} b_i e_i$$

In this equation, A_o denotes the attitude towards object O, b_i is the belief or subjective probability that the object possesses a certain attribute I, and e_i is the evaluation of that attribute. Only *salient* attributes enter the equation, i.e., those that a person considers relevant and attends to. The model can be illustrated by computing a person's attitude towards regular exercise on the basis of her individual beliefs and evaluations (see table 8.1). Composite attitude scores which are generated by summing belief-evaluation products usually correlate highly with more direct self-report measures of attitude (e.g., Fishbein & Coombs, 1974).

An important structural issue is *intra-attitudinal consistency*. Although summation models take into account various elements of an attitude, the degree to which these elements are consistent or inconsistent with each other is not reflected in the final sum. People may, however, evaluate an attitude object both favourably and unfavourably at the same time. Our example in table 8.1 shows how a mildly positive attitude can be made up of both beliefs with clearly positive and beliefs with clearly negative evaluation components. This coexistence of favourable and unfavourable beliefs is called *attitudinal ambivalence* (e.g., Kaplan, 1972). People often hold ambivalent attitudes towards health-related behaviours (see chapter 16). A typical example is provided by attitudes towards drinking alcohol. People may evaluate favourably the taste of a glass of wine and the social aspects of going out for a drink, but may be repelled by the prospect of a hangover and difficulty in concentrating on one's work.

TABLE 8.1 Conceptualizing attitude as the sum of belief × evaluation-products

Beliefs about the attitude object 'Regular exercise'	Subjective probability (i.e., belief or expectancy)	Evaluation	Expectancy × Value-product
leads to weight reduction	+3	+2	+6
prevents heart disease	+2	+3	+6
is time-consuming	+3	-2	-6
is painful	+1	-3	-3
is boring	+2	-1	-2
Attitude (sum of expectancy × value-products):			+1

Note: This hypothetical person believes that regular exercise most probably ($b_1 = +3$) leads to weight reduction, which she evaluates quite positively ($e_1 = +2$). Further, she thinks that exercise possibly ($b_2 = +2$) prevents heart disease ($e_2 = +3$), etc. When the five beliefs listed in the table are salient, her overall attitude is slightly positive.

PLATE 8.1   We may think favourably about going out for a drink, but not of getting a hangover

Consistency may also be defined as the relation of the overall attitude to its components. Although positive correlations are the rule, consistency varies in degree. An overall evaluation may be more or less consistent with its cognitive basis (evaluative-cognitive consistency), its affective basis (evaluative-affective consistency), or its behavioural basis (evaluative-behavioural consistency; see Eagly & Chaiken, 1998). Early studies on evaluative-cognitive consistency were conducted by Rosenberg (1960). He believed that low correlations between a person's beliefs and his or her overall attitude indicated the lack of a clear attitude or a 'vacuous attitude', which would lead respondents to answer attitude questions in an unreliable, erratic way (Rosenberg, 1968). However, more recent work has shown that attitudes low in evaluative-cognitive consistency may well have a strong affective basis. Research by Chaiken, Pomerantz and Giner-Sorolla (1995) showed that attitudes high in *either* evaluative-cognitive consistency *or* evaluative-affective consistency were highly accessible in memory and stable over time. Only attitudes low in *both* types of consistency showed low accessibility and stability, i.e., the somewhat 'erratic' pattern that had been described by Rosenberg (1960). The reason why high evaluative-affective consistency confers high *attitude strength* is that each encounter with the attitude object may elicit clear and strong feelings which can then be used as a basis for judgement.

Many other studies on structural aspects of attitudes have also invoked the concept of attitude strength. Factor-analytic studies indicate that attitude strength is a multidimensional construct (e.g., Krosnick, Boninger, Chuang, Berent, & Carnot, 1993; Prislin, 1996). Among its conceptual underpinnings are *non-ambivalence* of relevant beliefs (Thompson, Zanna, & Griffin, 1995) and high *consistency* among attitude components (Chaiken et al., 1995). Other conceptualizations emphasize the strength of the evaluative response itself, e.g., focusing on its *extremity* (Abelson, 1995) or *accessibility* (i.e., the ease with which an attitude comes to mind; Fazio, 1995). One can say that everything attitudes are assumed to do (e.g., to guide information processing; to cause behaviour), *strong* attitudes are assumed to do better. Commonly studied consequences of strength are thus attitudes' *resistance* against persuasive attack, *persistence* over time, and *consistency with behaviour* (e.g., Petty, Haugtvedt, & Smith, 1995).

Interestingly, research into attitude strength has shown that many attitudes are much weaker than the traditional view of attitudes as enduring knowledge structures might suggest. This was most pointedly demonstrated by Wilson and his colleagues, who found that simply asking people to think about the reasons why they hold a certain attitude often leads to dramatic change. For example, students who were asked to analyse reasons for their attitudes towards psychology courses changed their attitudes about these courses and, as a consequence, made poorer behavioural decisions. Specifically, they were less likely to enrol in high-quality (as opposed to low-quality) courses, whereas students who had not thought about reasons were more likely to choose the high-quality courses (Wilson & Schooler, 1991). Thus, various researchers have proposed that attitudes are best conceived of as context-dependent, temporary constructions (Schwarz & Bohner, in press; Wilson & Hodges, 1992).

Inter-attitudinal structure

How are attitudes towards different objects linked to each other in people's minds? This question has been analysed mainly in two ways. One approach highlighted the *hierarchical* aspect of thematically consistent cognitive structures, or *ideologies*, in which attitudes are embedded. From this viewpoint, an attitude towards a novel social or political issue may be derived from more central and general values a person holds in that area (see Kinder & Sears, 1985).

The other approach, Heider's (1946, 1958) **balance theory**, has been more influential in social psychology. Like other *cognitive consistency theories* (see Abelson et al., 1968), balance theory assumes that people strive for consistency among their cognitions. Of particular interest in Heider's analyses and subsequent research was how attitudes towards issues and attitudes towards people are related in a perceiver's mind (Heider, 1946). Assume that Patty loves her new partner Eric and dreams of joint vacations in the mountains. In determining the stability of each of these two cognitions, a third cognition needs to be considered, namely Patty's perception of Eric's attitude

Inter-attitudinal structure The way in which attitudes towards different attitude objects are organized in an individual's memory.

Balance theory A theory of cognitive consistency proposed by Heider that has been applied to attitude change and to explaining the relationship between attitudinal similarity and interpersonal liking. It assumes that individuals strive for maintaining and restoring equilibrium among their cognitions.

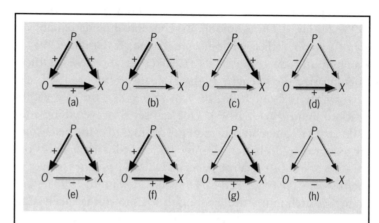

FIGURE 8.2   Balanced (a to d) and unbalanced (e to h) cognitive triads according to balance theory
(Heider, 1946)

towards mountain holidays. In Heider's terminology, these three cognitions form a *triad* involving the perceiver (*p*; e.g., Patty), another person (*o*; e.g., Eric), and some non-person object (*x*; e.g., mountain vacations). These elements may be linked by positive or negative relations which may reflect feelings (e.g., 'Patty loves Eric') or proximity (e.g. 'Patty and Eric are engaged'). A balanced (i.e., stable) state among the elements in a three-element structure exists when multiplying the signs of all three relations yields a positive sign. Balanced and unbalanced triads are depicted in figure 8.2.

As figure 8.2 shows, if Patty perceives that Eric hates the mountains (a negative *o-x*-relation), one relation would be negative and two positive (triad e). Thus, imbalance would exist. Patty should experience discomfort and be motivated to change her cognitive structure towards balance. She could do so in various ways: by change in the *p-x*-relation (i.e., herself adopting a negative attitude towards mountain holidays), by change in the *p-o*-relation (i.e., feeling less affection for Eric), or by change in the *o-x*-relation (e.g., Patty could persuade Eric that the mountains are more fun than he thought). In each of these cases, the resulting triad (b, c or a) would be balanced.

Research examined how participants rate hypothetical *p-o-x* triads for their pleasantness from *p*'s perspective. Most studies obtained high pleasantness ratings mainly for those balanced triads in which *p* likes *o* and agrees with *o* in the evaluation of *x* (triads a and b in figure 8.2), whereas the remaining six constellations were lower in pleasantness and did not differ much from each other (e.g., Jordan, 1953; Zajonc, 1968). This suggests that in addition to balance, attraction (sign of the *p-o* relation) and agreement (match of the *p-x* and *o-x* relations) predict the pleasantness of triads (see Eagly & Chaiken, 1993, pp. 133–44). Balance theory has been used to explain the positive relationship between attitudinal similarity and interpersonal liking (e.g., Newcomb, 1961; Cialdini, Trost, & Newsom, 1995; see chapter 12). Also, Zajonc and Burnstein (1965) showed that people are better able to encode and learn information that represents balanced rather than unbalanced states.

Determinants of Attitudes

What are the factors that determine a person's attitude?

In this section we discuss factors and processes that determine an individual's attitude. Although recent theorizing is addressing biological determinants of attitudes (see chapter 2; Tesser & Martin, 1996), the bulk of persuasion research has been concerned with the acquisition of attitudes during a person's lifetime through individual experiences. We will address the areas of persuasion and of attitude change resulting from changes in behaviour.

Persuasion

The area of **persuasion** addresses attitude change as a result of information processing, often in response to messages about the attitude object (for reviews see Chaiken, Wood, & Eagly, 1996; Petty & Wegener, 1998a). Theories of persuasion can be ordered according to the amount of cognitive effort involved in the change processes that they focus on (Petty & Cacioppo, 1981).

Persuasion Attitude formation or change, usually in response to arguments and/or other information about the attitude object.

Persuasion processes that require little cognitive effort

Attitude conditioning Starting from the assumption that attitudes are learned dispositions (Allport, 1935; Doob, 1947), early theorists tried to explain attitude change as a result of conditioning. In **classical conditioning**, an initially neutral stimulus is repeatedly paired with another stimulus that strongly evokes a certain response; learning is said to have occurred when the initially neutral stimulus alone suffices to evoke the response. Using this paradigm, attitude researchers showed that positive or negative evaluations can be created in humans if novel stimuli are repeatedly paired with stimuli that already elicit positive or negative responses (e.g., Berkowitz & Knurek, 1969; Staats & Staats, 1958; for a review, see Petty & Cacioppo, 1981). For example, Berkowitz and Knurek (1969) created favourable and unfavourable

Classical conditioning The process by which a neutral stimulus that initially does not elicit a particular response gradually acquires the ability to do so through repeated association with a stimulus that has already evoked that response.

attitudes, respectively, towards the names 'Ed' and 'George', by repeatedly presenting these names paired with positive and negative adjectives. Later, in an ostensibly unrelated experiment, each of their participants discussed with two confederates, who introduced themselves as Ed and George. After the discussion, both participants' ratings of the confederates and confederates' ratings of the participants' behaviour towards them reflected the valence of the previous conditioning.

In **operant conditioning**, learning occurs when responses increase in frequency because they have positive consequences (a process called reinforcement) or decrease in frequency because they have negative consequences (a process called punishment). Inspired by Skinner's (1957) account of human verbal behaviour as a result of operant conditioning, several studies applied principles of reinforcement to attitude statements. For example, Hildum and Brown (1956) interviewed students about their attitudes towards certain university policies. In one condition, every time a student responded favourably, the interviewer reinforced this response by saying 'good' or 'mm-hmm'; whereas in another condition, only unfavourable responses were reinforced. Students who were reinforced for unfavourable statements finally reported a less positive attitude than those who were reinforced for favourable statements.

> **Operant conditioning** Process of learning by reinforcement (i.e., responses increase in frequency because they have positive consequences) or punishment (i.e., responses decrease in frequency because they have negative consequences).

To summarize, it is possible to influence people's attitudes about objects by establishing a close connection in space and time (a) between these objects and positive or negative stimuli (classical conditioning) or (b) between evaluative responses to the attitude object and reinforcements (operant conditioning). In everyday experience, many attitude objects are indeed consistently associated with positive or negative contexts or consequences. For instance, children may observe displays of disgust in their caretakers each time they encounter members of certain ethnic groups (see chapter 15). Or, certain types of food always give rise to the experience of a repulsive taste. In both cases, this repeated experience should result in negative attitudes (towards the ethnic group or the food, respectively). The formation of attitudes that maximize rewards and minimize punishments is in line with a core postulate of the functional approach to attitudes (see above).

Feelings and other subjective experiences as information   But hedonic experiences may influence attitudes through other mechanisms as well. One economic strategy of making an evaluative judgement is to rely on the feelings that are apparently evoked by the attitude object. After all, things we like evoke positive feelings, and things we dislike cause us to feel bad – so why not use these affective responses as a shortcut to an evaluative judgement? Interestingly, however, it is not always easy to discriminate between feelings elicited by the attitude object and feelings one happens to experience at the time of judgement, but for irrelevant reasons. If people are unaware of the true cause of their affect, they may erroneously attribute it to attitude objects currently in their focus of attention (Schwarz, 1990b). In a test of this **mood-as-information hypothesis**, Schwarz and

Clore (1983) found that people who were interviewed on sunny days were in a better mood, which in turn caused them to evaluate their lives more positively, than others interviewed on rainy days. When respondents' attention was first drawn to the weather, its effect on mood persisted but judgements of life satisfaction were no longer influenced by it, suggesting that respondents corrected these judgements for the irrelevant affect (see also chapter 5).

Mood-as-information hypothesis The assumption that individuals use their mood as information in making evaluative judgements about an attitude object.

Mood effects on attitude judgements may be treated as a special case of individuals' relying on subjective experiences in attitude formation. Other examples include using the experienced *ease* with which information can be retrieved, generated or processed to judge its evidential quality (e.g., Howard, 1997; Reber, Winkielman, & Schwarz, 1998; Wänke, Bohner, & Jurkowitsch, 1997). For example, students who were exposed to an advertisement that suggested generating *one reason* to choose a BMW over a Mercedes, which they anticipated to be easy, judged BMW more favourably than students to whom a similar advert suggested generating *ten reasons*, which they anticipated to be difficult (Wänke et al., 1997). In a similar vein, students expressed greater liking for pictures when these pictures were easy rather than difficult to process due to higher contrast between figure and ground or longer exposure time (Reber et al., 1998).

Heuristic processing Assessing one's feelings and other subjective experiences as a basis of attitude judgements can be conceptualized as an example of **heuristic processing** (Chen & Chaiken, 1999). While these 'How do I feel about it?' heuristics (Schwarz, 1990b) make use of internal cues, persuasion researchers have usually highlighted heuristics that pertain to external cues (see Eagly & Chaiken, 1993, for a review). Heuristics are simple decision rules that can be applied to a judgement. Thus, people may use the heuristics 'Experts' statements are valid', 'I agree with people I like' or 'The majority is usually right', which leads them to agree with experts, likeable people and majorities more than with non-experts, dislikeable people and minorities. To do so, they must (a) perceive a relevant heuristic cue and (b) have an applicable heuristic accessible in memory (Chaiken, Liberman, & Eagly, 1989). As with conditioning and the use of feelings as information, a person need not necessarily be aware that she is applying a heuristic in generating an attitude judgement. Heuristics are particularly influential when an individual has little motivation or ability to engage in more extensive forms of processing; their use is guided by the 'principle of least cognitive effort' (Allport, 1954; see Bohner, Moskowitz, & Chaiken, 1995).

Heuristic processing Assessing the validity of a communication or the merits of an attitude object through reliance on heuristics, i.e., simple rules like 'the majority is right' or 'experts' statements are valid'.

Persuasion through effortful processing

Processing of message content and persuasion Note that none of the processes discussed so far involved any detailed consideration of the content of a persuasive message or specific aspects of the attitude object. The importance of processing

Message-learning approach
An eclectic approach to persuasion, featuring the assumption that attitude change is a function of the learning and retention of message content, and studying source, message, channel and recipient characteristics as variables in the persuasion process.

of message content was first emphasized in the **message-learning approach** to persuasion (Hovland, Janis, & Kelley, 1953). This approach can be understood as an eclectic set of working assumptions. Its proponents assumed that the learning and recall of message content, which would be facilitated by incentives to adopt the position advocated, mediates attitude change. Their research focused on various elements of the persuasion setting that would affect message learning, guided by the question 'Who says what to whom through which channel with what effect?' (B. L. Smith, Lasswell, & Casey, 1946).

Accordingly, the classes of independent variables examined were the message *source* ('who?', e.g., an expert or a non-expert), the *message* ('what?', including aspects of content and structure), *recipient characteristics* ('to whom?', e.g., self-esteem, intelligence), and the *channel* of the communication (e.g., written vs. spoken). Internal mediating processes that were studied include *attention* to the message, *comprehension* of its content, *rehearsal* of arguments and *yielding* to the message position. The dependent variables assessed ('with what effect?') were changes in *beliefs, attitudes* and *behaviour.*

By structuring the persuasion process in such a way, and by examining a host of interesting phenomena, the message-learning approach had a significant impact on later generations of persuasion research (for an overview of findings, see Petty & Cacioppo, 1981, ch. 3). However, owing to its lack of a unifying theory, it accumulated ad hoc explanations for a variety of effects, which were often contradictory and could not be meaningfully integrated.

A major tenet of the message-learning approach was that *reception* of a message, i.e., attention to and comprehension of its content, would mediate persuasion. As reception was assumed to be reflected in the recall of message content, high correlations of message recall and attitude change were expected to be the rule. Empirically, however, memory for message content turned out to be a poor predictor of persuasion (see Eagly & Chaiken, 1993). As a consequence, researchers shifted their attention to other cognitive mediators of attitude change, which emphasized the active transformation, elaboration and generation of arguments.

Active thought   Early research into active thought examined *role-playing* as a persuasion technique. King and Janis (1956) showed that students who actively improvised a speech based on arguments they had previously read showed greater attitude change than others who simply read externally generated arguments into a tape recorder or silently to themselves.

McGuire and Papageorgis (1962) proposed that *forewarning* recipients of the persuasive intent of a message might help them resist persuasion by stimulating the generation of their own counterarguments. Various studies supported this hypothesis (for an overview, see Eagly & Chaiken, 1993).

Mere thought   Thinking about an attitude object in the absence of external information which leads to extremization of the attitude.

Finally, work by Tesser (1978) revealed that even in the absence of a persuasive message, **mere thought** about an attitude object may lead to more extreme attitudes. This happens because people hold 'naive theories' or schemata, which make some attributes of an object more salient and facilitate inferences regarding related attributes. Thus schemata have a directive influence on thoughts and often produce changes in beliefs towards greater schematic consistency. Because attitudes vary as a function of a person's beliefs, a moderate initial attitude tends to change towards an extreme attitude under the guidance of mere thinking. For example, Sadler and Tesser (1973) introduced research participants to a likeable or dislikeable 'partner' (in fact, a tape recording). Later, some participants were asked to think about their partner, whereas others performed a distractor task. Finally, all participants rated their partner on various scales and listed their thoughts about him. Compared to distracted participants, non-distracted participants evaluated the likeable partner more favourably and wrote more positive thoughts about him, but rated the dislikeable partner more negatively and wrote more negative thoughts about him.

The cognitive response approach   The increasing evidence for the importance of active thought processes in attitude change led to the formulation of the **cognitive response approach** to persuasion (Greenwald, 1968; see Petty, Ostrom, & Brock, 1981). Its assumptions can be summarized as follows:

Cognitive response approach
A theoretical orientation assuming that attitude change is mediated by the overall favourability of thoughts or 'cognitive responses' that individuals generate when they are exposed to persuasive communications.

1   Individuals who are exposed to a persuasive message actively relate the content of this message to their existing knowledge and attitude towards the message topic, thereby generating new thoughts or *cognitive responses*.
2   Attitude change is mediated by these cognitive responses.
3   The degree and direction of attitude change are a function of the valence of the cognitive responses in relation to the message's position. In this sense, cognitive responses can be favourable, unfavourable or neutral.
4   The greater the proportion of favourable responses and the smaller the proportion of unfavourable responses elicited by a message, the greater is the attitude change in the direction advocated.

To assess the mediating role of cognitive responses in persuasion, researchers introduced a new method, the **thought-listing technique** (Cacioppo, Harkins, & Petty, 1981; Greenwald, 1968): research participants are asked to list any thoughts that have come to mind while they read or heard a persuasive message. These thoughts are later content-analysed and coded according to their favourability (see Petty and Cacioppo, 1986a, pp. 38–40). For example, students who listened to a message advocating an increase in tuition fees to improve library services may list thoughts like: 'I'll write better essays with better library resources' (a favourable thought); 'Stupid – many students can hardly pay the current fee' (an unfavourable thought); 'What will I have for lunch today?' (an irrelevant, neutral thought).

Thought-listing technique
Method used in persuasion research that has been popularized by proponents of the cognitive response approach. Research participants are asked to list the thoughts that came to mind while they were exposed to a persuasive message. These thoughts are later coded according to their favourability or other aspects and used as mediators in analyses of attitude change.

Dual-process models of persuasion Theories of persuasion (e.g., elaboration likelihood model; heuristic–systematic model) postulating two modes of information processing, which differ in the extent to which individuals engage in effortful thought about message arguments and other detailed information on an attitude object. The mode of information processing is assumed to depend on processing motivation and ability.

Elaboration likelihood model The elaboration likelihood model of Petty and his colleagues assumes that attitude change in response to persuasive communications can be mediated by two modes of information processing (see **dual-process models**). Elaboration denotes the extent to which a person engages in central-route processing of the issue-relevant arguments contained in a message rather than being influenced by processes that characterize the peripheral route to persuasion (e.g., classical conditioning; heuristic processing). Elaboration likelihood is determined by both processing motivation and ability.

Heuristic–systematic model The heuristic–systematic model of Chaiken and her colleagues assumes that attitude change can be mediated by two different modes of information processing, namely heuristic and systematic processing (see **dual-process models**). When individuals are unmotivated or unable to invest much cognitive effort, they are likely to rely on heuristic cues in forming an

To predict the impact that a variable will have on persuasion, it is crucial to know how this variable will affect cognitive responding to the message. Any factor that increases the likelihood of counter-arguing (e.g., forewarning) should decrease persuasion, and any factor that increases the likelihood of favourable responses should increase persuasion. Furthermore, if a person's dominant cognitive responses to a message can be expected to be favourable (e.g., a political party member listening to a speech of the party leader), then any factor reducing the overall amount of processing should decrease persuasion, whereas the opposite should hold if a person's responses are likely to be unfavourable. These assumptions have been incorporated and further developed in **dual-process models of persuasion**, so we address related findings in the next section.

Dual-process models of persuasion

Most persuasion research since the 1980s has been based on the **elaboration likelihood model** (ELM; Petty & Cacioppo, 1986a, b; Petty & Wegener, 1999) or the **heuristic–systematic model** (HSM; Bohner et al., 1995; Chaiken et al., 1989; Chen & Chaiken, 1999). Both models represent comprehensive frameworks of persuasion. They incorporate the assumptions of the cognitive response approach about active, effortful processing, but also address persuasion based on effortless processing. Each model distinguishes two prototypical modes of persuasion that form the poles of a continuum of processing effort.

The elaboration likelihood model In the ELM, these modes are called the **central route**, which involves effortful scrutiny of message arguments and other relevant information, and the **peripheral route**, which includes a variety of low-effort mechanisms such as conditioning, social identification and the use of heuristics. The two routes are conceived as antagonistic in their impact on persuasion outcomes (Petty & Cacioppo, 1986a, b). As people have limited time and resources, they cannot elaborate the details of every persuasive message they encounter – thus, peripheral-route processes should be the default. A person's *motivation* and *ability* to process a given message determine its 'elaboration likelihood'. The higher this likelihood, the greater should be the impact of central-route processing, mediated through the favourability of the recipient's cognitive responses, and the lower should be the impact of peripheral mechanisms on attitude change. Attitudes formed via the central route are assumed to be stronger (i.e., more persistent, resistant to attack and predictive of behaviour) than those formed via the peripheral route (Petty et al., 1995).

In the ELM, persuasion variables are thought to be capable of playing 'multiple roles' (for discussion, see Petty & Cacioppo, 1986a, ch. 8). This may be exemplified by the hypothesized effects of source attractiveness. An attractive model who promotes shampoo in a television advert may serve as a *peripheral cue* if elaboration likelihood is low, directly enhancing persuasion through peripheral mechanisms (e.g., conditioning). The model may serve as a *message argument* if elaboration likelihood is high, enhancing persuasion through issue-relevant cognitive responses ('If I use this shampoo, my hair will look as nice as hers'). Finally, the model's attractiveness may *enhance motivation* to centrally process the message ('Hey, look at the supermodel – I should pay attention to what she is saying'). Petty and Cacioppo propose that this latter effect should be most pronounced if elaboration likelihood was moderate to begin with; under these circumstances, source cues are assumed to indicate whether it is worthwhile paying attention to the message. In most empirical tests of the ELM, however, source and context variables were used to operationalize peripheral cues (e.g., expertise, liking, number of sources), whereas variations in message content were used to gather evidence on central-route processing.

attitude judgement; when motivation and ability are high, they also scrutinize message arguments and all other potentially relevant information to form a judgement.

Central route to persuasion   A person's careful and thoughtful consideration of the arguments presented in support of a position.

Peripheral route to persuasion Subsumes those persuasion processes that are not based on effortful issue-related thinking (e.g., classical conditioning, heuristic processing).

The *systematic variation of argument quality* to study influences on the degree of processing is a valuable innovation that Petty and his colleagues introduced. It is done by pilot-testing a pool of arguments regarding the kind of thoughts they evoke when carefully scrutinized. If arguments are strong, central-route processing should produce predominantly favourable cognitive responses and result in more positive attitudes; whereas if arguments are weak, central-route processing should evoke mainly unfavourable thoughts and lead to less positive attitudes (see Petty & Cacioppo, 1986a, ch. 2). In studies using argument quality as one experimental factor, the kind of influence that a variable has in the persuasion process can be inferred from the pattern of results it produces (Petty & Cacioppo, 1986a, b). Some of the possible patterns discussed in the ELM are depicted in figure 8.3.

Panel 1 of figure 8.3 shows the patterns we should observe if a treatment has no effect on persuasion. If this is the case and overall elaboration likelihood is high (panel 1 b), we observe only a main effect of argument strength, i.e., people exposed to strong arguments report more positive attitudes than people exposed to weak arguments. Under low elaboration likelihood (panel 1 a), this argument main effect should be smaller or absent. Panel 2 of figure 8.3 shows the effect of a treatment that can be characterized as a positive (panel 2 a) or a negative (panel 2 b) peripheral cue. Here we see a main effect of the treatment, which leads to either more positive or more negative attitudes, whereas any effect of argument strength is weak or absent. Panel 3 of figure 8.3 shows the effect of a treatment that either enhances (panel 3 a) or reduces (panel 3 b) the objective elaboration of a persuasive message. Here we observe an interaction effect of treatment by

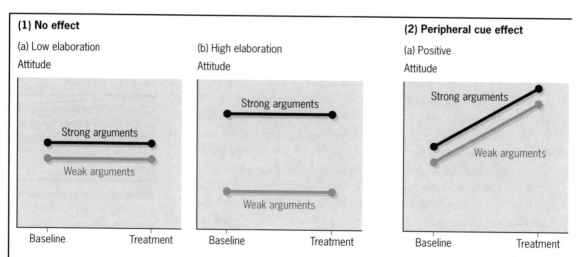

FIGURE 8.3   Some possible effects of a treatment variable in the ELM (adapted from Petty & Cacioppo, 1986a, figure 2–3, p. 34). The three panels show patterns for (1) a variable that has no effect; (2) a peripheral cue; (3) a variable that affects the motivation or ability to scrutinize a message

argument strength, i.e., the difference in attitudes that results from processing strong vs. weak arguments changes in magnitude depending on whether the treatment is present or absent.

This principle can be illustrated by research on *distraction*. Various studies had shown that distraction often reduces persuasion. But in some experiments the opposite effect occurred – recipients who were distracted while listening to a message changed their attitude *more* than non-distracted recipients (see Petty & Brock, 1981). The latter finding may seem surprising if one assumes that learning message content is the primary mediator of persuasion. From the viewpoint of the ELM, however, distraction should reduce recipients' ability for central-route processing, thus undermining the dominant cognitive responses that the message would otherwise have elicited. The dominant response to a message containing weak arguments should be counterarguing, and if this process is disrupted, resistance to persuasion should be weakened.

To test this disruption-of-counterarguing idea, Petty, Wells and Brock (1976, Exp. 1) varied both distraction (at four levels from no distraction to high intensity) and argument quality (strong vs. weak). Students were asked to listen to a message advocating an increase in tuition fees at their university. The strong message stated – among other arguments – that the fee increase was recommended after an intensive two-year investigation and that it would help to increase graduating students' starting salaries substantially; the weak message stated that the recommendation of a fee increase was based on a two-month study and that better lighting of classrooms was needed to reduce student headaches. To vary distraction, students were given a second task to perform while listening to the

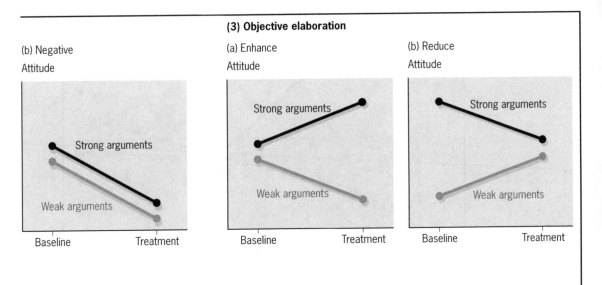

(3) Objective elaboration

(b) Negative
Attitude

Strong arguments

Weak arguments

Baseline   Treatment

(a) Enhance
Attitude

Strong arguments

Weak arguments

Baseline   Treatment

(b) Reduce
Attitude

Strong arguments

Weak arguments

Baseline   Treatment

message. They had to monitor and record the position of an X that was briefly flashed on a screen at varying time intervals. Depending on condition, the number of flashes per minute was 0, 4, 12 or 20.

Petty and his colleagues (1976) reasoned that the strong message would elicit predominantly favourable responses and thus distraction should reduce persuasion for this message, whereas the weak message would elicit mainly counter-arguing and thus distraction should enhance persuasion. These predictions were supported, as can be seen in figure 8.4. At higher levels of distraction, the difference in the effects of argument strength on participants' attitudes was clearly less pronounced than at lower levels of distraction. This means that distracted participants who listened to the weak message showed more agreement than non-distracted participants, and an opposite effect of distraction was observed for participants who had listened to the strong message. The favourability of particip-ants' cognitive responses showed a parallel pattern.

Generally, ELM-based research successfully readdressed areas that had been char-acterized by seemingly inconsistent findings. Similar interactions with argument quality were observed for other variables that affect processing via motivation or ability. The most prominent motivational factor studied is *personal involvement*. People who are highly involved in a topic should elaborate a message on this topic to a greater degree than people who are uninvolved. In an early experiment demon-strating this effect, Petty, Cacioppo and Goldman (1981) asked undergraduate students to listen to an audiotaped message about changes in the examination policy at their university. The message stated that all undergraduates would have to take comprehensive examinations in their major area of study as a requirement

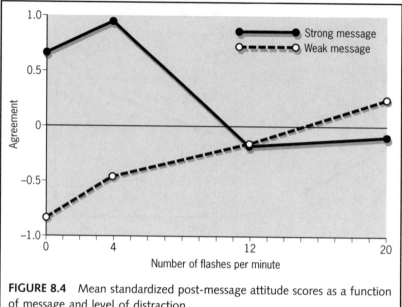

FIGURE 8.4   Mean standardized post-message attitude scores as a function of message and level of distraction

(Adapted from Petty, Wells, & Brock, 1976, Exp. 1. Copyright © 1976 by the American Psychological Association. Adapted with permission)

for graduation. Three experimental factors were varied in a 2 × 2 × 2 factorial design: involvement, source expertise and argument strength. To manipulate involvement, the students learned that the new exam policy would be implemented either in the following year (and thus affect them personally = high involvement) or ten years later (low involvement). To vary source expertise, the message was said to come either from 'the Carnegie Commission on Higher Education' (high expertise) or from a local high school class (low expertise). Finally, the comprehensive exam proposal was backed with arguments that were either weak or strong. After listening to the message, participants were asked to report their attitude towards comprehensive exams on several items that were later combined to form a standardized index.

Petty, Cacioppo and Goldman (1981) predicted that students for whom involvement was high would elaborate the message and would thus report more positive attitudes after listening to strong rather than weak arguments. Students for whom involvement was low, on the other hand, were not expected to engage in message elaboration but to form a judgement mainly on the basis of the peripheral cue, i.e., agree more with a source of high expertise than with a source of low expertise. As can be seen in figure 8.5, the results supported these predictions.

Other studies found that high *accountability* for one's judgements or *negative mood* also lead to increased message elaboration (for an overview, see Petty &

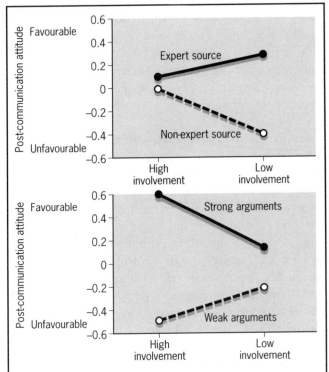

FIGURE 8.5 The effect of personal involvement on persuasion. Mean standardized post-message attitude is shown as a function of level of involvement, message strength and source expertise
(Adapted from a table presented by Petty, Cacioppo, & Goldman, 1981)

Wegener, 1998a). An individual difference variable affecting the degree of elaboration that was conceptualized and studied mainly in the context of the ELM is the **need for cognition** (NC; Cacioppo & Petty, 1982). Individuals high in NC enjoy engaging in effortful thinking across situations and topics, whereas individuals low in NC are generally unmotivated to expend much cognitive effort. High-NC (vs. low-NC) individuals have been found to show more central-route processing of messages but to be less susceptible to the impact of peripheral cues (for a review, see Cacioppo, Petty, Feinstein, & Jarvis, 1996).

In sum, the ELM provides a comprehensive framework of persuasion processes that can accommodate the effects of a wide range of variables and their interactions. It has been criticized, however, for its lack of predictive power (e.g., Eagly & Chaiken, 1993). Specifically, it is difficult to assess

Need for cognition An individual difference variable that differentiates individuals in terms of how much they engage in and enjoy thinking about topics and problems. When exposed to a persuasive message, individuals high in need for cognition engage in more content-related thinking than individuals low in need for cognition.

the level of elaboration likelihood independent of its effects (see figure 8.3); thus, one often cannot predict *a priori* in which of the multiple roles featured in the ELM a variable will serve. Furthermore, although Petty and his colleagues acknowledge that central and peripheral processes may co-occur (Petty & Wegener, 1998a), they do not specify the exact mechanisms and conditions of their interplay. These issues are more explicitly incorporated in the other current dual-processing framework of persuasion.

The heuristic–systematic model   The heuristic–systematic model (HSM) of persuasion features an effortless *heuristic* mode and an effortful *systematic* mode of processing (Bohner et al., 1995; Chaiken et al., 1989; Chen & Chaiken, 1999). The main similarities to the ELM lie in the HSM's concept of a processing continuum and the idea that processing effort is a function of motivation and cognitive capacity. **Systematic processing** is defined – much like central-route processing – as a comprehensive and analytic mode in which an individual accesses and scrutinizes all potentially relevant information and integrates all useful information in forming a judgement (Chaiken et al., 1989, p. 212). *Heuristic processing* is defined more narrowly and more specifically than the ELM's peripheral route. It entails the application of *heuristics*, simple rules of inference like 'consensus implies correctness' or 'experts' statements are valid' (see section on heuristic processing above). Although heuristic processing is thought to be an effortless, default mode, its occurrence does require the presence of a **heuristic cue** (e.g., a likeable or expert source), which signals the applicability of a heuristic that is accessible in a recipient's memory.

> **Systematic processing**
> Thorough, detailed processing of information (e.g., attention to and elaboration of the arguments contained in a persuasive message); this mode of processing requires a sufficient amount of both ability and motivation.

> **Heuristic cue**   Information present in a persuasion setting (e.g., a communicator's white lab coat) that indicates the applicability of a heuristic (e.g., 'experts' statements are valid').

Generally, systematic processing requires a certain degree of motivation and processing capacity; thus, at low levels of motivation and capacity, heuristic processing prevails. At higher levels of motivation and capacity, more effortful systematic processing comes into play, but heuristics continue to be used. Then, both processing modes jointly affect persuasion in an additive or interactive fashion (see the HSM's co-occurrence hypotheses for detail; Bohner et al., 1995). To illustrate this idea, we consider the HSM's predictions for the processing of an ambiguous message when a heuristic cue is present.

This kind of interplay is featured in the HSM's *bias hypothesis*: if message content is ambiguous or mixed (e.g., both strong and weak arguments or mixed evidence in favour of a position), initial heuristic-based inferences may bias the systematic evaluation of the message, leading to cognitive responses and attitudes that are in line with the implications of the heuristic applied. Chaiken and Maheswaran (1994) tested the bias hypothesis in a study that varied task importance, message ambiguity and source credibility. Participants were asked to evaluate information about a new answerphone, the 'XT 100'. High task importance participants learned that the XT 100 might soon be marketed in their region and believed that they were part of a select group of consumers whose individual judgements would affect the marketing decision. Low task importance participants, by contrast, were told that the XT 100 might be marketed in a different area and that their judgements would be aggregated with those of other consumers. Source credibility was varied by telling respondents that the product information came either from 'Consumer Reports', a prestigious product-testing magazine, or from a promotional pamphlet prepared by 'Kmart', a chain of discount stores. Participants then read the message, which – depending on condition – featured strong evidence in favour of the product (portraying the XT 100 as superior to the competition on important dimensions), weak evidence (portraying the XT 100 as inferior) or ambiguous evidence (portraying the XT 100 as superior on some dimensions and inferior on others). After reading the message, participants reported their attitudes towards the XT 100 and listed the thoughts that had come to mind while reading.

In the high task importance conditions, participants were expected to process systematically. In the case of unambiguously strong or weak evidence, we should mainly see an effect of message strength, with favourable thoughts and attitudes elicited by the strong message and unfavourable thoughts and attitudes evoked by the weak message. In the case of ambiguous message content, however, the source credibility heuristic was predicted to bias the systematic processing of content information, yielding more favourable thoughts and attitudes when the message ostensibly came from 'Consumer Reports' magazine rather than Kmart. This was exactly the pattern of results that Chaiken and Maheswaran (1994) observed – figure 8.6 shows the cognitive response data for the high importance conditions. Finally, in the low task importance conditions, heuristic processing prevailed, as there was only a main effect of source credibility on attitudes, whereas thoughts about the message were unaffected by either source credibility or argument quality.

The Chaiken and Maheswaran (1994) study illustrates how the HSM provides predictions about a complex interplay of processing modes under specifiable conditions. Although the ELM also allows for the co-occurrence of its processing modes, the exact nature of this co-occurrence is less clearly specified. Another area where the HSM aims at greater specificity are external criteria of processing motivation.

The HSM's **sufficiency principle** states that people strive for sufficient confidence in their attitudinal judgements. What is sufficient is determined by two constructs, the *sufficiency threshold* (ST) or desired confidence, and the *actual confidence* (AC). Whenever actual confidence is lower than the sufficiency threshold, the person will be motivated to process information, and the larger the gap between ST and AC, the more likely it is that closing it will require systematic processing (see Eagly & Chaiken, 1993). Both of these concepts vary between persons and situations. The ST may be raised under high task importance, personal relevance or accountability. For instance, if a topic is highly important to me, I will try to reach greater certainty in my judgement than if a topic is unimportant to me. Thus, under high importance the ST would be high and the potential gap between it and the

> **Sufficiency principle**
> Assumption in the heuristic–systematic model that people strive for sufficient confidence in their attitudinal judgements. When a person's *actual confidence* is lower than his or her desired confidence or *sufficiency threshold,* he or she will process information in order to close this gap.

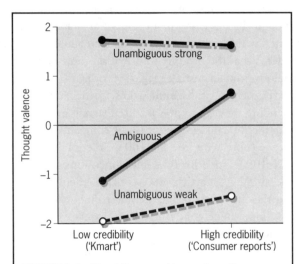

FIGURE 8.6 Heuristics may bias systematic processing. Thought valence is shown as a function of source credibility and message type (data from Chaiken & Maheswaran, 1994; high importance conditions only). The valence of product-related thoughts is biased by source credibility when message content is ambiguous

PLATE 8.2 Our attitudes towards different modes of transport involve a combination of different elements

AC would be large. A large gap between ST and AC may also be the result of a decrease in actual confidence. It has been shown that the AC may be decreased by a discrepancy in the valence of heuristic cues and content information, e.g., a majority of consumers favouring a product that is inferior to its competition (Maheswaran & Chaiken, 191). In recent studies, Bohner, Rank, Reinhard, Einwiller and Erb (1998) empirically demonstrated the mediating role of the sufficiency gap in effects of task importance on processing effort.

To summarize, both dual-processing models have had a tremendous impact on the field of persuasion. The ELM provides the more comprehensive framework, incorporating effortful processing as well as a variety of low-effort processes, and allowing distinctions between these processes and the various 'roles' a persuasion variable may play on an empirical basis. The HSM is more confined in its conceptualization of low-effort processing, but at the same time includes more specific assumptions about motivational processes and the interplay of its two processing modes. Both models fared well in empirical tests and helped to spur renewed interest in persuasion processes.

Change in behaviour can lead to attitude change

Rather than focusing on attitude change, interventions in many applied areas are directed at changing behaviour more immediately through *sanctions* or *incentives*

(see chapter 16). Legislators may increase the petrol tax with the aim of reducing individual car traffic; a health insurance company may offer reduced rates to people who participate in health promotion programmes. Thus, behaviour changes are brought about by changing the consequences of the behaviour. But would this behavioural change also result in any change of attitude? And if so, in what direction?

Reactance and overjustification

Psychological reactance An aversive state caused by restrictions to an individual's freedom of exerting choice over important behavioural alternatives, which in turn causes a motivational tendency to restore the restricted freedom.

Overjustification effect Rewarding individuals for performing a task they previously found interesting in itself (= overjustification) reduces their liking for the task.

Some research indicates that attitude change may often be opposite in direction to a change in behaviour. According to the theory of **psychological reactance** (Brehm, 1972), restricting a person's freedom of choice motivates the person to evaluate the eliminated alternatives more positively. Thus, the application of *sanctions* against smoking or other undesired behaviours may backfire, especially if the freedom to engage in the restricted behaviour is highly valued.

But offering *positive incentives* for engaging in desired behaviours may also have opposite consequences on attitudes, especially if those who receive the incentive have already been *intrinsically motivated* (i.e., held a positive attitude towards the behaviour). Even though the frequency or intensity of the behaviour may increase while the reward is applied, attitudes towards the behaviour may become *less* positive, a phenomenon known as the **overjustification effect** (Deci, 1971; Lepper, Greene, & Nisbett, 1973). For example, Lepper et al. (1973) provided preschoolers with an enjoyable new activity: drawing with 'magic markers'. After drawing for several minutes, some children were rewarded with a previously announced 'Good Player' certificate, others received the same reward unexpectedly, and still others received no reward. Two weeks later, the children were given the opportunity to play again with the markers. It was found that those children who had received the expected reward now spent only half as much time drawing compared with both the non-rewarded children and those who had been rewarded unexpectedly. These results have been explained in terms of self-perception theory (Bem, 1972). Those children who played with magic markers when a reward had been promised must have concluded that they did so *because* of the reward, and not so much because doing so was fun; the remaining children, who did not expect a reward, must have perceived themselves as drawing with the markers because they enjoyed doing so.

Cognitive dissonance Central construct in Festinger's theory of cognitive dissonance. An aversive state of arousal caused by cognitions (i.e., beliefs, attitudes, expectations) that are inconsistent with each other, motivating the individual to reduce dissonance by adding, subtracting or substituting cognitions to increase consistency.

Insufficient justification and cognitive dissonance

But there are also conditions under which attitudes are assimilated to a prior change in behaviour. The investigation of these conditions has been stimulated by the theory of **cognitive dissonance** (Festinger, 1957), the most famous cognitive consistency theory. According to dissonance theory, a person's thoughts, attitudes and beliefs ('cognitions') can be consonant, dissonant or irrelevant (i.e. unrelated) to each other. Holding dissonant beliefs creates *cognitive dissonance*, an unpleasant state of arousal which motivates the person to reduce the dissonance by adding, subtracting or substituting cognitions. For example, most employees would give up smoking at work after a ban on smoking had been introduced. Subsequently, the cognition 'I refrain from smoking at work' would be dissonant with the attitude 'I like to smoke' because, subjectively, the opposite of one would follow from the other (Festinger, 1957). One way of reducing dissonance is by adding further cognitions that make the cognitive system as a whole more consistent. In our example, the cognition 'If I smoked at work, I would lose my job' would reduce the dissonance and would thus enable the person to retain a positive attitude towards smoking. The non-smoking at work in spite of a positive attitude would be sufficiently justified by the expected sanctions connected with smoking. But what would happen if the person perceived that she *freely chose* to refrain from smoking, perhaps after a polite request from her co-worker? Under these conditions of **insufficient justification** of the attitude-discrepant behaviour, dissonance is likely to be reduced by substituting the dissonant attitude with an-other cognition that is more consonant: 'After all, I don't *really* like to smoke that much' – in other words, the person would be likely to change her attitude to justify her behaviour.

Insufficient justification The state of having shown an attitude-discrepant behaviour without perceiving an external reason for doing so; a special case of the conditions arousing cognitive dissonance.

This type of attitude change was first demonstrated by Festinger and Carlsmith (1959). In their experiment, students had to perform a lengthy series of extremely tedious tasks. Afterwards, a cover story was used to coax some participants into telling a lie – specifically, describing the experiment to a prospective participant (a confederate) as highly interesting. This *induced compliance* procedure was designed to create two dissonant cognitions: (a) 'I dislike this experiment' and (b) 'I just told the other student that it is interesting'. Furthermore, in one experimental condition, participants were promised 20 dollars – a small fortune at the time – for complying with the experimenter's request; in another condition, they were promised only one dollar. Festinger and Carlsmith reasoned that students in the one-dollar condition would experience a high level of cognitive dissonance, because they lacked sufficient external justification for their attitude-discrepant behaviour. In the 20-dollar condition, however, the high reward was predicted to keep the level of cognitive dissonance low ('OK, I've lied – but for 20 bucks, who wouldn't?'). As a consequence, students in the one-dollar condition would be likely to change their attitude about the experiment to bring it in line with their behaviour, thus reducing the dissonance, whereas students in the 20-dollar condition would not. Indeed, when students' post-behavioural attitudes towards the experiment were assessed, the 'one-dollar liars' reported that they found the experiment more enjoyable than did both the '20-dollar liars' and students in a control condition who had not been induced to lie.

In the decades that followed, hundreds of studies provided further evidence for dissonance effects; this research also delineated the conditions necessary for attitude-discrepant actions to produce attitude change (for an overview, see Cooper & Fazio, 1984; cf. Joule & Beauvois, 1998):

1 The person must perceive that the behaviour has *negative consequences* (e.g., Cooper & Brehm, 1971). This condition was given in the Festinger and Carlsmith study, as the confederate pretended that she had not made up her mind about participating and did so only after learning that the study would be interesting.

2 The person must take *personal responsibility* for the behaviour (e.g., Linder, Cooper, & Jones, 1967). In the Festinger and Carlsmith study, the experimenter's request was not perceived as part of the experiment proper, so participants could have refused to lie.

3 The person needs to *feel physiological arousal* and to *attribute this arousal to the attitude-discrepant behaviour*. Various studies showed that engaging in attitude-discrepant behaviour out of free will increases physiological arousal (e.g., Elkin & Leippe, 1986). In so-called 'misattribution' experiments (see chapter 7), some participants were led to believe that their arousal was caused by an unrelated event, for example a (placebo) pill, whereas other participants were not offered an unrelated explanation and thus were likely to attribute their arousal to its true cause: their attitude-discrepant behaviour. Only the participants not given the pill showed greater attitude change under high choice than under low choice (e.g., Zanna & Cooper, 1974).

Alternative interpretations of insufficient justification effects

Self-perception theory Theory proposed by Bem as an alternative to the theory of cognitive dissonance. Its main assumption is that individuals infer their own attitudes by engaging in attributional reasoning, just like an outside observer.

A major challenge for dissonance theory came from **self-perception theory** (Bem, 1965, 1972). Bem argued that internal cues are often weak or ambiguous. Thus, when people want to infer their own attitudes, they engage in attributional reasoning just like an outside observer. Generally, behaviour can have internal or external causes, and an internal cause (an attitude) will more likely be inferred to the extent that external causes cannot be identified (e.g., Kelley, 1972; see chapter 7). Thus, when students write an essay opposing freedom of speech and do not perceive a sufficient external reward for doing so (Linder et al., 1967), they are likely to infer that they really believe freedom of speech should be constrained. If, however, they are paid a large sum to write the essay, they should perceive their behaviour as externally caused and thus non-diagnostic of their true attitude.

Bem (1965) showed that participants to whom the procedures of induced-compliance experiments had merely been described made inferences about the true attitude of participants that replicated the actual result patterns. Bem concluded that for attitude change to occur, it was sufficient to have *information* about the behaviour and the conditions under which it occurred, whereas a *feeling* of negative arousal was not necessary. However, this alternative process assumption cannot accommodate the finding that misattribution of arousal to an irrelevant cause effectively undermined attitude change (e.g., Zanna & Cooper, 1974). A synthesis of dissonance and self-perception explanations was eventually proposed by Fazio, Zanna and Cooper (1977). They argued that self-perception theory better accounted for the effects of attitude-congruent advocacies (where the individual argues for a position close to their initial attitude), whereas dissonance theory was a better explanation for the effects of attitude-discrepant advocacies (involving positions clearly discrepant from initial attitudes).

Another alternative account of induced-compliance effects is *impression management theory* (Tedeschi, 1981). Impression management refers to the processes by which people try to create a desirable image of themselves in social interaction. The challenge for dissonance theory again lies in alternative assumptions about the processes which mediate attitude change. Impression management theorists assume that people strive for consistency in the image they create in others. Thus, as in dissonance theory, a consistency motive is invoked, but it is thought to operate at the public level of communicating the attitude to the experimenter, rather than at the level of the individual's private cognitions. In other words, participants are assumed to 'fake' an attitude which is in line with the discrepant behaviour, but do not 'really' change their attitudes.

According to impression-management logic, no change in the reported attitude should be found (a) if the attitude assessment is private and respondents are assured that their responses cannot be linked to them personally, or (b) if 'faking' responses is prevented by making participants believe that the experimenter can monitor their 'true attitude', no matter what their self-report may indicate. Studies that tested these assumptions yielded mixed evidence for impression management as a mediator of attitudinal responses (e.g., Gaes, Kalle, & Tedeschi, 1978; Stults, Messé, & Kerr, 1984). To conclude, it seems reasonable to assume that the accounts of cognitive dissonance and impression management complement rather than contradict each other. Concerns for self-presentation and the striving for cognitive consistency may both contribute to attitude change in varying degrees depending on the demands of the situation (Tetlock & Manstead, 1985). Having discussed the determinants of attitudes, we now turn to research on the consequences of attitudes.

The Consequences of Attitudes

How do attitudes influence attention, perception, elaboration and memory?
Under what conditions can we make a useful prediction of behaviour from people's attitudes?

Attitudes guide information processing

Attitudinal selectivity
Tendency to selectively attend to, process and remember information that is in line with one's attitude.

Work on **attitudinal selectivity** concerns the effects of attitudes on the selection and processing of new information. At the core of selectivity research has been the motivational assumption that people strive to maintain cognitive consistency by defending their attitudes (Festinger, 1957, 1964). This assumption was studied at all stages of the information-processing sequence (see chapter 5). We discuss effects of attitudes on attention and exposure, perception and judgement, elaboration and memory (see Eagly & Chaiken, 1998).

Selective attention and exposure

Selective exposure Dissonance theory assumes that people are motivated to search selectively for information that supports former decisions or existing attitudes, thereby actively avoiding opposing information.

Considering information that challenges one's attitudes may cause an unpleasant state of arousal (e.g., Festinger, 1964). Thus, people should actively seek out and direct their attention to information that is congruent with their existing attitudes (*congenial* information), and avoid or ignore information that is incongruent with these attitudes (*hostile* information). This **selective exposure** hypothesis has been tested in numerous studies (see Frey, 1986, for a review).

Most studies addressed an important qualification to the selective exposure hypothesis, namely that pronounced selectivity should mainly be observed when individuals are committed to their attitude by having made a behavioural decision, e.g., to buy a certain product (see Festinger, 1957). In such a situation, changing one's attitude to reduce dissonance should become less likely, and selective exposure more likely, than before a decision has been made. In one study by Frey and Rosch (1984), students were given information about a manager's work performance; then they were asked to judge his performance and to decide whether the manager's contract should be extended. Depending on experimental condition, this decision was said to be either definitive or reversible. After participants had made a decision about the manager's future, they got the opportunity to review additional information about him. These pieces of information were labelled in a way that unambiguously conveyed a positive or negative evaluation (e.g., '[The manager] has done a good job and therefore his contract should be extended'). Results supported the selective exposure hypothesis: students who had made an irreversible decision selected twice as many pieces of consonant as dissonant information, whereas students who had made only a tentative decision selected roughly equal amounts of congenial and hostile information.

According to Frey's (1986) review, available research supports the notion that selective exposure effects occur mainly for persons who are committed to their initial attitude through a behavioural decision. Frey further reports that there is weaker evidence for avoidance of hostile information than for exposure to congenial information. Finally, evidence for the operation of motives other than cognitive consistency was also observed. In particular, people sometimes prefer information that is useful for goal attainment as well as unfamiliar information, irrespective of its congruence with their attitudes (see Eagly & Chaiken, 1998).

Selective perception and judgement

In daily life, we cannot always avoid hostile information. However, Festinger (1957) suggested that under conditions of 'forced exposure', people perceive hostile information in a distorted way, whereas they perceive congenial information more accurately. Generally, the hypothesis that people disparage information that challenges their own position has received ample support. For instance, students who had read articles for and against capital punishment rated evidence that supported their own attitude towards capital punishment as more convincing than information that questioned their attitude. Furthermore, reading information on both sides led to a polarization of attitudes: those who were initially in favour of capital punishment became even more favourable, whereas those who were initially opposed became even more opposed (Lord, Ross, & Lepper, 1979). Such selective judgement effects seem to be more pronounced for stronger attitudes (e.g., Houston & Fazio, 1989) and to result from an active transformation of evidence, including biased elaboration and counterarguing (e.g., Cacioppo & Petty, 1979).

Selective elaboration and memory

Bartlett (1995 [1932]) proposed that recall may be selective due to the operation of attitudinal schemata, and other early researchers found evidence consistent with the view that congenial material would be remembered better than hostile material (e.g., Levine & Murphy, 1943). Mixed findings were reported in subsequent research, and quantitative reviews (e.g., Eagly, Chen, Chaiken, & Shaw-Barnes, 1999) concluded that there is a reliable albeit small congeniality effect in memory overall. Importantly, Eagly and her colleagues reported that the relationship between attitudes and the recall of attitude-relevant information varies widely in size and direction. Effects were smaller in more recent studies, and many studies even found better recall for hostile than for congenial information (e.g., Cacioppo & Petty, 1979). Furthermore, congeniality effects were moderated by the kind of issue studied. Issues for which value-relevant involvement was high (e.g., attitudes linked to important personal values or reference groups) were more likely to produce congeniality effects than issues low in value-relevant involvement. However, highly controversial issues were less likely to produce a congeniality effect than uncontroversial ones. These findings may be due to differences in the processing strategies people use when defending their attitudes. On one hand, people may try to ignore hostile information, especially if it threatens important values. But they may also actively confront and counterargue such information to the extent that the topic is controversial. The latter strategy would enhance rather than reduce memory for hostile information.

One of the conditions that facilitate or inhibit the operation of more active vs. more passive strategies of attitudinal defence may lie in the structure of attitude representations. As Pratkanis (1989) suggested, people can possess *unipolar* and *bipolar attitudes*, and more controversial topics are more likely to be represented in a bipolar structure. Thus, it may be easier to encode and actively counter-argue opposing information if the relevant attitude structure is bipolar rather than unipolar (see section on attitude structure above). Furthermore, research by Eagly and her colleagues (discussed in Eagly, 1998) showed that, although congenial and hostile information may be recalled equally well, the *processes* at both encoding and retrieval may differ substantially, with more effortful processing (including counterarguing) directed at recalling hostile information.

In sum, attitudes have been shown to influence the perception, interpretation, judgement and recall of attitude-relevant information. These influences seem to be more powerful for strong attitudes, which are easily accessible and based on an elaborate knowledge structure.

Attitudes as predictors of behaviour

One major reason why attitudes are studied is the belief that attitudes cause behaviour. This seems to be a highly plausible belief. Is it not obvious that people eat pizza because they like it or vote for politicians they like? It seems so, but research has shown that things are often not that simple. Research on attitude–behaviour relations is devoted to explaining the conditions under which attitudes predict behaviour, and the cognitive processes involved.

Is there an influence of attitudes on behaviour?

A seminal paper questioning the assumption that attitudes guide behaviour was published by LaPiere (1934). In the early 1930s, this author travelled across the USA in the company of a Chinese couple. Given the then-prevailing prejudice against people of Asian origin, LaPiere had expected that he and his Chinese companions would often be refused service by hotels or restaurants. To his surprise, however, this happened in only one of the 251 establishments they visited. Six months later, LaPiere mailed questionnaires to all the places visited, asking if they would accept 'members of the Chinese race' as guests. In line with the prevailing stereotype, but in stark contrast to their prior behaviour, 118 (92 per cent) of the 128 places who returned the questionnaire responded 'no'. LaPiere concluded that questionnaire responses do not validly reflect a person's true attitude.

Of course there are several flaws in LaPiere's (1934) study. To name a few: the people who answered the survey were usually not the ones who had admitted the guests; attitudes were assessed long *after* the behaviour in question; and the attitude object, an English-speaking couple accompanied by a white American, may not have been encoded as 'members of the Chinese race' when the behaviour was shown. Despite these problems, LaPiere's work and other studies, which also failed to find a clear relation of attitudes and behaviour, contributed to a generally pessimistic view on the possibility of predicting behaviour from attitudes (Wicker, 1969). In some studies, however, the prediction of behaviour from attitudes was quite successful (e.g., Fishbein & Coombs, 1974; for a review, see Ajzen & Fishbein, 1977). This variability in findings suggested that the question *whether* there exists a relationship between attitudes and behaviour was too undifferentiated. Thus, attitude researchers addressed more specific questions: 'Can improvements in measurement enhance prediction of behaviour from attitudes?'; 'What factors moderate the strength of attitude–behaviour relations?'; 'What are the mediating processes by which attitudes influence behaviour?' (Zanna & Fazio, 1982).

The correspondence principle One reason for failures to find strong attitude–behaviour relations lies in the lack of correspondence of the two measures. Both attitudes and behaviours can be specified with respect to four characteristics: (1) the *action* itself; (2) its *target*; (3) the *context* in which it is performed; and (4) the *time component* (Ajzen & Fishbein, 1977). It is unlikely that one can accurately predict any *specific* behaviour (e.g., 'attending a particular religious service next Sunday') from a *global* measure of attitude (e.g., a questionnaire on attitudes towards religion). But exactly this approach was taken in most early studies. According to Ajzen and Fishbein, a close relation between attitude and behaviour will obtain only if both measures agree in their degree of specification (**correspondence principle**). Reviewing relevant studies, these authors found that correlations between attitude and behaviour were indeed larger in those studies where specification of both measures was similar (see also Kraus, 1995).

> **Correspondence principle** (also **compatibility principle**) This principle states that a close relation between attitude and behaviour will obtain only if both measures agree in their degree of specification.

The correspondence principle was demonstrated directly by Davidson and Jaccard (1979), who predicted women's use of birth control pills over a two-year period from attitudinal measures varying in specificity. The attitude–behaviour correlation increased dramatically with increasing correspondence of measures, from $r = 0.08$ when a global attitude towards 'birth control' was used, to $r = 0.57$ when the attitude measure concerned 'using birth control pills during the next two years'. Note, however, that increasing the prediction of specific behaviours involves a shift on the predictor side from *attitudes towards objects* to the narrower concept of *attitudes towards behaviour*.

The aggregation principle Complementing the strategy of maximizing specificity, Fishbein and Ajzen (1974) proposed that researchers should use *multiple acts* to optimize prediction from global measures of attitude. Much as reliability increases with number of items in a scale (Cronbach, 1951), when aggregating across multiple behaviours, sampled over various contexts and points in time, any

Aggregation principle This principle states that global measures of attitude are better at predicting global measures of behaviour, which aggregate over a variety of situations and points in time, than any specific instances of behaviour.

determinants of these behaviours other than the attitude in question tend to cancel each other out in the aggregate score. A field study by Weigel and Newman (1976) illustrates the **aggregation principle**. These researchers assessed town residents' general attitudes towards the environment with a 16-item scale. Later, at different points in time, the respondents were given the opportunity to engage in various pro-environmental behaviours (e.g., signing a petition against off-shore oil drilling; participating in a kerbside recycling programme), and their participation was unobtrusively recorded. Even though the general attitude did not predict well most of the specific behaviours, its correlation with an *aggregated* behavioural measure was impressive (see table 8.2).

Conceptual correspondence From a conceptual point of view, other forms of attitude–behaviour correspondence have been discussed. For example, attitudes and behaviour are more closely related if those *functions of an attitude* that are salient at the time of attitude measurement are also salient at the time the behaviour is performed (Shavitt & Fazio, 1991; Tesser & Shaffer, 1990). Shavitt and Fazio (1991, Study 1) investigated students' attitudes and behavioural intentions towards each of two different drinks: Perrier mineral water and 7-Up lemonade. They reasoned that Perrier would be mainly liked based on the trendy 'image' or social impression it conveys, whereas 7-Up would be mainly liked for its taste. In

PLATE 8.3   'Image' vs. 'taste'?

TABLE 8.2 General attitude as a predictor of behavioural criteria varying in generality

Correlations of environmental attitude (16-item measure) with . . .					
Single behaviours[a]	r	Categories of behaviour	r	Fully aggregated behaviour index	r
Signing petitions:					
Offshore oil	0.41**	Petitioning behaviour scale	0.50**		
Nuclear power	0.36*				
Auto exhaust	0.39**				
Circulate petitions	0.27				
Roadside litter pick-up:				Behaviour index	0.62***
Participation	0.34*	Litter pick-up scale	0.36*		
Recruit friend	0.22				
Participation in kerbside recycling programme:					
Week 1	0.34*				
Week 2	0.57***				
Week 3	0.34*	Recycling behaviour scale	0.39**		
Week 4	0.33*				
Week 5	0.12				
Week 6	0.20				
Week 7	0.20				
Week 8	0.34*				

Note: Data from Weigel and Newman (1976). $N = 44$.
[a] The behaviours listed in the first column were each coded 0 (= not performed) or 1 (= performed) and then summed to form the respective indices.
* $p < 0.05$; ** $p < 0.01$; *** $p < 0.001$.

Shavitt and Fazio's experiment, either the image aspect or the taste aspect was made salient prior to judging the two drinks. This was done by asking some participants to rate 20 food items for their taste, whereas others were asked to rate the social impressions that each of 20 actions would create. Later, participants' attitudes towards Perrier and 7-Up as well as their intentions to buy each of these drinks were assessed. Shavitt and Fazio reasoned that buying intentions would be more strongly influenced by attitudes when the attitude function that was salient matched (rather than mismatched) the attitude function that is naturally served by the attitude object. Supporting these predictions, students' intentions to buy Perrier were more highly correlated with their attitudes towards Perrier when they had previously thought about social impression ($r = 0.87$) rather than taste

($r = 0.36$). By contrast, students' intentions to buy 7-Up were more highly correlated with their attitudes towards 7-Up when they had previously thought about taste ($r = 0.88$) rather than social impression ($r = 0.46$).

Findings implying that *thinking about the reasons why one holds a certain attitude* may increase or decrease the attitude–behaviour correlation (Wilson, Dunn, Kraft, & Lisle, 1989) can also be understood as an instance of variations in conceptual correspondence. Given that thinking about *reasons* emphasizes cognitive aspects of an attitude, it should increase attitude–behaviour correlations if the cognitive component is accessible at the time the behaviour is performed, but decrease correspondence if performing the behaviour is mainly based on the affective attitude component (see also Millar & Tesser, 1986).

Moderators of the attitude–behaviour relation

Various indicators of *attitude strength* have been proposed as moderators of the attitude–behaviour relation (see Petty & Krosnick, 1995). One general hypothesis guiding this approach is that strong attitudes are better predictors of behaviour than weak attitudes. We discuss strength in terms of *intra-attitudinal consistency*, *accessibility* and *cognitive effort in attitude formation*.

Intra-attitudinal consistency   Above we discussed how cognitive and affective components vary in their degree of consistency with attitude as an overall evaluation. (A person may believe that many actions of a government have harmful consequences, yet evaluate the government positively on the whole.) Rosenberg (1968) discovered that high evaluative–cognitive consistency (ECC) of an attitude is related to high temporal stability and resistance against persuasion attempts. This suggested the hypothesis that high ECC attitudes may also be better predictors of behaviour. Norman (1975) found support for this hypothesis when comparing attitude–behaviour correlations between groups of high vs. low ECC participants.

Accessibility   Fazio (1990) developed a theory that highlights the role of attitude accessibility as a moderator of attitude–behaviour consistency. This development was originally inspired by work on the role of *direct experience with the attitude object* in predicting behaviour. Regan and Fazio (1977) proposed that direct behavioural experience produces an attitude that is held with more clarity, confidence and stability than an attitude formed through indirect information about the attitude object. These attributes should render experience-based attitudes more accessible and should ultimately produce greater attitude–behaviour consistency. In one experiment, college students formed attitudes towards five types of intellectual puzzle, either through direct experience (by working through an example of each) or through indirect experience (by examining examples that had already been solved). When the students were later observed in a free-play situation, their attitudes towards each puzzle predicted the extent to which it was played more closely for students in the direct-experience condition than for students in the indirect-experience condition (Regan & Fazio, 1977; for a review, see Fazio & Zanna, 1981).

The process assumed to mediate this effect is the attitude's accessibility, operationally defined as the speed of attitude expression (Fazio, 1990). Conceptually, accessibility reflects the strength of association between the representation of the attitude object and an evaluation stored in memory. To guide behaviour, this evaluation needs to be activated. Indeed, Fazio and others have shown that attitudes based on behavioural experience are more accessible (e.g., Fazio, Chen, McDonel, & Sherman, 1982) and that greater attitude accessibility goes along with greater attitude–behaviour consistency (e.g., Fazio & Williams, 1986; for an application to consumer behaviour, see Kokkinaki & Lunt, 1997). Although it is plausible that attitude accessibility is an important mediator of attitudes' influence on behaviour, direct experience may bring about greater attitude–behaviour consistency through other mediating processes (Eagly & Chaiken, 1998), e.g., by increasing the temporal stability of an attitude (Doll & Ajzen, 1992). Further research is thus needed to disentangle the effects of accessibility from those of other aspects of attitude strength in mediating attitudes' impact on behaviour.

Cognitive effort in attitude formation   Variations in processing effort are at the core of dual-process models of persuasion (see above). According to these models, high motivation and ability lead to the formation of attitudes via effortful processing of relevant information, whereas low motivation or ability leads to lower processing effort and reliance on simple cues. Especially within the ELM, these routes to attitude formation have been linked to different degrees of attitude–behaviour consistency. Petty and Cacioppo (1986a, b) postulated that attitudes which were formed via the central route are more predictive of behaviour than attitudes formed via the peripheral route. Various research findings are compatible with this hypothesis by showing that the attitudes of individuals who processed under high-relevance conditions were more predictive of behaviour than those of people who processed under low-relevance conditions (for a review, see Petty et al., 1995; for applications to consumer behaviour, see Haugtvedt & Priester, 1997).

As we have already discussed, the *need for cognition* construct reflects individual differences in processing effort (Cacioppo & Petty, 1982; Cacioppo et al., 1996). As individuals high in NC engage in greater processing effort when forming an attitude, they should form stronger attitudes, which are highly predictive of behaviour. Consistent with this view, Cacioppo, Petty, Kao and Rodriguez (1986) found that attitudes towards US presidential candidates of students high in NC were better predictors of voting behaviour than attitudes of low-NC students.

Attitudes and behaviour: Interim summary and a note on causality   In sum, the correlation between attitude and behaviour is strong to the extent that both measures correspond in specificity or aggregation, and that similar aspects, functions and components of an attitude are salient at the time both attitude and behaviour are measured. Furthermore, indicators of attitude strength have been identified as moderators of the attitude–behaviour relation. It should be emphasized, however, that high *correlations* between attitude and behaviour are *not* sufficient to infer that attitudes *cause* behaviour. As we have seen, one alternative is that behaviour may influence attitudes, and another is that third variables, such as salient context-dependent beliefs, influence both attitude reports and behaviour. To the extent that the context remains stable, this would result in higher attitude–behaviour correlations without a direct causal link between the two constructs (Schwarz & Bohner, in press; Wilson & Hodges, 1992).

One possibility of establishing a causal link between attitude and behaviour is by experimentally manipulating the salience of an attitude before assessing a related behaviour. A causal influence of attitude on behaviour is indicated by a larger correlation in those conditions in which the attitude has been made salient, and thus more accessible. Using such a methodology, Snyder and Swann (1976) measured students' attitudes towards affirmative action. Two weeks later, the same students were asked to give their verdict in a sex-discrimination case (the behavioural measure). Some students were instructed to 'organize [their] thoughts and views about the affirmative action issue' (p. 1037), to increase the salience of their attitudes prior to the verdict; whereas others did not receive such an instruction. In the no-instruction condition, the favourability of the verdicts was unrelated to participants' attitudes, $r = 0.07$. In the condition in which attitudes had been made salient, however, the attitude–behaviour correlation was substantial, $r = 0.58$ (see also Bohner, Reinhard, et al., 1998; Snyder & Kendzierski, 1982).

Attitudes and other determinants of behaviour: expectancy-value models

Expectancy-value models
These models assume that decisions between different courses of action are based on two types of cognitions: (1) the subjective probabilities that a given action will lead to a set of expected outcomes, and (2) the valence of these outcomes. According to this approach, individuals will choose among various alternative courses of action the one that maximizes the likelihood of positive consequences and/or minimizes the likelihood of negative consequences.

Theory of reasoned action The most important classic theory

In the previous sections we have seen that attitudes are just one determinant of behaviour. Recognizing the importance of other determinants, a family of theories has been developed which placed attitudes in a network of predictor variables (e.g., Ajzen, 1991; Bentler & Speckart, 1979; Fishbein & Ajzen, 1975). They are called **expectancy-value models** (see Feather, 1982) because they define attitudes in terms of expectancy × value-products.

The initial formulation, Fishbein and Ajzen's (1975) **theory of reasoned action**, is displayed in figure 8.7 (top panel). According to the theory of reasoned action, the proximal cause of behaviour is *behavioural intention*, a conscious decision to engage in a certain behaviour. Any influences on behaviour that the theory accounts for are assumed to be mediated by this construct. The two major determinants of intention are attitude towards the behaviour and subjective norm. *Attitude towards the behaviour* is defined as the sum of expectancy × value-products. Each of these products consists of the subjective probability (= expectancy) that the behaviour has a certain consequence, multiplied by the value attached to this consequence.

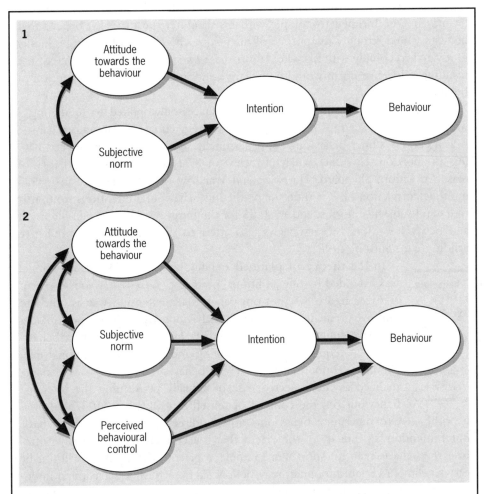

FIGURE 8.7   Schematic depiction of the theory of reasoned action (top panel) and the theory of planned behaviour (bottom panel). The theory of planned behaviour extends the theory of reasoned action by including perceived behavioural control as an additional predictor

(Adapted from Ajzen & Madden, 1986)

For example, a person may expect that by using the bus instead of driving she will certainly save money (a positive consequence with high likelihood), but may occasionally be late for work (a negative consequence with low likelihood). These two aspects combined would yield a moderately positive attitude towards using the bus.

The perceived social consequences of the behaviour are treated separately, forming the construct of *subjective norm*. This second determinant of behavioural intention is also defined as a sum of products, each product consisting of the belief that a significant other person thinks one should perform the behaviour, and the motivation to comply with this other person. For instance,

of the relationship between attitude and behaviour. Assumes that attitudes and subjective norms jointly predict behavioural intentions and thus behaviour.

a person may believe that his daughter thinks he should buy a sports car, but he may not be inclined to comply with his daughter; he may also believe that his wife would strongly disapprove of his buying the car, and he may be highly motivated to comply with his wife. If just these two referents are considered, the resulting subjective norm would be negative and would weaken the intention of buying the car.

The theory of reasoned action has been successfully applied to predicting a wide variety of behaviours, including simple strategy choices in laboratory games, health and consumer behaviours, and personally significant actions such as having an abortion. In a meta-analytic review of 87 studies testing the theory of reasoned action, Sheppard, Hartwick and Warshaw (1988) reported an overall multiple correlation of $R = 0.66$ for predicting behavioural intentions from attitudes and subjective norms, and $r = 0.53$ for the mean relation between intention and behaviour. More recent reviews also attest to the theory's high predictive validity (e.g., Sutton, 1998).

Theory of planned behaviour An extension of the theory of reasoned action. Besides attitudes and subjective norms, perceived behavioural control is included as a third predictor of behavioural intention and behaviour.

In the **theory of planned behaviour** (Ajzen, 1991), the model was extended by one additional predictor: *perceived behavioural control* (see figure 8.7, bottom panel). This extension was assumed to improve prediction especially for behaviours over which a person does not have complete voluntary control, for example, complex behaviours that require extensive planning and the right conditions (e.g., climbing a mountain). Perceived behavioural control was conceptualized as the expected ease of actually performing the intended behaviour (cf. the concept of self-efficacy; Bandura, 1977a). It was hypothesized to determine behaviour either indirectly, via influencing behavioural intention, or directly to the extent that it accurately reflects actual control over the behaviour in question. For example, a person who thinks it will not be easy to climb a certain mountain may be less likely to form a behavioural intention of doing so; she may also, however, be less likely to succeed once she has formed the intention to act, because it may indeed be difficult for her to perform the behaviour.

To illustrate research on expectancy-value models, let us look at a study conducted by Ajzen and Madden (1986, Experiment 2), which was designed to demonstrate the predictive superiority of the theory of planned behaviour over the theory of reasoned action. The participants were US business students; the target behaviour was getting an 'A' (the best grade) in a course. At two points in time – early in the semester and one week prior to final examinations – the researchers assessed students' attitudes towards 'receiving an "A" in this course', their subjective norms regarding this behaviour, and their perceived control over this behaviour. Specifically, attitude was measured by asking students to evaluate ten salient consequences of receiving an 'A' (e.g., raising one's grade point average; making friends feel awkward) on a *good–bad* scale, and also to rate the probability of each of these consequences from *unlikely* to *likely*. A belief-based measure of attitude was derived by summing the products of these two ratings over all ten consequences. To assess subjective norm, the participants indicated how much each of five referents (e.g., the course teacher; their family) would *approve* vs. *disapprove* of their getting an 'A', and how much they were motivated to comply with each referent (*very much* to *not at all*). A belief-based measure was formed by summing the products of these two ratings. Perceived behavioural control was measured by summing over eight beliefs that dealt with facilitating or inhibiting factors (e.g., involvement in extracurricular activities; the student's skills).

The main dependent variables in the analysis were behavioural intentions, measured with three items (e.g., 'I will try my best to get an "A" in this course'), and actual grades obtained. For each dependent variable at each time of measurement, two-step hierarchical regression analyses were performed. Their first step represented a test of the theory of reasoned action, and their second step represented a test of the theory of planned behaviour. Thus,

- behavioural intentions were predicted in a first step from attitude and subjective norm, and in a second step jointly from these two predictors and perceived behavioural control;
- behaviour (i.e., grade obtained) was predicted in a first step from intention and in a second step jointly from intention and perceived control.

Ajzen and Madden (1986) hypothesized that early in the semester perceptions of behavioural control would be quite inaccurate reflections of actual control. Therefore the inclusion of perceived behavioural control would improve the prediction of actual behaviour only indirectly via better prediction of behavioural intentions, but not directly. Late in the semester, however, students' perceptions of control should have become more accurate as they have gained experience with factors facilitating or inhibiting success; this would lead to improved prediction of actual behaviour both indirectly via intentions and directly.

These hypotheses were supported. When measured early in the semester, attitudes and subjective norm showed a substantial multiple correlation of $R = 0.48$ with behavioural intention, attesting to the validity of the theory of reasoned action. But the multiple correlation was significantly increased to $R = 0.65$ when perceived behavioural control was included as a further predictor. Furthermore, intention was correlated at $R = 0.26$ with the grade actually obtained, and including perceived behavioural control as a concurrent predictor did not increase the magnitude of this coefficient.

When measured late in the semester, attitude and subjective norm yielded a multiple correlation of $R = 0.49$ in predicting intentions; again, this was significantly improved to $R = 0.64$ when perceived behavioural control was included in the model. Also, when measured late in the semester, perceived control significantly improved the prediction of actual grade obtained: intention alone yielded $R = 0.39$; intention and perceived control together yielded $R = 0.45$. These results suggest that the theory of planned behaviour outperforms the theory of reasoned action in predicting behavioural intentions (and behaviour) when the behaviour under study is difficult to perform. However, other studies indicate that this is not the case for behaviours that can easily be performed, e.g., attending a meeting (Kelly & Breinlinger, 1995).

Other extensions of the theory of reasoned action have been proposed (see Eagly & Chaiken, 1993). Some theorists noted that behaviour can be influenced by *previous behaviour* or *habit*, and that these influences are not necessarily mediated by attitudes, subjective norms or intentions (e.g., Bentler & Speckart, 1979). A meta-analysis (Ouellette & Wood, 1998) indicates that past behaviour significantly contributes to the prediction of future behaviour along either of two pathways: well-practised behaviours in stable contexts (e.g., seatbelt use) recur because the processing that controls them becomes automatic; frequency of prior behaviour then reflects habit strength and *directly* affects future behaviour. Behaviours that are less well learned or occur in unstable contexts remain under the control of conscious processing; under these circumstances, past behaviour may influence future behaviour *indirectly via intentions*.

These findings relate to the more general criticism that both the theory of reasoned action and the theory of planned behaviour are limited in scope to conscious and deliberate behaviours, whereas they do not predict well behaviour that is not consciously intended and not based on deliberation about consequences (e.g., Fazio, 1990). Ajzen and Fishbein (1980) disputed this criticism by emphasizing that their model leaves room for the possibility that a behavioural intention has once been formed in the past, and that people may retrieve this previously formed intention rather than deliberating anew each time they engage in the behaviour in question.

MODE model The MODE (motivation and opportunity as determinants of how attitudes influence behaviour) model assumes that attitudes can influence behaviour either by the deliberate processing of the attitudinal implications for behaviour or by the automatic selective processing of attitude-relevant information.

Fazio (1990), however, delineated the conditions under which *attitudes toward targets* can activate behaviour immediately and automatically. In his **MODE model** ('motivation and opportunity as determinants'), *motivation* and *opportunity* deliberately moderate the processes through which behaviour is controlled (cf. the dual-process models of persuasion discussed above). When an individual lacks motivation or opportunity to decide deliberately about performing a behaviour, highly accessible attitudes about the target can automatically guide behaviour by affecting the perception of the situation. Although the assumption that only highly accessible attitudes can be automatically activated has been disputed (Bargh et al., 1992), Fazio's position is generally consistent with accumulating evidence showing that social behaviour may largely be subject to unconscious influences (for an overview, see Bargh, 1997; see also chapter 5).

In sum, expectancy-value theories have used a narrow definition of *attitude towards behaviour* (beliefs about the likelihood and value of behavioural consequences) and have relegated the attitude concept to the background as one among many predictors of behaviour. Through this increased specification they achieved considerable predictive power, especially in applied areas in which deliberate behaviours are studied (for reviews, see Ajzen, 1991; Sheppard et al., 1988; Sutton,

1998; for more empirical examples, see chapters 16 and 17). Conversely, in Fazio's (1990) MODE model, the broader concept of *attitude towards a target* is back at centre-stage when it comes to predicting behaviour under circumstances of low motivation or lack of opportunity to deliberate.

Summary and Conclusions

In this chapter we discussed basic issues in attitude research and reviewed theories and findings concerning the determinants and consequences of attitudes. Attitudes are summary evaluations of objects comprising affective, cognitive and behavioural components and serving important functions for the individual. The major determinants of attitudes that were studied by social psychologists are the processing of attitude-relevant information and prior behaviour. Striving for cognitive consistency, people often change their attitudes to bring them in line with their behaviour. Attitudes also change as people learn to associate the attitude object with pleasant or unpleasant contexts or consequences. But persuasion research in the last quarter of the twentieth century has focused on the thoughts that people actively generate – in response to the attitude object or information about it – as the main mediators of attitude change. Reflecting a general integrative trend in social psychology, dual-process models portray attitude change as an interplay of effortless and effortful processes, which are a function of cognitive, experiential and motivational factors.

Research on the effects of attitudes looked at information processing and, most importantly, behaviour. Attitudes were shown to influence all stages of the information-processing sequence, ranging from attention to recall. A congeniality bias is often found, but attitudes may also instigate active counterarguing of discrepant information rather than a simple preference for attitude-congruent information. Over the last three decades, research in the attitude–behaviour domain has more than dispelled the early pessimism that attitudes are poor predictors of behaviour. Attitudes do predict behaviour to the extent that the two constructs correspond in specificity and that similar aspects of the attitude object are salient at the time each construct is measured. Furthermore, the prediction of behaviour can be improved by taking into account other predictor variables as well as the processes involved in attitude formation and retrieval.

1   What functions do attitudes serve for the individual? Give examples for each attitude function.
2   In what sense can an attitude structure be more or less consistent?
3   According to balance theory, how are attitudes towards objects and attitudes towards other persons linked in a perceiver's mind?

DISCUSSION POINTS

4   Under what conditions is counter-attitudinal behaviour likely to result in attitude change?
5   Discuss the relationship between argument quality, source cues, motivation and ability to process in dual-process models of persuasion.
6   What is attitudinal selectivity?
7   Under what conditions are attitudes good predictors of behaviour?

FURTHER READING

Ajzen, I. (1991). The theory of planned behavior. *Organizational Behavior and Human Decision Processes*, 50, 179–211. This article presents the currently most popular theory on the attitude–behaviour relationship and reviews relevant empirical findings.

Chaiken, S., & Trope, Y. (Eds.). (1999). *Dual-process theories in social psychology*. New York: Guilford Press. This recently published reader presents state-of-the-art reviews of the dual-process approach, both within and beyond the attitudes domain, including recent critiques and controversies.

Eagly, A. H., & Chaiken, S. (1993). *The psychology of attitudes*. Fort Worth, TX: Harcourt Brace Jovanovich. The most comprehensive and integrative advanced-level textbook of attitude research.

Eagly, A. H., & Chaiken, S. (1998). Attitude structure and function. In D. T. Gilbert, S. T. Fiske, & G. Lindzey (Eds.), *The handbook of social psychology* (4th ed., pp. 269–322). New York: McGraw-Hill. An up-to-date reference chapter on issues of attitude structure and function.

Petty, R. E., & Wegener, D. T. (1998a). Attitude change: Multiple roles for persuasion variables. In D. T. Gilbert, S. T. Fiske, & G. Lindzey (Eds.), *The handbook of social psychology* (4th ed., Vol. 2, pp. 323–90). New York: McGraw-Hill. A recent reference chapter on the area of attitude change.

Tesser, A., & Martin, L. L. (1996). The psychology of evaluation. In E. T. Higgins & A. W. Kruglanski (Eds.), *Social psychology: Handbook of basic principles* (pp. 400–32). New York: Guilford Press. A multifaceted treatment of the concept of evaluation, addressing its sociocognitive, functional, biological and cultural aspects.

KEY STUDIES

Ajzen, I., & Madden, T. J. (1986). Prediction of goal-directed behavior: Attitudes, intentions, and perceived behavioral control. *Journal of Experimental Social Psychology*, 22, 453–74.

Petty, R. E., Cacioppo, J. T., & Goldman, R. (1981). Personal involvement as a determinant of argument-based persuasion. *Journal of Personality and Social Psychology*, 41, 847–55.

Social Interaction and Personal Relationships

PART III

CONTENTS

Prosocial Behaviour

9

Hans W. Bierhoff

OUTLINE

This chapter deals with 'prosocial behaviour', in which an actor tries to help another person. The actor is not motivated by the fulfilment of professional obligations, and the recipient is a person and not an organization. Related terms which have a slightly different meaning are 'helping behaviour' and 'altruism'. This chapter aims to answer the question: why do people help one another? Biological, individualistic, interpersonal and social-systems theory are taken into account. Two of the most important explanatory concepts are empathy and social responsibility. The theories complement each other and may be applied in combination in the prediction of prosocial behaviour. Pioneering studies on emergency intervention show that situational influences on prosocial behaviour are quite strong. The emphasis on situational influences must, however, be supplemented by an emphasis on individual differences which come into focus in the altruistic personality. Finally, the psychology of receiving help is discussed.

KEY CONCEPTS

- Diffusion of responsibility
- Empathy
- Evaluation apprehension
- Interpersonal guilt
- Just-world belief
- Pluralistic ignorance
- Reciprocity (norm of)
- Social responsibility (norm of)

Introduction

What is prosocial behaviour?

Consider the following story in a newspaper article. The director of the Bochum theatre in Germany knocked down his assistant director in the theatre's cafeteria. The director was obviously drunk. The fight ended when the assistant lay motionless on the floor. Although the fight lasted for several minutes, not one of the dozens of witnesses intervened.[1]

Today's altruist may be tomorrow's passive bystander; it all depends on the social situation. This is the message of Latané and Darley's (1969) well-known article on bystander apathy. If the first witnesses do not intervene, they encourage reserve and passivity on the part of other witnesses. In contrast, if a model acts altruistically, the chances are high that bystanders will do the same (Rushton, 1980).

The terms 'helping behaviour', 'prosocial behaviour' and 'altruism' describe interactions between helpers and help-recipients. While the helpers incur costs, the help-recipients receive rewards which are usually higher than the costs of the helpers. Whereas 'helping' is the broadest term, the definition of 'prosocial behaviour' is narrower in that the action is intended to improve the situation of the help-recipient, the actor is not motivated by the fulfilment of professional obligations, and the recipient is a person and not an organization. Finally, the term 'altruism' has an additional constraint, namely that the helper's motivation is characterized by perspective-taking and empathy. The overlap among these three terms is illustrated in figure 9.1. In general, prosocial behaviour may result either from the ultimate goal to benefit oneself (egoistically motivated behaviour) or from the ultimate goal to benefit another person (altruistically motivated behaviour). In this chapter, the middle-level term 'prosocial behaviour', which includes egoistically and altruistically motivated helping behaviour, is generally used because

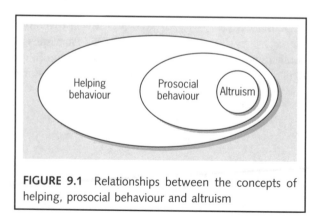

FIGURE 9.1   Relationships between the concepts of helping, prosocial behaviour and altruism

it refers to the central issues of this chapter. The term 'altruistic behaviour' is used only to emphasize the fact that a particular behaviour is altruistically motivated.

An example of helping is the stewardess who assists a passenger with her luggage. An example of prosocial behaviour would be a person who, expecting some help in the future in return, assists her neighbour with an insurance form. Finally, a classic example of altruism is the parable of the Good Samaritan. Many of those who saved Jews during the Nazi terror in Europe provide further examples of true altruists. Steven Spielberg's film *Schindler's List* recounts the true story of the dramatic rescue of more than 1,000 Jews from Nazi Germany by German industrialist Oskar Schindler. He took great personal risks and invested both time and money to find ways of helping Jews to escape from the Nazis.

Whereas the Samaritan's altruistic behaviour was not observed by bystanders, other forms of prosocial behaviour take place in public. Consider, for example, the emergency aid for Africa organized by Bob Geldof in 1985, or the Diana, Princess of Wales tribute CD. These modern examples of generosity make it clear that prosocial responses need not be without personal gain. For example, opera stars

PLATE 9.1 Net Aid – the global concert in aid of the starving in Ethiopia – is a modern example of altruism

such as Placido Domingo and pop stars like Rod Stewart might gain an advantage by sacrificing time and money for people in need, because acting prosocially might promote their records. In addition, many people will admire them for their unselfishness. In many cases, prosocial behaviour may be based on a mixture of egoistically motivated and altruistically motivated sources (Batson, Duncan, Ackerman, Buckley, & Birch, 1981).

Prosocial behaviour also varies with respect to the effort that is involved. On the one hand, people give small amounts of money to beggars sitting on the pavement or at the entrance to an underground station. They pick up fallen groceries or return an overpayment. On the other hand, they jump into a river to save a child's life or rush into a burning building to rescue the occupants. These examples illustrate the contrast between non-serious (low-cost) and serious (high-cost) helping (Smithson, Amato, & Pearce, 1983). While non-serious helping occurs on a daily basis, some of the serious helpers are honoured by the Carnegie Hero Fund Commission or by other institutions. In all examples of helping, the helpers invest effort, time or money, whether it is only a small amount or a great deal. Serious and non-serious helping may be distinct forms of prosocial behaviour, but they share common characteristics that are included in the major explanations of prosocial behaviour. These explanations form the main topic of this chapter, which also deals with help in emergencies, and the consequences of receiving help.

Why do People Help One Another?

The answer to this question depends on the level of analysis: biological, individualistic, interpersonal or social systems.

Biological approach

Under what conditions can prosocial behaviour be explained by evolutionary psychology?

The biological approach to altruism explains prosocial behaviour in terms of inborn or genetic tendencies. This raises the interesting question of how the process of natural selection could favour a gene that increases the tendency of an individual to help others. Prosocial behaviour can be understood as the result of natural selection if it increased rather than decreased an individual's (or her relatives') chance of reproducing (cf. chapter 2). Two general processes may have contributed to the development of prosocial behaviour: kin selection and reciprocity.

Consider kin selection first: the reproductive success of the individual (that is, the inclusive fitness) is dependent on the distribution of his or her genes in the next generation. Inclusive fitness is the sum of an individual's own reproduction success (direct fitness) and the proportion of the reproductive success of relatives that is elicited by the behaviour of the individual (indirect fitness; Hamilton, 1964). For example, the relatedness coefficient between siblings is 1/2. Therefore, one's own genes can be favoured by increasing the survival chances of brothers or sisters.

The theory of reciprocal altruism developed by Trivers (1971) explains prosocial behaviour on the basis of **reciprocity** among non-relatives. The basic tenet of the theory is that prosocial behaviour will be favoured by natural selection if it follows the principle of reciprocity and if the costs for the helper are lower than the benefits for the help-recipient. The principle of reciprocal altruism is based on the fact that it is worthwhile for Tania to protect Stephanie if it means that other persons (like Stephanie) will protect Tania. Cross-cultural evidence on giving and receiving help indicates that reciprocity is a universal phenomenon which is found in different cultures and that frequency of giving and receiving help is highly correlated (R. C. Johnson et al., 1989).

> **Reciprocity (norm of)**   The norm that we should do to others as they do to us. Reciprocity calls for positive responses to favourable treatment but negative responses to unfavourable treatment. Prosocial reciprocity occurs when people help in return for having been helped.

If the costs to the helper are low and the benefits to the help-recipient are high, reciprocal altruism may be advantageous. The problem with this type of altruism is that others may exploit it. Therefore, reciprocal altruism may be limited to certain circumstances: a high level of trust between helper and help-recipient, stability of group membership, longevity of the group, and a high degree of recognizability among the group members (Voland, 1993). Trust is often the result of familiarity and attitude similarity. In general, these are conditions which increase the likelihood of mutual support and decrease the danger that prosocial responses will be exploited.

Individualistic approach

Like the biological approach, the individualistic approach accounts for altruism in terms of individual tendencies to be helpful. However, these tendencies are not necessarily assumed to be genetically determined (although they can be), but acquired by social learning. There are basically two types of individualistic theories of altruism: one explains altruistic behaviour in terms of mood states, while the other assumes that altruism is determined by enduring personality characteristics.

Mood

What is the relationship between prosocial behaviour and mood states?

Empirical studies show that helping is fostered by a *positive mood*, which is induced by success or by thinking about happy experiences. For example, children who are in a happy mood tend to contribute more to charity (Isen, Horn, & Rosenhan, 1973) or share more with others (Rosenhan, Underwood, & Moore, 1974) than children in a neutral mood. The positive relationship between good mood and helping was confirmed in a meta-analysis by Carlson, Charlin and Miller (1988), based on 61 positive mood vs. neutral mood comparisons. In the studies covered (which encompass student and non-student samples), positive mood was induced by a variety of methods, including success on a task, finding a small amount of money and receiving a free gift. The mean amount of time that elapsed between the positive mood induction and the request for help was about 4 minutes. A significant coefficient of 0.54 was calculated, considered by conventional standards to be an indication of a medium effect size which is relevant in daily life.

The effects of good mood on helping are, however, relatively short-lived. In a field experiment, residents of Lancaster, Pennsylvania, received a packet of stationery as a gift at home (Isen, Clark, & Schwartz, 1976). Shortly afterwards they received a telephone call that was obviously a wrong number. Participants were asked to help the caller by making a phone call. The telephone rang 1, 4, 7, 10, 13, 16, or 20 minutes after the first contact. As illustrated in figure 9.2, the request was highly successful if it was made 1, 4 or 7 minutes after the presentation of the gift (on average, 83 per cent of participants performed the task). With a time delay of 10, 13 or 16 minutes, the response rate decreased to about 50 per cent. Finally, 20 minutes later only 12 per cent of participants made the phone call – a response rate that comes close to the results in the control condition, in which no gift was received.

These results can be explained in terms of an affect-priming model, which was developed by Bower (1981) and Forgas (1992). In this model, the informational

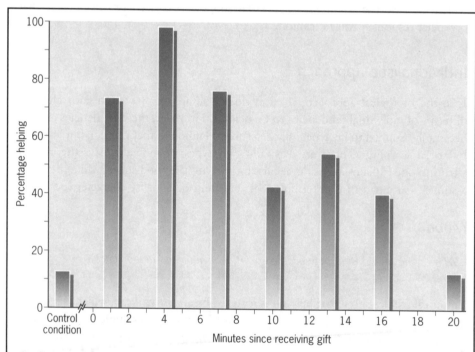

FIGURE 9.2 Percentage of helpful participants depending on timing of mood induction (Based on Isen, Clark, & Schwartz, 1976)

role of mood is explained as the selective activation and enhanced accessibility of mood-congruent memory contents. The good mood may arouse positive thoughts, which include positively toned activities such as prosocial behaviour.

A second approach which focuses on the informational role of moods is the affect-as-information model developed by Schwarz (1990b; see also chapter 5). In this approach, it is assumed that people follow a 'How do I feel about it?' heuristic, in the sense that they use current mood as a piece of information that is integrated into their overall judgement. In contrast to the affect-priming model, the affect-as-information model is primarily applied to simplified information processing on the basis of heuristics. For example, if a person is asked to evaluate another person, he or she might simply refer to his or her feelings about the other person.

From this perspective, feelings carry an informational value which may substitute for careful analytic reasoning. Specifically, positive feelings may inform the person that the current environment is a safe place (Schwarz, 1990b). The affect-as-information model simply implies that actors take their mood as an index of the safety of the given situation. Since prosocial responses are suppressed by danger signals (Cacioppo & Gardner, 1993), the relative absence of danger inferred from being in a good mood may encourage prosocial behaviour.

Forgas (1992) summarizes relevant research by pointing to an asymmetry of research findings with respect to positive and negative mood influences. The effects of a positive mood seem to be stronger and more consistent than the effects of negative moods. From an evolutionary perspective, it might be argued that *bad mood* signals problems and possibly danger (Schwarz, 1990b). Therefore, the conclusion is justified that when an individual is in a state of high self-focus, bad mood undermines altruistic intentions by increasing the perceived cost of intervention. Some research supports this prediction (Underwood, Froming, & Moore, 1977).

In their meta-analysis comparing negative-mood and neutral-mood conditions, Carlson and Miller (1987; see also Miller & Carlson, 1990) found that **interpersonal guilt**, as a special negative emotion, consistently increased helping (see also Bierhoff, Lensing, & Kloft, 1988). In general, guilt feelings as a response to transgression contribute to the maintenance of personal relationships (Estrada-Hollenbeck & Heatherton, 1998). The rate of prosocial behaviour is highest if the actor has harmed another person (interpersonal guilt), while it will be lowest if another person harms the actor (victimization).

Interpersonal guilt   Negative feelings about oneself which result from the knowledge that one is responsible for the distress of others or for damage done to them.

Prosocial personality

What are the main characteristics of the prosocial personality?

Personality influences on prosocial behaviour are especially likely when long-term commitments prevail, such as in volunteers who work for welfare organizations (Allen & Rushton, 1983; Penner & Finkelstein, 1998) and in blood donors (Piliavin

& Callero, 1991). But also in the case of spontaneous prosocial behaviour, trait dimensions labelled as prosocial personality are considered an important factor. Studies show that the same dimensions of personality exert an influence on both types of prosocial behaviour.

Elements of the prosocial personality include social responsibility, empathy and internal locus of control (Graziano & Eisenberg, 1997; Penner, Fritzsche, Craiger, & Freifeld, 1995; Staub, 1974). Whereas social responsibility and internal locus of control facilitate bystanders' feelings of obligation to help in emergency situations, high empathy contributes to a better understanding of the needs of other persons (Davis, 1994).

Social responsibility (norm of)
Social responsibility prescribes that people should help others who are dependent on them. It is contrasted with the norm of self-sufficiency, which implies that people should take care of themselves in the first place.

With respect to **social responsibility** as an element of the prosocial personality, the evidence is quite strong. Oliner and Oliner (1988) interviewed rescuers of Jews in Nazi Europe and found that, compared to a control group of people who did not help Jews, the rescuers were characterized by a higher degree of social responsibility. This result was replicated in a study of first aiders who intervened on behalf of injured traffic-accident victims (Bierhoff, Klein, & Kramp, 1991). Compared to a matched control group of potential non-helpers, helpers scored higher on the Social Responsibility Scale (Berkowitz & Daniels, 1964; Bierhoff, in press).

In addition, helpers expressed a stronger agreement with statements of the internal locus of control scale (Rotter, 1966) than non-helpers, as found by Bierhoff and colleagues (1991) and Oliner and Oliner (1988). Heckhausen (1989, p. 300) assumes that internality expresses generalized social responsibility. Empirically, social responsibility and internal locus of control correlate positively (Bierhoff et al., 1991). Both social responsibility and internal locus of control presuppose that the contingencies between own behaviour and its effects are high.

Just-world belief Generalized expectancy that people get what they deserve. Undeserved suffering of others threatens the just-world belief and motivates attempts to restore it. These include reducing the victims' suffering by helping, or devaluation of the victims.

Another characteristic of the prosocial personality is the **just-world belief** (Lerner, 1980), which refers to the generalized expectancy that people get what they deserve. Undeserved suffering of others is a strong threat to the belief in a just world. Therefore, behavioural and cognitive strategies are employed to restore the belief in a just world; these include either reducing the victims' suffering by helping them, or devaluing the victims. Both strategies are efficient when they reaffirm the belief in a just world by eliminating the impression of undeserved suffering. From a theoretical viewpoint, the relation between belief in a just world and prosocial behaviour depends on the expected effectiveness of prosocial behaviour. If prosocial behaviour is effective, in the sense that the problem is solved, just-world beliefs facilitate willingness to help. However, the same convictions have a negative influence on prosocial behaviour if the suffering of the victim will continue (since the continuing bad fate of the victim threatens the belief in a just world and devaluation of the victim is a better strategy for maintaining the just-world belief in this case).

Consistent with this analysis, Miller (1977b) showed that a strong belief in a just world was a positive factor in prosocial behaviour only when it was possible to solve the problem completely, otherwise it reduced helping. This pattern of results is consistent with the assumption that people may use two types of strategies to restore their threatened belief in a just world: they may offer help in order to remove the injustice, or they may devalue the victims in order to justify their bad fate. Only if the first strategy seems to be hopeless is the second, less humane strategy preferred (cf. Walster, Walster, & Berscheid, 1978). In the same vein, Bierhoff et al. (1991) found that helpers of accident victims scored higher on the belief-in-a-just-world scale than potential non-helpers. This is in agreement with Miller's analysis, since helpers of accident victims are confronted with a small number of victims and may reasonably expect that their attempt to help will be effective. The message is that belief in a just world has two faces: a prosocial one, if the expected effectiveness of intervention is high, and an apathetic one, if the expected effectiveness of intervention is low.

Whereas much research is devoted to spontaneous prosocial behaviour, less is known about volunteerism and long-term helping in general (cf. Clary & Snyder, 1991). The comparison of both kinds of helping suggests that volunteer work on an ongoing basis is determined by dispositional factors of the helpers to a greater extent than in the case of spontaneous helping (Allen & Rushton, 1983). In a study by Omoto and Snyder (1995), two groups of dispositional variables were taken into account: prosocial personality (measured by nurturance, empathic concern and social responsibility) and motivation for volunteering. Motivation for volunteering was measured by a questionnaire which contains scales for five kinds of motivation: values, understanding, personal development, community concern and esteem enhancement. These five scales were combined into a single indicator of motivation for volunteering. In an empirical study with members of an AIDS service organization, this indicator of motivation was positively related to length of service in the organization. In addition, prosocial personality positively influenced volunteer satisfaction, which in turn positively influenced length of service (see also Penner & Finkelstein, 1998).

A summary of empirical research indicates that dispositional **empathy** and prosocial behaviour are positively correlated (Davis, 1994; Eisenberg & Fabes, 1991). Dispositional empathy is understood as a vicarious emotion which is elicited by perceiving another in need. In the studies of Bierhoff et al. (1991) and Oliner and Oliner (1988), helpers expressed higher empathy than non-helpers.

Davis (1983) defined empathy as a set of separate but overlapping constructs. He developed the Interpersonal Reactivity Index as a multidimensional empathy questionnaire which contains 28 items distributed on four subscales: perspective-taking (e.g., 'I sometimes try to understand my friends better by imagining how things look from their perspective'), empathic concern (e.g., 'I often have tender, concerned feelings for people less fortunate than me'), fantasy (e.g., 'I really get involved with the feelings of the

> **Empathy** Affective state that is triggered when an individual witnesses the emotional state of another person. This feeling state results from adopting the perspective of the other and understanding his or her emotions.

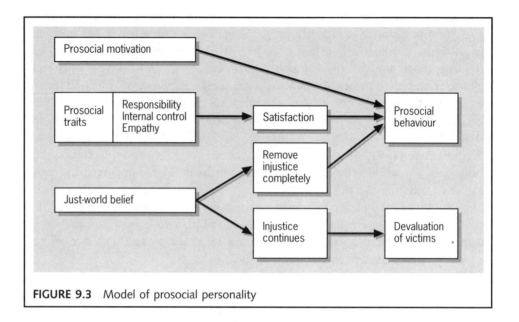

FIGURE 9.3   Model of prosocial personality

characters in a novel') and personal distress (e.g., 'Being in a tense emotional situation scares me'). Perspective-taking and empathic concern may be considered as measures of dispositional empathy, whereas personal distress is closely related to fearfulness, and fantasy is related to sensitivity to others. Dispositional empathy and personal distress may be contrasted with situational empathy and situational distress (Batson, Bolen, Cross, & Neuringer-Benefiel, 1986).

The model of the prosocial personality is illustrated in figure 9.3. It includes three components: prosocial motivation, prosocial traits and just-world belief. While it is assumed that prosocial motivation and prosocial traits exert a positive influence on prosocial behaviour in a variety of situations, the effect of the just-world belief depends on whether people expect that the injustice will be removed completely by helping.

Empathy-based altruism

What role does situational empathy play in explaining prosocial behaviour?

Much of the research by Batson (1991, 1995, 1998) has concentrated on the question of whether prosocial behaviour is motivated by altruistic or egoistic motives. The altruistic motive is equated with situational empathy, which elicits concern with the other's welfare.

How can an experiment offer an answer to the question of whether prosocial behaviour is motivated altruistically or egoistically? The basic idea is to confront people with a victim and offer them the possibility of leaving the situation. If

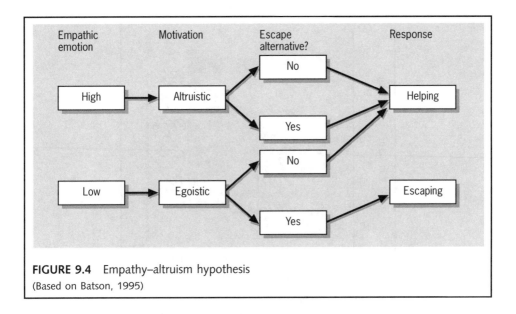

FIGURE 9.4   Empathy–altruism hypothesis
(Based on Batson, 1995)

people are egoistically motivated, they might prefer the escape alternative because it allows them to reduce any negative arousal that may have been elicited by the presence of the victim. In contrast, people who are motivated by empathy are not as likely to leave the situation since their desire to alleviate the suffering of the victim would still exist after they had left. This empathy–altruism hypothesis is depicted graphically in figure 9.4.

In an experiment by Batson and colleagues (1981), female students observed Elaine, an experimental confederate, who was apparently receiving electric shocks. In the second trial she acted as if she were suffering greatly from the shocks, as a result of which the experimenter asked the observer – the real participant in the experiment – whether she would be willing to continue with the experiment by taking Elaine's place. In one condition, participants believed that Elaine shared many attitudes with them. In another condition, participants were induced to think that Elaine held dissimilar attitudes. Batson and colleagues assumed that *high attitude similarity* would heighten altruistic motivation, whereas *low attitude similarity* would foster an egoistic motivation. In addition, difficulty of escape was manipulated. In the *easy escape condition* students knew that they could leave the observation room after the second trial, which meant that they would not be forced to continue observing Elaine's plight if the experiment continued with her. In the *difficult escape condition* students were instructed to observe the victim through to the end.

The hypothesis was that students would be reluctant to help Elaine if they were in the easy escape–dissimilar attitude condition. In all other conditions, the rate of helping should be high. The results confirmed this 'one-to-three' prediction: while the helping rate was 18 per cent in the easy escape–dissimilar condition, the proportion of helpers was much higher in the three other conditions

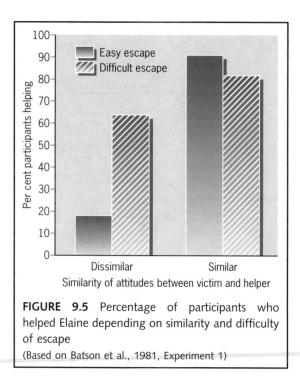

FIGURE 9.5 Percentage of participants who helped Elaine depending on similarity and difficulty of escape
(Based on Batson et al., 1981, Experiment 1)

(see figure 9.5). This pattern of results is typical of the findings of several experiments conducted by Batson and his co-workers (summarized by Batson, Fultz, & Schoenrade, 1987).

Cialdini, Brown, Lewis, Luce and Neuberg (1997) have proposed a new egoistic interpretation of the empathy–altruism hypothesis. They suggest that the very same conditions that promote true altruism in Batson's theory foster the experience of 'oneness', which is defined as 'a sense of shared, merged, or interconnected personal identities' (p. 483). Hamilton's (1964) concept of inclusive fitness suggests that people help others in their own self-interest on the basis of genetic commonality, which is derived from cues such as kinship, similarity and familiarity (see above). Cialdini and his colleagues point out that these cues are identical to the conditions which are mentioned by Batson (1991) as factors that elicit true altruism. They assume that such feelings of oneness are the functional cause of an increase in prosocial behaviour, whereas empathy is only a concomitant.

Their series of three studies provided evidence that the extent of felt oneness, and not empathic concern, is the primary factor that mediates the influence of closeness between potential helper and needy person on prosocial behaviour. Closeness was manipulated by preparing scenarios in which the person who needed help was a near stranger, acquaintance, good friend or close family member of the potential helper. Participants indicated which of seven options (from no help at all to a very substantial amount of helping) they would prefer. In addition, they rated the extent of oneness they felt with the needy person. In one study the need situation was that the other person was evicted from his or her apartment, while in the second study the need situation concerned two children whose parents had died in an accident. Results indicated that relationship closeness intensified feelings of empathy and feelings of oneness, which both correlated with prosocial behaviour ($r = 0.45$ and $r = 0.76$, respectively, in study 1). In the final step of the analysis, which took the combined effects of feelings of empathy and feelings of oneness on prosocial behaviour into account, the influence of empathic concern on prosocial behaviour diminished dramatically.

In response to this challenge, Batson et al. (1997) question the appropriateness of the manipulations of relationship closeness and severity of need in the scenario approach of Cialdini et al. (1997). However, they still have difficulty with the general finding that situational empathy does not predict willingness to help after controlling for feelings of oneness in the final step of the analysis (Neuberg et al., 1997).

Research on the empathy–altruism hypothesis is partially based on the distinction between two feeling states which might be aroused by a person in need (Batson, 1991). On the one hand, feelings of situational distress may be aroused. Situational distress is defined as a self-oriented vicarious emotion, which is described by adjectives such as 'alarmed', 'grieved', 'upset' and 'disturbed'. It is an unpleasant emotion which can be reduced by helping. It is also possible to reduce situational distress by leaving the situation because the escape reduces the impact of the suffering of the victim on the potential helper. Note that situational distress in this sense is situation-specific, not chronic personal distress.

The other feeling state that may follow from perceiving the other's need is termed situational empathy. It is described by adjectives such as 'sympathetic', 'moved', 'compassionate', 'warm' and 'soft-hearted'. Batson (1991) assumes that situational empathy is the result of adopting the perspective of another person who is in need. In addition, situational empathy is facilitated by attachment, which is developed in family relationships, friendships and romantic relationships (see chapter 12). Situational empathy is positively correlated with perspective-taking and empathic concern (as measured by the Davis scale; Batson et al., 1986). It is assumed in the empathy–altruism hypothesis that altruistic motivation is a direct function of the extent of situational empathy felt for a person in need (and not of chronic empathy; Batson et al., 1986).

Situational distress and situational empathy are defined as distinct vicarious emotions which are elicited by witnessing others' distress. The assessment of these emotions on the emotional response questionnaire shows that both scales are positively correlated (Batson et al., 1987). Participants who report feeling a high level of situational distress also tend to report a high level of situational empathy. It is not too far-fetched to assume that the relationship is the result of the unpleasant experience which distress and empathy have in common. At the same time, the results of factor analyses have indicated that assessments of vicariously experienced emotions in a given situation fall, as expected, on two orthogonal factors, which were called distress and empathy components.

Persons who primarily feel situational distress as a response to a person in need act situation-specifically, while those who predominantly report empathic concern act altruistically, independent of situational constraints. Toi and Batson (1982) provide evidence that situational empathy functions like manipulated empathy. Participants who are high on self-reported relative empathy (empathy index minus distress index) are willing to help a person in need with (71 per cent) or without (75 per cent) an escape option. In contrast, participants who express more situational distress than empathy are quite helpful when no escape option is available (81 per cent). But their willingness to help decreases substantially if an escape route is available (39 per cent). This pattern of results for persons who presumably are motivated mainly by situational distress mirrors the results that were obtained in the dissimilar attitude condition, whereas the pattern of results for persons who experience strong empathy relative to situational distress mirrors the results in the similar attitude condition (see above). The results of other studies with children (especially boys), which are summarized by Eisenberg and Fabes (1990), indicate that situational distress and prosocial behaviour are negatively related.

The attempt to identify conditions of true altruism is limited to low-cost helping. In a study on high-cost helping (Batson, O'Quinn, Fultz, Vanderplas, & Isen, 1983, experiment 3), the empathy–altruism hypothesis was not confirmed. This surprising result is explained by the assumption that increasing the cost of helping changes the underlying motivation from altruistic to egoistic among empathically aroused participants. Such a conclusion conflicts with the idea that altruistic behaviour is characterized by self-sacrifice (Krebs, 1975). Although one can speak of true altruism if people's self-reports indicate a predominance of empathy over personal distress, this kind of altruistic motivation fails if the costs of helping are high. Omoto and Snyder (1995) report that primarily egoistic motives (e.g., career development, understanding, esteem enhancement) are positively related to length of service in an AIDS organization, not altruistic motives (e.g., values, community concern; see also Neuberg et al., 1997).

In several studies, Eisenberg, Fabes and co-workers distinguished between personal distress and situational empathy in the study of children's prosocial behaviour. They showed that empathy (or sympathy) – and not distress – is positively related to prosocial behaviour in children. Eisenberg et al. (1993) used a 'baby cry helping task'. While the child was sitting in a room with the experimenter, the sound of a crying baby could be heard through a speaker in the room. The experimenter explained that the baby was in another room and tried to calm the baby down by talking to it via a microphone. In addition, the child was encouraged to do the same. Finally, in order to introduce an escape option, the child learned that it was possible to switch the speaker on or off. Afterwards the experimenter left the room, and the baby cry episode was repeated while the children's facial and behavioural responses were videotaped. Raters assessed the extent of situational distress from facial reactions. In addition, they rated the tone of voice in reference to its expression of comfort and irritation. Finally, the researchers measured the amount of time the child talked to the baby. Results indicated that facial distress was negatively correlated with time spent talking to the baby, whereas no significant relationship was found with tone of voice. Although these results were not completely replicated in a later study (Fabes, Eisenberg, Karbon, Troyer, & Switzer, 1994), these studies point to new directions of research on vicarious emotions experienced by potential helpers (e.g., the use of facial distress cues as a measure of vicariously experienced emotions).

Interpersonal approach

What does it mean when a person applies a prosocial transformation to the outcomes in a relationship?

The interpersonal approach focuses on the interdependence of people. For example, Jim and Keith, who are preparing for an upcoming examination, have decided to cooperate in their efforts. From that moment on, they are dependent on each other because their success depends at least in part on the quality of their cooperation. The structure of interpersonal relationships may be described on the basis of outcomes. For example, what are the advantages or disadvantages for Jim and Keith if they cooperate or if they compete? It is assumed that people strive to maximize rewards and to minimize costs. The most developed theory that explains interpersonal behaviour is exchange theory, which was originally for-mulated by Homans (1961), Thibaut and Kelley (1959) and Blau (1964). From this viewpoint, people are motivated in social situations to maximize the positive consequences to themselves (see chapters 11 and 12).

Kelley and Thibaut (1978) have extended the framework of exchange theory by developing a general theory of interdependence. Going beyond the original formulation of exchange theory, they allow for the possibility that interdependent persons transform the exchange relationship, which is based on the given rewards and costs, into a prosocial relationship. They explain that it may be mutually desir-able for interdependent persons to perform *prosocial transformations*. Such a trans-formation means that the person no longer acts on the basis of own consequences but substitutes the egoistic decision rule (do what is best for yourself) by a pro-social decision rule (do what is best for the other person). While the first type of decision rule is the basis of an exchange relationship, the second type constitutes a communal relationship (Clark & Mills, 1993).

The likelihood of prosocial transformations depends on many factors. As we all know, they do not occur all the time. But prosocial transformations may be expected if we consider a long-lasting relationship between friends. Therefore, one important cause for prosocial transformations lies in the extended time-perspective of the interdependence between persons. In the following section, the distinction between exchange and communal relationships is elaborated more systematically.

Exchange vs. communal relationships

What is the difference between communal and exchange relationships?

Interpersonal relations may be close or superficial. In close relationships (such as between friends), but not in superficial ones, people emphasize solidarity, inter-personal harmony and cohesiveness. In addition, in close relationships rewards for successful performance of a task are distributed according to the equality norm, whereas in superficial relationships rewards are distributed according to the con-tributions of each person to the task (on the basis of the equity norm; cf. Bierhoff, Buck, & Klein, 1986).

A similar distinction has been drawn by Mills and Clark (1982; see also Clark & Mills, 1993), who contrasted *exchange* and *communal* relationships. Examples for *exchange relationships* are those between strangers or acquaintances, whereas *communal relationships* refer to relationships between friends, family members or romantic partners. In exchange relationships people strive for maximal rewards, whereas in communal relationships people are concerned with the other's welfare. Therefore, it is plausible to assume that in exchange relationships people are motivated by egoistic motives, whereas in communal relationships they are motivated by the desire to alleviate the suffering of the victim.

In accordance with this description, empirical studies show that people in *exchange relationships* respond positively to repayments for benefits given and keep care-ful track of individual inputs into joint tasks (Clark, 1984). For *communal rela-tionships* a different pattern of results emerges (Clark, Mills, & Powell, 1986). In an experiment students were led to believe that another student might need their help. Students who were in a communal relationship with the other student paid more attention to the other's need when no opportunity to repay was expect-ed (in comparison with students who were in an exchange relationship). In contrast, when they expected that the other person would have an opportunity to reciprocate in kind in a later part of the experiment, the participants kept track of the needs of the other person with equal care in exchange and in communal relationships.

This pattern of results suggests that people in communal relationships are more helpful than in exchange relationships if no mutual give-and-take is expected. This conclusion is supported by the results of additional studies, which show that people are more helpful in communal than in exchange relationships and that this effect is stronger when the help-recipient is in a sad mood (Clark, Ouellette, Powell, & Milberg, 1987). Why does the recipient's sadness increase helping among potential donors with a communal orientation? Clark et al. (1987) sug-gest that communal observers are prone to attend to others' sadness (because they are disposed to keep track of others' needs) and, as a consequence, experience more feelings of empathy.

Social-systems approach

What does the social-systems perspective add to our understanding of prosocial behaviour?

The emphasis on situational determinants of prosocial behaviour has led to a relative neglect of the study of the impact of social systems or specific social settings. People spend most of their time with friends, classmates, colleagues or relatives in social settings in which social norms and interaction rituals have been established (Montada & Bierhoff, 1991). Appropriate behaviour in these social settings is learned during socialization in the family, in school, by viewing television and by the messages that are conveyed in literature and popular music (Rushton, 1980). Research indicates that instances of prosocial behaviour in children occur as early as in the second year of life (Bischof-Köhler, 1994; Zahn-Waxler, Radke-Yarrow, Wagner, & Chapman, 1992) and that older preschoolers show more prosocial behaviour than younger ones (Zahn-Waxler & Smith, 1992). While this emphasis on socialization is shared with the individualistic approach, since personality development is at least in part the result of social learning, the unique perspective of the social-systems approach is derived from the fact that social behaviour is influenced by factors that are inherent in social systems or settings. There are cultural norms, values and rituals that are shared by the whole community; there are reciprocal expectations among the holders of social roles; there are rights and obligations based on tradition, and general ethical principles, such as the declaration of Human Rights, which mould the behaviour of people in society.

Social responsibility

What are the elements of the process leading to the activation of prosocial behaviour? How can social responsibility be enhanced?

The *norm of social responsibility* prescribes that individuals should help other people who are dependent on their help. Berkowitz (1978) assumed that prosocial behaviour is a direct function of felt responsibility in a social situation. Earlier research had indicated that people worked harder on behalf of their partner the more dependent the partner was. It was assumed that perceived dependency elicited the norm of social responsibility, which in turn motivated prosocial responses. But prosocial activities require sacrifices, which can be avoided by passing the responsibility to others. The presence of other workers makes the **diffusion of responsibility** possible (see Berkowitz, 1978).

Diffusion of responsibility
Cognitive reinterpretation which divides responsibility among several persons, with the result that each person feels less responsible. As a consequence, each individual member in a

group feels less responsible than when alone. In groups of bystanders of emergencies, social inhibition of helping may be caused by weakened sense of responsibility among several bystanders.

Normative beliefs are learned during the socialization process (see chapter 3). In an attempt to differentiate between cultural rules and individual feelings, Schwartz (1977) contrasted social norms with personal norms. Because individuals differ with respect to their social learning of cultural values and rules, each person is characterized by a unique cognitive set of individual values and normative beliefs.

How are prosocial actions instigated? The activation of prosocial behaviour is described by Schwartz and Howard (1981), who propose a *process model of altruism*, which specifies five *successive* steps:

attention → motivation → evaluation → defence → behaviour

The first step of the process occurs when the person becomes aware that others need help. The attention phase includes recognition of other's distress, selection of an effective altruistic action, and self-attribution of competence. The next phase is related to the construction of a personal norm on the basis of social values (see below) and the subsequent generation of feelings of moral obligation (motivation phase). The third phase (evaluation of anticipated consequences of altruistic responses) centres around an assessment of potential costs and benefits. The expected costs include social costs (such as social disapproval), physical costs (pain, for example), self-concept distress (violation of the self-image) and moral costs (which result from violating personal norms). In the fourth phase the person may generate reasons for denial of responsibility, which are summarized by Montada (in press): the person may give priority to self-interest, or may refute the responsibility for others as an unjust demand. In addition, the responsibility may be perceived as conflicting with other obligations, or the person may conclude that relevant abilities or resources for intervention are lacking. The final step of the model refers to action or inaction depending on the result of the decision process.

The following example illustrates this model. People were asked to read schoolbooks to blind children (Schwartz, 1977). The recognition of the unfulfilled needs of blind children is the first part of the attention phase. This is followed by the question of whether effective actions to deal with the problem are possible and whether the potential helper feels competent to execute these actions (such as reading to blind children). If the answer is affirmative, feelings of moral obligation are generated on the basis of relevant values of benevolence and universalism (motivation phase). If strong feelings of moral obligation are generated, the potential helper will consider the expected consequences of helping (such as how much time must be invested, how much approval is gained by acting altruistically). If the evaluation is inconclusive (that is, if the pros and cons balance each other out), the potential helper may be inclined to deny personal responsibility (defence phase). A decision to read to the blind children (behaviour phase) is likely only if the anticipatory evaluation yields a positive result.

Norms are based on values that have several facets. Schwartz (1994, p. 20) defines values as beliefs that pertain to desirable end states, transcend specific situations, guide selection or evaluation of behaviour, people and events, and are ordered by relative importance. On the basis of data from 44 countries, Schwartz verified the existence of ten types of social values (e.g., achievement, conformity, security). Two values are immediately relevant for prosocial behaviour: benevolence, which is defined as 'preservation and enhancement of the welfare of people with whom one is in frequent personal contact' (p. 22), and universalism, which refers to 'understanding, appreciation, tolerance, and protection for the welfare of *all* people and for nature' (p. 22; emphasis in original). Whereas benevolence applies to personal relationships, universalism includes social justice and prosocial commitments on a wider social dimension. The two-dimensional structure of values, which was derived empirically (Schwartz, 1992), reveals that benevolence and universalism are closely related to each other. Feather (1995) demonstrated that values influence cognitive–affective appraisals of situations and the attractiveness of choice alternatives. In this sense, benevolence is related to responsible behaviour. In contrast, universalism is related to social justice.

Fairness norms

What connection exists between altruism and satisfaction of own aspirations? Which norms foster and which norms hinder prosocial behaviour?

People follow normative expectations about the level of rewards and costs that they themselves deserve. In addition, people subscribe to the *belief in a just world* (Lerner, 1980; see above). As a result, fairness norms are applied to one's own and to other's benefits and deprivations. Specifically, it is assumed that seeing that someone else has been deprived in some way elicits observers' empathic responses (Hoffman, 1990).

The relation between fair payment, overpayment and prosocial behaviour towards deprived people was studied in an experiment by Miller (1977a), which is also interesting because it sheds new light on the issue of altruistic motivation. Students had the opportunity to earn money by signing up for experimental hours in four conditions: (1) The pay for one hour was $2 (this payment corresponded to the department norm and therefore was appropriate within the given social system); (2) The pay for one hour was $3 (this amounted to relative overpayment compared to the norm of $2); (3) The pay for one hour was $2: $1 was paid to the student and $1 was donated to a needy family (therefore, the student received less than the norm prescribed while acting prosocially); (4) The pay for one hour was $3: $2 were paid to the student and $1 was donated to a needy family (in this condition, the student received what was deserved according to normative standards while at the same time acting altruistically). The mean response on the dependent variable – the number of hours for which the students

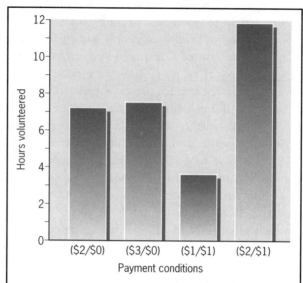

FIGURE 9.6 Willingness to volunteer depending on fair payment, overpayment and altruism. In the $2/$0 condition and the $3/$0 condition, each hour volunteered is paid with $2 and $3, respectively. In the $1/$1 condition, each hour volunteered is paid with $1 for the participant and $1 for a needy family; in the $2/$1 condition, each hour volunteered is paid with $2 for the participant and $1 for a needy family (Based on Miller, 1977a, Experiment 2)

volunteered – was significantly different in the four conditions: whereas willingness to cooperate was quite low in the third condition, it was quite high in the last condition (see figure 9.6).

These results lead to several conclusions. First, the additional incentive of one dollar in the overpayment condition increased the rate of cooperation only minimally. Second, the additional dollar increased the cooperation rate considerably if it served as an altruistic inducement that did not threaten the person's standard of deservingness. Altruism is a strong response if it does not violate the personal norm of fair payment for one's own efforts. Third, altruism was suppressed if it meant violating personal standards of deservingness. Receiving only one dollar for one's work seems to reduce cooperation, even if the second dollar goes to people in need.

Miller's (1977a) results may be summarized in a two-stage model of egoism–altruism: people first consider what their own fair share is. In addition, people experience empathic affect and act altruistically (under the condition that their standard of personal fairness is fulfilled) if the misfortune of others seems to be unjustified. Obviously, it is hard to act altruistically while one's own fair treatment is jeopardized. In contrast, people who perceive their own outcomes as fair seem to be very sensitive with respect to the perceived unfair treatment of others (cf. Hoffman, 1990). This model has important implications in applied settings. For example, willingness to be an unpaid blood donor should be higher among people who perceive their own fate as fair compared to those who believe that they are treated unfairly.

In addition, theoretical implications with respect to the issue of altruistic motivation suggest themselves. A genuinely altruistic motivation comes into play after the fulfilment of egoistic aspirations related to the fairness of one's own position in the social system. Outcomes that fall short of the level of the personal fairness standard elicit an egoistic orientation, which dominates altruistic inclinations.

From a social-systems viewpoint, facilitating and inhibiting influences on prosocial behaviour are taken into account. Inhibiting influences refer to norms that foster an egoistic orientation. For example, normative barriers against helping exist in many situations. Gruder, Romer and Korth (1978) describe a norm of self-sufficiency which implies that victims should have taken care of themselves in the first place. If victims act negligently, helping responses could be suppressed. The norm of self-sufficiency seems to prevail in many public places.

Several other social norms also tend to inhibit altruistic behaviour. For example, in many societies a strong ingroup/outgroup bias exists (cf. chapter 15). People usually show their own-community solidarity by contrasting their attitudes with those of people who are members of outgroups and who seem to deserve less help (Hoffman, 1990). A large body of research exists which indicates that helping is dependent on the race of the victim (cf. Gaertner, Dovidio, Anastasio, Bachman, & Rust, 1993). The typical result is that more help is offered if the victim is the same race as the helper. This result emerges only if the normative forces to help are weak or if it is easy to find an excuse for not helping. This pattern of results seems to indicate that people want to prevent being identified as prejudiced.

Up to this point nearly a dozen different explanations of prosocial behaviour have been discussed. As has been implied by the description of the theories, all of them are valid in the sense that they contribute to the explanation of prosocial behaviour, although on different levels of analysis. In addition, the theories mentioned are not mutually exclusive and may contribute to the explanation of a specific instance (e.g., emergency intervention) of prosocial behaviour in combination. For example, the effects of altruistic personality, communal relationship and norm of social responsibility may add to and intensify prosocial behaviour of a person who is confronted with a friend's emergency. This issue is considered again in the discussion section.

Emergency Intervention: When do we Help?

When do bystanders help, and when do they not?

Answers to the 'when' question refer to conditions under which individuals help. As we shall see, the situational control over prosocial behaviour is quite strong, which means that social and environmental conditions exert a strong influence on the likelihood of prosocial intervention in a given situation.

Darley and Batson (1973) conducted an experiment on emergency intervention. Participants in their study were students in a theological seminary. While some of the students were instructed to think about professional problems, others were asked to think about the parable of the Good Samaritan. As they left, the experimenter indicated that they would be either late ('Oh, you're late; they were expecting you a few minutes ago'), on time ('The assistant is ready for you, so please go right over'), or early ('If you would like to wait over there, it shouldn't be long').

On their way, students met a 'victim' who ostensibly had fallen on the floor. The percentage of participants who offered help constituted the dependent variable of the study. The results are summarized in figure 9.7. While the instruction to the students had a slight effect on altruism – those who were instructed to think about the parable tended to help more – the time-pressure manipulation exerted a much stronger influence. In general, participants were less helpful when they were in a hurry, although the reason for hurrying was not very serious.

This experiment shows that seemingly trivial situational variables can exert a profound effect on altruistic responses. The results of this experiment also illustrate what levels of altruism may be expected in emergency situations when only

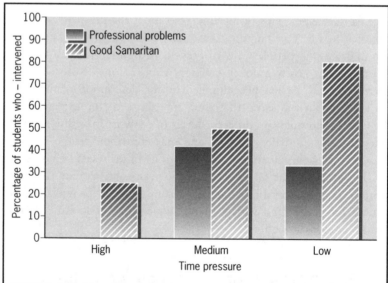

FIGURE 9.7 The effect of instruction and time pressure on prosocial responses in an emergency situation
(Based on Darley & Batson, 1973; Greenwald, 1975)

a single bystander is involved. The 42 per cent of participants in the professional-problems medium-time-pressure condition who helped may be more or less representative of the level of altruism that might be expected in comparable real-life situations (cf. Latané & Nida, 1981).

Numerous studies indicate that the willingness to intervene in emergencies is higher when a bystander is alone than when he or she is in the company of other bystanders (Latané & Nida, 1981). In one of the first experiments which showed this effect (Latané & Rodin, 1969), students overheard that a woman working next door in her office had climbed onto a chair, fallen on the floor and lay moaning in pain. This incident lasted 130 seconds. In one condition the student was alone. In a second condition another student (a confederate of the experimenter) was present, who was instructed to be passive. In a third condition two strangers were present at the time of the accident, and in a fourth condition two friends were present. Although two persons could have intervened in the third and fourth condition, in only 40 per cent of dyads of strangers and 70 per cent of dyads of friends did at least one student intervene. The *individual* likelihood of intervention was calculated according to a special formula as 22.5 per cent for strangers and 45.2 per cent for friends.[2] These corrected intervention rates are lower than in the alone-condition, but higher than in the passive-confederate condition (see figure 9.8). Additional analyses indicate that friends intervene faster than strangers within the 130 seconds of the emergency.

What are the processes which inhibit helping in groups of bystanders? The answer to this question is related to what was said about the explanations of prosocial

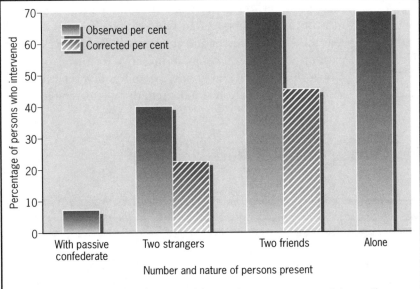

FIGURE 9.8 The effect of a second bystander on emergency intervention (Based on Latané & Rodin, 1969)

behaviour in the 'why' part of this chapter. To be motivated to help, one has to feel responsible, one has to define the episode as a helping situation, and one has to have the feeling that one's behaviour will result in approval rather than looking ridiculous. Consistent with this reasoning, empirical evidence indicates that three processes can cause social inhibition of helping (Latané & Darley, 1976; Schwartz & Gottlieb, 1976):

1   A single bystander feels that the responsibility for intervening is focused on him or her. With other bystanders present, the felt degree of responsibility is attenuated. The *diffusion of responsibility* leads to less altruism. This effect increases with the number of bystanders (Latané, 1981).

2   High situational ambiguity elicits feelings of uncertainty in the bystander. Because each bystander hesitates and tries to work out what is going on, the bystanders are models of passivity for each other. This social-comparison process leads to the erroneous conclusion that the other bystanders interpret the event as harmless. Thus, a social definition of the situation emerges which hinders prosocial responses. This process of **pluralistic ignorance** is discussed in more detail by Miller and McFarland (1991).

3   A third factor which presumably reduces the willingness to help is **evaluation apprehension**. The presence of the other bystanders elicits feelings of uneasiness because the others are observers of a potential intervention. This anxiety exerts its inhibiting influence especially in situations in which bystanders are in doubt about whether they will be able to intervene successfully. However, the process of evaluation apprehension can also increase the likelihood of an intervention. If bystanders believe that they are competent and able to perform very well, the presence of others may serve as an incentive for them to intervene. Under these special conditions, bystanders may feel that they are showing their superiority and strength by intervening.

Pluralistic ignorance   A belief that one's perceptions and feelings are different from those of others, while simultaneously one's visible behaviour is identical to that of others. In groups of bystanders of emergencies: the erroneous conclusion of each bystander that the other bystanders interpret the event as harmless.

Evaluation apprehension   The stressful experience of a person whose behaviour is observed by others. This experience may elicit anxiety and lead to deterioration of performance or high levels of performance, depending on the familiarity of the task and prior practice.

The Consequences of Receiving Help

How do the perspectives of helpers and help-recipients differ from each other? What are the possible negative consequences of help for the help-recipient?

In this section the emphasis turns from situational determinants of helping, which influence the helper, to the consequences of help, which are important for the help-recipient. The perspective of the help-recipient completes the analysis of prosocial episodes, since they always include helpers and help-recipients. In addition, the perspective of the help-recipient is important from a pragmatic point of view since it refers to one component of the success or failure of the helping act. While help may objectively constitute a 'success' in the sense that a problem is solved, it may nevertheless cause subjective experiences that deviate from its success.

People who offer help are usually convinced that if one helps somebody, that person is not only better off afterwards but also grateful. As many of us have learnt in daily life, this is not always the case. The same experience is associated with foreign aid, which is given to developing countries in the Third World. Many of these countries are harshly critical of those governments that support them. Why does this seemingly paradoxical response pattern emerge?

One reason for the mixed effects of help on the help-recipient lies in the negotiation of meaning: if Julia helps Michelle, she defines Michelle as a person who needs help. Gergen and Gergen (1983) argue that donor and recipient negotiate about the meaning of their interpersonal relationship. For example, on the one hand, the relationship could be interpreted as a mutual exchange. On the other hand, the relationship could also be understood as a long-lasting dependency of the help-recipient on the help-giver. If the altruistic act is defined as an instance of mutual exchange, the help-recipient could infer that both people involved are mutually dependent on each other. If, on the other hand, the altruistic act seems to underline the dependency of the help-recipients, they could infer that they are weak and passive.

Donors and recipients have different perspectives in the relationship (Dunkel-Schetter, Blasband, Feinstein, & Bennett, 1992). The donor profits from the fact that giving help is regarded as a desirable and fair thing to do. Although costs (time, money and effort, for example) are incurred, the positive consequences of giving help may outweigh the negative consequences. The recipient wants to prevent the other person from thinking that she was unable to take control of her fate. Because of the negative implications of weakness and inferiority associated with the role of a help-recipient, recipients will be inclined to redefine the altruistic relationship by emphasizing their own contributions.

The aid relationship comprises *four basic components* (Fisher, DePaulo, & Nadler, 1981). Donor characteristics (e.g., manipulative intent) and recipient characteristics (e.g., self-esteem) exert a modifying influence on the consequence of receiving help. In addition, aid characteristics (e.g., amount of help) and context characteristics (e.g., opportunity to reciprocate) influence feelings of indebtedness, evaluation of the donor and self-attributions by the recipient.

These components of the aid transaction influence the magnitude of self-threat and self-support inherent in the aid for the recipient (Nadler & Fisher, 1986). Negative responses by the recipient are predicted if self-threat prevails. Negative responses include negative feelings, negative evaluation of donor and aid, and high motivation for future improvement. On the other hand, positive responses on the part of the recipient are predicted if self-support prevails. Situational variables and dispositional factors exert an influence on the magnitude of self-threat and self-support, which in turn determines whether negative reactions or positive reactions of the recipient prevail.

Situational cues which emphasize the negative implications of receiving help (such as scornful comments) are especially threatening for recipients with high self-esteem (DePaulo, Brown, Ishii, & Fisher, 1981). In addition, the willingness to seek help depends on the self-threat associated with receiving help (Nadler, 1991), and this effect is especially pronounced for people with high self-esteem (Nadler, 1987). Seeking help is more common in reciprocal relationships (such as between friends; Wills, 1992).

Receiving help is especially important in educational settings, where students may sometimes need help to complete a difficult academic task. Successful self-regulated learning includes the ability to seek help when needed. Students who seek help with their academic work when needed are more successful at later tasks than students who do not seek help (Butler & Neumann, 1995). Nevertheless, many students avoid seeking help when they need it (Newman & Goldin, 1990). For example, they may avoid seeking help because they are worried about what their classmates will say. Avoidance of help-seeking is a function of low perceived benefits of help-seeking and perceived threats from peers and teachers (e.g., 'Other kids might think I'm dumb when I ask a question in maths'). Instrumental help-seeking is a function of focusing on learning and mastery and perceiving help-seeking as a beneficial strategy (Ryan, Gheen, & Midgley, 1998; Ryan & Pintrich, 1997).

Social support

Which forms of social support occur, and what is their effect on the help-recipient?

Social support focuses on giving and receiving help within relationships when coping with stressful life events and daily troubles (Morgan, 1990). Here we shall have more to say on the issue of help, which is supposed to have only positive consequences although it sometimes elicits negative consequences and side effects as well.

In general, a distinction between the perceived availability of social support (cognitive social support) and received support (behavioural social support) is drawn (Schwarzer & Leppin, 1992). Three conceptualizations of social support can be distinguished: the social-network or structural approach; the social-support-as-helping or functional approach; and the general-perception approach (Pierce, Sarason, & Sarason, 1990). The functional approach is of special importance for research on altruism since it allows an integration of theories and studies on social support and prosocial behaviour (Bierhoff, 1994).

Does social support protect the individual against the unfavourable consequences of negative life events? To answer this question with respect to mental health, data on general well-being and negative affects such as depression and sadness have been obtained. In general, social support seems to result in a certain amount of protection when stressful life events occur (Cohen & Wills, 1985). But it is still unclear whether the support–health relationship is caused by social support itself, or by other variables which are highly correlated with social support (e.g., neuroticism and hostility; Stroebe & Stroebe, 1997). Further research is needed to clarify this issue. In addition, more research is needed on the buffering hypothesis, which states that social support is especially effective when stressful life events occur. What are the mechanisms that mediate the positive effects of social support on well-being? Are the processes that lead from social support to stress-buffering dependent on specific personality types?

Social support may have negative as well as positive effects on the recipient (Nadler & Fisher, 1986). For example, it is important that the help given matches the needs of the recipients. In a study on the long-term effects of losing a child or a spouse in a road traffic accident, respondents identified giving advice and encouraging recovery as unhelpful (Lehman, Ellard, & Wortman, 1986). In addition, several problems can arise in social-support relationships: social supporters feel insecure about how to give their help appropriately; they usually have a short-term perspective; and if some kind of negative feedback from the recipient occurs, they may feel a threat to their self-esteem (Wortman & Conway, 1985). On the positive side, emotional support seems to contribute positively to well-being (Wills, 1991).

In general, when the relationship between provider and recipient is seen as reciprocal, it is less likely to elicit negative responses by the recipient, especially in exchange relationships. Social support could be understood from an exchange perspective since it is exchanged in interpersonal relations (Dunkel-Schetter et al., 1992). In social relationships which are not communal, people keep track of inputs and rewards (Clark & Mills, 1993). In an exchange context, one-sided support could have a negative impact. In contrast, in a communal context, high solidarity is congruent with one-sided help, and potential negative consequences of receiving help tend to be minimized.

Summary and Conclusions

Is it possible to combine several explanations of prosocial behaviour into a prediction of the likelihood of helping, or are the explanations mutually exclusive?

What are the main determinants of prosocial behaviour? In this chapter we have emphasized reciprocity, mood states, social responsibility, empathy and modelling effects.

A general principle is based on mutual give-and-take. A person who reciprocates a favour follows a normatively prescribed sequence of behaviour which is encouraged by natural selection. The perceived legitimacy of such behaviour sequences is relatively high, and negative implications for the help-recipients are avoided.

Positive mood enhances the likelihood of prosocial behaviour, while the effects of negative mood are more varied. But interpersonal guilt after transgressions is a strong predictor of prosocial behaviour, which might be interpreted as a process that facilitates the maintenance of personal relationships.

Diffusion of responsibility contributes to the inhibition of intervention in groups of bystanders, while the individual tendency to accept social responsibility is positively correlated with prosocial behaviour. Empathy is another individual-difference variable that is positively related to prosocial behaviour. Both dis-positional and situational empathy exert a positive influence on helping. Social responsibility and empathy constitute the core variables of the prosocial personality.

Finally, the phenomena of pluralistic ignorance and evaluation apprehension, which were observed in emergency situations among groups of passive bystanders, are examples of inhibiting influences of an audience on observers. While pluralistic ignorance is caused by passive bystanders who are taken as models of appropriate behaviour, evaluation apprehension is an expression of anxieties that emerge in many people when they are uncertain what to do and are considering taking action in public.

The theories developed as explanations of prosocial behaviour complement each other and may be applied simultaneously to reach a full understanding of the determinants of a specific example of help or passivity. For example, if a situation is not defined as a helping situation, if diffusion of responsibility occurs among bystanders, if the costs of helping are high, and if potential helpers feel that others will laugh at their inability to help in a competent way, the likelihood of intervention in an emergency is quite low.

NOTES

1 *Westdeutsche Allgemeine Zeitung*, Bochum, 219, 17 September 1997.
2 The formula for calculating the corrected individual likelihood of intervention is $P_I = 1 - \sqrt[N]{1 - P_G}$, where P_G is the likelihood that at least one person intervenes in the group and N is the number of group members. On the other hand, it is possible to calculate the corrected group likelihood of intervention on the basis of the individual intervention rate by the formula $P_G = 1 - (1 - P_I)^N$.

DISCUSSION POINTS

1 Many studies have found a good-mood effect on helping. How do you explain this result? Why does the good-mood effect dissipate quite quickly?
2 What are the characteristics of the prosocial personality?

3   What role does empathy play as a determinant of prosocial behaviour? Describe the difference between situational and dispositional empathy.

4   Is prosocial behaviour motivated by altruistic or egoistic motives? How can empirical studies be conducted to investigate this question?

5   How do you explain the fact that prosocial behaviour is reduced if personal standards of deservingness are violated?

6   In what ways do situational factors increase or decrease prosocial behaviour that is governed by the norm of social responsibility?

7   Is it possible to reduce the diffusion of responsibility that has often been observed in emergency situations?

8   Why is it appropriate to emphasize the reciprocity norm of prosocial behaviour, especially with regard to help-recipients who possess high self-esteem?

FURTHER READING

Batson, C. D. (1991). *The altruism question. Toward a social-psychological answer*. Hillsdale, NJ: Lawrence Erlbaum. On the basis of a historical overview of the altruism question, the empathy–altruism hypothesis is developed and research presented in support of the hypothesis.

Clark, M. S. (Ed.). (1991). *Prosocial behavior*. Newbury Park, CA: Sage. Covers developmental perspectives and social-psychological approaches.

Davis, M. H. (1994). *Empathy: A social psychological approach*. Boulder, CO: Westview Press. Focuses on that mediational variable of prosocial behaviour which has received the widest attention.

Eisenberg, N. (1986). *Altruistic emotion, cognition, and behavior*. Hillsdale, NJ: Lawrence Erlbaum. Origin and development of empathy and prosocial moral reasoning are emphasized.

Hunt, M. (1990). *The compassionate beast. What science is discovering about the human side of humankind*. New York: William Morrow. Using the relevant literature and interviews with a number of distinguished researchers, a journalist describes the main topics and controversies of research on prosocial behaviour.

Montada, L., & Bierhoff, H. W. (Eds.). (1991). *Altruism in social systems*. Lewiston, NY: Hogrefe. A collection of empirical studies and theoretical contributions which are written from a social-systems perspective.

Piliavin, J. A., & Callero, P. (1991). *Giving blood: The development of an altruistic identity*. Baltimore: Johns Hopkins University Press. An example of applied research on prosocial behaviour.

Schroeder, D. A., Penner, L. A., Dovidio, J. F., & Piliavin, J. A. (1995). *The psychology of helping and altruism*. New York: McGraw-Hill. The most comprehensive monograph on prosocial behaviour currently available.

Spacapan, S., & Oskamp, S. (Eds.). (1992). *Helping and being helped. Naturalistic studies*. Newbury Park, CA: Sage. A collection of contributions examining altruistic behaviour in everyday life.

KEY STUDIES

Darley, J. M., & Batson, C. D. (1973). From Jerusalem to Jericho: A study of situational and dispositional variables in helping behavior. *Journal of Personality and Social Psychology*, 27, 100–8.

Latané, B., & Rodin, J. (1969). A lady in distress: Inhibiting effects of friends and strangers on bystander intervention. *Journal of Experimental Social Psychology*, 5, 189–202.

Aggressive Behaviour

10

Amélie Mummendey
and Sabine Otten

OUTLINE

This chapter provides an overview of influential theoretical perspectives that try to explain the occurrence of and acquiescence in aggressive behaviour in general. It then focuses on aggression in specific social settings, namely family, school and workplace. Finally, more integrative models of aggression are introduced, which analyse aggression as behaviour which – from the actor's viewpoint – is both rational and functional. Evidence is presented indicating that the subjective decision-making process in favour of or against aggressive actions is shaped by social norms, and by attributions and interpretations specific to judgemental perspectives and individual response tendencies.

KEY CONCEPTS

- Catharsis
- Coercive power
- Cognitive neoassociationism
- Collective aggression
- Deindividuation
- Excitation-transfer theory

- Family aggression
- Frustration–aggression hypothesis
- Hostile attribution bias
- Modelling
- Social interactionist theory of coercive action
- Victimization (bullying, mobbing)

Introduction

On Wednesday, 21 April 1999, the Organization for Security and Cooperation in Europe (OSCE) reported on the most severe violations of human rights committed by Serbs in Kosovo against Albanians. They cut their throats, put out their eyes, cut off their noses, fingers, hands and feet. At the time of writing, this was not the only case of extreme aggression described in the newspaper. The previous day, another terrifying event was a shooting at a school in Littleton, Colorado, USA. And, sadly enough, there would have been similar examples if this chapter had been written at any other time. Aggression is committed continuously everywhere in the world.

For 1997, statistics report 186,447 cases of murder, manslaughter or serious physical aggression in Germany. The numbers for other European countries are comparable, and those for the United States even higher. The more spectacular the event, the more insistently we ask, 'why?'. What causes someone to insult, threaten, hit, torture or even kill another person? By identifying causes, people expect means of controlling and reducing aggression.

In this chapter we shall first present some of the influential theoretical attempts to explain aggressive behaviour, focusing on the *frustration–aggression hypothesis* and its successor theories, and on *aggression as learned behaviour*. Because of its prime importance in the discussion about the modelling of aggressive behaviour, we shall specifically consider the impact of *mass media*. The second section will deal with the role of different social settings in which aggression occurs, such as the family, school or workplace. In the third section, we shall reflect on some integrative approaches towards the problem of aggression, especially on *social-information processing* and *social influence*. Using this analysis of aggression as an interactional phenomenon, shaped by both the opponents' mutual contributions and the specific social context, we shall finally consider *collective aggression*, including such extreme forms as mass killing and genocide. Although individual differences may play a key role in understanding aggressive behaviour, their impact is not dealt with in a separate section, but touched upon in the scope of some of the sections mentioned above (for a more detailed review, see Geen, 1998).

Consider the following scenario, which takes place in a German city but could just as easily be imagined in many other cities in Europe or elsewhere. A crowd of young people are in a pub, most of them standing around the bar. Among them are two young men from Tunisia, studying physics at the local university. When the Tunisians leave the bar, a small group of Germans leave as well and follow them on their way to the bus station. The Tunisians walk faster, but the Germans gain on them. As the Tunisians start running, so do the Germans. Only a few metres from the bus station, the Germans catch up with the Tunisians and begin assaulting them. While one manages to escape, the other is thrown to the ground, kicked, punched and beaten with a baseball bat. After some minutes, the victim lies motionless as if dead and the Germans run away.

What theories can we reach for to identify the causes of the Germans' aggressive behaviour? In the course of this chapter, we shall try to analyse the scenario from different theoretical perspectives. However, before looking for answers to the question *why* aggression happens, we should answer the question of *what* aggression is.

Defining Aggression

In aggression research there has been an extended controversy concerning alternative definitions of aggression, but there seems to be consensus concerning two aspects. First, aggressive behaviour means infliction of harm or injury on another person or organism. Second, in order to exclude accidental harm or aversive stimulation administered for beneficial reasons, a definition must also include the actor's *intent* to create negative consequences for the victim. Both aspects are covered by the definition proposed by Baron (1977): 'Aggression is any form of behaviour directed toward the goal of harming or injuring another living being who is motivated to avoid such treatment' (p. 7) (see also Baron & Richardson, 1994, p. 7).

There are various ways in which people behave aggressively. Several authors have classified types of aggressive behaviour based upon different criteria, such as physical vs. verbal, or direct vs. indirect (Buss, 1961). Other classifications refer to the motives that might underlie a perpetrator's aggressive action: is it an instrument to reach a non-aggressive goal, or is it performed to cause harm as the ultimate goal? Distinctions have also been drawn between instrumental and 'angry aggression' (Buss, 1961), and between aggression that is defensive or offensive, provoked or unprovoked (Zillmann, 1979; see also Buss, 1971). Going back to the scenario described above, everybody would agree that the perpetrators act aggressively, that their behaviour is apparently hostile, offensive and unprovoked. However, a closer look at the description reveals that explicit information about provocation by the victims or about the perpetrators' goals and motives is missing. Parts of our impression of aggressive actions apparently go beyond pure descriptions or observations and rely on inferences instead. We shall come back to this issue in later sections of this chapter.

Theories of Aggression

What are the basic theoretical positions to explain aggressive behaviour?

Biological concepts about the causes of aggressive behaviour have been influential for a long time. These include discussions of aggression as instinct (McDougall,

1908), as drive (Freud, 1920), or as instinct-based behaviour (Lorenz, 1963; see Geen, 1998, and Tedeschi & Felson, 1994, for surveys). The experience of aggression as a ubiquitous phenomenon has also led to its analysis in terms of evolutionary functions of aggression. Shaped by natural selection, aggression is seen as a behavioural strategy with adaptive value in terms of the evolutionary purpose, which is reproductive success of one's own genes (Dawkins, 1989; Williams, 1966; see chapter 2 for the evolutionary approach to social psychology).

Frustration and aggression

What is the relation between frustration and aggression according to the frustration–aggression hypothesis?

In 1939 five authors, the so-called Yale Group, published a book entitled *Frustration and Aggression*, which initiated experimental research on aggression within social psychology (Dollard, Doob, Miller, Mowrer, & Sears, 1939). For several decades their **frustration–aggression hypothesis** was the theoretical core of research in this area. Their model of aggression assumes that a person is motivated to act aggressively by a drive induced by frustration. By frustration they mean the condition that arises when goal attainment is blocked, while aggression is action aimed at harming another organism. These two concepts are linked to the following two statements: (1) frustration always leads to some form of aggression, and (2) aggression is always a consequence of frustration. Aggression is not, however, always directed towards the cause of frustration and it can take different forms. If, for example, the person who is the source of frustration is physically strong or socially powerful, then the frustrated individual can turn his or her aggression against another, less dangerous person, or can express it in more indirect ways. Thus, after frustration both *target substitution* and *response substitution* are forms of displaced aggression. In line with the concept of **catharsis**, it is assumed that the tendency to act aggressively is reduced by showing aggressive behaviour or its substitutes.

Frustration–aggression hypothesis Aggression is always a result of frustration.

Catharsis Release of aggressive energy through the expression of aggressive responses, or through alternative forms of behaviour.

Immediately following its publication, the simple hypothesis concerning the causal relationship between frustration and aggression was questioned. Critics argued that frustration did not always lead to aggression, and that other reactions, such as fleeing or apathy, could also be observed. In addition, aggression often occurs without preceding frustration. A paid assassin, for example, may carry out his task without even knowing his victim, let alone being frustrated by him. Given these objections, the authors quite soon changed their original assumptions. Frustration was seen only as a stimulus to aggression; in an individual's hierarchy of possible response tendencies, aggression was seen as the *dominant* response tendency following frustration (Miller, Sears, Mowrer, Doob, & Dollard, 1941). Thus, frustration creates a readiness for aggression, but whether this manifests itself in actual behaviour depends on additional conditions.

It was Berkowitz (1964, 1969, 1974) with his cue-arousal theory who tried to define the relation between frustration and aggression more precisely. He inserted environmental conditions (or *cues*) for aggression as an intervening concept between the concepts of frustration and aggression. Frustration does not immediately evoke aggression, but generates a state of emotional arousal, namely *anger*, which in turn generates an inner readiness for aggressive behaviour. However, only if there are stimuli in the situation that have an aggressive meaning, that is, cues associated with anger-releasing conditions, or simply with anger itself, will aggression actually occur. Stimuli acquire their quality as cues for aggression through processes of classical conditioning; this way, in principle, any object or person can become a situational aggression cue.

How can aggressive cues influence aggressive behaviour?

Thus, an aggressive act has two distinct sources: the aroused anger within the harm-doer, and the cues within the situation. Berkowitz and his colleagues carried out a series of experiments to systematically test these assumptions of cue-arousal theory (Berkowitz, 1974; see also Gustafson, 1986, 1989). One experiment in particular evoked considerable interest, criticisms and both successful and unsuccessful replications of what has become known as the *weapons effect*.

According to Berkowitz, weapons are a prime example of a situational cue to aggression. Their presence should lead in general to more extreme aggression than the presence of objects with neutral connotations. Berkowitz and LePage (1967) tested exactly this hypothesis: if weapons function as aggression-arousing cues, do frustrated or angry people show more aggression in the presence of weapons? The participants (male college students) had to perform a task, and their performance was evaluated by an experimental confederate. This evaluation, consisting of a number of electric shocks, was independent of the actual performance, and served the purpose of generating different strengths of aroused anger. As expected, the participants who received a higher number of shocks reported more anger than those who had received only one shock. In a second phase of the experiment, both angered participants and non-angered participants had to evaluate the performance of the confederate, also by means of giving electric shocks. At this stage the situational aggression cues were manipulated. In one experimental condition, a shotgun and a revolver were placed on a nearby table; in another condition, no objects were present. The results were clearly in line with the hypotheses: for non-angered participants, aggressive cues had no effect on the number of shocks administered to the confederate. Angered participants, in contrast, gave more shocks in the presence than in the absence of weapons (see figure 10.1).

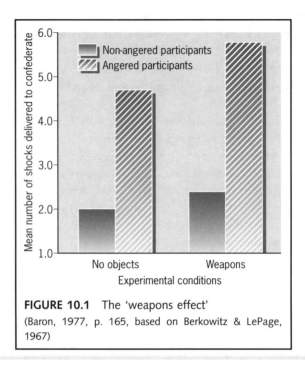

FIGURE 10.1 The 'weapons effect'
(Baron, 1977, p. 165, based on Berkowitz & LePage, 1967)

Although subsequent empirical tests on the weapons effect did not give un-equivocal support to Berkowitz's original assumptions, Carlson, Marcus-Newhall and Miller (1990) performed a meta-analysis on 56 studies assessing the extent to which aggression-related cues facilitate aggressive responses among negatively aroused participants. They presented strong evidence that aggression-cues did indeed increase aggressive responses in negatively aroused participants. However, differ-ent from the original cue-arousal hypothesis, the results implied that aggression-cues function as cognitive primes of aggression-related thoughts and images (see also Bushman, 1998, for videos as aggressive primes). Exposure to aggressive cues, independent of a preceding frustration or anger, can facilitate access to aggression-related schemata in memory.

Which factors affect the influence of non-specific arousal on aggressive behaviour?

Non-specific arousal and excitation transfer   Anger is the kind of arousal experi-enced from sources that are clearly associated with aggression. Physiological arousal in general is, however, also influenced by other stimuli such as physical exertion, sensational news stories, thrillers or erotic films. One assumption is that such non-specific or non-aversive sources of arousal probably supplement the anger or aversive arousal and, as a result, increase the readiness to behave aggressively. In this context, influenced by Schachter's (1964) two-factor theory of emotion, Zillmann (1971, 1988) developed his **excitation-transfer theory**. He assumes that residual arousal from a previous situation can be added to arousal elicited in a new situation.

Excitation-transfer theory
Sources of arousal not directly related to aggression may be added to aggression-specific arousal, thus intensifying aggressive responses.

The conditions for such excitation transfer and subsequently increased aggression are, first, that aggression is the dominant response tendency in the new situation, i.e., when an individual is already primed to act aggressively (e.g., Zillmann, Katcher, & Milavsky, 1972), and, second, that the arousal is interpreted or labelled in a way that is consistent with subsequent aggression. If, in response to a disparaging comment or an unjustified accusation, we feel our blood pressure and respiration rate increase, we interpret this state of arousal as anger and show increased readiness for aggressive behaviour. But the same signs of physiological arousal can also be felt in a situation where we are quite unexpectedly asked to deliver a short talk in front of a seminar group. Now the obvious interpretation of the same physiological state is embarrassment or fear, and an aggressive response is unlikely. When a given arousal can unambiguously be attributed to a non-aggressive stimulation, the arousal will be correctly interpreted and will have no effect on the extent or the likelihood of aggressive behaviour (see Rule & Nesdale, 1976; Tannenbaum & Zillmann, 1975). Hence, an increase in aggression due to general arousal is only to be expected when the individual lacks clear information about the causes of arousal (see Zillmann, Johnson, & Day, 1974).

What is the relation between aversive stimuli and affective reactions?

Cognitive neoassociationism The theoretical position described above sees the relation between arousal and aggression as a *sequence*. Different conditions lead to general arousal; depending on its perceived causes, this arousal is then labelled and leads to a specific emotion, such as anger. The kind of behaviour that is expected depends, in turn, on the type of emotion. Berkowitz (1989, 1990, 1993) criticized this view and proposed an alternative theory. His **cognitive neoassociationism** posits that there is no such thing as non-specific or neutral arousal. Aversive events have a direct negative effect and trigger directly aggression or flight behaviour; subjective emotional experiences like anger or fear may or may not accompany these forms of behaviour (see figure 10.2). Anger and aggression are not *sequential* but *parallel* processes (Berkowitz, 1983). Aggression (or flight) is the immediate impulsive response to aversive stimulation (Berkowitz & Heimer, 1989). This assumption is based upon associative network models of memory (see chapter 5).

Cognitive neoassociationism
The theory developed by Berkowitz that postulates a direct link between aversive events or negative affects and arousal of fight or flight behaviour. Denies the necessity of cognitive mediators for (emotional) aggression to occur.

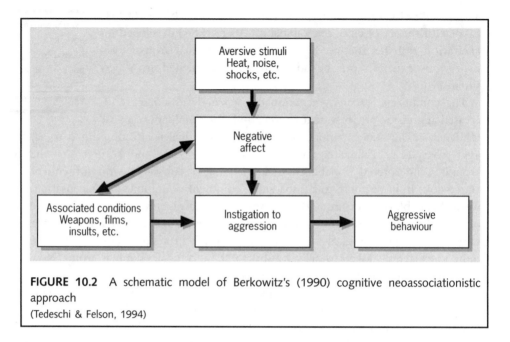

FIGURE 10.2   A schematic model of Berkowitz's (1990) cognitive neoassociationistic approach
(Tedeschi & Felson, 1994)

The more unpleasant the event, the greater the individual's readiness for aggression. A variety of conditions (such as insults, attacks, etc.) can become aversive events; physical pain is a prototypical condition for the triggering of negative affect (see Bell, 1992; Berkowitz, Cochran, & Embree, 1981). Besides, experiences of stressful environmental conditions such as noise, crowding and temperature can also heighten an individual's level of aversive arousal and increase the probability of aggression (e.g., Baron & Richardson, 1994; Donnerstein & Wilson, 1976), but only for individuals who have experienced anger and are therefore prepared to behave aggressively (Goldstein, 1994).

Back to our scenario. The Germans might have been frustrated; perhaps they got upset about something the Tunisians said in the bar. It is also conceivable that the Germans' anger stemmed from other events, but that the Africans were the most suitable target for their aggression. Likewise, as some Germans hold a stereotype of Africans or Muslims as violent, we can consider that – by association with this stereotype – the Tunisians might have activated an aggressive behavioural schema within their subsequent perpetrators. In any case, it is very likely that the Germans were in a state of aversive arousal and that they felt angry. The environment in the bar – hot and noisy – probably further heightened their arousal. But why did the Germans show this particular form of aggression, i.e., using baseball bats? How did they acquire their repertoire of behavioural alternatives, and their expectations about which action would be most expedient?

Aggression as learned behaviour

How is aggressive behaviour acquired by instrumental conditioning or by modelling?

The *frustration–aggression hypothesis* and its successor theories address processes regulating aggressive behaviour: they describe processes expected to operate in the individual organism, namely instigating aggressive responses. However, for these processes to elicit aggression, this type of action has to be available within the individual's behaviour repertoire. Learning theory addresses exactly this issue when asking the following questions: How does an individual acquire aggressive forms of behaviour? What determines whether such available forms of behaviour actually occur? Which factors are responsible for aggressive behaviour becoming habitual?

Instrumental conditioning

Individuals behave in order to reach desired goals. If a child really wants that bright red fire engine standing on the table, then he or she will go to the table and get it. But the situation becomes complicated if another child is playing with the toy. Somehow this other child must be made to give up the fire engine. One possibility is direct action: simply grab the toy. Different consequences can ensue from this behaviour. If this aggressive behaviour is successful (i.e., a useful way of obtaining an attractive object), then the child will use the same means in other, comparable situations. Through positive reinforcement, the tendency to behave aggressively will be strengthened. Indeed, it has been shown that people acquire different forms of aggressive behaviour through this process of instrumental conditioning. External environmental consequences control the acquisition and performance of aggression. Quite different forms of reinforcement can be effective in this way: obtaining attractive objects like toys, money or sweets (Walters & Brown, 1963); winning social approval or increased status (Geen & Stonner, 1971); and avoiding pain (Patterson, Littman & Bricker, 1967). Social support by a group or social norms may also reinforce expressions of hostility or aggressive responses to subsequent events (Buss, 1961, 1971).

Social learning theory

Bandura (1973) proposed that the first step towards acquiring a new form of aggressive behaviour is the process of **modelling**: individuals acquire new and more complex forms of behaviour by observing this behaviour, and its consequences, in other people or models. A typical experiment on modelling was carried out by Bandura, Ross and Ross (1961, 1963), in which children observed an adult playing with some toys. This adult showed very unusual and, for the

Modelling The tendency for individuals to acquire new (and more complex) forms of behaviour by observing this behaviour, and its consequences, in real-life or symbolic models.

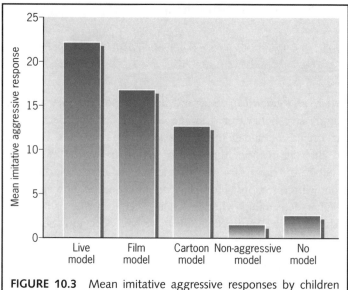

FIGURE 10.3 Mean imitative aggressive responses by children who were exposed to either aggressive models, non-aggressive models or observed no models
(Adapted from Bandura, 1973, p. 75)

children, quite new behaviours: he marched into the playroom, hit a large inflated toy (a 'Bobo doll') with a rubber hammer, kicked and yelled at it. Children in the control condition saw an adult who played quietly with the toys. In a second phase of the experiment, the model was either rewarded by the experimenter or experienced no positive consequences. Afterwards the children had a chance to play with the same toys. It was found that the children imitated the model's behaviour when they had seen it rewarded. The effect was found both when the model was seen in real life or only observed on video, and also with a comic figure as model (see figure 10.3).

Whereas many studies with children have emphasized the acquisition of new forms of behaviour (see Bandura, 1977b; Baron & Richardson, 1994), similar studies with adults have shown how a model could reduce inhibitions to behave aggressively in a certain situation (Baron, 1971; Epstein, 1966). For children, models for aggressive behaviour are supplied especially from two major social contexts, each of which is relevant for their everyday social interactions; namely, family and peer group (Bandura, 1973). Furthermore, mass media are constantly discussed and criticized for causing aggressive behaviour, particularly in young audiences. Taking into account both the large body of research and the increasing importance of media in shaping our social life, this issue will be dealt with in more detail in the following section.

Recall our scenario: the four Germans beat and kick their Tunisian victim. It is easy to imagine that such behaviour had been rewarded in the past, be it by the applause of their peers, or by access to valuable resources. Furthermore, if not directly then at least through mass media, it does not take us long to find models for xenophobic and brutal behaviour. It is not only the behaviour of the model that is observed, but also the way it is anchored in a social context. Media transmit behavioural norms and values, and they implicitly teach what justifies aggression.

Observing aggression in the media

What is the relation between aggressive behaviour and watching TV aggression?

In public discussion, one of the most accepted scapegoats for violence in our society is aggression in the media. Observation of aggressive media episodes is expected to increase aggression in the viewer. Accounting in this way for aggressive events not only sounds plausible, but also promises a relatively simple solution to the problem: just switching off the TV set.

From the perspective of social psychology, two questions are crucial: (1) whether exposure to violent media enhances aggression, and (2) which psychological processes underlie or mediate this possible media-exposure effect. Systematic overviews using meta-analytic techniques come to the conclusion that observation of aggression is often followed by an increase of aggressive responses (Andinson, 1977; Geen & Thomas, 1986; Hearold, 1986). Critics have questioned the ecological validity of these results, pointing to the artificial character of the laboratory studies the analyses were based upon. However, a more recent meta-analysis by Wood, Wong and Cachere (1991), based exclusively on field studies, reached the same conclusion, namely that media aggression has an enhancing effect on its consumers' aggressive behaviour.

In order to learn something about the possible long-term effects of viewing televised aggression, longitudinal studies have measured both viewing habits and observed aggression at several points in time. For example, Eron, Walder and Lefkowitz (1971; Eron, Huesmann, Lefkowitz, & Walder, 1972) tested their sample at the age of eight years and then again at the age of 18 years. The pattern of correlations obtained supported the hypothesis that a relatively high level of aggression at the age of 18 was linked to relatively frequent viewing of violent films at the age of eight (see figure 10.4). Other longitudinal studies report similar results (Eron & Huesmann, 1980; Groebel & Krebs, 1983; Huesmann, Lagerspetz, & Eron, 1984).

Comstock and Paik (1991) presented a meta-analysis based on more than a thousand tests of the effects of media aggression from various types of studies, i.e., experiments, field studies and longitudinal studies. They conclude that the picture is rather unequivocal. There is a pervasive short-term effect of TV aggression on viewers' behaviour and, concerning long-term effects, at least significant

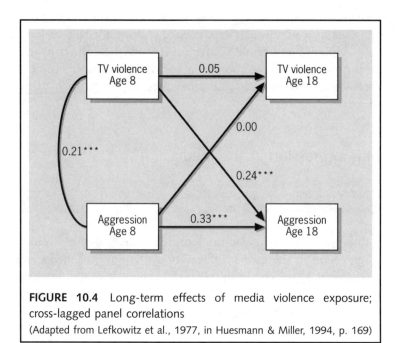

FIGURE 10.4 Long-term effects of media violence exposure; cross-lagged panel correlations
(Adapted from Lefkowitz et al., 1977, in Huesmann & Miller, 1994, p. 169)

positive correlations can be shown between the amount of TV aggression viewed and the strength of tendencies to behave aggressively. In addition, Comstock and Paik identified some factors which moderate the effect of TV aggression on aggressive behaviour (pp. 255ff.). Media aggression is more likely to increase the viewer's aggressive tendencies if the following conditions are present:

1 *Efficacy*: Aggression in the media is presented as an efficient instrument to achieve one's goals and/or remains unpunished.
2 *Normativeness*: Physical aggression or intentionally hurtful actions are shown without paying attention to their negative consequences on the part of the victim, his or her suffering, sorrow or pain. Moreover, aggression is often presented as being justified, that is, with 'good guys' like police officers as perpetrators.
3 *Pertinence*: The perpetrator is portrayed as similar to the viewer, he or she could imagine being in this role. Aggression is presented in a realistic manner rather than as fantasy or fiction.
4 *Susceptibility*: The portrayal of aggression is viewed in a state of emotional arousal (pleasure, anger, frustration), which prevents a more detached or critical attitude on the viewer's part.

Obviously, exposure to media aggression has an effect on viewers' real-world aggression. Which underlying processes could be assumed to explain this effect? From theoretical and empirical work in this domain, Gunter (1994) concludes that besides processes of excitation transfer and modelling, viewers' desensitization of emotional responsiveness towards brutal treatments and disinhibition of own aggressive actions can be the effect of continuous exposure to aggressive actors and mistreated victims. If TV protagonists enact aggressive behaviours without subsequently being subjected to negative sanctions, viewers' former inhibitions about performing such anti-normative behaviour might be weakened. In fact, male participants who saw an aggressive pornographic film daily for one week experienced decreased feelings of depression, annoyance and anxiousness in response to the films, but experienced them as more enjoyable, less violent and less degrading to women (Harris, 1994; Linz, Donnerstein, & Adams, 1989).

Frequent viewing of media aggression also influences attitudes towards aggression. People who learn from television that conflicts are often resolved aggressively, and that one aggressive act tends to be followed by another, may overestimate the likelihood that they themselves will be victims of aggression, they are more suspicious of others and suggest harsher sentences in the fight against crime (Gerbner, Cross, Morgan, & Signorelli, 1982). Though often overlooked, the relation between media aggression and behavioural aggression is not unidirectional. In real life, exposure to violent programmes is not typically imposed on children or adolescents, but instead they choose the channels, films or videos they want to watch (Gunter, 1985, 1994). Hence, the correlation between media exposure and aggressive behaviour might be confounded by individual preference for aggressive films.

Aggression in Social Settings

In the previous sections, we have dealt with different theoretical perspectives that explain the occurrence of aggressive behaviour in general. We now turn to more specific settings of everyday life in which aggression is expressed. Clearly, we cannot address the whole scope of social settings relevant for individual aggressive behaviour; instead we select only two settings that we think are important segments of the spectrum of individual aggression, namely family aggression, and aggression in school and at work.

Family aggression

What factors facilitate aggressive behaviour between family members?

Family means home and shelter, and support for its members, based on mutual affection between the generations. A family provides the warm and intimate environment in which children can develop and socialize to adjusted and competent members of society. However, Gelles (1997, p. 1) states: 'People are more likely to be killed, physically assaulted, hit, beat up, slapped, or spanked in their own homes by other family members than anywhere else, or by anyone else, in our society.' To combine these two very different faces of the family, we have to remember that, in relation to the total spectrum of behaviour, the frequency of aggressive actions is rather low. However, in relation to the total amount of aggressive behaviour, aggression in domestic contexts is apparently rather high. Worldwide, aggression in the family has to be conceived of as a severe social problem (Walker, 1999).

Family aggression According to the APA Task Force on Violence and the Family (APA, 1996), a pattern of violent and abusive behaviours, including a wide range of physical, sexual and psychological maltreatment, used by one person in an intimate relationship against another to gain power unfairly or maintain that person's misuse of power, control and authority.

Family aggression is conceived as a systematic pattern of abusive behaviours, which become increasingly frequent and severe over a period of time. It includes a wide range of physical, sexual and psychological maltreatment used by one person in an intimate relationship against another for the purpose of control, domination or coercion (APA, 1996; Shornstein, 1997). There are several myths concerning family aggression (Gelles, 1997) which have to be corrected, e.g., family aggression is not restricted to lower-class or mentally disturbed people, but occurs in all segments of society. Also, there is no gender difference concerning the frequency of initiated assaults in close relationships (Straus, 1993). There is, however, a difference concerning the severity of injury caused by aggressive attacks: here women cause far less severe injury than men. In any case, irrespective of gender, aggressive actions performed by adults in the family will be influential models for children (Jaffe, Wolfe, & Wilson, 1990; Straus, 1993).

Why is the family such a violent social setting? Gelles and Straus (1979) identified a number of factors which specify the family as a social group and which are responsible for both its intimate and supportive atmosphere and its aggressive and abusive potential (see Gelles, 1997). Family members interact frequently and engage in a broad range of activities that require a high degree of commitment and relevance for each participant, but which also imply the perceived right or even responsibility to influence the others' behaviour, beliefs and values. The family provides many occasions for negative interdependence. Over the extended periods spent together in the family, knowledge about the family members' strengths and vulnerabilities is accumulated, which can be used to attack the other in a conflict situation.

Gelles (1997) proposes a theory of intimate aggression which is based on exchange and interdependence theory (Blau, 1964; see chapter 11). Intimate aggression, like other social behaviours in social relations, is guided by the striving for rewards and the avoidance of costs. Aggression is used when the actor can expect the costs of this behaviour to be less than the rewards. The costs of the actor's aggression decrease with (1) absence of effective external social controls (here, the private nature of the family reduces the willingness for external parties to intervene); (2) power inequality between men and women; and (3) aggressiveness as a status-building, positively evaluated part of the image of the 'real man'.

Aggression in school and at work

> *What are the conditions which transform children at school and colleagues at work into perpetrators and victims of aggression?*

We have all met or at least heard about individuals who, either at school or at work, suffered from continuous harassment and attacks by classmates or colleagues. Often such situations lead to severe health problems; sometimes victims even commit suicide to escape their stressful and aversive situation. Although this specific form of aggression is certainly not limited to our modern times, it is only recently that systematic social-psychological research has begun, first in Scandinavia (Leymann, 1993; Olweus, 1973), and later in various other countries (see Smith & Sharp, 1994; Schuster, 1996; Zapf, 1999).

Olweus has defined **victimization** (synonymous with **bullying** or **mobbing**) as follows: 'A person is being bullied . . . when he or she is exposed, repeatedly and over time, to negative actions on the part of one or more other persons' (1994, p. 98). Negative actions are aggressive behaviours, such as physical or verbal, direct or indirect aggression. The imbalance in strength, status and power is specific to bullying or mobbing: the victim is inferior to the bully and therefore cannot easily defend him/herself against the attacks. Among victims' reactions are found psychosomatic symptoms, reduction in achievement levels and loss of self-esteem (Schäfer, 1997; Zapf, 1999). With regard to the perpetrators, bullies at school show a heightened risk of delinquency in adulthood (Lösel, Averbeck, & Bliesener, 1997); they are prone to continue bullying or mobbing later in their working life (Farrington, 1994).

Olweus (1994) distinguishes typical characteristics of victims and bullies in the context of schoolchildren which are quite similarly revealed by research on bullying among adult work colleagues (Niedl, 1995; Schuster, 1996; Zapf, 1999). Typically, victims are anxious, defensive, low in self-esteem, physically weak or look different from the majority. In contrast, bullies are often physically strong, behave aggressively in a variety of contexts, tend towards dominating others, are highly impulsive and have a secure self-esteem. Differential parental socialization styles have been shown to account for many of these personality differences (Schäfer, 1997). Gender and age differences are also relevant to the type of bullying: girls demonstrate more indirect attacks and less direct physical attacks than boys. With increasing age, however, this gender difference vanishes, due to a decrease in physical aggression for boys. In adult contexts, physical assaults cover only a very small part of the spectrum of bullying behaviour.

Victimization (synonymous with **bullying** or **mobbing**)   In social contexts, e.g. in schools or at work, individuals are sometimes singled out and frequently attacked or maltreated. Particular characteristics of this phenomenon are repeated and enduring inflictions of intended harm, using either direct or indirect aggressive means, mostly by more than one physically strong and/or high-status perpetrator against a physically weak and/or low-status victim, often deviating from the group's standard.

When does bullying occur? The *social misfit hypothesis* (see Schäfer, 1997) refers to the lack of compatibility between the more general social climate of the peer group and the individual's attitudes and behaviour. Dependent upon the type of group norms, identical behaviour styles can lead either to rejection and victimization or to acceptance (Wright, Giammarino, & Parad, 1986). In addition, based on 'referent cognition theory', Folger and Baron (1996) point to the function of perceived injustice on the perpetrators' side which may instigate bullying of suitable victims.

Altogether, research on bullying at school and in the workplace is still investigating various factors that might be relevant for the analysis of the phenomenon, and a theoretical framework of processes controlling the phenomenon has not yet been developed (Schuster, 1996). There is one aspect which differentiates research on bullying from other topics in aggression research. Usually, interest is directed towards the actor and his or her behaviours, but here, in contrast, perpetrator and victim are equally the focus of research. For integrative approaches to the analysis of aggression, however, this is not at all a special case. Moreover, aggression *always* means a contribution from (at least) two opponents, acting in a specific social context. It is this interaction that we consider in the next section.

Aggression: From Act to Interaction

What are the crucial concepts of aggression as social interaction?

The interpretation of individual behaviour as aggressive

When we appraise a behaviour as aggressive, we go beyond a simple description to make an evaluation. Such judgement by an observer or even a participant has social consequences; if a behaviour is judged to be aggressive, a negative sanction seems appropriate. A large-scale study of American men's attitudes to different forms of aggression found that the same behaviour (e.g., police assaulting students during a demonstration) can be seen positively or negatively, depending on whether the preceding action (e.g., a sit-in) is seen as legitimate or illegitimate (Blumenthal, Kahn, Andrews, & Head, 1972). Experiments dealing with the judgement of behaviour as aggressive indicate that *intention to harm*, *actual harm* and *norm violation* are the main criteria for labelling an act as aggressive (Ferguson & Rule, 1983; Löschper, Mummendey, Linneweber, & Bornewasser, 1984). If we agree that aggression is an interpretative construct rather than a descriptive one, then factors influencing or determining this interpretation become of

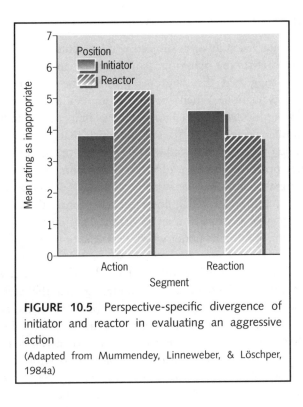

FIGURE 10.5 Perspective-specific divergence of initiator and reactor in evaluating an aggressive action

(Adapted from Mummendey, Linneweber, & Löschper, 1984a)

interest. First, the particular social normative context embedding the critical action will be of importance. Depending upon the context-specific validity of norms, a particular behaviour may be norm-violating or not. Second, attribution theory provides a viable line of thinking about what leads people to infer intent from the actions performed by another person (see chapter 7). Third, the perspective specific to the key positions in an aggressive interaction, i.e., actor, recipient or outside observer, plays an important role in determining the evaluation of a critical action.

Several studies performed by Mummendey, Linneweber and Löschper (1984a, b; also Felson, 1984) clearly show a perspective-specific divergence: actors evaluate their own action far more positively than recipients (and observers) do. This divergence occurs irrespective of whether the actor initiated the interaction sequence or only reacted to behaviour engaged in by the opponent (see figure 10.5). As Mummendey and Otten (1989) demonstrated in a further study, this was not due to perspective-specific differences in the perceptual representation of the interaction sequence, but was clearly based on a disagreement in evaluating one's own vs. the other's action (see also Mikula's (1994) research on determinants of everyday experience of injustice).

Social influence and coercive power

As we have seen, aggression involves subjective judgements about the actor's intentions and about whether the behaviour is normatively appropriate. Tedeschi and co-workers have suggested that aggression should be analysed by separating behaviour from evaluation. When viewed in an evaluatively neutral manner, aggressive behaviour involves a special form of social influence: an individual coerces another person to do something which that person would not have done otherwise. Aggression thus consists of the application of **coercive power** in the form of threat or punishment. By means of threat, we make clear that we want something special from someone, and that punishment will follow non-compliance. A punishment is any form of treatment that is aversive for the victim. The interesting research question is to define the conditions under which people seek to use this coercive form of influence.

Coercive power The use of threats and punishments in pursuit of social power.

Tedeschi and Felson (1994) have developed a **social interactionist theory of coercive action**, stating that the performance of a coercive action has to be seen as the result of a decision process: the actor, before engaging in threats or punishments, will have examined alternative means to achieve the relevant goals. Three major goals can be differentiated by which the choice of coercion is motivated: (1) to control others; (2) to restore justice; and (3) to assert or protect identities. The actor's decision whether or not to engage in coercion is influenced by the *expectancy* of how likely it is that the particular goal will be achieved by this means, by the *value* attached to the respective goal, and via estimation of *utilities* and *costs* associated with the behavioural alternatives (see figure 10.6).

Social interactionist theory of coercive action A theory to describe and explain aggression by separating its behavioural and judgemental aspects. In behavioural terms, aggression is defined as **coercive power**. Whether this coercion is perceived as aggressive depends on evaluative judgements held by the opponents of an outside observer.

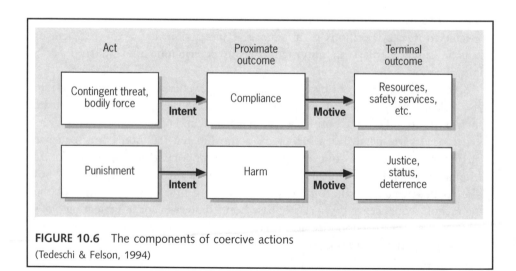

FIGURE 10.6   The components of coercive actions
(Tedeschi & Felson, 1994)

Above all, the performance of a coercive action is preceded or guided by a process of rationality. Rationality might vary with respect to the amount of elaboration and the extent of thought; it might be weak, especially if the situation is rather emotional, or if quick decisions have to be made. Rational decision is, however, the fundamental principle. Depending on the three different goals that are pursued by coercion, the outcomes of coercive actions acquire different values: if the goal is to achieve some positive resource, compliance by the target might be the intended outcome; if, however, the goal is to restore justice or to restore identity, the goal might be to harm or injure the target.

In this sense, the Germans' behaviour towards the Tunisians in our scenario could be described as the subjectively optimum alternative to achieve situationally relevant goals, possibly protection of their own identity as strong and dominant against a foreigner (see chapter 15), possibly restoration of justice, or both. The question of whether the coercive action is evaluated as *aggression* is quite independent of this description. It has less to do with the conditions for the occurrence of the behaviour than with the conditions under which certain behaviours are consensually *interpreted* as 'aggressive'.

Attribution and aggression

Actions in themselves do not contain the defining criteria mentioned above – intention to harm, actual harm and norm violation – but are actively constructed in these terms. That does not mean, however, that these perceptions happen by chance. On the contrary, everyday interactions are regulated by an impressive social consensus. Here lies an important challenge for social psychology, namely to figure out under which conditions people react to aversive events *as if* they were aggressive ones (Rule & Ferguson, 1984). Rule and Ferguson highlight two aspects of these attributions. First, one has to determine who, or what, is perceived as *responsible* for an aversive event. Second, attributions are constituents of an is–ought discrepancy with respect to the behaviour in question; that is, a perceived discrepancy between what the actor actually did, and what he or she should have done in a given situation.

The is–ought discrepancy is particularly important when the actor is held responsible for having caused aversive consequences. To attribute responsibility, we must decide whether the aversive consequences were *intended* by or at least *foreseeable* to the actor. Results from various studies indicate that a victim or an observer will be more angry (Averill, 1982; Mikula, 1994; Torestad, 1990) and more revengeful (Ohbuchi & Kambara, 1985), the more aversive the consequences are, and the greater the perceived is–ought discrepancy is.

Norms as regulators of aggression

What fuels and what interrupts the vicious circle of reciprocal aggression?

Perceived injustice and the norm of reciprocity

Parents typically tell their children that they should not hit, scratch or kick other children, and that if they are found behaving in these ways, they will be punished. But if their little son comes home in tears, claiming that someone took away his bike, or kicked him, the same parents will typically tell him: 'If someone kicks you, then kick back!' Gouldner (1960) proposes that the *norm of reciprocity* ('tit for tat') is a socially shared prescription that operates in many different societies (see chapters 11 and 12). If persons think they are victims of aggression, then, following the reciprocity norm, they can feel justified in retaliating. Experimental studies support this observation: while the initiator of a hostile act is perceived as aggressive, offensive and behaving unfairly, someone who physically attacks another in response to provocation is judged to be acting defensively and fairly (Brown & Tedeschi, 1976).

As we have seen, certain information increases the probability that an action will be labelled as aggressive and that, as a consequence, the aggression will be reciprocated or escalated. In the same way, information that weakens the attribution of responsibility or the perception of norm violation can have exactly the opposite effect on the unfolding of an interaction: the perpetrator is judged less negatively, and the victim's anger and tendency to retaliate is weaker (Ohbuchi, Kameda, & Agarie, 1989; Rule, Dyck, & Nesdale, 1978; Zumkley, 1981). We might learn, for example, that the Germans in our scenario had drunk too much alcohol; in other words, that they were not fully in control of their actions, and could not have foreseen the consequences of their behaviour. Such additional information can be used to *excuse* the actor. Another possibility is that the consequences of behaviour are re-evaluated, the act being seen as justified, unavoidable or even necessary: 'Finally, the Germans gave these Tunisians what they deserved! That's the way to treat people like them.' These kinds of accounts are classified as *justifications* (Tedeschi, Lindskold, & Rosenfeld, 1985).

Social information processing

How can perspective divergence be explained by social information processing?

The preceding sections have shown that aggression is a product that emerges from mutually divergent perspectives and interpretations of one's own and another's intentions and behaviour. Hence, social information processing plays a crucial role

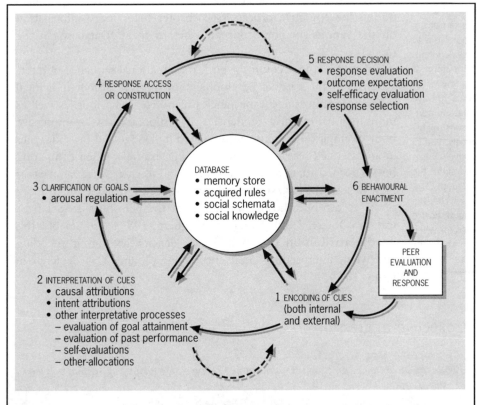

FIGURE 10.7 Social information-processing model of children's social adjustment
(Crick & Dodge, 1994, p. 76. Copyright © 1994 by the American Psychological Association.
Reprinted with permission)

in controlling the behavioural co-orientation between opponents in an aggressive
interaction sequence. Interesting work by Dodge (1986) has been concerned
with a deficient ability to perceive and/or interpret social cues sent out by other
individuals in an interaction episode. With their social information-processing model
of children's social adjustment, Dodge and his collaborators have developed an
integrative model (see figure 10.7) which identifies specific processing components of co-orientation processes in aggressive conflicts (Crick & Dodge, 1994;
Dodge, 1986).

In its reformulated version, the model describes six stages: (1) encoding of cues
(perception, attention, e.g., Thomas sees Michael taking his toy); (2) interpretation of these cues (e.g., 'Michael is intending to provoke me'); (3) clarification
of goals for one's own reaction (e.g., avoiding trouble, getting the toy back); (4)
access to a sample of responses (e.g., hitting Michael; complaining about Michael
to his mother); (5) decision in favour of one of those; and, finally, (6) behavioural enactment (e.g., Thomas hits Michael). Every process at each stage is
influenced by more ingrained concepts like norms and rules or social schemata.

Hostile attribution bias A crucial criterion for perceiving an action as aggressive is to infer the actor's hostile intent. According to the norm of reciprocity, the victim reciprocates by own aggressive actions. In contrast to non-aggressive persons, highly aggressive individuals tend to react more aggressively when the information about the actor's intent is ambiguous. This reaction coincides with the tendency to attribute hostile motives to the frustrator when clear information about the actor's intent is absent.

Conversely, these ingrained concepts are affected by actual experiences during the cognitive process (see chapter 6 for more information on the various memory concepts referred to as 'Database' in the model).

This model can account for both the situational sequence of inter-actions and the gradual development of more persistent individual differences concerning expectancies of others' behaviour, as well as more habitual response tendencies. It is supported by an impressive body of empirical evidence accumulated by Dodge and his colleagues in an extended research programme. For example, when comparing boys who, according to ratings by peers and teachers, were rated either high or low in aggression, the former turned out to be much more prone to attribute hostile intentions to the person causing a frus-tration (Dodge, 1980; Dodge & Somberg, 1987). Presumably, this **hostile attribution bias** is based on deficiencies during encoding and when interpreting social cues (stages 1 and 2 as depicted in figure 10.7).

Collective aggression

What are the different functions of norms in instigating and regulating aggression between social groups?

Violent riots during soccer games or brutal fights between police and demon-strators provide prominent examples of situations where people in groups behave in ways which, as individuals, they would probably never have dreamed of doing. In fact, some experimental studies indicate that individuals in groups show much more aggressive behaviour than they do when acting as individuals (Jaffe & Yinon, 1983; Mullen, 1986).

Deindividuation An individual state in which rational control and normative orientation are weakened, leading to greater readiness to respond in an extreme manner and to violate norms.

In the tradition of early mass psychology, associated with authors like LeBon, Tarde and Sighele, this group influence was analysed as follows: individuals in groups or masses behave more irration-ally, more impulsively and less normatively than they do as indi-viduals (see chapters 1 and 15). A modern version of this perspective is found in work on **deindividuation** (Diener, 1980; Zimbardo, 1969). Deindividuation refers to a special state in which the indi-vidual's control over his or her own behaviour is weakened, and concern about normative standards, self-presentation and the later consequences of one's behaviour decreases. Various factors contribute towards deindividuation, such as anonymity, diffusion of responsibility and a shortened time perspective. Though empirical evidence is mixed (e.g., Baron, 1970; Donnerstein, Donnerstein, Simons, & Dittrichs, 1972; Lange, 1971), in general, there is support for the idea that being in a group has a deindividuating effect on individuals, such that the usual inhibition to engage in aggressive behaviour is weakened (Prentice-Dunn & Rogers, 1983, 1989; Spivey & Prentice-Dunn, 1990).

Emergent-norm theory (Turner & Killian, 1972) stands in opposition to the basic assumptions of deindividuation theory. According to this view, extreme forms of behaviour are more likely in groups or crowds *not* because individuals lose their inhibitions or care less about norms, but because *new* norms arise. Reicher, Spears and Postmes (1995) propose in their social identity model of deindividuation (SIDE) that it is predominantly ingroup norms with which individuals comply (Postmes & Spears, 1998). For example, in situations of confrontation between the police and demonstrators, norms may develop that people should defend themselves against the police. Aggressive forms of behaviour such as throwing stones become possible not because individuals in groups or crowd situations conform less to norms, but rather because *the norms themselves* to which behaviour is oriented change. In a study designed to decide between the competing approaches of deindividuation and emergent norms, Mann, Newton and Innes (1982) found support for both theories: anonymous participants were more aggressive, but especially when aggressive behaviour was normative, and less so when it was normatively inappropriate.

Deindividuation theory leads to the prediction that more aggression can be expected in groups than in individual situations. However, again experimental findings are not clear-cut. It depends on the dominant norms within the group, whether its members will act in an extreme manner towards an opponent. Studies by Rabbie and colleagues (Rabbie, 1982; Rabbie & Horwitz, 1982; Rabbie & Lodewijkx, 1983) support this *norm-enhancement hypothesis*: groups behave more aggressively than individuals only when such behaviour can be defined as legitimate in terms of salient situational norms. Hence, it is not convincing to explain observable differences in interpersonal and **collective aggression** in terms of inner states and loss of rationality. If more extreme forms of aggression characterize group situations, then this might be due to the fact that group members mutually reinforce each other in the view that they are all behaving appropriately (Mummendey & Otten, 1993).

> **Collective aggression**
> Aggression performed simultaneously by a large number of people, groups or masses, either in a spontaneous way, like riots, or in a planned way, like wars.

Genocide (sometimes called 'ethnic cleansing') can be considered the most extreme form of collective aggression. Genocide implies a power hierarchy, with the perpetrators as the dominating and the victims as the dominated group. Aggression against the victim group is not negatively sanctioned; on the contrary, atrocities can be openly announced as they are justified by the dominant ideologies.

In his monograph *The Roots of Evil*, Staub (1989) argues that difficult living conditions are an important antecedent of genocide. In situations where the society is unstable and difficult to change through individual effort (e.g., as an extreme case, during war), ideologies that provide simple solutions can easily develop. Here, from the perspective of the perpetrators, ethnic cleansing fulfils social functions; the expulsion of the minority is assumed to solve societal problems.

Based on his analysis of four instances of mass killing or genocide, the most extreme one being the German Holocaust, Staub stresses that the atrocities of genocide develop gradually. In this process the norms provided by the society and demonstrated by bystanders, who either support or disapprove of aggression, play a crucial role. Beginning with less harmful behaviours, the perpetrators may gradually undergo psychological changes. Depending on the prevailing ideology, an aggressive act may imply both the victims' devaluation as well as the perpetrators' superior status. On these grounds, increasing levels of harm can be inflicted together with an increasingly firm sense of 'justification'. The superior group claims that it has to protect itself against the minority. For the sake of 'ethnic purity', repression, expulsion and, finally, mass killing become legitimized. According to Staub, the potential power of bystanders in this process is great; their action or inaction can either challenge or support the ideologies that fuel a progression of aggression.

Summary and Conclusions

At the beginning of this chapter we asked: What can cause a person to insult, hurt or even kill another person? Why do people treat others in ways that they would certainly never wish to be treated themselves? We have looked at a number of theoretical approaches and a variety of empirical findings in the field of aggression. We can summarize the picture as follows.

Aggression can be the reaction to the experience of frustration and anger, especially if the situation provides cues that elicit associations with aggression schemata. Aggressive behaviour can be learned through instrumental conditioning or modelling. The readiness to actually use this behaviour arises when it is seen as a useful means to an end – i.e., terminating a situation which is physically or psychologically aversive, and for which another person is held responsible.

We have also seen that the same behaviour can be judged as aggressive or not, depending on relevant norms, and on how the aggressive behaviour is attributed. Judgemental perspectives are also relevant. In particular, there are clear differences in the evaluation of identical behaviour from the perspective of harm-doer and victim.

Aggressive behaviour, whether between individuals or groups, is – like other forms of social behaviour – regulated by socially accepted and relevant situational norms. Looking for the causes of aggression, therefore, we should not concentrate on circumstances that energize individual drives or reduce the rational control of behaviour. Rather, we should focus on the conditions which – at least from the actor's perspective – make the intentional harm to another person seem both appropriate and justified.

1 Discuss the descriptive and evaluative constituents of the concept of 'aggression'.

2 In what ways do attributional processes influence aggressive tendencies and actions?

3 Compare the function of anger emotions as conceptualized in the approaches of Berkowitz and Zillmann.

4 The effects of media violence on aggression are well documented. How can different theories of aggression account for these effects?

5 Which are the specific conditions that increase the likelihood of family violence?

6 What are the typical characteristics of victims and perpetrators of bullying and mobbing?

7 Discuss the relation between aggression and coercive action.

8 'Intergroup aggression is irrational, impulsive and lacks normative concerns.' Discuss this statement in the context of current theoretical positions.

Baron, R. A., & Richardson, D. R. (1994). *Human aggression* (2nd ed.). New York: Plenum Press. Readable, wide-ranging introductory overview.

Berkowitz, L. (1993). *Aggression: Its causes, consequences, and control.* New York: McGraw-Hill. Comprehensive synopsis of the psychology of aggression, with main focus on the author's cognitive-neoassociationistic approach.

Geen, R. G. (1998). Aggression and antisocial behavior. In D. T. Gilbert, S. T. Fiske, & G. Lindzey (Eds.), *The handbook of social psychology* (4th ed., Vol. 2, pp. 317–56). New York: McGraw-Hill. Comprehensive review of current research on aggression; amongst others, covering the issue of gender differences and individual differences as moderators of aggression.

Goldstein, A. P. (1994). *The ecology of aggression.* New York: Plenum Press. Monograph analysing aggression as a person-environment event. Informative review on the ecology of aggression.

Staub, E. (1989). *The roots of evil. The origins of genocide and other group violence.* Cambridge: Cambridge University Press. Characterization of conditions and processes, both psychological and non-psychological, underlying various forms of mass violence.

Tedeschi, J. T., & Felson, R. B. (1994). *Aggression and coercive actions: A social interactionist perspective.* Washington, DC: American Psychological Association. A comprehensive monograph on the current state of psychological aggression research, a critical review of influential theoretical approaches, and an outline of a new social interactionist perspective on aggression and violence.

KEY STUDIES

Berkowitz, L., & LePage, A. (1967). Weapons as aggression-eliciting stimuli. *Journal of Personality and Social Psychology*, 7, 202–7.

Zillmann, D., Johnson, R. C., & Day, K. D. (1974). Attribution of apparent arousal and proficiency of recovery from sympathetic activation affecting excitation transfer to aggressive behavior. *Journal of Experimental Social Psychology*, 10, 503–15.

Social Interaction: Co-operation and Competition

11

Paul A. M. Van Lange and Carsten K. W. De Dreu

OUTLINE

How do people deal with conflicts between self-interest and collective interest? In particular, what makes people willing to forgo immediate self-interest and behave in a cooperative manner? The chapter discusses four key variables that promote cooperative behaviour: interpersonal dispositions, beliefs regarding other's behaviour, relationship-specific features (such as commitment and trust), and social norms (such as equality, reciprocity and equity). The chapter also considers the question of why cooperative behaviour declines with increasing group size, and why interactions between groups are less cooperative than interactions between individuals. We conclude by reviewing promising avenues for solving conflict, including third-party intervention and structural solutions that seek to change the decision or outcome structure of the situation.

KEY CONCEPTS

- Competition
- Cooperation
- Distributive justice
- Dual-concern model
- Experimental games
- Interdependence structure
- Mediation
- Mixed-motive situations
- Negotiation
- Procedural justice

- Social dilemma
- Social norms
- Social value orientation
- Structural solutions
- Team games
- Third-party intervention
- Transformation
- Trust
- Zero-sum situation

Introduction

What are mixed-motive situations?
How can the prisoner's dilemma be characterized in terms of correspondence of outcomes and basis for dependence?

Winter 1978/1979. Due to severe weather conditions, heavy snow in particular, a small village in the north of the Netherlands was completely cut off from the rest of the country, so that there was no electricity to use for light, heating, television, etc. However, one of the 150 inhabitants owned a generator that could provide sufficient electricity for everyone in this small community, if and only if they exercised substantial restraint in their energy use. For example, they should use only one light, refrain from using heated water, the heating should be limited to about 18 degrees Celsius, and the curtains should be kept closed. As it turned out, the generator collapsed because most people were in fact using heated water, living comfortably at 21 degrees Celsius, watching television and burning several lights simultaneously. After being without electricity for a while, they were able to repair the generator, and this time inspectors were appointed to check whether people were using more electricity than they had agreed upon. But even then, the generator eventually collapsed due to overuse of energy. And again, every inhabitant suffered from the cold, the lack of any light, and of course the inability to watch television.

The situation described above may be rather unusual and extreme. Yet conflicts between self-interest and collective interest pervade everyday life. For example, the division of household chores among relationship partners can take cooperative or non-cooperative forms, as can **negotiations** such as the dispute between seller and buyer over the price and services relevant to a product, or discussions among colleagues concerning who gets the best office. Such conflicts can also be found at the societal level. While we may at times be tempted to evade taxes, or to pollute the environment, society as a whole is of course better served when most members do not evade taxes and do not pollute the environment. Various media remind us of such interdependence situations, as well as of intense conflicts between groups, including the many examples of non-cooperative – and often violent – interactions among ethnic groups (e.g., conflicts of interests in the Middle East), or the ways in which trade unions negotiate with business companies (e.g., negotiations regarding salaries and working conditions). In fact, conflicts between self-interest and collective interests are so pervasive in everyday life that one can go so far as to claim that the most challenging task governments, organizations and even partners in a relationship face is to manage conflicts successfully between self-interest and collective interest.

Negotiation Discussion between two or more parties with the apparent aim of resolving divergence of interest.

The theme of **cooperation** and **competition** has been a prominent domain of theory and research within a variety of disciplines, including philosophy, political science, economics, sociology, biology and
psychology. It was explicitly addressed by the philosopher Thomas
Hobbes (1651), who asked: how are collectivities able to function at
all, if – so he believed – humans tend to be primarily concerned with
pursuing their immediate personal interest? Some scientists, such as
the economist Adam Smith, responded to the Hobbesian problem
by assuming that collectivities function quite well *because*, if everybody pursues
his or her self-interest, society would benefit as an unintended consequence. In
other words, Adam Smith in many respects denied the existence of conflicts between
self-interest and collective interest.

Cooperation Behaviour that
maximizes the outcomes (or
well-being) of a collective.

Competition Behaviour that
maximizes relative advantage
over others.

Many or most scientists now believe that Adam Smith's view is too narrow,
if not simply wrong. Indeed, as illustrated earlier, conflicts between self-interest
and collective interest are an everyday reality. Therefore, it is of clear practical
interest to understand how people behave in such situations, and how cooperative
behaviour might be promoted. In addressing this issue, many theorists assume
that humankind is rationally self-interested. People are assumed to enhance their
own outcomes (self-interest), with little or no regard for others' outcomes. This
assumption of 'rational self-interest' has dominated many of the traditional theories
relevant to interpersonal and intergroup behaviour, including early formulations
of game theory (Luce & Raiffa, 1957) and social exchange theory (Homans, 1961).
More recently, these theories have been extended and complemented by models
which assume that human behaviour is often guided by broader considerations
than direct self-interest. In addition to emphasizing long-term considerations,
more recent theories and models assume that individuals may also wish to enhance
the well-being of others, the well-being of the collective, or achieve equality in
outcomes.

This chapter focuses on such broader considerations, which are needed to fully
comprehend and analyse the ways in which we interact with others, and how individuals may or may not solve conflicts of interest. Social psychologists are not the
only scientists who stress the importance of these broader considerations. For
example, such views have also been developed in the context of the biological
sciences and in evolutionary theory. However, social-psychological theory and
research focus more directly on the intrapersonal and situational determinants of
such broader considerations, which in turn help us understand behaviours and interaction phenomena such as cooperation and competition. Throughout
this chapter, we use *interdependence theory* (Kelley & Thibaut, 1978;
for a recent overview, see Rusbult & Van Lange, 1996) as a conceptual framework for reviewing and illustrating several key phenomena
and psychological mechanisms relevant to understanding cooperation
and competition. As we shall see, this theory emphasizes **interdependence structure**, situations in which personal outcomes are partially

Interdependence structure
Situations in which personal
outcomes are partially or
completely determined by the
actions of one or more others.

or completely determined by the actions of one or more others, and the ways in which individuals might transform such situations and pursue broader goals.

Mixed-motive situations

Mixed-motive situations
Situations characterized by the conflict between personal goals and collective goals.

To fully understand cooperation and competition, it is important to analyse the features of situations that permit cooperative and competitive behaviour. Through situational analysis, game theory 'discovered' several so-called **mixed-motive situations** (Schelling, 1960); that is, situations in which the individual's interest partially corresponds and partially conflicts with the interests of others. The most famous mixed-motive situation following from game theory is the *prisoner's dilemma*, which represents a specific yet intense conflict between self-interest and collective interest. Consider, for example, two neighbours living in apartments with thin walls who may wish to play their favourite music at high volume, but together they would probably be better off playing it at a somewhat lower volume. Figure 11.1 presents a prisoner's dilemma involving two individuals, whereby a *cooperative choice* (C-choice) stands for playing music at moderate volumes, and a non-cooperative, or *defecting choice* (D-choice), stands for playing it at high volume. If John plays his music at high volume, and Sarah does not, the outcomes for John are very good (16), but those for Sarah are poor (4); the reverse occurs when Sarah plays her music at full blast, whereas John does not (Sarah 16; John 4). If both listen at moderate volumes, the outcomes for both are fairly good (12 and 12), and considerably better than if both listen at high volumes (8 and 8). The prisoner's dilemma represents a conflict between acting in an individually rational manner (i.e., a non-cooperative choice yields greater outcomes than a cooperative choice, irrespective of the other's choice) and acting in a collectively rational manner (i.e., outcomes for each individual are greater when both cooperate than when both do not cooperate).

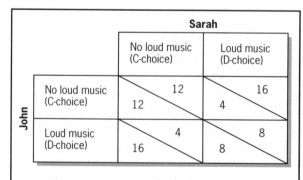

FIGURE 11.1 Example of a prisoner's dilemma for Sarah and John

	Percentage of others who are members				
	0	25	50	75	100
Being a member (C-choice)	−25	−15	−5	+5	+15
Not being a member (D-choice)	−15	−5	+5	+15	+25

FIGURE 11.2 An example of an N-person prisoner's dilemma

The conflict between individual and collective rationality apparent in the prisoner's dilemma can be extended to situations involving many individuals, often referred to as *N-person prisoner's dilemmas*. For example, it is attractive for many individuals to commute in their own cars – they can sit comfortably and quietly listen to their choice of music, and avoid other people's mobile phones (individual rationality). However, at the level of the collective or group, each individual may be better off if he or she succeeds in coordinating a carpooling or ridesharing system so as to minimize traffic congestion and environmental pollution (collective rationality). Similarly, trade unions can function considerably better to the extent that a greater number of individuals become members; however, membership requires fees and time and thus is a costly option from an individual perspective. Using this latter example, figure 11.2 presents an N-person prisoner's dilemma, revealing that an individual's outcomes are always better by not being a member (D-choice) than by being a member (C-choice), while at the same time his or her outcomes are better when all or most are members than when very few are members. In this example, being a member is always more costly than not being a member by 10 outcome units, irrespective of the percentage of others who are members (because of the money and time it takes). At the same time, the individual's outcomes are greater to the degree that more others are members. And, if all are members, each member would be better off (an outcome of +15; see top right cell) than if there were no members at all, including the individual himself or herself (an outcome of −15; see bottom left cell). Thus, like the two-person prisoner's dilemma, this N-person prisoner's dilemma represents a conflict between individual rationality and collective rationality.

The concept of **social dilemma** refers to situations in which self-interest and collective interest are at odds (for a recent review, see Komorita & Parks, 1995). Social dilemmas may differ in terms of the specific conflict of interest they represent; that is, social dilemmas do not necessarily take the form of a prisoner's dilemma. Implicitly or explicitly, most of the remainder of this chapter will focus on prisoner's dilemmas

Social dilemma Situation in which self-interest and collective interest are at odds.

because they have received most empirical attention and because this specific structure shares important features with many everyday-life situations in which self-interest and collective interests are at odds (e.g., negotiations).

Disregarding structural differences between social dilemmas, these situations can differ in terms of 'what it takes' to solve such social dilemmas fruitfully: some social dilemmas call for a decision whether or not to forego personal benefits, whereas other social dilemmas call for a decision whether or not to engage in costly actions. In this regard, one may distinguish between social traps and social fences (for an overview, see Messick & Brewer, 1983).

Social traps are social dilemmas in which actions that are attractive to each individual in the short run result over time in costs that are shared by all individuals involved (i.e., long-term collective costs). An interesting example of a social trap is provided by Hardin's (1968) description of the 'tragedy of the commons'. It describes how herdsmen in little villages utilized a publicly owned resource – public pasture. Most herdsmen increased their herd size using the pasture. After all, the greater the herd size, the greater their profits. 'And what difference does it make when one adds a few animals?', so they must have thought. As it turned out, this *did* make a big difference because most or all herdsmen thought the same way, and added animals to the pasture. The collective result of these individual actions was that the exceptionally large number of cows and sheep led to overgrazing, exceeding the natural replenishment rate of the pasture, and ultimately leading to the loss of the entire herd that grazed on it. This problem is also often referred to as a *resource dilemma*. Other examples of such situations are energy conservation, environmental pollution and depletion of natural resources (e.g., overfishing).

Social fences are social dilemmas in which actions that are unattractive to each individual in the short run result over time in benefits to the collective (long-term collective benefits). Examples are so-called *public good dilemmas*, such as the provision of health care, public television, recreation and sport facilities. These public good dilemmas pose an interesting problem, especially because often individuals who do not contribute to the public good will profit from it. This gives rise to the temptation to free-ride on the contributions of others (Stroebe & Frey, 1982). For example, it is tempting to profit from the activities of student unions (e.g., greater computer facilities for students at universities), while not contributing any money, time or effort to these unions.

Under some circumstances, individuals may be less likely to cooperate in public good dilemmas than in resource dilemmas because cooperation in public goods requires immediate losses, whereas cooperation in resource dilemmas requires foregoing immediate benefits. Losses tend to inflict greater pain than equivalent gains yield pleasure, rendering cooperation less likely in public good dilemmas than in resource dilemmas. However, this effect occurs to the extent that one evaluates gains and losses from an individual perspective (i.e., in terms of '*my* own gains and losses'). When evaluated from a collective perspective (i.e., in terms of '*our* gains and losses'), public goods dilemmas may evoke an even greater level of cooperation (De Dreu & McCusker, 1997).

The domain of interdependence structure

Mixed-motive situations, such as the prisoner's dilemma, the N-person prisoner's dilemma and the social dilemma, represent only *one* type of interdependence situation. That is, they represent only one of the various interdependence situations that are logically possible. For example, two presidential candidates are also interdependent in enhancing the odds of becoming the president of the United States. The strategies that they might use to increase their votes might be quite diverse, emphasizing one's own strengths, emphasizing the other's limitations, or both. But the underlying structure is probably quite different from a prisoner's dilemma, as it resembles some basic features of a **zero-sum situation**, whereby the gain for the one person implies an equal loss to the other, and vice versa. Thus, there is an exceptionally strong conflict of interest. Alternatively, when two colleagues need each other's expertise to perform well on a task – and both are motivated to perform really well – then such individuals face a situation in which they need each other to accomplish their goals, and they can both succeed or both fail. Here, there is interdependence as well, but no conflict of interest; rather, a perfect correspondence between one another's interests.

> **Zero-sum situation** A situation in which an individual's own interest is completely conflicting with a partner's interest.

What are the key features of outcome interdependence? What are the primary 'dimensions' underlying outcome interdependence? Interdependence theory (Kelley & Thibaut, 1978) provides a comprehensive framework for understanding four features of outcome interdependence: (1) degree of dependence; (2) mutuality of dependence; (3) correspondence of outcomes; and (4) basis for dependence.

The first feature, *degree of dependence*, refers to the degree to which an individual's ability to attain good outcomes is influenced by the actions of an interdependent other. A strong degree of dependence, especially a strong degree of interdependence, is often associated with subjective feelings of dependence and long-term orientation (e.g., commitment to a relationship). Commitment has been demonstrated to be a powerful determinant of prosocial behaviour in the context of personal relationships and formal organizations (e.g., Rusbult & Farrell, 1983; Rusbult, Verrette, Whitney, Slovik, & Lipkus, 1991; Van Lange, Rusbult, et al., 1997; see chapters 9 and 12). In contrast, increasing independence tends to be associated with reduced prosocial behaviour. For example, the presence of good alternatives (which reduces dependence) tends to be associated with a stronger orientation to one's own outcomes, this being the case in the context of both ongoing relationships and specific interactions, such as in negotiation.

The second feature, *mutuality of dependence*, refers to the degree to which two individuals are mutually or unilaterally dependent on each other for attaining good outcomes. This feature of interdependence is directly relevant to symmetric and asymmetric power relations. When mutuality of dependence is high (i.e., symmetric power relations), the potential for exploitation on the part of one or both individuals is low. Such interactions and relationships tend to be associated with stability and mutual cooperation. When mutuality of dependence is low, the potential for exploitation is greater, which tends to be associated with less stability and less cooperation. This would appear particularly true when there is some conflict of interests. Conversely, when there is little conflict of interest, greater weakness and dependence on the part of the 'needy' individual can actually increase the likelihood of receiving help (e.g., Schopler & Bateson, 1965). Mutuality of dependence is also relevant to understanding social information processing. The more dependent individual is likely to engage in thorough, systematic information processing to find out 'what the other is like', whereas the less dependent person is likely to engage in shallow information processing and stereotyping (Fiske, 1993).

A third feature, labelled *correspondence of outcomes*, refers to the degree to which preferences correspond vs. conflict. The example of the two presidential candidates represents very low correspondence (i.e., a strong conflict of interest), whereas the two partners who would benefit from each other's expertise are in a situation involving very high correspondence of outcomes (i.e., no conflict of interest). This feature, already identified in classic theories of cooperation and competition (Deutsch, 1949b), 'sets the stage' for the elicitation of important motives. When outcomes are quite correspondent, cooperative motives are activated, feelings of trust are enhanced, and over time individuals tend to obtain mutual cooperation. In contrast, when outcomes are quite non-correspondent, non-cooperative or competitive motives are activated, feelings of distrust are enhanced, and over time individuals tend to obtain mutual competition (e.g., Kelley & Grzelak, 1972). At the same time, when individuals are confronted with an increase in non-correspondence (i.e., the individuals' interests become gradually more conflicting over time), then they are likely to develop strong norms and even formal agreements to protect the well-being of all individuals involved (e.g., Thibaut & Faucheux, 1965).

Finally, a fourth feature of interdependence is labelled *basis for dependence*, and refers to the degree to which a person's outcomes are unilaterally influenced by another person's actions vs. jointly influenced by both own and other person's actions. When my outcomes are unilaterally influenced by a partner, control over my outcomes is in the hands of the partner, which is termed *fate control*. For example, a person who is in a position to do you an important favour has unilateral control over your outcomes. In contrast, when an individual's outcomes are *jointly* influenced by own and other's actions, control is in the hands of *both* partners. A trivial but illustrative example of behaviour control can be derived from traffic situations, in which the outcomes (potentially drastic ones in this case, no collision vs. collision) are determined by whether or not both drivers drive on the correct side of the road. It is the combination of own and other's behaviour which determines the outcomes for both individuals. This is called *behaviour control*, because an individual can influence the other's behaviour in the here and now by making a particular choice. For example, in conversations, we influence the behaviour of the other by starting to talk vs. quietly waiting for the other to start talking. When behaviour control is mutual, such situations call for *coordination*, an example being the alternation of talking and listening in conversations, or the passing of two individuals on a pavement.

Exchange is linked to motivation (e.g., is John willing to give up some of his interest to benefit Sarah?), whereas coordination is more strongly linked to individual and collective 'ability' (e.g., are John and Sarah able to match or mismatch each other's choices to their joint benefit?). The distinction between fate control (exchange) and behaviour control (coordination) is quite useful to understanding why dyads, groups or organizations do not function as well as they could. For example, as described in chapter 14, productivity in organizations is often a function of (1) loss due to insufficient motivation to contribute to group performance (motivation loss), and (2) loss due to poor coordination of individual efforts (coordination loss; Steiner, 1972; see also Kerr & Bruun, 1983).

The four features of outcome interdependence discussed above allow one to categorize and define each interdependence situation. The two-person prisoner's dilemma, for example, is a situation that is characterized by fairly low correspondence of outcomes, and often accompanied by high levels of mutuality of dependence. The primary basis of dependence is fate control (and not behaviour control), thus calling for exchange (i.e., exchanges of cooperative behaviours, which serve collective well-being), rather than coordination. Hence, from an interdependence perspective, the two-person prisoner's dilemma represents a motivational problem (are individuals willing to enhance each other's interests at some cost to self?), suggests the importance of beliefs about other's behaviour (is the other likely to make a cooperative choice?), and evokes norms that serve to protect the well-being of both individuals ('Isn't the cooperative choice the morally appropriate choice?'). These are three key issues relevant to why individuals may make a non-selfish choice in prisoner's dilemmas and related mixed-motive situations.

Beyond Direct Self-Interest: Transformation of Situations

What is social value orientation? What are the main types of social value orientation? What are four sources of transformation?

Is our behaviour always guided by direct self-interest? Do we always act in such a manner as to enhance own immediate outcomes? As alluded to earlier, the answer is 'no'. Frequently, we act in a manner so as to obtain good personal outcomes in the future, and take a long-term orientation to a concrete situation in the here and now. Alternatively, we may take account of the outcomes of other individuals with whom we are interdependent. Just as we wish to enhance outcomes for ourselves, we may wish to enhance the outcomes for others. Or we may wish that self and other get equally good outcomes. In either case, people go 'beyond direct self-interest'.

The notion that people go beyond direct self-interest is formulated in interdependence theory (Kelley & Thibaut, 1978), which makes a distinction between *the given matrix* and *the effective matrix*. The given matrix is largely based on hedonic, self-interested preferences, and summarizes the consequences of the individual's own actions and the partner's actions on the individual's outcomes. In the example discussed earlier, John's given matrix is based on the immediate consequences of own and other's behaviours for his outcomes. Presumably, John's best outcome would be when Sarah plays her music at moderate volume while John plays his music at high volume; the second best outcome would be when both play their music at moderate volume; the third best outcome is when both play their music at high volume; and John's worst outcome would be when Sarah plays her music at high volume while John plays his music at moderate volume. In the light of these preferences, John 'should' be very likely to play his music at a high volume.

However, John may actually play his music at moderate volume rather than high volume. How can one understand such behaviour? According to interdependence theory, John is *transforming* the given matrix into an *effective matrix*, a matrix which summarizes John's broader preferences than the simple pursuit of direct self-interest. For example, John may assign value to the well-being of Sarah, seeking to enhance *joint outcomes* rather than his own outcomes with no regard for Sarah's outcomes. Thus, interdependence theory assumes that the pursuit of direct immediate outcomes often provides an incomplete understanding of interpersonal behaviour. That is why this theory introduces the concept of **transformation**, defined as a movement away from preferences of direct self-interest by attaching importance to longer-term outcomes or outcomes of another person (other persons or groups).

Transformation A movement away from preferences of direct self-interest by attaching importance to longer-term outcomes or outcomes of another person (other persons or groups).

The concept of transformation was based in part on the literature on **social value orientation** (McClintock, 1972; see also Griesinger & Livingston, 1973), which distinguishes among eight distinct preferences or orientations, including altruism, cooperation, individualism, competition, aggression, as well as nihilism, masochism and inferiority (we shall not discuss the latter three since they are exceptionally uncommon). As shown in figure 11.3, in this typology, *cooperation* is defined as the tendency to emphasize positive outcomes for self and other ('doing well together'). In contrast, *competition* is defined as the tendency to emphasize relative advantage over others ('doing better than others'), thereby assigning positive weight to outcomes for self and negative weight to outcomes for other. *Individualism* is defined by the tendency to maximize outcomes for self, with little or no regard for outcomes for other; *altruism* is defined by the tendency to maximize outcomes for other, with no or very little regard for outcomes for self (see chapter 9); and *aggression* is defined by the tendency to minimize outcomes for other (see chapter 10). Cooperation, individualism and

Social value orientation Preference for particular patterns of outcomes for self and others.

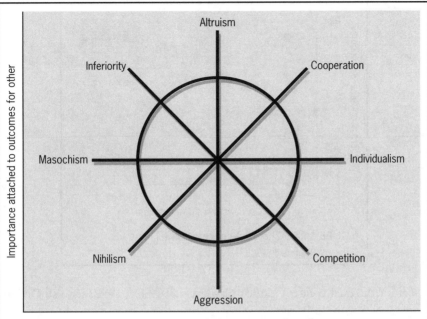

FIGURE 11.3 Typology of social value orientations
(McClintock, 1972; Griesinger & Livingston, 1973)

competition represent common orientations in that most of us probably have repeated experience with each of these tendencies, either through introspection or through observation of other's actions. Thus, the eight outcome transformations can be schematically represented by two dimensions, including (1) the importance (or weight) attached to outcomes for self, and (2) the importance (or weight) attached to outcomes for other.

Similar models have been developed by other researchers. The most notable model is the **dual-concern model** (Pruitt & Rubin, 1986), developed in an attempt to understand the values or concerns that might underlie negotiation. As in the model described above, the dual-concern model assumes two basic concerns: (1) concern about own outcomes, and (2) concern about other's outcomes. The dual-concern model assumes that each of these concerns can run from weak to strong (see figure 11.4). This model delineates four negotiation strategies based on high vs. low concern about own outcomes and high vs. low concern about other's outcomes. As can be seen in figure 11.4, according to the dual-concern model, *problem-solving* is a function of high self-concern and high other-concern; *yielding* is a function of low self-concern and high other-concern; *contending* is a function of high self-concern and low other-concern; and *inaction* is a function of low self-concern and low other-concern. Negotiation research has yielded good

Dual-concern model Two-dimensional model that specifies several actions in terms of concern for self and concern for other.

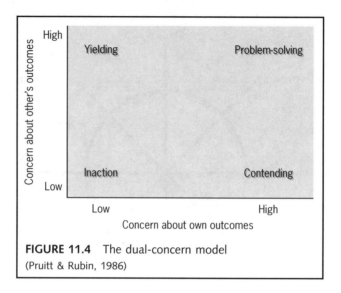

FIGURE 11.4   The dual-concern model
(Pruitt & Rubin, 1986)

support for the dual-concern model (Carnevale & Pruitt, 1992; see also De Dreu, Weingart, & Kwon, in press).

Recently, the model of social value orientation and the dual-concern model have been extended to include a third orientation (or concern), the pursuit of equality in outcomes. It appears that individuals who tend to enhance joint outcomes (cooperation, problem-solving) are also strongly concerned with equality in outcomes, whereas individuals who are more individualistic or competitive are not very strongly concerned with equality in outcomes (Van Lange, 1999). The implication is that individuals who were concerned with joint outcomes might not act cooperatively if they think that such actions create injustice, either to their own disadvantage or the other's disadvantage.

Sources of transformation

What is it that leads individuals to 'go beyond direct self-interest'? In this section, we discuss four basic sources of transformation, including (1) interpersonal dispositions; (2) beliefs regarding other's behaviour; (3) features of the relationship; and (4) **social norms**. These sources of transformation are far from absolute, but in many ways stand as key sources for understanding why individuals do or do not tend to make cooperative choices, why individuals do or do not tend to engage in constructive negotiation, and so on. The empirical research that we review is often derived from findings obtained with **experimental games**, a research tool for examining social interaction that is derived from game theory, as well as from research on behaviour in ongoing relationships, negotiation situations and organizations.

Social norms   Broadly shared guidelines for appropriate behaviour in social contexts.

Experimental games   A research tool for examining social interaction, derived from game theory.

Interpersonal dispositions

One disposition which is very closely linked to the concept of outcome trans-formation is *social value orientation* (McClintock, 1972), defined as the preference for specific patterns of outcomes for self and others. Individuals differ in the prob-ability with which they seek to enhance joint outcomes and equality in outcomes (*prosocial* orientation), own outcomes (*individualistic* orientation) and relative out-comes (*competitive* orientation). Thus, 'prosocials' are oriented towards maximizing what is best for all and minimizing differences in outcomes for self and others ('What do we get? Do we get an equal share?'); 'individualists' are oriented towards maximizing own outcomes in an absolute sense ('How much do I get?'); and 'competitors' are oriented towards maximizing own outcomes in a relative sense ('How much do I get in relation to what the other gets?'). Relative to individual-ists and competitors, prosocials are more prone to make cooperative choices in prisoner's dilemma games, large-scale social dilemmas, negotiation situations as well as in several social dilemmas in real life, such as willingness to sacrifice in ongoing relationships (De Dreu & Van Lange, 1995; Liebrand & Van Run, 1985; Van Lange, Agnew, Harinck, & Steemers, 1997).

Interestingly, by approaching others in a non-cooperative manner, competitors and individualists are likely to elicit non-cooperative behaviour from others, which may account for the fact that these individuals tend to hold individualistic or competitive beliefs regarding humankind. Prosocials, in contrast, tend to approach others cooperatively, and may elicit either cooperative or non-cooperative behavi-our from others (i.e., some people reciprocate cooperation, whereas others do not). The ultimate result of such *self-fulfilling prophecies* is that prosocials tend to develop heterogeneous beliefs regarding humankind (e.g., 'the world is peopled by cooperative as well as selfish individuals'), whereas individualists and com-petitors may develop fairly homogeneous beliefs regarding humankind (e.g., 'most people are selfish'). Competitors, in particular, tend to believe that people are not be trusted, and that they seek to exploit others. In the light of such a gloomy view of human nature, which they often confirm through their own competitive behaviour, it is 'understandable' that competitors are not inclined to behave cooperatively.

Evidence in support of these lines of reasoning comes from a classic study by Kelley and Stahelski (1970). They first assessed participants' goals with a ques-tionnaire, and classified participants as either 'cooperative' or 'competitive'. On the basis of these classifications, three pairs of participants were created: (1) co-operative pairs, (2) cooperators paired with competitors and (3) competitive pairs. The pairs played 40 trials of a two-person prisoner's dilemma, and after each block of 10 trials, participants were asked about the goals and intentions of the other person. They found that the inferences made by cooperators were more accurate overall than those made by competitors. Indeed, competitors interpreted the competitive behaviour that they themselves elicited from cooperators in terms of competitive goals. In contrast, cooperators elicited cooperation from cooperators and competition (or non-cooperative choices) from competitors, and made parallel inferences.

Several other dispositions may relate to transformation. One such variable is **trust**, defined as the general belief in the honesty and co-operative intentions of others (Yamagishi, 1988). Another dispositional variable has been developed more recently: *concern with future consequences* (Strathman, Gleicher, Boninger, & Edwards, 1994). This disposition is especially relevant in situations with an extended time horizon such as the earlier-described social traps and social fences (Messick & Brewer, 1983). While most individuals tend to prefer immediate rather than longer-term outcomes, there appears to be considerable individual variability in the weight assigned to immediate outcomes vs. future outcomes. Individuals who are more strongly inclined to adopt a long-term orientation in general are also more likely to take a long-term perspective towards interaction, and may take into account how one's own and other's actions here and now influence own and perhaps other's outcomes in the future.

> **Trust** The general belief in the honesty and cooperative intentions of others.

Finally, one might ask: Where do these interpersonal dispositions come from? While genetic influences and differences in biological make-up are plausible, there is also evidence in support of the assumption that dispositions such as social value orientation and trust are partially shaped by prior interaction experiences and further shaped by future interaction experiences. For example, prosocial orientation tends to be more prevalent among individuals raised in large families rather than small families, and the prevalence of prosocial orientation tends to increase with age (Studies 3 and 4; Van Lange, Otten, De Bruin, & Joireman, 1997). Thus, there is good reason to believe that dispositions, which are relevant to transformations, are rooted in social interaction experiences.

Beliefs regarding other's behaviour

Other's behaviour – or beliefs regarding other's behaviour – is a strong determinant of transformations and subsequent own behaviour. A pervasive effect is that the observation or expectation of non-cooperative behaviour evokes non-cooperative behaviour in the interdependent other. An observation or expectation that the interdependent other makes a cooperative choice tends to elicit (or maintain) cooperative behaviour among some (but not all) of us, especially individuals with a prosocial orientation (Kuhlman & Marshello, 1975). At the same time, it is good to realize that the link between expectations and own cooperative behaviour may be bidirectional. Expectations may cause choice, as described above. But at the same time, choice may also determine expectations. For example, individuals may base their expectations on their own inclinations (i.e., projection), or may tend to justify their behaviour by their expectation (e.g., 'I chose non-cooperatively because I thought nobody else would cooperate'; Dawes, McTavish, & Shaklee, 1977; Messé & Sivacek, 1979).

An important issue is how to approach someone with whom one wishes to develop a cooperative, mutually beneficial relationship. Should one cooperate and risk being exploited by a non-cooperative response, or should one make a non-cooperative move to demonstrate that one is not to be trifled with? Research suggests that an effective strategy is tit-for-tat (TFT). This strategy begins with a cooperative choice and subsequently imitates the other person's previous choice. It is an effective means for eliciting stable patterns of mutual cooperation (Axelrod, 1984; McClintock & Liebrand, 1988). TFT is nice, as it begins with a cooperative move. TFT is clear and predictable, and it is fair as it rewards cooperation by acting cooperatively in turn, and punishes non-cooperation by acting non-cooperatively in turn.

In an interesting experiment, Kuhlman and Marshello (1975) compared three strategies followed by the partner in a two-person prisoner's dilemma, including (1) 100 per cent cooperation, (2) tit-for-tat and (3) 100 per cent non-cooperation. In addition to the partner's strategy, they examined the social value orientation of the participant, comparing prosocials, individualists and competitors. As can be seen in figure 11.5, partners who consistently exhibited cooperation (100 per cent cooperation) elicited more than 90 per cent cooperation in prosocial participants. In contrast, individualists (38 per cent) and competitors (15 per cent) exhibited little cooperation. Partners following tit-for-tat elicited fairly high levels of cooperation in both prosocials (80 per cent) and individualists (65 per cent), but failed to promote cooperation in competitors (17 per cent). Partners who

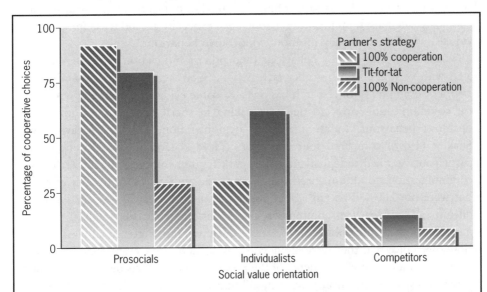

FIGURE 11.5 Percentage of cooperative choices as a function of individual's own social value orientation (prosocial vs. individualist vs. competitor) and partner's strategy (100 per cent cooperation vs. tit-for-tat vs. 100 per cent non-cooperation)

(Kuhlman & Marshello, 1975. Copyright © 1975 by the American Psychological Association. Reprinted with permission)

consistently exhibited non-cooperation elicited very little cooperation in pro-socials, individualists and competitors. The interesting conclusion following from this work is that tit-for-tat is quite effective in eliciting cooperation, even among individuals who are primarily or exclusively interested in pursuing self-interest. Yet tit-for-tat is unable to elicit cooperation in competitors. This may be because competitors cannot 'beat' tit-for-tat; that is, competitors cannot receive greater outcomes than the tit-for-tat partner by making cooperative choices. More recent evidence indicates that, if they can, competitors tend to withdraw from others pursuing tit-for-tat (Van Lange & Visser, 1999). Indeed, if people cannot accomplish their primary interaction goals (in this case, receiving better outcomes than others), they are likely to 'move away' from others.

Beliefs about other's behaviour are central in the so-called *goal-expectation theory* advanced by Pruitt and Kimmel (1977). This theory argues that cooperation is likely to be effectively promoted when two conditions are met: (1) the individual must pursue cooperative *goals*, and (2) the individual must *expect cooperation* from the interdependent other. The goal/expectation logic has received good support in several social dilemma studies, including ones examining real-life social dilemmas such as whether to commute by car or by public transport. Thus, expectations regarding other's cooperation are especially important to individuals who seek to accomplish mutual cooperation. The important point is that individuals who actually hold cooperative goals may not exhibit cooperation if they fear that others will not cooperate. Therefore, according to Yamagishi (1986), it is important to establish a sanctioning system that punishes people who do not cooperate; such a system promotes cooperative expectations and trust among individuals, which in turn may promote cooperative behaviour.

Beliefs regarding other's behaviour (and other's motivation) are often associated with or influenced by other factors. One such factor is verbal *communication*. For example, prior research has revealed some evidence that the opportunity for communication prior to decision-making in social dilemmas promotes cooperative behaviour. In an interesting demonstration, Dawes, McTavish and Shaklee (1977) compared four conditions: (1) a no-communication condition: participants worked independently on a task for ten minutes; (2) an irrelevant-communication condition: participants discussed several topics for ten minutes but were not allowed to talk about issues relevant to their choices in the social dilemma; (3) a relevant-communication condition: participants talked for ten minutes about future choices in the social dilemma, but were not allowed to disclose the choice that they were intended to make; and (4) relevant communication with non-binding announcements of their intended choices. As figure 11.6 shows, percentages of cooperation were only 30 and 33 in the no-communication and irrelevant-communication conditions, and 72 and 73 in the two conditions in which participants discussed the social dilemma. Accordingly, this study revealed that communication can be quite effective in promoting cooperation, but for such communication to be effective it should deal with issues relevant to the social dilemma task at hand. Subsequent research has also revealed that communication appears to be especially effective if it results in promises by all of its members to

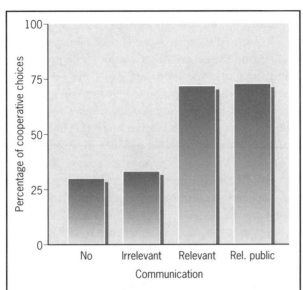

FIGURE 11.6 Percentage of cooperative choices in five-person groups who did not communicate (no communication), communicated about an irrelevant topic (irrelevant communication), communicated about the social dilemma (relevant communication), or communicated about their intended choices and made those intended (but non-binding) choices public (relevant and public communication)
(Dawes, McTavish, & Shaklee, 1977)

cooperate (Orbell, Van de Kragt, & Dawes, 1988). Although there are still several specific explanations that might account for the beneficial effects of communication, it is plausible that communication enhances building trust in one another's cooperative behaviour, which in turn promotes cooperation.

Expectations or beliefs regarding another's behaviour are also importantly influenced by impressions of the other's personality (see chapter 5). Especially in social dilemma situations, people are strongly motivated to form impressions, whereby they tend to focus on morality-related impressions ('Is the other a good person?'; Van Lange & Kuhlman, 1994) rather than other impressions. Also, people base their decision to cooperate on information about other's group membership, and cooperate less when others belong to groups that are stereotypically seen as competitive and opportunistic (e.g., business students), rather than as nice and cooperative (e.g., religion students) (De Dreu, Yzerbyt, & Leyens, 1995).

Features of the relationship

Outcome transformations may be guided by features of the relationship. One important example is the degree of *satisfaction* one derives from being involved in that relationship – a greater degree of satisfaction stimulates a prosocial transformation and is likely to produce cooperative behaviours such as constructive problem-solving, accommodating to the other's needs and willingness to sacrifice. Interestingly, above and beyond the degree of satisfaction, such prosocial transformations are greater to the extent that the individual (1) perceives his or her *quality of alternatives* to be poor (e.g., the perceived quality of specific partners, or of having no involvement with others), and (2) has *invested* more in that relationship (e.g., shared friends, shared mortgage, shared secrets). Higher satisfaction, poorer alternatives and larger investment together produce the experience of *commitment*, defined in terms of strong desire to continue the relationship, long-term orientation and feelings of attachment. Commitment tends to promote several relationship-maintenance mechanisms, including (1) accommodation, the willingness to respond constructively rather than destructively to a partner's destructive behaviour, and (2) willingness to sacrifice (Rusbult et al., 1991; Van Lange, Rusbult, et al., 1997). Commitment may also motivate individuals to derogate alternative, potentially tempting partners and to develop overly positive images of their own partner and relationship (Rusbult & Van Lange, 1996; see chapter 12). There is a good deal of support for the strong influence of commitment on such behaviours and perceptions, in the domain of both close relationships and employee–organization relationships. For example, individuals are less likely to engage in absenteeism and more likely to engage in organizational citizenship and extra-role behaviour (i.e., efforts that serve organizational well-being) to the degree that they are committed to the organization (Rusbult & Farrell, 1983).

A second variable relevant to ongoing relationships is *trust*. Although trust is sometimes considered a dispositional variable (see above), it often develops in the context of the relationship between two interdependent individuals (Holmes & Rempel, 1989). Through the exchange of cooperative behaviours, partners in a relationship not only fruitfully solve the potential problems at hand, but also communicate trust to one another. Trust is presumably associated with long-term orientation, believing that their partner will reciprocate favours and sacrifices. In contrast, lack of trust is likely to guide somewhat less benevolent interpretations of partner's behaviour, and can instigate a negative cycle of reciprocity up to escalation of conflict. As we have seen for commitment, trust too is a key concept in the context of close relationships as well as relationships among colleagues in organizations and business (De Dreu, Giebels, & Van de Vliert, 1998; Kramer & Tyler, 1995).

Social norms

Outcome transformations may also be rooted in social norms that define rules for dealing with specific interdependence problems and opportunities. Such norms often serve to (1) enhance the functioning of groups and societies, even the more micro-level forms of functioning, such as everyday rules of civility and decency, and (2) protect the 'weak' from being exploited by the powerful and provide help to individuals who are in strong need of such help. Social norms deal with the distribution and allocation of outcomes, or they deal with procedural issues.

Three types of distribution norms have received most theoretical and empirical attention. The norm of **distributive justice** promotes distributions of outcomes such that each member gets an equal share (equality norm), or a share that is proportional to his or her invest- ment and contributions – the larger the relative contribution, the larger one's share (equity norm; Adams, 1965). More generally, distributive justice refers to criteria of fairness used to evaluate the

Distributive justice Criteria of fairness used to evaluate the quality of one's own outcomes by linking it to the quality of others' outcomes.

quality of one's own outcomes by linking it to the quality of others' outcomes. Whether it is equality, equity or some other distributive criterion, it is clear that people tend to respond strongly to such norms. For example, research shows that people derive most satisfaction from outcomes that are distributed according to equity or equality norms, and are least satisfied with outcomes that do not comply with these principles, even when it is to their own advantage (Messick & Sentis, 1985). Second, the *reciprocity norm* (Gouldner, 1960) states that behaviour – whether generous and cooperative or self-centred and non-cooperative – should be matched. Third, the norm of *social responsibility* states that outcomes of indi- viduals who are relatively weak, dependent or otherwise less capable of pursuing good outcomes for themselves should be assisted. This norm to some degree resembles the so-called '*need principle*' (Deutsch, 1975), which prescribes that greater outcomes should be provided to those who need those outcomes the most.

Norms also influence the procedures used for allocating outcomes among individuals. Indeed, **procedural justice**, or criteria of justice used to evaluate the quality of the decision-making process for distributing outcomes between people (Thibaut & Walker, 1975), appears to be quite important to feelings of fairness. That is, it is not only the distribution *per se* that determines fairness, but the fairness of the procedures may in some situations be just as important, if not

Procedural justice Criteria of justice used to evaluate the quality of the decision-making process for distributing outcomes between people.

more important (Lind & Tyler, 1988). For example, whether or not people are allowed an opportunity to voice their opinion determines how fair they perceive a situation to be, largely irrespective of whether the outcomes are good or bad, fair or unfair (e.g., Van den Bos, Lind, Vermunt, & Wilke, 1997). At the same time, when procedures are fair, violation of distribution norms is far less import- ant than when procedures are unfair (Brockner & Wiesenfeld, 1995).

Norms are applicable to a great variety of situations and, when violated, tend to result in disapproval by observers and guilt in the actor. At the same time, different, conflicting norms may operate simultaneously, resulting in normative ambiguity which is often resolved by adhering to norms that best serve one's per- sonal interest. For example, individuals who have contributed less than average to a group's well-being tend to favour the norm of equality, whereas those who contributed more than average to the well-being of a group favour equity, claim- ing a proportionally greater benefit from the group in return. As such, norms are an important source of disagreement and conflict among group members (Pruitt,

1981). It is also true that violation of prominent norms (e.g., violation of equality) is more likely to take place when such violation is hard to observe by oneself and others. And when a resource cannot be distributed equally, individuals are prone to take the bigger share for themselves (Allison, McQueen, & Schaerfl, 1992).

Beyond Dyads and Small Groups

What are the psychological differences when one moves from dyadic relationships through small groups to large groups?

What are the psychological differences when one moves from cooperation within a group to cooperation between groups?

So far we have discussed four basic sources of transformations, which may lead individuals to pursue broader goals than the simple pursuit of direct self-interest. These sources – interpersonal dispositions, (beliefs regarding) other's behaviour, features of relationships and social norms – are applicable to a wide variety of interdependent relationships. However, it is important to keep in mind that there are important psychological differences as one moves from dyadic relationships through small groups to large groups. Next, we discuss psychological differences when one moves (1) from dyads through small groups to large groups, and (2) from cooperation within a group to cooperation between groups.

From dyads to large groups

There are at least three qualitative differences between dyadic relationships and larger-group relationships (see Dawes, 1980). First, in dyadic relationships the harm of non-cooperation is focused on one other person rather than spread out over many others. Second, in dyadic relationships individuals are often able to shape the other's behaviour by their own behavioural strategy. Third, in dyadic relationships it is practically impossible to make a completely anonymous choice, in that there is only one other person. For these reasons, it is not surprising that individuals exhibit more cooperation in, for example, two-person prisoner's dilemmas than in eight-person prisoner's dilemmas.

At the same time, it is interesting that even when one compares relatively small groups (e.g., groups of three up to ten persons), there appears to be a fairly linear decline in cooperation (e.g., Fox & Guyer, 1977). This may be because, first, anonymity is still greater in larger groups. Second, with increasing group size, individuals become more pessimistic about the efficacy of their efforts to promote collective outcomes (Kerr, 1996; see chapter 14). And third, people tend to feel less personally responsible for good collective outcomes in larger groups. Nevertheless, cooperation in large groups can still be promoted, particularly by (1) strengthening social norms prescribing cooperation; (2) effective communication, that is, communication about the intended choice to which group members commit themselves; and (3) enhancing feelings of identity with the group or a sense of 'we-ness' (e.g., Brewer & Kramer, 1986).

From interpersonal to intergroup relations

Interestingly, interactions between groups are characterized by lower levels of cooperation and higher levels of competition than are interactions between individuals (Schopler & Insko, 1992). This so-called *individual–group discontinuity effect* is due to (1) lower levels of trust in intergroup relations, eliciting fear of being exploited by the other group; (2) stronger levels of support that group members give to each other for pursuing the interest of their own group (and each member's self-interest) at the expense of the other group; and (3) lower levels of identifiability, in that responsibility for self-centred behaviour is often shared in intergroup settings, but not in interpersonal settings. Evidence for individual–group discontinuity has been observed in experimental as well as in non-laboratory contexts (Pemberton, Insko, & Schopler, 1996). Similarly, intergroup negotiation becomes more competitive when the number of team members on each side increases. Moreover, recent evidence suggests that the discontinuity effect is markedly reduced when one or both groups adopts a tit-for-tat strategy; thus, under some conditions, tit-for-tat seems quite effective in promoting cooperation between groups (Insko et al., 1998).

Recently, Bornstein (1992) has developed **team games**, that is, situations in which the interdependent relationship both within a group and between groups is specified. This research suggests that cooperation within a group (i.e., the ingroup) is enhanced when the outcomes for the ingroup are negatively related to outcomes for the outgroup; that is, when the ingroup gains what the outgroup loses (zero-sum interdependence). Conversely, cooperation within a group tends to be modest or low when both the ingroup and the outgroup profit from such cooperation. This suggests that one key to cooperation within a group is the underlying interdependence between ingroups and outgroups (cf. Rabbie & Horwitz, 1988). Sometimes, within-group cooperation can be detrimental to the well-being of the entire collective, consisting of ingroups and outgroups. For example, during war soldiers exhibit within-group cooperation by fighting, yet the ingroup and outgroup together, or the larger collective, are better off when they do not engage in any aggressive behaviour. Above and beyond the nature of the interdependent relationship between groups, research reveals that categorization in terms of 'we' and 'they' can yield *ingroup bias*, allocating greater resources or benefits to the own group than to the other group (e.g., Tajfel, 1978; see chapter 15).

Team games Games representing interdependent relationships among the individual, the own group and another group.

Solutions for Conflict

What are the possible roles of a third party?
Why should structural solutions be quite effective?

Quite often, individuals within dyads and groups are able to obtain collectively desirable outcomes through establishing stable patterns of mutual cooperation. Of course, in such cases, individuals utilize the mixed-motive situation in a manner beneficial to all members involved, and the 'dilemma' has been fruitfully solved. Alternatively, it is easy to imagine that a group or dyad fails to establish a cooperative, mutually beneficial pattern of interaction. In fact, as we have seen, it may take just one member who continues to behave in a selfish manner for two people to develop a non-cooperative relationship. Patterns of non-cooperation, real or even anticipated, can be resolved or prevented through (1) **third-party intervention**, that is, the intervention of a third party to help solve a conflict of interest between two or more people, or (2) **structural solutions**, that is, effectively changing situations so as to overcome the detrimental effects of non-cooperative behaviour. These two solutions are discussed in turn.

Third-party intervention The intervention of a third party to help solve a conflict of interest between two or more people (or groups of people).

Structural solutions Solutions aimed at promoting collectively desired behaviour through altering aspects of the interdependence structure underlying relationships between people.

Third-party intervention

Third-party intervention can take the form of emergent intervention or contractual intervention. Emergent intervention usually has no formally defined role, and the third party usually has an ongoing relationship with one or both parties to the conflict. Examples are third-party interventions by parents, neighbours or friends, fellow group members, or colleagues. In the case of emergent intervention, third parties volunteer to offer services which the dyad or group can either accept or reject. Alternatively, in the case of contractual third-party intervention, members of the dyad or group invite a third party to offer services to solve the conflict. Examples are third-party interventions by a police officer, a judge, a personnel officer, or some external agency specialized in conflict resolution (e.g., the United Nations).

Third parties assume a variety of roles and strategies. Building on the pioneering work by Thibaut and Walker (1975), Sheppard (1984) distinguished between (1) *process control*, a third party's control over the presentation and interpretation of evidence relevant to the dispute, and (2) *decision control*, a third party's control over the outcome of the dispute. As can be seen in figure 11.7, these two dimensions jointly produce four distinct roles a third party adopts when intervening in a conflict between two or more people: (1) an impetus role, (2) an

		Process control	
		Absent	Present
Decision control	Absent	Impetus role	Mediational role
	Present	Adjudicative role	Inquisitorial role

FIGURE 11.7 Type of role as a function of the availability of process control and decision control (Based on Sheppard, 1984)

inquisitorial role, (3) an adjudicative role and (4) a mediational role. When third parties lack process and decision control, they assume *an impetus role*, providing advice and suggestions. Examples of such third parties are personnel advisers or job counsellors in organizations; but such third parties could also be friends or colleagues. These people often provide relevant information, or suggest how to approach the conflict, without actually controlling the process or the outcome. When, on the other hand, third parties exercise both process and decision control, they assume *an inquisitorial role*. An example is a manager who intervenes in a conflict between two subordinates fighting over office space. In such a situation, the manager controls both the process (when do we talk about it, who talks first) and the outcome (who gets the nice desk at the window).

When third parties only exert decision control, they assume *an adjudicative role*. A good example is the judge, who listens to each party, or his or her representative, and then makes a decision. In the example of the two colleagues disputing a desk near the window, their manager may adopt (and often does) an adjudicative role – listening to each side and then making a decision. Finally, third parties adopt *a mediational role* when they exercise process control only (**mediation**). Consider, for example, a colleague assisting two disputants fighting over office space. This colleague is 'involved' and controls the process, but is unable to enforce a solution and decide who will get the desk near the window.

> **Mediation** Assistance of a third party to help solve a conflict of interest, often through communication with both parties.

Of the four roles third parties may assume, the role of the mediator is most popular (Karambaya & Brett, 1989; Lewicki & Sheppard, 1985). The first reason is that, contrary to the inquisitorial and adjudicative roles, mediators leave decision control to the disputants. This feeling of control over the final outcome is understandably important to conflict parties. The second reason is that mediation more often than any other role produces stable agreements which are acceptable to both parties. As such, mediation may improve the relationship between the parties, and may help them to (re-)establish a mutually beneficial future.

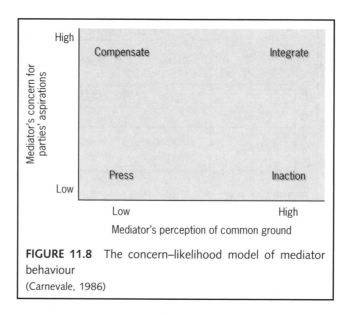

FIGURE 11.8   The concern–likelihood model of mediator behaviour
(Carnevale, 1986)

Recently, a model has been developed to account for how mediators may intervene. According to the *concern–likelihood model of mediation* (Carnevale, 1986; Carnevale & Pruitt, 1992), mediation activities are guided by two features, including (1) the mediator's concern for the parties' aspirations, and (2) the mediator's perception of common ground (i.e., the likelihood that parties will reach agreement). As can be seen in figure 11.8, when concern for parties' aspirations is low and perceived common ground is high, mediators are predicted to remain inactive and to let the parties handle the dispute themselves. When, in contrast, concern for aspirations is high and perceived common ground is high, mediators are likely to choose an integrating, problem-solving strategy. In this case, mediators will ask questions to understand the underlying desires and interest each of the conflict parties brings to the table, and propose solutions that satisfy the needs and desires of all parties involved. A famous example is the mediation by former US president Jimmy Carter in the conflict between Egypt and Israel concerning the Sinai. Israel occupied large parts of the Sinai and refused to return it to Egypt, which had sound historical claims. As a mediator, Jimmy Carter discovered that Israel held onto the Sinai because it desired safety and protection, while Egypt held onto the Sinai because of territorial desires. The integrative solution Jimmy Carter proposed was for Israel to return the Sinai to Egypt, with Egypt allowing for a large demilitarized zone – this way, both disputants had their basic desires fulfilled.

When concern for aspirations is high and perceived common ground is low, mediators are predicted to use compensation to entice parties to make concessions. For example, a manager mediating a conflict between two office mates about who gets the window desk may ask one subordinate to concede and leave the desk to her colleague. In return, the manager compensates this concession by giving her subordinate a new computer. Finally, when concern for aspirations is low and perceived common ground is high, mediators may be tempted to press parties into a solution. In this case, mediators use persuasive arguments to reduce the disputants' aspirations, or threaten to expose the disputants' (childish) behaviour to the mass media if they do not give in.

In both contractual and emergent mediation, mediators usually need to steer a precise course between the disputants lest they alienate one side and lose their credibility and acceptability. There is always the danger that one or both parties will come to believe that the mediator is hostile and biased against them (Pruitt & Carnevale, 1993). In terms of the strategic choice model discussed above, (suspected) mediator bias would express itself in the mediator placing stronger emphasis on one of the parties' aspirations, either before the mediation starts or during the process of conflict resolution (Van de Vliert, 1992). Mediator bias may be merely perceptual (i.e., in the heads of the parties), but sometimes it may be real. For example, mediators may in fact side with more powerful parties, especially when this powerful party also has substantial capacity to sanction the mediator. Although mediator bias is often a threat to constructive conflict resolution, several authors argue that a biased mediator is sometimes the only one available to mediate the conflict. Also, disputants are more willing to accept a biased mediator if he or she is believed to exhibit this bias before the mediation starts and not during conflict resolution (e.g., Pruitt & Carnevale, 1993).

Structural solutions

When individuals are unable to obtain collectively desirable outcomes in a given situation, they may consider structural solutions by altering the structure of the situation in such a manner as to stimulate cooperative behaviour (Messick & Brewer, 1983). Whereas third-party intervention is a line of theory and research developed in the literature of negotiation, the psychology following from structural solutions is strongly embedded in the social dilemma literature. There are at least two distinct forms of structural solutions, including (1) changes in the *outcome structure* underlying a mixed-motive situation, and (2) changes in the *decision structure* underlying a mixed-motive situation.

First, structural changes in *outcome structure* can focus on either rewarding cooperation or punishing non-cooperation. A concrete example of the former is the implementation of the carpool lane. In an attempt to promote carpooling and discourage individual car use, the Dutch government decided to reward carpooling by implementing a carpool priority lane, a lane on a highway near Amsterdam that could only be used by carpoolers which was thus less congested, and therefore much faster than the other lanes. (Unfortunately, carpooling was not effectively promoted by the implementation of the carpool priority lane, in part because solo drivers felt they were unable to change to carpooling; see Van Vugt, Van Lange, Meertens, & Joireman, 1996). Another solution involves punishing non-cooperation to make it less attractive. For example, governments might implement a system by which car drivers have to pay for using the highway during rush hour (cf. Yamagishi, 1986). Clearly, reward and punishment are frequently used to promote collectively desirable behaviour, not just by governments (such as taxes and subsidies) but also by employers, colleagues, relationship partners, and so on.

Changes in the outcome structure generally are quite effective in promoting cooperation, for two broad reasons. First, such solutions change the outcome structure in such a manner that the mixed-motive nature of the situation is diminished (i.e., when cooperation becomes almost as attractive to individuals as non-cooperation) or remove altogether the mixed-motive nature (i.e., when cooperation becomes more attractive to individuals than non-cooperation). Second, such structural solutions tend to enhance people's expectations regarding other's willingness to cooperate, thereby removing one important barrier for cooperation (Yamagishi, 1986). At the same time, there are often several barriers to overcome to be able to implement such a structural solution. Structural solutions are more likely to be accepted if they are perceived as efficient (i.e., they should be perceived as effective in promoting collective well-being) and fair (i.e., the costs for realizing such collectively desirable outcomes should be distributed fairly among the participants in the group or community; Samuelson, 1993). And, as alluded to earlier, all or most individuals must feel that they are able to make a co-operative choice, which certainly is not always the case in real-life social dilemmas (see Van Vugt et al., 1996).

Structural solutions can also entail changes in the *decision structure* underlying a mixed-motive situation. For example, negotiators may opt for a judge who will eventually make a decision. In group contexts, individuals may elect a leader from their group who would make decisions for the entire group. As is often the case with other structural solutions, individuals are more strongly motivated to elect a leader when they repeatedly fail to obtain stable patterns of mutual cooperation (e.g., Samuelson, Messick, Rutte, & Wilke, 1984; Wilke, 1991). Indeed, the major task of governments, managers and leaders in organizations and private business is to manage mixed-motive situations in a manner beneficial to the well-being of the collective (i.e., the organization). This is in essence what Hobbes (1651) argued several centuries ago. Yet a strong central authority is unable to regulate all forms of interpersonal and intergroup behaviour. And – as we hope to have demonstrated – humans have probably evolved to approach mixed-motive situations in such a manner that humans themselves are quite able to pursue and accomplish relatively stable patterns of mutual cooperation. That humans are not always able to reach such solutions themselves is self-evident, particularly for large-scale social dilemmas, such as maintaining a healthy environment, and for intergroup relations, such as international conflict. And these are exactly the domains where third-party intervention and structural solutions are most urgent.

Summary and Conclusions

How do people seek to solve conflicts between self-interest and collective interest? Social-psychological theory – and interdependence theory, in particular – stresses the importance of broader considerations that extend the pursuit of direct self-interest. Such broader considerations, or transformations, include, for example, desire to enhance long-term outcomes, desire to enhance collective outcomes, and desire to enhance equality in outcomes. This chapter identified four major sources of transformation, including (1) interpersonal dispositions, such as pre-existing individual differences in prosocial, individualistic and competitive value orientations; (2) beliefs regarding other's behaviour; (3) relationship-specific features, such as commitment and trust; and (4) social norms, such as equality, reciprocity and equity. Next, we discussed the psychological differences that emerge when one moves from dyads to large groups and when one moves from interpersonal relationships to intergroup relationships. In both cases we see a decline in co-operation. Finally, we reviewed promising avenues for solving conflict, including third-party intervention, in which an external agent seeks to solve escalation of conflict, and structural solutions, in which the situation is altered in terms of decision structure and/or outcome structure in an attempt to enhance collectively desirable outcomes.

DISCUSSION POINTS

1 When electricity is scarce in a small village, how should the local gov-ernment manage the situation to ensure that everyone is able to use a sufficient amount of electricity to satisfy their basic needs?
2 Suppose that a particular country, where the public transportation is quite good, is faced with incredible congestion and unhealthy air due to excessive car use. How should the government manage this large-scale social dilemma and promote the use of public transportation?
3 Imagine that John and Mary have a conflict about what to watch that night on television. Mary wishes to watch an important soccer game, whereas John wants to relax and watch a film on another chan-nel. As the night progresses, Mary tells John that he can watch the film, and that she will read commentaries about the soccer game in the newspaper the next day. John accepts this proposal. What would theoretically be the most plausible explanation for Mary's act of generosity?
4 Ann thinks that Peter, who is inclined to behave in a very forgiving and generous manner, is likely to be exploited by others. Susan, on the other hand, thinks that Peter's style might be somewhat costly in the short term, but that in the long run Peter will get back what he's done for others, and more. Who is right? And might such beliefs tell us something about the personalities of Ann and Susan?

5   Two colleagues are having a fight over who should get the larger office. What might be the possibilities for their boss to solve this conflict in a satisfactory and effective manner?

6   John argues that almost all generous acts, including anonymous donations to noble causes (e.g., donations to Third World countries), are ultimately driven by self-interest. Is he right? If so, why? If not, why not?

7   John and Mary fell in love with a house, and John is directly negotiating with the owner. He tells Mary that the best thing to do is to focus primarily on the price because that is what is relevant to them. Moreover, he argues, other issues (e.g., when they move out, whether or not to buy things that they might leave in the house or take with them) are simply irrelevant in view of the amount of money involved. John's initial offer is 200,000 Euros, but the owner's initial demand was 240,000 Euros. John would actually be willing to pay 240,000 Euros for the house (after all, he and Mary love the house, and they are able to afford it), yet hopes that they reach an agreement of about 220,000 Euros (an equal split between initial demand and offer). How should John proceed?

FURTHER READING

Axelrod, R. (1984). *The evolution of cooperation*. New York: Basic Books. Provides a very convincing demonstration of the effectiveness of tit-for-tat through the author's computer tournament studies.

Kelley, H. H., & Thibaut, J. W. (1978). *Interpersonal relations: A theory of interdependence*. New York: Wiley. This classic book advances interdependence theory, a comprehensive theory of interdependence and social interaction.

Komorita, S. S., & Parks, C. D. (1995). Interpersonal relations: Mixed-motive interaction. *Annual Review of Psychology*, 46, 183–207. Provides a comprehensive overview of decades of research and theory relevant to prisoner's dilemmas, social dilemmas and related mixed-motive situations.

Messick, D., & Brewer, M. B. (1983). Solving social dilemmas: A review. In L. Wheeler & P. Shaver (Eds.), *Review of personality and social psychology* (Vol. 4, pp. 11–44). Beverly Hills, CA: Sage. Provides a theory-based overview of social dilemma research, outlining differences among social dilemmas and why they are important.

Pruitt, D. G., & Carnevale, P. J. (1993). *Negotiation in social conflict*. London: Open University Press. Provides a comprehensive overview of research, models and theory relevant to negotiation, mediation and solutions to conflict.

Rusbult, C. E., & Van Lange, P. A. M. (1996). Interdependence processes. In E. T. Higgins & A. W. Kruglanski (Eds.), *Social psychology: Handbook of basic principles* (pp. 564–96). New York: Guilford Press. Provides an overview of decades of research relevant to Kelley and Thibaut's (1978) interdependence theory, and extensions of this theory.

Thibaut, J. W., & Walker, L. (1975). *Procedural justice: A psychological analysis*. New York: Wiley. Provides a theory-based overview of the importance of procedural justice, which subsequently became a prominent area of research.

Dawes, R. M., McTavish, J., & Shaklee, H. (1977). Behavior, communication, and assumptions about other people's behavior in a common dilemma situation. *Journal of Personality and Social Psychology*, 35, 1–11.

Kuhlman, D. M., & Marshello, A. (1975). Individual differences in game motivation as moderators of preprogrammed strategic effects in prisoner's dilemma. *Journal of Personality and Social Psychology*, 32, 922–31.

KEY

STUDIES

Affiliation, Attraction and Close Relationships

12

Bram P. Buunk

As human beings almost of all us need, and seek out, others at certain times and for certain reasons. We are social beings, and the presence of others, especially when they provide us with social support, can be crucially important when we are faced with adversity such as stress and illness. This chapter begins with a discussion of *affiliation*, the motives for and conse-quences of seeking out the company of other people. This is followed by a section on *attraction and friendships*, focusing on the factors that make individuals like other people and become friends with them. Next, the nature of *romantic attraction* is dealt with, and finally, we discuss the development of *close relationships*, such as those involved in marriage.

OUTLINE

KEY CONCEPTS

- Affiliation
- Attachment theory
- Attraction
- Buffer effect of social support
- Commitment
- Emotional contagion
- Equity theory
- Evolutionary theory

- Intimacy
- Investment model
- Loneliness
- Passionate love
- Reciprocity
- Self-fulfilling prophecy
- Social comparison theory
- Social support

Introduction

Carl is in general a happy man. He enjoys having fun and spending time with his friends. Recently, he fell in love with Carin, a beautiful woman whom he had known for some time; however, Carin does not reciprocate his feelings. Since then, Carl has felt quite unhappy and at times lonely. Although he needs company because of his unhappiness, even being with his friends hardly improves his mood. Carin likes Carl, but just does not have romantic feelings for him. She feels that Carl lacks ambition, and is not the type of man she is looking for. Her closest girlfriend, with whom she discusses everything, agrees that Carl is not right for her.

Humans are a very social breed. They seek each other's company in a variety of situations, they make friendships with other people, and they seem to find their ultimate happiness and despair in their intimate relationships. But what is it that drives us to engage in contact with others? What determines the fact that we often quite rapidly find ourselves liking some people more than others? Why do some relationships end quite soon, and why do others remain close during a lifetime? These issues are dealt with in the present chapter.

Affiliation – The Need for Social Contact

Which conditions affect the wish to be in the company of others?

Situations fostering affiliation: when do people affiliate?

Affiliation   The tendency to seek out the company of others, irrespective of the feelings towards such others.

Humans have a general need to affiliate with others, and they spend a considerable part of their life in the company of other people. For example, using the experience-sampling method, O'Connor and Rosenblood (1996) examined **affiliation** motivation and actual social behaviour in naturally occurring situations. Student volunteers were asked to record for half a week their actual and their desired state of social contact (i.e., being together with others) in response to electronic signals from a beeper. The electronic signal was programmed to beep intermittently at an average interval of one hour. Respondents were in social contact 47 per cent of the time, and wanted to be in social contact 51 per cent of the time. Thus, although people choose to spend a great deal of time with others, they are also, by their own choice, alone a great deal of the time. The authors interpret these findings as indication for a homoeostatic model. Like hunger, for instance, the desire to affiliate appears to function as a *drive*, in that people look

PLATE 12.1   Why do we fall in love?

for an optimal range of social contact. When individuals experience too much solitude, they seek out social contact until their affiliative drive is satiated, and when they experience excess social contact, they seek out solitude to restore the optimum level of affiliation.

It is generally assumed that the human desire for affiliation stems in large part from the fact that in our evolutionary past, joining others when facing a threat such as predators and aggressors enhanced our chances for survival. The notion that a threat induces a desire for affiliation has received special attention from social psychologists, beginning with Schachter's (1959) pioneering experiments. In these experiments, female students in the experimental condition were welcomed by someone who introduced himself as Dr Gregor Zilstein of the Medical School's Department of Neurology and Psychiatry. He had the outward appearance of a doctor, with a white coat and a stethoscope, and behind him was an impressive array of electrical equipment. Dr Zilstein gave a lecture on the importance of research on the use of electroshock therapy, and told the participants that they would receive a series of painful electric shocks that would hurt, although there would be no permanent damage. In the control condition, the same experimenter appeared, but without all the electrical equipment, and the participants were told that they would receive a series of very mild shocks, which would not be at all painful, and that they would in fact enjoy the experiment. Next, all participants were told that they had to wait ten minutes, and they were asked to indicate if they wanted to wait either alone or in the company of others. In line with the expectations, the results showed that about twice as many participants wanted to be in the company of others in the high-anxiety condition than in the low-anxiety condition. The results of this pioneering research have been replicated a number of times, and have been followed up by studies among populations experiencing stress in real life. For instance, in a study among Dutch disabled individuals, Buunk (1995) showed that those high in anxiety had a relatively higher need to talk with other disabled individuals about their situation.

Motives for affiliation: what do people look for when they affiliate under stress?

But why do people affiliate when confronted with a stressful situation? Although one can think of various reasons, such as seeking reassurance or support, simple curiosity, and a desire to express one's emotions, research has indicated that three motives especially play a role in this regard – *social comparison*, *anxiety reduction* and *information seeking*.

Social comparison

> How is the desire to seek out the company of others under stress motivated by the wish to compare one's feelings with those of others?

Social comparison theory A theory which emphasizes that individuals assess their attitudes, abilities and emotions by comparing themselves with similar others, and that they do so especially when they are uncertain about themselves.

According to Schachter (1959), when individuals are confronted with the prospect of receiving an electric shock, they may not know how to feel and respond: 'Am I too worried?', 'Should I be really nervous?', 'Am I the only one who is afraid?' According to **social comparison theory** (Festinger, 1954), in such an ambiguous situation affiliation with others facing the same situation would give one the opportunity to compare one's responses with those of others, and thus to assess the appropriateness of one's feelings. In line with this theory, Schachter found that individuals under threat of an electric shock preferred to be in the company of someone also waiting to undergo the same experiment, rather than in the company of others who were in a quite different situation, such as waiting for a professor. As Schachter concluded:

'Misery doesn't love just any kind of company, it loves only miserable company' (p. 24). In a similar vein, Gump and Kulik (1997) found that individuals who were faced with a threat (i.e., the prospect of undergoing experimentally ischaemic pain similar to that experienced by those with coronary heart disease) spent more time looking at how another individual responded who would undergo the same threat than at an individual who would participate in a very different experiment. Additional evidence supporting the social comparison interpretation comes from studies showing that, as Festinger's (1954) theory would predict, especially *uncertainty* about one's own feelings and responses enhances affiliative desires (e.g., Buunk, 1994; Gerard, 1963).

Anxiety reduction

How is seeking the company of others motivated by a desire to reduce anxiety?

Probably more than a desire to reduce uncertainty through social comparison, a desire for anxiety reduction plays an important role in affiliation under stress. A host of evidence indicates that individuals in threatening and stressful circumstances do often turn to sympathetic others who may offer them reassurance, comfort and emotional support (e.g., Stroebe & Stroebe, 1997; Wills, 1991). According to **attachment theory**, such behaviours concern an innate tendency that is also apparent in other primates such as rhesus monkeys and chimpanzees, as well as in infants who, in response to clues to danger, seek close contact with their mother (Reis & Patrick, 1996; Shaver & Klinnert, 1982). Childhood experiences in caregiver–child interactions will lead to the development of a certain *attachment style* (see figure 12.1). Individuals who have had caregivers who were always available for them, and responsive to their needs when they were in distress, will most likely develop a secure attachment style. They will view others as trustworthy, dependable and helpful. In contrast, individuals whose caregivers showed a lack of responsiveness, rejection or physical and emotional abuse are more likely to develop an insecure attachment style. They may adopt an 'avoidant' style, characterized by distance from others and a cynical view of others as untrustworthy and undependable. They may also develop an 'anxious/ambivalent' style, characterized by a strong desire to be close to others, combined with a fear that others will not respond to this desire (Hazan & Shaver, 1987; Mikelson, Kessler, & Shaver, 1997; Reis & Patrick, 1996). Simpson, Rholes and Nelligan (1992) showed that when confronted with an anxiety-provoking situation, women with a secure attachment style sought *more* support from their partner the higher their level of anxiety, whereas avoidant women sought *less* support from their partner as their anxiety was higher.

> **Attachment theory**   A theory that proposes that the development of secure infant–caregiver attachment in childhood is the basis for the ability to maintain stable and intimate relationships in adulthood.

> Question: Which of the following best describes your feelings?
>
> Secure: I find it relatively easy to get close to others and am comfortable depending on them and having them depend on me. I don't often worry about being abandoned or about someone getting too close to me.
>
> Avoidant: I am somewhat uncomfortable being close to others; I find it difficult to trust them completely, difficult to allow myself to depend on them. I am nervous when anyone gets too close, and often, love partners want to be more intimate than I feel comfortable being.
>
> Anxious/Ambivalent: I find that others are reluctant to get as close as I would like. I often worry that my partner doesn't really love me or won't want to stay with me. I want to merge completely with another person, and this desire sometimes scares people away.

FIGURE 12.1   Measure of attachment styles used by Hazan & Shaver (1987)

Information seeking

> How does seeking the company of others when under stress fulfil a need for information about the nature of the threat?

On the basis of the same attachment theory, Shaver and Klinnert (1982) pointed out that young children not only seek out a parent for direct emotional comfort, but also to get clues about how serious the situation is, thus to obtain information about the nature of the threat. According to Shaver and Klinnert, this applies to adults as well. Individuals faced with a threat will seek out someone knowledgeable who may provide information to assess the danger implied by this threat. Kulik and Mahler (1989) examined this issue in an interesting natural setting, i.e., among patients who had to undergo an operation, a situation usually evoking a considerable amount of anxiety. In line with the analysis of Shaver and Klinnert (1982), most patients preferred on the night before their operation to be with someone who had already had an operation – thus someone who could provide information about the exact nature of the threat, rather than with someone who was also about to undergo an operation.

The three motives discussed here are not mutually exclusive: it seems rather likely that in many situations all three motives are present. Thus, individuals under stress may affiliate with similar others who may provide them with social comparison information to evaluate their emotions, with calm others who may reduce their anxiety, and with well-informed others who may provide objective information about the nature of the threat. Nevertheless, anxiety does not always lead to a desire to affiliate. For example, Molleman, Pruyn and Van Knippenberg (1986) found among cancer patients a curvilinear relationship between anxiety and desire

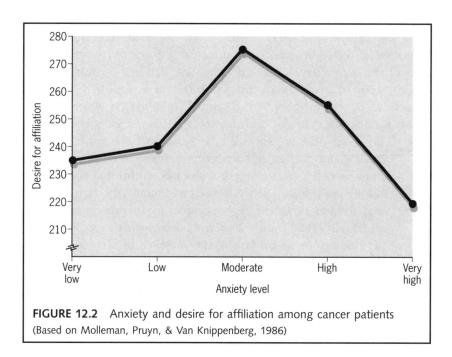

FIGURE 12.2 Anxiety and desire for affiliation among cancer patients
(Based on Molleman, Pruyn, & Van Knippenberg, 1986)

for affiliation: those with a low level of anxiety, as well as those with a very high level of anxiety, felt a lesser need to interact with other patients than those with an intermediate level of anxiety (see figure 12.2). Probably, extreme forms of anxiety and upset lower the desire for affiliation because individuals are worried that by talking about their feelings with others, their fears may be increased.

Effects of affiliation

Do people under stress find what they are looking for?
Does affiliation help in reducing uncertainty and stress?
Do people who are under stress change their feelings as a consequence of social comparisons?

Such questions have been addressed by many different disciplines and from divergent theoretical perspectives, a few of which will be discussed below.

Affiliation and anxiety reduction

How does the company of others reduce anxiety?

Some experiments have provided evidence for the beneficial effects of affiliation *per se* on anxiety. In a well-known study by Amoroso and Walters (1969), participants received electric shocks as part of a learning experiment, resulting in increased heart rate. When they were told to wait a while until the next trial, those who were joined for eight minutes by three other participants, who were confederates of the experimenter, showed a dramatic decrease in heart rate and in subjectively reported anxiety, even though no talking was allowed. These effects were much stronger than those in the control condition, in which participants had to wait alone. Despite the evidence for a stress-reducing effect of affiliation, often the presence of others may enhance rather than reduce anxiety and distress, in particular when the other person present is nervous rather than calm. In such cases, **emotional contagion** may occur: individuals often unconsciously mimic the facial expressions and feelings of others. For example, in an experiment by Gump and Kulik (1997, Study 2), female participants were faced with the prospect of performing a stressful task in the presence of a confederate of the experimenter who, through smiles, looks and frowns, behaved either calmly or nervously. Participants showed emotional contagion: they became more anxious when confronted with the nervous than when confronted with the calm confederate.

> **Emotional contagion** The unconscious mimicking of the facial expressions and feelings from another individual.

Social support and stress reduction

> When does support from others help and when does it not help in alleviating stress?

The literature on **social support** provides a great deal of evidence for the stress-reducing features of affiliation. Social support refers to the feeling of being supported by others and is usually divided into four components, i.e., *emotional* support (feeling cared for, loved and appreciated); *appraisal* support (feedback and social comparison on how to evaluate things); *informational* support (such as information about how to handle things); and *instrumental* support (receiving concrete aid and help) (House, 1981). The first three of these components correspond to the three functions of affiliation under stress that were mentioned before, i.e., social comparison, anxiety reduction and information seeking. In numerous studies, social support has been found to be beneficial in terms of stress reduction, an effect that has been observed with respect to such divergent stressors as the transition to parenthood, financial strain, health problems and work stress (see Stroebe & Stroebe, 1997, for a review).

> **Social support** The feeling of being supported by others, usually divided into four components, i.e., emotional support, appraisal support, informational support and instrumental support.

Social-support researchers have been particularly interested in the so-called **buffer effects of social support**, i.e., those instances where people who perceive that they are supported are less affected by stressful events and conditions than those who feel unsupported. An example of the buffering role of social support comes from a study by Cohen and Hoberman (1983). As figure 12.3 indicates, this

> **Buffer effect of social support** The effect that those who perceive that they are supported are less affected by stressful events and conditions than those who feel unsupported.

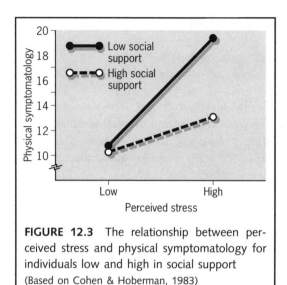

FIGURE 12.3 The relationship between perceived stress and physical symptomatology for individuals low and high in social support (Based on Cohen & Hoberman, 1983)

study showed that individuals who felt their life was very stressful had many more physical symptoms, such as headaches, insomnia and weight loss, when they perceived low support from others than when they perceived high support. There is also experimental evidence for a buffer effect of social support. For instance, Sarason and Sarason (1986) found some evidence that people who were informed they *could* turn to the experimenter for help (but actually never did) were able to perform better on a task that required considerable cognitive effort than people who did not have this opportunity.

Although there is substantial evidence that discussing one's feelings with others may be good for one's health (Pennebaker, 1989), in some cases sharing one's feelings may enhance one's fears. In an interesting experiment by Costanza, Derlega and Winstead (1988), people were asked to engage in a brief discussion with other participants before they had to guide a tarantula through a maze. Participants who were instructed to talk about their fears, feelings and anxieties experienced *more* negative affect and kept the spider at a greater distance than participants who had been instructed to engage in problem-solving conversation.

There is also evidence that for individuals with an insecure attachment style, social support may have adverse effects. In an experiment by Carpenter and Kirkpatrick (1996), participants were subjected to the prospect of undergoing a stressful experience. Among individuals with an avoidant or anxious/ambivalent attachment style, this evoked more stress as apparent from a higher heart rate and blood pressure when their partner was present than when their partner was absent. According to the investigators, this is due to the fact that individuals with an insecure attachment style *do* have a need for support, but are concerned that their partners might reject them while expressing such a need.

Lack of affiliation and loneliness

How is a lack of affiliation associated with loneliness?

Loneliness   A complex
affective response stemming
from felt deficits in the number
and nature of one's social
relationships.

One of the most direct and obvious signs of a lack of affiliation and satisfying social relationships is **loneliness**. Loneliness is a complex affective response stemming from a felt deficit in the number and nature of one's social relationships. In a study by Shaver and Rubinstein (1980), loneliness was found to constitute four clusters of feelings and experiences: (1) *desperation* (feeling desperate, panicky, helpless and abandoned); (2) *depression* (feeling sad, depressed, empty, sorry for oneself and alienated); (3) *impatient boredom* (feeling uneasy, impatient and bored; unable to concentrate); and (4) *self-deprecation* (feeling unattractive, stupid and insecure). According to Weiss (1975), two distinct forms of loneliness exist: *emotional loneliness*, which results from the absence of an intimate partner, and *social loneliness*, which is a consequence of the absence of supportive friends and ties to a social network. Attachment theory assumes that the absence of an intimate partner cannot be compensated for by supportive friends, and that one may experience emotional loneliness without experiencing social loneliness. Stroebe, Stroebe, Abakoumkin and Schut (1996) found indeed that widowed individuals experienced much more emotional loneliness, but not more social loneliness, than married people and that individuals with little social support experienced more social loneliness, but not more emotional loneliness, than individuals who had much social support available in their social network.

Lack of affiliation and health

Is a lack of affiliation bad for your health?

A lack of involvement in relationships not only leads to loneliness, but may also have serious health consequences. In a pioneering study, Berkman and Syme (1979) examined which individuals in a sample that was questioned first in 1965 had died nine years later. Those who had passed away appeared to have been socially isolated: they were more often unmarried, had fewer good and frequent contacts with friends and families, and were less often members of church and other organizations. Whereas for men, being married was more important for survival, for women having intense relationships with friends and family played a key role. These differences in mortality were directly due to effects of affiliation as such, and not caused by the fact that those less socially connected lived more unhealthily, or that those with a disability were less well able to establish and maintain

social ties. Since this pioneering study, there have now been over a dozen different epidemiological studies in various countries showing mortality effects of a lack
of social integration, particularly for men (Stroebe & Stroebe, 1997).

Attraction and the Development of Friendships

Why do people feel attracted to each other, and when do they become friends?

In many situations we affiliate without making a conscious choice for the company of specific others (Berscheid, 1985). For example, we may join a sports club
without feeling particularly attracted to the members of that club, and we usually
move to a new neighbourhood without even knowing who our neighbours will
be. Interestingly however, there is ample evidence that affiliation may foster friendship. We shall first discuss how this might occur, and next we shall
deal with the important impact of attitude similarity upon **attraction**.
Finally, attention is paid to the fact that attraction does not necessarily lead to friendship, but that friendship implies more, i.e., an
interdependent relationship that includes a willingness to coordinate
actions and to take the interests of the other into account.

Attraction   Positive feelings
towards another individual,
including a tendency to seek
out the presence of the other.

The physical environment

*How does the physical environment affect interpersonal attraction and the development
of friendships?*
What role does familiarity play in interpersonal attraction?

We like those we are with – many studies have shown that simply being in the
physical presence of another individual will enhance the probability of becoming
friends with that individual. The pioneering study on this issue was done half a
century ago by Festinger, Schachter and Back (1950) in Westgate West, a housing complex for student couples, consisting of 17 buildings, each with ten apartments on two floors. Couples were assigned to them on the basis of a waiting
list. After a number of months, *more than ten times as many* friendships appeared
to have developed with others within the same building than with others in
different buildings. But even within one's own building, physical *propinquity*
appeared to play a major role. More friendships had developed with others
on the same floor than with others on different floors, and the more doors away
another couple lived on the same floor, the less often a friendship had developed
with the other couple (see figure 12.4)!

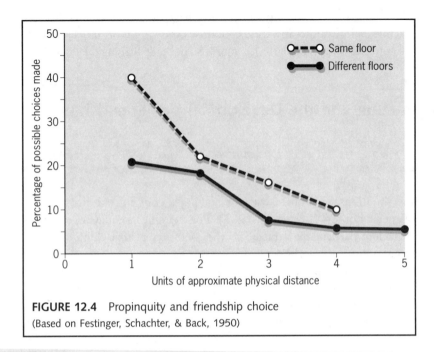

FIGURE 12.4 Propinquity and friendship choice
(Based on Festinger, Schachter, & Back, 1950)

There may be several reasons why propinquity leads to attraction, as many other studies have shown. First, there are simply fewer barriers to developing a friendship with someone close by. Even climbing a stairway to see someone on a different floor is more trouble than just seeing the people next door. Second, by being regularly in the company of another, we obtain more information about the other person, and have the opportunity to discover mutual interests and common attitudes. For example, in a study in a housing project, Athanasiou and Yoshioka (1973) found that for people living close to each other (e.g., same building), similarities in leisure time interests were more likely to influence friendship choice. Third, propinquity may lead to attraction through the so-called *mere exposure effect*. This was shown in a study by Saegert, Swap and Zajonc (1973), who manipulated frequency of exposure unobtrusively by having each participant spend a different number of trials of about 40 seconds with each of five other participants. The more often one had met another participant in the experiment, the more the other was liked.

A study by Yinon, Goldenberg and Neeman (1977) in an Israeli university showed that mere exposure may indeed lead to the development of friendships. The dormitories in this university differed in the amount of interaction they allowed the participants, from low to very high. For example, in the dormitory providing low interaction, rooms had private showers and sinks, whereas very high interaction was provided in an isolated unit with all facilities communally shared, including toilet, showers, sink and kitchen. The results showed that the higher the level of interaction allowed, the higher the proportion of friends chosen within the living unit.

It must be noted that the role of environmental propinquity in fostering attraction may depend on various other factors. First, the effects of propinquity are especially pronounced when the participants are quite similar. For instance, in the Festinger et al. (1950) study, all participants were war veterans and students. Second, propinquity may also decrease attraction by making the unpleasant characteristics of others more noticeable. For example, in a study in Southern California, Ebbesen, Kjos and Konecni (1976) found that not only the most liked others lived close by, but also the most *dis*liked others. These others were disliked because they exhibited annoying behaviours such as parking in front of the driveways and making a noise at night.

The similarity of attitudes

Do people like others more who have the same attitudes as they have? If so, why is that?

Similarity is, in general, a potent factor fostering attraction and friendships. Friends have been found to be more similar to one another than non-friends in, for instance, age, marital status, race, personality traits and intelligence (Hays, 1988). *Attitude similarity*, in particular, appears to lead to attraction. In Byrne's (1971) well-known *attraction paradigm*, participants fill out an attitude questionnaire such as the one presented in figure 12.5. A few weeks later they are given an attitude questionnaire which they assume has been filled out by another person. In fact, it has been completed by the experimenter so as to express attitudes of varying degrees of similarity or dissimilarity to the participant. Such experiments consistently show that attraction is a direct linear function of proportion of similar attitudes (i.e., the number of similar attitudes divided by the total number of similar and dissimilar attitudes). This so-called *law of attraction* has also been found to occur when one meets the other in person. For example, Griffit and Veitch (1974) studied the development of attraction among male volunteers who were confined to a simulated fall-out shelter environment for a period of ten days. Before the beginning of the experiment, attitudes towards 44 topics were assessed. During and at the end of the stay, participants were asked to indicate the names of three people they would like to keep in the shelter, and three names of people they would like to be evicted. Those who were chosen to remain had attitudes more similar to those of the participants than those chosen to be removed.

Why is attitude similarity so important? According to *social comparison theory*, when comparing our opinions on new issues, we might benefit more from talking to others who hold the same attitudes as we do than from talking to others who hold quite different views. Although this process undoubtedly plays a role, the major explanation given by Byrne (1971) is based upon *classical conditioning*.

Classical Music (check one)

- ❏ I dislike classical music very much.
- ❏ I dislike classical music.
- ❏ I dislike classical music to a slight degree.
- ❏ I enjoy classical music to a slight degree.
- ❏ I enjoy classical music.
- ☒ I enjoy classical music very much.

Sports (check one)

- ❏ I enjoy sports very much.
- ❏ I enjoy sports.
- ❏ I enjoy sports to a slight degree.
- ❏ I dislike sports to a slight degree.
- ☒ I dislike sports.
- ❏ I dislike sports very much.

Welfare Legislation (check one)

- ❏ I am very much opposed to increased welfare legislation.
- ☒ I am opposed to increased welfare legislation.
- ❏ I am mildly opposed to increased welfare legislation.
- ❏ I am mildly in favour of increased welfare legislation.
- ❏ I am in favour of increased welfare legislation.
- ❏ I am very much in favour of increased welfare legislation.

War (check one)

- ☒ I feel strongly that war is sometimes necessary to solve world problems.
- ❏ I feel that war is sometimes necessary to solve world problems.
- ❏ I feel that perhaps war is sometimes necessary to solve world problems.
- ❏ I feel that perhaps war is never necessary to solve world problems.
- ❏ I feel that war is never necessary to solve world problems.
- ❏ I feel strongly that war is never necessary to solve world problems.

Strict Discipline (check one)

- ❏ I am very much against strict discipline of children.
- ❏ I am against strict discipline of children.
- ❏ I am mildly against strict discipline of children.
- ❏ I am mildly in favour of strict disciplining of children.
- ☒ I am in favour of strict disciplining of children.
- ❏ I am very much in favour of strict disciplining of children.

Divorce (check one)

- ❏ I am very much opposed to divorce.
- ❏ I am opposed to divorce.
- ☒ I am mildly opposed to divorce.
- ❏ I am mildly in favour of divorce.
- ❏ I am in favour of divorce.
- ❏ I am very much in favour of divorce.

FIGURE 12.5 Profile of attitudes of stranger
(Based on Byrne, 1971)

Byrne showed that hearing someone express similar attitudes evokes positive affect, and that hearing someone express dissimilar attitudes evokes negative affect. Next, Byrne showed that such affective responses can be conditioned to other persons. A person whose picture was present when participants were simultaneously listening to the expression of similar attitudes was liked more than when the same picture was presented while participants were listening to someone expressing dissimilar attitudes. Of course, one could argue that this could be the result of thinking that the person in the picture was the one expressing the attitudes. However, in a subsequent experiment, Byrne showed that conditioning also occurred when the statements could not be attributed to the person in the picture, because he or she was of the opposite sex to the person expressing the attitudes.

Although the link between attitude similarity and attraction is a very robust one, there are a number of qualifications to this general pattern. First, attitude similarity affects attraction particularly for attitudes that are *important* for an individual (Byrne, London, & Griffit, 1968). Second, individuals tend to assume that others have attitudes similar to their own, and when no information is provided about another, they may feel as attracted to him or her as when they learn the other has similar attitudes. Indeed, individuals may feel more repulsed by dissimilar others than attracted to similar others (Rosenbaum, 1986). Third, not attitude similarity as such, but rather similarity of preference for free-time activities may be important for friendship (Werner & Parmelee, 1979), casting some doubt upon Byrne's (1971) assumption that attitude similarity leads to attraction because it is intrinsically rewarding. Finally, when it concerns interpersonal styles, such as dominance and submissiveness, complementarity is more important than similarity. For example, Dryer and Horowitz (1997) found that dominant individuals were most satisfied interacting with individuals who were instructed to play a submissive role, whereas submissive individuals were more satisfied interacting with individuals who were instructed to play a dominant role.

Friendship as a relationship

What are the main characteristics of friendship?

Even when the environmental factors are conducive, and even when a high degree of attitude similarity exists, a friendship between two people may still not develop. Characteristic of the beginning of a friendship is *mutuality* of attraction, and this may give rise to the *voluntary interdependence* that is characteristic of friendships (Hays, 1988). Individuals involved in such relationships are motivated to invest in their relationship, to coordinate their behaviours, and to take the interests of the other into account. In friendships throughout the life cycle, and in all social

Reciprocity   The basic rule in interpersonal relationships that one can expect to obtain assets such as status, attractiveness, support and love to the degree that one provides such assets oneself.

Equity theory   Assumes that satisfaction is a function of the proportionality of outcomes to inputs of the person as compared with those of a reference other, and that individuals will try to restore equity when they find themselves in an inequitable situation.

groups, such interdependence implies in general **reciprocity** in terms of, among others, helping, respecting and supporting each other (Hartup & Stevens, 1997). For example, working-class women have friendships that are very reciprocal with respect to goods and services they provide to each other (Walker, 1995).

According to **equity theory**, those who have the feeling of giving more to their friends than they receive – the deprived – as well as those who feel they receive more than they give – the advantaged – will be less happy in their friendships than those who perceive a reciprocal exchange (Walster, Walster, & Berscheid, 1978). For example, in one study those who felt advantaged as well as those who felt deprived with respect to the giving and receiving of help and support in the relationship with their best friend were more lonely than those who felt this relationship was reciprocal (Buunk & Prins, 1998). According to Buunk and Prins, the development of friendships requires a subtle feeling for the appropriate way to establish and maintain reciprocity in relationships. The importance of reciprocity for friendships is also apparent from the most important rules in friendship: volunteering help in time of need, respecting the friend's privacy, keeping confidences, trusting and confiding in each other, standing up for the other in his or her absence, and not criticizing each other in public (Argyle & Henderson, 1985). In general, the sensitivity to reciprocity in friendships and other relationships seems to be the result of the evolution of the human species in which maintaining mutually supportive relationships was crucial for survival (Buunk & Schaufeli, 1999; chapter 2).

Gender and friendship

How do male and female friendships differ?

There are important differences between male and female friendships. In general, women want others as friends to whom they can talk about intimate issues such as feelings and problems. Women also disclose more intimate things in their relationships with friends than men do. In contrast, men look for friends with similar interests, emphasize more the joint undertaking of activities, and do not give a high priority to discussing feelings (Sherrod, 1989).

Why are friendships between men less intimate than those between and with women? Reis, Senchak and Solomon (1985) examined a number of different explanations, and showed that most explanations could be excluded. First, the difference is not due to the fact that men apply different *criteria* for intimacy than women, because men appeared to judge video fragments differing in intimacy in the same way as women did. Second, the difference appeared not to be due to a reluctance of men to *label* their interactions as intimate, because con-

PLATE 12.2 Friendships between women tend to be more intimate than those between men

versation narratives that could not be identified as being written by a man or woman were judged as more intimate when they in fact came from a female than when they were written by a male. Finally, and perhaps most importantly, the gender differences in intimacy in friendship are not due to *social skills*, because when men are asked to have an intimate conversation with their best friend, they are, according to judges, able to do so as well as women. Reis et al. concluded that the main reason men have less intimate interactions with their friends is not because they cannot do so due to their socialization, but because they simply *prefer* not to have intimate interactions on many occasions, even though they know quite well how to have these. But why do these differences then exist? Evolutionary theorists point to the similarities between gender differences in friendship found among humans and primates such as chimpanzees. They argue that evolution has favoured a male preference for instrumental friendships in groups, because men had to collaborate in hunting and fighting. In contrast, women had to establish and maintain a network of nurturing relationships aimed at taking care of and raising children (de Waal, 1983).

Romantic Attraction

What characterizes and stimulates romantic attraction?
Is attitude similarity as important here as in friendships?

No one will doubt that falling in love with another individual and feeling sexually attracted to someone is experienced quite differently from liking someone and developing a friendship with him or her. Although most individuals are heterosexual and fall in love only with someone of the opposite sex, some individuals are exclusively homosexual and develop romantic feelings only for same-sex others. Moreover, some people – women more so than men – may fall in love with individuals of both their own and the opposite sex (Buunk & Van Driel, 1989). Heterosexual as well as homosexual romantic relationships are, especially in the beginning, often characterized by **passionate love**. This experience includes a strong longing for union with the other, and is characterized by high arousal and an interplay between intense happiness and despair. Furthermore, passionate love is usually accompanied by a preoccupation with the partner and idealization of the other, and by the desire to know the other as well as the desire to be known by the other (Hatfield, 1988). Berscheid and Walster (1974) proposed that passionate love requires two components. The first is a state of physiological arousal, due to either positive emotions such as sexual gratification and excitement, or negative emotions such as frustration, fear and rejection. The second component of passionate love consists of labelling this arousal as 'passion', or 'being in love' (see the discussion of 'misattribution' in chapter 7). Whether such labelling occurs depends on a number of factors, including general notions about what one should feel in the case of passionate love, beliefs about what constitute appropriate partners and circumstances, knowledge about which situations produce which emotions, and self-perceptions as a romantic person.

> **Passionate love**   A state of intense longing for union with another individual, usually characterized by intrusive thinking and preoccupation with the partner, idealization of the other, and the desire to know the other as well as the desire to be known by the other.

Much research in this tradition has focused upon the non-obvious prediction that negative emotions may fuel passion. For example, White, Fishbein and Rutstein (1981, Experiment 2) showed that not only seeing a comedy, but also watching a film depicting killing and mutilation, enhanced romantic attraction to a woman seen subsequently on a videotape. In an experiment by Dutton and Aron (1974), men who had been frightened, by being given the prospect of receiving an electric shock, found a woman with whom they were supposed to participate in a learning experiment much sexier and more attractive than did men who had learned they were just going to receive a barely perceptible tingle of a shock. Not only arousal due to negative feelings, but also neutral arousal has been found to be linked to passionate attraction. In one experiment, White et al. (1981, Experiment 1) showed that men who had been involved in two minutes of exercise found a video of an attractive woman whom they were supposed to meet more attractive, and an unattractive woman less attractive, than men who had only been involved in 15 seconds of exercise.

According to Foster, Witcher, Campbell and Green (1998), the intensifying effect of arousal on attraction is not so much due to the misattribution of arousal, but reflects an automatic process that occurs immediately, without awareness of the person involved. Some authors have argued that the fact that romantic attraction is an automatic and usually quite intense emotional experience is due to the evolutionary importance of sexual reproduction. Although affiliation and friendship may also have fostered survival, had sexual attraction between males and females not existed, we would not have been on earth (Kenrick & Trost, 1989).

Nevertheless, to some extent the chances of developing a romantic relationship with someone else are determined by the same factors that are important for the development of friendship. Propinquity makes the beginning of romantic attraction more likely, and similarity is also important for love relationships. For example, Frazier, Byer, Fischer, Wright and DeBord (1996) found that individuals were most attracted to others who had the same attachment style – secure, avoidant or anxious – as they had. There is also considerable evidence for the role of attitude similarity in romantic attraction. Byrne, Ervin and Lambert (1970) administered an attitude questionnaire to a large group of students, and selected from this group 24 pairs who were very similar in attitudes, and 24 pairs who were very dissimilar (with the restriction that the male had to be as tall or taller than the female). The participants were asked to go on a 'date' in the university cafeteria of about 30 minutes, and even after this brief encounter, attitude similarity appeared to have a clear effect upon attraction, including perceived desirability as a date and as a marriage partner. However, in this experiment, the perceived *physical attractiveness* of the 'partner' was as important in determining attraction as the proportion of similar attitudes. The importance of physical attractiveness as a determinant of romantic attraction was also demonstrated in a classic study by Walster, Aronson, Abrahams and Rottman (1966), who invited students for a 'computer dance' in which they were paired with another individual. Physical attractiveness as assessed by independent judges had a strong effect upon attraction for men as well as for women, regardless of one's own level of attractiveness. In a similar study, homosexual men who participated in an 'afternoon tea date' liked their partner more and wanted to date him more, the more physical attractive the partner was, independent of one's own level of attractiveness and assertiveness (Sergios & Cody, 1985/86).

The physical attractiveness stereotype

Why is physical attractiveness so important?

Physical attractiveness affects romantic attraction through a positive stereotype: when someone is beautiful, we automatically attribute, in general, many other

PLATE 12.3   The physical attractiveness stereotype: we attribute many positive characteristics to someone who is beautiful

positive characteristics to him or her (Feingold, 1992). Although attractive people are viewed as somewhat less modest, they are especially perceived as sexually warmer and more socially skilled than unattractive people, but also as more sociable (e.g., more extravert and friendly), more dominant (e.g., more assertive) and mentally healthier (including happier and emotionally more stable). Both male and female attractive targets are viewed in a more positive light, although there is a stronger tendency to attribute sexual warmth to attractive women than to attractive men.

Self-fulfilling prophecy   When an originally false social belief leads to its own fulfilment. Social belief refers to people's expectations regarding another group of people. When a self-fulfilling prophecy occurs, the perceiver's initially false beliefs cause targets to act in ways that objectively confirm those beliefs.

These stereotypes are not completely unfounded. Although the personality and behavioural characteristics of attractive people are in general not very different from those of unattractive people, attractive people have been found to be less lonely, less socially anxious, more socially skilled and more popular with the opposite sex. Among women attractiveness is, more than among men, correlated with self-esteem, opposite-sex popularity and sexual permissiveness (Feingold, 1992). Probably, from the beginning of their life, attractive people receive more positive attention and will, through a so-called **self-fulfilling prophecy**, become more self-confident in their social life. This process was shown in a study by Snyder, Tanke and Berscheid

(1977). These investigators led male participants to believe that they were conducting a 'getting acquainted' telephone conversation with an attractive vs. an unattractive woman. Remarkably, the women who were *believed* to be attractive (though they were not actually more attractive) became, as a consequence of the more positive behaviours of the males towards them, more friendly and sociable, whereas the women assumed to be physically unattractive became cool and aloof during the conversation.

Gender differences in preferences for physical attractiveness and status

Do women find physical attractiveness as important as men do?
Do heterosexuals and homosexuals differ in this respect?

Although both men and women value physical attractiveness, physical attractiveness is in general a more important determinant of romantic attraction for males than it is for females. Buss (1989) found in a study in 37 cultures that, although both genders rated physical attractiveness as important, in most cultures men found this more important than women did. The higher value placed by males upon physical attractiveness is in line with **evolutionary theory** (Buss, 1994; see also chapter 2). According to this perspective, males have been selected to prefer women who are likely to produce healthy babies and who are likely to raise such children successfully. Therefore, men would have become particularly sensitive to signs of youth, health and reproductive value. Signs of youth are indeed in all cultures important cues for female attractiveness. For instance, Cunningham (1986) showed that males are attracted more to females possessing young, so-called *neonate*, features – large eyes, a small nose area, a small chin and widely spaced eyes. The criteria for physical attractiveness are remarkably consistent across cultures (Cunningham, Roberts, Barbee, Druen, & Wu, 1995).

> **Evolutionary theory** A theory that explains human behaviour, including differences in partner preferences according to gender, from their reproductive value, i.e., their value in producing offspring in our evolutionary past.

According to the evolutionary perspective, given the long period that human offspring are dependent upon parental care, females had more chances of having their offspring survive when they were choosy in selecting male partners, that is, selecting males who would provide the necessary resources during the long period that the children needed care, and women would thus have become particularly sensitive to signs of status and dominance. There is indeed considerable evidence showing that women more often seek partners with a high socio-economic status than men do (Feingold, 1992). This gender difference has been quite stable over the past 50 years, and Buss (1989) also found that women in 37 cultures placed a higher value upon social status and wealth than men.

Women, more than men, are attracted to others of the opposite sex who display non-verbally dominant behaviour (i.e., choosing a chair close to another, gesturing a lot and not nodding the head too much; Sadalla, Kenrick & Vershure, 1987); tall (but not too tall) men with athletic features are considered attractive (Hatfield & Sprecher, 1986); and the attractiveness of males is, more than that of females, related to mature features such as prominent cheekbones and a long and wide chin, as well as a large smile area, including a high and wide smile and a higher-status clothing style (Cunningham, Barbee, & Pike, 1990).

Studies examining personal ads in which partners are sought have shown that the differences in mate preferences between homosexual men and women are in many ways similar, or even more pronounced than among heterosexual men and women. Compared to lesbian women, gay men more often state an age preference, seek information about physical characteristics (such as hair and eye colour, height, physique), show more interest in attractiveness (e.g., by requesting a photograph), and express specific sexual interests. In general, this emphasis on physical and sexual characteristics is stronger among homosexual than among heterosexual men. In contrast, lesbian women more often than gay men provide personality information about themselves – such as about their sincerity, intelligence, hobbies and interests – and seek specific personality characteristics such as a sense of humour. While such self-descriptions and preferences of lesbians are more pronounced than those of heterosexual women, compared to men of both sexual orientations, homosexual and heterosexual women have a similar preference for mates with expressive characteristics such as being affectionate, caring, empathic and sensitive (e.g., Gonzales & Meyers, 1993; Hatala & Prehodka, 1996).

Beginning and developing a romantic relationship is – maybe even more than a friendship – contingent upon reciprocal attraction, which is most likely to occur when both partners are about equally attractive. With discrepancies in attractiveness, the relationship will be dissatisfying for both partners as well as unstable. Therefore, although in general the most attractive people are preferred as a partner, in line with *equity theory* – a theory that was mentioned above (Walster et al., 1978) – most individuals will adapt their standards for a partner to their own level of attractiveness. Indeed, compared to attractive individuals, less attractive individuals judge their dates less harshly, are more likely to be willing to date less attractive others, and are less likely to consider dating attractive others (Stroebe, Insko, Thompson, & Layton, 1971; Walster et al., 1966). Due to this process of adapting one's criteria to one's own 'market value', individuals will tend to end up with partners of approximately their own attractiveness level. This is referred to as the *matching principle*. When there are differences in attractiveness level, according to equity theory these will be compensated for by other assets. A 'classic' example of this is that attractive women sometimes marry less attractive though higher-status men (Buss, 1994).

Close Relationships: Satisfaction and Dissolution

Satisfaction in relationships

Which factors make a close relationship happy and satisfying?

Once individuals have established a mutual attraction, they may begin to develop a voluntary interdependent relationship by increasing their mutual involvement. Some relationships will become happy, satisfying and stable, others will be filled with conflicts and problems, and are likely to end sooner or later. Whether it concerns unmarried cohabitation or marriage, or gay and lesbian relationships, a high degree of **intimacy** is characteristic for happy couples. According to Reis and Patrick (1996), interactions are experienced as intimate when three conditions are met: (1) *Caring*: feeling that the other loves us and cares about us. As noted by Reis and Patrick, most people mention this as a central component of intimacy, and individuals will feel reluctant to be open to someone whom they feel does not care for them. (2) *Understanding*: one must feel that the other has an accurate view of how one sees oneself, that the partner knows one's important needs, beliefs, feelings and life circumstances. For example, Swann, de la Ronde and Hixon (1994) found that married individuals were most satisfied with their relationship when their partner perceived them in line with their self-perceptions, although marital satisfaction is particularly high for those whose partner perceives them in a more positive way than they see themselves (Murray, Holmes, & Griffin, 1996). (3) *Validation*: the communication of acceptance, acknowledgement and support by the other partner for one's point of view. Indeed, one of the most prominent features in terms of which happy and distressed couples appear to differ is the extent to which their communication is characterized by validation. For example, couples are happier the more they show affection and understanding, the more they let the other know that they empathize with his or her feelings, and the better they are at taking the perspective of the partner. In contrast, couples are less happy the more they show conflict avoidance (for example, not wanting to discuss problematic issues, making indirect references to a conflict issue), soothing (ignoring and covering up differences) and destructive communication (for example, criticizing, disagreeing, complaining and sarcastic remarks) (see Noller & Fitzpatrick, 1990; Schaap, Buunk, & Kerkstra, 1988).

> **Intimacy** A state in interpersonal relationships that is characterized by sharing of feelings, and is based upon caring, understanding and validation.

Individuals with insecure attachment styles, in particular, have problems with developing intimacy: they display higher levels of withdrawal and verbal aggression during conflict, are less likely to engage in cooperative problem-solving, and are less effective in providing the partner with comfort and emotional support (Reis & Patrick, 1996). For example, Gaines et al. (1997) examined how individuals responded when faced with a potentially destructive behaviour of the partner – for example, the partner says something crude or inconsiderate, yells at the individual, or behaves in a cold, rejecting manner. Those with a secure attachment style responded much more by actively attempting to resolve the problem by, for example, discussing the situation and suggesting solutions to problems. In contrast, those with an avoidant and anxious attachment style responded more with destructive responses, including actively harming the relationship by yelling at the partner and threatening termination, or by passively harming the relationship by refusing to discuss problems. Throughout the life cycle, attachment styles are related to marital communication and satisfaction (Feeney, 1994).

A typical feature of individuals with unhappy close relationships is that they tend to interpret the partner's behaviours and characteristics in a negative way. For example, those low in satisfaction tend to engage in maladaptive attributions. They tend to blame the problems in the relationship on their partner, and tend to see their own and their partner's problem-related behaviour as global (affecting also other behaviours in marriage), as well as stable (likely to occur in the future). Put differently, individuals in distressed relationships do not see problems arising as issues that should be resolved in their own right, but as issues typical of severe and stable problems in their relationship. Research has shown that such a maladaptive attributional pattern predicts a decline in marital satisfaction (Fincham & Bradbury, 1991). Individuals satisfied with their relationship tend to give the partner more credit for resolving conflict, and tend to blame themselves more for inconveniencing the other (Thompson & Kelley, 1981; see chapter 7).

Happy couples also tend to interpret *social comparisons* with other couples in such a way that they feel better about their own relationship, whereas unhappy couples mainly look more at the negative implications of such comparisons. For example, a study by Buunk, Collins, VanYperen, Taylor and Dakoff (1990) showed that unhappily married individuals felt envious when they saw others having a better marriage, and worried that the same might happen to them when they encountered couples with more serious marital problems than they had. In general, partners in happy couples tend to perceive their own partner and their own relationship in a very positive light compared to other partners and relationships. For example, Buunk and Van den Eijnden (1997) showed that individuals who felt that their own relationship was better than that of most others exhibited a higher level of satisfaction. In a similar vein, Murray and Holmes (1997) found that dating and marital couples with high levels of satisfaction, love and trust perceived their partner much more positively than the typical partner, felt they had much more control over potential difficulties than people in the typical relationship, and were more optimistic about the future of their relationship. Such perceptions predicted whether or not dating couples remained together over the course of the year.

A final aspect that distinguishes happy from unhappy couples is the degree of *equity*. As noted above, equity theory assumes that individuals in close relationships expect a reciprocal and equal exchange. In evaluating this exchange,

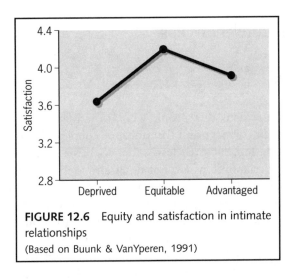

FIGURE 12.6   Equity and satisfaction in intimate relationships

(Based on Buunk & VanYperen, 1991)

individuals may consider a variety of inputs in and outcomes from the relationship, including love, support, financial contributions and household tasks (VanYperen & Buunk, 1991). Numerous studies have shown that distress occurs among the advantaged, who feel guilty because they receive more from the relationship than they believe they deserve, but especially among the deprived, who feel sad, frustrated, angry and hurt because they receive less than they believe they deserve. As shown in figure 12.6, a study by Buunk and VanYperen found that those perceiving equity were most satisfied, followed by those feeling advantaged, with those feeling deprived experiencing the lowest level of satisfaction (cf. Sprecher & Schwartz, 1994). Interestingly, even more than in heterosexual relationships, equity is important in lesbian relationships where equality and reciprocity are particularly valued (Schreurs & Buunk, 1996). Furthermore, inequity can have quite serious consequences for the relationship. Prins, Buunk and VanYperen (1992) found that women (but not men) in inequitable relationships had not only a stronger desire to engage in extramarital relationships, but they had also actually been involved more often in such relationships than women in equitable relationships.

Despite the importance of equity for satisfaction in close relationships, the role of this variable should not be overstated. First, the level of rewards seems a better predictor of satisfaction in love relationships than fairness: it is more important to feel our partner is rewarding us in terms of providing love, status, information and sexual satisfaction than to perceive perfect equity in the exchange of rewards with our partner (Cate, Lloyd, & Long, 1988). Second, a number of studies indicate that equity does not predict the quality and stability of the relationship in the future (e.g., Lujansky & Mikula, 1983; VanYperen & Buunk, 1990).

Commitment in relationships

What is commitment, and how does it come about?

It would seem self-evident that people who are satisfied with their relationship will also stick to their partners, and that unhappy couples will eventually end their relationship. Nevertheless, social scientists have long observed that happy relationships are not necessarily stable relationships, and that stable relationships are not necessarily happy relationships (Rusbult & Buunk, 1993). Rusbult (1983) proposed the **investment model** to explain what makes people motivated to maintain their relationships, i.e., what factors enhance **commitment** to these relationships. According to Rusbult, commitment refers to the individual's tendency both to maintain a relationship and to feel psychologically attached to it. Such commitment is based upon three factors: (1) A high *satisfaction*, i.e., an individual loves a partner and has positive feelings about the relationship. (2) A low perceived *quality of alternatives*, i.e., the best imagined alternative relationship for the present relationship, the appeal of living alone, what is simultaneously available in addition to the present relationship (such as an interesting job, or good friends), and the actual presence of an alternative partner (Buunk, 1987). When developing a relationship, individuals will gradually close themselves off, behaviourally and cognitively, from attractive alternatives. Johnson and Rusbult (1989) found a strong tendency to derogate attractive individuals from the opposite sex among highly committed individuals who were required to engage in interaction with them as part of a study on computer dating.

Many relationships suffer unhappy periods, and even when the alternatives are quite attractive, that does not necessarily mean they fall apart. Therefore, the investment model proposes a third variable: (3) *investment size*. This refers to the variety of ways in which individuals become linked to their partner, by investing time and energy, by making sacrifices, by developing mutual friends, by developing shared memories, and by engaging in activities, hobbies and possessions that are integrated in the relationship. According to recent research, during the course of a relationship the selves of both partners begin to overlap and become interconnected. Benefiting the other is seen as benefiting oneself and, through identification, the traits and abilities of the other become vicariously shared (Aron, Aron, & Smollan, 1992; Aron, Aron, Tudor, & Nelson, 1991).

A substantial number of studies have shown that all three factors – satisfaction, alternatives and investments – are necessary to predict commitment and the likelihood of breaking up a relationship, and this applies to heterosexual as well as to gay and lesbian relationships (Rusbult & Buunk, 1993). Moreover, commitment has been found to affect a wide variety of behaviours, in particular the

Investment model   A theory that assumes that commitment to a relationship is based upon a high satisfaction, a low quality of alternatives, and a high level of investments.

Commitment   The individual's tendency both to maintain a relationship and to feel psychologically attached to it.

tendency to give one's own interests priority over that of the relationship. For instance, highly committed individuals are more willing to make sacrifices for their relationship: they are more likely to continue their relationship when it would be necessary to give up the most important activities in their life, other than their relationship, such as parents, career, religion, friends or pastimes, in order to maintain their relationship (Van Lange, Rusbult, et al., 1997). In addition, Rusbult and Martz (1995) found that battered women who sought refuge at a shelter were, despite the often serious abuse, more likely to return to their partner after departure from the shelter when they had a high commitment to their partner prior to entering the shelter. Another rather dramatic effect of commitment was found in a study by Buunk and Bakker (1997), who showed that those with low levels of commitment were inclined to engage in unprotected sex outside the relationship, without informing the partner about this and without taking precautions to protect the steady partner against the possible risk of this behaviour.

The consequences of break-ups

What consequences do break-up and divorce have for mental and physical well-being?

The break-up of a relationship, and especially a divorce, may have serious consequences. With the increased divorce rate, such consequences affect large numbers of individuals in the Western world. The mental and physical health of divorced people has been found to be worse than that of married individuals, and even worse than that of people who have been widowed or those who never married. One of the reasons for this is that obtaining a divorce may in some cases be a consequence, instead of a cause, of mental problems (Cochrane, 1988; Stroebe & Stroebe, 1986). Nevertheless, ending a marriage through divorce is in itself a painful process. As attachment theory suggests, spouses usually develop – even in the face of the most serious hostility and fights – an emotional attachment that cannot easily be dissolved even if one wants to. Indeed, many people who have divorced or separated remain emotionally attached to their ex-partner, as is manifest from a variety of obvious, seemingly irrational indications of continued attachment between spouses, including spending a lot of time thinking about the former relationship, wondering what the ex-partner is doing, doubting that the divorce has really happened, and feeling one would never recover from the marital breakdown (Ganong & Coleman, 1994; Kitson, 1982). In addition to having to relinquish the attachment to the former spouse, divorced people are often confronted with the transition from being married to being single. Living alone, after having lived with a partner for a long time, usually requires considerable adjustment. It is often difficult to maintain earlier, couple-based friendships and, consequently, new relationships have to be initiated and built. Moreover, adapting to a different, lower social status can be a painful process, especially because there is still some stigma attached to being divorced. In addition, divorcees usually receive less support than widowed people, because friends may side with the former spouse. Furthermore, divorcees often have to deal with feelings of failure and rejection. Nevertheless, adjustment to divorce is for some individuals easier than for others. For example, individuals who took the initiative to divorce, who are embedded in social networks, and who have a satisfying, intimate relationship, are relatively better off. In addition, certain personality characteristics, including high self-esteem, independence, tolerance for change and egalitarian sex-role attitudes, facilitate coping with the situation of being divorced (Price-Bonham, Wright, & Pittman, 1983). Although most divorced individuals will eventually remarry, many are reluctant to remarry and just cohabit with a partner or stay single, while a minority develops a gay or lesbian relationship after the divorce (Buunk & Van Driel, 1989; Ganong & Coleman, 1994).

Summary and Conclusions

Humans are social animals. The need to affiliate with others is a basic human drive that is particularly enhanced in stressful situations, when people seek out others to compare their feelings, to reduce their anxiety, and to obtain information about the nature of the threat. Especially those with a secure attachment style affiliate when under stress, and benefit from the support and presence of other people. Although sometimes affiliation may increase rather than reduce stress and anxiety, those with deficiencies in their social relationships experience relatively more loneliness and health problems. The physical proximity of others as well as similarity in attitudes promote the development of relationships such as friendships and love relationships. Reciprocity, interdependence and, particularly for women, intimacy are characteristic for all personal relationships. More than friendships, love relationships are fostered by physiological arousal and physical attractiveness, with men paying more attention to signs of youth and health, and women more to signs of status. Satisfying love relationships are characterized by constructive communication, positive interpretations of the partner's behaviour, equity and favourable perceptions of one's own relationship in comparison with that of others. Commitment develops on the basis of a high satisfaction, combined with increasing investments in the relationship, and with a decreasing attention to alternative options. Due to the strong attachment that usually develops in intimate relationships, break-ups and divorces are painful processes. Although affiliation with strangers and friends may be quite important for well-being, happy intimate relationships are probably the most important source of satisfaction for most individuals in our society. They provide many of the benefits of affiliation, including not only emotional support, opportunities for social comparison and instrumental help but also a social identity. Without doubt, close intimate relationships are the most far-reaching form of affiliation individuals engage in in the course of their life.

1 How could one design an apartment building in such a way that interaction and the development of friendships within the building would be stimulated?

2 In what different ways may social support foster survival? Why may support be related to health?

3 Think of as many conditions as possible under which talking to others will increase stress.

4 What could people do to alleviate loneliness without seeing others?

5 Think of as many features as possible that make a friendship different from a love relationship.

6 Derive from the findings in this chapter a situation in which there would be a strong likelihood that two people (i.e., a heterosexual man and woman, two gay men or two lesbian women) would become romantically attracted to each other. Think, among other things, of the spatial context, the characteristics of the two people, and the activities they might engage in.

7 Think about a possible cross-cultural study that would test socio-evolutionary notions about physical attractiveness.

8 Come up with a number of situations to which individuals with different attachment styles might show different responses.

9 Suppose a heterosexual or homosexual couple feel they are not as committed to their relationship as they were before. What can you suggest, on the basis of the investment model, that they could do to enhance commitment?

DISCUSSION POINTS

Buss, D. M. (1994). *The evolution of desire: Strategies of human mating*. New York: Basic Books. An interesting, well-written book on the socio-evolutionary approach to romantic attraction and close relationships.

Buunk, B. P., & Van Driel, B. (1989). *Variant lifestyles and relationships*. Newbury Park, CA: Sage. Deals with close relationships outside marriage, including relationships of singles, unmarried cohabitation, extramarital relationships, homosexual and lesbian relationships and communal groups.

Hatfield, E., & Sprecher, S. (1986). *Mirror, mirror . . . The importance of looks in everyday life*. New York: SUNY Press. A somewhat dated but good review of research on physical attractiveness.

Hinde, R. A. (1997). *Relationships. A dialectical perspective*. Hove: Psychology Press. A very thorough, broad and in-depth review of all aspects of close relationships.

Lerner, M. J., & Mikula, G. (Eds.). (1994). *Entitlement and the affectional bond: Justice in close relationships*. New York: Plenum Press. A useful reader on equity, social exchange and justice in dating, marital and family relationships.

Noller, P., & Fitzpatrick, M. A. (Eds.). (1988). *Perspectives on marital interaction*. Clevedon/Philadelphia: Multilingual Matters. A

FURTHER READING

well-composed reader of chapters dealing particularly with marital communication.

Sarason, B. R., Sarason, I. G., & Pierce, G. R. (Eds.). (1990). *Social support. An interactional view.* New York: Wiley. An excellent volume on all aspects of and approaches to social support.

Sternberg, R. J., & Barnes, M. L. (Eds.). (1988). *The psychology of love.* New Haven, CT: Yale University Press. Chapters review various approaches to love.

KEY STUDIES

Hazan, C., & Shaver, P. (1987). Romantic love conceptualized as an attachment process. *Journal of Personality and Social Psychology,* 52, 511–24.

Rusbult, C. E. (1980). Commitment and satisfaction in romantic associations: A test of the investment model. *Journal of Experimental Social Psychology,* 16, 172–86.

Social Groups PART IV

CONTENTS

Social Influence in Small Groups

13

Eddy Van Avermaet

OUTLINE

Beginning with majority and minority influence, this chapter looks at instances where people change their opinions following exposure to the opinions of others. When and how do judgements expressed by a majority or a minority influence the judgements of other group members? And can these effects be accounted for by a single explanatory model? Group polarization constitutes a second topic. We try to explain why, after discussion, a group's position is often more extreme than the average initial position of its members prior to the discussion. We show that in some cases distinctly negative outcomes result from this group mode of thinking. The final section of the chapter is devoted to an analysis of a set of famous studies on obedience to authority. It tries to unravel the factors that make people willing to inflict harm upon an innocent other merely because a figure of authority ordered them to do so.

KEY CONCEPTS

- After-image
- Autokinetic effect
- Compliance
- Conformity
- Consistency
- Conversion
- Group polarization
- Groupthink
- Informational influence

- Innovation
- Majority influence (conformity)
- Minority influence (innovation)
- Normative influence
- Obedience
- Self-categorization theory
- Social comparison
- Social influence

Introduction

What is social influence?

Imagine you are one of a group of seven people who represent the student body at departmental meetings. The forthcoming meeting will discuss and take a vote on a proposed change in the curriculum: several applied courses are to be dropped and replaced by more theoretically oriented subjects. Before the meeting the student representatives get together to try to reach a common position on the issue. You have given the issue a lot of thought and you favour the departmental proposal. At the student meeting you then learn that some people share your view but that others do not. You try to convince them of your viewpoint, and they try to convince you of theirs. What will be the outcome? Most likely you will reply: it all depends on the circumstances! In giving that reply, you concur with social psychologists, who for many years now have been systematically studying the factors that determine social influence in small groups.

Social influence A change in the judgements, opinions and attitudes of an individual as a result of being exposed to the views of others.

Broadly speaking, the study of **social influence** coincides with social psychology itself, because the entire field deals with the influence of social factors on behaviour. Typically, however, the concept of social influence is given a more restricted meaning: social influence refers to a change in the judgements, opinions and attitudes of an individual as a result of being exposed to the judgements, opinions and attitudes of other individuals (de Montmollin, 1977). With this restricted definition in mind, the present chapter will introduce you to some of the more important phenomena that have been studied concerning social influence in group settings. One should keep in mind that this restricted definition also covers the area of persuasive communication and attitude change, described in chapter 8. It would appear instructive for the student of this book to search explicitly for elements of similarity and integration between these two separate chapters.

Majority influence (conformity) Social influence resulting from exposure to the opinions of a majority, or the majority of one's group.

The first topic is **conformity**, or **majority influence**. Do individuals change their opinions when they learn that the majority of the members of a group to which they belong hold a different opinion? Do they perhaps only give in overtly and maintain their own conviction in private, or does majority influence really change people's minds? Under which conditions do individuals manage to resist majority influence? Next we turn our attention to the reverse phenomenon, namely

Minority influence (innovation) Social influence resulting from exposure to the opinions of a minority group, or the minority of one's group.

innovation, or **minority influence**. Can a minority in a group bring about changes in the opinions of a majority? Which characteristics should a minority have in order to produce an effect? Do minorities exert their influence through the same mechanisms as majorities? And is there a difference in quantity or quality of influence?

The third and fourth sections will deal respectively with the phenomena of group polarization and obedience. **Group polarization** refers to the fact that, under certain conditions, the outcome of a group discussion is more extreme than the initial average position of the individual group members. We will look into some of the theories and experiments that have been set up to account for this most remarkable phenomenon. Finally, we will pay attention to a special case of social influence: when and why will individuals, merely at the persistent request of an authority, show **obedience** to orders which they themselves consider unethical and which they are, in principle, unwilling to execute?

Group polarization A change in the average position of a group, following group discussion, in the direction of the initially dominant pole.

Obedience Carrying out the orders given by a person invested with authority.

Conformity, or Majority Influence

Sherif and the autokinetic effect

How do others' opinions influence our judgements?

In an early social-influence experiment, Muzafer Sherif (1935) placed participants alone or in groups of two or three in a completely darkened room. At a distance of about 5 metres, a single and small stationary light was presented to them. As you may already have experienced yourself, in the absence of reference points a stationary light appears to move rather erratically in all directions. This perceptual illusion is known as the **autokinetic effect**. Sherif asked his participants to give an oral estimate of the extent of movement of the light, obviously without informing them of the autokinetic effect. Half of the participants made their first 100 judgements alone. On three subsequent days they went through three more sets of trials, but this time in groups of two or three. For the other half of the participants the procedure was reversed. They underwent the three group sessions first and ended with a session alone. Participants who first made their judgements alone developed rather quickly a standard estimate (a personal norm) around which their judgements fluctuated. This personal norm was stable, but it varied highly between individuals. In the group phases of the experiment, which brought together people with different personal norms, participants' judgements converged towards a more or less common position – a group norm. With the reverse procedure this group norm developed in the first session and it persisted in the later session alone. Figure 13.1 illustrates both kinds of findings. The funnel effect in the left panel reveals the convergence in the (median) judgements of three participants who first judged alone (I), and later in each other's presence (II, III, IV). The right panel shows the judgements of a group of three participants who

Autokinetic effect The illusion of movement of a stationary point of light when viewed in a totally dark environment.

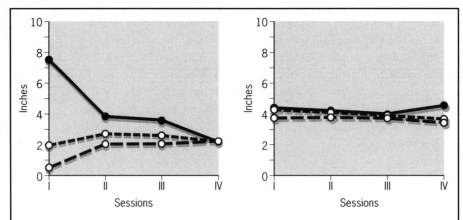

FIGURE 13.1   Median judgements of movement under alone (I) or group (II, III, IV) conditions (left), and under group (I, II, III) or alone (IV) conditions (right) in Sherif's (1935) study on norm formation

went through the procedure in the reverse order. Here the convergence is already present in the first group session and there is no sign of funnelling out in the final alone session.

This famous experiment shows that, where confronted with an unstructured and ambiguous stimulus, people nevertheless develop a stable internal frame of reference against which to judge the stimulus. However, as soon as they are confronted with the different judgements of others, they quickly abandon this frame of reference so as to adjust it to that of others. On the other hand, a joint frame of reference formed in the presence of others continues to affect a person's judgements when the source of influence is no longer present.

We have described conformity as a change in an individual's judgement in the direction of the judgements expressed by the majority of the members of a group to which the individual belongs. Strictly speaking, Sherif's study is not a conformity or majority-influence experiment because he merely brought together two or three people who held different opinions. To turn it into a conformity study, one would have to replace all the participants but one by confederates who unanimously agree upon a particular judgement. Jacobs and Campbell (1961) did just that and in addition, after every 30 judgements, they replaced a confederate by a naive participant until the whole group was made up of naive participants. Their results indicated that the majority had a significant effect on the participants' judgements, even after they had gradually been removed from the situation.

Up to this point you may not be too surprised. After all, it is normal and even adaptive that people are influenced by or conform to the judgements of others when the judgemental stimulus is ambiguous or when they feel uncertain about their own judgement. But would you also conform to the judgements of others when they appear to be patently wrong, when their judgements are completely at odds with what your senses and physical reality tell you? Would social reality prevail, or would you, as the saying goes, 'call them as you see them'?

The surprise of Solomon Asch

Will others influence our judgements, even when these others are obviously incorrect?

The question raised above constituted the starting point of a series of famous conformity experiments conducted by Solomon Asch in the early 1950s (Asch, 1951, 1952, 1956). In his first study, Asch invited seven students to participate in an experiment on visual discrimination. Their task was simple enough: 18 times they would have to decide which of three comparison lines was equal in length to a standard line. On each trial one comparison line was in effect equal in length to the standard line, but the other two were different (for an example, see figure 13.2). On some trials these were both longer or shorter, or one was longer and the other shorter. Also, trials differed in terms of the extent to which the two incorrect lines were different from the standard line. All in all, the task was apparently very easy, as is shown by the fact that in a control group of 37 participants, who made their judgements in isolation, 35 people did not make a single error, one person made one error and one person made two errors. Hence, summing over participants and trials, a negligible 0.7 per cent errors were made in the control condition. In the experimental condition participants, who were seated in a semicircle, were requested to give their judgements aloud, in the order in which they were seated, from position 1 to position 7. Actually, there was only one real participant, seated in position 6. All the others were confederates of the experimenter and, on each trial, they unanimously gave a predetermined answer. On six 'neutral' trials (the first two trials, and four other trials distributed over the remaining set), the confederates gave correct answers. On the other 12 'critical' trials, they unanimously agreed on an incorrect line. The neutral trials, particularly the first two, were added to avoid suspicion on the part of the real participant

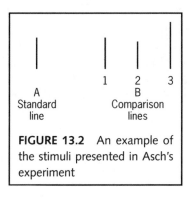

FIGURE 13.2 An example of the stimuli presented in Asch's experiment

and to try to ensure that the confederates' responses were not attributed to their poor eyesight. It should be pointed out that, throughout the experiment, both the experimenter and the confederates acted in a rather impersonal and formal manner, not showing any surprise or negative reaction to the answers given. As a matter of fact, as you might expect, only the real participants showed explicit signs of being uncomfortable and upset, giving the experimenter and the other participants nervous looks, sweating and gesticulating.

The results reveal the tremendous impact of an 'obviously' incorrect but unanimous majority on the judgements of a lone participant. In comparison with the control condition, which you will remember yielded only 0.7 per cent errors, the experimental participants made almost 37 per cent errors. Not every participant made that many errors, but it is instructive to observe that out of Asch's 123 participants, only about 25 per cent did not make a single error (compared with 95 per cent in the control condition), another 28 per cent gave eight or more (out of 12) incorrect answers, and the remaining participants made between one and seven mistakes (see figure 13.3 for the exact frequency distribution). From a methodological point of view, it is important to grasp clearly the distinction between percentage of errors and percentage of influenced participants. Students (and even textbooks) sometimes confuse the two measures by asserting that 37 per cent errors means that 37 per cent of the participants were influenced. The above distinction is also important from an interpretational viewpoint, because just by itself the error percentage presents only an incomplete picture of the amount of influence exerted (it says nothing about the distribution of this influence).

Asch's experiment, with its astonishing results, provided the groundwork for a rich tradition of theoretical speculations and empirical studies, directed at

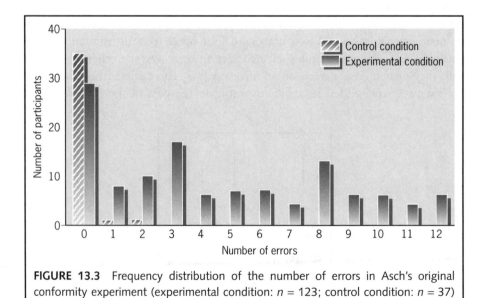

FIGURE 13.3   Frequency distribution of the number of errors in Asch's original conformity experiment (experimental condition: $n = 123$; control condition: $n = 37$)

determining the boundaries of the phenomenon, the conditions under which conformity increases and decreases, and whether conformity is only public or also private. The next paragraphs present a selection of this research against the background of the major theoretical perspective within which it can be situated. Most of this research has made use of a paradigm, modelled after Asch's, but far more economical. Using the so-called 'Crutchfield' technique (Crutchfield, 1955), participants typically are placed in separate cubicles where they see the responses of (simulated) confederates appear electronically on a panel. The savings in time and confederates are great, but some of the realism of the original Asch procedure is lost in the process.

Why people conform: normative and informational influence

What are the major mechanisms through which groups influence their members?

When people have to express a judgement about some aspect of reality in the presence of others they have two major concerns: they want to be right, and they want to make a good impression on the others. To determine what is right, individuals have two sources of information: what their perceptions of physical reality indicate, and what others say. Throughout life individuals have learned to appreciate the value of both sources of information. On numerous occasions they have experienced the adaptive value of founding their judgements and behaviours on their own view of reality. On the other hand, a lot of what they have learned about reality is based on information provided by others, and in their experience relying on others' judgements had proved adaptive as well. Moreover, in most instances both their own judgements and those of others have coincided, providing people with a stable view of their environment. The conformity situation, however, opposes these two sources of information and confronts the individual with the conflict of choosing between two – in principle – reliable bases of information. If, in this perspective, individuals conform, they are said to have undergone **informational influence**: they yield to others because they trust their judgement more than their own. There is, however, also another reason why a person might yield to group pressure. Because we are dependent on others for the satisfaction of a variety of needs, it is important that we maximize their liking for us. To the extent that disagreeing with others can be anticipated to lead to dislike or even outward rejection, and that agreeing will lead to more positive evaluations and continued group membership, people are induced to conform to others' judgements for normative reasons. Hence, conformity caused by the desire to be liked and by the aversion to being disliked is due to **normative influence**.

Informational influence
Influence based on the informational value of opinions expressed by others, on what they tell a person about an aspect of reality.

Normative influence
Influence based on the need to be accepted and approved by others.

Informational and normative influence (Deutsch & Gerard, 1955) are then the major general mechanisms through which groups have an impact on their members. Of course, the relative weight of these two mechanisms varies from situation to situation. In some instances, people will conform more because of the information others provide, whereas in others they will conform mainly for normative reasons. Moreover – and this is an equally important distinction – normative and informational influence processes can be expected to produce effects at different levels. If a person conforms mainly because of what others will think of her, she will change her overt behaviour while privately maintaining her prior conviction; but if she trusts the information provided by others, she will in addition also change her private opinion. Hence a distinction should be made between public conformity, or **compliance**, and private conformity, or **conversion**. As a matter of fact, researchers in this field have used public and private response modes in conformity settings as a means of assessing whether normative or informational influence is the more important change mechanism. Results of these experiments have shown that, at least as far as the original Asch experiment is concerned, normative influence is more important than informational influence. This can be inferred from the observation that public responses are far more influenced by the group's judgement than are responses given in private (for a review, see Allen, 1965).

In a more general sense, and through the manipulation of various characteristics of the influence situation, social psychologists have attempted to collect evidence for the theoretical proposition that conformity will increase or decrease as a function of the amount of informational and/or normative dependence of an individual on the group.

> **Compliance**   A change in overt (public) behaviour after exposure to others' opinions.

> **Conversion**   A change in covert (private) behaviour after exposure to others' opinions; internalized change; a change in the way one structures an aspect of reality.

Normative and informational influence: experimental evidence

Under which conditions are the normative and informational influence mechanisms engaged?

Beginning with normative influence, Endler (1965) showed that direct reinforcement for conforming responses leads to an increment in conformity. Deutsch and Gerard (1955) increased the interdependence of the group members by promising a reward (tickets to a Broadway play) to the five groups that made the fewest errors of judgement in the Crutchfield version of the Asch task. Setting this goal for the group, which clearly made the members very dependent on each other for obtaining a desired effect, produced twice as much conformity as a baseline condition (see also Thibaut & Strickland, 1956). As a different illustration of the role of normative influence, via a meta-analytic comparison of conformity effects in individualist vs. collectivist cultures, Bond and Smith (1996) observed more conformity in cultures that place a high value on harmony in person-to-group relations. Their meta-analysis also showed that, at least within the United States, the size of the conformity effects observed has decreased over the years. This finding might reflect the reduced impact groups have over their members nowadays compared to fifty years ago.

Turning to the role of informational influence, it has been shown that the participant's perceived competence at the judgement task relative to others, as well as his or her self-confidence, determine the amount of conformity (e.g., Mausner, 1954). Di Vesta (1959) showed that there was more conformity on later trials if the early trials contained many neutral trials (where the majority gives correct answers), because under these conditions the participant is more likely to attribute competence to the other group members. Task difficulty or stimulus ambiguity is another variable which, through the informational mechanism, influences conformity. Baron, Vandello and Brunsman (1996) observed that an increase in task difficulty, which makes people more uncertain, in effect had them turn more to a group of unanimous others for information about the correct response, especially so when answering correctly resulted in a tangible material reward. Interestingly, when the task was very easy, the introduction of a monetary reward for correct responses reduced conformity. Under these latter conditions the motive to be accurate easily outweighs any influence that could result from normative group pressure.

The size of the majority is yet another example of a relevant variable in this context. Asch (1951) ran groups in which the size of the 'majority' varied from one to 16. One person had no effect, but two persons already produced 13 per cent errors (see figure 13.4). With three confederates the conformity effect

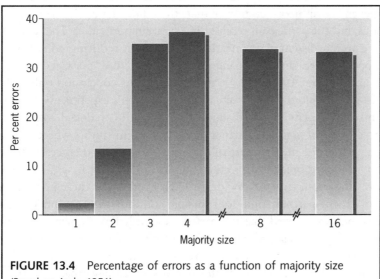

FIGURE 13.4   Percentage of errors as a function of majority size (Based on Asch, 1951)

reached its full strength with 33 per cent errors. The addition of even more confederates did not lead to further increments in conformity. Later studies by Gerard, Wilhelmy and Connolley (1968) and by Latané and Wolf (1981) have questioned this conclusion and suggest that adding more members to the majority will, in effect, lead to more conformity but with diminishing increments per added member. The exact nature of the function relating majority size to conformity remains an issue of debate between those who posit a linear relationship vs. those who favour one or another form of non-linear relationship (Bond & Smith, 1996). Aside from size *per se*, the degree of perceived independence of the influence sources is also important. Adding more members to the majority will only lead to more influence if the majority members are perceived as independent judges and not as sheep following the others or as members of a group who have arrived jointly at a judgement. Wilder (1977) showed that two independent groups of two people have more impact than four people who present their judgements as a group, and three groups of two have more effect than two groups of three, who in turn yield more conformity than one group of six. Clearly, independent sources of information are more reliable than a single aggregated information source.

Finally, a fascinating series of studies, excellently summarized by Allen (1975), has looked at the effects of replacing one of the confederates by another person who deviates from the majority position. When Asch gave the participant a 'supporter', in the form of a confederate who answered before the participant and who gave correct answers on all trials, the conformity of the real participant dropped dramatically to a mere 5.5 per cent. In trying to find out whether the reduced conformity was caused by the break in the unanimity of the majority or by the fact that participants now had a social supporter (for their own private opinion), Asch added a condition in which the confederate deviated from the majority but gave an even more incorrect answer than they did. Hence the majority was not unanimous, but the participant received no social support either. The results showed that the extreme dissenter was nearly as effective in reducing conformity as the social supporter. Breaking the unanimity would therefore appear to be crucial but, as Allen and Levine (1968, 1969) later showed, this conclusion only holds with respect to unambiguous stimulus situations, as in Asch's experiments. With opinion statements only a genuine social supporter will lead to reduced conformity.

The role of *social support* is further demonstrated in studies where the participant has a partner for the first part of the experiment, who then ceases to respond owing to an alleged breakdown in the equipment (Allen & Bragg, 1965), or who then leaves the room (Allen & Wilder, 1972). Even under these non-responding-partner or absent-partner conditions, people continue to resist influence, at least as long as they are assured that the partner responded in the same setting (under pressure) as they do. Also, when a participant is given a partner who then deserts by switching to the incorrect majority responses, she will not maintain her prior 'independence'. Rather, she will conform as if she had never had a partner (Asch, 1955).

Although the social support effects can also partially be interpreted in terms of normative influence, it is instructive to look at them from an informational point of view. Looking at the desertion effect first, it is understandable that a person, upon learning that someone whose judgements he trusts (because they coincide with his own) changes sides, will be strongly influenced by that person's behaviour. 'Here is an intelligent person changing his position; I'd better do as he does because he can be relied on!' In a similar vein, the other social support effects would tend to indicate that the participant's refusal to conform is caused by the fact that, as Allen puts it, the social supporter provides an independent assessment of reality, which is sufficient to outweigh the potential informational value of the majority's responses. This interpretation is strongly supported by the data of an experiment by Allen and Levine (1971). Here too the participant was given a supporter, but in one of their two support conditions the social support was invalid. The supporter, although giving correct answers, could not possibly be perceived as a valid source of information because the participant knew that the supporter had extremely poor vision (as was evident from a pre-experimental eye examination and from his eyeglasses with thick lenses). The results, shown in figure 13.5, indicate that, although invalid social support is sufficient to reduce the amount of conformity significantly, compared with a unanimous-majority condition, the valid social supporter has much more impact. One lesson to be learned from all these studies is obvious: if you are afraid of being influenced by

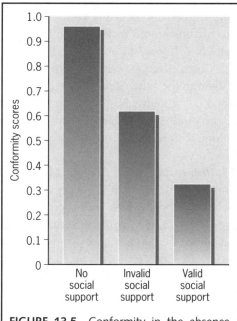

FIGURE 13.5 Conformity in the absence and in the presence of social support (Based on Allen & Levine, 1971)

a group (at least publicly – and that is often what counts!), make sure you bring a partner along, and preferably one you can count on to stick by your position!

Clearly then, the addition of a person sharing an isolated individual's viewpoint makes him or her resist that influence. But is resisting the only behavioural option open to the individual (and his or her supporter)? Can he or she not try actively to attempt to persuade the majority that they might be wrong and that he or she is right? Just look around and you will say 'yes'. However, it was not really until the late 1960s that social psychologists, mainly under the impetus of the French psychologist Serge Moscovici, began seriously to study the conditions under which a minority can do more than merely resist and itself become an active source of influence.

Innovation, or Minority Influence

The power of a consistent minority

How can a minority influence a majority?

In the film *Twelve Angry Men*, 12 jurors have to decide over the guilt or innocence of a young man charged with the murder of his father. At the outset of the deliberation all but one are convinced of the youth's guilt. Does the lone juror (Henry Fonda) yield to the unanimous majority? No! Does he only passively resist their influence attempts? No! Instead he actively attempts to persuade the others of the correctness of his own position, standing firm, committed, self-confident and unwavering. One by one the other jurors change sides, until in the end they all agree that the accused is not guilty. History and present-day social life provide ample examples of minority influence: Galileo, Freud, new forms of art, the growing impact of the ecological movement, and the women's movement are but a few examples.

In his book *Social Influence and Social Change*, Moscovici (1976) argues that most instances of minority influence or innovation cannot be accounted for by the mechanisms which traditionally have been proposed to explain majority influence. Indeed, if you think of it, minorities do not have a lot going for them: they are few in number; they often do not have normative control over the majority; at first they are more often ridiculed than taken seriously; they are perceived as 'dummies' and 'weirdoes'. In other words, they do not seem to have access to the informational and normative means of control, explicitly or implicitly available to a majority. How can they then have influence? Moscovici answers that the core of their impact is to be found in their own *behavioural style*. A minority has to propose a clear position on the issue at hand and hold firmly to it, withstanding all the time the pressures exerted by the majority. The most important compo-

PLATE 13.1   Henry Fonda wins over a previously unanimous majority of other jurors in the film *Twelve Angry Men*

nent of this behavioural style is the **consistency** with which the minority defends and advocates its position. This consistency entails two components: intraindividual consistency or stability over time (**diachronic consistency**) and interindividual consistency within the minority (**synchronic consistency**). Only if minority members agree amongst each other and continue to do so over time can they expect

Consistency A behavioural style indicative of maintenance of position. **Diachronic**: consistency over time; **synchronic**: consistency between individuals.

the majority to begin to question its own position, consider the correctness of the minority position, and eventually be influenced.

The key role of consistency has been demonstrated in many experiments, only two of which shall be described in detail (for overviews, see Maass & Clark, 1984; Wood, Lundgren, Ouellette, Busceme, & Blackstone, 1994). In what is essentially a reversed Asch experiment, Moscovici, Lage and Naffrechoux (1969) had students participate in a study on colour perception in groups of six. Participants first underwent a test for colour blindness. Upon passing this test they were then shown 36 slides, all clearly blue and only differing in intensity. Their task was simply to judge the colour of the slides by naming *aloud* a simple colour. Two of the participants, seated in the first and second position, or in the first and fourth position, were actually confederates of the experimenter. In the consistent condition they answered 'green' on all trials, which made them diachronically as well as synchronically consistent. In the inconsistent condition they answered 'green' 24 times and 'blue' 12 times. The experiment also contained a control condition, where the groups were made up of six naive participants. As figure 13.6 shows, in the control condition only 0.25 per cent green responses were given, revealing the obviousness of the correct response. Out of 22 naive participants only one person gave two green responses. In the inconsistent-minority condition 1.25 per cent responses were green, only slightly and insignificantly more than

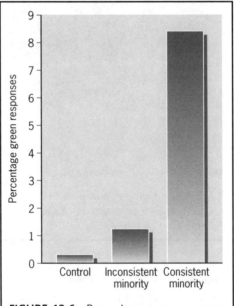

FIGURE 13.6   Percentage green reponses given by majority participants in the experiment by Moscovici, Lage and Naffrechoux (1969)

in the control condition. In the consistent-minority condition, however, green responses were made 8.42 per cent of the time.

This experiment clearly shows that a consistent minority can have a distinct effect on the public judgements of the members of a majority group. Before proceeding it is instructive to compare Moscovici's setting with that of Asch. In the Asch study one participant is opposed by a consistent majority of six; in Moscovici's experiment a group of four naive participants stands against a consistent minority of only two confederates. In Asch's study the conflict confronting the participants is induced by the majority; in Moscovici's experiment a similar conflict is induced by a minority. Although the minority does not have 'the numbers', its consistent behavioural style makes it influential – at least after a while, when the majority participants begin to observe that the minority maintains its position in spite of their opposition. It is indeed a typical observation that, in contrast to conformity studies, the minority effect only begins to show after a certain period (Nemeth, 1982). The impression of potential correctness of the minority position is further advanced when majority members notice that one or more of their own group members begin to answer like the minority – a finding reminiscent of what happens in a conformity setting when a social supporter of the participant deserts to the majority. The picture that begins to unfold, then, is that a consistent minority sets in motion a variety of intra- and interpersonal processes in the majority which ultimately result in influence.

Let us now look at a second experiment which demonstrates that consistency need not necessarily take the form of repetition of the same response, but can also be expressed through a clear pattern in the responses of the minority. Nemeth, Swedlund and Kanki (1974) essentially replicated Moscovici's earlier experiment, but they added two conditions in which the confederates said 'green' on half of the trials and 'green-blue' on the other half. In a random condition the green and green-blue responses were randomly distributed over the trials, but in a correlated condition the confederates said 'green' to the brighter slides and 'green-blue' to the dimmer slides (or vice versa). In the latter condition the confederates were definitely not repetitive in their answers, yet they were consistent in that their responses were patterned after a characteristic of the stimulus (its brightness). The results showed that, compared to a no-influence control condition, the random condition had no effect. The correlated condition, on the other hand, produced almost 21 per cent influenced responses. Interestingly, and in contrast to Moscovici's findings, a repetitive and consistent 'green' minority did not significantly affect the participant's responses. Nemeth gives an interesting clue as to why this happened. Her participants were allowed to respond with all the colours that they saw in the slides, whereas Moscovici's participants could only respond with a single colour. If a minority does not show any flexibility in its behaviour (when the context allows for it), it has no effect in spite of its consistency, because under these circumstances it also tends to be perceived as rigid and unrealistic. A series of studies by Mugny and Papastamou (Mugny, 1982) provided direct evidence for this interpretation. Using opinion statements rather than a perceptual task, they observed that minority proposals presented to participants in written form were far less effective in inducing change when they were formulated in slogan-like and uncompromising terms than when expressed in more moderate language. Importantly, the rigid and the flexible messages were perceived as equally consistent. Mugny (1982) feels that a minority will only be effective if it consistently provides a distinct alternative perspective on reality and yet shows its willingness to negotiate a kind of compromise. Of course, beyond a certain point this willingness to compromise may take away some of the perception of consistency and result in less influence (Turner, 1991).

Nemeth's and Mugny's experiments again show that consistency is a necessary condition for minority influence, but at the same time they indicate that whether or not consistency leads to effective influence depends on how it is interpreted by the majority. The image one forms of the minority and the nature of the attributional processes activated jointly by the minority's behavioural style, by the context in which it emits these behaviours, and by the behavioural reactions of the members of one's own group, appear crucial mediating variables in determining the minority's ultimate effect on the judgements of a person (for an overview and discussion of the role of attributional processes, see Maass & Clark, 1984; Chaiken & Stangor, 1987; Wood et al., 1994).

Majority and minority influence: two processes or one?

Do majorities and minorities have the same or different effects?
Are the influence mechanisms of majorities and minorities identical?

Dual-process explanations

At this point you might raise the important question: at what level does this influence occur? Perhaps under certain conditions a minority may not lead to public influence (because of normative pressures from the majority), but it could still be influential at a more latent, private level. In our discussion of majority influence we argued that, in a conformity setting, normative pressures lead to public influence and informational pressures lead to public and private influence, but do not forget that in that setting all others are opposed to the participant. In the minority setting, on the other hand, participants have to deal with two groups – the opposing minority and their own majority group. It is plausible to assume that the minority has less normative control over the participant than does a majority. As a matter of fact, research shows that minorities are strongly disliked (Moscovici & Lage, 1976). For this reason one might expect minorities to have less public influence on a participant, at least when other resisting majority members are also present. But what about private influence? Could it be that a minority has a more profound impact on one's private opinion than a majority, whose answers one might simply accept because 'if so many people agree, they must be right and I must be wrong' without really having given a lot of thought to the issue at hand?

Precisely these thoughts led Moscovici (1980) to formulate some very striking propositions about the *differences* in process and effect between majority and minority influence. These propositions have generated a lot of research and quite a bit of controversy, because other researchers have emphasized the *similarities* between the two influence modalities (Latané & Wolf, 1981; Tanford & Penrod, 1984; Kruglanski & Mackie, 1990). The question itself is fascinating and yet very complicated, and we can therefore only present you with an introduction to it (for an excellent discussion, see Maass & Clark, 1984; Wood et al., 1994; De Vries, De Dreu, Gordijn, & Schuurman, 1996). Before doing so, it is perhaps helpful to keep in mind that Moscovici essentially deals with the contrast between a situation in which a unanimous majority confronts a single person and a situation where a minority group stands against a majority group. You should be careful not to generalize from this situation to all conceivable minority–majority interaction settings, where the impact of intra- and interpersonal processes and the direct vs. indirect effects of minorities and majorities might be different.

Moscovici proposes that the majority, in the conformity paradigm, activates a **social comparison** process in which the participant compares his response to that of others, 'concentrates all his attention on what others say, so as to fit in with their opinions and judgements' (1980, p. 214) without giving a lot of attention or thought to the issue itself. Add to that the role of the normative pressures exerted by the majority, and only public compliance in their presence is expected. Any private effects would be short-lived because once the person, freed from the presence of the majority, focuses again on the issue at hand, he will return to his prior opinions.

Social comparison The act of comparing own behaviour to others' behaviour in order to evaluate the correctness and adequacy of own behaviour.

In contrast, a minority will evoke a *validation* process – cognitive activity aimed at understanding why the minority consistently holds on to its position. Attention will be focused on the object, and in the process the participant – to some extent without even being aware of it – may begin to look at the object as the minority does and become privately (or latently) converted to its position. The majority's normative pressures (at least if they overtly resist) will however prevent this effect from being shown publicly. Therefore, relatively speaking, minorities will lead to conversion (without compliance) and majorities will lead to compliance (without conversion).

To test this theory, various kinds of experiments have been designed. As an example we will describe one very ingenious and provocative experiment conducted by Moscovici and Personnaz (1980). Participants (taking part in pairs) were first shown a series of five blue slides. In private they wrote down the colour of the slide as well as the colour of the after-image of the slide (on a rating scale going from 1 = yellow to 9 = purple). The **after-image** is what one sees on a white screen after having fixed a colour for a while, and it is the complementary colour of the

After-image The colour seen on a white surface after exposure to another colour; it is the complementary colour of the original colour.

original one. The after-image of blue is yellow-orange, and the after-image of green is red-purple. To manipulate the majority or minority status of the responses, participants were then informed that their colour response was shared by 81.8 per cent (or by only 18.2 per cent) of the people who had previously participated. The other 18.2 per cent (or 81.8 per cent) had judged the slides green. During the next phase (15 trials), the colour responses had to be given publicly, but no judgements of the colour of the after-image were asked for. The first person to respond, a confederate, always said green. In view of the information received prior to this phase, the real participant perceived this green response as a minority or a majority response. The third phase (15 trials) was again private, the confederate and the participant writing down both the colour of the slide and the rating of the after-image. The experiment concluded with a fourth phase in which the participant answered again in private, but in the absence of the confederate. Moscovici felt that if the influence source had brought about a real change in the perception of the participant, this ought to result in a shift of the judged colour of the after-image towards the complementary colour of green (the higher end of the response scale), even though there had never been a direct influence attempt by the confederate with respect to this judgement. The results, shown in figure 13.7, indicate that, compared with a no-influence control condition, the majority source produced no changes in this judgement, whereas the minority source did.

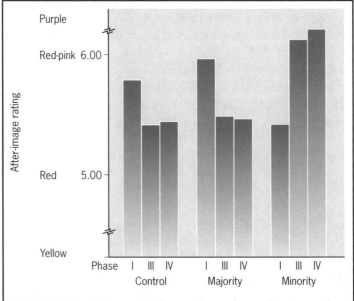

FIGURE 13.7 Judgements of the colour of the after-image during each of the phases of Moscovici and Personnaz's experiment (Data from Moscovici, 1980)

Using a somewhat different methodology – a spectrometer on which partici-pants had to adjust the colour so that it matched the slide and the after-image they had previously seen – Personnaz (1981) replicated this differential effect of a majority- and a minority-influence source. Other replications were less success-ful, however. Sorrentino, King and Leo (1980) and Martin (1998) failed to find overall evidence for a conversion effect. Doms and Van Avermaet (1980) did find a conversion effect, but this effect was equally strong in the majority as in the minority condition. Apparently, then, there are major methodological difficulties with this paradigm (Martin, 1998). The major merit of the after-image studies would therefore appear to have less to do with their empirical support (or lack thereof) for Moscovici's theory, and more to do with the fact that they led researchers to examine more closely levels of social influence and the underlying cognitive processes. Largely due to their provocativeness, these studies inspired researchers in the field to look at majority and minority influence in a novel fash-ion, which in turn inspired them to design their own, more appropriate tests of the valuable theoretical ideas underlying the paradigm. Indeed and fortunately, the value of a theory is not dependent upon any single experimental paradigm.

Single-process explanations

Another interesting perspective on the comparison between majority and min-ority influence was offered by Latané and Wolf (1981). In contrast to Moscovici, they view influence as a unitary process regardless of its source. Social influence, or social impact as they call it, is a multiplicative function of the strength (power, expertise), immediacy (proximity in space and time) and size (number) of the influence source. This implies that the effect of any one of these variables will be greater as the value of another variable increases. Regarding the effect of size, the variable of most interest to them, they postulate a *power function*, with each addi-tional influence source having less impact than the previous one. Fifty people have more impact than five people, but adding one extra person will make less of a difference in the first case than in the second. This principle of marginally decreasing impact is expressed through the equation

$$\text{impact} = sN^t$$

where s is a scaling constant which reflects the impact of a single source, t is an exponent with a value of less than one, and N is the number of influence sources (people). This implies that impact increases as some power of the size of the influence source. Against this background it is already understandable why Latané and Wolf expect minorities to have less impact than majorities. In addition, in the case where an individual stands with others as the object of social influence, the source's impact will be divided over the target members. Each target will experience less impact than when it is alone. As the size of the target group increases, the source's impact on each target member will decrease. There are therefore two major reasons why minorities are less powerful than majorities as influence sources: they have smaller numbers, and their impact is divided (diffused) over more targets.

In a meta-analysis of the data of many related studies Tanford and Penrod (1984), who proposed a refinement of Latané's social impact theory, reached basically similar conclusions. However, as Maass and Clark (1984) have remarked, the social impact models (and the studies cited in their support) deal mainly with public influence and they have little to say about the processes through which the antecedent factors of strength, immediacy and size operate. It is precisely to process and to level of influence that Moscovici's model speaks the most.

The relative value of single- and dual-process models

In assessing the relative value of dual-process models of influence (Moscovici, 1980) vs. that of single-process models (Latané & Wolf, 1981; see also Turner, 1991, for another example), a number of other important points should be kept in mind. First, at the level of research designs, studies cited in support of either kind of model use widely discrepant operationalizations of the majority and minority status of the source (in terms of sheer numbers or in terms of the societal dominance of a position). The majority/minority variable is manipulated on a between- or on a within-participants basis, and participants take part in actual groups or as individuals who learn about majority and minority positions only through written or taped accounts. Dependent measures of influence vary from public compliance over private change on direct measures to change on indirect measures (e.g., on a related topic). Second, at the level of process analysis, the evidence should be judged not only by the extent to which the actual influence effect is in line with the predictions of a given model, but also by the presence or absence of direct evidence for the assumed mediators of the effect. A number of studies have in effect looked for direct evidence of differential cognitive activity in reaction to minorities and to majorities and have tested its role as a mediator of influence effects. By and large, the results of these studies indicate that cognitive activity mediates the influence effects, but differences between majority- and minority-source conditions are minor or even absent (Maass & Clark, 1983; Mackie, 1987).

Third and finally, in a very insightful chapter Kruglanski and Mackie (1990) argue that more or less stringent criteria can be distinguished to determine whether majority and minority influence differ *per se*. At a very stringent level, they can only be considered as different if an antecedent factor, which can be manipulated independent of the nature of the source, shows a statistical interaction with the nature of the source and/or if the nature of the source interacts with the nature of the influence measure. At a less stringent level, one might already agree on differences if they are caused by a factor which 'typically' covaries with the nature of the source. Perceived extremity of position is a good example. Although minorities may take more extreme stands typically, in instances where a majority takes a comparably extreme stand it may produce the same effect.

Kruglanski and Mackie doubt whether variables like consistency, extremity, involvement and the like operate differently in the majority and minority case *per se*, but it is plausible to argue that they are often correlated with source status. In line with this perspective, the meta-analysis by Wood and colleagues (1994) shows that, compared to a control condition, minorities *and* majorities can in effect produce influence at *each* of the three levels of public change, direct private change and indirect private change. This fact argues against an exclusive relationship between the nature of the source and the kind of influence effect. At the same time, however, this meta-analysis shows stronger overall public and direct private effects for majorities, but stronger indirect private influence effects for minorities. Apparently, and contrary to Moscovici's original ideas, normative considerations influence public and private direct judgements alike. Not only does one not want to be publicly aligned with a minority (for fear of losing face), one does not even want to face a private alignment with this group. This is especially true when the influence situation is experienced face-to-face and when minorities and majorities are defined in terms of real social groups.

In concluding, there does appear to be a privileged relationship between the nature of the source and the size (quantity) and kind (quality) of influence effects, but to a large extent this relationship appears due to the fact that minority and majority status of the source is itself typically correlated with some other characteristics. Moreover, when minorities or majorities have an effect at a given level, essentially identical normative and informational processes seem at work.

Majority and minority influence: imitation vs. originality

Can minorities instigate more creative thinking?

Moscovici's and Latané's models and many of the studies described above depart from the traditional definition of influence in terms of movement towards the position of the influence source. Nemeth has proposed broadening the concept of influence to refer to any change in thought processes, opinions and decisions, independent of the direction of these changes (Nemeth, 1986). Her perspective has led to a refreshing insight into comparing and distinguishing majority and minority influence.

With Moscovici, she shares the view that minorities induce more cognitive effort than majorities and that the nature of the thought processes itself is also different. But whereas Moscovici stresses that the message-relevant thoughts concentrate on the position espoused by the minority, which then eventually is adopted, Nemeth proposes that thought becomes issue-relevant rather than position-relevant. The distinction is important, because it implies that minorities would induce more divergent attention and thinking and the consideration of a multitude of alternatives, including alternatives not proposed explicitly by the minority source. As

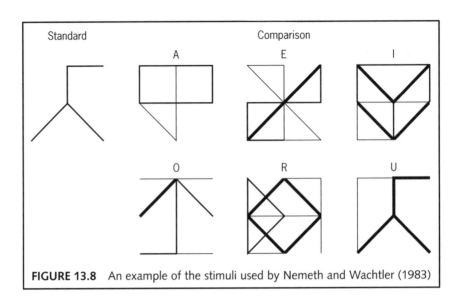

FIGURE 13.8   An example of the stimuli used by Nemeth and Wachtler (1983)

a consequence, the presence of a minority viewpoint, even when it is objectively incorrect, would contribute to judgements which are at the same time more original and qualitatively better, because more alternatives are weighted against each other. Majorities, on the other hand, would produce a restriction of attention, convergent thinking and the mere imitation of the alternative proposed.

A nice illustration of the above perspective was offered in a study by Nemeth and Wachtler (1983). Participants in groups of six were shown slides which contained a standard figure and a set of six comparison figures (see figure 13.8). Their task was to detect the standard figure in as many of the comparison figures as possible. Either two or four people, confederates of the experimenter, named two of the comparison figures. One of these was easy (U in figure 13.8), the other was difficult (e.g., E). The difficult figure indicated was either correct (E) or incorrect (e.g., A). Results showed that, regardless of the correctness of the choices made by the confederates, participants exposed to a majority of four were more likely to imitate responses than those exposed to a minority of two. Most pertinent to Nemeth's thesis, however, was the observation that participants confronted with a minority, again regardless of the correctness of the proposals, produced a higher percentage of novel responses in general and, more specifically, a higher percentage of correct responses (I and R in figure 13.8). It appears therefore that a minority stimulated a more active and differentiated examination of the stimulus field, leading to the detection of novel and correct solutions. More generally, results of this nature point to the positive contribution of minority viewpoints to creativity in problem-solving (Nemeth & Kwan, 1987; Nemeth, 1995).

The positive impact of a minority on the quality of thought processes was also nicely illustrated in a mock jury study by Nemeth (1977). Questioning the wisdom of the US Supreme Court, which had ruled that states could allow juries to render verdicts based on majority support rather than on unanimous agreement, Nemeth asked students as members of mock juries to reach a verdict about the guilt or innocence of a defendant accused of murder. Some of her juries had to deliberate until they reached a unanimous verdict, for others a two-thirds majority was sufficient. The juries were composed such that initially some members favoured a conviction and some favoured acquittal. In the unanimity condition, where the jurors had no choice but to consider the minority point of view, the deliberations lasted longer, jurors recalled more of the evidence, a wider range of considerations was brought into the picture, more alternative ways of looking at the evidence were developed, and the jurors felt more confident about their decisions. In contrast, when the unanimity requirement was dropped, the quality of the deliberations suffered (see also Hastie, Penrod, & Pennington, 1983).

An integrating perspective: the differential processing model

Can the influence of majorities and minorities be integrated in a common theoretical framework?

At this stage, you may experience a sense of feeling lost between the different types of models that have been proposed. An integration of the various perspectives in an overall framework would appear in order. Such is the ambition of the differential processing model of persuasion recently advanced by De Vries et al. (1996). Theoretically, this model draws on both Moscovici's and Nemeth's ideas, but it integrates them with a general theory of persuasion, the heuristic–systematic model (see chapter 8). In terms of its reference to empirical findings, it departs from and tries to do justice to Wood et al.'s (1994) conclusion that, under specifiable conditions, majorities and minorities can produce similar or different effects.

As explained in chapter 8, heuristic information processing leads one to accept (or reject) the validity of a persuasive message merely on the basis of simple decision rules, such as 'if most others agree, they must be right', or 'if only few people feel this way, they must be wrong'. A careful analysis of the message itself is not undertaken, and any resulting opinion change is only superficial and short-lived. Systematic processing, on the other hand, involves a careful analysis of the argumentation itself. If the arguments are found convincing, stable attitude change will result and eventually also encompass one's attitude on related issues. In general, two preconditions have to be met for systematic processing to occur. People should have the ability to process the information and they should be motivated to process the information. This motivation will go up or down dependent on a person's confidence in his or her own position.

Applying these ideas to persuasion settings characterized by differential amounts of numerical support for a particular position, De Vries et al. (1996) argue that, in general, a large number of supporters for a position different from one's own will evoke a higher motivation to process information systematically, for the simple reason that the more others disagree with you, the less confident you will feel of your own position. Minority support *per se* is clearly not as unsettling as majority support. In principle, therefore, the probability of attitude change following majority influence is higher than following minority influence, if at least – upon systematic processing – the arguments are accepted as valid. Even in the absence of this motivation to process information systematically, it can still be argued that the majority will have a stronger, although possibly only a short-lived, effect on the attitude, due to the operation of the consensus heuristic.

In spite of the above, minorities are also capable of motivating their audience towards a systematic examination. This occurs when a minority manages to capture the audience's attention, e.g., by displaying a high degree of consistency over time in defending its position, or by presenting its arguments in an original manner, or when the issue at stake is itself very involving. Hence, majorities and minorities can both induce systematic processing, but the thought process evoked will differ as a function of the nature of the influenced source. In line with Nemeth's ideas, De Vries et al. assume that majorities induce convergent processing, whereas minorities will induce divergent processing. As a result, majorities are most likely to have an (enduring) effect on direct measures of influence, whereas minorities are more likely to have an (enduring) effect on indirect measures or related issues.

Decision-making in Groups

Group polarization

Will discussion of an issue by a group of like-minded individuals make the conclusion more or less extreme?

Consider again the hypothetical student meeting we mentioned at the beginning of this chapter. Suppose that at the outset all the student representatives are opposed to the departmental proposal, but with a certain amount of variation as to the extremity of their opposition. In an attempt to reach a consensual position, they engage in a discussion, each student presenting his or her own arguments and reacting to those of others. If you guess that the decision will be resolved through a compromise around the average of the initial individual positions, you are probably wrong. In situations of this sort, people tend to converge on a position which is more extreme than this average.

As an illustration, Moscovici and Zavalloni (1969) had French high-school students first write down in private their attitudes towards President De Gaulle (or towards North Americans) by indicating the extent of their agreement with statements such as: 'De Gaulle is too old to carry out successfully his difficult political job' (or 'American economic aid is always used to exert political pressure'). Next, as a group, they had to reach a consensus on each item; and finally, they made another private attitude rating. As a result of the discussion, participants became more extreme in their attitudes. As figure 13.9 shows, the attitude towards De Gaulle, which was slightly positive before the discussion, became more positive after the group discussion; this change was maintained during the post-discussion private measurement. The attitude towards the Americans shows a similar polarization pattern, but in the negative direction; the original slightly negative attitude became more negative after the discussion.

The phenomenon at hand is a very general one. On any judgemental dimension, groups tend to shift in the direction of the pole which they, on the average, favoured initially. Hence, *group polarization* refers to an enhancement of an initially dominant position due to group discussion (Myers, 1982). An excellent summary by Lamm and Myers (1978) documents this phenomenon in a wide variety of contexts: stereotypes, interpersonal impressions, gambling behaviour, prosocial and antisocial behaviour, negotiations, jury decisions, group counselling and religious social support systems. To cite but one example in a jury context,

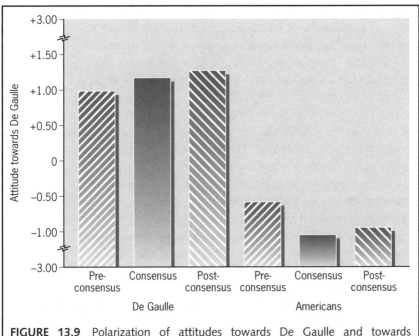

FIGURE 13.9 Polarization of attitudes towards De Gaulle and towards Americans

(Data from Moscovici & Zavalloni, 1969)

Myers and Kaplan (1976) formed mock juries that had to determine the guilt of defendants. Via a manipulation of the strength of the evidence, some groups already initially favoured conviction, while other groups initially favoured acquittal. Discussions within each of these kinds of groups led to a polarization of these initial tendencies (see also Hastie et al., 1983).

Explaining group polarization

> *How can the phenomenon of group polarization be explained?*
> *Can the normative and informational mechanisms of majority influence be used to explain group polarization?*
> *Can group polarization be accounted for by self-categorization theory?*
> *How does the repeated expression of one's own viewpoint affect group polarization?*

Self-categorization theory A general theory of group behaviour emphasizing the impact of self-definitions at different levels of abstraction (individual, group, humanity) on judgement and behaviour.

To account for group polarization, for many years explanations in terms of normative and/or informational influence processes dominated the scene. These explanations are very similar to those proposed earlier as underlying the conformity effect. They were later joined by a new contender, **self-categorization theory**, a general social-psychological theory put forth by Turner, Hogg, Oakes, Reicher and Wetherell (1987). It aspires to account for many group-related behaviours, of which polarization is but one case.

The *normative* or *social comparison* point of view departs from Festinger's theory of social comparison (1954), which holds that because of a need to evaluate one's own opinions (and abilities), people will compare their opinions with those of others. Furthermore, because people want to have a positive self-image and also want to be perceived positively by others, this comparison process will be biased in the direction of viewing oneself as 'better' or 'more correct' (i.e., closer to the norm) than others. The implication of this theory is therefore that when, during the group discussion, you discover that others hold opinions more in the direction of the valued alternative, you will yourself become more extreme in order to differentiate yourself positively from the others. Indirect support for this explanation is found in studies indicating that people indeed think that they are closer to the normative position than others (Codol, 1975), but at the same time they admire views that are even more extreme than theirs, in the valued direction of course (Jellison & Davis, 1973). Direct support would be obtained if one could show that merely knowing the others' position on an issue, without having heard any of their arguments, would be sufficient to produce a polarization effect. Experiments have in fact supported that prediction (e.g., Myers, 1978; Sanders & Baron, 1977; Cotton & Baron, 1980).

The *informational influence or persuasive arguments* perspective suggests that the group discussion generates a number of arguments, most of which are in support of the position already favoured by the group members. To the extent that these arguments coincide with ones you have already considered yourself, they should already serve to strengthen your own position. But the group is also likely to produce arguments you had not thought of before, making your reaction even more extreme. The group polarization phenomenon basically becomes then a process of *mutual persuasion*, whereby the extent of the shift is a function of the proportion of the arguments favouring one side as opposed to another, their cogency and their novelty (Myers, 1982). In this perspective, the *arguments presented* rather than the *positions communicated* would cause polarization. Support for this viewpoint is found in studies which have shown that there is a positive correlation between the relative number of pro and con arguments presented by group members and the amount and direction of the post-discussion polarization (Madsen, 1978). Experimental studies, in which the relative frequency of pro and con arguments were manipulated, produced comparable results (e.g., Ebbesen & Bowers, 1974; Vinokur & Burnstein, 1978).

A critical review and a meta-analysis of 33 experiments that speak to either one of the two explanations presented above suggests that social comparison and persuasive argumentation processes each produce sizeable polarization effects, although the argumentation effects tend to be stronger (Isenberg, 1986). Based on this review, it can be argued that the two processes can contribute independently to group polarization. Outside the laboratory they will very often co-occur, but specific decision parameters may moderate the extent to which one or the other process dominates. In this respect, Isenberg (1986) suggests that for factual issues rationality, informational influence and persuasive argumentation will dominate, whereas emotionality, normative influence and social comparison will be more prominent for value-laden and ego-involving issues.

In spite of their obvious value, neither social comparison theory nor persuasive arguments theory can adequately explain the additional observation that, when holding position information and persuasive arguments constant, more or less polarization will result depending on the social context within which the information is provided (Wetherell, 1987). *Self-categorization theory*, derived from social identity theory, has emerged as a powerful general approach to group behaviour that does account for these and other observations (Turner et al., 1987). According to this theory, which will also be touched upon in chapter 15, people use a system of concepts to define themselves. These concepts include self-categorizations as individual persons different from others and self-categorizations as members of social groups different from other groups. When a social self-categorization becomes salient, it acquires normative properties in that it focuses and orients people on what binds them together and what distinguishes them from other groups. Turner and colleagues then advance the crucial assumption that this group norm is not simply the average position of the group members, but rather the prototypical position of the group. The *prototype* is the position that corresponds the best to what the group has in common *and* to what differentiates it from another group. Hence the person who differs the least from ingroup members and the most from outgroup members acts as the group's prototype. This person is the normative reference point whose arguments will therefore also be perceived as most informational and persuasive. Within this conception the notion of 'norm' is no longer exclusively tied to pleasing others (as in the conformity literature), but rather it relates to an ideal social self-categorization. The definition of the prototype also implies that its position will vary with contexts, specifically with the distribution of opinions within one's own group and with the differences between own group and other groups. Because the ratio between the two is crucial, the prototype will be more extreme when an outgroup is made salient in the first place, but especially when this outgroup is very different from the ingroup. More group polarization can therefore be expected in the presence than in the absence of an outgroup or when a different as compared to a similar outgroup is present. The importance of the social context was shown in a study by Hogg, Turner and Davidson (1990), who found that the direction of polarization can actually be reversed by a change in the social context. Confronted with a decision task in which they could opt for caution or risk, participants perceived the ingroup norm as more cautious than their pre-test mean when confronted with a riskier outgroup, but they perceived the norm as riskier when confronted with a more cautious outgroup.

Persuasive arguments theory, social comparison theory, self-categorization theory and the studies designed to test these theories all focus on the impact of communications received from others in the course of group discussions. But what about the communications expressed by the participants themselves? Would they not also affect the amount of group polarization? Based on the general observation that, outside a discussion context, the repeated expression of an attitude by itself induces an extremization of position, Brauer, Judd and Gliner (1995) began to investigate the role of repeated expression in the production of group polarization. They had each member of a group of four participants engage in a series of brief dyadic encounters with each other group member, instructing them each time about which of five preselected issues they could express their own and hear the other's opinion. In total, each participant was made to participate in 15 different dyadic exchanges according to a prearranged schedule that determined who would be in the dyad and which issue had to be talked about. Through careful counterbalancing, this procedure allowed for the independent manipulation of the frequency with which each member expressed an attitude (between 0 and 6) and the frequency with which each member heard others express their opinion (between 0 and 5). The results showed a reliable effect of the frequency of attitude *expression* on polarization over and above the effect of the frequency of *hearing* others' attitude expressions. Moreover, and very interestingly, the authors also observed that the magnitude of the self-expression effect was correlated with the extent to which a participant's conversation partner used the participant's own arguments again in a latter exchange with him. A follow-up study provided experimental evidence for this latter effect. In groups where a participant had been encouraged to use and integrate others' arguments, the polarization effect of frequency of attitude expression was significantly greater than in groups where integration had been discouraged. Two mechanisms appear at work, then, and they reinforce each other. First, as participants repeat themselves, a process of conversational simplification sets in: over time, expressions become less elaborate, more unqualified and therefore more extreme. Second, this tendency is reinforced if one receives social validation from others, when over time they in turn make use of the participant's progressively simpler and more extreme statements. In other words, others' behaviour contributes to the perceived persuasiveness of one's own arguments.

Relating the above findings and interpretations to the three dominant explanations of group polarization, Brauer and Judd (1996) argue that they can be fitted most easily within the persuasive arguments perspective, if at least one extends this approach by also incorporating the persuasive effect of one's own arguments and their validation by others. Integrating the effects of repeated expression in social comparison theory or self-categorization theory is less evident. Moreover, Brauer et al. (1995) additionally observed that repeated expression does not affect the perceived averaged position of the other individuals in the group or the position perceived as prototypical of the group as a whole. This absence of a shift in the standard of comparison is problematic for these two theories, for which polarization depends crucially on social comparison. The social validation findings, however, are consistent with self-categorization theory, because they point to the impact of a group's reaction on one's sense of identity as a group member.

Groupthink: an extreme example of group polarization

What is groupthink and how can it be explained?

In view of the frequency with which, in reality, decisions are made by groups composed of like-minded participants (councils, committees, juries, governments), the research on group polarization has far-reaching implications. The processes involved may indeed lead such groups to advocate decisions which are incorrect, unwise or, in the worst case, disastrous.

Irving Janis (Janis, 1972, 1982a) has described a number of instances of political and military decision-making which provide dramatic illustrations of the utmost stupidity shown by groups, in spite of the superior 'intelligence' of their members. The Bay of Pigs invasion in 1961 is perhaps the best-known example. President Kennedy and a small group of advisers had decided to send a relatively small group of Cuban exiles to invade the coast of Cuba with the support of the American air force. Everything went wrong, and within a matter of days the invaders were killed or captured. How, as a group, could Kennedy and his advisers have been so stupid, as they later admitted themselves? As a more recent example, the dramatic explosion of the space shuttle Challenger in 1986 similarly appears to have been the result of a number of ill-made decisions (Esser & Lindoerfer, 1989).

Janis, who undertook a most careful analysis of all the available documents in the Bay of Pigs case and in other similar cases, speculates that the decision-makers became the victims of an extreme form of group polarization, which he calls **groupthink**. Groupthink obtains when the decision process of a highly cohesive group of like-minded people becomes so overwhelmed by consensus seeking that their apprehension of reality is undermined. As Janis contends, this process is encouraged when a number of conditions are fulfilled: when the decision group is highly cohesive; when it is isolated from alternative sources of information; and when its leader clearly favours a particular option. Against the background of these antecedent conditions, the group discussions that evolve are likely to be characterized by an illusion of one's own invulnerability, and by attempts at mutually rationalizing actions which are in line with the proposed option while at the same time ignoring or discounting inconsistent information. These processes occur both at the intraindividual (self-censorship) and at the interindividual (conformity pressures) level. Even though some members of such groups may at one time or another have their private reservations about the proposals made, they are not likely to express them overtly. The ultimate outcome of these processes is a decision endorsed by all, but far removed from what might be expected if rational and balanced information-seeking and information-providing processes had operated. Although Janis' analysis is more penetrating than this brief presentation can show, the above material should be sufficient for you to grasp the essentials of this analysis – and to suggest some cures for groupthink. How should the leader behave? What would you think of a devil's advocate in the group? Which benefits can be gained by having the group members write down their personal thoughts and arguments independently and individually?

> **Groupthink** A group decision process, strongly oriented towards consensus, among like-minded and cohesive individuals, emanating in one-sided and incorrect conclusions.

Undoubtedly, the eye-catching characteristics of the groupthink phenomenon itself, combined with Janis' own superb gift at sketching a masterly vivid account of real-life cases, have contributed greatly to the widespread acceptance of his model. Moreover, other authors have provided similar analyses of other cases (Hensley & Griffin, 1986; 't Hart, 1990). On the other hand, laboratory studies and conceptual analyses of decision-making situations have definitely not confirmed all the links of Janis' model. Amongst others, the central variable of cohesiveness has not been observed to affect group decision-making in a consistent way (Flowers, 1977; McCauley, 1989). Moreover, many studies fail to make the methodologically wise comparison between the nature and outcome of group functioning in situations where Janis' antecedents are present and those where they are not. Based on a critical analysis of the literature, Aldag and Fuller (1993) have proposed a more general group problem-solving model. Its essential features are that it presents the elements of decision-making processes in less pejorative and value-laden terms (e.g., lack of procedural norms is replaced by procedural requirements), and it adds a number of antecedent process and outcome variables. In this latter respect, political motives and outcomes play a key role, testifying to the idea that decisions that may be thoughtless and ill-conceived from a rational efficiency point of view can also result from deliberate and planned political strategies.

Obeying Immoral Orders: The Social Influence of an Authority

Milgram's obedience experiment

Which situation did Milgram create to study obedience to authority?

The various social influence phenomena described in the previous sections have a number of characteristics in common. The most important of these are that influence sources and targets typically have equal status; the pressure exerted by the influence source is more implicit than explicit; and the source makes no attempt at directly controlling or sanctioning the resistance that targets of influence attempts might eventually show. For example, in Asch's experiment all the participants were students, the majority only exerted pressure by stating an opinion that was different from the participant's, and the participant's responses never led to any explicit negative reactions on the part of the majority. An entirely different influence context is created when an influence source has high status, explicitly orders a person to behave in a way which he or she would not spontaneously do, or would even have strong feelings against, and continuously monitors whether the person indeed carries out the orders given. Precisely this setting was created in a famous and, at the same time, notorious series of studies on *obedience* carried out by Stanley Milgram and dramatically captured in his best-selling book *Obedience to Authority* (Milgram, 1974). The essential components of Milgram's basic experiment as well as some of its variants were already introduced in chapter 4. However, for the sake of clarity and vividness in the context of the present chapter, a more integrated and detailed presentation of these studies is necessary.

Through a newspaper advertisement Milgram recruited volunteers to participate, for a payment of $4, in a study on learning and memory. The participants in the experiment were aged between 20 and 50, and they represented almost the entire range of professional levels. Upon arriving at the laboratory, the participant was met by the experimenter, actually a biology teacher in his early thirties, and another 'participant', a confederate of the experimenter who in fact was a sympathetic middle-aged accountant. The experimenter explained that the study dealt with the effects of punishment on learning, and that one of the participants would be the teacher and the other the learner. Lots were drawn and the participant would be the teacher. Teacher and learner were taken to an adjacent room, where the learner was strapped into a chair and electrodes were fixed to his wrists – because the punishment to be applied was electric shock. The experimenter explained that the shocks could be extremely painful, but they would cause no permanent damage.

Next the teacher was taken to his own room, where he received his orders. The learning task was a paired associates task; each time the learner gave an incorrect answer, the teacher had to punish him with an electric shock, beginning at 15 volts (V), and increasing the shock intensity by 15 V with every new mistake. To this end the teacher had to use a shock generator with a row of 30 pushbuttons, each marked by the appropriate intensity (from 15 V to 450 V). Several verbal labels gave the participant a clear sense of the meaning of successive groups of shock levels: the labels went from slight shock (to 60 V), through moderate shock (to 120 V), strong shock (to 180 V) and very strong shock (to 240 V), to intense shock (to 300 V), extreme intensity shock (to 360 V) and 'danger: severe shock' (to 420 V). The two final shock levels were marked 'XXX'. Various additional features of the shock generator gave the apparatus a distinctly 'real' appearance. Moreover, to demonstrate the reality of the shocks, the teacher received a sample shock of 45 V.

The learning task could then begin. By prior arrangement, the confederate made numerous errors, thereby 'forcing' the teacher to administer increasingly stronger shocks. Each time the participant hesitated or refused, the experimenter prodded him to go on by means of at most four graded orders: 'Please continue'; 'The experiment requires that you continue'; 'It is absolutely essential that you continue'; 'You have no other choice, you must go on'. The experiment was terminated when, in spite of the experimenter's prods, the teacher refused to continue, or when three shocks of the highest intensity had been administered. Before presenting the results, we should add that the participant was not only exposed to the explicit influence attempt by the experimenter, but was also confronted with an increasingly explicit appeal by the learner. Whereas at first the participant could hear the victim react with only a minor grunt (from 75 V to 105 V), at 120 V he began to shout that the shocks became very painful. Later in the sequence he started screaming in agony; he shouted to be let out and that he could not stand the pain. From a given point on he refused to provide more answers – but the participant still had to shock because 'no answer is an incorrect answer'.

How did Milgram's participants, faced with the conflict between the pressures emanating from the authority, from the victim and from their own inner self, react in this situation? Very much to his own surprise, Milgram observed that 62.5 per cent of his participants continued to administer shocks to the highest level. The average maximum shock level was 368 V. The authority of 'the man of science', who never threatened with any sanctions, let alone held a gun to the person's head, was sufficient to override the inner (conscience) and outer (the victim's cries) forces that could have made the participant disobey. A frightening perspective. Were Milgram's participants perhaps 'evil' people? All the evidence speaks against it. For one thing, the participants' behaviour during the experiment clearly testifies to the strong conflict they experienced: they were extremely tense and nervous, they perspired, bit their lips and clenched their fists. Moreover, a control condition in which participants were allowed to choose any shock levels they themselves considered appropriate showed that only two out of 40 people exceeded the 150 V level, and 28 never even went beyond 75 V. Clearly, Milgram's participants were not sadists; they apparently were caused to behave the way they did by the powerful role of situational factors. In variations of his basic experiment, Milgram has looked at the difference a number of these situational factors make. Some of these variations, as they relate to characteristics of the authority, the closeness of the victim and the behaviour of the participant's peers, are briefly summarized in the next paragraphs.

Situational determinants of obedience

How do different aspects of the situation affect the degree of obedience?

The physical (and emotional) proximity of the victim was manipulated by means of four different conditions. In a first condition, the victim heavily pounded on the wall separating his room from the teacher's; in the second, he was heard crying and shouting (as described earlier). In two other conditions, the teacher and the victim were actually in the same room. In one of these the teacher not only heard but also saw the victim. In the final condition, the teacher had to hold the victim's hand on a shock plate. The obedience rates corresponding to these four conditions of increasing contact are shown in figure 13.10. Maximal obedience went from a high of 65 per cent of the participants to a low (if one can call it that) of 30 per cent. Data such as these should invite you to speculate about the differences between traditional and modern warfare in terms of the differential resistance to orders they would induce.

The authority of the experimenter and the amount of control he had was varied in a number of ways. When the experiment was carried out in a less scientific and prestigious environment – a rundown office building rather than Yale University, where the original study took place – obedience did not drop significantly. However, when – in the original setting – the experimenter was absent from the participant's room and gave his orders over the telephone, maximal obedience dropped to 21 per cent (a number of participants said over the phone that they were giving higher shocks than they in fact did!). The fact that the authority patently violated a promise made to the learner did not reduce obedience greatly. In one of the experimental variations the learner, who had said earlier that he had a heart condition, only agreed to the experiment 'on the condition that you let me out when I say so'. From the tenth shock on (150 V), he demanded that the experiment be stopped, but the experimenter ignored him and insisted that the teacher had to go on. The percentage of participants

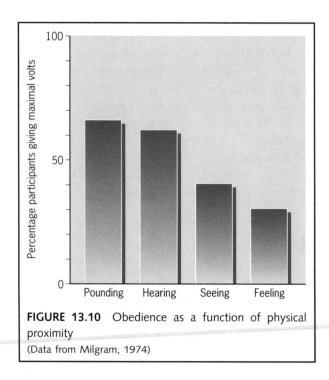

FIGURE 13.10   Obedience as a function of physical proximity
(Data from Milgram, 1974)

showing maximal obedience in this frightening setting was reduced by only 10 per cent, compared with a baseline condition. A final relevant variation is one in which the experimenter, before and therefore without instructing the participant to increase shock levels, had to leave the room. He carried over his authority to a second participant present, who at first would only have to register the learner's reaction times. This second participant then came up with the idea of increasing the shock level with every error and, throughout the learning session, he insisted that the teacher applied his rules. The results speak for themselves. Twenty per cent of the participants obeyed the equal-status authority to the end. In addition, when a participant refused and the 'authority' decided that he would administer the shocks himself, a number of participants physically attacked the 'torturer' or pulled out the plug of the shock generator. Such heroism was unfortunately never shown when the authority was 'the man of science in his white coat'!

In a final pair of experimental variations presented here, Milgram investigated the role of peer pressure. In the first there were three co-teachers, the participant and two confederates. The first confederate presented the task, the second registered the learner's responses, and the participant administered the shocks. At 150 V the first confederate refused to continue and took a seat, away from the shock generator. At 210 V the second confederate refused. The effect of their behaviour on the participants was dramatic: only 10 per cent were maximally obedient (see figure 13.11). In contrast, if the teacher, who administered the learning task, was accompanied by a co-teacher, who gave the shocks, 92 per cent of

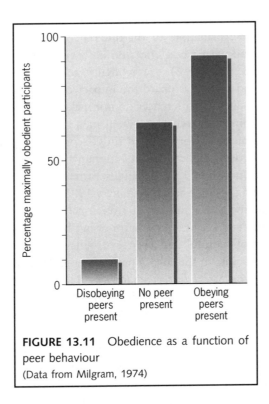

FIGURE 13.11   Obedience as a function of peer behaviour
(Data from Milgram, 1974)

the participants participated in the experiment to the end. Of course, they did not have to give the shocks themselves; but what kept them from protesting as the confederates had done in the prior condition? In view of the fact that peer behaviour can produce either 10 per cent or 92 per cent obedience, the powerful role of interpersonal rather than intrapersonal factors is evident. Again, these experiments should make you think of real-life examples whereby you protest or do not protest against acts of violence, merely as a function of what others do.

What would you have done?

Why do people underestimate the occurrence of obedient behaviour?

While reading the above paragraphs you probably constantly said to yourself: 'I would not have obeyed!' For your comfort, that is how most people react upon hearing a description of the Milgram experiments. Milgram himself and others (e.g., Bierbrauer, 1979) asked people from all walks of life, including psychiatrists, how many people would obey the experimenter. Invariably, they all expected low obedience rates (with a maximal average shock of 130 V). Only with a very vivid and lengthy re-enactment of the experiment could Bierbrauer get students to expect an average maximal shock of 260 V, which is still an underestimation of what real participants did. One explanation for the difference between what we think we and others will do and what we in effect do is to be found in the *fundamental attribution error* (see chapter 7) – a tendency to underestimate the role of situational factors and to overestimate the impact of personality factors. In the Milgram situation, individual differences do not make a lot of difference: his analyses revealed only minor differences between men and women, between people holding different professions, or between those scoring differently on personality inventories. Moreover, replications of Milgram's study in different countries and cultures have demonstrated the generality of the effect (e.g., Mantell, 1971, Meeus & Raaijmakers, 1986; Shanab & Yahya, 1978).

Notwithstanding the grave impact of situational factors on obedience to a malevolent authority and the resultant harm-doing behaviours, research on various extreme forms of harmful and even evil behaviour (genocide, rape, child abuse, murder) also points to the role of person-related factors. In a recent special issue of *Personality and Social Psychology Review*, Bandura (1999) notes that the persistence of harm-doing behaviour, which may well have been instigated by situational factors initially, demands self-regulation processes that definitely involve the actor-person him- or herself. In addition, Baumeister and Campbell (1999) and Berkowitz (1999) make a strong case that, for some individuals, evil may have an intrinsic appeal. These latter findings should protect us against the overly simplistic conclusion that 'it is all in the situation', and against a resulting morally condoning attitude towards perpetrators (Miller, Gordon, & Buddie, 1999).

The dynamics of obedience

Which processes are at work in the Milgram studies?
What can be learnt from the obedience studies?
Is obedience always the only alternative?

According to Milgram, three interlocking factors are at work in these situations. First, participants in his experiments and people at large have had a life-long history of being rewarded for obedience to authority and they have come to expect authorities to be trustworthy, credible and legitimate. Second, in the experiments, and in everyday life, 'binding' and 'entrapping' factors come into operation. Aside from the fact that there are psychological barriers to disobey right away, people only gradually slip into committing acts of graver and graver consequences. The subtle progression and escalation of more and more extreme behaviours play a crucial role in helping us understand why ethically concerned individuals end up committing unquestionably evil deeds (Darley, 1992; Kelman & Hamilton, 1989). As a third explanatory concept, Milgram introduced the notion of agentic shift, to refer to the subjective experience (justification) of: 'I am not responsible,

PLATE 13.2   At the Nuremberg War Trials, after the Second World War, many prominent Nazis tried to use 'obedience to authority' as a defence

because I was ordered to do so!' These words are reminiscent of the ultimate defence of soldiers, officers and the like upon being brought to trial for acts in which they were involved. The defence of senior Nazi officers after the Second World War, of Argentinian military personnel after the downfall of the junta, and of members of the former East German border patrol after the unification of Germany are cases in point.

As a whole, and as mentioned earlier, the facts themselves and the above conceptual analysis testify to the overriding impact of situational factors and how they are perceived by most people over personality-based determinants. The lessons of Milgram's research cannot therefore be ignored, although it is equally dangerous and overly simplistic to try to reduce dramatic historical cases of torture and killing exclusively to the processes of obedience to authority (Miller, Collins, & Brief, 1995). Still, the observation that, in the absence of these other factors, such as a deep sense of frustration, perceived threat or strong negative feelings towards an outgroup, people can already be made to inflict severe harm on others, strengthens rather than weakens the lessons that can be drawn from Milgram's studies.

Experiments such as Milgram's raise serious ethical concerns, and so they should. Does the scientific benefit and the moral lesson learned from them outweigh the costs and the potential harm to participants (Baumrind, 1964; Miller, Collins, & Brief, 1995)? Regardless of your answer to this question, however, ask yourself if your ethical concerns would be as great if these studies had shown that people actually disobey the immoral orders given them by an experimenter.

In concluding, and as an antidote, notwithstanding the pessimistic perspective raised by our description of the Milgram studies, people do not always obey mal-evolent authorities. Rochat and Modigliani (1995) describe the fascinating case of the citizens of the French village of Le Chambon who, during the Second World War, defied the efforts of the authorities to have them engage in the persecution of war refugees and who – in spite of terror – collectively participated in actions which saved thousands of refugees. One of the factors that played a key role in setting and keeping people on this track was the fact that resistance against the authorities' orders was initiated immediately, inspired by a sermon of one of the village's pastors. In the best of cases, such early 'whistleblowing' can even inter-rupt unfolding chains of events before it is too late, as was shown in an organ-izational context by Miceli and Near (1992). The role of immediacy of resistance as a factor decreasing the probability of later obedience is also shown in a reana-lysis of some of Milgram's own data by Modigliani and Rochat (1995), who subjected the audio recordings of the conversations between the experimenter and the teacher to a content analysis. Of the participants who showed signs of verbal protest early in the experiment, only 17 per cent ended up delivering more than 150 volts (mean: 129 volts), and not a single person was obedient till the end. In contrast, of the participants who began to demonstrate protest only later, 58 per cent delivered shocks between 150 and 450 volts, and 42 per cent were fully obedient (450 volts). These results, and our own earlier detailed account of what went on in Milgram's experiments, reveal that an adequate understanding of 'obedience to authority' requires a careful analysis of the dynamic interplay between the fixed and structural characteristics of the situation and the evolving pattern of interactions between the authority, the participant and the victim.

Summary and Conclusions

Following a definition of social influence as a change in judgements and opinions following exposure to the judgement and opinions of others, this chapter first treated majority and minority influence in groups. Many experiments testify to the fact that isolated individuals are influenced easily by a unanimous majority, even when this majority is incorrect. The size of this conformity effect depends on a number of variables, the role of which can be understood by relating them to the mechanisms of informational and normative influence. Under the proper circumstances, however, the majority itself can be influenced by an active minority. Along with a number of other variables, a behavioural style of consistency on the part of the minority plays a key role in producing this effect. Hence, majorities and minorities can each be influential, but they do so through partly different mechanisms and with partly different effects. As explained in the chapter, majorities would induce convergent thinking, whereas minorities produce divergent thinking. As a result, majorities produce more direct influence on the target at hand, while minorities produce more creative responding and more indirect influence on related issues.

Group polarization was discussed next. It refers to the observation that, following a group discussion, the average responses become polarized in the direction of what was already the inclination of the group prior to the discussion. Two of the explanations presented resemble those given earlier for conformity effects. Group polarization obtains because people want to move towards the valued group norm or because they become persuaded by the informational value of the arguments given by other group members. A final explanation, based on self-categorization theory, attempts to integrate both of these perspectives and in addition demands attention for the intergroup context in which group discussions take place. In extreme cases, the processes involved in group polarization can orient a group towards a very one-sided analysis of the topic of discussion and thereby result in incorrect and unrealistic judgements and decisions. The section on 'groupthink' outlined the mechanisms that come into play in producing this negative effect of group discussions.

Obedience to an authority constituted the final topic of this chapter. A description of Milgram's famous studies, in which people are made to inflict harm on an innocent other 'because the experiment requires you to do so', was followed by an analysis of the impact of predominantly situational factors on this behaviour, and by a discussion of the mediating mechanisms.

Although imperfections of some of the 'little' experiments conducted in social-psychological laboratories may leave you with some doubts and questions, the different lines of research sketched in this chapter offer valuable perspectives towards understanding both everyday and major historical as well as contemporary events. The political landslides during the late 1980s in the countries of Eastern Europe, the abolition of apartheid in South Africa, and the mass killings in Rwanda, Bosnia, Kosovo and other places, and the group suicide of the members of a sect in Switzerland, are but a few examples of the more dramatic events in which social influence in one form or another played a key role. At the same time, and perhaps less notably so, social influence is an essential ingredient of our everyday social life: what determines which line of clothing we wear, what guides us in our choice of vacation spots, which films do we see? In the final analysis, can you think of any behaviour, thought or feeling which would not be at least partly the result of social influence processes?

DISCUSSION POINTS

1 Why does normative influence provide only a partial explanation of majority influence?

2 Compared to 37 per cent errors observed by Asch in his conformity study, do you feel that 8 per cent errors observed by Moscovici in his innovation study constitutes a substantial or minor effect?

3 What was the 'after-image' study of Moscovici and Personnaz supposed to show? What conclusions can actually be drawn?

4 If you were asked to advise a minority group as to what strategies it might use to exert influence on a majority, what would you tell them?

5 What do you see as the major advantages of Turner's self-categorization explanation of group polarization over earlier theories?

6 What precautions can a group take to prevent the occurrence of 'groupthink'? Which strategies would be more or less effective?

7 How can we explain why Milgram's experimental participants were so obedient?

8 Do you agree that Milgram's experimental situation captures the essentials of the real-life situations with which it is often compared?

FURTHER READING

Allen, V. L. (1975). Social support for nonconformity. In L. Berkowitz (Ed.), *Advances in experimental social psychology* (Vol. 8, pp. 1–43). New York: Academic Press. A detailed account of theory and research with respect to the factors leading to a reduction in conformity to a majority.

Asch, S. E. (1956). Studies of independence and conformity: A minority of one against a unanimous majority. *Psychological Monographs*, 70 (9, Whole No. 416). This text presents Asch's own account of his famous conformity experiments. The best way to learn about these studies is to read them first hand.

Janis, I. L. (1972). *Victims of groupthink*. Boston. MA: Houghton Mifflin. This book contains Janis' theory of groupthink, amply illustrated with case materials.

Milgram, S. (1974). *Obedience to authority*. New York: Harper & Row. Milgram's own dramatic, best-selling story of his many experiments on obedience to authority.

Miller, A. G., Collins, B. E., & Brief, D. E. (Eds.). (1995). Perspectives on obedience to authorities: The legacy of the Milgram experiments. *Journal of Social Issues*, 51, 1–212. A special issue of the *Journal of Social Issues* devoted entirely to the reactions drawn by Milgram's obedience research and to novel insights in understanding obedient and defiant behaviour.

Moscovici, S. (1980). Toward a theory of conversion behaviour. In L. Berkowitz (Ed.), *Advances in experimental social psychology* (Vol. 13, pp. 208–39). New York: Academic Press. A presentation of Moscovici's propositions with respect to the relationship between influence source (majority or minority) and level of effect (compliance or conversion), supplemented by an overview of relevant experimental studies.

Turner, J. C. (1991). *Social influence*. Buckingham: Open University Press. A provocative analysis of a wide spectrum of social influence phenomena from the perspective of self-categorization theory.

Milgram, S. (1963). Behavioral study of obedience. *Journal of Abnormal and Social Psychology*, 67, 371–8.

Moscovici, S., Lage, E., & Naffrechoux, M. (1969). Influence of a consistent minority on the responses of a majority in a color perception task. *Sociometry*, 32, 365–80.

KEY

STUDIES

Group Performance

Henk Wilke and
Arjaan Wit

14

OUTLINE

Performing in task-oriented groups rather than as separate individuals may have advantages and disadvantages. At an individual level, group members' performance is either facilitated or impaired by working in the presence of others. At a group level, combining group members' individual contributions into a group product may also yield process losses and gains. To illustrate this, we focus on three specific collective task activities: idea generation, information sampling and decision-making.

The chapter deals with how process losses can be explained. Moreover, it aims to provide some preliminary guidelines on how to ensure that group members gain from working together as a group rather than as separate individuals. Making optimal use of group members' resources requires measures to counteract coordination losses, motivation losses and dysfunctional status-organizing processes, and these are also discussed.

KEY CONCEPTS

- Additive task
- Brainstorming
- Common knowledge effect
- Competitive interdependence
- Conjunctive task
- Cooperative interdependence
- Coordination losses
- Diffuse status characteristics
- Disjunctive task
- Dominant responses
- Eureka task
- Evaluation apprehension
- Free-riding
- Hidden profile

- Interaction process analysis (IPA)
- Mixed-motive interdependence
- Motivation losses
- Nominal group technique
- Non-dominant responses
- Process losses
- Production blocking
- Social compensation
- Social decision scheme
- Social facilitation
- Social inhibition
- Social loafing
- Specific status characteristics
- Sucker effect

Introduction

A large part of our lives is spent in groups. We live in families, work in organizations and quite often spend our leisure time in joint activities with others. To some extent, all these activities imply some kind of group performance. This chapter focuses on performance in task-oriented groups, in particular on processes that have to do with problem-solving, productivity and goal attainment. The basic idea is that among the various reasons why people can and do get together in groups, one major attraction is the collaborative pursuit of common goals. Industrial work groups, music bands, boards of directors, sports teams and brainstorming groups are just a few examples of such task-oriented groups. Or take, for instance, a group of students working on a research project or as members of an advisory committee charged with the task of formulating proposals to update the current curriculum. This chapter will address how group members' individual performance is affected by working in each other's presence, how their contributions should be combined into a group product, how their own task motivation depends on fellow group members' efforts, and how role and status differentiation among the members affect group productivity. Before elaborating on these issues, however, we will first introduce some of the leading concepts of this chapter.

Determinants of Group Performance

How are task demands, available resources, and the social processes of combining the available resources into a group product, related to potential and actual group performance?

Potential group performance refers to the way that a group should perform if it made optimal use of its available resources – such as relevant knowledge, abilities, skills, tools, time and money – to meet the demands of the task. If members of a group, together or individually, possess the required resources, the group has a greater potential than when the group lacks some of the resources to meet the task demands. From everyday life, however, we know that the availability of all the required resources does not guarantee a high actual group performance. Why is high potential performance not always attained?

Process losses and gains

Individual members of task groups may make all kinds of errors or omissions. When, for some reason or another, such cases of negligence are not rectified by knowledgeable co-workers, group performance falls below its potential. Imagine, for instance, that you gave a few people one minute to solve the following problem individually: 'A man bought a horse for $60 and sold it for $70. Then he bought it back for $80 and again sold it for $90. How much money did he make in the business?' Further, imagine that you thereafter formed small groups of these people to discuss the same problem. You would then discover that almost all groups would reach consensus about the solution. Most groups would offer the correct solution ($20). However, in groups, in which only a few members had initially solved the problem correctly, the final group solution would be incorrect (Thomas & Fink, 1961). Thus, during the process of consensus seeking, the available resources in the group are not always combined optimally. This example of how **process losses** cause actual group performance to fall short of its potential may be expressed by the following equation (Davis, 1969; Laughlin, 1980; Steiner, 1972, 1976):

Process losses Group processes that prevent a group from reaching its potential productivity. Such losses include coordination losses and motivation losses.

actual performance = potential performance − process losses

Despite the danger of process losses, many people prefer working together on a task, since they generally assume that cooperative interaction is fun, enjoyable, interesting (as it very often is!), and may yield various gains in effectiveness and creativity. It is a widely shared conviction, for instance, that generating ideas in interactive brainstorming sessions elicits more fruitful proposals than when people do not share their unique thoughts and ideas. Furthermore, experienced athletes may tell you that performing in the presence of others, either a passive audience or actively participating team members, facilitates feats of strength and endurance, surpassing their own and others' expectations. Later on in this chapter we will return to these examples, which suggest that task performance in groups may not only suffer from process losses, but may sometimes also yield gains in productivity. For now, it suffices to present the more appropriate equation (Hackman & Morris, 1975):

actual performance = potential performance − process losses + process gains

This chapter deals with the question of how process losses in a task group can be explained and how they should be prevented. Moreover, this chapter aims to provide some tentative guidelines on how to ensure that a group gains from working as a group instead of as single individuals. Before elaborating on the group processes involved when group members interact in order to combine their individual resources into a group product, however, we will first address the inhibitory and facilitatory effects of performing in each other's presence.

Individual Performance in a Social Context

How does working in each other's presence, rather than alone, affect group members' individual task performance?

As early as 1898, Triplett observed that cyclists rode faster when racing together than when racing alone. In the years that followed, numerous experiments were carried out with a wide variety of tasks. Some studies showed performance improvement as a result of the presence of others, while other studies showed performance impairment. For instance, Travis (1925) found that when working in front of an audience compared to working alone, well-trained experimental participants clearly improved their performance on simple eye–hand coordination tasks. In Pessin's (1933) study, in which experimental participants had to learn lists of nonsense syllables alone or in front of a passive audience, facilitatory *and* inhibitory effects of the presence of others were found. Pessin showed that, on average, learning a sequence of seven nonsense syllables was faster and the mean number of errors during acquisition was smaller when the experimental participants worked alone than when in front of an audience. Pessin tested the same experimental participants again later. In the later testing, their task was to relearn the original list alone or in front of an audience. This time, however, the results showed that substantially fewer trials were required to relearn and reproduce the lists correctly in the audience condition than in the alone condition. These and other research findings left scientists for many years with the conclusion that an individual performing in the presence of others is sometimes likely to do better than when alone, and sometimes likely to do worse. It remained for Zajonc (1965) to advance an explanation for these conflicting research findings.

Mere presence

Dominant responses
Responses that take precedence in a person's response repertoire, such as well-learned or instinctive responses.

Non-dominant responses
Novel, complicated or untried responses that the individual has never (or only infrequently) performed before.

Zajonc suggested that the mere presence of others leads to improved performance on well-learned or easy tasks, but to impaired performance on tasks which are not (yet) well learned and which may therefore be perceived as difficult or complex. The mere presence of others facilitates the emission of responses that take precedence in an individual's behavioural repertoire (so-called **dominant responses**, having a higher likelihood of elicitation than other responses), but inhibits the emission of novel and complicated responses that the individual has never or only infrequently performed before (so-called **non-dominant responses**). If the enhanced emission of well-learned responses (**social facilitation**) and the inhibition of novel responses (**social inhibition**) are appropriate for successful task completion, then people will perform better when others are present than when they are working alone. Thus, differences in task difficulty – on the basis of people's skills or previous experience with the task – may explain the seemingly conflicting results obtained by the early studies of Triplett (1898), Travis (1925) and Pessin (1933). Pedalling a bicycle, exhibiting other well-learned physical motor skills, or relearning an already well-learned list of nonsense syllables should result in higher performance in the presence of others than when working alone. If, however, the facilitation of dominant responses and the inhibition of non-dominant responses are inappropriate for successful task completion, the presence of others will impair task performance. In complex reasoning or problem-solving tasks requiring concentration and complex cognitive activity, there is a high probability of giving ill-considered responses. If strong (and multiple) inappropriate response tendencies prevail at the expense of the required non-dominant responses, the presence of others interferes with successful task completion.

> **Social facilitation**   Increased emission of dominant responses, resulting from the presence of others.

> **Social inhibition**   Decreased emission of non-dominant responses, resulting from the presence of others.

Why does the mere presence of others enhance the emission of dominant responses? On the basis of the Hull–Spence drive theory (see Spence, 1956), Zajonc (1980) assumes that others' physical presence leads to an innate increase in arousal, i.e., a readiness to respond to whatever unexpected action the others might undertake, resulting in an increased emission of dominant responses at the expense of non-dominant responses. The relationship between the presence of others, arousal, the appropriateness of the socially facilitated or inhibited responses and the level of performance is shown in figure 14.1. The subsequent literature, however, offers alternative explanations for social facilitation and inhibition (SFI), as we will discuss below.

Evaluation apprehension

Cottrell (1968, 1972) was among the first to amend Zajonc's explanation, by suggesting that increased arousal constitutes a learned response to the presence of

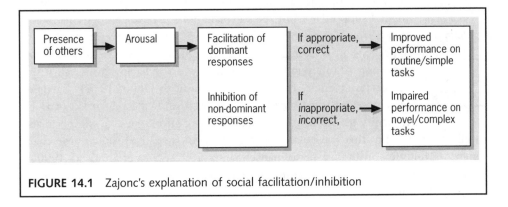

FIGURE 14.1   Zajonc's explanation of social facilitation/inhibition

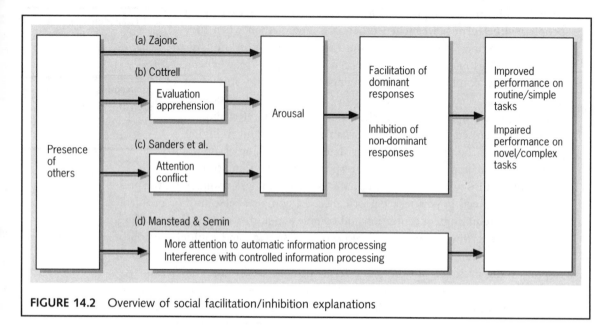

FIGURE 14.2   Overview of social facilitation/inhibition explanations

others, rather than an innate response. According to Cottrell, task performers have learned to associate the presence of other people with performance evaluation, which, in turn, is linked to the anticipation of positive or negative outcomes. The presence of others will not elicit arousal and the accompanying facilitation of dominant responses (and inhibition of non-dominant responses) *unless* task performers anticipate being evaluated by these others. The difference between these two explanations is depicted in panels (a) and (b) of figure 14.2.

    Although one may have difficulty in applying Cottrell's concept of **evaluation apprehension** to cockroaches, ants and chickens, which have also shown SFI effects (Clayton, 1978; Zajonc, Heingartner, & Herman, 1969), or to tasks that involve little threat of evaluation, such as eating and drinking (Markus, 1978), there is some experimental support for Cottrell's explanation. It has been demonstrated that SFI effects are often eliminated when the salience of evaluation apprehension is decreased by allowing task performers to give their responses privately rather than publicly, or by having non-evaluative audiences (Henchy & Glass, 1968; Sasfy & Okun, 1974). Further evidence has been provided by research, showing that it is not task difficulty *per se*, but the subjective expectation that one will perform well (poorly) and that one will receive positive (negative) outcomes, that improves (interferes with) task performance (Sanna, 1992; Sanna & Shotland, 1990). Thus, people's concern about being evaluated clearly is part of the explanation of SFI phenomena.

Evaluation apprehension   The stressful experience of a person whose behaviour is observed by others. This experience may elicit anxiety and lead to deterioration of performance or high levels of performance, depending on one's own familiarity of the task and prior practice.

Attention conflict

Another explanation of why the presence of others may be arousing has been suggested by Sanders, Baron and Moore (1978; Sanders, 1981). The presence of others may evoke a response conflict between attending to the task itself vs. attending to these others. Others' presence may be distracting because of noises or gestures, anticipated approving or disapproving reactions, and people's tendency to make social comparisons. Since some of the attention needed to meet the task demands will be directed at the other people, one may expect a general impairment of task performance on all kinds of tasks, either well learned or not well learned. This distraction interferes with the attention given to the task and creates an internal response conflict that can only be overcome with greater effort. The attention conflict enhances arousal, resulting in the facilitation of dominant responses and inhibition of non-dominant responses (see figure 14.2, panel (c)). The hypothesized attention conflict also explains why not only the presence of other people, but also other forms of distraction such as noises or flashing lights, produce SFI effects.

Manstead and Semin (1980) also focused on information-processing aspects of task performance. Building on Shiffrin and Schneider's (1977) distinction between 'automatic' vs. 'controlled' information processing, Manstead and Semin assume that the presence of an evaluative audience motivates a task performer to devote more attention to the progress of the automatic task sequences, which generally results in improved performance on routine tasks. When the task requires cognitively controlled processing, however, the presence of others interferes with performance because attention devoted to the audience subtracts from the already demanding task demands (see panel (d) in figure 14.2).

A multi-faceted approach

In the past decade, the idea that one single explanation might account for SFI effects seems to have been abandoned in favour of a multi-faceted approach to explain why the effect of the presence of others on individual task performance moves from benign to harmful as the perceived complexity of the task increases (Guerin, 1993). The presence of others may interfere with learning tasks, since learning implies that the most likely (dominant) responses are not yet the correct ones. However, once the required responses have become well learned and routine, the presence of others may improve performance. Given that most tasks in everyday life involve routine as well as non-routine activities, it is important to mention the results of a comprehensive meta-analysis of 241 SFI studies by Bond and Titus (1983). They concluded that the process gains on simple well-learned tasks are often not as great as the process losses on complex, not well-learned tasks. Their meta-analysis also suggests, however, that mere presence of others accounts for only 3 per cent of variation in individual productivity. As such, SFI may be only part of the explanation for why actual group performance may fall short of its potential. In order to address other sources of losses and gains in productivity, we will now shift our attention from non-interactive performance contexts to interactive contexts, in which successful task completion requires co-ordination, a division of labour and a combination of group members' inputs into a group product.

Combining Individual Resources into a Group Product

Which factors determine group performance when group members are not only working in each other's presence, but when they also have to combine their individual resources into a group product?

Having described how individual group members' task performance can be affected by the mere presence of others, we now go one step further to look at the interactions between group members who depend on one another to achieve group success.

Interdependence

In task groups, a group member's outcomes typically do not depend only on his or her own performance, but also on the performance of his or her co-workers. Deutsch (1949a; see also chapter 11 of this volume) distinguished between two basic types of interdependence, namely cooperative and competitive interdependence. To the extent that one group member's successful performance promotes the success of fellow group members, they are **cooperatively interdependent**. As long as their private interests coincide, group members will be motivated to contribute their individual resources such as effort, knowledge, time or money to serve their common interests. Cooperation requires coordinated action. For example, if the chairperson of the earlier mentioned educational committee solicits written proposals from its members, it is in their common interest to submit individual proposals in time. No one benefits from being late. Coordination is promoted by unambiguous communication about the timing of collective action, about deadlines, and about the order in which group members' resources should be combined. The interactions between the group members should be organized in such a way that the available resources are combined optimally into

Cooperative interdependence A task situation in which the success of any one member of the group improves the chances of other members succeeding.

a group product. If the group falls short in this respect, the group suffers from a first type of process loss, so-called **coordination losses** (Steiner, 1972).

Working in a group almost always involves a mixture of cooperative *and* competitive motives, however. Group members are **competitively interdependent** to the extent that positive outcomes for one group member entail negative outcomes for the other group member(s). For instance, electing a chairperson, dividing the group budget or allocating the collective workload among the members of the group may evoke competitive motives. The mixture of cooperative and competitive interdependence in almost any task group (**mixed-motive interdependence**) motivates group members to serve their common interests, but meanwhile motivates them also to act in their self-interest, since what is to be gained by oneself (e.g., higher status, a larger share of the budget, a smaller share of the collective workload) can only be obtained at the expense of fellow group members. Even when cooperative motives prevail in a certain task group, the mixture of cooperative and competitive motives may still lead group members to (un)consciously reduce their own efforts on behalf of the group and to take advantage of fellow group members' cooperation. This constitutes a second type of process loss, namely **motivation losses** (Steiner, 1972).

The occurrence of coordination losses and motivation losses is strongly affected by the way in which individual resources have to be combined into a group product, as well as by the number of people in the group, as we will see below.

Coordination losses
Deterioration in group productivity in comparison to individual productivity due to group members' inability to combine their resources in an optimal way.

Competitive interdependence
A task situation in which any one member of the group will succeed only if other member(s) of the group fail.

Mixed-motive interdependence
A task situation in which group members are cooperatively as well as competitively interdependent.

Motivation losses   Inefficiency that results from more or less conscious reductions in the motivation to do one's very best on behalf of the group.

Assembly rules

How should the available resources of the participating group members be combined to produce the best possible group product? Steiner (1972, 1976) distinguished between various assembly rules. Three of these rules, namely additive, disjunctive and conjunctive assembly rules (see table 14.1), are particularly relevant with respect to the occurrence of coordination losses and motivation losses.

Additive tasks

In **additive tasks** the group product consists of a simple addition of all members' contributions, as in the case of rope-pulling, cheering, stuffing envelopes, raking leaves and shovelling snow. In these tasks each group member performs the same act and actual group performance can be expressed as the total amount of work done. The

Additive task   A group task that can be completed by adding together all individual members' inputs.

TABLE 14.1 Typology of assembly rules

Type of assembly rule	Potential group productivity	Examples
Additive	Group outperforms its best-performing member	Rope-pulling, cheering, stuffing envelopes, shovelling snow
Disjunctive (Eureka)	Group performance matches the performance of the best-performing member	Tasks with an obviously correct solution: simple calculations, word puzzles, anagrams
Disjunctive (non-Eureka)	Group performance can match the performance of the best-performing member, but often falls short	Tasks without an obviously correct solution: complex problems and puzzles
Conjunctive (non-divisible)	Group performance matches the performance of the worst-performing member	Climbing a mountain peak with all members of the group, regardless of individual ability
Conjunctive (divisible)	Group performance may exceed the performance of the worst-performing member, if subtasks are properly matched to the abilities of the members	Climbing a mountain peak with only the most able climbers, leaving easier jobs (supply of goods and food) to the less able group members

Source: Adapted from Steiner (1972, 1976)

additive assembly rule implies that the group as a whole outperforms its best-performing member. Assuming no process losses, a four-person group should produce twice as much as a dyad, and four times as much as a single individual. The recipe for group success seems rather simple: all group members should do as much as they can, while maintaining the necessary coordination with their co-workers.

In some of the first social-psychological experiments on task performance in groups, it has already been demonstrated, however, that even though a group working on an additive task outperforms a single individual working alone, such a group does not make optimal use of its members' resources. In his research between 1882 and 1887, Ringelmann had young men pull a rope, either alone or in groups of two, three or eight people (see Kravitz & Martin, 1986). He measured the momentary force exerted by means of a recording dynamometer. When the participants worked alone, they pulled with an average force of 63 kilograms, but when working as a group they did not reach their full potential: two men did not pull with a force of 126 kilograms, nor did three men pull with a force of 189 kilograms. It appeared that a two-person group had an average pull of 118 kilograms (8 kilograms below its potential), a three-person group pulled with an average of 160 kilograms (29 kilograms below its potential), while an eight-person group exerted a force of even 256 kilograms *below* its potential. Why did productivity losses increase with group size?

The fact that actual performance did not equal potential performance in Ringelmann's groups may have been due to coordination losses as well as motivation losses. In the first place, group members may not have coordinated their efforts optimally. For instance, they may not have pulled in exactly the same direction or, when they did, they may not have exerted their maximum force at exactly the same moment. Reaching optimal coordination between all group members' inputs clearly becomes more difficult as group size increases, since it requires that all group members receive, understand and follow any given instructions about the right time, the right direction and the right modality of their individual inputs.

In addition to coordination losses, the members of Ringelmann's groups may also have suffered from motivation losses. The tendency to reduce one's own efforts may be due to the fact that as group size increases, the responsibility for successful task completion is diffused and the identifiability of one's own inputs is decreased (Latané 1986; Latané & Darley, 1970; Leary & Forsyth, 1987). Given the mixture of cooperative and competitive motives, any group member in a large group may hide in the crowd and still share in the positive outcomes associated with group success. Group success becomes less likely, however, the more group members reduce their own efforts.

Subsequent studies show that coordination and motivation losses play an important role not only in rope-pulling groups (Ingham, Levinger, Graves, & Peckham, 1974), but also in other additive tasks. In their classic study, Latané, Williams and Harkins (1979) requested experimental participants (who were blindfolded and wearing headsets that played loud noise) to shout loudly, purportedly to assess 'the effects of sensory feedback on the production of sound in groups'. They were asked to shout as loudly as they could as a single individual, or as a member of a dyad or as a member of a six-person group. Under each of these three conditions, individual performance was recorded by a sound level meter. Consistent with Ringelmann's earlier observations, groups produced more noise than single individuals, but group productivity failed to reach its full potential. The observed productivity losses as a function of group size are depicted in figure 14.3. The horizontal line along the top represents potential productivity to be expected if there were no coordination or motivation losses (i.e., productivity of 100 per cent of a group member's individual potential, measured when tested alone). The line marked 'real groups' shows that experimental participants

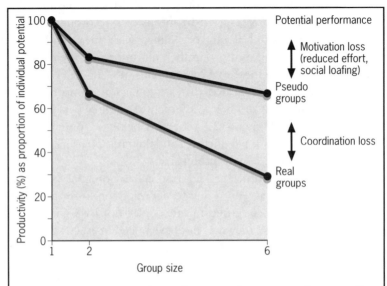

FIGURE 14.3   Intensity of sound generated per person (as proportion of individual potential), when cheering as a single individual or as a member of a real or pseudo two-person group or six-person group
(Based on Latané, Williams, & Harkins, 1979)

produced only 66 per cent of their individual potential when working in dyads, while they produced only 36 per cent of their individual potential in six-person groups.

To disentangle productivity losses due to faulty coordination from those due to reduced motivation, Latané et al. had some of their experimental participants perform the cheering task in 'pseudo-groups'. While participants in real groups were cheering in each other's presence, participants in pseudo-groups were merely *led to believe* that they were cheering with one or with five fellow participants, while in actuality they were shouting alone. The blindfolds and headsets made this deception possible. Thus, any productivity loss observed in the pseudo-groups could be attributed only to reduced motivation, not to faulty coordination, since there were no co-workers to coordinate one's cheering with. The line marked 'pseudo-groups' in figure 14.3 shows that participants who were led to believe that they were cheering with only one co-worker shouted at 82 per cent of their individual potential, while those who thought that they were shouting with five co-workers reached 74 per cent of their individual potential.

Thus, actual group performance is obviously lower than its potential, and productivity losses increase with larger group size. In real-life groups, such productivity losses can almost always be attributed to coordination as well as motivation losses. Latané et al.'s (1979) experimental introduction of pseudo-groups allowed the estimation of the relative impact of these two types of productivity loss. In this particular cheering experiment, it appeared that actual performance in real groups is equal to potential performance minus process losses due to faulty coordination (about half of the total productivity loss) and due to reduced motivation (the other half of the total productivity loss). These findings suggest that even if a task group did manage to prevent all possible coordination losses by efficient tuning of group members' inputs, the group would still not reach its full potential owing to motivation losses. This so-called **social loafing** phenomenon, i.e., reduced individual effort expenditure the larger the size of the group, is not limited to simple physical tasks such as rope-pulling and cheering. It also prevents a group from reaching its potential when working on vigilance tasks, memory search tasks, monitoring tasks, creativity problems, brainstorming and decision-making tasks (Hoeksema-VanOrden, Gaillard, & Buunk, 1998; Jackson & Harkins, 1985; Jackson & Williams, 1985).

> **Social loafing** Reduced effort expenditure (motivation loss) in large groups, mainly due to the fact that one's own contributions are not identifiable and cannot be evaluated.

Given the generality of social loafing in group tasks, groups should find ways to counteract its underlying motivational bases. Several studies have shown that social loafing is minimized when group members are working on challenging and involving tasks and believe that their own inputs can be fully identified and evaluated through comparison with fellow group members' inputs (Brickner, Harkins, & Ostrom, 1986; Harkins & Jackson, 1985; Williams, Harkins, & Latané, 1981) or through comparison with another group (Harkins & Szymanski, 1989). The motivation to present oneself in a favourable way in order to remain a well-respected member of a successful group may ensure that actual group performance comes closer to its potential. As long as the task is not too cognitively demanding (cf. Cottrell's, 1972, and Sanna's, 1992, approaches to social facilitation and inhibition), evaluation apprehension may facilitate group members' individual performance so that actual group performance approximates its potential. Under such circumstances, people working on important tasks in groups which are important to them, may even work harder collectively than alone in order to compensate for anticipated loafing by their co-workers. In contrast to the pessimistic view that groups will invariably fall short of their potential, this instance of **social compensation** illustrates that, under particular circumstances, people may work harder in groups than alone (Guzzo & Dickson, 1996; Williams, Karau, & Bourgeois, 1993; Zacarro, 1984).

> **Social compensation** Increased effort on a group task in order to compensate for co-workers' actual, perceived or anticipated lack of effort or ability.

Increasing the identifiability of group members' individual inputs to prevent them from hiding in the crowd may not be a panacea, however. While reduced individual effort in groups of increasing size (social loafing) may be more or less unconscious (Harkins, 1987; Harkins & Petty, 1982), motivation losses may also be strategically inspired by group members' self-interest (Baron, Kerr, & Miller, 1992; Kerr & Bruun, 1981; Stroebe & Frey, 1982). Working in a group may lead some group members to conclude that their own efforts are dispensable, given fellow group members' resources and/or efforts. Such feelings of dispensability may lead to the temptation to take a **'free ride'** on fellow group

> **Free-riding** Strategy of leaving it to other group members to contribute to the group product, because the individual considers his or her own contribution to be dispensable.

members' cooperative efforts. In the following discussion about disjunctive and conjunctive assembly rules, we will elaborate on such strategically inspired motivation losses.

Disjunctive tasks

Disjunctive task An either/or group task that can be completed by selecting one single group member's input to stand as the group product.

Eureka task A disjunctive task with a solution that, once suggested, seems obviously correct to all group members.

In contrast to additive tasks in which all contributions are summed, **disjunctive tasks** require that the group selects one specific contribution from a pool of members' contributions to stand as the group product. In the earlier mentioned study by Thomas and Fink (1961) on group performance on the horse-trading problem, for instance, only one particular solution serves as the group product. One may suppose that groups working on a disjunctive intellectual task will generally outperform individuals working alone, since 'two know more than one'. This line of reasoning assumes that truth always wins: if there is just one group member offering the obviously correct answer, it is very likely that the group will adopt it as the group solution. Ideally, group performance in such so-called **Eureka tasks** matches the performance of the most competent or best-performing group member (see table 14.1).

Having one highly competent group member is no guarantee of group success, however, as Thomas and Fink (1961) have shown. Individual members of task groups may make various kinds of errors. When, for some reason or another, knowledgeable co-workers hold back during the group discussion and do not provide the correct solution, group performance will fall below its potential. Furthermore, a correct solution offered by a single highly competent member will not always be supported by his or her co-workers when it is not generally accepted as the only, obviously correct, solution. In complex tasks having no single, obviously correct, solution (non-Eureka tasks), a single knowledgeable group member will have a hard time persuading the co-workers to adopt his or her own solution as the correct one. Therefore, in many complex intellectual tasks, group performance can match the performance of the most competent member, but often falls short. Group performance will only reach its potential when a significant proportion of the group members (finally) supports the correct solution (Hastie, 1986; Stasser, Kerr, & Davis, 1989). Later in this chapter, we will elaborate on the interpersonal influence processes necessary to arrive at a mutually agreed-upon solution (see also chapter 13 of this volume). In our present discussion, we merely focus on the occurrence and prevention of coordination and motivation losses.

Disjunctive tasks require sufficient coordination to designate the most competent group member(s) to take the lead in task completion. If the group fails to allocate (sub)tasks and duties to individual group members in accordance with their specific abilities, the group runs the risk that the group interactions will be dominated by the most assertive group members, who are not necessarily the most competent ones.

With respect to the occurrence and prevention of motivation losses, disjunct-ive tasks clearly differ from additive tasks. Earlier in this chapter, we saw that when working on additive tasks, *all* group members may lose some of their mot-ivation, either unconsciously (social loafing) or strategically (free-riding), since they may all consider their own efforts equally dispensable for group success, the more so as group size increases. In disjunctive tasks, however, particularly the *low-competent* group members may be strategically motivated to reduce their own efforts and free-ride on others' contributions. Even if their contributions will be fully identifiable (making it impossible for them to hide in the crowd), the low-competent members may hold back, keep themselves in the background and stick uncritically to the solutions offered by those who are assumed to be the experts and who may therefore dominate the interaction. Such strategically driven mot-ivation losses in disjunctive tasks are more likely the larger the size of the group (Kerr & Bruun, 1983). They may be especially harmful in non-Eureka tasks, which have no single, obviously correct, solution. If reduced motivation and lowered task involvement keep potentially fruitful contributions beneath the surface, many valuable resources in the group remain unused. To prevent such motivation losses, steps should be taken to counteract feelings of dispensability. If in one way or another ordinary group members can be led to believe that their own cooperation really matters, they are less likely to take a free ride on their more competent co-workers' cooperation.

Conjunctive tasks

Whereas disjunctive tasks require that at least *one* group member fulfils the task successfully, **conjunctive tasks** require that *all* group mem-bers contribute as much as they can to successful task completion.

Conjunctive task A group task requiring that all members complete it successfully.

In *non-divisible* conjunctive tasks, groups invariably perform at the level of the group member with the worst performance (see table 14.1). For instance, the speed at which a party of mountain climbers can ascend a moun-tain peak is determined by its slowest member. Similarly, a group working on a research project, or an advisory panel such as the earlier mentioned educational committee, can in many cases not proceed until all members have thorough know-ledge of the latest results and developments. Since the perceived probability of having a very slow or incompetent member increases with group size, actual group performance often falls further short of its potential as the number of group members increases (Kerr & Bruun, 1983).

Some conjunctive group tasks, however, are *divisible* and can be broken down into subtasks which can be allocated to individual members in accordance with their specific abilities. For example, climbing a mountain can be divided into several subtasks, such as rope-leader and followers. When the most able group members perform the most difficult subtasks and leave easier subtasks to the less able members, group performance is more likely to exceed the performance of the least able member. Thus, conjunctive tasks require sufficient coordination, not

PLATE 14.1   Mountain climbing as a group is a conjunctive task: the speed of the party is determined by the slowest member

only properly to match the (sub)tasks to the abilities of the group members (as in the case of a disjunctive task), but also to provide support for the slowest or least able members of the group.

Whether or not the conjunctive task can be divided into subtasks is particularly important with respect to the occurrence and prevention of strategically driven motivation losses. The larger the size of the group working on a non-divisible conjunctive task, the greater the likelihood that the *most competent* group members will lose their task motivation out of frustration at being impaired by the (s)low performance of low-competent co-workers (Kerr & Bruun, 1983). Demotivation of the most competent members may result in serious productivity losses, since group performance on conjunctive tasks often depends on the extent to which more competent group members provide help and assistance to their less competent co-workers. If the latter do not reach their potential, the group as a whole will also fall short of its potential.

It should be noted that many group tasks in everyday life do not fit neatly into this taxonomy of additive, disjunctive and conjunctive assembly rules. In most cases, group tasks include many subtasks, which can be identified with one of the three discussed assembly rules. Nevertheless, the above analysis of the role of perceived dispensability on individual effort expenditure implies that in disjunctive (sub)-tasks, less competent group members may lose their motivation to do their very best because they believe that their own efforts will not really affect group performance. In conjunctive (sub)tasks, however, highly competent group members may doubt whether their own efforts matter, given the low performance of their less competent co-workers.

These instances of strategically driven motivation losses may not only harm group productivity in itself, but may also set the stage for another type of strategically driven motivation loss. When an individual group member actively contributes to the group and then learns that (some) co-workers do not take their share of the collective workload, this individual may also lose his or her task motivation, not wanting to carry free-riders. This so-called **sucker effect** (Kerr, 1983) refers to the situation in which a group member with capable co-workers, who could have contributed but actually refrain from doing so, reduces his or her own efforts too in order to escape the inequitable role of being exploited by less co-operative fellow group members.

> **Sucker effect**   A reduced motivation to do one's very best for the group, if one learns that fellow group members withhold their contributions.

Process Losses in Three Task Activities

How do coordination losses and motivation losses affect actual group performance during collective idea generation, information sampling and decision-making?

To illustrate the occurrence and prevention of coordination and motivation losses, we will now focus on three specific collective task activities. Some task activities require that group members exert their efforts simultaneously and act in concert. For instance, problem-solving groups whose members are properly tuned to focus simultaneously on one and the same activity – such as defining the main problem, thinking about possible solutions, evaluating proposals, implementing solutions – generally perform better than groups whose members' contributions are less well tuned in time (Harper & Askling, 1980; Tschan, 1995). However, we shall see below that group performance will not invariably benefit from simultaneity in members' actions, nor from coordinated efforts to align their contributions.

Idea generation

The question of how coordination and motivation losses can be minimized in order to combine individual resources optimally into a group product is very salient when a group has to generate creative ideas about possible ways to solve a problem. In an attempt to promote process gains from working as a group rather than as single individuals, an advertising executive (Osborn, 1957) suggested the so-called **brainstorming** technique. To start a typical interactive

> **Brainstorming**   A group technique aimed at enhancing creativity in groups by means of uninhibited generation of as many ideas as possible concerning a specified topic.

brainstorming session, group members receive instructions to generate as many ideas as possible and to 'piggyback' on ideas from their fellow group members in order to generate even more ideas. One person records all the expressed ideas, which have to be presented and placed before the group as rapidly as possible without discussion, clarification or comment. Evaluation and selection of the most fruitful ideas are to be done later. Osborn claimed that groups who follow these instructions generate more ideas than single individuals, and that the quality of these ideas is also superior. The empirical evidence does not support this optimistic claim, however. According to McGrath (1984), group members in interactive brainstorming groups generate fewer and less creative (as rated by judges) ideas than the same number of individuals working separately (Bond & Van Leeuwen, 1991; Mullen, Johnson, & Salas, 1991).

Diehl and Stroebe (1987; see also Stroebe & Diehl, 1994) investigated three possible explanations for productivity losses in interactive brainstorming groups. The first explanation builds on the additive assembly rule of the brainstorming task. Given that all individual ideas will be pooled, participants may lose their motivation to do their very best and may hide in the crowd or strategically free-ride on others' creative efforts. To test this hypothesis, Diehl and Stroebe instructed participants of brainstorming groups to expect either *individual* or *pooled* assessment of their ideas. It appeared that productivity was indeed somewhat higher among group members who had been led to expect individual as opposed to pooled assessment of the generated ideas.

The second explanation suggests that, despite the instructions not to evaluate one another's ideas, the fear of negative evaluations from their co-workers prevents participants from freely presenting their own unique ideas. As we discussed earlier in this chapter, evaluation apprehension (Cottrell, 1968, 1972; Sanna, 1992) may result in social inhibition of non-dominant responses. Thus, when participants perceive the task as cognitively complex, i.e., with a high probability of their giving inappropriate responses, evaluation apprehension may lead to productivity losses. To test this hypothesis, Diehl and Stroebe's brainstorming groups either followed the *usual* brainstorming procedure or were *videotaped*, ostensibly for the purpose of presentation to a class that was attended by most of the participants. It appeared that the prospect of being evaluated by classmates indeed reduced actual productivity, but again, the observed negative effects were not very strong.

Searching for a more powerful explanation for the observed productivity losses in interactive brainstorming groups, Diehl and Stroebe investigated a third explanation. Due to the informal coordination rule that only one group member may speak at a time, other group members, who meanwhile have to keep silent, may be distracted by the content of the group discussion, forget their own ideas, or may be impaired from developing new ideas. To test this hypothesis, Diehl and Stroebe had some participants brainstorm in real interacting four-person groups ('interactive group' condition). By contrast, participants in four other conditions were physically separated from one another in different cubicles. Even though participants in these conditions were seated alone, they were instructed to express their ideas vocally via a clip-on microphone in order to have their expressed ideas tape-recorded. In the 'alone, individual, no communication' condition, participants were brainstorming individually. In the three remaining 'alone' conditions, each cubicle contained an intercom and a display with lights, each light representing one specific group member. These lights functioned like a set of traffic lights. As soon as one member of the four-person group started to speak, a voice-activated sensor switched his or her light to green in all of the other three cubicles. Meanwhile, the other three lights on the display were red. As soon as that person stopped talking for 1.5 seconds, these red lights were switched to green, indicating that somebody else could speak. When this happened, the red lights went on for the remaining three group members. By these technical devices, three different 'alone' conditions were created. In the 'alone, blocking, communication' condition, the display with lights regulated participants' turn-taking in their communication with one another via the intercom. All of them heard through the earphones what was being said by the other participants. Since only one person could speak at any moment, they could make their contributions only when their own light switched to green. In the 'alone, blocking, no communication' condition, participants also had to wait for their turn before expressing their ideas, but could not hear each other's ideas via the intercom. In the 'alone, no blocking, no communication' condition, participants were instructed to disregard the lights and the intercom and to express their ideas whenever they wanted to.

In all five conditions, participants had 15 minutes to make suggestions about the question 'How can unemployment be reduced in Germany?'. In order to compare the productivity of participants working under these different conditions afterwards, Diehl and Stroebe had to pool the ideas expressed by the four individuals who brainstormed alone and without communication, to make a 'nominal group' product. Since the same idea may be suggested several times by four people working alone, without communication, whereas such repetition would not be allowed in free communication, redundant ideas were eliminated from the pooled set of ideas that constituted the 'nominal group' product. Table 14.2 presents the average number of non-redundant ideas expressed in each of the five conditions. The results show that participants generated approximately twice as many ideas when they were allowed to express their ideas as they occurred (i.e., in the two non-blocking conditions) than when they had to wait their turn (i.e., in the three blocking conditions). These results suggest that '**production blocking**' is indeed an important factor explaining the inferiority of interactive brainstorming groups.

> **Production blocking** Reduction in individual productivity and creativity in generating ideas due to interruptions and turn-taking in interactive brainstorming sessions.

One other result in table 14.2 deserves our attention. The finding that preventing participants from overhearing each other's ideas did not significantly affect brainstorming productivity is important, for at least two reasons. First, a comparison between the 'alone, blocking, *no* communication' condition and the 'alone, blocking, communication' condition pertains to the earlier mentioned evaluation apprehension explanation for productivity losses. Apparently, it made little (only

TABLE 14.2   Average number of non-redundant ideas expressed by four-person groups working under blocking and non-blocking conditions

Condition	Number of ideas
Blocking:	
Interactive group	55.7
Alone, blocking, communication	37.7
Alone, blocking, no communication	45.7
Non-blocking:	
Alone, no blocking, no communication	102.7
Alone, individual, no communication	106.0

Source: Adapted from Diehl & Stroebe (1987)

8 per cent) difference whether or not participants anticipated that their own expressed ideas could be overheard – and evaluated – by fellow group members. Second, the same comparison clearly shows that overhearing one another's ideas did not *in*crease brainstorming productivity. In contrast to Osborn's (1957) optimistic claim, participants who could 'piggyback' on the ideas expressed by fellow group members did *not* generate more non-redundant ideas than participants who could not overhear others' ideas.

One may wonder why traditional brainstorming is still so popular, despite the overwhelming evidence that interactive brainstorming groups suffer from serious productivity losses. Why do so many people have the illusion that they are more productive in a group setting than when working alone? According to Stroebe and Diehl (1994; Stroebe, Diehl, & Abakoumkin, 1992), participants in interactive brainstorming groups have difficulty in differentiating between their own and others' contributions. They are inclined to claim some of the proposed ideas as being generated by themselves, while these ideas actually have been proposed by fellow group members. Thus, the popularity of the traditional interactive brainstorming technique may reside in participants' overestimation of the number of ideas that have been proposed by *themselves.*

Information sampling

Besides the importance of generating innovative ideas, task performance often merely requires the sampling and usage of already available information from the group members. Members enter a task group with a large range of idiosyncratic ideas and unique pieces of information, which may differ widely from one member to another owing to personal expertise, ability and previous experience. A group can really gain from working together if its members feel free to express their unique opinions. Two types of social influence may prevent them from doing so, however (Deutsch & Gerard, 1955; Jones & Gerard, 1967; see also chapter 13 of this volume). In the first place, group members want to be liked and respected as a group member. In their eagerness to maintain group membership and to avoid being a deviant (Schachter, 1951), they may focus primarily on information and knowledge that they have *in common* (normative pressures). Second, group members want to end up with *correct* information. When they withhold their own unique ideas because they trust others' information and expressed judgements more than their own, we speak of informational pressures to yield to others' opinions. Owing to these two types of conformity pressures, group members will focus primarily on information that they know others possess, instead of concentrating on expressing information that only they possess.

When all members of a group have exactly the same pieces of information at their disposal, the motives 'to be liked' and 'to be correct' coincide. By exchanging and discussing their shared information, group members will reach consensus, making optimal use of all available resources. However, even when group members have different perspectives on the task and its completion, which often occurs since they are usually recruited as members of a task group on the basis of their specific expertise, normative and informational pressures will motivate them mainly to consider the information that they have *in common* (Stasser, Kerr, et al., 1989; Stasser, Taylor, & Hanna, 1989; Stewart & Stasser, 1998). Unshared pieces of information or opinions which may contradict the emerging group consensus often remain unused.

A strong focus on common knowledge may inhibit a fruitful exchange of unique pieces of information available in the group. The sampling advantage of shared information over unshared information in group discussions may incur a serious process loss in the case of a so-called **hidden profile**, i.e., when the collective profile of information available to the group at large favours one choice option, but the pattern of information possessed by individual mem-

> **Hidden profile** Problem where the best solution will go unrecognized because relevant information that is dispersed among group members does not receive sufficient attention.

bers favours another option. As an example, imagine a four-person group being faced with two alternative options to deal with a given task, option A and option B (see figure 14.4). The four group members I to IV share three arguments in favour of option A, and only one argument in favour of option B. In addition, on the basis of personal expertise, each group member has one unique argument in favour of option B. In this particular information profile, all four group members are likely to express their support for option A, given their three shared arguments in favour of option A and only one shared argument in favour of option B, while the hidden profile supports option B. If the four group members had expressed all their available arguments, it would have become apparent that five arguments (i.e., one shared argument plus four unique arguments) supported option B. Thus, a premature focus on option A would leave valuable resources (four unique arguments in favour of option B) unused, and this is what actually happens in many groups.

Group members	I	II	III	IV
Share three arguments in favour of option A	1A 2A 3A	1A 2A 3A	1A 2A 3A	1A 2A 3A
Share one argument in favour of option B	1B	1B	1B	1B
Each have one unique argument in favour of option B	2B	3B	4B	5B

FIGURE 14.4   A hidden profile: group members tend to focus on shared information (three arguments in favour of option A, one in favour of option B), but do not discuss the four unique arguments in favour of option B

Common knowledge effect
The tendency of group members to focus merely on commonly shared (rather than unique) pieces of information.

In sum, although essential for successful coordination of group members' contributions, subtle mutual pressures to align individual contributions into a commonly shared task perspective may have drawbacks when it comes to information sampling and vigilant decision-making. As such, this so-called **common knowledge effect** (Gigone & Hastie, 1993, 1997) constitutes a negative side-effect of group members' efforts to coordinate and align their individual contributions.

Decision-making

Informational and normative conformity pressures may operate simultaneously, although to varying degrees. When finding a *correct* task solution is most important, such as 'How many hands are needed to move this pile of bricks?', informational influence processes may predominate. However, when the desire to express a *shared identity* is high, such as in highly cohesive groups, normative pressures may be relatively strong (Festinger, 1950; Kaplan & Miller, 1987).

Social decision scheme   A probabilistic model, specifying the process by which individual inputs are combined into a group decision.

Strong normative pressures may appear, for instance, in judgemental discussions about ethical issues such as 'Which of the many groups of asylum seekers deserve our support?'. Research by Davis (1973, 1996; see also Kerr, 1992; Laughlin & Ellis, 1986) shows that in judgemental tasks the 'majority rule' often serves as an implicit **social decision scheme** to determine what the ultimate group decision will be. Given that the sheer *number* of group members supporting a specific judgement, rather than the validity of their arguments, accounts for the final group decision, normative pressures are stronger than informational pressures. The majority rule may yield a negative side-effect, however, by focusing group members primarily on the normative requirement to reduce any discrepancy between their own opinion and the opinion held by the majority. The fear of being rejected by fellow group members may impede creative and divergent thinking and cause group members to overlook crucial information. As a result, they may make poor decisions (Janis, 1982b).

In contrast to such judgemental tasks, intellectual tasks have a more or less convincing solution. In Eureka tasks having one single, obviously correct, solution (see table 14.1), the earlier mentioned 'truth wins rule' may serve as the social decision scheme. The proposal of the correct solution by even one single group member may serve as an informational cue, which immediately convinces fellow group members. Non-Eureka tasks, having no single, obviously correct, solution, leave room for many different interpretations, however, and the social influence process involves the exchange of arguments to persuade one another of the correctness of one's own solution. The constructive cognitive conflict evoked by a persistent group member (or minority) may promote careful consideration of the reasons for the apparent discrepancy, laying the ground for innovative and divergent thinking (Nemeth, 1994; see also chapter 13 of this volume). Given a single group member's lack of numerical support, his or her influence mainly relies on informational rather than on normative pressure.

Preventing process losses

Given the importance of open-mindedness to alternative perspectives at various stages of task completion, groups should find ways to optimally combine group members' resources into a group product.

As we have seen, the generation of novel ideas in interactive brainstorming sessions may be seriously inhibited by production blocking. It may be more effective to ask group members to develop their ideas separately, and only thereafter have these ideas expressed, discussed and evaluated in a joint meeting. The **nominal group technique** (NGT; Delbecq, Van de Ven, & Gustafson, 1975) involves such a two-stage procedure. To prevent production blocking in the idea-generation stage, group members are required not to exchange their ideas with their co-workers but to write their ideas down privately. The second stage involves the evaluation of the privately developed perspectives. Comparisons between NGT and traditional brainstorming show that NGT produces superior results, suggesting that idea generation by members of a task group, such as the earlier mentioned educational committee, may be most fruitful if the participants

Nominal group technique
An alternative to interactive brainstorming, which calls for combining individuals' inputs (developed in isolation) into a group product.

have first generated their ideas individually before the exchange of these ideas takes place (Van de Ven & Delbecq, 1974). An alternative coordination device to prevent production blocking may be computerized brainstorming (Valachich, Dennis, & Connolly, 1994). As in the NGT, the lack of face-to-face interaction minimizes production blocking, which may be particularly important when novel and creative ideas have to be generated in task groups with many participants.

In the process of sampling unique pieces of already available information, task groups should also find ways to promote process gains from working as a group. The explicit announcement that the search and exchange of all pieces of information may prove valuable in finding the correct solution (Stasser & Stewart, 1992) and the awareness that any group member may possess unique pieces of information (Stasser, Stewart, & Wittenbaum, 1995) may ameliorate the sampling disadvantage of unshared information. The assignment of group members to expert roles may help groups to coordinate their information processing more efficiently. Mutually recognized personal expertise may evoke more discussion about unshared pieces of information because adopting an expert role may make group members accept responsibility for expressing information within their own area of expertise. It may also make them feel that their contributions are less dispensable. As a result, the assigned experts may volunteer unshared information and the co-workers may explicitly solicit unshared information from the experts.

To test this hypothesis, Stewart and Stasser (1995) analysed audio recordings of experimental groups during their discussions concerning which candidate (out of three candidates) was most qualified for the position of student council president. Each member of a discussion group had received information about the three candidates in a private booklet. For any one discussion group, some subsets of information pertaining to a candidate were given to all group members (shared information), while other subsets were given to only one member (unshared information). During their discussions, group members had to record on a group information sheet as much accurate information as they could about the three candidates and to reach consensus about which candidate was best suited for the position. Participants in the 'expertise not assigned' condition were only informed that group members may not have received identical sets of information about the candidates. In the 'expertise assigned' condition, by contrast, each participant was informed that he or she had received extra information about a specific candidate that other group members did not receive. Thus, in front of the other group members, each member was identified as being an expert about a particular candidate.

The proportions of shared and unshared information mentioned during the decision-making process are depicted in figure 14.5. In the 'expertise not assigned' condition, unshared pieces of information were not very likely to be mentioned (only 7 per cent of all items that were mentioned) in comparison with shared pieces of information (18 per cent). Apparently, the goal of reaching

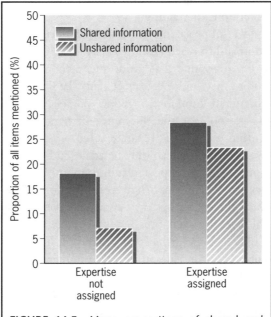

FIGURE 14.5 Mean proportions of shared and unshared pieces of information mentioned during the group discussions
(Based on Stewart & Stasser, 1995)

consensus without assigned expertise may have kept the perceived need to explore systematically unshared information very low. The assignment of expert roles resulted in more discussion about unshared pieces of information, but did not eliminate the sampling disadvantage for unshared information about the candidates. Even under strong demands to adopt expert roles, group members were still inclined to mention more shared (28 per cent) than unshared pieces of information (23 per cent). Related research by Stasser and Titus (1985, 1987) suggests that group members in discussion groups remain reluctant to express unshared pieces of information, unless they detect some signs of social support that confirms the veracity of their own unique ideas.

Training a group to avoid biased information sampling may yield only limited effects (Larson, Christensen, Abbott, & Franz, 1996; Larson, Foster-Fishman, & Keys, 1994). From these studies it appeared that trained groups did not differ from untrained groups in their focus on commonly shared information. The only difference was that untrained groups first elaborately discussed their shared information before they started their (brief) discussion about unshared information, while trained groups did not show such a shift over time. Thus, the tendency to neglect unshared information during group discussions cannot easily be overcome by procedural interventions or training.

Are there more powerful procedures to cope with normative pressures to focus on shared information and to reach an early decision? One way to stimulate divergent thinking may be to arrange that group members meet in *subgroups* before the discussion in a joint meeting (Wheeler & Janis, 1980). The presence of these subgroups in a subsequent combined meeting may elicit discussion and critical examination of the reasons for the difference in perspectives that have been developed earlier within each of the separate subgroups. If the subgroups eventually come to agree, which often can only be achieved by exchanging arguments to persuade the members of the opposing subgroup, it is less likely that the combined group will overlook any important considerations. The common frame of reference on which the subgroups may eventually come to agree on the basis of exerting mutual informational pressure may then be adopted with more confidence than if only a single group had worked on it.

Another intervention to stimulate an unbiased inquiry of alternative perspectives may be to install a so-called *devil's advocate*, having as his or her role to present any information that may lead to the disqualification of the prevailing perspective (Herbert & Estes, 1977). Unlike the lone dissenter in a task group without such a formally installed devil's advocate, this dissenting group member's popularity in the group will not be harmed since his or her deviant role is mutually agreed upon. Moreover, the role should be shifted regularly from one group member to another and severe cognitive conflicts should be avoided by instructing the devil's advocate to present any counter-argument in a low-key, non-threatening manner to set the stage for a fruitful exchange of information. This procedural intervention, like the other ones mentioned above, is aimed at making optimal use of all the available resources in the group by pushing its members past the bounds of restrictive thinking along the lines of the prevailing group norm.

Group Structure

How is actual group performance affected by emerging role and status differentiation and by the prevailing pattern of communication?

Although members of a task group share group membership, this does not imply that they are all equal. Successful completion of a task requires sufficient coordination of their inputs. One of the main functions of organization is to avoid process losses. When the task is divisible, subtasks can be allocated to individual members in accordance with their specific abilities and interests. As we shall see below, role differentiation implies status differentiation, which may yield process gains, but also process losses, however.

TABLE 14.3 Interaction process analysis (IPA)

Observation categories

Relationship-oriented behaviour (positive)
  1 Shows solidarity
  2 Shows tension release
  3 Agrees

Attempted task solutions
  4 Gives suggestion
  5 Gives opinion
  6 Gives orientation

Task-related questions
  7 Asks for orientation
  8 Asks for opinion
  9 Asks for suggestion

Relationship-oriented behaviour (negative)
  10 Disagrees
  11 Shows tension
  12 Shows antagonism

Source: Bales (1950); Bales & Slater (1955)

Role differentiation

Elaborate observations of task groups, and coding of group members' behaviour by means of the so-called **interaction process analysis (IPA)** scheme, shown in table 14.3, reveals that one can distinguish between group members specializing in relationship-oriented behaviour and other group members specializing in task-oriented behaviour (Bales, 1950; Bales & Slater, 1955). These two kinds of expertise are rarely fulfilled by one and the same person.

Interaction process analysis (IPA) A formal observational measurement system devised by Bales for coding the interactions of members of small social groups into task-oriented and relationship-oriented categories.

In terms of the IPA categories, relationship specialists, more often than other group members, initiate positive relationship-oriented behaviours (categories 1 to 3) and ask task-related information from fellow group members (categories 7 to 9). In contrast, task specialists more frequently initiate task-related behaviours (categories 4 to 6) and they are more often addressed by other group members to provide task-related information (categories 7 to 9). At the same time, however, these task specialists are often the recipients of negative relationship-oriented expressions (categories 10 to 12).

Status differentiation

Although relationship specialists may be most liked in the group, task specialists are usually perceived as the ones who contribute most to successful goal achievement. When successful goal achievement is vital to the group, group members will try to identify those individuals among them who are expected to contribute most. Expectation states theory (Berger, Rosenholtz, & Zelditch, 1980) assumes that *a priori* expectations about one another's contributions to group success set the stage for status differentiation. Group members who are assumed to possess superior task-related abilities are addressed more often, are encouraged to take initiatives, and may even be formally designated to take the lead. Meanwhile, ordinary group members are more likely to comply with the influence attempts of the designated few. As a result, a status structure develops in which the behaviour of each is determined by certain rules, standards of conduct or norms, which specify acceptable behaviour. Group performance often gains from such a co-ordination process of dividing roles and duties amongst the group members.

Specific status characteristics
Information about a person's abilities that is directly relevant to the group task.

Diffuse status characteristics
Information about a person's abilities that is only obliquely relevant to the group's task, deriving mainly from large-scale category memberships (age, ethnicity, sex) outside the task group.

Personal characteristics of group members lay the ground for *a priori* expectations, and thus for emerging status differentials. **Specific status characteristics** refer to the abilities and skills of group members which are considered of direct relevance to goal attainment (for instance, proven expertise in mathematics when the task demands computational skills). In addition to specific status information, or in the absence of it, group members may also develop mutual expectations by considering one another's **diffuse status characteristics**, i.e., any personal qualities they consider of indirect relevance to successful attainment of the group goals. For instance, in the earlier mentioned educational committee charged with the task of formulating proposals to update the current curriculum, group members' gender, age, ethnicity and status in other groups may all serve as (diffuse) status characteristics, on the basis of which some group members are expected to contribute more to group success than others. In addition to stable personal characteristics, behavioural style (assertiveness, participation rate and degree of group orientation) may also serve as a cue for status differentiation (Lee & Ofshe, 1981; Mazur, 1983; see chapter 17 of this volume for more details on leadership). A summary of these findings is presented in figure 14.6.

Ideally, status differentiation in task groups should be based on task-specific status characteristics. For instance, an older woman might play a minor role when her group is competing with other teams in a sports tournament, but may emerge as the key figure in an interteam quiz where her broad knowledge about local history is valued. However, diffuse status characteristics such as gender, age and ethnicity often generalize across tasks, irrespective of their true task relevance. For instance, an older female member of an ethnic minority may have a hard time gaining true influence in the earlier mentioned educational committee. Overcoming negative stereotypes in a task group is also difficult for people having

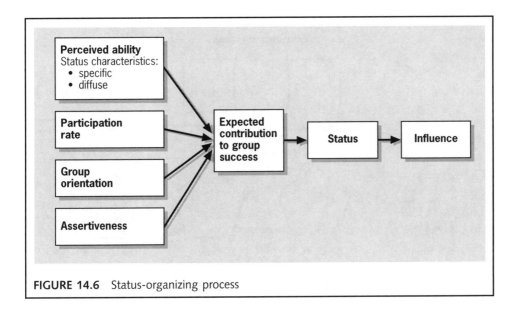

FIGURE 14.6 Status-organizing process

low socio-economic status. Given that group members with higher-ascribed task ability are often allowed to exert more influence in the interactions than group members with a lower-ascribed task ability (Berger & Zelditch, 1993; De Gilder & Wilke, 1994; Greenstein & Knottnerus, 1980), the crucial question is whether group members' mutual expectations about each other's contributions to group success are correct or biased. Group performance may be impaired by role- and status-differentiation processes if the group overlooks the valuable contributions offered by members who actually are competent, but who are not considered worthy of high status (Kirchler & Davis, 1986).

That status differentiation does not always lead to improved group performance is illustrated by Torrance's (1954) study, in which pilots, navigators and gunners served as the experimental participants working on the earlier mentioned horse-trading problem. It appeared that a person higher in military rank (a diffuse status characteristic) was allowed to exert more influence in the group discussion than persons lower in rank. Of the pilots (highest rank) who had reached the correct answer on the horse-trading problem before the group discussion, only one-tenth failed to persuade their co-workers to accept it, while one-fifth of the navigators (lower rank) and one-third of the gunners (lowest rank) failed to do so. Thus, a correct solution is more likely to prevail as the group solution when it is offered by a high-status member than when it is offered by a member having a lower status. Moreover, Torrance's results also show that the same regularity holds true for *in*correct solutions: high-status members who advocate an incorrect solution appear to be more successful in persuading their co-workers to accept their incorrect solution than are members with lower status. A high-status member who is on the wrong track may therefore pose a more serious threat to group success than an equally mistaken low-status member.

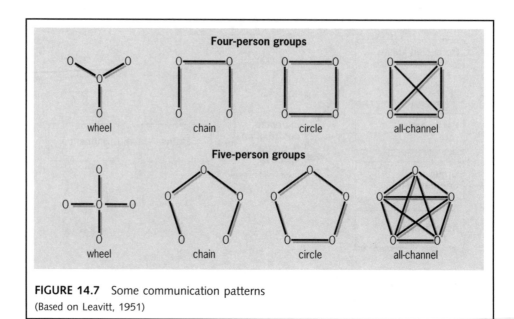

FIGURE 14.7   Some communication patterns
(Based on Leavitt, 1951)

Communication patterns

As we saw above, members of a task-oriented group address task specialists more often than other group members (Bales & Slater, 1955). By doing so, task groups may develop a communication pattern in which a central role is assigned to the task specialist(s). How does the communication pattern as such affect group performance?

To study the effects of communication patterns, Leavitt (1951) had experimental participants seated around a circular table, being separated from each other by vertical partitions. Slots that could be opened and closed by the experimenter allowed participants to pass information to (some of the) other group members. Figure 14.7 shows a number of communication patterns. Of these communication patterns, the wheel is most centralized since any group member on the periphery must send information to his or her co-workers via the single person occupying the central position. By contrast, in the all-channel pattern, no one regulates the distribution of information and any group member can communicate directly with any other member without having to rely on someone else.

Employing very simple experimental tasks, which merely required the gathering of specific pieces of information from the participants, Leavitt found that groups with centralized communication patterns made fewer errors than groups with decentralized patterns. Job satisfaction, however, was higher in a decentralized group, because its members, unlike most participants in a centralized group, did not feel like outsiders. Particularly those in the outlying positions felt dispensable and left the work to a more centrally positioned co-worker. Such motivation losses in the peripheral group members may cause the group to fall short of its potential.

In a review of 18 communication experiments, Shaw (1964) discovered that in groups working on more complex tasks (arithmetical problems, sentence constructions and discussion-type problems), decentralized communication patterns were superior, at least for the first of a series of tasks. In comparison with simple tasks, complex tasks require much more information to be integrated. Since this coordinating duty typically falls on one person in a centralized communication pattern, this centrally positioned person is very likely to suffer from information overload. As a result, group performance is impaired. In decentralized communication patterns, by contrast, the information load can be shared more evenly among the group members, resulting in higher group performance *and* higher job satisfaction.

Given that groups in everyday life may learn from experience, however, it is important to note that after working some time on the complex problems, centralized communication patterns may become less inefficient (Shaw, 1964; Mackenzie, 1976). Whereas group performance on simple tasks may immediately profit from the coordinated efforts of the centrally positioned group member(s), in complex tasks the coordinating advantages of a centralized communication pattern only begin to pay off after a while. Being faced with the double task load of solving a complex task *and* organizing the communication between the members of the educational committee, for instance, may be too difficult for the group to handle in the early stages of task completion. After gaining experience with the task and with the participating people, however, this double task may be dealt with more efficiently.

Overcoming dysfunctional aspects of group structure

The tasks faced by real-life groups are many times more complex than the ones used in laboratory research. Therefore, it seems safe to suggest that centralizing the communication early may result in coordination losses (information overload of centrally positioned group members) as well as motivation losses (dissatisfaction and feelings of dispensability among the peripheral group members). Without delegation of many of their duties to their co-workers, the centrally positioned group members may be unable to process all the relevant task information necessary for optimal group performance. Problems arising from sub-optimal participation of the ordinary group members can only be overcome if low-status members look past their co-workers' negative expectations and can be motivated to put extra effort into demonstrating their true abilities to promote successful completion of the group task. Research has shown that demonstrating the right to high status through fruitful contributions indeed seems to be more effective than claiming a high-status position otherwise (Freeze & Cohen, 1973; Martin & Sell, 1985; Pugh & Wahrman, 1983). It appears, for instance, that a low-status member who shows a strong group-oriented motivation to contribute to successful task completion is more likely to gain influence in the group than another low-status member who apparently pursues mainly his or her private interests (Ridgeway, 1978).

An alternative way to cope with dysfunctional role and status differentiation may be to arrange that group members occupying central and/or leading positions do not make their opinions clear at the outset of the group discussion. A procedure that induces high-status members to wait until ordinary group members have expressed their views may promote a more elaborate inquiry of alternative perspectives. It is a well-known fact in hierarchically structured organizations, such as the military for instance, that the best way to elicit the true opinions of a group of differently ranked group members is to start with the lowest rank and end with the highest. Otherwise, it is very likely that potentially valuable resources will remain unused.

Summary and Conclusions

Working in a group rather than as separate individuals may have its pros and cons. This chapter has looked at actual group performance as a function of potential group performance minus process losses plus process gains. Taking individual task performance as a starting point, it appeared that the mere physical presence of others may improve group members' individual performance on simple, well-learned tasks. However, when tasks are more complex and less routine, as is most often the case in real life, social facilitation of inappropriate responses and social inhibition of the required non-dominant responses may wipe out any beneficial effects of working in each other's presence.

Process losses and gains at the level of interacting groups may also inhibit or facilitate group performance. Making optimal use of group members' resources requires clearly communicated coordination rules. Some tasks (process-planning, for instance) require simultaneity in group members' efforts, while in other tasks (such as generating new creative ideas) simultaneous contributions may result in production blocking. In comparison with coordination losses, however, motivation losses are even more difficult to overcome. The mixture of cooperative and competitive motives in almost any task group makes group members susceptible to the temptation to leave the work to their co-workers. Motivation losses can be prevented by the mutual exertion of normative pressures, which put less cooperative group members at risk of being rejected by the group. Although crucial for concerted action towards group success, enhancing group members' concern about receiving social approval and being a well-respected group member may also have negative side-effects, however. Out of reluctance to express their true private opinions or unique pieces of information that might contradict the emerging group consensus, group members often focus on common knowledge. Some procedural interventions have been suggested to minimize the likelihood of biased information sampling and decision-making. For instance, making group members aware of, and responsible for, specific domains of knowledge may promote group discussion about unshared information.

To keep group members motivated to do their very best to make the group succeed, each of them should be matched with (sub)tasks according to their individual abilities and interests, if possible. One should be aware, however, that the associated emergence of status differentials and communication patterns may result in yet another type of process loss. Status-organizing processes are dysfunctional if they generate self-fulfilling prophecies, so that people conform to the performance level expected of them even though their actual abilities may be lower or higher than those ascribed to them. For instance, high-status members occupying the central positions in the communication pattern run the risk of being overloaded with coordinating duties, while the resources of ordinary group members may remain unused. To gain from potentially valuable contributions from group members who are not considered worthy of high status and who may feel 'left out' in their peripheral positions, the group should find ways to overcome negative status-generalization biases.

DISCUSSION POINTS

1   Evaluation apprehension plays an important role in social facilitation and inhibition processes. How can members of a task group promote its beneficial effects (process gains), and how should they prevent its harmful effects (process losses)?

2   Explain why task groups are rarely characterized by *purely* cooperative interdependence, but almost always by mixed-motive interdependence.

3   Baron et al. (1992) draw a distinction between 'social loafing', when individuals' own contributions to the group cannot easily be identified and evaluated, and 'free-riding', when the individual believes that his or her own contributions to the group are dispensable. Discuss why increasing the identifiability of group members' contributions to the group may prove beneficial to counteract social loafing, but that additional (any suggestions?) interventions are needed to prevent free-riding.

4   Explain why making people believe that their fellow group members are very willing to cooperate is a double-edged sword if one aims to promote cooperation in a task group.

5   Imagine a stage race in the Tour de France, with three participating cycling teams, each containing four members. Suppose that the finishing times of the four members of team A are as follows: 1 hour and 46 minutes, 1h47, 1h47 and 1h49. The finishing times of the members of team B are 1h44, 1h45, 1h49 and 1h53. The finishing times of the members of team C are 1h45, 1h45, 1h46 and 1h51. Who is the winner, if the stage race is set up as a competition between individuals? Which team wins the stage race in the case of a competition between teams under an additive assembly rule? And under a disjunctive assembly rule? And under a conjunctive assembly rule? Under the latter two assembly rules, how will a cycling team respond when half-way through the race one of its members gets a flat tyre?

6   Discuss beneficial *as well as* harmful effects of strong normative conformity pressures in task groups.

7   Discuss research findings concerning role differentiation in task-oriented groups in relationship to expectation states theory.

FURTHER READING

Baron, S., Kerr, N. L., & Miller, N. (1992). *Group process, group decision, group action.* Buckingham: Open University Press. This book gives an excellent review of theory development and empirical studies in the area of group performance.

Cartwright, P., & Zander, A. (Eds.). (1968). *Group dynamics: Research and theory.* New York: Harper & Row. This collection of classic articles presents much of the seminal research and thinking in the area of group dynamics. The introductory chapters provide excellent reviews of the basic ideas expressed in the collected articles.

Forsyth, D. (1999). *Group dynamics.* Belmont, CA: Wadsworth. A well-written and comprehensive introduction to group dynamics.

Paulus, P. B. (Ed.). (1983). *Basic group processes.* New York: Springer. A collection of sophisticated reviews on group dynamics.

Worchel, S., Wood, W., & Simpson, J. A. (Eds.). (1992). *Group process and productivity.* London: Sage. Collected readings on small-group decision-making, status differentiation, group development and group norms.

Wilke, H., & Meertens, R. W. (1993). *Group performance.* London: Routledge. An up-to-date and comprehensive text about cognitive, reflective and communicative processes affecting task performance in groups.

Witte, E. H., & Davis, J. H. (Eds.). (1996). *Understanding group behaviour* (Vols. 1 and 2). Mahwah, NJ: Lawrence Erlbaum. A recent collection of studies on social-psychological processes in small groups.

KEY STUDIES

Diehl, M., & Stroebe, W. (1987). Productivity loss in brainstorming groups: Toward the solution of a riddle. *Journal of Personality and Social Psychology*, 53, 497–509.

Latané, B., Williams, K., & Harkins, S. (1979). Many hands make light work: The causes and consequences of social loafing. *Journal of Personality and Social Psychology*, 37, 822–32.

Intergroup Relations

Rupert Brown

15

OUTLINE

Intergroup behaviour occurs when members of one group act towards another in terms of their group membership rather than for personal or idiosyncratic reasons. It can be distinguished from interpersonal behaviour. In this chapter the major theories of intergroup behaviour are introduced and the key discoveries in the field are presented. Research from deliberately artificial 'minimal' settings is discussed alongside evidence from naturalistic contexts. The chapter concludes by discussing the ways in which intergroup discrimination and prejudice can be reduced.

KEY CONCEPTS

- Authoritarian personality
- Categorical differentiation
- Contact hypothesis
- Frustration–aggression
- Ingroup
- Intergroup behaviour
- Interpersonal–(inter)group continuum
- Intragroup homogeneity
- Minimal group paradigm
- Outgroup
- Prejudice
- Social identity
- Superordinate goal

Introduction

ULSTER PREPARES FOR ITS SADDEST MARCH: BEHIND THREE SMALL COFFINS

Today Northern Ireland witnesses the big Orange parades and the continuation of the Drumcree confrontation. Tomorrow it will witness the heart-rending journey of three under-sized coffins to premature graves, the victims of sectarianism. The Quinn boys – Richard, 11, Mark, 9, and Jason, 7 – [. . .] whose mother is Catholic, died in the flames when their County Antrim home was petrol-bombed by loyalists at 4 a.m. yesterday. (A tragic incident in Northern Ireland, as reported in *The Independent*, 13 July 1998)

FRANCE GOES WILD AT WORLD CUP VICTORY

Hundreds of thousands of exultant French people of all races poured onto the streets of Paris last night in wild celebration of France's stunning 3–0 victory over Brazil in the World Cup final. The Avenue des Champs Elysées was blocked with dancing, singing crowds within minutes of the final whistle at the Stade de France. (Post-victory celebrations in Paris, as reported in *The Independent*, 13 July 1998)

What is Intergroup Behaviour?

Intergroup behaviour Actions by members of one group towards members of another group.

Even the most casual reader of newspapers cannot help but notice headlines such as these, which frequently appear at our breakfast tables. The events referred to – occurring just a few hours apart in two European countries – are both instances of **intergroup behaviour**: that is, actions by members of one group towards members of another group. Coincidentally, the incidents concerned exemplify the negative and positive aspects of intergroup encounters: on the one hand, the latest act of violence in a long saga of sectarian conflict; on the other, a joyous multi-ethnic occasion in which previous intergroup tensions between French people of white European and North African origin were superseded by the national team's sporting success against another country. The national recategorization, about which we will have more to say later, was undoubtedly facilitated by the prominent presence in the French team of several ethnic minority group members.

This chapter will consider some of the ways intergroup behaviour can be understood from a social-psychological perspective. It begins by briefly examining some popular theories that attempt to explain intergroup conflict and prejudice, either as the expression of some particular personality type or as the result of temporary or chronic levels of frustration. As will be shown, these ideas are rather limited in their application. A much more fruitful approach is to see intergroup behaviour as a response to real or imagined group interests, and this is the subject of the second section. The third section takes up a question that arises out of the second: namely, does group membership in and of itself give rise to discriminatory behaviour? As we shall see, there are good grounds for thinking

PLATE 15.1   Positive intergroup behaviour: French football supporters of different ethnic groups unite to celebrate their team's victory

that it does; this leads naturally to the fourth section, where the link between group membership and social identity processes is explained. A central idea that emerges out of this is the importance for the individuals of being able to see their group as positively distinct from other groups. Finally, factors likely to lead to a reduction of intergroup conflict are discussed.

Popular Notions of Intergroup Conflict and Prejudice

What is involved in understanding prejudice?
How can we distinguish between interpersonal and group behaviour?

Prejudice as personality type

More common than the outright manifestation of intergroup conflict with which we began this chapter are various forms of **prejudice**

> **Prejudice**   A derogatory attitude or set of attitudes towards all or most of the members of a group.

PLATE 15.2 Negative consequences of intergroup behaviour: Protestant and Catholic funerals of victims of sectarianism in Northern Ireland

– that is, the holding of derogatory attitudes about the members of a social group (racism, sexism and so on). Such intergroup attitudes are commonly associated with the kind of violent encounter described earlier. The question is: where do these prejudiced attitudes originate? (See also chapter 3.)

One popular view is that prejudice is primarily a personality problem; the most influential example of this type of theory was that proposed by Adorno, Frenkel-Brunswick, Levinson and Sanford (1950). Their hypothesis was that an individual's social attitudes were 'an expression of deep-lying trends in personality' (Adorno et al., 1950, p. 1). Working from a Freudian perspective, they believed that most people's personality development involved the repression and redirection of various instinctive needs by the constraints of social existence. The parents were considered to be the main agents of this socialization process, and in 'normal' development they usually struck a balance between discipline and allowing the child self-expression. The problem with the bigot, argued Adorno et al., was that this balance was upset by the parents adopting an excessively harsh disciplinary regime and by being overanxious about the child's conformity to social mores. The effect of this, they believed, was that the child's natural aggression towards the parents (an inevitable consequence of being subjected to constraints)

was displaced on to alternative targets because of the feared consequences of displaying it directly. The likely choice of targets would
be those seen as weaker than or inferior to oneself – for example,
members of deviant groups or ethnic minorities. The end result,
therefore, was someone overdeferential towards authority figures
(since these symbolize the parents) and overtly hostile towards non-
ingroup members – the so-called '**authoritarian personality**'.

Authoritarian personality
A particular type of personality
– oversubmissive to authority
figures – which is also thought
to be particularly susceptible
to prejudice.

Adorno et al. developed a personality inventory – the F-scale – which was designed to distinguish between those with potentially fascist (or racist) tendencies
and those with more 'democratic' leanings. High-scoring adults on this scale had
rather different childhoods and more dogmatic attitudes than low scorers. The
association between authoritarianism and various forms of prejudice has been
confirmed in several intergroup contexts: for example, prejudice against ethnic
groups in the United States (Campbell & McCandless, 1951), against Muslims
in India (Sinha & Hassan, 1975), generalized ethnocentrism in the Netherlands
(Meloen, Hagendoorn, Raaijmakers, & Visser, 1988), antipathy towards mentally
ill people or sufferers of AIDS (Hanson & Blohm, 1974; Witt, 1985), and sexual
aggression of men towards women (Walker, Rowe, & Quinsey, 1993).

In the 1950s this approach attracted much criticism, with the F-scale itself coming under the closest scrutiny (Brown, 1965; Christie & Jahoda, 1954). The various controversies need not detain us here. However, it is important to note the limitations of this kind of 'individual differences' perspective (see also Billig, 1976; Brown, 1995). First, by locating prejudice in the dynamics of the individual personality, it underestimates the importance of current social situations in shaping people's attitudes. For example, in joining an organization or group, we are invariably influenced by the norms prevailing in it. Siegel and Siegel (1957) found that students who had been randomly assigned to liberal student dormitories showed a significant decrease in authoritarianism after a year, whilst those allocated to a more conservative sorority changed little. Second, extending this argument to the societal level, it tends to neglect socio-cultural determinants of prejudice. Pettigrew (1958) demonstrated this clearly in his study of prejudice in South Africa. Not surprisingly, he found that white South Africans showed very high levels of anti-black prejudice and yet they did not appear to have particularly high levels of authoritarianism. In other words, in terms of personality type, they were rather similar to 'normal' populations; so their overtly racist attitudes probably derived much more from the then prevailing societal norms in South Africa than from any personality dysfunction.

A third problem is the inability of the personality approach to explain the widespread *uniformity* of prejudice in certain societies or subgroups within societies. If prejudice is to be explained via individual *differences* amongst people, how can it then be manifested in a whole population, or at least in a vast majority? In prewar Nazi Germany – and in many other places since – consistently racist attitudes and behaviour were shown by hundreds of thousands of people who must have differed on most other psychological characteristics. A research illustration of this point is provided by Davey's (1983) study of interethnic attitudes amongst English children. In one task, involving sharing out sweets between unknown members of different ethnic groups shown in photographs, nearly 60 per cent of the white children discriminated in their sweet distribution – that is, they gave more to the white children shown in the photographs than to the others. It is hard to imagine that all these children had been exposed to the special kind of family dynamics alleged to cause prejudice.

A fourth problem concerns the *historical specificity* of prejudice. As an example, consider the increased incidence of attacks against migrant workers in Germany and against Asian groups in Britain in the early 1990s. These increases in racism took place over the space of just a few years, much too short a time for whole generations of German or British families to have adopted new forms of child-rearing practices giving rise to authoritarian and prejudiced children. (See Altemeyer, 1988, and Doty, Peterson, & Winter, 1991, for examples of research which has documented temporal changes in authoritarianism.) Examples such as these strongly suggest that the attitudes held by members of different groups towards each other have more to do with the objective relations between the groups – relations of political conflict or alliance, economic interdependence and so on – than with the familial relations in which they grew up.

The 'scapegoat' theory of prejudice: intergroup aggression as a result of frustration

Between 1882 and 1930 there were nearly 5,000 reported cases of lynchings in the United States. The vast majority of these involved black victims and occurred in southern states. Hovland and Sears (1940), who first brought these gruesome statistics to psychologists' attention, noticed that there was a remarkable correspondence between the annual variation in these killings and various farming economic indicators (farming being the principal industry in southern states): as the economy receded and times got hard, so the number of lynchings increased (see also Hepworth & West, 1988).

What might account for this correlation of economic recession with anti-black violence? Hovland and Sears (1940) believed it was caused by frustration. Drawing upon Dollard, Doob, Miller, Mowrer and Sears' (1939) **frustration–aggression** theory, they hypothesized that the hardships experienced in a depressed economy raised people's levels of frustration, which, in turn, led to increased aggression. According to frustration–aggression theory, aggression is often not directed at the true source of the frustration (e.g., the capitalist system that caused the recession), but is often diverted onto vulnerable and easily accessible targets such as members of minority groups.

Frustration–aggression (hypothesis) Aggression is always a result of frustration.

Attempts to confirm this so-called 'scapegoat' theory of prejudice have met with mixed success. Miller and Bugelski (1948) conducted an experiment in which young men in a camp, eagerly anticipating a night on the town, were suddenly told that their evening out was cancelled. Before this frustrating event the men's attitudes towards two national groups were measured, and again afterwards. These attitudes became significantly less favourable after the frustration, a clear confirmation of the frustration–aggression 'displacement' hypothesis since these two groups could have had no conceivable responsibility for the men's plight. On the other hand, other experiments have yielded more equivocal results (e.g., Burnstein & McRae, 1962; Stagner & Congdon, 1955).

It was inconsistencies like these, as well as some other conceptual and empirical difficulties, which led to the decline in the popularity of frustration–aggression theory as an explanation of prejudice (Billig, 1976; Brown, 2000). Perhaps the most serious of these problems was the consistent finding that *absolute* levels of hardship and frustration often seemed to be less potent instigators of aggression than a sense of *relative* deprivation. We return to this idea later in the chapter. Another criticism of the frustration–aggression approach is that it assumes that intergroup behaviour is primarily emotionally driven (i.e., by frustration) rather than being goal directed. As we shall see, this assumption is rather questionable.

Interpersonal vs. group behaviour

In attempting to explain intergroup behaviour by means of variations in personality types or levels of frustration, the above approaches make the assumption that people's behaviour in group settings is essentially similar to their behaviour in all other situations. Thus, whether we are alone, or interacting with one or two other close friends, or participating in some event involving a group which is important to us, our behaviour is still seen to be mainly determined by the same psychological variables.

There are, however, a number of difficulties with this hypothesis. First, it cannot easily account for the widespread uniformity of behaviour which is so typical of situations where groups are psychologically salient. This is particularly problematic for any personality-type explanations, as we saw earlier. A second, and closely related, problem concerns situations where several thousand members of different groups are involved – like French victory celebrations described at the start of this chapter. Here, the number of different possible interpersonal relationships between the protagonists must have been enormous, and yet the behaviour was observably predictable and uniform. Finally, people's behaviour, besides being more uniform in group settings, is also often qualitatively different. For example, in research on bargaining it has been found that during the course of union–management negotiations, there are differences between exchanges involving *interparty* interaction and those involving *interpersonal* discussion. In general, the former are characterized by more references to the two groups' objectives, a 'tougher' bargaining stance, and a greater influence of the relative strengths of the two sides' cases. During interpersonal encounters, on the other hand, there are more positive references to one's opponents, the social orientation is of a more 'problem-solving' kind, and the outcome is less predictable from objective features of the groups' negotiating position (Stephenson, 1978). Similarly, the effects of attitudinal similarity, which at the interpersonal level nearly always seem to promote attraction (Byrne, 1971; see chapter 12), are more complex at the intergroup level since *either* attraction *or* repulsion can result under the appropriate conditions (Brown, 1984a; Diehl, 1988).

It was considerations like these which led Tajfel (1978) to suggest that it is important to distinguish between interpersonal and intergroup behaviour and, consequently, to argue that theories addressing problems at the one level might not easily be extrapolated to explain phenomena at the other. *Interpersonal behaviour* means acting as an *individual* with some idiosyncratic characteristics and a unique set of personal relationships with others (e.g., J. Smith of certain physical appearance, intelligence and personality, and with various friendships). *Intergroup behaviour*, on the other hand, means acting as a *group member* (e.g., behaving as a *sectarian terrorist*). In the first case the various social categories one belongs to are less important than the constellation of individual and interpersonal dynamics. In the second case the reverse is true; *who* one is as a person is much less important than the religious groups you and your targets happen to belong to.

TABLE 15.1   The interpersonal–group continuum

Factor	Interpersonal	Group
Presence of two or more social categories?	Obscured or not relevant	Clearly visible and salient
Uniformity of behaviour and attitudes within one group?	Low	High
Stereotyped or uniform treatment of other group members?	Low	High

What Tajfel proposed, therefore, was that any sequence of social behaviour can be depicted as falling somewhere along a *continuum* defined by the two extremes of interpersonal and intergroup behaviour. Quite where it falls depends on three factors. The first is the clarity with which different social categories can be identified. Where social divisions like black and white, man and woman, are clearly discernible, this will tend to locate the behaviour towards the intergroup end. Where the category differences are less clear or less relevant, the behaviour is more likely to be interpersonal. The second is the extent to which the behaviour within each group is variable or uniform. Interpersonal behaviour will show the normal range of individual differences; when groups are salient, people's behaviour becomes more similar. The third factor is how far one person's treatment of or attitude towards others is idiosyncratic or uniform and predictable. In our interpersonal dealings we negotiate a variety of ways of responding to those we know; intergroup encounters, on the other hand, are marked by stereotyped perceptions and behaviours.

It is worth noting that these three criteria do not just distinguish interpersonal behaviour from *intergroup* behaviour. Turner (1982) pointed out that behaviour within the group (*intragroup* behaviour) is also often marked by an awareness of category boundaries, uniformity of behaviour and stereotypical perceptions. For this reason, Brown and Turner (1981) proposed that the continuum which Tajfel (1978) had identified should be extended and relabelled as the **interpersonal–group continuum** (see table 15.1).

Interpersonal–(inter)group continuum   A continuous dimension of social behaviour distinguishing between actions performed as an individual and actions performed as a group member.

Intergroup Behaviour as a Response to Real or Imagined Group Interests

How is intergroup behaviour related to the goals of the group involved?

Instead of regarding intergroup prejudice as a problem associated with a particular personality type or level of frustration, it may be more useful to view it as the 'normal' response of ordinary people to the intergroup situation confronting them. One factor that seems to be particularly important is the nature of the respective goals of the groups concerned: are the goals *incompatible*, so that what one group is seeking will be at the expense of another; or are they *concordant*, so that both groups are working towards the same objective and may even need each other for its attainment? An example of the former case would be the relationship between workers and their employers where the one's wages are at the expense of the other's profits. An example of concordant goals would be when minority political parties form coalitions to achieve political power (e.g., the right-wing parties in Italy in 1994, or Labour and the Liberal Democrats in Scotland in 1999).

Within social psychology the best-known proponent of this approach is Sherif (1966). At the heart of Sherif's theory is the proposition that group members' intergroup attitudes and behaviour will tend to reflect the objective interests of their group *vis-à-vis* other groups. Where these interests conflict, then their group's cause is more likely to be furthered by a competitive orientation towards the rival group, which is often easily extended to include prejudiced attitudes and even overtly hostile behaviour. At the same time, the success of the **ingroup** in achieving the goal is likely to be furthered by very positive attitudes towards other ingroup members, thereby engendering high morale and cohesion. Where, on the other hand, the groups' interests coincide, then it is more functional for the group members to adopt a cooperative and friendly attitude towards the **outgroup**. If this is reciprocated, then a positive joint outcome is more probable.

Ingroup   A group to which a person belongs, or thinks he or she belongs.

Outgroup   A group to which a person does not belong, or thinks he or she does not belong.

Sherif's summer-camp studies

To demonstrate the validity of this perspective Sherif, together with his colleagues, conducted three longitudinal field experiments which have become classics in the literature (Sherif & Sherif, 1953; Sherif, White, & Harvey, 1955; Sherif, Harvey, White, Hood, & Sherif, 1961). The full design included three stages: group formation, intergroup conflict and conflict reduction. To effect this design, Sherif and his colleagues arranged for the experiments to be conducted in the context of a boys' summer camp. The boys themselves, aged around 12 years, had all been carefully screened before being invited to the camp, and only those who seemed to be psychologically well adjusted were accepted. In addition, none of the boys knew each other before coming to the camp. Although this was a highly select and unrepresentative sample, it did ensure that any behaviour they subsequently exhibited could not be attributed to a prior history of social or psychological deprivation, or to pre-existing personal relationships between the boys.

Group formation

In the first stage, the large group of 22 to 24 children was split up into the two experimental groups of the study. In the first two experiments, in addition to matching on various physical and psychological characteristics, it was also arranged to have the majority of each boy's best friends in the *outgroup* (these friendships had formed in the first few days of the camp). In the third experiment, the boys never actually met each other prior to the groups being formed, and were initially camped some distance from each other, unaware of the other group's presence. For some days the children engaged in various activities in these groups without, however, having much to do with the other group. Although the other group did not figure much in their thinking, it is interesting to note that in the first two experiments the observers did record some instances of comparisons between the groups; in these comparisons 'the edge was given to one's own group' (Sherif, 1966, p. 80). Furthermore, in the third study, where the groups did not know of each other's existence initially, on being informed of the presence of the other group several boys spontaneously suggested that the other group be challenged to some sporting contest. As we shall see, it is significant that these expressions of ingroup favouritism occurred before the intergroup conflict phase of the experiment had actually been introduced.

Intergroup competition

A series of intergroup contests was then announced (e.g., softball, tug-of-war, etc.). The overall winner of these contests would receive a cup and each member of this successful group would be given a gleaming new penknife – just the kind of prize every 12-year-old boy covets. The losers would receive nothing. In this way, an objective conflict of interest was introduced between the groups. In technical terms, they had moved from being independent of one another to being negatively *interdependent*: what one group gained, the other lost. With the advent of this conflict stage the boys' behaviour changed dramatically. Whereas in the first stage the two groups had coexisted more or less peaceably, they were now transformed into two hostile factions, never losing an opportunity to deride the outgroup and, in some instances, physically attack it. In a variety of micro-experiments, disguised as games, Sherif and his associates observed consistent ingroup favouritism in judgements, attitudes and sociometric preferences. An example of one of these was the 'bean toss' contest, where members of the groups had to collect up as many beans as possible in one minute from an area of grass where they had been scattered. Each boy's collection was purportedly projected onto a screen for a brief exposure and his fellow team members had to estimate his performance (in fact, a standard number of beans was projected each time). As can be seen from figure 15.1, each group judged fellow group members' performance to be superior to that from members of the outgroup.

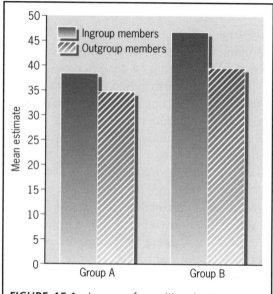

FIGURE 15.1 Ingroup favouritism in group performance estimates during intergroup competition (Sherif et al., 1961, table 5)

These behaviours were all the more remarkable when it is remembered that in the first two studies at least, every boy's best friends had been placed in the *other* group. How fragile those initial interpersonal relationships proved to be in the face of the changing intergroup relationship!

Conflict reduction

Superordinate goal A goal desired by two or more groups but which can only be achieved through the groups acting together, not by any single group on its own.

Having so easily generated such fierce competition, the researchers attempted to reduce the conflict by introducing a series of **superordinate goals** for the groups – that is, goals which both groups desired but which were unattainable by one group by its own efforts alone. One such superordinate goal was engineered by arranging for the camp truck to break down some miles from the camp. Since it was nearly lunchtime, the children had a clear common interest in getting the truck started to return them to camp. However, the truck was too heavy to be push-started by one group on its own. Only by both groups pulling on the tug-of-war rope attached to the front bumper – the same rope which they had used in *contest* only days earlier! – could the truck be moved. After a number of scenarios like this, a marked change was observed in the boys' behaviour. They became much less aggressive towards members of the other group, and on a number of quantitative indices showed a clear reduction in the amount

PLATE 15.3   A tug-of-war *between* groups is an example of negative interdependence

of ingroup favouritism. For example, the boys were asked to rate each group on a series of evaluative traits ('tough', 'friendly', 'sneaky', etc.). Figure 15.2 portrays the proportion of negative traits that were attributed to the outgroup before and after the engagement with superordinate goals. As can be seen, these underwent a sharp decline in the third phase of the experiment.

On the face of it, these experiments seemed to provide strong support for Sherif's theory. The behaviour of these ordinary, well-adjusted children was shown to vary systematically with the changing intergroup relationship. More-over, the changes in the boys' behaviour were too widespread and too rapid to be attributable to any enduring personality disposition. The intergroup hostility was just as evident in the 'winning' groups as it was in the presumably more frus-trated 'losing' groups. Both the popular theories considered earlier, then, were shown up as deficient by these findings. These deficiencies were underlined by later research. In a variety of studies it has been invariably found that groups which either adopt or have imposed on them 'win–lose' orientations show more inter-group discrimination or outgroup aggression than those with more collaborative orientations (e.g., Brown, Condor, Matthews, Wade, & Williams, 1986; Ryen & Kahn, 1975; Struch & Schwartz, 1989).

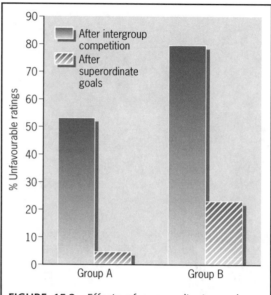

FIGURE 15.2 Effects of superordinate goals on negative stereotypes of the outgroup (Sherif et al., 1961, table 4)

PLATE 15.4 An example of a superordinate goal: both groups *pull together* to move a broken-down truck

Mere Group Membership as a Source of Intergroup Discrimination

Why is intergroup discrimination so easy to elicit?

In the previous section we saw how important intergroup goal relationships were in shaping group members' attitudes and behaviour towards both their own group and various outgroups. However, an important question remains unanswered from all this research: does the mere fact of belonging to one group have consequences for our attitudes towards other groups? Does being of one nationality (or religion or ethnicity or class), in and of itself, generate predictable orientations towards members from another country (religion and so on)? It is this question we address in this section.

Minimal group experiments

Rabbie and Horwitz (1969) were the first to investigate this issue. Following Lewin (1948), they reasoned that the essential condition for the arousal of group feelings was the perception of some interdependence of fate amongst the group members. Accordingly, they arranged for schoolchildren who did not know each other to be divided at random into two groups of four persons. Members of the two groups were given identification badges (green or blue), and were initially seated either side of a screen so that they could see only members of their own group. In the control condition, that was the extent of their group experience. In the experimental conditions, on the other hand, the groups further experienced a 'common fate' by being given – or by being deprived of – some new transistor radios. Subsequently in all conditions, the screen separating the groups was removed and each person was asked to stand up and read out some personal biographical details about himself or herself, while the other children rated him or her on a number of scales. Rabbie and Horwitz (1969) found that in the experimental conditions these impressionistic ratings were markedly affected by the person's group affiliation: ingroup members were consistently rated more favourably than outgroup members. In the control condition, however, no such ingroup bias was observed, although in a subsequent extension of the experiment (which increased the sample size), some biases were observed on two of the scales (Horwitz & Rabbie, 1982). Nevertheless, the conclusion from this experiment seemed to be that classification into a group *by itself* exerted little influence on group members' judgements. Only when that classification coincided with some common experience of reward or deprivation did group-related perceptions emerge.

That conclusion proved to be premature, however. Tajfel, Flament, Billig and Bundy (1971) took the **minimal group paradigm** one stage further and showed that mere categorization *was* sufficient to elicit intergroup discrimination. Like Rabbie and Horwitz, they assigned schoolboys to one of two groups on a very arbitrary basis – their alleged preference for one of two abstract artists Paul Klee and Vassilij Kandinsky. However, in this experiment the children knew only which group they themselves had been assigned to; the identities of their fellow ingroup and outgroup members were kept hidden by the use of code numbers. Then, under the general pretext of the experiment ('a study of decision-making'), the children were asked to allocate money to various recipients using specially prepared booklets of decision matrices (see table 15.2 for an example). The identity of the recipients on each page was unknown, but their group affiliation was revealed. To eliminate self-interest as a possible motive in the allocations, the children were never able to award money to themselves.

The results were clear. Although they made some effort to be fair in their allocations, the children showed a persistent tendency to award more money to ingroup recipients than to those whom they believed belonged to the other group. This was true even when, in absolute terms, the ingrouper might be worse off. For example, in the matrix shown in table 15.2, the mean response from people in the Kandinsky group was somewhere between the [11,12] and [13,13] options. Notice that this choice results in the Kandinsky recipient actually receiving 6 or 7 points *less* than he might otherwise have done, but, crucially, he thereby receives more than the Klee recipient. The results are rather surprising when one

TABLE 15.2   A sample matrix from the Tajfel et al. (1971) minimal group experiment

Numbers are rewards for:												
Member 74 of Klee group	25	23	21	19	17	15	13	11	9	7	5	3	1
Member 44 of Kandinsky group	19	18	17	16	15	14	13	12	11	10	9	8	7

Note:

(a) On each page participants must choose one box.

(b) This is one of several different types of matrix used. It was designed to measure the tendency to *maximize the difference* (MD) between ingroup and outgroup recipients. In the experiment, this matrix would be presented to each participant at least twice: once as shown, and once with the group affiliations of the two recipients reversed.

(c) In the original experiments, 1 point = 0.1 p. Given that each booklet contained some 16 pages (each with point values ranging from 1 to 29), the total amount of money that each person thought he was dispensing was not inconsiderable. In 1970 this probably amounted to about £0.50 which, at today's prices, is equivalent to more than £3.00.

considers how sparse this social setting really was. The children were allocated to two meaningless groups on a flimsy criterion. They never interacted with members of their own or the other group. The two groups had no current or past relationship with each other. And yet, when asked to allocate sums of money to anonymous others, the children consistently favoured ingroup members over outgroupers. Simply being assigned to a group can, after all, have predictable effects on intergroup behaviour.

Intergroup discrimination in this minimal group situation has proved to be a remarkably robust phenomenon. In more than two dozen independent studies in several different countries using a wide range of experimental participants of both sexes (from young children to adults), essentially the same result has been found: the mere act of allocating people into arbitrary social categories is sufficient to elicit biased judgements and discriminatory behaviour (see Brewer, 1979; Tajfel, 1982).

Despite this empirical consensus, the minimal group paradigm has attracted controversy. Space does not permit a discussion of all the contentious issues. However, it is worth making the following observations on some of the more important ones. The first concerns whether participants in these experiments are really showing ingroup favouritism or, alternatively, are displaying behaviour better described as some form of *fairness* (Branthwaite, Doyle, & Lightbown, 1979; Turner, 1980). It seems clear that people do show a propensity towards equalizing ingroup and outgroup outcomes in these situations. However, it is also true that they are nearly always more 'fair' to ingroupers than to outgroupers. In other words, although people's choices cluster around the centre or 'fair' point (e.g. [13,13] in table 15.2), when an ingroup member is the recipient on the top line the responses tend to be to the left of centre; when an outgroup member is the beneficiary on the same line, the responses move to the *right* of centre. Furthermore, the evidence for this persistent bias is derived not just from particular reward-allocation matrices but from a variety of other dependent measures, which have also shown that ingroup members or products receive more favourable ratings than equivalent outgroup stimuli (Brewer, 1979; Brown, Tajfel, & Turner, 1980).

A second issue concerns whether the pervasive discrimination observed in the allocation of rewards can be generalized to the distribution of penalties or aversive stimuli. Hewstone, Fincham and Jaspars (1981) modified the normal paradigm by asking group members to *subtract* money from ingroup and outgroup recipients (who had previously been allocated an initial sum). Although some evidence of ingroup bias was observed as a consequence of categorization, the levels were lower than those obtained with the standard measures. Mummendey et al. (1992) extended this principle by asking participants to distribute (what they thought would be) durations of an unpleasantly high-pitched tone to ingroup and outgroup members. This seemed to eliminate completely ingroup favouritism, and strategies of equalizing outcomes (or fairness) or minimizing the total amount of aversive stimulation were much more in evidence.

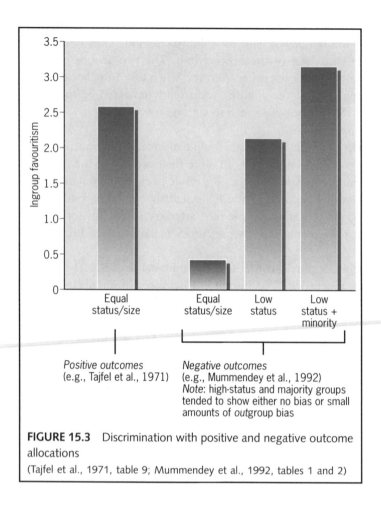

Positive outcomes
(e.g., Tajfel et al., 1971)

Negative outcomes
(e.g., Mummendey et al., 1992)
Note: high-status and majority groups
tended to show either no bias or small
amounts of *out*group bias

FIGURE 15.3   Discrimination with positive and negative outcome
allocations
(Tajfel et al., 1971, table 9; Mummendey et al., 1992, tables 1 and 2)

Intergroup discrimination re-emerged only in certain circumstances – for
example, when the participants were in a subordinate or minority status group
(figure 15.3, and Otten, Mummendey, & Blanz, 1996). The explanation for this
difference between positive and negative outcomes is still not clear (Mummendey
& Otten, 1998). It could simply be that in the relatively aseptic laboratory
conditions in which such experiments are carried out, there are strong social
desirability norms against penalizing or harming a fellow participant. This would
have the effect of raising the threshold for displaying ingroup favouritism. On
the other hand, it could be that being asked to do something so socially 'inappropriate' as inflicting discomfort on their peers places participants in a common
predicament, reducing the significance of the original minimal categories and
making more salient some new superordinate grouping ('we the participants in
the experiment'; Mummendey & Otten, 1998). Such a cognitive restructuring
of the situation, as we shall see later, could cause a change in discriminatory
behaviour.

Explanations of intergroup discrimination in minimal groups

It is one thing to establish a phenomenon; it is quite another to explain it. What underlies the apparently gratuitous discrimination in these most minimal of groups? One explanation is in terms of norms (Tajfel et al., 1971). According to this view, being made aware that one is a member of a group might, in most of the cultures in which the experiments have been conducted, evoke associations with teams and team games. These might make a competitive norm highly salient and lead to the unequal allocation of money between the groups in an attempt to 'win'. That this competitiveness is not full-blown might be explained by a countervailing norm of fairness – another value attribute in Western cultures. This form of explanation is supported by the findings from a cross-cultural study, which found variations in the extent of minimal group discrimination among children of European, Samoan and Maori origin (Wetherell, 1982). All three groups showed clear ingroup favouritism, although the latter two showed somewhat less than the first.

Attractive though such an account may be, it has at least two shortcomings that have inhibited its widespread adoption (Turner, 1980). First, such an explanation needs to be able to predict in advance which of a number of norms will predominate in any particular situation. After all, there are a variety of cultural norms that might be relevant: fairness, as we have seen, is one; profit maximization – surely salient in most Western countries – is another; equity is yet another. Without some theory of norm salience, we are only able to explain after the event why a particular pattern of discrimination occurred. A second and related criticism is that normative accounts are by their nature rather too general. They do not really permit one to predict the systematic variations in response to the minimal group situation which it is possible to observe even *within one culture* (Turner, 1981). For example, introducing group-status or size differences, or changing the nature of the recipients, all have reliable effects on levels of discrimination (Brown & Deschamps, 1980–1; Mummendey et al., 1992; Sachdev & Bourhis, 1987).

A second explanation offers some hope of avoiding these problems; this explanation is in terms of categorization processes (e.g., Doise, 1976). Some earlier work had shown that if a simple categorization (e.g., A/B) is imposed on a set of physical stimuli (e.g., lines of different lengths) such that the shorter lines all fall into group A and the longer ones into group B, then judgements of stimuli falling into different classes will become distorted, with the effect that perceived differences *between* the two categories become exaggerated (Tajfel & Wilkes, 1963). A similar phenomenon has been observed with more social stimuli: attitude statements which are categorized as having come from one of two sources may be seen as more different from one another than those which have not been so classified (McGarty & Penny, 1988). Doise (1976) argues that these judgemental biases are the result of a fundamental cognitive process, that of

Categorical differentiation
The exaggeration of real differences between two categories.

categorical differentiation. He suggests that in order for social categories to be useful ordering and simplifying devices, it is important that they discriminate clearly between class and non-class members. Thus, the function of the differentiation process is to sharpen the distinctions between the categories – and, relatedly, to blur the differences *within* them – so as to better organize and structure our mental and social worlds. If we apply this analysis to the minimal group context, it suggests that the situation confronting the experimental participants is sufficiently ill defined for them to latch on to the previously meaningless categories (Klee and Kandinsky) and use them to make sense of it. Once that particular (and only) classification has been adopted, the inevitable categorical differentiation occurs, and occurs in the only way possible here – by allocating different amounts to ingroup and outgroup recipients.

Intragroup homogeneity   The extent to which members of a group are seen as similar to each other on various attributes.

Directly related to these categorization processes is another phenomenon, that of perceived **intragroup homogeneity** (see chapter 5 for a fuller discussion of categorization). As noted earlier, categorization does not only result in the accentuation of differences between categories, it also causes members of the same category to be seen as more similar to one another. This perception of homogeneity is often not a symmetrical process: one group is usually seen as more homogeneous than the other (Devos, Cornby, & Deschamps, 1996). A common finding is that outgroups are seen as more homogeneous than ingroups: 'They' are all the same, but 'We' are all different (Quattrone & Jones, 1980). Why might this be? Linville, Fischer and Salovey (1989) have suggested it is caused by our different knowledge of and familiarity with members of the ingroup and the outgroup: because we are likely to know more ingroup members, our perception of the ingroup should be more complex and differentiated. This is unlikely to be the whole explanation, however. Greater perceived homogeneity in the outgroup is not always correlated with the numbers of people known (Brown & Smith, 1989; Jones, Wood, & Quattrone, 1981), and can also be observed even in minimal group settings where no one is known in the ingroup or the outgroup (Wilder, 1984). An alternative explanation is that it is not the numbers of people known that is important, but the nature of ingroup and outgroup categories themselves (Park, Judd, & Ryan, 1991). According to this view, perceptions of groups are not based on a tally of specific ingroup and outgroup acquaintances but are derived from the prototypical member of each and some estimate of variability around this typical person. The reason that the ingroup is sometimes seen as more variable is that it is more important (because it contains the self), more concrete (again, because at least one member is very well known), and consists of a greater number of meaningful subgroups (Park, Ryan, & Judd, 1992).

This explanation cannot be the complete story either because it fails to account for the opposite phenomenon: the perception that the ingroup is more homogeneous than the outgroup (Simon, 1992a). This tends to happen when the ingroup is much smaller than the outgroup (Brown & Smith, 1989; Simon & Brown,

1987), and on judgemental dimensions which are important to the ingroup (Brown & Wootton-Millward, 1993; Kelly, 1989; Simon, 1992b). Underlying this effect may be processes of social identification (Simon, 1992a; see below).

The categorization model offers a simple and powerful explanation of intergroup biases in terms of a single cognitive process. However, there is one important limitation to such an explanation: it cannot readily account for the asymmetry which is such a pervasive feature of intergroup differentiation. In other words, why does the ingroup (and not the outgroup) come off best in intergroup perceptions, judgements and resource allocations? The categorization approach can account for the fact that groups are made more distinctive from one another, but it cannot explain why that distinctiveness is often valued positively for the ingroup and negatively for the outgroup. To understand what underlies that *positive* distinctiveness we need a new concept, that of *social identity*. This idea will be discussed shortly, but before doing so another explanation for minimal intergroup discrimination will be briefly considered.

Rabbie, Schot and Visser (1989) have suggested that what really motivates people's discriminatory behaviour in minimal group experiments is self-interest. At first glance this seems paradoxical, since the paradigm was designed specifically to eliminate self-interest as a possible motive by preventing participants from ever allocating rewards directly to themselves. However, Rabbie et al. argue that, while such *direct* self-interest considerations may be eliminated, they could still be operative if participants believe that the members of each group will tend to favour each other. Hence, they too may try to follow this implicit norm so as to maximize the benefits to fellow ingroup members and hence, by reciprocity, themselves. To test this idea, Rabbie et al. (1989) added two variations to the normal minimal group paradigm. In one condition they specified that participants would only receive what other ingroup members gave them; in another they would only get what *outgroup* members allocated. Altering the participants' perceived dependence on others in this way had a predictable effect on their own reward distributions: those dependent solely on the ingroup increased their ingroup favouritism somewhat compared to the normal condition, while those dependent wholly on the outgroup sharply decreased it, and even showed *outgroup* favouritism. Locksley, Ortiz and Hepburn (1980) also found evidence that when participants believed ingroup members had given less and outgroup members more than expected, the usual ingroup favouritism disappeared.

These experiments show that people are sensitive to self-interest considerations when these are made more explicit. However, they do not demonstrate conclusively that participants' expectations of others' behaviour are the sole determinant of their own allocation decisions. Indeed, Diehl (1989) showed that the link between reciprocity expectations and actual behaviour may not be a simple one. In this experiment, participants were given false feedback about outgroup members' *intended* (and not actual) allocation strategies. Subsequently, they were asked to indicate their own intentions and then actually distribute the rewards. There was some correlation between participants' own intentions and their assumptions about what outgroup members would do. However, when it came to their *actual* behaviour, there was no reliable difference between those who expected the outgroup to be fair and those who anticipated it to be discriminatory. Thus, perceptions of interdependence and mutual reciprocity, while they clearly play a role in guiding group members' behaviour, seem not to provide a complete explanation for intergroup discrimination; other motives seem to be at work, too (Bourhis, Turner, & Gagnon, 1997).

Group Membership and Social Identity

What is social identity and what are its consequences for intergroup behaviour?

Who am I? Who are we?

Segmenting the world into a manageable number of categories does not just help us to simplify and make sense of it; it also serves one other very important function – to define who we are. Not only do we classify others as members of this or that group, but we also locate *ourselves* in relation to those same groups. Our sense of identity, in other words, is closely bound up with our various group memberships. As a simple demonstration of this, readers may ask themselves the following question: 'Who am I?' Analysis of people's answers to that question (repeated a number of times) usually reveals several (if not the majority) of the self-descriptions referring to group affiliations, either explicitly (e.g., 'I am a member of the Orange Order') or implicitly through reference to the occupation of social roles (e.g., 'I am a student'), to gender (e.g., 'I am a woman') or to nationality (e.g., 'I am French') (Kuhn & McPartland, 1954).

Social identity A person's sense of who he or she is, derived from his or her group membership(s).

This idea that **social identity** derives from group membership has a long history (e.g., Mead, 1934), but it was not until more recently that it was realized that social identity processes might have implications for intergroup behaviour (Tajfel, 1978; Tajfel & Turner, 1986). This can happen if we assume, with Tajfel and Turner (1986), that by and large people prefer to have a positive self-concept rather than a negative one. Since part of our self-concept (or identity) is defined in terms of group affiliations, it follows that there will also be a preference to view those ingroups positively rather than negatively. But how do we arrive at such an evaluation? Tajfel and Turner (1986) extend Festinger's (1954) social comparison theory and suggest that our group evaluations are essentially relative in nature; we assess our own group's worth by comparing it with other groups. The outcome of these intergroup comparisons is critical for us because indirectly it contributes to our own self-esteem. If our own group can be perceived as clearly superior on some dimension of value (like skill or sociability), then we too can bask in that reflected glory. Cialdini et al. (1976) provided a nice illustration of this phenomenon amongst college football supporters. After their college's successes in football games, supporters were more likely to be seen wearing college insignia and clothing than after defeats. Their willingness to be identified as belonging to the group seemed to be associated with the group's fortunes in intergroup encounters (see also Snyder, Lassegard, & Ford, 1986). Because of our presumed need for a positive self-concept, it follows that there will be a bias in these comparisons to look for ways in which the ingroup can, indeed, be distinguished favourably from outgroups. Tajfel calls this 'the establishment of positive distinctiveness' (Tajfel, 1978, p. 83).

How can this theory – social identity theory, as it is known – help to explain the persistent tendency for people to display intergroup discrimination, even in as barren a context as the minimal group paradigm? Consider again the situation facing the experimental participants. They have been allocated to one of two equally meaningless groups. Indeed, so meaningless are they that there is literally nothing to differentiate them except the group labels and the fact that they themselves are in one group and not the other. They are referred to by code numbers, thus leading to feelings of anonymity. Given this anonymity, the only possible source of identity, primitive though it may be, is their ingroup. However, that group is initially indistinguishable from the other group and hence, according to the theory, contributes little positive to its members' self-esteem. Accordingly, the pressures of distinctiveness come into play and the members of both groups seek to differentiate their own group positively from the other by the only means which the experimenters have provided – by allocating more money to fellow ingroupers than to outgroupers. Recall, also, that they will often do this even at the cost of some absolute gain to the ingroup (the maximizing difference strategy).

Social identity theory, then, presumes some direct causal connection between intergroup discrimination and self-esteem. Abrams and Hogg (1988) have pointed out that this link could take either or both of two forms. It could be that people show intergroup discrimination in order to enhance their social identity (and hence raise their self-esteem), simply on the grounds that positive self-regard is generally to be preferred to a neutral or negative self-concept. Alternatively, it could be that prior low self-esteem, perhaps deriving from membership in a low-status group, causes intergroup discrimination in order to raise it to 'normal' levels. The evidence for both of these processes is somewhat equivocal although, on balance, the first has received more support than the latter (Rubin & Hewstone, 1998). Thus, studies have found that in minimal group situations, participants who were denied the usual opportunity to display intergroup discrimination showed lower self-esteem than those who were not (Lemyre & Smith, 1985; Oakes & Turner, 1980). This suggests that discrimination causes self-esteem to rise. On the other hand, studies which have investigated the opposite direction of causality have usually produced less supportive evidence. For example, several studies have found that it is groups with *enhanced* status or power or individuals with higher self-esteem who seem to show greater ingroup favouritism (Crocker & Luhtanen, 1990;

Crocker, Thompson, McGraw, & Ingermann, 1987; Sachdev & Bourhis, 1985, 1987). The more general effects of status on intergroup behaviour will be discussed further below, but, at the very least, the available evidence suggests that the hypothesis that self-esteem plays a causal role in controlling intergroup discrimination can no longer be sustained.

Social identity theory, then, has sought to provide an account of people's readiness to favour these most minimal of ingroups. But its applicability is not limited to these rather contrived experimental situations; part of its attraction has been its ability to make sense of a wide range of phenomena in naturalistic contexts. We shall describe just two examples; for others, see Tajfel (1982) and Brown (1984b).

Intergroup differentiation in naturalistic contexts

There is a common tendency for groups of workers in industrialized countries to be concerned about the size of wage relativities *vis-à-vis* other groups of workers. This was particularly prevalent in the British engineering industry in the 1970s but, historically, examples of disputes centring on differentials go back at least as far as the early nineteenth century. What is interesting about these industrial conflicts is that they may have little 'realistic' basis in the sense that there is rarely an explicit conflict of interest between the groups concerned. The other important aspect of differentials disputes is – as the words imply – that they are about the *difference* between groups rather than about their levels of wages in absolute terms. These two points were borne out very clearly in a study of an aircraft engineering factory by Brown (1978). He showed, using matrices adapted from the minimal group laboratory, that shop stewards from one department in the factory would be prepared to sacrifice as much as £2 per week in absolute terms in order to increase their differential over another group to £1. That this intergroup differentiation cut across the group's 'real' interests was confirmed in another part of the study, where the same stewards were asked to respond to a hypothetical superordinate goals scenario involving factory-wide redundancies. Only a minority of those interviewed responded to this scenario by proposing cooperative strategies involving other groups. These findings seemed much more explicable by social identity theory than by Sherif's theory, which was described earlier.

A second illustration is provided by children's stereotypes and friendship preferences. It might be thought that children, especially of primary school age or younger, might be unlikely to show much sign of intergroup discrimination because they have had so little exposure to the 'tainting' influence of societal norms and prejudices. Unfortunately, the evidence shows that they, like their adult caretakers, are prone to display rather marked ingroup favouritism and outgroup stereotyping. Take gender, for instance. From as early as three years of age – or even younger in girls – children show a strong preference to play with same-sex

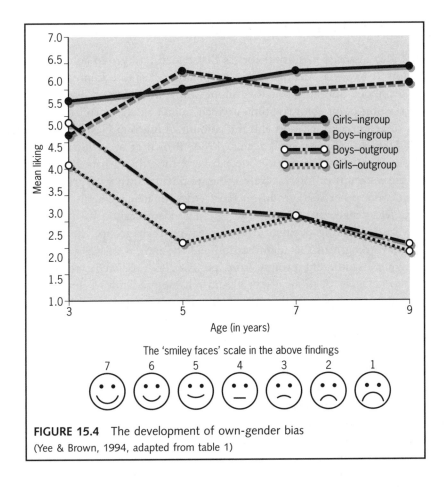

FIGURE 15.4 The development of own-gender bias
(Yee & Brown, 1994, adapted from table 1)

peers (Harkness & Super, 1985; La Freniere, Strayer, & Gauthier, 1984; Maccoby & Jacklin, 1987). This gender segregation, as it is called, is typically accompanied by some clear-cut attitudes and stereotypes in which the child's own gender is viewed much more positively than the other (Hayden-Thompson, Rubin, & Hymel, 1987). In one study, children were asked to use a simple scale of 'smiley faces' to show how much they liked boys and girls. From the age of five years in boys, and three years in girls, there was very strong ingroup bias in these ratings (see figure 15.4; Yee & Brown, 1994). Ethnic bias has also been observed in children as young as seven years. Davey (1983) asked British primary school children of white, West Indian or Asian origin to attribute positive and negative traits to their own and other ethnic groups. The children's stereotypical views of the ingroup were nearly always more positive than about one or other outgroups, sometimes attributing twice as many positive traits to it than to the others. Other studies have observed similar biases in other contexts (see Aboud, 1988). The prevalence of biases in these domains, where conflicts of interest are not obviously present, strongly suggests that identity-differentiating processes are at work.

Ingroup bias and group identification

A central idea in social identity theory is that biased intergroup comparisons are directly linked to social identification. Presumably, the more important a group is to its members, the more bias they should show in its favour. This hypothesis was the starting point for two studies which examined the correlation between strength of group identification and the amount of ingroup bias shown in inter-group judgements (Brown & Williams, 1984; Brown et al., 1986). Both were carried out in industrial settings – one a bakery, the other a paper mill. In both studies, the ingroups of interest were the respondents' own workgroup, and the outgroups were other workgroups in the factory, or management. On a variety of indices, clear ingroup bias was observed. The identification with the ingroup was also predominantly positive. And yet, within each group, the relationship between the strength of this identification and the indices of bias was very vari-able, ranging in different groups from positive (as predicted), through non-existent, to negative. A more powerful and reliable predictor of intergroup bias in both studies was perceived conflict with the outgroup – a finding more in keeping with the Sherif approach considered earlier.

The rather unstable correlation between group identification and ingroup bias has been confirmed in other studies (Hinkle & Brown, 1990). In an attempt to account for this variability, Hinkle and Brown suggested that the psychological processes proposed by social identity theory may not be operative in all groups. They hypothesized that this would depend on two factors: the prevailing level of individualism or collectivism in the group or group members (Triandis, Bontempo, Villareal, Asai, & Lucca, 1988), and their inclination to engage in inter-group comparisons or, instead, a preference for group evaluations of a more abstract or autonomous kind (Hinkle & Brown, 1990). Hinkle and Brown argued that a strong link between group identification and favouritism would only be expected in those groups simultaneously characterized by a *collectivist* orientation – i.e., where there was an emphasis on intragroup cooperation and group achievements – and a *relational* orientation – i.e., a concern with one's group's standing or per-formance relative to other groups. In three studies, some support was found for this idea: group members classified as collectivist and relational showed positive associations between identification and bias; those designated as individualist and autonomous showed no association at all (Brown et al., 1992; see figure 15.5).

Subordinate status, intergroup comparisons and social unrest

The examples chosen to illustrate social identity processes had one other feature in common, a feature characteristic of nearly all real-world intergroup relation-ships: they involved groups of unequal status. The three groups in the aircraft engine factory formed a clear hierarchy among themselves and, of course, all enjoyed

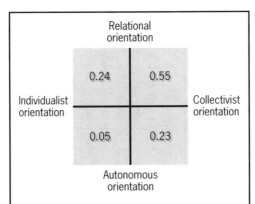

FIGURE 15.5 The association between group identification and ingroup bias, as moderated by different social orientations (Brown et al., 1992, from tables 2, 3 and 5)
Note: Figure shows mean correlations between identification and bias across three independent studies.

much less power and status than their employers (Brown, 1978). Minority groups and the two genders seldom enjoy equal status in most societies. Let us now consider what the consequences of belonging to a low-status group might be.

At first glance these seem negative. Members of such groups will frequently discover that they have lower wages (if they have a job at all), poorer housing, fewer educational qualifications, and are consensually regarded as being inferior on a whole host of criteria. Thus, not only are they worse off in a direct material sense, but psychologically, too, they may well be disadvantaged. If identity is indeed maintained through intergroup comparisons, as social identity theory suggests, then the outcome of the available comparisons is unremittingly negative for their self-esteem.

Leaving the group

One reaction to this state of affairs is simply to try to leave the group, as Tajfel (1978) has suggested. Examples of members of 'inferior' groups distancing themselves physically or psychologically from their group are not hard to find. In their classic studies of ethnic identification, Clark and Clark (1947) found that black children in the United States showed identification with and preference for the dominant white group – a finding replicated with minority groups in other countries (Aboud, 1988). Disidentification with the ingroup is by no means a phenomenon restricted to children, as Lewin (1948) noted of American Jews who attempt to 'pass' into Gentile society. Ellemers et al. (1988) studied this experimentally by creating high- and low-status groups between which mobility

TABLE 15.3 Responses to a negative social identity

	Individualistic strategy	Collective strategies	
Aim	Change one's personal standing in society	Change standing of one's group in society	
Method	Leave the group, e.g., blacks attempting to 'pass' as whites	(1) Restrict comparison to other subordinate groups, e.g., concern by workers over worker–worker wage differences; neglect of worker–employer disparities	(2) Change the dimensions of comparison, e.g., adoption of new cultural and musical forms by 'punks' in Britain	(3) Direct confrontation with dominant group, e.g., demands for social change by feminists in industrialized countries
Possible outcomes	Some individuals may benefit, but many unable to; position of groups unchanged	Some changes may occur among subordinate groups: major status differences between groups unchanged	May create climate for change if new dimensions achieve social recognition	May lead to change if society is unstable and dominant group's position under challenge from other directions

was permitted or not. This 'permeability' factor had its effects primarily on the low-status group members: where they saw a chance to escape to the higher-status group, identification with the ingroup decreased. This effect was particularly noticeable amongst the 'more able' members of the subordinate group, presumably because they believed they had a better chance of upward mobility. However, this is not a universal or necessary consequence, as is revealed by studies in different historical contexts which have failed to find such disidentification (Hraba & Grant, 1970; Vaughan, 1978). We return to this point shortly.

Social comparisons

Nevertheless, such individualistic strategies may not always be possible, especially if the group boundaries are relatively fixed and impermeable, as is the case with many ethnic and religious groups. In cases like these, Tajfel and Turner (1986) suggest that a number of other avenues may be pursued. One is to limit the comparisons made to other similar or subordinate status groups so that the outcome of these comparisons is then more favourable to the ingroup. Such was the case in Brown's (1978) factory study mentioned above, where the workers' concern was over differentials amongst themselves rather than with the much larger difference between themselves and management. In another context, Rosenberg and Simmons (1972) found self-esteem to be higher amongst blacks making comparisons with other blacks than in those who compared themselves with whites. Another strategy is to sidestep the main dimensions of comparison (on which the subordinate group is regarded as inferior) and either invent new dimensions or change the value of those existing dimensions. Thus, Lemaine (1966) found that in a children's camp those groups whose hut constructions were poorer than others (because they had not had the same access to building materials) found new attributes to emphasize (e.g., the hut's garden). Similarly, the lifestyle of subcultural groups like the 'punks' of the 1980s or the 'ecowarriors' of the 1990s is characterized by a complete negation of the dominant society's values in fashion, music and morality. Still a third route is to confront directly the dominant group's superiority by agitating for social and economic change. Such were the goals of the black movement in the United States in the 1960s, and such are currently the demands of feminist groups in many industrialized societies. These different strategies – the individualistic and the three collective – are summarized in table 15.3.

Cognitive alternatives

Which of these tactics will be chosen may well depend on the prevailing social climate. If it is such that no real alternatives to the status quo may be conceived, then the first two options seem more likely; without some sense that the power relations can be changed, it is difficult for subordinate groups openly to challenge the existing order (the third strategy). Tajfel and Turner (1986) have proposed that for such 'cognitive alternatives' to exist, some perception of instability and illegitimacy is necessary. The system must be seen to be changing and to be based on arbitrary principles of justice. Experimental studies support this idea. Where laboratory groups coexist in stable and justifiable status relations, subordinate groups show little sign of throwing off their inferiority. If, however, the status hierarchy is implied to be flexible or unfair, subordinate groups respond by displaying strong ingroup identification and favouritism, and hostility towards the dominant group (Brown & Ross, 1982; Caddick, 1982; Ellemers, Wilke, & Van Knippenberg, 1993). Once again, the likelihood of these reactions translating themselves into collective action aimed at changing the status quo may depend on the permeability of group boundaries. Wright, Taylor and Moghaddam (1990) showed that where group boundaries are completely closed, group members are more likely to respond to disadvantage by some kind of rebellious collective strategy. If, on the other hand, there is the slightest possibility of upward mobility, even if this only results in a few 'token' subordinate group members being allowed to move, then individualistic strategies are more likely.

Relative deprivation

A rather similar conclusion is reached by Runciman (1966) and Gurr (1970). They argue that a key factor in generating social unrest amongst subordinate groups is a sense of relative deprivation. *Relative deprivation* arises from a perceived discrepancy between what one has and what one feels entitled to. This discrepancy can arise from comparison either with one's own group in the past (Davies, 1969) or, more often, with other groups (Runciman, 1966). Where these comparisons reveal a gap between achievements and aspirations, then people will often feel sufficiently motivated to attempt social change. This will be especially true, as Walker and Pettigrew (1984) have argued, where the comparisons are made on an intergroup basis rather than between self and others.

The significance of relative deprivation as a factor generating unrest is supported by a number of studies. Vanneman and Pettigrew (1972) found that amongst whites in the United States, the holding of racist attitudes and support for conservative political candidates was related to the white respondents' feelings of relative deprivation, thus showing that relative deprivation can be experienced by dominant groups as well as by subordinate groups. Grant and Brown (1995), in an experimental study, found that groups, who were unexpectedly deprived of an anticipated reward because of the negative judgements of their task performance by an outgroup, showed markedly higher levels of ingroup bias, aggression and protest than groups not so deprived. Finally, Guimond and Dubé-Simard (1983) found that intergroup, but not interpersonal, deprivation was reliably correlated with support for political change in Canada, a finding later replicated by Walker and Mann (1987) amongst young unemployed people in Australia. A recurring theme in all these studies is the importance of the distinction between personal and group deprivation in generating collective dissatisfaction with the status quo.

The Reduction of Intergroup Conflict and Changing Negative Stereotypes

How can intergroup discrimination and negative stereotyping be lessened?

Most of the theory and research we have considered thus far has been concerned with what might be termed the negative side of intergroup relations, the processes that give rise to ingroup favouritism, intergroup hostility and the like. What of the other side of the coin, the factors that are likely to facilitate the reduction of intergroup conflict?

Superordinate goals

One obvious strategy, as we saw from the earlier discussion of Sherif's realistic group conflict theory, is to try to arrange for the conflicting groups to cooperate with one another in the pursuit of superordinate goals. As Sherif's own summer-camp studies found, and other research subsequently confirmed, in such circumstances formerly antagonistic relationships can be transformed into something approaching mutual tolerance (Brown, 1995).

However, cooperation over superordinate goals may not always be an effective panacea for the improvement of negative intergroup relations; indeed, it may even increase antagonism towards the outgroup. Worchel, Andreoli and Folger (1977) noted that in Sherif's studies the cooperation over superordinate goals always proved successful. They showed, in contrast, that when that cooperation did not achieve its aims and had been preceded by a competitive episode, liking for the outgroup diminished. In addition, it may be important for groups engaged in cooperative ventures to have distinctive and complementary roles to play. When this does not occur and the groups' contributions are not easily recognizable, liking for the other group decreases, perhaps because the group members are concerned for the integrity of the ingroup (Brown & Wade, 1987; Deschamps & Brown, 1983). However, the positive effects of distinguishing task roles very clearly may be restricted to cooperative encounters at an intergroup level; when the interaction is more personalized, the beneficial effects of clear-cut role assignment may be diminished (Marcus-Newhall, Miller, Holtz, & Brewer, 1993).

Redrawing the category boundaries

Social categorization, as we have seen, has the potential to instigate discriminatory behaviour and judgements. But the same processes which are thought to underlie those biases can be harnessed in the service of conflict reduction. Turner (1981) noted that if members of two groups could redefine themselves as belonging to a single superordinate category, then the erstwhile 'outgroupers' would be recategorized as fellow members of the new, larger, ingroup and a more favourable attitude towards them should ensue. An example of this strategy would be when political leaders appeal to societal subgroups to sink their differences in the cause of national unity.

The effectiveness of this 'recategorization' approach has been demonstrated by Gaertner and his colleagues. In a laboratory setting, they arranged for an intergroup encounter to occur under conditions which led to the perception of participants as belonging to a single group, two separate groups, or as discrete individuals. As predicted, the 'one group' perception was reliably associated with a more favourable rating of the former outgroup, and more so than in either the 'individual' or 'two group' cases (Dovidio et al., 1997; Gaertner, Dovidio, Anastasio, Bachman, & Rust, 1993; Gaertner, Rust, Dovidio, Backman, & Anastasio, 1994). The recategorization strategy has proved to be a useful tool for the reduction of intergroup bias in laboratory settings, perhaps because the artificial groups typically used there can easily be subsumed into a new and larger entity. Outside the laboratory, where members of real groups may have more invested in retaining their original identities, it may be important to combine the 'one group' approach with devices that allow the subgroups to maintain some distinctiveness. There is experimental evidence which supports this idea (Dovidio, Gaertner, & Validzic, 1998; Gonzalez & Brown, 1999).

Another way ingroup biases can be reduced is to arrange for two or more social categories (e.g., ethnicity and gender) to cut across one another. Categorization principles would suggest that in 'criss-cross' situations like this, the discrimination observed in terms of either of the original categories will be reduced because the simultaneous processes of between-category differentiation and within-category assimilation effectively cancel one another out (see figure 15.6). Deschamps and Doise (1978) and Deschamps (1977) have found evidence of such reduced differentiation when categories (both real and artificial) are crossed. Note, however, that if the two crossing categories result in a double ingroup in juxtaposition with a double outgroup (e.g., in figure 15.6, black men vs. white women), then there is evidence that this results in enhanced rather than reduced differentiation (Brown & Turner, 1979; Migdal, Hewstone, & Mullen, 1998; Urban & Miller, 1998; Vanbeselaere, 1991).

Outside the laboratory, where the categories may be psychologically much more meaningful and where they may differ in status and size, such superimposition of categories can have more complex effects. In addition, because of contextual factors, one category dimension can sometimes dominate over others, thus weakening any effects associated with their criss-crossing. This was shown clearly in a study conducted in Bangladesh, where the relevant dimensions were religion (Muslim and Hindu), nationality (Bangladesh and Indian), and language (Bengali and Hindi) (Hewstone, Islam, & Judd, 1993). Consistent with an earlier study conducted in India (Hagendoorn & Henke, 1991), Hewstone et al. (1993) found

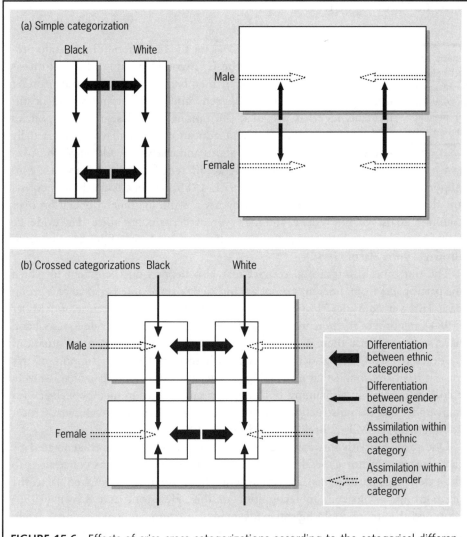

FIGURE 15.6 Effects of criss-cross categorizations according to the categorical differentiation model: (a) simple categorization; (b) crossed categorizations

that respondents' intergroup evaluations were strongly determined by religion, rather less so by nationality, and almost not at all by whether the stimulus group spoke the same language or not. The net result of this was that people of a different religion *and* nationality were strongly derogated by respondents, especially in comparison to compatriots of the same religion. Thus, while the crossed-categorization strategy clearly has some positive implications for conflict reduction, it cannot be relied on to eliminate all manifestations of ingroup favouritism.

The contact hypothesis

Contact hypothesis The idea that contact between members of different groups under certain conditions lessens intergroup prejudice and hostility.

One of the most influential ideas for the reduction of intergroup prejudice is the **contact hypothesis**. Broadly speaking, this hypothesis suggests that contact between members of different groups, under the appropriate conditions, lessens intergroup prejudice and hostility. This idea has provided the rationale for desegregation policies in housing, employment and education which have been partially implemented in the United States and elsewhere. Although the contact hypothesis has been proposed in several different forms over the years (e.g., Allport, 1954; Cook, 1962; Pettigrew, 1971, 1986), on one issue these theorists are all agreed: contact between groups by itself, without some cooperation over common goals, will not reduce, and may even exacerbate, prejudice. The evidence from studies of ethnic relations largely confirms this (Amir, 1976; Hewstone & Brown, 1986; Slavin, 1983).

The outcome of intergroup contact may also depend on the extent to which the participants from different groups are interacting on an interpersonal or a group basis (Brewer & Miller, 1984; Hewstone & Brown, 1986). Brewer and Miller (1984), mindful of the potentially divisive effects of making social categories salient, have suggested that there are advantages in personalizing intergroup situations by de-emphasizing categorical differences wherever possible. In support of this idea, it has been found that instructing people to focus on interpersonal issues in a cooperative group containing both ingroup and outgroup members elicits less ingroup bias than an instruction to focus on the task (Bettencourt, Brewer, Croak, & Miller, 1992; Miller, Brewer, & Edwards, 1985).

One problem with this approach is that any change of attitude generated by the contact may not generalize to other members of the groups concerned; to the extent that participants are seen as individuals, then the cognitive link to the prior groups is blocked. In recognition of this, Hewstone and Brown (1986) proposed that there could be some advantages in maintaining the original group boundaries so long as the two groups were still positively interdependent and able to cooperate with one another on an equal footing. In this way, the interaction would be of a more intergroup nature, the participants would be likely to be seen as more representative of their groups, and hence any positive change would have more widespread effects. Consistent with this, Wilder (1984) found that contact between members of different college groups who were seen as typical of their group produced more positive intergroup attitudes than contact between atypical members. The beneficial effects of contact with typical outgroup members have been confirmed in the contexts of contact between members of stigmatized and non-stigmatized groups and between members of different countries (Brown, Vivian, & Hewstone, in 1999; Desforges et al., 1991; Maras & Brown, 1996; Van Oudenhouven, Groenewond, & Hewstone, 1996).

Further support for this conclusion is provided by a recent development of the contact hypothesis called the extended contact effect (Wright, Aron,

McLaughlin-Volpe, & Ropp, 1997). This proposes that knowledge that one's fellow ingroup members have close friendships with outgroup members can help to reduce prejudice towards the outgroup. A likely reason for this is that the ingroup 'exemplars' provide normative information for how one should behave and also may contribute to a redefinition of the intergroup relationship as less negative. There is emerging both correlational and experimental evidence in support of this idea: those knowing of or observing ingroup–outgroup friendships typically show less prejudice or ingroup bias than those who do not (Liebkind & McAlister, 1999; Wright et al., 1997). Underlying this model is the idea that both ingroup and outgroup role models should been seen as typical or representative of their groups and not exceptions to the rule.

Although the Hewstone and Brown model offers a promising way of tackling the generalization problem, it is not without its difficulties. One of these follows from the same argument that provided the rationale for the model in the first place. If intergroup (rather than interpersonal) contact permits greater generalization of attitude change, then, in principle, both positive *and* negative attitudes can be generalized. Thus, if the cooperative encounter goes wrong, then structuring the interaction at an intergroup level could make matters worse. Furthermore, intergroup interactions may be more anxiety-provoking than interpersonal ones, and anxiety may not be conducive to harmonious social relations (Stephan & Stephan, 1985). Islam and Hewstone (1993a), in a study of Muslim–Hindu contact in Bangladesh, found that features indicative of intergroup relationships were correlated with increased anxiety, which, in turn, was linked with less favourable attitudes towards the outgroup.

There is, then, a fine line to be drawn in designing situations of intergroup contact. Enough category salience must be retained to permit the positive change to be generalized; but not so much as to allow the regression into the familiar and destructive patterns of prejudice that are associated with too firmly drawn category divisions.

Summary and Conclusions

This chapter began with two intergroup encounters. In the pages that followed, various social-psychological theories were examined which have been proffered as explanations of scenes such as these. How successful are they in doing this? It is not difficult to see that, taken singly, not one of the approaches can plausibly claim to have provided the whole – or even most of – the answer, if by 'the answer' we mean being able to explain why the events happened where, when and as they did. Mainly this lack of explanatory power has to do with a point that is often overlooked by social psychologists. Social events have historical precursors, and are often controlled by economic and political processes far beyond the reach of any purely social-psychological analysis. This means that, as social psychologists, we ought to be suitably modest in our ambitions to be able to explain them.

But, even with this caveat firmly in mind, it seems that none of the approaches by itself really provides an adequate explanation of what happened in Ireland or France. To be sure, some of these protagonists were more involved than others, and doubtless there were variations in personality types and levels of frustration which predisposed some individuals to greater activity than others. But when one observes the active and simultaneous involvement of such large numbers of people – as in the Champs Elysées on that July evening – it seems unlikely that everyone involved was so individually predisposed. On the other hand, both events contain elements of 'realistic conflicts' – the type described by Sherif. For centuries Protestants and Catholics have been disputing control over different parts of Ireland, and the World Cup competition is, by definition, a win–lose event. But even this analysis, useful though it is, takes for granted the groups concerned and the psychological significance of those groups for their members. Being a Protestant (or a Catholic) in Ireland is important for those involved far beyond that immediate tragic incident. For many of them, their whole lives – or, as we might say in psychological language, their whole *identities* – are dominated by the fortunes of their group. What happens to the group matters to them, and they are often prepared to commit brutal violence in its name. In short, therefore, a viable social-psychological explanation of intergroup behaviour is likely to draw on more than one of the theories considered here. On their own, each has its weaknesses; taken together, their strengths provide us with, if not the end of the story, then at least a promising beginning.

DISCUSSION POINTS

1   How far can intergroup behaviour be explained by personality variables or internal drive states such as frustration?
2   How can intergroup and interpersonal behaviour be distinguished, and why is this distinction important?
3   How far can intergroup behaviour be explained solely by examining groups' material interests?
4   What seem to be the most plausible explanations for discrimination in the minimal group paradigm?
5   Assess the contribution which social identity theory has made to the understanding of the intergroup behaviour of different status groups.
6   What seem to be the most promising avenues for the reduction of intergroup conflict?

FURTHER READING

Brewer, M. B., & Brown, R. J. (1998). Intergroup relations. In D. T. Gilbert, S. T. Fiske, & G. Lindzey (Eds.), *The handbook of social psychology* (4th ed., Vol. 2, pp. 554–94). New York: McGraw-Hill. A concise overview of the field.

Brewer, M. B., & Miller, N. (1996). *Intergroup relations.* Buckingham: Open University Press. A detailed account of the area from two of its leading researchers.

Brown, R. J. (1995). *Prejudice: Its social psychology.* Oxford: Blackwell. A thorough review of social-psychological theory and research on prejudice.

Hewstone, M., & Brown, R. J. (Eds.). (1986). *Contact and conflict in intergroup encounters.* Oxford: Blackwell. A collection of chapters examining the contact hypothesis in several international contexts, and developing a new 'intergroup' approach.

Mackie, D. M., & Hamilton, D. L. (Eds.). (1993). *Affect, cognition, and stereotyping: Interaction processes in group perception.* San Diego, CA: Academic Press. A collection of chapters examining the interplay of affective and cognitive processes in intergroup perceptions, concentrating mainly on North American research.

Macrae, N., Stangor, C., & Hewstone, M. (1996). *Stereotypes and stereotyping.* London: Guilford Press. Recent theoretical and empirical work on stereotyping.

Sherif, M. (1966). *Group conflict and co-operation: Their social psychology.* London: Routledge & Kegan Paul. A concise account of Sherif's theory and a summary of his summer-camp studies.

Tajfel, H. (1981). *Human groups and social categories: Studies in social psychology.* Cambridge: Cambridge University Press. Contains all Tajfel's major theoretical and empirical writing, from his early research on the categorization of physical stimuli to his more recent work on social identity.

Lemyre, L., & Smith, P. M. (1985). Intergroup discrimination and self esteem in the minimal group paradigm. *Journal of Personality and Social Psychology,* 49, 660–70.

Wilder, D. A. (1984). Intergroup contact: The typical member and the exception to the rule. *Journal of Experimental Social Psychology,* 20, 177–94.

KEY

STUDIES

Applications PART

V

CONTENTS

Health Psychology: A Social-Psychological Perspective

16

Wolfgang Stroebe and Klaus Jonas

OUTLINE

The chapter focuses on the contribution of social-psychological theories and research to the study of two major psychological sources of health and illness, namely patterns of health behaviour and psychosocial stress. What we try to demonstrate in this chapter is how social-psychological knowledge can be used to change health behaviour patterns and to reduce the impact of psychosocial stress. The major questions we address are why people continue to engage in these behaviours, even if they know that they are damaging to their health, and whether there is any way to influence them. With regard to the health consequences of psychosocial stress, one major issue we discuss is how critical life events can impair the mental and physical health of an individual. The second major issue is whether certain coping strategies are more effective than others in reducing the impact of stressful life events and whether the availability of certain resources (e.g., social support) can protect the individual against the negative impact of stressful life events.

KEY CONCEPTS

- Adrenaline
- Buffering hypothesis of social support
- Catecholamines
- Cognitive appraisal
- Coping
- Coping resources
- Cortisol
- Critical life events
- Defence motivation
- Emotion-focused coping
- Endocrine system
- Epidemiology
- Fear-arousing communications
- Functional measures of social support
- Health belief model

- Health education
- Immune system
- Modification of incentive structure
- Noradrenaline
- Placebo control group
- Precaution adoption process model
- Problem-focused coping
- Prospective study
- Protection motivation theory
- Self-efficacy
- Social support
- Stage models of health behaviour change
- Stress
- Structural measures of social support
- Transtheoretical model

Introduction

The fact that smoking, drinking too much alcohol, eating a diet rich in animal fats or leading a sedentary lifestyle can result in serious health impairments is so widely accepted today that one easily forgets that these health risks were practically unknown before the second half of the twentieth century (Dawber, 1980). For the same reason, it is hard to believe that the concept of stress was made popular only in the late 1940s through the work of Selye (1956) on patterns of bodily responses that occur when an organism is exposed to a stressor.

This chapter will focus on the contribution of social psychology to the study of health behaviour and psychosocial stress. Both these research topics offer challenging opportunities for our discipline. As experts in strategies of attitude and behaviour change, social psychologists can make major contributions to the study of health behaviour and health behaviour change. The same is true for the area of stress research. Many of the most stressful life events (e.g., divorce, bereavement) involve break-ups of social relationships. Furthermore, the health impact of stressful life events also depends on individuals' ability to cope with a crisis and on the extent to which they receive social support from relatives and friends. Finally, the impact of stress on health is partly mediated by negative changes in health behaviours, such as increased smoking or alcohol consumption.

Behaviour and Health

The impact of behaviour on health

No single set of data can better illustrate the fact that our health is influenced by the way we live than the findings of a **prospective study** of the association of certain health behaviours with longevity, conducted in the United States (e.g., Breslow & Enstrom, 1980). Prospective studies are longitudinal studies where a group of people (a cohort) is observed for a certain period of time. The suspected causal factors (e.g., health behaviours) are measured at the beginning of the study, and the outcome variables (e.g., health) are assessed at the end.

Prospective study Longitudinal study where the suspected causal factors (e.g., stressful life events) that predict a certain future outcome (e.g., depression or heart disease) are measured first, and the outcome variables are then assessed at some future point in time.

In this study, participants were asked in 1965 whether they engaged in the following seven health practices: sleeping seven to eight hours daily, eating breakfast almost every day, never eating between meals, currently being at or near prescribed height-adjusted weight, never smoking cigarettes, moderate use of alcohol and regular physical activity. In 1965, it was found that good health practices were positively associated with good health. More importantly, however, when this sample was revisited nine and a half years later, it was discovered that those who had engaged in these health practices in 1965, and usually had continued to do so over the years, tended to live longer. The men who had followed all seven health practices had a death rate that was only 28 per cent of that of men who followed three or fewer of these practices. The rate for women who followed all the practices was 43 per cent of those who followed three or fewer. Since then, further research has confirmed the association between most of these health behaviours and longevity (for a review, see Stroebe, 2000).

Determinants of health behaviour

What are the major determinants of health behaviour according to the health belief model and according to protection motivation theory?
What are the weaknesses of the health belief model and of protection motivation theory?

Why do people continue to engage in health-impairing behaviours even if they know that they are damaging their health? Is there any way to influence them? This section will present theoretical models that provide a framework for the analysis of the cognitive determinants of health behaviour. We have to know why people behave the way they do in order to be able to influence them. In the subsequent section, we will discuss strategies of health behaviour change.

Health belief model

Health belief model   The model assumes that people's health behaviour is determined by their perception of the threat of illness or injury and the advantages and disadvantages of taking action.

The **health belief model** has been developed by social psychologists working for the US Public Health Service to explain why people fail to perform preventive behaviours such as having vaccinations or screening tests (Becker & Maiman, 1975; for a recent review, see Sheeran & Abraham, 1996). The health belief model focuses on health-related cognitions (health beliefs) because these are thought to represent the major causal determinants of preventive health behaviours.

At the same time, health beliefs are considered to be the appropriate targets for persuasive communications because they can be influenced by relevant information (e.g., mass media appeals), whereas other predictors of health behaviour, such as demographic variables, are clearly not amenable to change.

According to the health belief model (figure 16.1), an individual's decision to adopt a certain health behaviour is determined by the following four health beliefs:

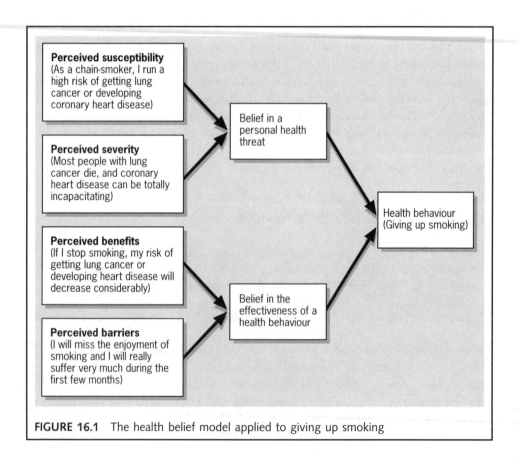

FIGURE 16.1   The health belief model applied to giving up smoking

1   *Perceived susceptibility* (vulnerability): the subjective perception of the risk of getting a disease, if no protective measures are taken.
2   *Perceived severity*: the evaluation of physical or social consequences of contracting the disease, such as, for example, pain, deterioration of family life.
3   *Perceived benefits*: the degree to which a particular health recommendation is regarded as reducing the perceived susceptibility or severity of the health risk.
4   *Perceived barriers*: negative aspects of the recommended behaviour, such as, for example, side-effects of a medication, the pain expected as a result of undergoing some medical procedure, financial costs, effort.

The model further assumes that the decision-making process involving these health beliefs is triggered by 'cues to action'. Such cues can be internal (e.g., perceptions of symptoms) or external (e.g., a mass media campaign).

The extent to which individuals believe they are susceptible to a health threat and the extent to which they perceive this threat as severe will determine the extent of their *belief in a personal health threat*. Individuals who feel threatened will search for ways to reduce the threat. Their willingness to accept an action recommendation will be determined by the cost–benefit analysis by which they weigh the perceived benefits of a recommended action against the costs or perceived barriers. The outcome of this analysis will determine their *belief in the effectiveness of a health behaviour* recommended to them. For example, a middle-aged woman, who has been chain-smoking for many years, might become worried about the risk of developing lung cancer and coronary heart disease (*perceived susceptibility*). She knows that both illnesses are extremely serious (*perceived severity*). She therefore begins to consider giving up smoking. She knows that if she succeeded, her risk of developing heart disease or lung cancer would begin to decrease (*perceived benefits*). However, she hesitates, because she enjoys smoking very much, and she is worried about the withdrawal symptoms she is likely to experience (*perceived barriers*). She might continue to ponder over this decision until she learns that a friend of hers who is also a smoker has suddenly died. This cue to action might tip the balance and trigger a decision.

Despite its plausibility, the health belief model suffers from a number of weaknesses. First, it does not contain rules specifying the combination of predictors. In most studies, therefore, an additive combination of the four health beliefs is assumed. In the case of a health threat, an additive combination would imply that the threat of a disease is a function of the sum of 'perceived susceptibility' and 'perceived severity'. Thus, individuals should perceive a moderate health threat if one of the two variables is perceived as high, even if the other approaches zero. But why would one feel personally threatened by a disease, however severe, if one was convinced that one did not run the slightest risk of getting it?

Second, the model focuses only on beliefs related to *health* concerns. This focus is too narrow. Many health behaviours are popular for reasons unrelated to health. For example, people who exercise regularly may do so to have contact with other individuals or for general 'excitement'. Similarly, people may go on a diet because of their desire to look good rather than to be healthy. Finally, their decision to exercise or to diet may be the result of social pressure from partners or friends (i.e., subjective norms).

The health belief model also fails to incorporate two cognitive variables which have been recognized as major determinants of behaviour during the last few decades. One important omission is that of **self-efficacy** (Bandura, 1997). This refers to the individual's perceived ability to carry out the respective behaviour. The concept is thus related to that of perceived behavioural control used in the model of planned behaviour (Ajzen, 1988; chapter 8). Many empirical studies have demonstrated that self-efficacy is one of the strongest predictors of health behaviour (for a review, see Schwarzer, 1992). As Rosenstock, Strecher and Becker (1988) argued, this omission was due to the original focus of the model on simple behaviours that did not require a great degree of personal skills or self-efficacy, such as vaccinations or having a physical check-up.

> **Self-efficacy** Refers to beliefs in one's ability to carry out certain actions required to attain a specific goal. For example, the belief that one is capable of giving up smoking or going on a diet.

A second important omission is that of *behavioural intention*. For example, the various health beliefs of the smoker described earlier are likely to influence her intention with regard to stopping, and this intention *in turn* will influence her behaviour. The importance of incorporating behavioural intentions as a theoretical component which *mediates* between health beliefs and health behaviour has been shown in several studies (e.g., Wurtele, 1988; Wurtele, Roberts, & Leeper, 1982).

Whereas the omission of behavioural intention is an omission at the theoretical level, there are also omissions at the methodological level. Thus, applications of the health belief model typically relate the four health beliefs directly to behaviour, without assessing the belief in a personal health threat or in the effectiveness of a recommended health behaviour, even though these beliefs are assumed to be the most direct determinants of behaviour.

To put this criticism of the health belief model into perspective, it has to be remembered that this model predates all the other cognitive models of behaviour discussed in this chapter. At the time it was developed (i.e., 1950), it was a major innovation. The model specified cognitive determinants of health behaviour that were plausible to health professionals and lay persons alike. These variables were also significantly related to a variety of health behaviours (for reviews, see Harrison, Mullen, & Green, 1992; Janz & Becker, 1984). Finally, by helping to identify the cognitive determinants of health behaviour, the model formed a basis for the design of effective mass media campaigns. However, the failure of the health belief model to specify the combination of its cognitive variables was soon recognized as a serious shortcoming.

AIDS CAN AFFECT ANYONE

PLATE 16.1   This poster subtly raises fears, but also includes a recommendation

Protection motivation theory

The original version of **protection motivation theory** constituted an attempt to specify the algebraic relationship between the core components of the health belief model and was mainly used to understand the impact of **fear-arousing communications** (Rogers, 1975; Rogers & Mewborn, 1976; for a recent review, see Boer & Seydel, 1996). Fear-arousing communications consist of two parts, namely a fear appeal and an action recommendation. The fear appeal contains information about some health threat (e.g., AIDS) and about the vulnerability of certain target populations (e.g., men who have sex with men; drug users who inject). The action recommendation presents a protective action, which reduces or eliminates the risk (e.g., condom use; no needle-sharing, or cleaning of shared needles, to avoid transmission of infected blood). Fear-arousing communications are essential components of most *health education* campaigns.

Protection motivation, that is, the intention to engage in some kind of health-protective behaviour, was assumed to depend on three factors: (1) the subjective probability of the occurrence of a noxious event (*vulnerability*); (2) the evaluation of the event (*perceived severity*); and (3) the perceived efficacy of a given protective action in averting the danger (*response efficacy*). The model assumes that the three factors combine multiplicatively to determine the intensity of protection motivation. This assumption followed from the plausible consideration that protection motivation should not be aroused if any

Protection motivation theory
Originally an attempt to specify the algebraic relationships between the components of the health belief model. In its most recent version, the model assumes that the motivation to protect oneself from danger is a positive function of four beliefs: the threat is severe, one is personally vulnerable, one has the ability to perform the coping response, and the coping response is effective in reducing the threat. Two further beliefs are assumed to decrease protection motivation: the rewards of the maladaptive response are great, and the costs of performing the coping response are high.

Fear-arousing communications
Persuasive communications that attempt to motivate recipients to change behaviour deleterious

to their health by inducing fear about the potential health hazards and providing a recommendation for an action that would reduce or eliminate the threat.

___

of the three factors was zero. Why should somebody take protective action against a health threat if he or she did not feel vulnerable, or if the threat was not severe, or if the protective action was totally ineffective? However, even though the assumed multiplicative combination has been investigated in several studies (e.g., Kleinot & Rogers, 1982; Maddux & Rogers, 1983; Rogers & Mewborn, 1976), almost none of these investigations obtained evidence consistent with it (for exceptions, see Rogers, 1985; Rogers & Mewborn, 1976).

A major reformulation of protection motivation theory turned it into a general theory of behaviour in the face of potential threats (Rogers, 1983). Protection motivation is aroused when individuals are exposed to a health threat. For example, a young and sexually active bachelor may read that people who engage in unprotected sex with a variety of different partners are increasingly at risk of contracting AIDS (vulnerability), that there is still no cure for AIDS (severity), and that therefore the use of condoms is strongly recommended. According to the revised theory (figure 16.2), exposure to a health threat initiates two appraisal processes known from stress theory, namely threat appraisal and coping appraisal (Lazarus & Folkman, 1984). In the course of *threat* appraisal, individuals evaluate the severity of the threat and their vulnerability to the threat (i.e., the health risk) and weigh them against the rewards that would come from maladaptive responses, such as continuing to have sex without condoms. In the course of the *coping* appraisal, the costs of carrying out the recommended adaptive behaviour are weighed against the perceived efficacy of the recommended action (i.e., response efficacy) and the perceived ability to perform the recommended behaviour (i.e., self-efficacy). The relative outcomes of these appraisal processes determine the amount of protection motivation, that is, the extent to which the individual forms the intention to take a specific protective action. Thus, even though this theory incorporates many of the same predictor variables as the theory of planned behaviour, the two models are derived from vastly different theories, namely stress theory (e.g., Lazarus & Folkman, 1984) as compared to attitude theory (e.g., Fishbein & Ajzen, 1975). Furthermore, even though threat appraisal and coping appraisal are assumed to be the most direct determinants of protection motivation, they are usually not measured directly in tests of the model.

In his revision, Rogers (1983) dropped the assumption of a multiplicative combination of vulnerability, severity and response efficacy. Instead, he suggested that the factors *within* a given appraisal process combine additively. For example, vulnerability, perceived severity and the rewards of the maladaptive response are assumed to summate algebraically to produce the final appraisal of threat (vulnerability + severity − rewards). Similarly, coping appraisal is a summation of the appraisals of response efficacy, self-efficacy and any 'costs' of adopting the recommended action (response efficacy + self-efficacy − costs). However, *between* appraisal processes, a multiplicative combination has been postulated. This latter assumption has been introduced to specify the impact of the two efficacy appraisals. Increasing threat appraisal is assumed to increase protection motivation only if the individual believes that he or she is able to perform a coping response

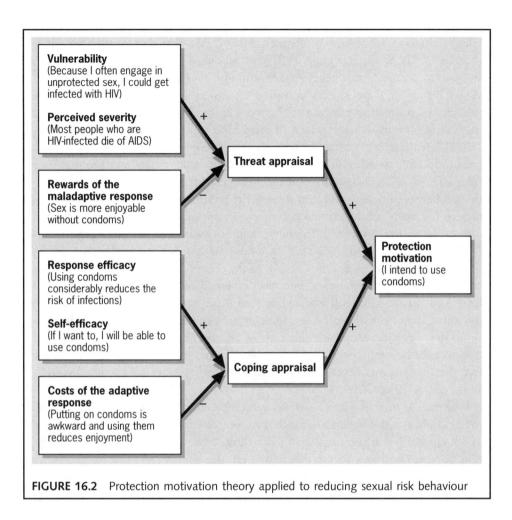

FIGURE 16.2   Protection motivation theory applied to reducing sexual risk behaviour

and that this is effective in reducing or eliminating the danger (i.e., if self-efficacy and response efficacy are both high). If individuals believe that they are unable to perform the protective action or if the action would be ineffective in reducing or eliminating the danger, an increase in the threat should not increase protection motivation.

Given these complexities, it is hardly surprising that evidence for the combinatorial rules suggested by Rogers (1983) has been inconsistent (Jonas, 1993). Although there was some support for the assumption that only variables belonging to different classes would combine multiplicatively (e.g., Kleinot & Rogers, 1982; Self & Rogers, 1990), findings from other studies did not support this hypothesis (e.g., Maddux & Rogers, 1983; Mulilis & Lippa, 1990; Rippetoe & Rogers, 1987). Thus, to date, the relationship between the diverse protection motivation theory variables is far from being clear.

Like the health belief model, protection motivation theory has been investigated within the context of a wide range of diverse health-related behaviours, for example exercise (Fruin, Pratt, & Owen, 1991; Wurtele & Maddux, 1987), breast self-examination (Rippetoe & Rogers, 1987), AIDS-related health behaviour (Van der Velde & Van der Pligt, 1991) and smoking (Maddux & Rogers, 1983). In contrast to the health belief model (and also to the theory of planned behaviour), many of these studies consisted of experimental manipulations of the variables of protection motivation theory. The findings of these studies offered support for the main assumptions of protection motivation theory. Thus, behavioural intentions were often found to be positively related to the dimensions of the model such as self-efficacy, response efficacy, vulnerability and severity. As a rule, self-efficacy turned out to be the strongest predictor of behavioural intentions, whereas obtaining an effect for severity proved to be difficult at times. This pattern has been confirmed in a recent meta-analysis of 27 studies of protection motivation theory, with 29 independent samples and a total of 7,694 participants (Milne, Sheeran, & Orbell, 2000). In an assessment of the association between the components of protection motivation theory and behaviour (measured concurrently or prospectively), intention emerged as the strongest predictor of behaviour, followed by self-efficacy and the other coping appraisal variables. Of the threat appraisal variables, vulnerability was more strongly associated with behaviour than severity. However, this lack of consistent evidence for severity does not necessarily imply that severity is unimportant; it may rather be due to the fact that participants show little variability in their ratings of severity (Salovey, Rothman, & Rodin, 1998).

How do the health belief model and protection motivation theory compare with the model of planned behaviour, which is a more general model of behaviour (Ajzen, 1988; chapter 8)? A comparison of these three models as predictors of the intention to use condoms found that although the theory of planned behaviour explained a higher proportion of the variance in intentions to use condoms than either of the other two models, the predictive power of protection motivation theory was only slightly lower than that of the theory of planned behaviour (Bakker, Buunk, & Siero, 1993). This is not so surprising, given the overlap in predictors between the two models.

Stage models

One limitation of the theories of health-related behaviour – and also of the more general theories, such as the theory of planned behaviour – is that they focus on the determinants of the individual's *motivation* to perform a certain behaviour, and assume that people behave in line with their intention. The fact that behavioural intentions are the best predictors of behaviour supports the validity of this assumption. However, research on health behaviour provides many examples of intention–behaviour inconsistencies, such as smokers who want to stop but either never do or relapse after a few days, and dieters who break their diet. Sometimes these inconsistencies arise because individuals change their intentions, but often people want to go through with their intentions but do not possess the skills necessary to engage in the intended behaviour. For example, condom use requires several skills, from the technical skill of putting on the condom properly to the social skill of discussing this issue with a partner. Similarly, skills are needed to maintain smoking cessation, or to control one's eating or drinking. If people are aware of their lack of skills, low self-efficacy may prevent them from even forming an intention. However, often people discover these limitations only when they prepare for action. A second limitation of the models of health-related behaviour as well as of the more general models of behaviour is that they are relatively static. To predict behaviour, these theories combine the postulated determinants of behaviour according to some algorithm, assuming that the numerical value of the equation places the individual along a single continuum that indicates the probability of action. Any intervention that increases the value of the prediction equation is presumed to enhance the prospects for behaviour change (Weinstein & Sandman, 1992).

In contrast, **stage models of health behaviour change** assume that individuals go through a sequence of stages from decision-making to action, and that different predictors become important at transition points between different stages. The different stages are assumed to represent qualitatively different patterns of behaviour, beliefs and experience, and factors which produce transitions between stages vary, depending on the specific stage transition being considered. Two stage models will be presented here, namely the precaution adoption process model (e.g., Weinstein & Sandman, 1992) and the transtheoretical model of behaviour change (e.g., Prochaska, DiClemente, & Norcross, 1992).

> **Stage models of health behaviour change** Theories (e.g., transtheoretical model; precaution adoption process model) which assume that health behaviour change involves progression through a discernible number of stages, from ignorance of a health threat to completed preventive action.

The starting point of Weinstein's **precaution adoption process model** (figure 16.3) is the individual who is totally unaware of a given health threat (Stage 1). An individual moves to Stage 2 when he or she has learned about some threat but is not yet really concerned about it. Further information may convince the individual that the risk is serious and that he or she is personally vulnerable. This would move him or her to Stage 3 of the precaution adoption process, the stage at which decisions are being considered. This process can result in the decision either to take action or not to take action. If people have decided not to take action, the precaution adoption process ends, at

> **Precaution adoption process model** A stage model of health behaviour change which describes the stages individuals are assumed to move through in adopting some health-protective measure. It has originally been developed as a dynamic version of the health belief model.

least for this particular point in time. This outcome represents a separate stage (Stage 4). If individuals have decided to adopt a precaution (Stage 5), the following step is to initiate action (Stage 6). Stage 7 reflects a 'maintenance' stage, which is only required for lifestyle changes such as taking up physical exercise or stopping smoking, but not for precautions such as having a chest X-ray or some other medical procedure.

Despite some overlap, the stages of change distinguished by the **transtheoretical model** differ in several aspects from those of the precaution adoption process model. The starting point of the transtheoretical model is the *precontemplation* stage. An individual in this stage has no intention of changing the respective maladaptive beha-

> **Transtheoretical model** A stage model of behaviour change developed to understand how people intentionally change their

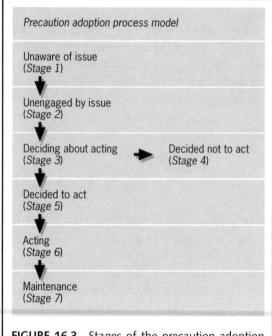

FIGURE 16.3   Stages of the precaution adoption process model

behaviour. The model is called transtheoretical because it is based on an integration of theoretical constructs from diverse theories of psychotherapy.

viour such as cigarette smoking and does not find this behaviour to be problematic. Respondents are classified as precontemplators if they reply 'no' to the question whether or not they intend to change their respective behaviour within the next six months. Since individuals may have different reasons for not intending to change (e.g., ignorance of a health threat vs. low self-efficacy as a result of repeated failures in achieving change), the stage of precontemplation is likely to contain a rather heterogeneous group of individuals. In the *contemplation* stage, the individuals realize that there are problems associated with the maladaptive behaviour. They indicate that they intend to change (e.g., to quit smoking) sometime within the next six months, but that they are not yet committed to taking specific action. In the *preparation* stage, the individual forms the intention to change. This stage is operationalized by indicating the intention to change within the next month and having undertaken at least one unsuccessful attempt within the last year. The *action* stage is operationalized by having managed to change one's behaviour successfully for at least one day or for a maximum of six months. The last stage, the *maintenance* stage, begins when the individual has been able to change for more than six months consecutively. Figure 16.4 presents a spiral pattern to reflect the fact that most people relapse and then regress to an earlier stage.

The strength of these stage models of behaviour change is that they offer a systematic analysis of the factors that influence people as they move from stage

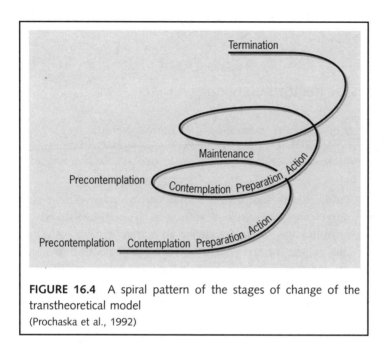

FIGURE 16.4   A spiral pattern of the stages of change of the transtheoretical model
(Prochaska et al., 1992)

to stage. For example, fear appeals which combine novel information about a risk factor and about the respondents' vulnerability with a recommendation on how to reduce or eliminate these health risks should be effective in moving individuals through the initial stages of change. By the time these respondents reach the decision point (Stage 3 or contemplation stage), information should be added to the persuasive communication, which boosts the individuals' confidence in their ability to perform this action (i.e., self-efficacy). Once individuals have decided to abandon health-impairing and to adopt health-promoting behaviour, information on health risks and on the effectiveness of the recommended action will no longer induce change. What individuals need now is information which improves their ability to change their behaviour and helps them to maintain, or even increase, confidence in their ability to do so.

The two major implications for interventions to be derived from these stage models are, first, that persuading individuals to form the *intention* to change their behaviour is often not enough, and second, that the nature of the arguments contained in a persuasive communication has to be *matched* to the stage of change of the target individual. There is limited systematic evidence with regard to these hypotheses. For example, in one of the few studies to assess predictions from the transtheoretical model with regard to matching, Dijkstra, De Vries, Roijackers and Van Breukelen (1998) found only limited support for the assumed superiority of persuasive communications that were stage-matched rather than unmatched. More consistent support for stage models comes from cross-sectional studies which assess the importance of different predictor variables (e.g., beliefs about health outcomes, self-efficacy) at different stages of change (e.g., Blalock et al., 1996;

Prochaska, Velicer, Guidagnoli, Rossi, & DiClemente, 1991; but see also Herzog, Abrams, Emmons, Linnan, & Shadel, 1999).

Strategies of health behaviour change

Which effects do dual-process models predict for fear appeals?
Do strategies of persuasion also work outside the laboratory, in the 'real world'?

Health education The provision of knowledge and/or training of skills which facilitate voluntary adoption of behaviour conducive to health.

Modification of the incentive structure Refers to strategies of behaviour change that influence behaviour by increasing the 'costs' of undesirable (e.g., health-impairing) behaviour, and decreasing the 'costs' of desirable (health-promoting) behaviour. Governments often use fiscal (e.g., tax increases on cigarettes and alcoholic beverages) or legal measures (e.g., laws enforcing use of seatbelts or crash helmets) to influence behaviour.

Public health interventions designed to achieve large-scale behaviour change rely on two strategies, namely **health education** and **modification of the incentive structure**. Health education involves the transfer of knowledge or skills. It provides individuals, groups or communities with knowledge about the health consequences of certain lifestyles and the skills to enable them to change their behaviour. This 'transfer of knowledge' usually involves exposure of people to persuasive messages designed to motivate them to adopt health-enhancing behaviour patterns and to change health-impairing behaviours. Strategies that rely on modification of relevant incentives increase the costs of engaging in certain unhealthy practices, or decrease the costs of healthy behaviours. For example, governments may increase the tax on cigarettes or alcohol, or introduce a fine for people who do not use seatbelts, or they may offer free inoculations or free health check-ups to certain risk groups. Since health education constitutes an application of social-psychological strategies of attitude and behaviour change, we will first review the theoretical bases of some of these techniques and the research testing these theories under controlled laboratory conditions. Only then will we review studies of the effectiveness of strategies of health education and of the modification of incentives.

Persuasion in the laboratory

The major difficulty in persuading people to abandon health-impairing habits and to adopt health-enhancing behaviours is that this usually involves *immediate* effort (e.g., jogging) or renunciation of gratification (e.g., stopping smoking) in order to achieve greater rewards (or to avoid worse punishment) in the *remote future*. It is therefore not surprising that fear-arousing communications have become the mainstay of most mass media health education programmes.

Early research on fear arousal has been guided by the assumption that fear is a drive or motivator of attitude change (for a review, see Leventhal, 1970). Drive models assume that fear appeals induce fear, which is then reduced by the performance of the recommended action (or the rehearsal of the action recommendation). When a response reduces fear, it is reinforced and becomes part of the individual's permanent response repertory. If the performance of the recommended action (or rehearsal of the recommendation) does not decrease fear, because the action provides insufficient protection, the individual is assumed to reduce fear by derogating the communication. With the development of the health belief model and protection motivation theory, the behaviouristic assumption that the protective action taken by an individual was reinforced by fear reduction was replaced by the cognitive assumption that individuals accepted a recommendation if they perceived it as effective in averting negative consequences, which were otherwise likely to happen to them.

Empirical support for these predictions was mixed. The vast majority of experiments on the impact of fear appeals have found that higher levels of threat lead to greater persuasion than lower levels (Boster & Mongeau, 1984). However, studies of many of the variables assumed to moderate the impact of fear appeals resulted in inconsistent findings. For example, studies which combined the manipulation of fear levels with that of the effectiveness of the recommended action failed to find the moderating effects of response efficacy. Although individuals were less willing to accept an action recommendation if the protective action was described as ineffective rather than effective in averting a threat, this effect was independent of the level of threat (e.g., Rogers, 1985). This pattern is inconsistent with drive theory and protection motivation theory. Both theories would have predicted that manipulations of response efficacy should result in greater differences in acceptance of a recommendation when threat was high rather than low. If there is no threat, an action recommendation is unlikely to be accepted, regardless of the efficacy of the recommended action. Similarly, studies which assessed the impact of fear appeals for individuals who differed in vulnerability often revealed patterns that were inconsistent with theoretical predictions. Differences in the level of fear induced by a communication resulted in smaller differences in willingness to accept the recommendation for individuals who were vulnerable to the health risk than for those who were not vulnerable (e.g., Berkowitz & Cottingham, 1960). Both theories would have predicted a greater impact of the fear manipulation for high rather than low vulnerability.

Interest in the study of fear arousal had eclipsed before the rise of dual-process theories of persuasion (chapter 8). The number of studies which assessed the impact of fear appeals on message processing is therefore rather limited (e.g., Gleicher & Petty, 1992; Jepson & Chaiken, 1990; Kuppens, De Wit, & Stroebe, 1996; Liberman & Chaiken, 1992). According to *dual-process theories*, fear-arousing communications can have one of two effects: (1) they can increase the motivation to accurately and systematically process the arguments contained in the communication, or (2) they can induce defence motivation. **Defence motivation** reflects the desire to hold attitudes and beliefs that are consistent with existing central attitudes and values. Defence motivation leads to a directional bias to accept a specific belief,

Defence motivation The desire to defend and maintain certain beliefs or attitudinal positions that are consistent with existing central attitudes and values.

for example the belief that one is healthy and safe. Thus, when defence motivation is induced by a health threat, individuals will selectively process the information, trying to derogate cues which indicate that they are at risk and overemphasize reassuring information.

In predicting the type of motivation likely to be induced by a fear-arousing communication, it is important to distinguish between health threat and fear response. A health threat is reflected by the information that there is a risk of certain health consequences. For example, a health threat would be implied by the information that there is a deadly epidemic in Africa, or that driving without seatbelts increases the risk of serious injuries in the event of a road accident. Fear is one of the potential emotional reactions to such information. One of the important factors determining whether or not a health threat will arouse fear is personal vulnerability. As long as individuals do not feel vulnerable (i.e., as long as the threat is not personally relevant), they should not feel threatened, even by a potentially severe health threat. Therefore, little fear should be aroused in the case of the epidemic in Africa.

For individuals who do *not* feel vulnerable to the health threat, increasing the threat level of the message (e.g., by describing the health consequences as more severe) should *increase the motivation to accurately process* the health information. Their motivation to engage in argument-relevant thinking, which should be low if the health threat is minor, is likely to increase with increasing severity of a threat. After all, it may be worthwhile to be informed about some serious health threat, even if the information is not personally relevant at the moment. Increasing the severity of the threat should therefore motivate them to scrutinize *both* the threatening message *and* the action recommendation. As a result of this differential scrutiny, respondents should be the more likely to recognize weak arguments (and appreciate strong arguments) in messages describing health risks, if the threat is described as severe rather than weak. Given that respondents accept the validity of a threat, the effect of differential levels of threat on attitudes towards the action recommendation will depend on the quality of the arguments contained in the action recommendation. Increases in the severity of the threat should improve their attitude towards the recommended action if the action recommendation is soundly argued, and decrease attitudes if the recommendation contains weak arguments.

If individuals feel *personally vulnerable*, information about a serious health threat is likely to arouse defence motivation. Under defence motivation, the overriding processing principle becomes selectivity (Chaiken, Giner-Sorolla, & Chen, 1996). Individuals will selectively process information in the way that best meets their defensive needs. In predicting the consequences of defensive processing of fear-arousing communications, it is important to remember that these communications consist of two parts, a fear appeal which describes the risk, and an action recommendation which informs individuals on how to take protective action. Vulnerable individuals should be reluctant to accept that they are at risk. They should therefore carefully scrutinize the information that conveys the risk, searching for inconsistencies and logical errors. In doing this, they should act similarly to individuals who are not vulnerable, but feeling threatened, they should be mainly motivated to search for weaknesses in the argumentation. However, once individuals have accepted that the threat is severe and that they are personally vulnerable, they should be *less* motivated to scrutinize the arguments contained in the action recommendation and more willing to accept the action recommendation. After all, by accepting the action recommendation, they can feel safe again.

Given these complex predictions, it is not surprising that research resulted in a complex pattern of findings. However, if one orders studies into those that focus on processing of *fear appeals* and those that focus on processing of the *action recommendation*, a more orderly pattern emerges. Evidence for selective processing of fear appeals has been presented by Liberman and Chaiken (1992), who exposed individuals to messages which either supported (high threat) or disconfirmed (low threat) a purported link between coffee drinking and fibrocystic disease, described as a serious breast disease. Vulnerability was determined by whether participants in this experiment drank coffee or did not drink coffee. Thus, the high-threat version of the message should induce fear in coffee drinkers because it made them feel *vulnerable* to a serious health threat. It should not induce fear in respondents who never drank any coffee. The low-threat version, which claimed that this link had been disconfirmed, should not be fear-arousing for either group. These manipulations resulted in two main effects on beliefs in the negative health consequences of caffeine consumption, but no interaction (figure 16.5): participants were more confident in the link between caffeine and fibrocystic disease after having received a high- rather than low-threat message. More interestingly, however, individuals who drank a lot of coffee, and therefore felt vulnerable, were less willing to accept the link than those who did not drink a great deal of coffee and therefore did not feel vulnerable. Defensive processing was first indicated by the fact that vulnerable individuals were less willing to accept the caffeine–illness link. It was also indicated by various processing measures taken in this study, which showed that vulnerable individuals processed threatening information in a biased fashion. That this apparent defensiveness emerged even for the low-threat message suggests that even the low-threat message may have been sufficiently threatening to coffee drinkers to arouse defensive processing.

Several studies have shown that individuals who feel vulnerable to a serious health threat are more willing to accept a recommendation aimed at reducing the threat without critical scrutiny than are individuals who did not feel vulnerable (e.g., Jepson & Chaiken, 1990; Kuppens et al., 1996). For example, Jepson and Chaiken (1990) reported that individuals who were chronically fearful about cancer detected fewer logical errors that were planted in a message about the effectiveness of cancer check-ups for adults, and also listed fewer issue-relevant thoughts than participants who were not fearful. Moreover, fearful participants also indicated more agreement with the message.

In conclusion, findings from laboratory research indicate that fear appeals are quite effective in influencing health attitudes and even behaviour, and that higher levels of threat result in greater change (Boster & Mongeau, 1984). However, as we will see below, the effectiveness of fear appeals may be limited to the types of

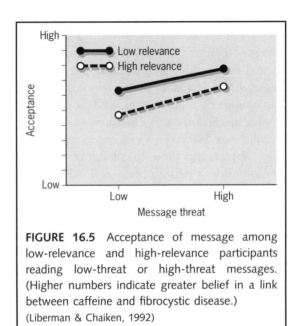

FIGURE 16.5 Acceptance of message among low-relevance and high-relevance participants reading low-threat or high-threat messages. (Higher numbers indicate greater belief in a link between caffeine and fibrocystic disease.) (Liberman & Chaiken, 1992)

situations that have typically been used in these studies, namely novel threats and protective actions that do not require a great deal of skill (i.e., respondents had the ability to perform these actions). Information on health threats is unlikely to result in attitude or behaviour change if respondents are already familiar with this information or if they do not possess the necessary skills to perform the recommended action. Since this lack of skills is likely to be reflected in low self-efficacy, it may already prevent the formation of an intention.

Persuasion in the field

There can be little doubt that extensive national campaigns which emphasize the risk of engaging in health-impairing behaviours can produce substantial change in attitudes and behaviours. For example, the anti-smoking campaign that began with the US Surgeon General's first report in 1964 had great impact in the United States (figure 16.6). The percentage of people who smoked decreased from 42.4 per cent in 1965 to 25.5 per cent in 1994 (Sorensen, Emmons, Hunt, & Johnston, 1998). Yet even with such apparently clear-cut data, it is difficult to decide how much of the behaviour change is due to the information campaign, and how much to other causes. For example, the average price of cigarettes in the United States increased from 27.9 cents in 1965 to 169.3 cents in 1994 (Sorensen et al., 1998). Since even smokers react to price increases with a reduction in consumption, these price increases offer an alternative interpretation for the decrease in smoking. To assess the impact of a media campaign on smoking behaviour, one would therefore need a control group which was in every respect comparable to the US population but was not exposed to the campaign.

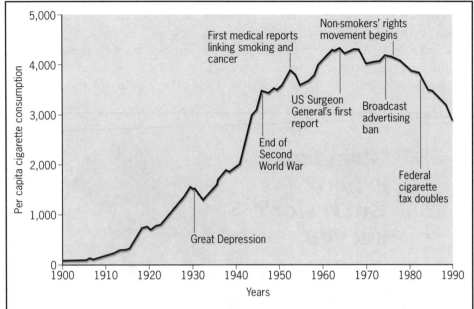

FIGURE 16.6   Per capita cigarette consumption among adults before and after the US Surgeon General's first report about the health risks of smoking

Fortunately, such controlled studies have been conducted as community-based quasi-experiments (e.g., Farquhar et al., 1977; Puska et al., 1985). The first was the Finnish 'North Karelia Project' launched in 1972. This large-scale community study used the province of North Karelia as the intervention site, and the neighbouring province of Kupio as non-intervention control group (Puska et al., 1985). The intervention consisted of an intensive educational campaign through the news services, physicians and public health nurses who staffed the community health centres. The campaign not only informed about the health risks involved in various health-impairing behaviours, but great efforts were also made to teach practical skills for change, such as smoking-cessation techniques, or ways of buying and cooking healthier food. Risk factors were measured at baseline and at two follow-up assessments five and ten years after the start of the intervention. An assessment of the effectiveness of these programmes based on self-report data showed that, compared to the control group, there was a considerable improvement in several dietary habits in North Karelia. There was also a net reduction in smoking, as well as a small but significant net reduction in serum cholesterol levels and blood pressure. Most importantly, however, there was a 24 per cent decline in cardiovascular deaths in North Karelia, compared with a 12 per cent decline nationwide in Finland.

Almost concurrently with the Finnish project, a second large-scale project, the Stanford-Three-Community Study, was started in the United States. This study exposed several communities to a massive media campaign concerning smoking, diet and exercise over television, radio, newspapers, posters and printed materials sent by mail (Farquhar et al., 1977). In one of the communities, the media campaign was supplemented by face-to-face counselling for a small subset of high-risk individuals. A control community was not exposed to the campaign. The media campaign increased people's knowledge about cardiac risk and resulted in modest improvements in dietary preferences and other cardiac risk factors. Only

Giving up is hard. But it won't kill you.

NHS

www.givingupsmoking.co.uk

Don't give up giving up.
For information and support call 0800 169 0 169.

PLATE 16.2 Anti-smoking campaigns, like this poster, have helped to increase the perceived health risks of smoking and led to a decline in this habit

the intervention community which received face-to-face, intensive instruction in addition to the media exposures achieved a significant reduction in smoking rates when compared to the control group (Farquhar et al., 1977). In the late 1970s, three more large-scale community intervention trials aimed at reducing coronary risk factors, including high blood pressure, elevated serum cholesterol levels, cigarette smoking and obesity, were started (Carleton et al., 1995; Farquhar et al., 1990; Luepker et al., 1994). However, results were disappointing. The effects of these interventions were even weaker than those of the Stanford-Three-Community Study.

There has been much speculation about the reasons for the rather modest impact, particularly of these more recent interventions. One factor is that these studies were conducted during a time when major efforts were made by governmental institutions all over the United States to change health-impairing lifestyle patterns in the US population. That these efforts were successful is demonstrated by the pervasive health improvements that were observed in the non-intervention, control cities in all three studies. Once people know about the health risks associated with a given health-impairing behaviour pattern, those who continue to engage in this behaviour do so either because they are unable to change, or because they have other powerful motives which make them disregard these risks. Survey data on smoking showed that many of the people who still smoked in the United States in the late 1970s would have liked to stop, but felt unable to do so (Leventhal & Cleary, 1980). What people needed at that stage was information on *how* rather than *why* to change. To still have an impact, the interventions used in these studies should have focused on information that boosted self-efficacy and taught people how to change, rather than emphasizing once more the health risks resulting from various behaviour patterns.

The risk of the failure of an intervention can be substantially reduced by basing the design of the persuasive communication on an analysis of the factors which determine a given health behaviour. A minimal criterion for a given belief to be a determinant of health behaviour is that it *varies* with the behaviour in question. Because there is overwhelming evidence that smokers and non-smokers alike accept that smoking is unhealthy, arguments aimed at persuading smokers that smoking is unhealthy are unlikely to influence their behaviour (Stroebe, 2000). Similarly, a recent meta-analysis of the determinants of heterosexual condom use indicated that neither the perceived severity of HIV-infections nor perceived vulnerability was significantly associated with condom use (Sheeran, Abraham, & Orbell, 1999). Because beliefs relating to one's 'self-efficacy with regard to condom use', or behaviours such as 'carrying a condom' and 'discussions of condom use with partners' showed strong associations with condom use, these variables would be more promising targets for interventions aimed at reducing sexual risk behaviour. In line with these assumptions, evidence indicates that studies which combine skill training (i.e., with regard to condom use or sexual negotiations) with health education about risk factors are very effective in decreasing sexual risk behavior (for a review, see Stroebe, 2000).

Beyond persuasion: changing the incentive structure

Governments often combine health education with fiscal or legal measures which change the contingencies affecting individuals as they engage in health-impairing behaviour. It is one of the most basic assumptions of economic theory that, everything else being equal, the demand for a good should decrease if the price of that good is increased. Studies of the impact of cigarette price on demand for smoking have estimated that a 10 per cent increase in the price of cigarettes would result in a 14 per cent decrease in demand for cigarettes in adolescents, and a 4 per cent decrease in adults, who have more disposable income than adolescents (Lewit & Coate, 1982). Thus, a 10 per cent increase in the tobacco taxes in the United States would save over 6,000 lives a year (Moore, 1996). Similar arguments can be made for increases in the tax on alcoholic beverages.

Legal measures are effective to the extent that they succeed in linking new incentives to a given behaviour. Thus, seatbelt laws introduce a new incentive for seatbelt use, namely the avoidance of paying a fine. When Swedish drivers could not be persuaded to use their seatbelts, the government introduced a law that made seatbelt use compulsory for front-seat passengers in private cars. This law increased the frequency of seatbelt use from 30 to 85 per cent within a few months (Fhanér & Hane, 1979). A meta-analysis comparing the impact of seatbelt education programmes with legal measures indicated that legal measures resulted in substantially greater changes than education (Johnston, Hendricks, & Fike, 1994).

The usefulness of strategies which influence behaviour via changes in the incentive structure seems limited owing to the tendency for changes in the 'price' of a given behaviour to influence mainly the attitude towards *purchasing* the product rather than the attitude towards the product itself. Thus, although marked increases in the price of alcoholic beverages might induce people to buy less alcohol, they might drink at their old level whenever drinks are free. However, high prices of cigarettes or alcoholic beverages might prevent adolescents from even developing bad habits in the first place. Furthermore, there are a number of conditions under which incentive-induced behaviour change could result in more general change. First, behaviour becomes habitual if it is performed frequently and regularly and under environmental conditions that are stable (Ouellette & Wood, 1998; Verplanken & Aarts, 1999). Thus, once people get used to putting on their seatbelts, it becomes a habit, being automatically elicited by environmental cues like entering the car, or closing the car door, and incentives are no longer necessary to maintain the behaviour. Second, after having been induced through legal sanctions to use their seatbelts, individuals might realize that this experience is much less unpleasant than they had anticipated. Third, the incentive-induced compliance might have aroused cognitive dissonance (chapter 8). After all, the fines for non-compliance with seatbelt laws were often minimal, and the law was not enforced very strictly. Thus, people who disliked seatbelts and had never used them before might have felt that the legal sanctions were really insufficiently severe to justify their compliance. The knowledge that they behaved contrary to their attitudes without really sufficient reason would have produced dissonance. They might have reduced this unpleasant state by changing their attitudes towards seatbelt use to bring it in line with their behaviour.

Conclusions

We discussed two strategies of health behaviour change, namely health education and the modification of incentives through fiscal or legal measures. Because health education relies mainly on persuasion, the first step in designing an effective education programme is the identification of the beliefs that determine a given health behaviour. However, the important lesson we learned from stage theories of behaviour change is that messages will have to be matched to the stage of change of the target individuals. It is likely not only that different beliefs will have to be targeted for different segments of the population, but also that the target beliefs will change over time.

   Given these complexities, it is tempting to rely exclusively on legal or fiscal strategies instead of persuasion. However, there are limitations to the use of monetary incentives or legal sanctions to influence health behaviour which do not apply to persuasion. First, these strategies cannot be applied to all health behaviours. Whereas it is widely accepted that governments should control the price of tobacco products and alcohol, a law forcing people to jog daily would be unacceptable and difficult to enforce. Furthermore, the use of monetary incentives or legal sanctions to control behaviour might weaken internal control mechanisms that may have existed beforehand. Research on the effects of extrinsic rewards on intrinsic motivation has demonstrated that performance of an intrinsically enjoyable task will decrease once people are offered a reward for performing that task (e.g., Lepper & Greene, 1978). However, as the war on smoking has shown, health education and modification of incentive structures are used as complementary rather than competing strategies. The health education campaign initially alerted people about the health risks of smoking and resulted in a non-smoking ethos that was probably responsible for both the large increases in federal taxes on tobacco and legislative successes of the non-smokers' rights movements during the 1970s and 1980s.

Stress and Health

Like smoking or eating a fatty diet, leading a stressful life can make you sick. The concept of stress has been made popular through Selye's (1956) research on patterns of bodily responses that occur when an organism is exposed to a stressor such as intensive heat or infection. These ideas were then adopted by psychiatrists, who began to study stressful life events as factors contributing to the development of a variety of physical and mental illnesses. Basic to this work was the idea that psychosocial stress, caused by **critical life events** such as loss of a partner or unemployment, leads to the same bodily changes observed as a result of tissue

Critical life events Events that represent major changes in an individual's life, which range from short-term to enduring and which are potentially threatening.

Stress The condition that arises when individuals perceive the demands of a situation as challenging or exceeding their resources and endangering their well-being.

damage. Numerous definitions of the concept of **stress** have since been suggested. The common element is their emphasis on a process in which 'environmental demands tax or exceed the adaptive capacity of an organism, resulting in psychological and biological changes that may place persons at risk for disease' (Cohen, Kessler & Gordon, 1995, p. 3).

The measurement of critical life events

What are the strengths and weaknesses of self-report measures of life events?

The negative health impact of psychosocial stress has been studied in the context of critical life events. The majority of this research related self-report measures of cumulative life events to measures of health and illness. These life-event measures, which have been pioneered by Holmes and Rahe (1967), typically consist of lists of potentially stressful life events (for a review, see Turner & Wheaton, 1995). Respondents are requested to indicate which of these events they have experienced during a given time period. The 'social readjustment rating scale' of Holmes and Rahe (1967) lists 43 items which describe 'life-change events', defined as events which require a certain amount of social readjustment from the individual (table 16.1). Because it was assumed that any event which forced individuals to deviate from their habitual pattern would be stressful, pleasant as well as unpleasant events were included in the list. However, only negative events were later found to be related to ill health (Turner & Wheaton, 1995). The cumulative score consists either of the number of life events experienced during a specific period of time, or the sum of weights which reflect the severity of these events. Surprisingly, using weighted scores rather than mere frequency does not improve the prediction of health problems (Turner & Wheaton, 1995).

The ease of administration of these checklists made it feasible to screen large numbers of people. This enabled researchers to conduct prospective studies in which life events were assessed *before* the onset of illness. For example, Rahe (1968) related the life-change scores of 2,500 navy personnel, measured before their six-month tour of duty, to shipboard medical records. During the first few months of the cruise, high-risk individuals (with life-event scores in the top 30 per cent) had nearly 90 per cent more first illnesses than the low-risk group of individuals, whose scores fell into the lowest 30 per cent.

After an initially enthusiastic reception, the checklist approach came under methodological scrutiny (for a review, see Stroebe, 2000). It was argued that the relationship observed between life stress and health could reflect a reporting bias. People who perceived every little event as major might also be more likely to consult their doctor for minor illnesses. Along similar lines, Watson and Pennebaker (1989) suggested that studies which related life-event measures to self-report

TABLE 16.1   The social readjustment rating scale

Rank	Life event	Mean value
1	Death of spouse	100
2	Divorce	73
3	Marital separation	65
4	Jail term	63
5	Death of close family member	63
6	Personal injury or illness	53
7	Marriage	50
8	Fired at work	47
9	Marital reconciliation	45
10	Retirement	45
11	Change in health of family member	44
12	Pregnancy	40
13	Sex difficulties	39
14	Gain of new family member	39
15	Business readjustment	39
16	Change in financial state	38
17	Death of close friend	37
18	Change to different line of work	36
19	Change in number of arguments with spouse	35
20	Mortgage over US$10,000	31
21	Foreclosure of mortgage or loan	30
22	Change in responsibilities at work	29
23	Son or daughter leaving home	29
24	Trouble with in-laws	29
25	Outstanding personal achievement	28
26	Wife begins or stops work	26
27	Begin or end school	26
28	Change in living conditions	25
29	Revision of personal habits	24
30	Trouble with boss	23
31	Change in work hours or conditions	20
32	Change in residence	20
33	Change in schools	20
34	Change in recreation	19
35	Change in church activities	19
36	Change in social activities	18
37	Mortgage or loan less than US$10,000	17
38	Change in sleeping habits	16
39	Change in number of family get-togethers	15
40	Change in eating habits	15
41	Vacation	13
42	Christmas	12
43	Minor violations of the law	11

Source: Holmes & Rahe (1967)

measures of illness might reflect a stable personality disposition to experience negative affect. While this type of 'negative affectivity' is highly correlated with measures of symptom reporting, it seems unrelated to objective health indicators (e.g., blood pressure, immune system functions). Finally, it was argued that by containing items which reflected health symptoms (e.g., personal injury or illness, sex difficulties), the checklist measures contaminated stress and illness measures.

One strategy to address these problems has been the development of interview-based measures, which allow the extensive probing of event reports to assess whether the event was really severe in emotional impact, and to gain information about the circumstances surrounding the event (Wethington, Brown, & Kessler, 1995). It assumed that this additional information would be helpful in deciding whether a given event was 'really' major or merely 'perceived' as major by the respondent. Underlying this procedure is the questionable assumption that the perception of the researcher is more real than the perception of the person experiencing the event. A second strategy has been to relate objectifiable life events (e.g., death of a partner, unemployment), to objective health indicators (e.g., disability, mortality). For example, Parkes, Benjamin and Fitzgerald (1969) compared the death rates of a sample of widowers for the nine years following their loss to that of a matched sample of men who were still married. As figure 16.7 shows, these widowers suffered a 40 per cent increase in mortality during the first six months of bereavement. These findings have since been replicated in numerous studies (Stroebe & Stroebe, 1987).

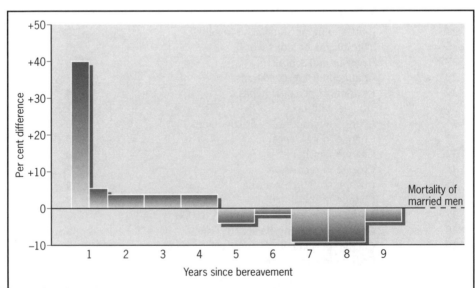

FIGURE 16.7 Percentage difference between the mortality rates of widowers over the age of 54 and those of married men of the same age by number of years since bereavement

What makes critical life events stressful?

Which dimensions of coping can be distinguished?
What is the role of coping resources in determining the experience of stress?

By relating the incidence of illness to specific stressful events, research on the health impact of critical life events evaded the thorny issue of specifying why certain psychological experiences are stressful, how the organism recognizes stressful events, and how interindividual differences in reactions to stress can be explained. These issues have been addressed by psychological approaches to stress which analyse the cognitive processes that mediate between life events and stress (e.g., Lazarus & Folkman, 1984).

According to the cognitive stress theory of Lazarus and Folkman (1984), which has dominated stress research for several decades, 'psychological stress is a particular relationship between the person and the environment which is appraised by the individual as taxing or exceeding his or her resources and endangering his or her well-being' (p. 19). The two central processes that determine the extent of stress experienced in a given situation are **cognitive appraisal** and **coping**. Lazarus and Folkman (1984) distinguish three forms of appraisal, namely primary appraisal, secondary appraisal and reappraisal. Whereas primary appraisal serves to distinguish stressful situations from those that are harmless, secondary appraisal weighs the potential threat against coping resources and also decides on coping options. Reappraisal refers to a changed appraisal on the basis of new information from the environment. One function of reappraisal is to monitor the changes in the environment that may have resulted from individuals' problem-focused coping.

Coping encompasses both the cognitive and behavioural strategies which individuals use to manage both a stressful situation and the negative emotional reactions elicited by that event. Lazarus and Folkman (1984) distinguished two forms of coping, namely **problem-focused coping** and **emotion-focused coping**. Problem-focused coping is instrumental behaviour directed at reducing or eliminating the threat. It is the type of behaviour predicted by models of health behaviour. Emotion-focused coping is aimed at reducing emotional distress. In coping with their emotions, individuals may use cognitive strategies, such as reappraising the situation as less threatening, or engaging in wishful thinking. But they may also try 'to calm their nerves' by taking tranquillizers, drinking alcohol or lighting a cigarette.

Cognitive appraisal   The evaluative process that determines why, and to what extent, a particular situation is perceived as stressful.

Coping   The cognitive and behavioural strategies which individuals use to manage both a stressful situation and the negative emotional reactions elicited by that event.

Problem-focused coping   Refers to instrumental behaviour aimed at reducing or eliminating the risk of harmful consequences which might result from the stressful event.

Emotion-focused coping   Coping strategies which do not focus on the stressful event but on ameliorating the distressing emotional reactions to the event.

A second dimension of coping which frequently emerges from research is approach vs. avoidance (Roth & Cohen, 1986). An individual can confront his or her emotions (e.g., by reappraising the situation or confiding to a friend); but he or she can also avoid the confrontation using strategies such as denial, distraction or wishful thinking. Similarly, the individual can confront a health threat by undergoing some diagnostic procedure, but he or she might also decide that it would be better to avoid seeking a diagnosis. These two dimensions would thus result in a simple fourfold category system of coping strategies, namely problem-approach, problem-avoidance, emotion-approach and emotion-avoidance.

Coping resources The extrapersonal (e.g., social support) and intrapersonal resources (e.g., optimism) available to the individual for coping with the demands of a critical event.

The extent to which a situation is experienced as stressful, as well as the individual's success in mastering it, will depend on his or her **coping resources**. Lazarus and Folkman (1984) distinguish resources which are primarily properties of the person, and resources which are primarily environmental. The intrapersonal resources include physical resources such as good health and energy, psychological resources such as optimism or a positive self-concept, and competencies such as problem-solving and social skills. Examples of extrapersonal or environmental resources are financial resources or social support, that is, the availability of others who can help the individual in coping with the stress situation.

How does stress affect health?

What are the mechanisms by which stress can affect health?

Endocrine system The system of glands and other structures that produces and secretes hormones into the bloodstream.

Catecholamines Summary term which subsumes the hormones adrenaline and noradrenaline (also dopamine).

Adrenaline A hormone secreted by the adrenal medulla which stimulates the sympathetic nervous system. It stimulates the heart action and raises the blood pressure, releases glucose and increases its consumption, increases the circulation of the blood in the muscles, relaxes air passages and stimulates breathing. It prepares the body

There are two types of mechanisms through which stress can affect health. Stress can affect health directly through changes in the body's physiology, or indirectly through changes in individual behaviour. Much of the direct impact of stress on health is mediated by the **endocrine system**, a system of glands and other structures that produces and secretes hormones into the bloodstream. Hormones are messenger substances which, once released into the bloodstream, act on distant target sites. The major stress hormones are the **catecholamines adrenaline** and **noradrenaline**, which are secreted by the adrenal medulla and/or sympathetic nerve endings, and the corticosteroid **cortisol**, which is secreted by the adrenal cortex (Cohen et al., 1995). The release of catecholamines stimulates cardiovascular activity and raises blood pressure. Cortisol is important for energy mobilization of the body. It promotes the synthesis of glucose from the liver. Cortisol also mobilizes the fat stores from fat depots and increases the level of serum lipids, that is, fat-like substances in the blood such as triglycerides and cholesterol. These hormones have also been implicated in the modulation of the **immune system**.

The second pathway from stress to health is through health-impairing behaviours. Individuals under stress tend to engage in these behaviour patterns in order to reduce the threat or to cope with the emotions aroused by the potentially aversive experience. For example, when the workload becomes so extreme that people abandon regular meals and just 'grab a quick bite' whenever there is time, when they resort to tranquillizers, cigarettes or alcohol to help them calm down or go to sleep, coping behaviour can become deleterious to one's health. In line with this reasoning, a survey reported by Cohen and Williamson (1988) found small but statistically significant correlations between perceived stress and shorter periods of sleep, infrequent consumption of breakfast, increased quantity of alcohol consumption and greater frequency of usage of illicit drugs. Marginally significant relations were also found between stress and smoking and lack of physical exercise.

Stress and illness

The impact of stress on infectious disease has been demonstrated in experimental studies. For example, Cohen, Tyrell and Smith (1993) exposed volunteers to either a cold virus or a saline solution (i.e., **placebo control group**). Psychological stress was measured beforehand by self-report measures. Whereas none of the individuals in the saline-control group developed an infection, there was a clear association between level of stress and health outcome for those who were exposed to the virus: highly stressed individuals had a significantly higher risk of infection and of developing a cold than persons who were less stressed. Controlling for health practices did not reduce the association between stress and susceptibility to illness. Similar findings were reported by Cohen and colleagues (1998).

The impact of stress on coronary heart disease has been demonstrated in studies which used prospective designs on individuals who were already at high risk. For example, Byrne, Whyte and Butler (1981) assessed stress experiences in a cohort of survivors of heart attacks in an interview that took place one to two weeks after the attack. The individuals who had a non-fatal or fatal recurrence of the disease within the following eight months had reported significantly more worries at the first interview than people who had not suffered a recurrence. These findings have been replicated in other prospective studies of high-risk groups (e.g., Ruberman, Weinblatt, Goldberg, & Chaudhary, 1984). Finally, there is evidence which implicates stress in the development of depression (for a review, see Kessler, 1997).

for physical action and at the same time inhibits digestion and excretion.

Noradrenaline A hormone secreted by the adrenal medulla and by the nerve endings of the sympathetic nervous system. Whereas adrenaline prepares the body for physical action, noradrenaline deals with the routine jobs such as maintaining an even blood pressure.

Cortisol A hormone secreted by the adrenal cortex which promotes the synthesis and storage of glucose, suppresses inflammation and regulates the distribution of fat in the body.

Immune system The organs and structures that protect the organism against foreign substances. Its major function is to combat infectious micro-organisms (bacteria, viruses and parasites). It does so through the production of infection-fighting cells and chemicals.

Placebo control group Control group used to check whether the effect of a treatment is due to the active ingredient of the treatment or some other effect. Placebo control groups receive apparently the same treatment as the intervention group, except that the administered treatment lacks the active ingredient.

Moderators of the stress–health relationship

What coping strategies are effective?
What is the difference between the direct-effect and the buffering hypothesis of social support?

Anybody who has interviewed individuals who have undergone a critical life event will be impressed by the vast differences in their reactions. It is therefore hardly surprising that an abundance of factors have been suggested as moderators of the stress–health relationship. We will briefly discuss three such moderators, namely coping strategies, dispositional optimism and social support. The role of social support will be discussed most extensively because it is the variable that is most relevant to social psychologists (see chapter 12).

Strategies of coping

Research on the effectiveness of different coping strategies in reducing stress has so far resulted in unclear results (for reviews, see Stroebe, 2000; Terry & Hynes, 1998). A major problem with much of the early research on coping is that it assessed coping effectiveness in relation to a range of *different* stressful events (e.g., Aldwin & Revenson, 1987; Folkman, Lazarus, Dunkel-Schetter, DeLongis, & Gruen, 1986). The decision to adopt a procedure which essentially averages measures of coping effectiveness across different encounters and thus disregards the *nature* of the stressful event is inconsistent with the general consensus in the literature that the effectiveness of a given coping strategy is dependent on the nature of the stressful event with which the individual tries to cope.

This problem has been recognized in more recent studies of coping effectiveness which identified the degree to which individuals have control over a stress situation as the one factor most likely to moderate the effectiveness of their coping strategies. More specifically, it was predicted that problem-focused coping strategies would be most effective in situations over which the individual has a great deal of control, whereas emotion-focused coping strategies would be more effective in stress situations over which the individual has very little control. However, despite the plausibility of this hypothesis, empirical support has been rather mixed (for a review, see Terry & Hynes, 1998).

The only general guideline we can offer at this point is that chronic use of avoidant coping has been found to be associated with poorer adjustment than use of emotion-focused coping strategies in which individuals confront their emotions (e.g., Carver et al., 1993; Nolen-Hoeksema & Larson, 1999). In one prospective study, avoidance measured at the time of diagnosis was even found to be associated with cancer progression one year later (Epping-Jordan, Compas, & Howell, 1994). Evidence that confrontation of one's emotions is associated with better adjustment than avoidance is also consistent with research by Pennebaker on the positive health impact of disclosure of previously undisclosed traumatic events. Pennebaker consistently found that people who had been instructed to write about past traumatic events (e.g., Pennebaker, Kiecolt-Glaser, & Glaser, 1988) or recent upsetting experiences (Pennebaker, Colder, & Sharp, 1990) reported fewer health centre visits following the experiment when compared with controls who wrote about trivial events (for a review, see Pennebaker, 1989).

But even though confrontational varieties of emotion-focused coping appear to be more effective than avoidance coping, this association may be curvilinear. There is evidence to suggest that rumination, that is, thinking too much about one's emotions, is also a poor coping strategy (e.g., Nolen-Hoeksema & Larson, 1999; Nolen-Hoeksema, McBride, & Larson, 1997). Ruminators tend to focus passively on their symptoms of distress and the meaning and consequences of these symptoms instead of actively working through their emotions. Ruminative response styles therefore prolong depression by enhancing the effects of negative mood on cognition and by interfering with instrumental behaviour.

Dispositional optimism

It would seem plausible that an optimistic nature helps people to cope with major life events (Scheier & Carver, 1985). The crucial factor in optimism is that optimists will be more likely than pessimists to see desired outcomes as within their reach. Because people who see desired outcomes as attainable should continue to exert effort at reaching these outcomes, even when doing so is difficult, one would expect optimists to be more persistent than pessimists in their effort to attain desirable outcomes. Dispositional optimism can be measured with the life orientation test, a test designed to measure the extent to which individuals hold the general expectation that good things are likely to happen to them (typical item: 'In uncertain times, I usually expect the best'; Scheier, Carver, & Bridges, 1994).

Evidence for optimism-related differences in coping has been reported in numerous studies (e.g., Aspinwall & Taylor, 1992; Chang, 1998; Scheier, Weintraub, & Carver, 1986). Optimism has been found to be associated with more use of problem-focused coping, seeking of social support and emphasizing the positive aspects of a stressful situation. In contrast, pessimism was associated with denial and distancing, and with focusing on the goal with which the stressor was interfering (e.g., Scheier et al., 1986).

There is also evidence to suggest that optimists are more effective in coping with stressful life events. For example, studies of coronary bypass patients and of women who underwent surgery for breast cancer demonstrated that optimists recover more quickly from major surgery (Scheier et al., 1989). Optimists recovered faster from the effects of the bypass surgery and there was also a positive relationship between optimism and post-surgical quality of life six months later, with optimists doing substantially better than pessimists. Comparable findings were reported from a longitudinal study of women with early-stage breast cancer.

Finally, it has also been demonstrated that the better adjustment of optimists to stressful life events is at least partially mediated by differences in coping styles (e.g., Aspinwall & Taylor, 1992; Chang, 1998). For example, a longitudinal study of college students who were interviewed twice, once shortly after entering college and again three months later, found that optimists made less use of avoidant coping (Aspinwall & Taylor, 1992). Avoidant coping in turn predicted less successful adjustment to college life three months later. Greater optimism was also related to greater use of active coping. This in turn predicted better adjustment to college.

Social support

Social support reflects the information from others that one is loved and cared for, esteemed and valued, and part of a network of communication and mutual obligation (Cobb, 1976). Research distinguishes between structural and functional measures of social support. **Structural measures of social support** assess the individuals' network of social relationships (e.g., marital status, number of friends). The information is relatively objective, and easy to obtain either through self-reports or from records. **Functional measures of social support** assess whether interpersonal relationship serve a particular function. Various typologies of support functions have been proposed (e.g., House, 1981). Most distinguish between *emotional support* (providing empathy, care, love; typical item: 'If I feel depressed and lonely, there is somebody I can talk to who will understand me'); *instrumental support* (tangible help; typical item: 'If I became ill, there is somebody whom I could ask to take care of me'); *belonging support* (social contacts; typical item: 'If I decided to go out of town for a day, I would have somebody I could ask to come with me'); and *appraisal support* (feedback useful for self-appraisal; typical item: 'If I feel uncertain about whether I have acted correctly, there is somebody whose opinion I can rely on').

Much of the impetus for the work on social support and health came from the field of **epidemiology**. In an impressive early survey, Berkman and Syme (1979) demonstrated a relationship between social support and mortality (see chapter 12). However, whereas Berkman and Syme (1979) had to rely on self-reports of physical health, some of the later studies used more objective biomedical health measures. For example, House, Robbins and Metzner (1982) measured a wide range of health indicators (e.g., levels of blood pressure, cholesterol, respiratory functions, electrocardiograms) at the start of their prospective study of 2,754 men and women in 1967. At the same time, several classes of social relationships and activities were assessed. Again, an overall index of these social relationships was

Social support Reflects the information from others that one is loved and cared for, esteemed and valued, and part of a network of communication and mutual obligation. Such information can come from a spouse, a lover, children, friends, or social and community contacts such as churches or social clubs.

Structural measures of social support Reflect the social integration or social embeddedness of individuals by assessing the existence or quantity of their social relationships.

Functional measures of social support Measures that assess the extent to which interpersonal relationships serve particular support functions (e.g., emotional, instrumental, belonging and appraisal support).

Epidemiology The study of the distribution and determinants of health-related states or events in specified populations.

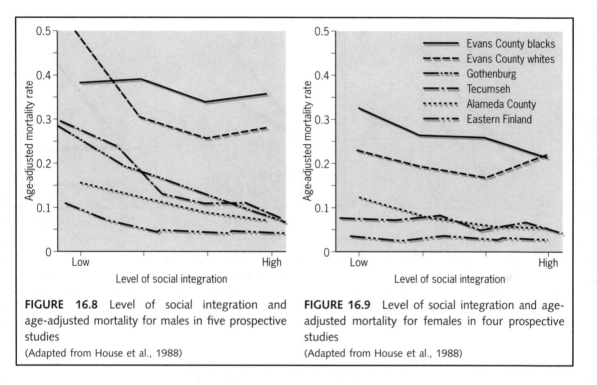

FIGURE 16.8 Level of social integration and age-adjusted mortality for males in five prospective studies

(Adapted from House et al., 1988)

FIGURE 16.9 Level of social integration and age-adjusted mortality for females in four prospective studies

(Adapted from House et al., 1988)

inversely related to mortality over the 10- to 12-year follow-up period, even after adjustment for initial health status. People with low levels of social relationship had approximately twice the mortality risk of those with high levels.

These findings have since been replicated in several studies conducted in different countries (for a review, see House, Landis, & Umberson, 1988). Although the levels of mortality vary greatly across studies, the patterns of prospective association between social support and mortality are remarkably similar. This can be seen from figures 16.8 and 16.9, which show the age-adjusted mortality rates for males and females, respectively, from studies from which parallel data could be extracted (House et al., 1988).

Less dire consequences of the lack of social support have also been established. There is empirical evidence not only that the extent to which individuals experience social support lowers their risk of developing coronary heart disease (e.g., Williams et al., 1980), but also that social support facilitates recovery from coronary artery bypass surgery (a procedure in which the narrow passage is bypassed by surgically grafted pieces of artery). For example, King, Reis, Porter and Norsen (1993), who followed a cohort of patients for a year after a bypass operation, found that the more patients reported before surgery that their spouse esteemed them, the higher was their emotional well-being one year later and the less likely they were to experience a recurrence of symptoms of angina pectoris (i.e., periodic attacks of chest pain caused by brief and incomplete blockages of

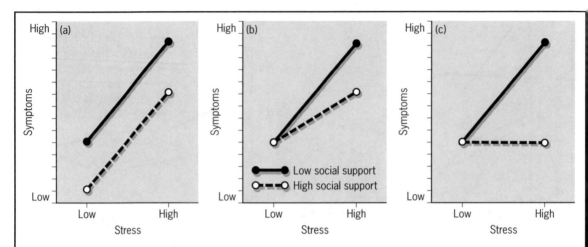

FIGURE 16.10   An illustration of the two ways in which social support is assumed to benefit health: the direct effect (panel a) hypothesis proposes that the health benefits of social support occur irrespective of the level of stress; the buffering effect hypothesis proposes that social support protects individuals to some extent (panel b) or totally (panel c) against the negative impact of stress on health

the blood supply to the heart). The recurrence of angina symptoms was also reduced by the perceived availability of belonging and instrumental support.

That these findings are not atypical can be seen from a meta-analysis of more than 100 studies of the relationship between social support and health which appeared between 1976 and 1987 (e.g., Schwarzer & Leppin, 1989). Schwarzer and Leppin found that social support was significantly related not only to mortality but also to self-report measures of health status, physiological reactivity (e.g., blood pressure, heart rate) and – most strongly – to depression.

Because levels of stress were not assessed in these studies, it is unclear whether these findings reflect a generalized beneficial effect of social support, independent of stress, or whether social support merely moderates the impact of stress (i.e., 'buffering', see below). Both effects are discussed in the literature. Figure 16.10 illustrates the two ways in which social support can benefit health and well-being. A *direct effect* of social support on health could occur because large social networks provide persons with regular positive experiences and a set of stable, socially rewarded roles in the community (Cohen & Wills, 1985). For example, individuals with high levels of social support may have a greater feeling of being liked and cared for. The positive outlook this provides could be beneficial to health, independent of the stress experience. A high level of social support may also encourage people to lead a more healthful lifestyle.

Buffering hypothesis of social support   The hypothesis that social support protects the individual against the negative health impact of high levels of stress.

In contrast, the **buffering hypothesis** suggests that social support affects health by protecting the individual against the negative impact of high levels of stress. This protective effect can best be understood by analogy with inoculation. Just as a difference in health of individuals who are, or are not, inoculated should emerge only when they are exposed to the infectious agent, the protective function of social support is only effective when the person encounters a strong stressor. Thus, under low-stress conditions, no differences would be expected in the health and well-being of groups enjoying differential levels of social support.

Buffering could operate through two types of processes. First, individuals who experience a high level of social support may *appraise* a stressful event as less stressful than people with little social support, because they know that there are people to whom they can turn for advice or who would even be willing to support them financially. A second way in which social support might buffer the negative impact of stress is by improving people's *ability to cope* with the stressor. Thus somebody who is experiencing a crisis might be better able to cope if she or he knows people who can give advice or perhaps even provide a solution to the problem.

To differentiate between the direct effect (i.e., main effect of social support on health) and the buffering effect (i.e., interaction of social support and stress) of social support, studies have to assess the impact of differential levels of social support under differential levels of stress on health and well-being. The pattern that has emerged from this type of research is less than clear-cut. Some studies reported only main effects, while others found interactions between stress and social support. In a review of this literature, Cohen and Wills (1985) argued that these differences in findings are related to the type of measure that was used in a given study. They reasoned that for a buffering effect to occur, the type of social support that is available should be closely linked to the specific coping needs elicited by a stressful event. Since only functional measures assess different types of social support, only studies using functional measures should yield evidence of buffering effects. The use of structural measures, which assess the existence or number of relationships but not the functions actually provided by those relationships, should only result in main effects. Their review supported this hypothesis.

Ultimately, the impact of social and psychological variables on physical health must be transmitted through *biological* processes. In a recent review of the relationship between social support and physiological processes, Uchino, Cacioppo and Kiecolt-Glaser (1996) focused particularly on mechanisms underlying the association between social support and physical health. This review revealed evidence linking social support to aspects of the functioning of the cardiovascular, endocrine and immune systems. It is interesting to note that the observed association between social support and cardiovascular, endocrine and immune functions did not appear to have been mediated in any substantial way by health behaviour. Thus, whereas there is support for the assumption that social support affects health through biological processes, there is little evidence that it operates by encouraging healthier behaviour patterns. This latter finding is surprising, because there is evidence that individuals who are socially integrated (e.g., married rather than single) adopt more healthy lifestyles (Stroebe & Stroebe, 1987).

Conclusions

Research on the stress–health relationship has linked psychosocial stress to increases in the risk of death and of mental and physical illnesses, such as depression, infectious disease or coronary heart disease. The association between stress and health is assumed to be mediated by two types of mechanisms. The first is the direct effect of stress on health, which is mainly mediated by the endocrine system. The second refers to the indirect effects through changes in health-impairing behaviour patterns. There is empirical support for both types of mechanism.

We also discussed coping strategies and coping resources (optimism, social support) as moderators of the impact of stress on health. Research on the effectiveness of different coping strategies in alleviating health-impairing consequences of stress has resulted in few generalizeable findings. The only consistency which tends to emerge is that avoidant coping strategies such as denial, distancing or escape, though probably sometimes effective in the early stages of coping with traumatic events, may be a risk factor for adverse health consequences if used chronically. Optimism was discussed as a personality variable which moderates the impact of stress on health and well-being. It has been assumed that the greater stress resistance of optimists is mediated by differences in coping strategies. Evidence was presented to support this assumption. Finally, the beneficial effect of social support on health was discussed. There is consistent evidence that individuals with low levels of social support have higher risks of morbidity and mortality. There is also evidence that the perceived availability of social support buffers individuals against the impact of stressful life events. Since the health impact of most of these factors appears to be mediated by either cognitive appraisal or coping processes, this research raises the possibility that one could direct interventions towards the modification of style of appraisal or coping.

Summary and Conclusions

There are three distinct phases in research on the health impact of risk factors, namely the *identification* of a factor as a health risk, the *explanation* of the mechanisms by which the risk factor affects health, and the development of *interventions* aimed at reducing or eliminating this risk. The contribution of behavioural health-risk factors to the development of cardiovascular disease was discovered through large-scale epidemiological studies conducted after the Second World War. The findings of these studies motivated governments in many industrial countries to institute health education campaigns aimed at persuading people to change their lifestyles. Most of the past changes in risk behaviour were the result of the diffusion of novel information, that behaviour, which had previously been considered harmless, carried substantial health risks. Although this information had great impact, it was probably the novelty of the information rather than the sophistication of the techniques of health education that was mainly responsible. Many individuals changed their lifestyle once they realized that smoking or having unprotected sex endangered their health. However, some people did not. Sometimes the problem was that these people were not reached by these campaigns, but more often they were not persuaded by these messages or they were unable to change. Designing campaigns to reach groups that are notoriously difficult to reach (e.g., ethnic minorities) to convince them of the need to change their behaviour, and to provide them with the skills to do so successfully, is one of the major challenges for social psychologists working in the health area.

With a substantial proportion of deaths each year attributable to modifiable lifestyle factors, strategies that are effective in changing people's health behaviour make a valuable contribution to primary prevention. During the last decades there has been a great deal of progress in social-psychological understanding of processes of persuasion and attitude change. Health psychology constitutes a worthwhile field of application of this knowledge. Social psychologists can help to design effective mass media campaigns to inform people of the health hazards involved in health-impairing behaviour patterns.

The study of the impact of stress on health is in an earlier phase than research on behavioural risk factors. Although stress has been suspected as a cause of ill health for many decades, the accumulation of evidence demonstrating the health impact of stress is only now becoming convincing. We are also making progress in our understanding of the processes by which psychosocial stress affects health. However, despite these advances, progress in designing interventions to alleviate the health consequences of stress has been slow. Since it is difficult to reduce exposure to stress, interventions will have to rely on factors that protect those who are at high risk against the deleterious effects of stressful events. Social psychology provides many of the theories which guide stress research and help us to improve our understanding of these processes.

1 Why do people engage in health-impairing behaviours even if they know that they are damaging their health?

2 To what extent does protection motivation theory constitute an improvement over the health belief model?

3 How do stage models of health behaviour change differ from the traditional models of behaviour such as the health belief model or the theory of planned behaviour (chapter 8)?

4 What steps would you take if you had to design an effective mass media campaign aimed at changing health-impairing lifestyles? What role can models of behaviour play in designing a mass media campaign?

5 Discuss the reasons for the failure of more recent community interventions to achieve major lifestyle changes.

DISCUSSION
POINTS

6   Discuss the methodological weaknesses of studies which relate stress measures based on self-reports of critical life events to self-reports of health.

7   Under what conditions are emotion-focused coping strategies more effective than problem-focused coping, and why?

8   Contrast the direct-effect hypothesis with the buffering hypothesis of social support. How do studies have to be designed to test buffering effects?

FURTHER READING

Berkman, L. F., & Syme, S. L. (1979). Social networks, host resistance, and mortality: A nine-year follow-up study of Alameda County residents. *American Journal of Epidemiology*, 109, 186–204. The classic epidemiological study which demonstrated for the first time the association between social support and longevity.

Boer, H., & Seydel, E. R. (1996). Protection motivation theory. In M. Conner & P. Norman (Eds.), *Predicting health behaviour* (pp. 121–62). Buckingham: Open University Press. A detailed presentation of protection motivation theory and an extensive review of the research that has been conducted to test the theory.

Cohen, S., Kessler, R. C., & Gordon, L. U. (Eds.). (1995). *Measuring stress*. New York: Oxford University Press. This edited book contains chapters from leading experts on psychological methods of assessing stress in humans. It also provides a good overview of research on stress and on the relationship between stress and a variety of disorders.

Cohen, S., Tyrell, D., & Smith, A. (1993). Negative life events, perceived stress, negative affect, and susceptibility to the common cold. *Journal of Personality and Social Psychology*, 64, 131–40. A fascinating experimental study assessing the role of psychosocial stress in increasing the risk of catching a cold.

Cohen, S., & Wills, T. A. (1985). Stress, social support, and the buffering hypothesis. *Psychological Bulletin*, 98, 310–57. This is a classic review and theoretical analysis of the research on social support and health. On the basis of their analysis and review, the authors established that buffering effects of social support can only be expected in studies that use functional measures of social support.

Lazarus, R. S., & Folkman, S. (1984). *Stress, appraisal, and coping*. New York: Springer. This classic monograph by two of the leading figures of psychological stress research reviews the cognitive stress theory of Lazarus and Folkman. It presents an integrative theoretical analysis of two decades of research on psychological stress.

Sheeran, P., & Abraham, C. (1996). The health belief model. In M. Conner & P. Norman (Eds.), *Predicting health behaviour* (pp. 23–61). Buckingham: Open University Press. A detailed presentation of the health belief model and an extensive review of the research that has been conducted to test this model.

Stroebe, W. (2000). *Social psychology and health* (2nd ed.). Buckingham: Open University Press. The book reviews the epidemiological research on the health impact of health-impairing behaviours (e.g., smoking, drinking excessive alcohol, eating too much, sexual risk behaviour) and of psychosocial stress. It discusses each of these topics in the light of social-psychological theories that have been used in studying stress and in influencing health behaviour.

KEY STUDIES

Cohen, S., Tyrell, D., & Smith, A. (1993). Negative life events, perceived stress, negative affect, and susceptibility to the common cold. *Journal of Personality and Social Psychology*, 64, 131–40.

Liberman, A., & Chaiken, S. (1992). Defensive processing of personally relevant health messages. *Personality and Social Psychology Bulletin*, 18, 669–79.

Social Psychology in Organizations

17

*Nico W. VanYperen
and
Evert Van de Vliert*

OUTLINE

To show how social psychology can be applied in organizational psychology, three social-psychologically oriented process theories of work motivation are introduced: goal-setting theory, social justice theory and productive conflict theory, followed by a brief review on leadership theories. First of all, however, organizational outcomes (i.e., job satisfaction, commitment, turnover, health-related outcomes and job performance) are discussed. This chapter concludes with a list of theory-based conditions leaders should create to motivate their subordinates to do well in their jobs.

KEY CONCEPTS

- Assessment centre technique
- Benchmarking
- Burnout
- Communal orientation
- Communal relationship
- Ego orientation
- Employee-oriented behaviour
- Exchange relationship
- Extra-role behaviour

- In-role behaviour
- Learning orientation
- Least-preferred co-worker
- Maturity of subordinates
- Tension level
- Problem-solving
- Task-oriented behaviour
- Transformational leader
- Turnover

Introduction

How can theories in social psychology be applied to organizations?

A police captain faced serious problems with his officers (formerly called sergeants). A reorganization initiated by the central government forced him to apply a participative management approach in which a high degree of decision-making and job control was placed within newly formed work teams. He supported the reorganization, but in the meantime, he was worried about the implications for his sergeants losing most of their leadership tasks and formal power. Wages were not cut, but each sergeant was supposed to operate as a regular team member and to do regular police work, with only a few additional, coordinating tasks. Although the reorganization had led to a higher level of involvement among the majority of the police officers, the sergeants felt unfairly treated and were very unhappy with their new jobs. Their motivation and performance on the job decreased, absenteeism nearly doubled, and they reacted more aggressively towards officers, colleagues and the public.

The police captain's problem is quite typical for managers in both private and public organizations: how to obtain and maintain – within the specific constraints of the situation – a motivated workforce to achieve overall organizational effectiveness? To learn how to lead and motivate his sergeants and maintain their morale, the police captain needs to be aware of the relevant organizational-psychological dynamics. From organizational psychology, he could learn about what satisfies and motivates people, about the causes of good and bad job performance, and about the reasons why people lose their commitment, skip work or do an inadequate job.

Organizational psychology is defined in terms of its area of application, which means that it deals with human behaviour in organizations and builds heavily upon theories and models adopted from the four basic subdisciplines of psychology: social psychology, personality psychology, developmental psychology, and physiological and cognitive psychology (see figure 17.1). However, considering that organizations are human creations consisting of people who influence each other, social psychology is a major contributor to this interdisciplinary field. A social-psychological perspective improves our understanding of a variety of themes dealing with the social determinants and consequences of individual job experience and behaviour (e.g., attitudes, motivation, stress, performance, satisfaction), group functioning (e.g., communication, leadership, joint decision-making, conflict, team-building), and organizational viability (e.g., strategic mission, structural design, cultural fit, human resource practices, organizational change).

This chapter will focus on one of the most important topics in organizational psychology, that is, the topic of *motivation at work*, which also has salient social-psychological roots. Motivation represents a highly complex phenomenon that affects, and is affected by, variations in other organizational phenomena such as leader-

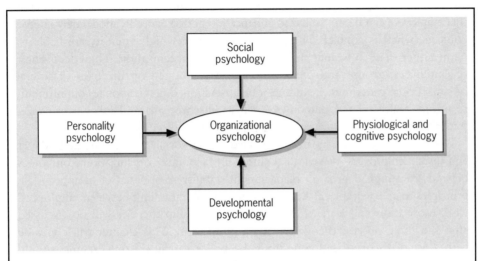

FIGURE 17.1 The relationship between organizational psychology and the four basic subdisciplines of psychology: social psychology, personality psychology, developmental psychology, and cognitive and physiological psychology

ship style, job design and salary systems, as well as organizational outcomes such as job satisfaction, organizational commitment and job performance. Another reason why the topic of motivation has received considerable and sustained attention among both practitioners and scholars is that every organization needs motivated and well-trained people in order to improve, or at least to maintain, their effectiveness and efficiency (Steers, Porter, & Bigley, 1996).

The intense interest in the key concept of work motivation has resulted in many theories that deal with the question of how employees' work motivation can be increased. These theories can be grouped into two general classes: content theories and process theories. The *content theories* of work motivation assume that factors exist within the individual (e.g., instincts and needs) that energize, direct and sustain behaviour. These factors may be either innate psychological characteristics, such as physiological needs and the need for safety and security (e.g., Maslow, 1954), or socially acquired attributes, such as the need for achievement and the need for power (e.g., McClelland, 1961).

In contrast to content theories, *process theories* of work motivation attempt to describe *how* behaviour is energized, directed and sustained. To show how social psychology can be applied in organizational psychology, we will organize this chapter around three social-psychologically oriented, mutually complementary *process theories* of work motivation and resulting effectiveness. These three theories are goal-setting theory, social justice theory and productive conflict theory. Goal-setting theory postulates that specific and difficult goals that are accepted by the employee motivate him or her to put time and effort into his or her job. Social justice theory postulates that perceptions of distributive and procedural fairness are particularly important in this regard. Finally, productive conflict theory maintains that employees can be motivated to enhance job performance by moderately intense conflicts, whereas conflicts of either too low or too high intensity are liable to harm rather than to benefit the parties and their organization. The effectiveness of employees, groups and organizations can be judged on the basis of several organizational outcomes, including job satisfaction, organizational commitment, turnover, health-related outcomes (such as absenteeism) and job performance. Accordingly, these organizational outcomes will be discussed first.

Whether performance goals, social justice and social conflict energize, direct and sustain employees' behaviour required for favourable organizational outcomes depends to a high degree on management's ability to apply a set of appropriate principles in the workplace. Because of this inseparable link between employees' work motivation and leadership behaviour, leadership theories will be discussed after the three process theories of work motivation. This chapter will conclude with a list of theory-based conditions the police captain in our example should create to motivate his sergeants to do well in their jobs.

Organizational Outcomes

What are some of the main 'outcomes' that should be investigated in organizational psychology?

Job satisfaction, organizational commitment and turnover

The important outcomes of job satisfaction and organizational commitment are the most widely studied *attitudes* in organizational psychology (see chapter 8). There is general agreement that *job satisfaction* 'is an affective (that is, emotional) reaction to a job that results from the incumbent's comparison of actual outcomes with those that are desired (expected, deserved, and so on)' (Cranny, Smith, & Stone, 1992, p. 1). This definition is consistent with Thibaut and Kelley's (1959) notion of satisfaction in their influential social exchange theory as well as with Adams' (1965) equity theory (see chapter 12). There is rather strong evidence that increasing worker participation, enriching jobs, setting difficult and specific goals, treating employees with dignity and respect, etc., all lead to positive outcomes, including higher levels of job satisfaction and job performance (for a review, see Steers et al., 1996). An interesting question is whether these and similar interventions satisfy employees and motivate them to perform at a higher level, or whether they lead to a higher performance level resulting in more satisfaction with the job. We will return to this point later.

Organizational commitment is generally defined as *'the relative strength of an individual's identification with and involvement in a particular organization'*

(Mowday, Steers, & Porter, 1979). According to Meyer and Allen (1991), how-ever, this definition refers to only one component of organizational commitment, namely affective commitment. Employees high on affective commitment *want* to stay with the organization. The second component Meyer and Allen differen-tiate in their three-component model of commitment is normative commitment. Employees high on normative commitment feel that they ought to remain with the organization because they believe that it is the right and moral thing to do. Finally, employees with a high level of continuance commitment continue employment with the organization because they *have to* do so. They lack employ-ment alternatives and if they did have any, they would meet insurmountable barriers because they would lose too many valuable investments. Examples of investments leavers may lose are time and effort that are put into job-related skills and knowledge, friends at work, extraneous benefits uniquely associated with the job, good retirement benefits, status and job security. Self-evidently, length of service is positively related to continuance commitment. The longer the period of time employees work for the organization, the more investments they would lose when terminating the relationship with the organization.

Research on employee **turnover** has shown that job dissatisfac-tion is not the only predictor of voluntary turnover. In their review article on the employee turnover process, Mobley and his associates (Mobley, Griffeth, Hand, & Meglino, 1979) concluded that only a weak negative correlation exists between job satisfaction and volunt-ary turnover. The reason why dissatisfied employees stick with their job may be high levels of continuance commitment: they lack altern-atives (for example, due to macroeconomic effects) or meet too many barriers that keep them from leaving (cf. Hulin, 1991). On the other hand, satisfied employees may terminate the relationship with the organization because they find alternatives even more attractive and because there are no barriers that keep them from leaving (they are low on continuance commitment). Similar predictors of employee turnover have been proposed by Farrell and Rusbult (1981) in their investment model (see also chapter 12).

> **Turnover** Employee quitting; turnover is deleterious to organizations when good performers leave (dysfunctional turnover), but beneficial when poor performers leave (functional turnover).

Health-related organizational outcomes

Health-related organizational outcomes include **burnout** (which will be discussed later) and temporary job withdrawal or *absenteeism* (e.g., Johns, 1997; Rhodes & Steers, 1990). Organizational psycho-logists are particularly interested in the frequency of short-term absences (usually less than five days), that is, the number of times an employee reports sick in a certain time interval. The frequency of short-term absences is presumed to reflect voluntary absences. When there are, for example, conflicts at work, a heavy workload or difficult work conditions, employees may be more inclined to report sick, and also when their

> **Burnout** A specific consequence of occupational stressors, characterized by three aspects: emotional exhaustion, depersonalization and reduced personal accomplishment.

complaints are not objectively verifiable. Absence behaviour can be considered as one of the adaptive responses available to employees in coping with their work environment (Hagedoorn, VanYperen, Van de Vliert, & Buunk, 1999; Hulin, 1991; Rosse & Miller, 1984). Thus, research and subsequent interventions should be considered when a particular department or entire organization faces a high frequency of short-term absences.

Job performance

The organizational outcome of *job performance* will be discussed more extensively because for practitioners in particular, actual job performance is probably the most important criterion for judging the effectiveness and efficiency of employees, groups and organizations. However, the problem with this organizational outcome is that it is often quite difficult to define the behaviours required for a job. For example, in an attempt to describe behaviours that are formally expected from managers, Mintzberg (1973) presented three global categories. *Informational roles* are con-

PLATE 17.1 A manager is expected to perform informational, decisional and interpersonal roles

cerned with the acquisition of information and the transmission of information to subordinates, other units in the organization, or relevant individuals or groups outside the organization, such as customers and suppliers. *Decisional roles* include initiating, designing and implementing innovative changes, handling disturbances, allocating resources and negotiating. Finally, *interpersonal roles* focus primarily on the manager's position in the group and his or her interpersonal relationships with others within and outside the group. If these roles are performed well, the manager contributes to organizational effectiveness in terms of collective goal accomplishment, chances of future cooperation and favourable individual consequences (e.g., Guzzo & Dickson, 1996; Hackman, 1990).

In-role vs. extra-role behaviour

In-role behaviour is defined as those aspects of job performance that are explicitly expected and rewarded. Although the link between role prescription and corresponding reward is quite obvious and most prevalent, employees are sometimes punished for doing as desired (Kerr, 1995). For example, professors are expected to teach and to do research (e.g., to write articles for scientific journals), and they often have to choose between these two activities when allocating their time. Professors who devote more time to teaching rather than research activities will be punished in professional terms for meeting these job expectations. At the university, teaching is generally considered as less prestigious, and salary increases and promotions are often based on research output (i.e., the number of publications in high-quality journals), which also has to do with the fact that research output is easier to document and quantify than teaching quality. In a reward system in which only research and publications are rewarded (and the failure to produce publications is punished), even to the detriment of teaching and at the expense of students, the time and effort professors devote to teaching depends very much on how conscientious they are and their interest in teaching.

In-role behaviour Those aspects of job performance that are explicitly expected and rewarded.

Extra-role behaviours are those aspects of job performance that are not specified in advance by role prescriptions, that are not directly or explicitly recognized by the formal reward system, and that are not a source of punitive consequences (Van Dyne, Cummings, & McLean Parks, 1995). Evidently, organizations cannot formalize the entire array of behaviours needed for achieving organizational effectiveness. Examples of extra-role behaviour are helping others with heavy workloads, providing constructive suggestions regarding changes that might be made in one's department or company, skipping breaks and taking steps to prevent problems with co-workers. Extra-role behaviour is interesting because the occurrence of this type of activity is much more under the control of the individual than in-role behaviour, and is therefore determined more by social-psychological variables and individual difference characteristics.

Extra-role behaviour Those aspects of job performance that are not specified in advance by role prescriptions, that are not directly or explicitly recognized by the formal reward system, and that are not a source of punitive consequences when refrained from by job incumbents.

Job satisfaction and job performance

A number of theories and models have attempted to show that satisfied employees perform well on their jobs, and that dissatisfied employees are inherently unproductive. Their basic assumption is that *if the employee really wants to perform better, his or her in-role job performance will naturally go up* (Staw, 1986). However, there are several dispositional and situational factors that may serve to constrain satisfied employees from performing in-role behaviour, for example mental and physical abilities, energy level, self-confidence, technical procedures, lack of financial support, and dependency on machines (e.g., assembly-line work) or colleagues (e.g., administrative jobs). Indeed, it might be that a secretary enjoys her work because she gets along well with with her colleagues, but she performs quite poorly because she lacks the skills a competent secretary needs.

Research has demonstrated unequivocally that no strong link exists between job satisfaction and in-role job performance. In the mid-1960s, Vroom (1964) published a review that showed that satisfaction and in-role job performance are hardly related to each other ($r = 0.14$), a result that appears highly replicable (Iaffaldano & Muchinsky, 1985). Similar correlations have been found between satisfaction and other specific organizational outcomes, including voluntary turnover and temporary job withdrawal (such as lateness and voluntary absenteeism; e.g., Hackett, 1989; Tett & Meyer, 1993). Apparently, satisfied employees sometimes do a poor job, or withdraw permanently or temporarily, whereas in some cases dissatisfied employees stick to their job and do very well.

Another reason for the low correlation between job satisfaction and specific work and non-work behaviours (e.g., in-role job performance, turnover and absenteeism) is that there is no reason to assume that dissatisfied employees enact the same identifiable behaviour under all circumstances. Attitude theorists (see chapter 8) have made a strong case against the wisdom of expecting general attitudes (such as job satisfaction) to predict specific behaviours. Most likely, general attitudes will match general behavioural measures, whereas attitudes towards specific acts will be related to specific behaviours. Indeed, research has shown that the intention to leave is the best predictor of actual turnover (e.g., Tett & Meyer, 1993). For example, in a recent study by VanYperen (1998a), intention to quit was the single direct predictor of actual turnover several months later. The general attitude of job satisfaction, on the other hand, is a better predictor of a global category of activities, such as extra-role behaviours, that are much more under employees' control. In a meta-analytic review of 55 studies, Organ and Ryan (1995) found that job satisfaction and extra-role behaviour were more strongly related than were job satisfaction and in-role job performance. Thus, we may conclude that the intuitively appealing idea of a satisfied and productive employee has received some empirical support.

PLATE 17.2   Are they also productive?

Understanding Organizational Outcomes

To show how social psychology can help us to understand organizational outcomes, three process theories of work motivation (goal-setting theory, social justice theory and productive conflict theory) will be discussed next. Whether the principles suggested by the three theories really help to reach favourable organizational outcomes depends largely on the quality of the manager, or more precisely, on the contingency between the manager's qualities and environmental conditions, including the characteristics and qualities of his or her subordinates. Accordingly, leadership theories that may be used to identify and train competent managers will be discussed after the three theories of work motivation.

Goal-setting theory

What sort of goals should employees be set?

To improve the disappointing performance of the company's sales representatives, the managing director of an electrical wholesale company decided to try out a new

Benchmarking A company benchmarks when it rates itself against others with better business practices in order to identify factors that will enable it to perform as well as, or better than, competitors.

management technique: **benchmarking**. *In a pilot study, the sales growth of 31 branches of the company (the benchmarking treatment group) would be compared with the sales growth of 35 other branches within the company (the control group). In the benchmarking treatment group, all branch managers were given a challenging but achievable target of 10 per cent sales improvement at the end of a four-month period, compared to the same period of the previous year. At the beginning of each month, from month 2, each branch was sent a 'League Ladder' showing the percentage of improvement and ranking of all the branches in that group for the past month. In addition, they were sent a list of ideas and suggestions about techniques and practices used to improve performance, provided by managers of the best-performing branches. These hints included: provision of after-hours contact numbers on business cards; a 'win-back' initiative to recover at least two former customers each month; personalized training of sales representatives to understand and use customer-trend reports. In contrast to the control group, which achieved negligible growth over the four-month period, the benchmarking treatment group achieved an average increase of 5.6 per cent in sales, which translates into a large financial gain over the baseline period* (Mann, Samson, & Dow, 1998).

The managing director of this company felt that work motivation and job performance could be improved by challenging employees with clear, achievable performance goals. In a similar vein, the basic premise of goal-setting theory is that employees' conscious objectives influence their work behaviours. The core finding of the research on goal-setting is that specific and difficult goals that are accepted by the individual result in a higher level of performance than do either specific but easy goals, or difficult but vague goals (Locke & Latham, 1990). As illustrated in the example of the electrical wholesale company, the performance of the sales representatives improved because they accepted the specific and difficult goal of 10 per cent sales improvement, whereas the control group only marginally improved because they had either a vague 'do-your-best' goal, or even no goal at all. Note, however, that an important circumstance that influences the relationship between goals and performance is *feedback*. The combination of goal-setting and feedback (e.g., a 'League Ladder') is more effective than either one of these alone. The example further shows that ideas and suggestions *how to improve* are crucial to achieve growth.

Goal-setting studies in the area of organizational psychology typically use outcome goals, i.e., goals to obtain a particular performance score. The logical starting point for setting one's goal on a task is *previous performance*, that is, a self-referenced outcome goal. However, Locke and Latham (1990) additionally assume, albeit not very explicitly, that outcome goals may also be formulated in terms of social or normative comparisons, that is, the goal may be to outperform others or to reach a normative standard. In the above example, the managing director formulated an outcome goal in terms of both a self-referenced standard (10 per cent sales improvement) and social comparison (by introducing a 'League Ladder').

Ego and learning orientation

In line with this differentiation between other-referenced and self-referenced goals, the social-psychological literature on motivation and achievement using a goal-perspective analysis differentiates between the orientation towards *other-referenced* outcome goals (denoted as an **ego orientation**, competitive orientation or performance goal orientation) and *self-referenced* learning goals (referred to as a **learning orientation**, task orientation or mastery orientation). An ego orientation reflects the individual's goal of establishing his or her superiority over others, whereas a learning orientation involves gaining skill and performing to the best of one's ability. Studies using this theoretical perspective suggest that an exclusive ego orientation is maladaptive. Specifically, an ego orientation, compared to a learning orientation, is accompanied by less persistence, less satisfaction, less perceived competence, less intrinsic motivation and the tendency to choose subjectively less difficult tasks. An ego orientation also has a negative effect on how employees explain their failure, resulting in attributions to external, uncontrollable factors, such as lack of ability, innate talent and luck (Duda, 1992; Farr, Hofmann, & Ringenbach, 1993). This pattern of attributions can have a negative impact on motivation, future orientation and self-esteem (see chapter 7). Furthermore, because the main purpose of ego-oriented individuals is to outperform others, they perceive less control over their success because they do not have control over the performance of their comparison targets or external referents. That is, when they are outperformed by others, they feel bad about themselves. However, when they have performed to their potential or even more, they should feel good about themselves and take the others' better performance for granted. In contrast to Festinger's (1954) assumption in the formulation of his social comparison theory (see chapter 12), ego-oriented individuals *do not* engage in social comparisons mainly for reasons of self-evaluation. Rather, their orientation towards others is particularly inspired by a self-enhancement motive, that is, a need to accomplish or to preserve a positive self-concept. Ego-oriented individuals lose their interest in social comparison information when they are quite certain that their performance is inferior to that of others.

> **Ego orientation** Reflects the individual's goal of establishing his or her superiority over others.

> **Learning orientation** Reflects the individual's involvement in gaining skill and performing one's best.

Particularly in the long term, a learning orientation leads to better task performance and more improvement than an ego orientation (e.g., VanYperen & Duda, 1999). How can this finding be reconciled with the consistent findings in the goal-setting literature suggesting that goal-setting leads to better task performance, irrespective of the content of the goal? A meta-analysis by Utman (1997), primarily based on experimental studies with children, suggests that the advantage of being learning oriented is limited to relatively complex tasks. Similar patterns have been found in adult samples. For example, Winters and Latham (1996) showed that an ego orientation increased performance on simple tasks through its straightforward effect on effort and persistence. By contrast, on complex tasks, where learning was the primary issue, a learning orientation increased perform-ance. In a similar vein, Kanfer and Ackerman (1989) conducted a study among Air Force trainees mastering a complex task (a flight simulation). Their results suggest that an ego orientation is dysfunctional at the initial learning stage. However, an ego orientation enhanced performance when the individual had the requisite skill and knowledge to perform a task. In the learning stage, individuals need to devote their attention to the task itself rather than to con-cerns about the consequences of failing to attain the task. An ego orientation, more so than a learning orientation, is accompanied by obtrusive thoughts during task performance (see also chapter 13: effects of presence of others on task performance).

Determinants of goal orientations

The literature has predominantly treated the goal orientation adopted by the individual as an individual difference variable. Ego orientation and learning ori-entation have been found to be independent factors; it is possible to be simul-taneously high or low on both dimensions (e.g., Button, Mathieu, & Zajac, 1996; Duda, 1992). However, the individual's goal orientation also has situational and cultural determinants, suggesting that organizations and other environments where individuals are involved in learning activities, skill development and per-formance evaluation have an important role in developing and reinforcing goal orientations. As illustrated by the case of the electrical wholesale company, man-agement can create an organizational climate that is high on both goal dimen-sions, overruling or strengthening the dispositional goal orientation. In a similar vein, an ego orientation was found to be dominant among Anglo-Americans, where-as a learning orientation emerged as the more powerful factor among Chinese, suggesting that cultural influences also play a role in the development of goal orientations (Xiang, Lee, & Solmon, 1997).

The obvious implication for managerial practice is that a learning climate may affect employees' level of intrinsic motivation, their willingness to particip-ate in training programmes, their beliefs about the causes of success, and their perseverance to accomplish a task successfully. It should be recognized, however, that organizational life, as well as our Western societies in general, tend to be governed by competition and normative evaluation: there are far more potential leaders than positions in companies, employees are confronted with perform-ance standards, and pass and fail designations on personnel selection tests are based upon the results of others. Nonetheless, the electrical wholesale company case clearly demonstrates that the maladaptive effects of an organizational ego climate are not likely to occur when there is a corresponding learning climate in which individual or team improvement is emphasized simultaneously (Button et al., 1996).

Social justice theory

What is meant by 'distributive' and 'procedural' justice, and how do they affect employees' motivation?

The president of an American company was forced to reduce its payroll by temporarily cutting wages by 15 per cent. At the end of the work week, he called a meeting lasting approximately 15 minutes. He told the employees that the pay reduction was effective the following week, for a period expected to last ten weeks. The only additional information he provided indicated that lost contracts dictated the need for the pay cut. No expressions of apology or remorse were shared, and the basis for the decision was not clearly described. Within the ten-week period that followed, he faced an almost 300 per cent increase in the employees' theft rate of tools, supplies, etc. (Greenberg, 1990).

What did the company president do wrong? How could he have prevented employees from stealing in the current emergency situation, in which pay reduction was unavoidable? According to social justice theory, it is not only the pay reduction itself that leads to employee theft, but particularly the manner in which

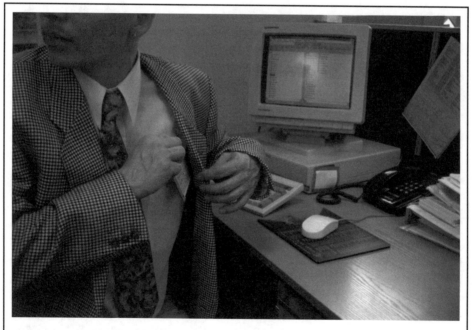

PLATE 17.3 How can we prevent this behaviour?

the decision is communicated. To understand good or bad job performance from a social justice perspective, two separate notions of justice should be taken into account: distributive and procedural justice (Cropanzano & Folger, 1996).

Distributive justice and equity theory

Distributive justice exists when inputs and outcomes are fairly distributed among participants. It is important to note that the objective characteristics of the situation are of less importance than how the individual assesses the value and relevance of the various participants' inputs and outcomes. In other words, justice is in the eye of the beholder (Walster, Berscheid, & Walster, 1973). Moreover, the rule underlying the perception of distributive justice may differ between individuals. Some people perceive a distribution of outcomes as fair when everyone receives similar outcomes, irrespective of inputs (*equality rule*), whereas others feel that individuals with greater needs should receive higher outcomes (*needs rule*) (Leventhal, 1980). However, most research on distributive justice in organizational settings has been conducted from the perspective of *equity theory* (Adams, 1965; see chapter 12). According to the *equity rule*, fairness exists whenever the ratio of the individual's outcomes (O) to inputs (I) is perceived to be equal to the ratio of comparison targets: individuals with greater inputs (e.g., 14 hours vs. 7 hours) should receive higher outcomes (e.g., €140 vs. €70):

$$\frac{O_{person}}{I_{person}} = \frac{O_{target}}{I_{target}}$$

Adams (1965) enumerated a list of inputs from the side of employees that may be relevant, including intelligence, education, experience, training, skill, seniority and effort expended on the job, as well as a list of outcomes employees may receive from the organization, including pay, rewards intrinsic to the job and job status. According to equity theory, individuals are less satisfied with their job when they perceive their investments as not proportional to their outcomes. Hence, a basic assumption of equity theory is that a similarity exists between the process through which individuals evaluate their social relationships and economic transactions in the market. Other assumptions are that individuals try to maximize their outcomes, but also that only equitable relationships will survive in the long term (Walster et al., 1973).

According to equity theory, individuals find themselves inequitably treated when their own ratio and the ratio of the comparison target are unequal. Rather than maximizing their own outcomes, individuals prefer equity for securing themselves with reasonable long-term material and immaterial outcomes (such as establishing and maintaining relationships). Feelings of inequity are of two types: feeling disadvantaged and feeling advantaged. Both situations evoke feelings of distress (particularly disadvantaged inequity) and will therefore be avoided. When individuals find themselves in an inequitable situation, they have several options to cope with this lack of reciprocity, including restoration of actual or psychological equity, altering the comparison target and leaving (e.g., VanYperen, Hagedoorn, & Geurts, 1996).

Mowday (1996) reviewed the research on behavioural reactions of employees who were dissatisfied because of inequitable payment. Reactions to underpayment vs. overpayment were summarized under two conditions: hourly compensation vs. piece-rate compensation. Underpaid employees are inclined to restore equity by decreasing their inputs (e.g., reducing effort) when their outcome is a constant (hourly payment). However, when payment is variable and depends on quantity (piece-rate payment), they are apt to restore equity by increasing their outcome by producing more in the same time, which obviously results in poorer-quality output. In the case of overpayment, the reversed pattern is likely to emerge. Overpaid employees will put more effort into the job when they are paid by the hour, and will produce less and have a higher-quality output when there is a piece-rate reward system.

The tendency to restore equity at the behavioural level will be lower for employees who have restored equity psychologically. Equity can be restored psychologically by altering the importance and the relevance of one's own or the other's inputs or outcomes. For example, an employee who works more hours than his colleagues but who is not proportionally rewarded may convince himself that it is fair that he spends more hours in the company because he has more time available than his colleagues, which brings about less perceived inequity.

Long-term inequity and burnout

When employees feel that it is impossible to restore actual or even psychological equity, and when an alternative is more attractive than the currently held job (for example, an alternative job or taking care of the children), they will resign. However, if no alternative jobs are available, or employees find alternative activities less attractive, resignation is less likely to occur, even if employees feel inequitably treated. Employees who do not successfully restore equity in the long run are likely to develop burnout symptoms (VanYperen, Buunk, & Schaufeli, 1992; VanYperen, 1998b). Burnout is a specific consequence of occupational stressors and is characterized by three aspects: emotional exhaustion, depersonalization, and reduced personal accomplishment (Maslach & Jackson, 1981). Emotional exhaustion refers to depletion of energy resources as a result of the emotional demands of a job. Depersonalization is the development of negative, cynical attitudes and feelings about one's work, whereas reduced personal accomplishment is defined as the tendency to evaluate oneself negatively with regard to one's job. Initially, burnout was defined in terms of one's relationship with recipients (e.g., cynical attitudes and feelings about recipients), which has limited the research of this phenomenon to helping professions, including nursing, teaching, police work and social work.

Exchange relationship A relationship in which there are two parties who understand that one benefit is given in return for another benefit, and each party is able to maintain equity in the relationship.

In helping professions, two equity considerations can be distinguished: the relationship with the organization for which one works, and the relationship with the recipients with whom one works (VanYperen, 1996). The relationship between employee and employer is typically an **exchange relationship**, i.e., a relationship in which there are two parties who understand that one benefit is given in return for another benefit, and each party is able to maintain equity in the relationship. By contrast, in the relationship between helping professional and recipient, equity maintenance is virtually impossible (see chapter 9 on the helper–recipient relationship). Perceived underbenefit in relationships with recipients is a basic job characteristic of human service professions: helping professionals are supposed to give, while recipients are supposed to receive. Clark and Mills (1993) argued that the relationship between helping professional and recipient is therefore an example of a one-sided **communal relationship**. In communal relationships, the norm is to give benefits in response to needs or to demonstrate a general concern for the other person. For example, the exchange relationship between the nurse and the nursing home provides the basis for the one-sided communal relationship the nurse has with patients.

Communal relationship A relationship in which the norm is to give benefits in response to needs or to demonstrate a general concern for the other person.

Nevertheless, helping professionals may feel that they invest too much in their relationships with recipients. VanYperen and colleagues (1992) found that 37 per cent of the nurses in their sample perceived an imbalance in their relationships with patients. Apparently, among these nurses the rewards on the part of the patients (positive feedback and appreciation, patients' health improvement) were not enough to compensate the high investments nurses made.

Communal orientation The desire to give and receive benefits in response to the needs of, and out of concern for, others.

In case of perceived inequity in the relationship between helping professionals and recipients, disadvantaged helping professionals will not necessarily experience burnout symptoms. Their experience depends on their **communal orientation**, which refers to the desire to give and receive benefits in response to the needs of, and out of concern for, others. Persons high in communal orientation are more apt to help another individual than persons low in communal orientation (Clark & Mills, 1993). Caregivers high in communal orientation appear to be less vulnerable to burnout symptoms in the case of perceived inequity in the relationship with recipients (VanYperen et al., 1992). As shown in figure 17.2, individual differences in communal orientation differentiated when nurses felt they invested much in the relationships with patients: low-communally oriented nurses with high investments felt most emotionally exhausted.

Procedural justice

Procedural justice refers to the process that has led to reward allocation. Leventhal (1980) proposed six criteria or rules an allocation procedure should satisfy to accomplish procedural justice (see table 17.1), although in some

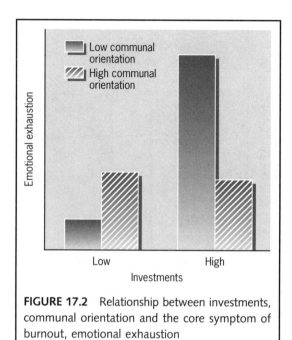

FIGURE 17.2 Relationship between investments, communal orientation and the core symptom of burnout, emotional exhaustion
(VanYperen et al., 1992)

TABLE 17.1 The six procedural rules to define the criteria of procedural justice (after Leventhal, 1980)

The consistency rule:	Allocations should be consistent across persons and over time.
The bias-suppression rule:	Personal self-interest and blind allegiance to narrow preconceptions should be prevented at all points in the allocation process.
The accuracy rule:	The allocation process should be based on as much good information and informed opinion as possible.
The correctability rule:	Opportunities should exist to modify and reverse decisions made at various points in the allocation process.
The representative rule:	All phases of the allocation process must reflect the basic concerns, values and outlook of important subgroups in the population of individuals affected by the allocation process.
The ethicality rule:	Allocation procedures should be compatible with the fundamental moral and ethical values accepted by the individual.

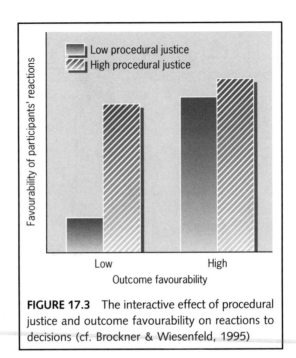

FIGURE 17.3 The interactive effect of procedural justice and outcome favourability on reactions to decisions (cf. Brockner & Wiesenfeld, 1995)

situations one or more particular rules have greater weight than others (e.g., VanYperen, Van den Berg, & Willering, 1999). According to the *two-component model of justice* (Cropanzano & Folger, 1996), negative or unfair outcomes such as an unfair pay reduction or perceived inequity only energize behaviour. The perceived fairness of the procedure determines the beneficial or detrimental direction of the behavioural reaction. Indeed, results from 45 samples suggest that if the distribution is unfair, employees react less negatively, or even positively, as long as they perceive the procedure that has led to the undesired outcome as fair (Brockner & Wiesenfeld, 1995). Employees' reactions are most favourable when they perceive either distributive justice or procedural justice, or both (see figure 17.3).

Specifically, Greenberg (1990) demonstrated that a fair procedure mitigates aggressive reactions, such as theft, to pay cuts. No increase in the employees' theft rate was observed in a similar company (company B) to company A described at the beginning of this section. In company B, the president was also forced to reduce its payroll by temporarily cutting wages by 15 per cent. In contrast to the president of company A, he followed a procedure in which the criteria of procedural justice, enumerated in table 17.1, were met. Specifically, the president of company B called a meeting at the end of the work week which lasted approximately 90 minutes (instead of 15 minutes). He also told the employees that the pay reduction was effective the following week, for a period expected to last ten weeks. The difference compared with the president of company A was the additional information he provided. The basis for the decision was clearly explained and justified by presenting charts and graphs detailing the temporary effects of the lost contracts on cash-flow revenues. Projections verified that the cash-flow problem dictating the need for the pay cuts was only temporary, and this was clearly explained. The tone of the presentation was such that a great deal of respect was shown for the employees, and all questions were answered with sensitivity. Approximately one hour was spent answering all questions. Furthermore, the employees were told that company management seriously regretted having to reduce their pay, but that doing so would preclude the need for any layoffs. They were further assured that all plant employees would share in the pay cuts and that no favouritism would be shown (Greenberg, 1990). Although we must be extremely cautious in concluding from two cases (there could be many other differences between the two companies), Greenberg's study suggests that a fair procedure can change the perception of a negative outcome, thus keeping employees from reacting aggressively to the negative outcome.

Productive conflict theory

Is conflict good or bad for organizations?

Two executives, Eric and Diane, form a selection committee to hire a capable candidate as their joint assistant. Because of illness during a vacation in a foreign country, Eric has been absent for three weeks. When Eric returns, it appears that Diane has continued the procedure and that there are only two candidates left. Both Eric and Diane feel frustrated and motivated to do something about it because things have not proceeded satisfactorily. Diane believes that Eric let her do all the work alone. Eric feels bypassed by Diane because the two remaining candidates do not meet the requirements that Eric finds most important. Eric and Diane have made an appointment to talk things over.

This conflict situation represents a world of daily organizational conflict between individuals or groups, or between individuals and groups. Typical *conflict issues* in organizations are scarce resources (money, equipment, space, manpower, information, attention, prestige, social power), disagreements about collective policies or procedures, or about individual role behaviours, and social-emotional conflicts whereby a group member's personal or social identity comes into question (Van de Vliert, 1997a; Walton, 1969). In cases of sexual harassment, for example, the victim's personal identity rather than an available resource or a work activity is at stake. All such situations, in which organizational members feel obstructed or irritated by others, influence the parties' work motives and subsequent job performance for the following reason. Almost by definition, a conflict makes an issue salient and some objectives and corresponding courses of action more important and feasible than others. Importance in conjunction with feasibility does motivate, whereas importance without feasibility (as well as feasibility

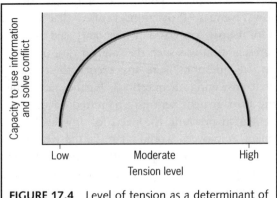

FIGURE 17.4   Level of tension as a determinant of the individual's capacity to use information and solve conflict
(Van de Vliert, 1996)

without importance) does not motivate a conflict party to undertake a certain course of action (Van de Vliert, 1997a). Note that this statement is empty in that it does not yet specify whether the conflict issue will be avoided, negotiated or battled out. What conflict behaviour follows? And how beneficial or detrimental is this particular conflict behaviour in terms of its substantive and relational outcomes for the organization, including job satisfaction and performance, and health-related consequences? Walton's (1969) productive conflict theory (for recent overviews, see De Dreu, 1997; Van de Vliert, 1997b) provides some classic and still viable answers to those questions by taking into account the level of tension.

The intriguing core proposition argues that organizational conflict with a moderate **tension level** is better than no conflict at all.

Tension level   In productive conflict theory, the operationalization of need level which is curvilinear related to compromise or to solve a conflict.

Problem-solving   A way of handling conflict in which there is high concern for everyone's goals, and complete satisfaction of all parties involved is achieved at the end.

Walton (1969) discerned three levels of tension in conflict (low, moderate, high) with differential effects on the motivational capacity to utilize information and to produce beneficial conflict outcomes for the organization (see figure 17.4). *Low-tension-level* conflicts lead to neglect of information, inactivity and avoidance, and low joint performance, as it is insufficiently important to confront the issue. In the case of a *moderate level of tension*, the parties will consider it relatively important and feasible to seek and integrate more information and more alternative courses of action; they will experience a stronger impulse to improve the situation. Conflict management in the form of **problem-solving** and compromising now increases the organization members' satisfaction, commitment and joint performance. *High-tension-level* conflicts reduce the motivational capacity to perceive, process and evaluate information; reconciliation and settlement are deemed undesirable, impracticable, or both. This produces aggressive and defensive interactions that result in less effective or downright destructive organizational consequences, including poor performance and health problems.

Taken together, conflicts of either too low or too high intensity are liable to harm rather than to benefit the parties and their organization, while moderately intense conflicts are likely to do the reverse. Consequently, a low level of tension requires limited conflict escalation to optimize motivation in order to enhance job performance and well-being. In moderately escalated conflicts, it is best to initiate negotiation or mediation if one wants to secure productive and satis-factory outcomes. Finally, when the level of tension is high, temporary inhibition of action and accommodative moves to de-escalate the conflict seem most appro-priate to further optimal motivation and substantive as well as relational effect-iveness. So, according to productive conflict theory, conflict is both an enemy and a friend on the perpetual expedition to organizational effectiveness.

In line with Walton's (1969) model, a cross-organizational study shows that organizations with many minor disagreements have few major clashes and instances of serious escalation (Corwin, 1969). Likewise, social influence research repeatedly shows that too little or too much disagreement between source and target in-duces less systematic and thorough scrutiny of issue-relevant information than a moderately conflictual relationship (De Dreu & De Vries, 1993; Nemeth & Staw, 1989; see chapter 14). Because productive conflict theory is less clear about the specific relationship between behaviour and performance than about the overall relationship between tension level, performance motivation and performance, Van de Vliert, Nauta, Giebels, & Janssen (1999) initiated a series of field experiments, including the following one.

In one-day workshops on conflict management, the above role script about Eric and Diane's selection problem was acted out by co-working dyads from a variety of industries, consultancy firms and governmental institutions. Each simulation was videotaped and then used for training, and later for research by rating the conflict behaviour and the effectiveness. The videotape-based training uncovered a variety of tension levels and related motivational orientations and behaviours. Though some dyad members tried to avoid open confrontation, most of them were fighting in order to win, or were seeking to resolve the discord. In line with productive conflict theory, low and high levels of tension were primarily asso-ciated with non-confrontation and aggressive reactions, respectively, whereas compromising and problem-solving flourished at moderate levels of tension. The actual interaction was considered less effective to the extent that it resulted in a stalemate or produced a winner and a loser, and more effective to the extent that it resulted in better joint outcomes for the dyad, a better mutual relation-ship between its members, or both. Most interestingly, mixtures of fighting and problem-solving were even more effective than pure problem-solving, especially if fighting preceded problem-solving. Indeed, the series of field experiments (Van de Vliert et al., 1999) repeatedly demonstrated that mixtures of fighting and problem-solving, to be located at the top of the inverted U-curve in figure 17.4, enhance the organization's performance and affective viability most.

Leadership Theories

To what extent is leaders' behaviour determined by their personal traits, the behaviours they enact, or the situations they find themselves in?

All three theories on work motivation discussed in this chapter strongly suggest that leadership in organizations affects employees' job performance. Managers set goals, whether or not in collaboration with their subordinates. Additionally, one of the roles a manager plays is that of resource allocator. In this role, a manager makes decisions about which subordinates get which resources (distributive justice). A manager also plays a part in developing organizational procedures and implementing these procedures (procedural justice). Last but not least, managers handle conflicts with their superiors, same-level colleagues and subordinates in a more or less destructive or constructive way.

Leadership has been defined broadly as a social influence process through which an individual intentionally exerts influence over others to structure the behaviours and relationships within a group or organization (Yukl, 1994). However, considerable variation exists between specific definitions of leadership as outlined in different theoretical perspectives. Traditionally, these definitions can be categorized on the basis of *trait, behavioural* and *situational* perspectives on leadership.

Trait approach to leadership

At the beginning of the twentieth century, the so-called 'great man' leadership theories asserted that leadership qualities were inherited (it was apparently assumed that the Y-chromosome was indispensable for 'born leaders'). These theories evolved into trait theories that did not make assumptions about whether leadership characteristics were inherited or acquired. The basic assumption of the trait approach to leadership was that a finite set of individual difference variables exists that can be used to distinguish successful from unsuccessful leaders. However, the list of potential biographical, personality, emotional, physical, intellectual and other personal characteristics of successful leaders appeared to be endless, although the classic review of Stogdill (1948) suggests that leaders are only somewhat taller and somewhat more intelligent than non-leaders. On the basis of his review, Stogdill concluded that situational factors were also influential. Indeed, business leaders, political leaders, military leaders and church leaders do not have identical traits. Another problem with the trait approach is the low analytical and predictive value of traits. *Even if it were possible* to describe current leaders in terms of traits, it is difficult to predict whether a person with particular characteristics will become a successful leader.

Despite these recognized problems of the trait approach, many people still believe that individual characteristics predict leadership behaviours, as is illustrated by the popularity of the **assessment centre technique**. An assessment centre is an employee evaluation technique that uses multiple methods to assess the skills and traits known to be related to success in a particular function (e.g., supervisor). Kirkpatrick and Locke (1991) mentioned six core traits on which leaders differ from non-leaders, namely drive, the desire to lead, honesty/integrity, self-confidence, cognitive ability and knowledge of the business. However, these authors note that such traits alone are not sufficient for successful leadership; they are only a precondition. Leaders who possess the requisite traits must competently take certain actions to become successful.

A contemporary trait approach is the framework of charismatic or transformational leadership. **Transformational leaders** act to change or transform their followers' needs and redirect their thinking (Bass, 1985). Followers of a transformational leader feel that their leader is endowed with exceptional personal qualities. Bass (1985) maintains that transformational leaders:

> **Assessment centre technique** An employee evaluation technique that uses multiple methods to assess the skills and traits known to be related to success in a particular function (e.g., supervisor).

> **Transformational leader** A person who is seen by followers as a leader endowed with exceptional personal qualities and who works to change or transform his or her followers' needs and redirect their thinking.

- arouse strong emotions in followers, resulting in the identification of the followers with their leader;
- inspire followers by articulating an appealing vision, by using symbols to focus followers' efforts, and by modelling appropriate behaviour;
- stimulate intellectually by encouraging followers to be creative problem-solvers;
- individualize by providing special support to followers.

Hence, subordinates of transformational leaders in organizations are assumed to transcend their own short-term self-interest for the sake of their work group or the organization. Transformational leadership is seen as giving meaningfulness to work by infusing work and organizations with moral purpose and commitment rather than by affecting the task environment of subordinates, or by offering material incentives and the threat of punishment (Shamir, House, & Arthur, 1993). Findings indicate that subordinates of transformational leaders are more satisfied with their jobs and organizational procedures, and more frequently exert extra-role behaviours on their jobs (Bass, 1985). However, it should be noted that transformational leadership is not necessarily good. In contrast, it can easily be imagined that this type of leadership leads to blind fanaticism in the service of megalomaniacs and dangerous values. The risks involved in following charismatic leaders are at least as large as the promises (Conger, 1990; Shamir et al., 1993).

Behavioural approach to leadership

Employee-oriented behaviour
Refers to a leadership style that includes behaviours such as showing concern for subordinates, acting in a friendly and supportive manner, showing appreciation for subordinates' contributions and recognizing their accomplishments.

Task-oriented behaviour
Refers to a leadership style that includes planning and scheduling work, establishing communication networks, providing necessary supplies, equipment and technical assistance, and evaluating job performance.

During the 1950s, dissatisfaction with the trait approach led researchers to adopt a new, behavioural focus on the study of leadership. The main question became: what do leaders do and how are these behaviours related to employees' job performance? Through the studies conducted in the 1950s (for a review, see Steers et al., 1996), two independent leadership styles were identified, suggesting that leaders can be high (or low) on both dimensions simultaneously (Blake & Mouton, 1970). **Employee-oriented behaviour** (also denoted as relationship-oriented behaviour or consideration) refers to behaviours such as showing concern for subordinates, acting in a friendly and supportive manner, showing appreciation for subordinates' contributions and recognizing their accomplishments. **Task-oriented behaviour** (or initiating structure) includes planning and scheduling work, establishing communication networks, providing necessary supplies, equipment and technical assistance, and evaluating job performance. A general finding is that an employee-oriented leadership style is accompanied by more satisfaction among subordinates. Similar to leadership traits, however, the effectiveness of leadership style depends on the work context. Certain traits or behaviours may be helpful and effective in some situations. These same traits and behaviours, however, may be unimportant, or even detrimental, in other situations. Accordingly, contingency theories of leadership evolved that turned the attention of researchers to situational aspects of leadership.

Contingency theories of leadership

The perspective that the most effective way to lead depends on the situation is clearly social psychological. It implies that diagnosing and evaluating the situation before applying a particular leadership style is a crucial step for effective leaders. The first coherent, and probably most famous, situational approach to leadership was developed by Fiedler (1968). In his contingency theory, he postulated that group performance is determined by the interaction between leadership style and three aspects of situations in which group members work interdependently towards a common goal that influence the leader's role. These three aspects are:

1   *Leader–member relations,* referring to the degree of confidence, trust and respect subordinates have for the leader. The group atmosphere is classified as either good or poor.

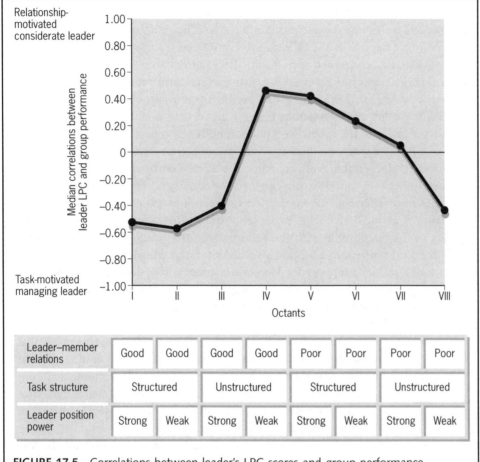

FIGURE 17.5   Correlations between leader's LPC scores and group performance
(Fiedler, 1968)

2   *Task structure.* A structured task has a clear, specified goal and can be easily
    evaluated (e.g., painting a door), whereas an unstructured task is complex and
    does not have one correct solution (e.g., writing an essay).
3   *Leader position power* is the power inherent in the leadership position, includ-
    ing the rewards and punishments that are officially or traditionally at the leader's
    disposal. Position power is classified as either high or low.

Groups can now be located in a three-dimensional space, and within each of the eight octants (see figure 17.5), Fiedler computed correlations between the leader's attitude towards his **least-preferred
co-worker** (LPC) and group performance. This attitude was assessed
by asking the leader to describe on a 20-item semantic differential
(pleasant vs. unpleasant, friendly vs. unfriendly, etc.) the person with

Least-preferred co-worker   In
Fiedler's theory of leadership,
the attitude towards the
person with whom the leader
has worked least well in
accomplishing some task.

whom he or she has worked least well in accomplishing some task. A leader with a high LPC score tends to see even a poor co-worker in a relatively favourable manner and is therefore characterized as a relationship-motivated considerate leader. On the other hand, a low-LPC leader is considered to be a task-motivated managing leader, i.e., concerned with productivity rather than with interpersonal relations. Fiedler's analyses revealed a negative correlation (about − 0.45) between leadership style (low LPC) and group performance in, for example, a situation in which the quality of the relations between leader and members is poor, the task is unstructured, and the supervisor's position power is weak (see figure 17.5: Octant VIII). Note that when the quality of the relations between leader and members improves, and everything else remains the same (unstructured task and weak position power: Octant IV), an employee-oriented leadership style (high LPC) becomes most effective (the correlation between leadership style and group performance is about 0.45). This example illustrates that a wrong diagnosis of the quality of the relationship with the subordinates may result in group ineffectiveness due to the manager adopting an inappropriate leadership style.

Although research support for Fiedler's contingency leadership model is weak, its basic idea that the impact of leadership style on group effectiveness depends on a set of situational factors has endured. Situational theories of leadership have intuitive appeal; it is quite obvious that effective leadership depends on the interaction between trait-like and situational factors. However, the problem is that the list of potential traits as well as relevant situational factors is endless. Similar to the trait approaches that differ with regard to the traits they illuminate, contingency theories differ with regard to the situational factors they focus on. For example, Hersey and Blanchard's (1982) theory of leadership, which also lacks empirical support but is popular among practitioners, highlights the **maturity of subordinates**. In the development process of a group from immaturity to maturity, the leadership style shifts away from entirely task-oriented (supervisor tells subordinates what to do) to entirely relationship-oriented (subordinates' self-direction and self-control or delegation).

Maturity of subordinates In Hersey and Blanchard's theory of leadership, the development phase of a group that determines the style the leader has to adopt.

Other contingency leadership models are more sophisticated: more factors are included, such as subordinate characteristics, leader behaviour, goal congruence, leader's information, subordinate and leader expectancies, etc. But more factors make it even more difficult to test the theory appropriately. At best the theory considers the effects of the various factors separately, even though the factors under consideration may interact. The strength of contingency theories of leadership is that important traits, behaviours and situational variables are specified which should be considered in almost any organizational setting. Thus, these theories can be used by leaders to guide the search for satisfactory solutions in a particular situation.

The romance of leadership

Reasoning that there are so many dispositional, group, organizational and cultural factors that have an influence on leadership behaviour, one might question the viability of the leadership concept. It might be that in traditional leadership research the amount of control leaders exert is overestimated. An alternative, provocative conceptualization to this romanticized conception of leadership is that leadership is a perception that plays a part in the way people attempt to make sense out of organizationally relevant phenomena. Meindl, Ehrlich and Dukerich (1985) observed that leaders are made scapegoats for poor organizational performance and praised for excellent performance. Hence, they hypothesized that there is a growing preference for using leadership as an attribution category (see also chapter 7) in understanding organizational outcomes with increasingly large magnitudes of effects. In one of their experimental studies, they confronted undergraduate business students with one of six different versions of a brief organizational performance-related scenario. The scenarios differed only in terms of the information they provided on performance outcomes, which were defined in terms of either sales increase (2 per cent/10 per cent/25 per cent) or sales decrease (2 per cent/10 per cent/25 per cent). As predicted, the results indicated that extreme performances lead to a proportional increase in attributing the outcome to the leader. Meindl et al. (1985) concluded that perhaps leadership is not as important as we normally think and that '*the romance and the mystery surrounding leadership concepts are critical for sustaining follower-ship and that they contribute significantly to the responsiveness of individuals to the needs and goals of the collective organization*' (p. 100).

Summary and Conclusions

In this chapter, we have addressed two of the most fundamental and critical behavioural topics facing today's work organizations: work motivation and leadership. Both topics represent highly complex phenomena that affect, and are affected by, variations in other organizational factors, including organizational outcomes. Furthermore, both topics deserve considerable and sustained attention from both practitioners and organizational researchers because every organization needs motivated employees and competent leaders in order to reach its goals.

It has been shown how organizational psychology benefits from social-psychological theories such as goal-setting theory, social justice theory, productive conflict theory and leadership theories. Specifically, the police captain we introduced at the beginning of this chapter may learn from this chapter that he should create or restore the following conditions to motivate his sergeants to do well in their job:

- Set mutually agreed goals that are specific and difficult.
- Establish an organizational climate in which individual and team improvement is emphasized.
- Distribute outcomes fairly among employees.
- Make employees feel fairly treated by satisfying the six criteria of procedural justice.

- De-escalate high-intensity conflict and escalate low-intensity conflict.
- Mix fighting and problem-solving when managing conflict.
- Inspire employees to transcend their own short-term self-interest for the sake of the collective.
- Vary the management style with the situational demands.

DISCUSSION POINTS

1 Can you explain why some professors do not devote a lot of time to teaching?
2 Why is the average correlation between job satisfaction and job performance almost zero? From the viewpoint of organizational effectiveness, do you prefer satisfied or dissatisfied employees? Why?
3 What should managers do to create an ego climate, and what should they do to create a learning climate?
4 How may the following employees react to distributive injustice?

- The sergeant who perceives the procedure that has led to the undesired outcome as unfair.
- The communally oriented nurse who feels she invested more in the relationships with her patients than she received in return.

5 Under what conditions does conflict enhance organizational effectiveness?
6 Why is Fiedler's theory considered a situational approach to leadership? Describe a situation in which a task-oriented leadership style is most effective (according to Fiedler's contingency theory).
7 Do you think that leadership is important for the effectiveness of an organization? Or is leadership a romanticized concept? Why?

FURTHER READING

Brockner, J., & Wiesenfeld, B. M. (1995). An integrative framework for explaining reactions to decisions: Interactive effects of outcomes and procedures. *Psychological Bulletin*, 102, 189–208. A review of studies on the interactive effects of distributive justice and procedural justice on individuals' reactions to a decision.

Farr, J. L., Hofmann, D. A., & Ringenbach, K. L. (1993). Goal orientation and action control theory: Implications for industrial and organizational psychology. In C. L. Cooper & I. T. Robertson (Eds.), *International Review of Industrial and Organizational Psychology*, 8, 193–232. This chapter describes the implications of the goal orientation approach for some selected topics of interest for social and organizational psychologists.

Locke, E. A., & Latham, G. P. (1990). *A theory of goal setting and task performance.* Englewood Cliffs, NJ: Prentice-Hall. This book represents the culmination of a 25-year intensive study of goal-setting theory. Research findings gathered from nearly 500 studies are reviewed and discussed.

Steers, R. M., Porter L. W., & Bigley, G. A. (1996). *Motivation and leadership at work.* McGraw-Hill. This book is an excellent integration of papers on motivation and leadership authored by leading academic scholars.

Van de Vliert, E. (1997). *Complex interpersonal conflict behaviour: Theoretical frontiers.* Hove: Psychology Press. This monograph is about reactions to interpersonal conflict, which are viewed as components of complex conflict behaviour that influence each other's impact on the substantive and relational outcomes.

Van Dyne, L., Cummings, L. L., & McLean Parks, J. (1995). Extra-role behaviors: In pursuit of construct and definitional clarity (A bridge over muddied waters). In L. L. Cummings & B. M. Staw (Eds.), *Research in Organizational Behavior*, 17, 215–85. This chapter clarifies the similarities and differences among four specific extra-role behaviours: organizational citizenship behaviour, prosocial organizational behaviour, whistle-blowing and principled organizational dissent.

KEY STUDIES

Greenberg, J. (1990). Employee theft as a reaction to underpayment inequity. The hidden costs of pay cuts. *Journal of Applied Psychology*, 75, 561–8.

Mann, L., Samson, D., & Dow, D. (1998). A field experiment on the effects of benchmarking and goal setting on company sales performance. *Journal of Management*, 24, 73–96.

Glossary

Accessibility The ease and speed with which information in memory can be found and retrieved.

Activation A heightened state of the central and particularly the autonomous nervous system. Some authors use the term to refer specifically to the sympathetic branch of the autonomous nervous system.

Actor–observer difference The claim that actors attribute their actions to situational factors, whereas observers tend to attribute the same actions to stable personal dispositions. The effect is confined to a difference in situational attribution, and appears due to differences in information, perceptual focus and linguistic factors.

Adaptation The possession of characteristics which enable the organism to survive and reproduce better than those with other characteristics. It is implied that these characteristics are better designed for the particular environment than are alternatives.

Additive task A group task that can be completed by adding together all individual members' inputs.

Adrenaline A hormone secreted by the adrenal medulla which stimulates the sympathetic nervous system. It stimulates the heart action and raises the blood pressure, releases glucose and increases its consumption, increases the circulation of the blood in the muscles, relaxes air passages and stimulates breathing. It prepares the body for physical action and at the same time inhibits digestion and excretion.

Affect Often used synonymously with emotion. Some social psychologists restrict the use to the valence aspect, pleasant vs. unpleasant or positive vs. negative, of feelings.

Affiliation The tendency to seek out the company of others, irrespective of the feelings towards such others.

After-image The colour seen on a white surface after exposure to another colour; it is the complementary colour of the original colour.

Aggregation principle This principle states that global measures of attitude are better at predicting global measures of behaviour, which aggregate over a variety of situations and points in time, than any specific instances of behaviour.

Altruistic behaviour In evolutionary terms, this is defined as behaviour which helps another individual's fitness despite a fitness cost for the donor. In social psychology, it refers to behaviour characterized by perspective-taking and empathy, which is undertaken with the intention of benefiting another person where the donor has a choice not to do so.

Anchoring and adjustment Judgemental heuristic that leads to characteristic biases: quantitative tendency to be biased towards the starting value or anchor. The subsequent adjustment process is typically incomplete.

Appraisal Evaluation of the significance of an object, event or action to a person, including an evaluation of one's coping activities. Can occur at various levels of the central nervous system and need not be conscious.

Assessment centre technique An employee evaluation technique that uses multiple methods to assess the skills and traits known to be related to success in a particular function (e.g., supervisor).

Assimilation A shift in the frame of reference caused by a context stimulus such that judgements of other stimuli are biased towards the context stimulus (e.g., in the context of humour, other utterances may appear more humorous).

Attachment   An enduring emotional tie between one person and another one.

Attachment theory   A theory that proposes that the development of secure infant–caregiver attachment in childhood is the basis for the ability to maintain stable and intimate relationships in adulthood.

Attitude   A psychological tendency that is expressed by evaluating a particular entity with some degree of favour or disfavour.

Attitudinal selectivity   Tendency to selectively attend to, process and remember information that is in line with one's attitude.

Attraction   Positive feelings towards another individual, including a tendency to seek out the presence of the other.

Attribution theory   The conceptual framework within social psychology dealing with lay, or common-sense, explanations of behaviour.

Attributional biases   A bias occurs if the perceiver systematically distorts (e.g., over- or underuses) some otherwise correct procedure, or indeed if the result of the procedure itself is distorted.

Attributional style   The tendency to make a particular kind of causal inference across different situations and across time.

Augmentation principle   The augmentation principle (originally invoked in relation to causal schemata) implies that the role of a given cause is increased if an effect occurs in the presence of an inhibitory cause. This idea has also been used to explain the social influence exerted by minorities.

Authoritarian personality   A particular type of personality – oversubmissive to authority figures – which is also thought to be particularly susceptible to prejudice.

Autokinetic effect   The illusion of movement of a stationary point of light when viewed in a totally dark environment.

Availability   Judgemental heuristic for judging the frequency or probability of events on the basis of the ease with which relevant memories come to mind.

Balance theory   A theory of cognitive consistency proposed by Heider that has been applied to attitude change and to explaining the relationship between attitudinal similarity and interpersonal liking. It assumes that individuals strive for maintaining and restoring equilibrium among their cognitions.

Benchmarking   A company benchmarks when it rates itself against others with better business practices in order to identify factors that will enable it to perform as well as, or better than, competitors.

Bottom-up processing   Information processing driven by new stimulus input rather than abstract knowledge structures in memory.

Brainstorming   A group technique aimed at enhancing creativity in groups by means of uninhibited generation of as many ideas as possible concerning a specified topic.

Buffering hypothesis of social support   The hypothesis that social support protects the individual against the negative health impact of high levels of stress.

Burnout   A specific consequence of occupational stressors, characterized by three aspects: emotional exhaustion, depersonalization and reduced personal accomplishment.

Catecholamines   Summary term which subsumes the hormones adrenaline and noradrenaline (also dopamine).

Categorical differentiation   The exaggeration of real differences between two categories.

Category   Grouping of two or more distinguishable objects that are treated in a similar way. Classes of objects in the world.

Catharsis   Release of aggressive energy through the expression of aggressive responses, or through alternative forms of behaviour.

Causal attribution   The inference process by which perceivers attribute an effect to one or more causes.

Causal schemata   Abstract, content-free conceptions of the way certain kinds of causes interact to produce an effect (e.g., multiple necessary cause schema; multiple sufficient cause schema).

Central route to persuasion   A person's careful and thoughtful consideration of the arguments presented in support of a position.

Classical conditioning The process by which a neutral stimulus that initially does not elicit a particular response gradually acquires the ability to do so through repeated association with a stimulus that has already evoked that response.

Coefficient of relatedness (r) The proportion of shared genes above those shared by unrelated individuals.

Coercive power The use of threats and punishments in pursuit of social power.

Cognitive appraisal The evaluative process that determines why, and to what extent, a particular situation is perceived as stressful.

Cognitive dissonance Central construct in Festinger's theory of cognitive dissonance. An aversive state of arousal caused by cognitions (i.e., beliefs, attitudes, expectations) that are inconsistent with each other, motivating the individual to reduce dissonance by adding, subtracting or substituting cognitions to increase consistency.

Cognitive neoassociationism The theory developed by Berkowitz that postulates a direct link between aversive events or negative affects and arousal of fight or flight behaviour. Denies the necessity of cognitive mediators for (emotional) aggression to occur.

Cognitive response approach A theoretical orientation assuming that attitude change is mediated by the overall favourability of thoughts or 'cognitive responses' that individuals generate when they are exposed to persuasive communications.

Collective aggression Aggression performed simultaneously by a large number of people, groups or masses, either in a spontaneous way, like riots, or in a planned way, like wars.

Commitment The individual's tendency both to maintain a relationship and to feel psychologically attached to it.

Common knowledge effect The tendency of group members to focus merely on commonly shared (rather than unique) pieces of information.

Communal orientation The desire to give and receive benefits in response to the needs of, and out of concern for, others.

Communal relationship A relationship in which the norm is to give benefits in response to needs

or to demonstrate a general concern for the other person.

Competition In interdependence theory, behaviour that maximizes relative advantage over others. In evolutionary biology, the process whereby an animal obtains greater or fewer resources necessary for survival and reproduction than another individual.

Competitive interdependence A task situation in which any one member of the group will succeed only if other member(s) of the group fail.

Compliance A change in overt (public) behaviour after exposure to others' opinions.

Confederate An accomplice or assistant of the experimenter who is ostensibly another participant but who in fact plays a prescribed role in the experiment.

Conformity *See* **majority influence**.

Confounding A variable that incorporates two or more potentially separable components is a confounded variable. When an independent variable is confounded, the researcher's ability to draw unambiguous causal inferences is seriously constrained.

Conjunctive task A group task requiring that all members complete it successfully.

Consistency A behavioural style indicative of maintenance of position. **Diachronic**: consistency over time; **synchronic**: consistency between individuals.

Construct An abstract theoretical concept (such as social influence).

Construct validity The validity of the assumption that independent and dependent variables adequately capture the abstract variables (constructs) they are supposed to represent.

Contact hypothesis The idea that contact between members of different groups under certain conditions lessens intergroup prejudice and hostility.

Contrast A shift in the frame of reference caused by a context stimulus such that judgements of other stimuli tend away from the context stimulus (e.g., other people appear rather poor in contrast to an extremely rich person).

Control group A group of participants who are typically not exposed to the independent variable(s) used in experimental research. Measures of the dependent variable derived from these participants are compared with those derived from participants who are exposed to the independent variable (i.e., the **experimental group**), providing a basis for inferring whether the independent variable determines scores on the dependent variable.

Conversion   A change in covert (private) behaviour after exposure to others' opinions; internalized change; a change in the way one structures an aspect of reality.

Cooperation   Behaviour that maximizes the outcomes (or well-being) of a collective. In evolutionary biology, when two animals pursue an action which enables them to obtain resources of benefit to both.

Cooperative interdependence   A task situation in which the success of any one member of the group improves the chances of other members succeeding.

Coordination losses   Deterioration in group productivity in comparison to individual productivity due to group members' inability to combine their resources in an optimal way.

Coping   The cognitive and behavioural strategies which individuals use to manage both a stressful situation and the negative emotional reactions elicited by that event.

Coping resources   The extrapersonal (e.g., social support) and intrapersonal resources (e.g., optimism) available to the individual for coping with the demands of a critical event.

Correspondence bias   The tendency to infer an actor's personal characteristics from his or her observed behaviours, even when the inference is unjustified because other possible causes of the behaviour exist (*see* **fundamental attribution error**).

Correspondence principle (also **compatibility principle**)   This principle states that a close relation between attitude and behaviour will obtain only if both measures agree in their degree of specification.

Cortisol   A hormone secreted by the adrenal cortex which promotes the synthesis and storage of glucose, suppresses inflammation and regulates the distribution of fat in the body.

Covariation principle   In Kelley's theory of causal attribution, a perceiver with sufficient time and motivation can make attributions by perceiving the covariation of an observed effect and its possible causes. The effect is attributed to the condition that is present when the effect is present, and absent when the effect is absent.

Cover story   A false but supposedly plausible explanation of the purpose of an experiment. The intention is to limit the operation of demand characteristics.

Critical life events   Events that represent major changes in an individual's life, which range from short-term to enduring and which are potentially threatening.

Crowd psychology   The study of the mind (cf. **group mind**) and the behaviour of masses and crowds, and of the experience of individuals in such crowds.

Cuckoldry   When a male cares for his female partner's offspring that are not his own.

Debriefing   The practice of explaining to participants the purpose of the experiment in which they have just participated, and answering any questions the participant may have. It is especially important to debrief participants when the experimental procedure involved deception – in which case, the debriefing should also explain why the deception was considered to be necessary.

Decentration   The ability to take account simultaneously of different aspects of a task rather than to centre exclusively on one.

Defence motivation   The desire to defend and maintain certain beliefs or attitudinal positions that are consistent with existing central attitudes and values.

Deindividuation   An individual state in which rational control and normative orientation are weakened, leading to greater readiness to respond in an extreme manner and to violate norms.

Demand characteristics   Cues that are perceived as telling participants how they are expected to behave or respond in a research setting, i.e., cues that 'demand' a certain sort of response.

Dependent variable   The variable that is expected to change as a function of changes in the independent variable. Measured changes in the dependent variable are seen as 'dependent on' manipulated changes in the independent variable.

Developmental instability The extent to which development has been influenced in a direction other than bilateral symmetry by genetic abnormalities and environmental disruptions such as toxins and parasites.

Diffuse status characteristics Information about a person's abilities that is only obliquely relevant to the group's task, deriving mainly from large-scale category memberships (age, ethnicity, sex) outside the task group.

Diffusion of responsibility Cognitive reinterpretation which divides responsibility among several persons, with the result that each person feels less responsible. As a consequence, each individual member in a group feels less responsible than when alone. In groups of bystanders of emergencies, social inhibition of helping may be caused by weakened sense of responsibility among several bystanders.

Discounting principle The discounting principle (originally invoked in relation to causal schemata) implies that the role of a given cause in producing an effect is decreased if other plausible causes are present.

Discrete emotions The theoretical notion that there is a limited number of highly differentiated basic or fundamental emotions that are common to different species and cultures.

Disjunctive task An either/or group task that can be completed by selecting one single group member's input to stand as the group product.

Display rules Modern term denoting the old observation that there are socio-cultural norms that govern the type of emotional expressions that are acceptable in specific situations.

Distributive justice Criteria of fairness used to evaluate the quality of one's own outcomes by linking it to the quality of others' outcomes.

Dominant responses Responses that take precedence in a person's response repertoire, such as well-learned or instinctive responses.

Dual-concern model Two-dimensional model that specifies several actions in terms of concern for self and concern for other.

Dual-process models of persuasion Theories of persuasion (e.g., elaboration likelihood model; heuristic–systematic model) postulating two modes of information processing, which differ in the extent to which individuals engage in effortful thought about message arguments and other detailed information on an attitude object. The mode of information processing is assumed to depend on processing motivation and ability.

Ease of recall The subjective feeling that information pertaining to some topic can be easily found and retrieved from memory; not to be confused with objective recall success.

Ego orientation Reflects the individual's goal of establishing his or her superiority over others.

Elaboration likelihood model The elaboration likelihood model of Petty and his colleagues assumes that attitude change in response to persuasive communications can be mediated by two modes of information processing (*see* **dual-process models**). Elaboration denotes the extent to which a person engages in central-route processing of the issue-relevant arguments contained in a message rather than being influenced by processes that characterize the peripheral route to persuasion (e.g., classical conditioning; heuristic processing). Elaboration likelihood is determined by both processing motivation and ability.

Emotion Earlier often used synonymously with feeling or affect. Modern usage assumes emotion to be a hypothetical construct denoting a process of an organism's reaction to significant events. Emotion is generally presumed to have several components: physiological arousal, motor expression, action tendencies and subjective feeling.

Emotion-focused coping Coping strategies which do not focus on the stressful event but on ameliorating the distressing emotional reactions to the event.

Emotional contagion The unconscious mimicking of the facial expressions and feelings from another individual.

Emotional reaction triad *See* **emotion**; the three response components: physiological arousal, motor expression and subjective feeling.

Empathy Affective state that is triggered when an individual witnesses the emotional state of another person. This feeling state results from adopting the perspective of the other and understanding his or her emotions.

Employee-oriented behaviour   Refers to a leadership style that includes behaviours such as showing concern for subordinates, acting in a friendly and supportive manner, showing appreciation for subordinates' contributions and recognizing their accomplishments.

Endocrine system   The system of glands and other structures that produces and secretes hormones into the bloodstream.

Epidemiology   The study of the distribution and determinants of health-related states or events in specified populations.

Equity theory   Assumes that satisfaction is a function of the proportionality of outcomes to inputs of the person as compared with those of a reference other, and that individuals will try to restore equity when they find themselves in an inequitable situation.

Eureka task   A disjunctive task with a solution that, once suggested, seems obviously correct to all group members.

Evaluation apprehension   The stressful experience of a person whose behaviour is observed by others. This experience may elicit anxiety and lead to deterioration of performance or high levels of performance, depending on one's own familiarity of the task and prior practice.

Evaluative priming   Presenting a positive vs. negative stimulus facilitates the subsequent perception and processing of another stimulus of the same positive vs. negative valence.

Evolutionary psychology   An approach to psychology based on the principle of natural selection. The emphasis is placed more on psychological mechanisms and flexibility than is the case for sociobiology.

Evolutionary theory   A theory that explains human behaviour, including differences in partner preferences according to gender, from their reproductive value, i.e., their value in producing offspring in our evolutionary past.

Exchange relationship   A relationship in which there are two parties who understand that one benefit is given in return for another benefit, and each party is able to maintain equity in the relationship.

Excitation-transfer theory   Sources of arousal not directly related to aggression may be added to aggression-specific arousal, thus intensifying aggressive responses.

Exemplar-based representation   Memory representation of a concept (group, category) in terms of concrete exemplars rather than abstracted features.

Expectancy-value models   These models assume that decisions between different courses of action are based on two types of cognitions: (1) the subjective probabilities that a given action will lead to a set of expected outcomes, and (2) the valence of these outcomes. According to this approach, individuals will choose among various alternative courses of action the one that maximizes the likelihood of positive consequences and/or minimizes the likelihood of negative consequences.

Experiment   A method in which the researcher deliberately introduces some change into a setting to examine the consequences of that change.

Experimental games   A research tool for examining social interaction, derived from game theory.

Experimental group   A group of participants allocated to the 'experimental' condition of the experiment, i.e., the condition in which participants are exposed to that level of the independent variable that is predicted to influence their thoughts, feelings or behaviour.

Experimental scenario   The 'package' within which an experiment is presented to participants. In field experiments it is, ideally, something that happens naturally. In laboratory experiments it is important to devise a scenario that strikes the participant as realistic and involving.

Experimenter effects (sometimes referred to as **experimenter expectancy effects**)   Effects unintentionally produced by the experimenter in the course of his or her interaction with the participant. These effects result from the experimenter's knowledge of the hypothesis under test, and they increase the likelihood that the participants will behave in such a way as to confirm the hypothesis.

Expression Muscular actions in the face, the vocal organs, the hands and the skeletal musculature generally that are linked to internal states of the organism and thus provide indices of such states, thereby serving communicative purposes. As a consequence, expression is often manipulated to produce appropriate signals in social interaction.

Extended identity The awareness that social judgements of us may reflect our associations with other people.

External validity Refers to the generalizability of research findings to settings and populations other than those involved in the research.

Extra-role behaviour Those aspects of job performance that are not specified in advance by role prescriptions, that are not directly or explicitly recognized by the formal reward system, and that are not a source of punitive consequences when refrained from by job incumbents.

Facial feedback hypothesis *See* **proprioceptive feedback**; here specifically the notion that amplification or inhibition of facial expression of emotion will modify the intensity and possibly the nature of subjective feeling.

Factorial experiment An experiment in which two or more independent variables are manipulated within the same design.

Family aggression According to the APA Task Force on Violence and the Family (APA, 1996), a pattern of violent and abusive behaviours, including a wide range of physical, sexual and psychological maltreatment, used by one person in an intimate relationship against another to gain power unfairly or maintain that person's misuse of power, control and authority.

Fear-arousing communications Persuasive communications that attempt to motivate recipients to change behaviour deleterious to their health by inducing fear about the potential health hazards and providing a recommendation for an action that would reduce or eliminate the threat.

Feeling Earlier used synonymously with emotion. Modern use restricted to the component of subjective experience of emotional arousal, often conscious and verbalizable by using emotion words or expressions.

Field experiment A true randomized experiment conducted in a natural setting.

Fitness The ability of an organism to leave a greater proportion of its genes in succeeding generations than other individuals (*but see also* **inclusive fitness**).

Fluctuating asymmetry The degree to which an individual deviates from perfect bilateral symmetry.

Free-riding Strategy of leaving it to other group members to contribute to the group product, because the individual considers his or her own contribution to be dispensable.

Frustration–aggression (hypothesis) Aggression is always a result of frustration.

Functional measures of social support Measures that assess the extent to which interpersonal relationships serve particular support functions (e.g., emotional, instrumental, belonging and appraisal support).

Fundamental attribution error The tendency for perceivers to underestimate the impact of situational factors and to overestimate the role of dispositional factors in controlling behaviour. This bias can be explained in terms of cognitive, cultural and linguistic factors (*see* **correspondence bias**).

Group mind The concept of the supra-individual nature and independence of the collective mind of a social group.

Group polarization A change in the average position of a group, following group discussion, in the direction of the initially dominant pole.

Groupthink A group decision process, strongly oriented towards consensus, among like-minded and cohesive individuals, emanating in one-sided and incorrect conclusions.

Hawthorne effect A term used to describe the effect of participants' awareness that they are being observed on their behaviour.

Health belief model The model assumes that people's health behaviour is determined by their perception of the threat of illness or injury and the advantages and disadvantages of taking action.

Health education The provision of knowledge and/or training of skills which facilitate voluntary adoption of behaviour conducive to health.

Hedonism (psychological) The doctrine that every activity is motivated by the desire for pleasure and the avoidance of pain.

Helping behaviour In its biological meaning, it is equivalent to **altruistic behaviour** in the most general sense.

Heuristic cue Information present in a persuasion setting (e.g., a communicator's white lab coat) that indicates the applicability of a heuristic (e.g., 'experts' statements are valid').

Heuristic processing Assessing the validity of a communication or the merits of an attitude object through reliance on heuristics, i.e., simple rules like 'the majority is right' or 'experts' statements are valid'.

Heuristic–systematic model The heuristic–systematic model of Chaiken and her colleagues assumes that attitude change can be mediated by two different modes of information processing, namely heuristic and systematic processing (*see* **dual-process models**). When individuals are unmotivated or unable to invest much cognitive effort, they are likely to rely on heuristic cues in forming an attitude judgement; when motivation and ability are high, they also scrutinize message arguments and all other potentially relevant information to form a judgement.

Hidden profile Problem where the best solution will go unrecognized because relevant information that is dispersed among group members does not receive sufficient attention.

Hostile attribution bias A crucial criterion for perceiving an action as aggressive is to infer the actor's hostile intent. According to the norm of reciprocity, the victim reciprocates by own aggressive actions. In contrast to non-aggressive persons, highly aggressive individuals tend to react more aggressively when the information about the actor's intent is ambiguous. This reaction coincides with the tendency to attribute hostile motives to the frustrator when clear information about the actor's intent is absent.

Hypothesis A proposed explanation for an observed relationship between events.

Illusory correlation An overestimation of the strength of a relationship between two, usually distinct, variables (e.g., 'crime' and 'immigrants'); a possible cognitive basis of stereotyping.

Immune system The organs and structures that protect the organism against foreign substances. Its major function is to combat infectious micro-organisms (bacteria, viruses and parasites). It does so through the production of infection-fighting cells and chemicals.

Implicit attitudes Evaluative tendencies that may influence judgements or behaviours without the individual being aware of their influence.

Implicit measures Measures of constructs such as attitudes and stereotypes that are derived from the way respondents behave (such as how long they take to make a decision or to answer a question) rather than from the content of their answers to explicit questions about these constructs. They are a class of **unobtrusive measure**.

Implicit verb causality The tendency to infer causes within the sentence subject from action verbs and causes within the object from state verbs.

Inclusive fitness This refers to the representation of an individual's genes in succeeding generations when help given to relatives is balanced against reproduction.

Independent variable The variable that an experimenter manipulates or modifies in order to examine the effect on one or more dependent variables.

Individualism The doctrine that emphasizes the rights, values and interests of the individual from which all rights and values of society have to be derived and justified (ethical and political individualism). The doctrine that all explanations of individual or social phenomena are to be rejected unless they are expressed wholly in terms of individuals (methodological individualism).

Individuo-centred approach Any approach to the study of social behaviour and social functions relying exclusively or largely on the study of individual experience and behaviour.

Informational influence Influence based on the informational value of opinions expressed by others, on what they tell a person about an aspect of reality.

Ingroup A group to which a person belongs, or thinks he or she belongs.

Innovation *See* **minority influence**.

In-role behaviour Those aspects of job performance that are explicitly expected and rewarded.

Insufficient justification The state of having shown an attitude-discrepant behaviour without perceiving an external reason for doing so; a special case of the conditions arousing cognitive dissonance.

Interaction effect A term used when the combined effects of two (or more) independent variables in a factorial experiment yield a pattern that differs from the sum of the **main effects**.

Interaction process analysis (IPA) A formal observational measurement system devised by Bales for coding the interactions of members of small social groups into task-oriented and relationship-oriented categories.

Inter-attitudinal structure The way in which attitudes towards different attitude objects are organized in an individual's memory.

Interdependence structure Situations in which personal outcomes are partially or completely determined by the actions of one or more others.

Intergroup behaviour Actions by members of one group towards members of another group.

Internal validity Refers to the validity of the inference that changes in the independent variable result in changes in the dependent variable.

Interpersonal–(inter)group continuum A continuous dimension of social behaviour distinguishing between actions performed as an individual and actions performed as a group member.

Interpersonal guilt Negative feelings about oneself which result from the knowledge that one is responsible for the distress of others or for damage done to them.

Intimacy A state in interpersonal relationships that is characterized by sharing of feelings, and is based upon caring, understanding and validation.

Intra-attitudinal structure Comprises aspects of an attitude's representation in memory, such as its polarity, its dimensionality and the degree of consistency among the components of an attitude (*see* **three-component model of attitude**).

Intragroup homogeneity The extent to which members of a group are seen as similar to each other on various attributes.

Investment model A theory that assumes that commitment to a relationship is based upon a high satisfaction, a low quality of alternatives, and a high level of investments.

Judgemental heuristic Rules-of-thumb that allow quick and economic judgements, even under high uncertainty.

Just-world belief Generalized expectancy that people get what they deserve. Undeserved suffering of others threatens the just-world belief and motivates attempts to restore it. These include reducing the victims' suffering by helping, or devaluation of the victims.

Knowledge function An attitude's function of guiding, organizing and simplifying information processing.

Learned helplessness A state characterized by learning deficits, negative emotion and passive behaviour when organisms learn that their responses are independent of desired outcomes.

Learning orientation Reflects the individual's involvement in gaining skill and performing one's best.

Least-preferred co-worker In Fiedler's theory of leadership, the attitude towards the person with whom the leader has worked least well in accomplishing some task.

Likert scale A technique for measuring attitudes developed by Rensis Likert. The key feature of this method is that respondents are asked to rate the extent of their agreement or disagreement with a set of statements about the attitude object.

Linguistic categories Different types of verbs and adjectives that can take the role of predicates in behaviour descriptions.

Linguistic intergroup bias The tendency to use more abstract linguistic categories to describe positive ingroup and negative outgroup behaviour than to describe negative ingroup and positive outgroup behaviour.

Loneliness A complex affective response stemming from felt deficits in the number and nature of one's social relationships.

Main effect A term used to refer to the separate effects of each independent variable in a **factorial experiment**.

Majority influence (conformity) Social influence resulting from exposure to the opinions of a majority, or the majority of one's group.

Manipulation check A measure of the effectiveness of the independent variable.

Maturity of subordinates In Hersey and Blanchard's theory of leadership, the development phase of a group that determines the style the leader has to adopt.

Mediating variable A variable that mediates the relation between two other variables. Assume that independent variable X and dependent variable O are related. If a third variable Z is related to both X and O, and if the X–O relation disappears when we take the role of Z into account, then Z is said to mediate the relation between X and O.

Mediation Assistance of a third party to help solve a conflict of interest, often through communication with both parties.

Memory-based judgement Typically, unexpected judgements that have to rely on whatever relevant information can be retrieved from memory.

Mental contagion The hypothetical mechanism underlying the spread of affect and of ideas in crowds.

Mere thought Thinking about an attitude object in the absence of external information which leads to extremization of the attitude.

Message-learning approach An eclectic approach to persuasion, featuring the assumption that attitude change is a function of the learning and retention of message content, and studying source, message, channel and recipient characteristics as variables in the persuasion process.

Meta-analysis A set of techniques for statistically integrating the results of independent studies of a given phenomenon, with a view to establishing whether the findings exhibit a pattern of relationships that is reliable across studies.

Minimal group paradigm A set of experimental procedures designed to create ad hoc groups on essentially arbitrary criteria with no interaction within or between them, and with no knowledge of who else belongs to each group. Once such a situation has been created, people's perceptions of or reward allocations to the groups may be measured.

Minority influence (innovation) Social influence resulting from exposure to the opinions of a minority group, or the minority of one's group.

Mixed-motive interdependence A task situation in which group members are cooperatively as well as competitively interdependent.

Mixed-motive situations Situations characterized by the conflict between personal goals and collective goals.

MODE model The MODE (motivation and opportunity as determinants of how attitudes influence behaviour) model assumes that attitudes can influence behaviour either by the deliberate processing of the attitudinal implications for behaviour or by the automatic selective processing of attitude-relevant information.

Modelling The tendency for individuals to acquire new (and more complex) forms of behaviour by observing this behaviour, and its consequences, in real-life or symbolic models.

Modification of the incentive structure Refers to strategies of behaviour change that influence behaviour by increasing the 'costs' of undesirable (e.g., health-impairing) behaviour, and decreasing the 'costs' of desirable (health-promoting) behaviour. Governments often use fiscal (e.g., tax increases on cigarettes and alcoholic beverages) or legal measures (e.g., laws enforcing use of seatbelts or crash helmets) to influence behaviour.

Monogamy A mating system comprising one male and one female. It can apply to human marriages.

Mood Major differences to emotion are a diffuse origin (rather than a specific eliciting event), a much longer duration and a lower overall intensity.

Mood-as-information hypothesis The assumption that individuals use their mood as information in making evaluative judgements about an attitude object.

Mood congruency The tendency to perceive, encode, store and recall information more efficiently that is effectively congruent with one's emotional state. Also refers to the tendency to give more positive (negative) judgements in positive (negative) mood states.

Motivation losses Inefficiency that results from more or less conscious reductions in the motivation to do one's very best on behalf of the group.

Mutuality model A model of socialization which assumes that caregiver and child have reciprocal effects on each other's behaviour.

Natural selection The process whereby individuals with certain characteristics are more frequently represented in succeeding generations as the result of being better adapted for that environment.

Need for cognition An individual difference variable that differentiates individuals in terms of how much they engage in and enjoy thinking about topics and problems. When exposed to a persuasive message, individuals high in need for cognition engage in more content-related thinking than individuals low in need for cognition.

Negotiation Discussion between two or more parties with the apparent aim of resolving divergence of interest.

Nominal group technique An alternative to interactive brainstorming, which calls for combining individuals' inputs (developed in isolation) into a group product.

Non-dominant responses Novel, complicated or untried responses that the individual has never (or only infrequently) performed before.

Noradrenaline A hormone secreted by the adrenal medulla and by the nerve endings of the sympathetic nervous system. Whereas adrenaline prepares the body for physical action, noradrenaline deals with the routine jobs such as maintaining an even blood pressure.

Normative influence Influence based on the need to be accepted and approved by others.

Normative model Standard, optimally correct way of making an inference or judgement (e.g., Kelley's ANOVA model).

Obedience Carrying out the orders given by a person invested with authority.

One-shot case study A research design in which observations are made on a group after some event has occurred or some manipulation has been introduced. The problem is that there is nothing with which these observations may be compared, so one has no way of knowing whether the event or manipulation had an effect.

On-line judgement Judgements formed immediately upon presentation of stimulus information.

Operant conditioning Process of learning by reinforcement (i.e., responses increase in frequency because they have positive consequences) or punishment (i.e., responses decrease in frequency because they have negative consequences).

Operationalization The way in which a theoretical **construct** is turned into a measurable **dependent variable** or a manipulable **independent variable** in a particular study.

Outgroup A group to which a person does not belong, or thinks he or she does not belong.

Overjustification effect Rewarding individuals for performing a task they previously found interesting in itself (= overjustification) reduces their liking for the task.

Parental investment The contribution in terms of time and energy to feeding, incubating and protecting developing offspring.

Participant observation A method of observation in which the researcher studies the target group or community from within, making careful records of what he or she observes.

Passionate love A state of intense longing for union with another individual, usually characterized by intrusive thinking and preoccupation with the partner, idealization of the other, and the desire to know the other as well as the desire to be known by the other.

Peripheral route to persuasion Subsumes those persuasion processes that are not based on effortful issue-related thinking (e.g., classical conditioning, heuristic processing).

Persuasion Attitude formation or change, usually in response to arguments and/or other information about the attitude object.

Placebo control group Control group used to check whether the effect of a treatment is due to the active ingredient of the treatment or some other effect. Placebo control groups receive apparently the same treatment as the intervention group, except that the administered treatment lacks the active ingredient.

Pluralistic ignorance A belief that one's perceptions and feelings are different from those of others, while simultaneously one's visible behaviour is identical to that of others. In groups of bystanders of emergencies: the erroneous conclusion of each bystander that the other bystanders interpret the event as harmless.

Polyandry A mating system comprising one female and several males. It can also refer to human marriages.

Polygyny A mating system comprising one male and several females. It can also refer to human marriages.

Positivism The doctrine according to which knowledge should be based on natural phenomena and their temporal and spatial relationships as identified and verified by the methods (methodology) of empirical science.

Post-experimental enquiry A technique advocated by Orne for detecting the operation of demand characteristics. The participant is carefully interviewed after participation in an experiment, the object being to assess perceptions of the purpose of the experiment.

Post-test only control group design A minimal design for a true experiment. Participants are randomly allocated to one of two groups. One group is exposed to the independent variable; another (the control group) is not. Both groups are assessed on the dependent variable, and comparison of the two groups on this measure indicates whether or not the independent variable had an effect.

Precaution adoption process model A stage model of health behaviour change which describes the stages individuals are assumed to move through in adopting some health-protective measure. It has originally been developed as a dynamic version of the health belief model.

Prejudice A derogatory attitude or set of attitudes towards all or most of the members of a group.

Primacy effect The tendency for information received early to have a stronger influence than later information on one's judgements or memory about persons, objects or issues.

Priming effect The finding that a schema is more likely to be activated if it has recently been presented or used in the past.

Problem-focused coping Refers to instrumental behaviour aimed at reducing or eliminating the risk of harmful consequences which might result from the stressful event.

Problem-solving A way of handling conflict in which there is high concern for everyone's goals, and complete satisfaction of all parties involved is achieved at the end.

Procedural justice Criteria of justice used to evaluate the quality of the decision-making process for distributing outcomes between people.

Process losses Group processes that prevent a group from reaching its potential productivity. Such losses include coordination losses and motivation losses.

Production blocking Reduction in individual productivity and creativity in generating ideas due to interruptions and turn-taking in interactive brainstorming sessions.

Proprioceptive feedback Proprioception refers to the capacity of internal organs to provide sensory information about changes in the body. Proprioceptive feedback refers to changes in one internal system upon detection of changes in another system.

Prosocial behaviour In its biological sense, this is equivalent to altruistic behaviour. In its social-psychological sense, it is narrower than helping behaviour in that the action is intended to improve the situation of the recipient, and the actor is not obliged to help the person receiving help.

Prospective study Longitudinal study where the suspected causal factors (e.g., stressful life events) that predict a certain future outcome (e.g., depression or heart disease) are measured first, and the outcome variables are then assessed at some future point in time.

Protection motivation theory Originally an attempt to specify the algebraic relationships between the components of the health belief model. In its most recent version, the model assumes that the motivation to protect oneself from danger is a positive function of four beliefs: the threat is severe, one is personally vulnerable, one has the ability to perform the coping response, and the coping response is effective in reducing the threat. Two further beliefs are assumed to decrease protection motivation: the rewards of the maladaptive response are great, and the costs of performing the coping response are high.

Prototype The best exemplar of a given category; an abstract representation of the attributes associated with a category, which is stored in memory and used to organize information.

Psychological reactance An aversive state caused by restrictions to an individual's freedom of exerting choice over important behavioural alternatives, which in turn causes a motivational tendency to restore the restricted freedom.

Quasi-experiment An experiment in which participants are not randomly allocated to the different experimental conditions (typically because of factors beyond the control of the researcher).

Quota sample A sample that fills certain pre-specified quotas and thereby reflects certain attributes of the population (such as age and sex) that are thought to be important to the issue being researched.

Reactivity A measurement procedure is reactive if it alters the nature of what is being measured (i.e., if the behaviour observed or the verbal response recorded is partly or wholly determined by the participant's awareness that some aspect of his or her behaviour is being measured).

Reciprocal altruism Altruistic behaviour shown by an animal or person when the recipient is likely to behave altruistically to the donor in the future.

Reciprocity (norm of) The norm that we should do to others as they do to us. Reciprocity calls for positive responses to favourable treatment but negative responses to unfavourable treatment. Prosocial reciprocity occurs when people help in return for having been helped. In interpersonal relationships, the basic rule that one can expect to obtain assets such as status, attractiveness, support and love to the degree that one provides such assets oneself.

Reliability A measure is reliable if it yields the same result on more than one occasion or when used by different individuals.

Representativeness Judgemental heuristic used to estimate event probabilities on the basis of crude similarity principles. For instance, a symptom is taken as evidence for a threatening disease even when the objective base-rate of the disease is extremely low.

Reproductive strategies Consistent patterns of sexual and parenting behaviour which typically lead to the production of viable offspring.

Salience The distinctiveness of a stimulus relative to the context (e.g., a male in a group of females; a group of people, one of whom is in the spotlight).

Sample survey A research strategy that involves interviewing (or administering a questionnaire to) a sample of respondents who are selected so as to be representative of the population from which they are drawn.

Sampling The process of selecting a subset of members of a population with a view to describing the population from which they are taken.

Script Knowledge structure representing routinized action episodes in particular domains.

Secure base The feeling of security and trust associated with a specific person or place, such as a child's orientation towards his or her primary caregiver.

Selective exposure Dissonance theory assumes that people are motivated to search selectively for information that supports former decisions or existing attitudes, thereby actively avoiding opposing information.

Self-categorization theory A general theory of group behaviour emphasizing the impact of self-definitions at different levels of abstraction (individual, group, humanity) on judgement and behaviour.

Self-efficacy Refers to beliefs in one's ability to carry out certain actions required to attain a specific goal. For example, the belief that one is capable of giving up smoking or going on a diet.

Self-esteem maintenance function An attitude's function of setting the self apart from negative objects and aligning it with positive objects.

Self-fulfilling prophecy When an originally false social belief leads to its own fulfilment. Social belief refers to people's expectations regarding another group of people. When a self-fulfilling prophecy occurs, the perceiver's initially false beliefs cause targets to act in ways that objectively confirm those beliefs.

Self-handicapping A subtle form of self-serving bias, whereby someone manipulates causes of their failure before it happens to obscure the link between performance and evaluation.

Self-monitoring A personality trait. Individuals high in self-monitoring tailor their behaviour to fit situational cues and the reactions of others, whereas individuals low in self-monitoring act more in accordance with their internal states and dispositions.

Self-perception theory Theory proposed by Bem as an alternative to the theory of cognitive dissonance. Its main assumption is that individuals infer their own attitudes by engaging in attributional reasoning, just like an outside observer.

Self-serving bias People are more likely to attribute their successes to internal causes such as ability, whereas they tend to attribute failures to external causes such as task dif-ficulty. This bias appears due to cognitive and motivational factors, varying across public and private settings.

Semantic differential A technique for measuring attitudes (among other things) developed by Charles Osgood and his colleagues. The key feature of this method is that respondents are asked to rate the attitude object on several bipolar adjective scales.

Sexual selection A form of natural selection which involves selection of, and access to, sexual partners.

Simple random sample A sample in which each member of the population has an equal chance of being selected and in which the selection of every possible combination of the desired number of members is equally likely.

Simulation heuristic Outcomes or events are judged to be likely to the extent that they can be mentally simulated or imagined.

Social comparison The act of comparing own behaviour to others' behaviour in order to evaluate the correctness and adequacy of own behaviour.

Social comparison theory A theory which emphasizes that individuals assess their attitudes, abilities and emotions by comparing themselves with similar others, and that they do so especially when they are uncertain about themselves.

Social compensation Increased effort on a group task in order to compensate for co-workers' actual, perceived or anticipated lack of effort or ability.

Social constructivism Notion that social and cultural factors create reality for the individual, independently of biological processes, providing a language for the definition of self and experience in the world.

Social decision scheme A probabilistic model, specifying the process by which individual inputs are combined into a group decision.

Social desirability A term used to describe the fact that participants are usually keen to be seen in a positive light and are therefore reluctant to report on their negative qualities.

Social dilemma Situation in which self-interest and collective interest are at odds.

Social exchange theory A general theoretical model that views relationships in terms of rewards and costs to the participants. It emphasizes that individuals expect certain levels of outcomes on the basis of their standards, which are in part derived from previous experiences, the outcomes of their partners and the outcomes of comparable others.

Social facilitation Increased emission of dominant responses, resulting from the presence of others.

Social hypothesis testing Verifying or falsifying propositions through socially motivated processes of attention, information search, logical reasoning and (often selective) memory.

Social identity A person's sense of who he or she is, derived from his or her group membership(s).

Social identity function An attitude's function of expressing an individual's values and of establishing identification with particular reference groups.

Social influence A change in the judgements, opinions and attitudes of an individual as a result of being exposed to the views of others.

Social inhibition Decreased emission of non-dominant responses, resulting from the presence of others.

Social interactionist theory of coercive action A theory to describe and explain aggression by separating its behavioural and judgemental aspects. In behavioural terms, aggression is defined as **coercive power**. Whether this coercion is perceived as aggressive depends on evaluative judgements held by the opponents of an outside observer.

Social loafing Reduced effort expenditure (motivation loss) in large groups, mainly due to the fact that one's own contributions are not identifiable and cannot be evaluated.

Social norms Broadly shared guidelines for appropriate behaviour in social contexts.

Social representation A collective belief that is shared among many members of a society (e.g., concerning science, religion, individualism) and which involves both the representation and transformation of knowledge.

Social responsibility (norm of) Social responsibility prescribes that people should help others who are dependent on them. It is contrasted with the norm of self-sufficiency, which implies that people should take care of themselves in the first place.

Social support The feeling of being supported by others, usually divided into four components, i.e., emotional support, appraisal support, informational support and instrumental support.

Social value orientation Preference for particular patterns of outcomes for self and others.

Socialization The process whereby people acquire the rules of behaviour and the systems of beliefs and attitudes that equip a person to function effectively as a member of society.

Sociobiology The application of Darwin's theory of natural selection to explaining the origins and maintenance of social behaviour.

Socio-centred approach Any approach to the study of individual and social behaviour emphasizing the conditioning functions of the social/societal structural context.

Socio-cognitive conflict The communication of discrepancies between the perspectives of two or more participants in a task, which promotes opportunities for the participants to become more aware of deficiencies in their individual understanding.

Sociology The social science dealing with social systems/structures such as social relationships, social institutions, whole societies.

Specific status characteristics Information about a person's abilities that is directly relevant to the group task.

Stage models of health behaviour change Theories (e.g., transtheoretical model; precaution adoption process model) which assume that health behaviour change involves progression through a discernible number of stages, from ignorance of a health threat to completed preventive action.

Standard of comparison Position of an anchor or comparison stimulus on a judgement scale.

Stereotype Shared beliefs about personality traits and behaviours of group members. By stereotyping we overlook individuality.

Stooge *See* **confederate**.

Strange Situation A standardized procedure used in attachment research to test infants' reactions to separation from their caregiver and responsiveness to strangers.

Stress The condition that arises when individuals perceive the demands of a situation as challenging or exceeding their resources and endangering their well-being.

Structural measures of social support Reflect the social integration or social embeddedness of individuals by assessing the existence or quantity of their social relationships.

Structural solutions Solutions aimed at promoting collectively desired behaviour through altering aspects of the interdependence structure underlying relationships between people.

Subtyping Stereotypes can be maintained by attributing disconfirming observations to a subtype of people who are separated from the stereotyped group.

Sucker effect A reduced motivation to do one's very best for the group, if one learns that fellow group members withhold their contributions.

Sufficiency principle Assumption in the heuristic–systematic model that people strive for sufficient confidence in their attitudinal judgements. When a person's *actual confidence* is lower than his or her desired confidence or *sufficiency threshold*, he or she will process information in order to close this gap.

Suggestion The technique and/or process by which another person is induced to experience and behave in a given way, i.e., as determined by the suggesting agent, e.g., a hypnotist.

Superordinate goal A goal desired by two or more groups but which can only be achieved through the groups acting together, not by any single group on its own.

Sympathetic arousal *See* **activation**.

Systematic processing Thorough, detailed processing of information (e.g., attention to and elaboration of the arguments contained in a persuasive message); this mode of processing requires a sufficient amount of both ability and motivation.

Task-oriented behaviour Refers to a leadership style that includes planning and scheduling work, establishing communication networks, providing necessary supplies, equipment and technical assistance, and evaluating job performance.

Team games Games representing interdependent relationships among the individual, the own group and another group.

Tension level In productive conflict theory, the operationalization of need level which is curvilinear related to compromise or to solve a conflict.

Theory A set of abstract concepts (i.e., constructs), together with propositions about how those constructs are related to one another.

Theory of planned behaviour An extension of the theory of reasoned action. Besides attitudes and subjective norms, perceived behavioural control is included as a third predictor of behavioural intention and behaviour.

Theory of reasoned action The most important classic theory of the relationship between attitude and behaviour. Assumes that attitudes and subjective norms jointly predict behavioural intentions and thus behaviour.

Third-party intervention The intervention of a third party to help solve a conflict of interest between two or more people (or groups of people).

Thought-listing technique Method used in persuasion research that has been popularized by proponents of the cognitive response approach. Research participants are asked to list the thoughts that came to mind while they were exposed to a persuasive message. These thoughts are later coded according to their favourability or other aspects and used as mediators in analyses of attitude change.

Three-component model of attitude This model assumes that attitudes are a combination of three distinguishable modes of experience and reactions to an object: affective, cognitive and behavioural.

Top-down processing Information processing driven by abstract, superordinate knowledge structures in memory (e.g., schema, expectation) which influence the perception and interpretation of new stimuli.

Transformation A movement away from preferences of direct self-interest by attaching importance to longer-term outcomes or outcomes of another person (other persons or groups).

Transformational leader A person who is seen by followers as a leader endowed with exceptional personal qualities and who works to change or transform his or her followers' needs and redirect their thinking.

Transtheoretical model A stage model of behaviour change developed to understand how people intentionally change their behaviour. The model is called transtheoretical because it is based on an integration of theoretical constructs from diverse theories of psychotherapy.

True randomized experiment An experiment in which participants are allocated to the different conditions of the experiment on a random basis.

Trust The general belief in the honesty and cooperative intentions of others.

Turnover Employee quitting; turnover is deleterious to organizations when good performers leave (dysfunctional turnover), but beneficial when poor performers leave (functional turnover).

Universality Psychobiological notion assuming that evolved behavioural mechanisms should be found all over the world, independent of culture (although culturally determined modifications are always considered possible).

Unobtrusive measures (also called non-reactive measures) Measures that the participant is not aware of, and which therefore cannot influence his or her behaviour.

Utilitarian function An attitude's function of maximizing rewards and minimizing punishments in guiding behaviour.

Utilitarianism The doctrine that the determining condition of individual and social action is the (expectation of the) usefulness of its consequences (psychological utilitarianism). The doctrine that the aim of all social action should be the greatest happiness of the greatest number (ethical utilitarianism).

Validity   A measure is valid to the extent that it measures precisely what it is supposed to measure.

Variable   The term used to refer to the measurable representation of a construct (*see also* **independent variable** and **dependent variable**).

Victimization (synonymous with **bullying** or **mobbing**)   In social contexts, e.g. in schools or at work, individuals are sometimes singled out and frequently attacked or maltreated. Particular characteristics of this phenomenon are repeated and enduring inflictions of intended harm, using either direct or indirect aggressive means, mostly by more than one physically strong and/or high-status perpetrator against a physically weak and/or low-status victim, often deviating from the group's standard.

Völkerpsychologie (German = psychology of peoples)   An early (nineteenth- to twentieth-century) form of a historical and comparative socio-cultural psychology dealing with the cultural products (language, myth, custom, etc.) resulting from social interaction.

Zero-sum situation   A situation in which an individual's own interest is completely conflicting with a partner's interest.

Zone of proximal development   The distance between what the child can do unaided and what he or she can do in collaboration with, or under the guidance of, others.

References

Abelson, R. P. (1981). The psychological status of the script concept. *American Psychologist*, 36, 715–29.

Abelson, R. P. (1995). Attitude extremity. In R. E. Petty & J. A. Krosnick (Eds.), *Attitude strength: Antecedents and consequences* (pp. 25–41). Mahwah, NJ: Erlbaum.

Abelson, R. P., Aronson, E., McGuire, W. J., Newcomb, T. M., Rosenberg, M. J., & Tannenbaum, P. H. (Eds.). (1968). *Theories of cognitive consistency: A sourcebook*. Chicago: Rand McNally.

Aboud, F. (1988). *Children and prejudice*. Oxford: Blackwell.

Abrams, D., & Hogg, M. (1988). Comments on the motivational status of self-esteem in social identity and intergroup discrimination. *European Journal of Social Psychology*, 18, 317–34.

Abramson, L. Y., Metalsky, G. I., & Alloy, L. B. (1989). Hopelessness depression: A theory-based subtype of depression. *Psychological Review*, 96, 358–72.

Abramson, L. Y., Seligman, M. E. P., & Teasdale, J. (1978). Learned helplessness in humans: Critique and reformulation. *Journal of Abnormal Psychology*, 87, 49–74.

Adams, J. S. (1965). Inequity in social exchange. In L. Berkowitz (Ed.), *Advances in experimental social psychology* (Vol. 1, pp. 267–99). New York: Academic Press.

Adorno, T. W., Frenkel-Brunswick, E., Levinson, D. J., & Sanford, R. N. (1950). *The authoritarian personality*. New York: Harper.

Ainsworth, M. D. S., & Bell, S. M. (1970). Attachment, exploration and separation: Illustrated by the behaviour of one-year-olds in a strange situation. *Child Development*, 41, 49–67.

Ainsworth, M. D. S., Blehar, M., Waters, E., & Wall, E. (1978). *Patterns of attachment*. Hillsdale, NJ: Erlbaum.

Ajzen, I. (1988). *Attitudes, personality and behaviour*. Buckingham: Open University Press.

Ajzen, I. (1991). The theory of planned behavior. *Organizational Behavior and Human Decision Processes*, 50, 179–211.

Ajzen, I., & Fishbein, M. (1977). Attitude–behavior relations: A theoretical analysis and review of empirical research. *Psychological Bulletin*, 84, 888–918.

Ajzen, I., & Fishbein, M. (1980). *Understanding attitudes and predicting social behavior*. Englewood Cliffs, NJ: Prentice-Hall.

Ajzen, I., & Madden, T. J. (1986). Prediction of goal-directed behavior: Attitudes, intentions, and perceived behavioral control. *Journal of Experimental Social Psychology*, 22, 453–74.

Akhtar, N., Dunham, F., & Dunham, P. J. (1991). Directive interactions and early vocabulary development: The role of joint attentional focus. *Journal of Child Language*, 18, 41–9.

Aldag, R. J., & Fuller, S. R. (1993). Beyond fiasco: A re-appraisal of the groupthink phenomenon and a new model of group decision making processes. *Psychological Bulletin*, 113, 533–52.

Aldwin, C. M., & Revenson, T. A. (1987). Does coping help? A reexamination of the relation between coping and mental health. *Journal of Personality and Social Psychology*, 53, 337–48.

Allen, M. J., & Rushton, J. P. (1983). Personality characteristics of community health volunteers: A review. *Journal of Voluntary Action Research*, 12, 36–49.

Allen, V. L. (1965). Situational factors in conformity. In L. Berkowitz (Ed.), *Advances in experimental social psychology* (Vol. 2, pp. 133–75). New York: Academic Press.

Allen, V. L. (1975). Social support for non-conformity. In L. Berkowitz (Ed.), *Advances in experimental social psychology* (Vol. 8, pp. 1–43). New York: Academic Press.

Allen, V. L., & Bragg, B. W. E. (1965). The generalization of nonconformity within a homogeneous content dimension. Unpublished manuscript. (Cited in Allen, 1975.)

Allen, V. L., & Levine, J. M. (1968). Social support, dissent and conformity. *Sociometry*, 31, 138–49.

Allen, V. L., & Levine, J. M. (1969). Consensus and conformity. *Journal of Experimental Social Psychology*, 4, 389–99.

Allen, V. L., & Levine, J. M. (1971). Social support and conformity: The role of independent assessment of reality. *Journal of Experimental Social Psychology*, 7, 48–58.

Allen, V. L., & Wilder, D. A. (1972). Social support in absentia: Effect of an absentee partner on conformity. Unpublished manuscript. (Cited in Allen, 1975.)

Allison, S. T., McQueen, L. R., & Schaerfl, L. M. (1992). Social decision making processes and the equal partitionment of shared resources. *Journal of Experimental Social Psychology*, 28, 23–42.

Alloy, L. B. (1982). The role of perceptions and attributions for response-outcome noncontingency in learned helplessness. A commentary and discussion. *Journal of Personality*, 50, 443–79.

Alloy, L. B., & Tabachnik, N. (1984). Assessment of covariation by humans and animals: The joint influence of prior expectations and current situational information. *Psychological Review*, 91, 112–49.

Allport, F. H. (1924). *Social psychology*. Boston: Houghton Mifflin.

Allport, G. W. (1935). Attitudes. In C. Murchison (Ed.), *Handbook of social psychology* (Vol. 2). Worcester, MA: Clark University Press.

Allport, G. W. (1954). *The nature of prejudice*. Reading, MA: Addison-Wesley.

Altemeyer, B. (1988). *Enemies of freedom: Understanding right-wing authoritarianism*. San Francisco: Jossey-Bass.

Amir, Y. (1976). The role of intergroup contact in change of prejudice and ethnic relations. In P. A. Katz (Ed.), *Towards the elimination of racism*. New York: Pergamon.

Amirkhan, J. H. (1998). Attributions as predictors of coping and distress. *Personality and Social Psychology Bulletin*, 24, 1006–18.

Amoroso, D. M., & Walters, R. H. (1969). Effects of anxiety and socially mediated anxiety reduction on paired-associate learning. *Journal of Personality and Social Psychology*, 11 (4), 388–96.

Anderson, C. A. (1983). The causal structure of situations: The generation of plausible causal attributions as a function of the type of event situation. *Journal of Experimental Social Psychology*, 19, 185–203.

Anderson, C. A. (1991). Attributions as decisions: A two stage information processing model. In S. L. Zelen (Ed.), *New models – new extensions of attribution theory* (pp. 12–54). New York: Springer Verlag.

Anderson, J. R. (1976). *Language, memory, and thought*. Hillsdale, NJ: Sage.

Andinson, F. S. (1977). TV violence and viewer aggression: A cumulation of study results 1956–1976. *Public Opinion Quarterly*, 41, 314–31.

Anolli, L., & Ciceri, R. (1997). The voice of deception: Vocal strategies of naive and able liars. *Journal of Nonverbal Behavior*, 21 (4), 259–84.

APA Public Communications (1996). *Raising children to resist violence: What can you do*. Washington, DC: American Psychological Association.

Archer, J. (1996). Sex differences in social behavior: Are the social role and evolutionary explanations compatible? *American Psychologist*, 51, 909–17.

Argyle, M., & Henderson, M. (1985). *The anatomy of relationships*. Harmondsworth: Penguin.

Aristotle (1941). *Ethica Nicomachea*. In R. McKeon (Ed.), *The basic works of Aristotle*. New York: Random House.

Arnold, M. B. (1960). *Emotion and personality. Vol. 1: Psychological aspects*. New York: Columbia University Press.

Aron, A., Aron, E. N., & Smollan, D. (1992). Inclusion of the other in the self scale and the structure of interpersonal closeness. *Journal of Personality and Social Psychology*, 63, 596–612.

Aron, A., Aron, E. N., Tudor, M., & Nelson, G. (1991). Close relationships as including the other in the self. *Journal of Personality and Social Psychology*, 60, 241–53.

Aronson, E., Ellsworth, P. C., Carlsmith, J. M., & Gonzales, M. H. (1990). *Methods of research in social psychology* (2nd ed.). New York: McGraw-Hill.

Aronson, E., & Mills, J. (1959). The effects of severity of initiation on liking for a group. *Journal of Abnormal and Social Psychology*, 59, 177–81.

Aronson, E., Wilson, T. D., & Brewer, M. B. (1998). Experimentation in social psychology. In D. T. Gilbert, S. T. Fiske, & G. Lindzey (Eds.), *The handbook of social psychology* (4th ed., Vol. 1, pp. 99–142). New York: McGraw-Hill.

Asch, S. E. (1946). Forming impressions of personality. *Journal of Abnormal and Social Psychology*, 41, 258–90.

Asch, S. E. (1951). Effects of group pressure on the modification and distortion of judgements. In H. Guetzkow (Ed.), *Groups, leadership and men*. Pittsburgh: Carnegie.

Asch, S. E. (1952). *Social psychology*. New York: Prentice-Hall.

Asch, S. E. (1955). Opinions and social pressure. *Scientific American*, 193, 31–5.

Asch, S. E. (1956). Studies of independence and conformity: A minority of one against a unanimous majority. *Psychological Monographs*, 70 (9, Whole No. 416).

Ash, M. G. (1985). Gestalt Psychology: Origins in Germany and reception in the United States. In C. Buxton (Ed.), *Points of view in the modern history of psychology* (pp. 293–344). New York: Academic Press.

Ashforth, B. E., & Humphrey, R. H. (1995). Emotion in the workplace: A reappraisal. *Human Relations*, 48 (2), 97–125.

Aspinwall, L. G., & Taylor, S. E. (1992). Modeling cognitive adaptation: A longitudinal investigation of the impact of individual differences and coping on college adjustment and performance. *Journal of Personality and Social Psychology*, 63, 989–1003.

Athanasiou, R., & Yoshioka, G. A. (1973). The spatial character of friendship formation. *Environment and Behavior*, 43–65.

Averill, J. R. (1980). A constructivist view of emotion. In R. Plutchik & H. Kellerman (Eds.), *Emotion. Theory, research, and experience* (pp. 305–40). New York: Academic Press.

Averill, J. R. (1982). *Anger and aggression: An essay on emotion*. New York: Springer.

Axelrod, R. (1984). *The evolution of cooperation*. New York: Basic Books.

Azmitia, M. (1996). Peer interactive minds: Developmental, theoretical, and methodological issues. In P. B. Baltes and U. M. Staudinger (Eds.), *Interactive minds: Life-span perspectives on the social foundation of cognition* (pp. 133–62). New York: Cambridge University Press.

Bakker, A. B., Buunk, B. P., & Siero, F. (1993). Condoomgebruik door heteroseksuelen: Een vegelijking van de theorie van gepland gedrag, het health belief model en de protectie-motivatie theorie. [Condom-use among heterosexuals: A comparison of the theory of planned behaviour, the health belief model and protection motivation theory]. *Gedrag & Gezondheid*, 21, 238–55.

Bales, R. F. (1950). *Interaction process analysis: A method for the study of small groups*. Chicago: Chicago University Press.

Bales, R. F., & Slater, P. E. (1955). Role differentiation in small decision-making groups. In T. Parson & R. F. Bales (Eds.), *Family, socialization and interaction process*. Glencoe: Free Press.

Baltes, P. B., & Staudinger, U. M. (Eds.). (1996). *Interactive minds: Life-span perspectives on the social foundation of cognition*. New York: Cambridge University Press.

Bandura, A. (1973). *Aggression: A social learning analysis*. Englewood Cliffs, NJ: Prentice-Hall.

Bandura, A. (1977a). Self-efficacy: Toward a unifying theory of behavioral change. *Psychological Review*, 84, 191–215.

Bandura, A. (1977b). *Social learning theory*. Englewood Cliffs, NJ: Prentice-Hall.

Bandura, A. (1997). *Self-efficacy: The exercise of control*. New York: Freeman.

Bandura, A. (1999). Moral disengagement in the perpetration of inhumanities. *Personality and Social Psychology Review*, 3, 193–209.

Bandura, A., Ross, D., & Ross, S. A. (1961). Transmission of aggression through imitation of aggressive models. *Journal of Abnormal and Social Psychology*, 63, 575–82.

Bandura, A., Ross, D., & Ross, S. A. (1963). Imitation of film-mediated aggressive models. *Journal of Abnormal and Social Psychology*, 66, 3–11.

Banse, R., & Scherer, K. R. (1996). Acoustic profiles in vocal emotion expression. *Journal of Personality and Social Psychology*, 70 (3), 614–36.

Bargh, J. A. (1989). Conditional automaticity: Varieties of automatic influence in social perception and cognition. In J. S. Uleman & J. A. Bargh (Eds.), *Unintended thought* (pp. 3–51). New York: Guilford Press.

Bargh, J. A. (1996). Automaticity in social psychology. In E. T. Higgins & A. W. Kruglanski (Eds.), *Social psychology: Handbook of basic principles* (pp. 169–83). New York: Guilford Press.

Bargh, J. A. (1997). The automaticity of everyday life. In R. S. Wyer & T. K. Srull (Eds.), *Advances in social cognition* (Vol. 10, pp. 1–61). Mahwah, NJ: Erlbaum.

Bargh, J. A., Chaiken, S., Govender, R., & Pratto, F. (1992). The generality of the automatic attitude activation effect. *Journal of Personality and Social Psychology*, 62, 893–912.

Bargh, J. A., & Chartrand, T. L. (in press). Studying the mind in the middle: A practical guide to priming and automaticity research. In H. T. Reis & C. M. Judd (Eds.), *Handbook of research methods in social psychology*. New York: Cambridge University Press.

Bargh, J. A., Chen, M., & Burrows, L. (1996). Automaticity of social behavior: Direct effects of trait construct and stereotype activation on action. *Journal of Personality and Social Psychology*, 71, 230–44.

Bargh, J. A., & Pietromonaco, P. (1982). Automatic information processing and social perception: The influence of trait information presented outside of conscious awareness on impression formation. *Journal of Personality and Social Psychology*, 43, 437–49.

Bargh, J. A., & Pratto, F. (1986). Individual construct accessibility and perceptual selection. *Journal of Personality and Social Psychology*, 71, 230–44.

Bargh, J. A., & Thein, R. D. (1985). Individual construct accessibility, person memory, and the recall-judgment link: The case of information overload. *Journal of Personality and Social Psychology*, 49, 1129–46.

Barkow, J. H., Cosmides, L., & Tooby, J. (1992). *The adapted mind*. New York & Oxford: Oxford University Press.

Baron, R. A. (1970). Anonymity, de-individuation and aggression. Unpublished doctoral dissertation, University of Minnesota.

Baron, R. A. (1971). Exposure to an aggressive model and apparent probability of retaliation as determinants of adult aggressive behavior. *Journal of Experimental Social Psychology*, 7, 343–55.

Baron, R. A. (1977). *Human aggression*. New York: Plenum Press.

Baron, R. A., & Richardson, D. R. (1994). *Human aggression* (2nd ed.). New York: Plenum Press.

Baron, R. M., & Kenny, D. A. (1986). The mediator-moderator variable distinction in social psychological research: Conceptual, strategic, and statistical considerations. *Journal of Personality and Social Psychology*, 50, 869–78.

Baron, R. S., Vandello, J. A., & Brunsman, B. (1996). The forgotten variable in conformity research: Impact of task importance on social influence. *Journal of Personality and Social Psychology*, 71, 915–27.

Baron, S., Kerr, N. L., & Miller, N. (1992). *Group process, group decision, group action*. Buckingham: Open University Press.

Baroni, M. R., & Axia, G. (1989). Children's meta-pragmatic abilities and the identification of polite and impolite requests. *First Language*, 9, 285–97.

Barrows, S. (1981). *Distorting mirrors: Visions of the crowd in late nineteenth century France*. New Haven, CT: Yale University Press.

Barsade, S. G., & Gibson, D. E. (1998). Group emotion: A view from top and bottom. In D. H. Gruenfeld (Ed.), *Composition. Research on managing groups and teams* (Vol. 1, pp. 81–102). Stamford, CT: Jai Press.

Barsalou, L. W. (1985). Ideals, central tendency, and frequency of instantiation as determinants of graded structure in categories. *Journal of*

Experimental Psychology: Learning, Memory, and Cognition, 11, 629–54.

Barsalou, L. W. (1990). On the indistinguishability of exemplar memory and abstraction in category representation. In T. K. Srull & R. S. Wyer, Jr. (Eds.), *Advances in social cognition. Vol. 3. Content and process specificity in the effects of prior experiences* (pp. 61–88). Hillsdale, NJ: Erlbaum.

Bartlett, F. C. (1932/1995). *Remembering: A study in experimental and social psychology.* Cambridge: Cambridge University Press.

Bass, B. M. (1985). *Leadership and performance beyond expectations.* New York: Free Press.

Batson, C. D. (1991). *The altruism question. Toward a social-psychological answer.* Hillsdale, NJ: Lawrence Erlbaum.

Batson, C. D. (1995). Prosocial motivation: Why do we help others? In A. Tesser (Ed.), *Advanced social psychology* (pp. 333–81). New York: McGraw-Hill.

Batson, C. D. (1998). Altruism and prosocial behavior. In D. T. Gilbert, S. T. Fiske, & G. Lindzey (Eds.), *The handbook of social psychology* (4th ed., Vol. 2, pp. 282–316). New York: McGraw-Hill.

Batson, C. D., Bolen, M. H., Cross, J. A., & Neuringer-Benefiel, H. E. (1986). Where is the altruism in the prosocial personality? *Journal of Personality and Social Psychology,* 50, 212–20.

Batson, C. D., Duncan, B. D., Ackerman, P., Buckley, T., & Birch, K. (1981). Is empathic emotion a source of altruistic motivation? *Journal of Personality and Social Psychology,* 40, 290–302.

Batson, C. D., Fultz, J., & Schoenrade, P. A. (1987). Distress and empathy: Two qualitatively distinct vicarious emotions with different motivational consequences. *Journal of Personality,* 55, 21–39.

Batson, C. D., O'Quinn, K., Fultz, J., Vanderplas, M., & Isen, A. (1983). Self-reported distress and empathy and egoistic versus altruistic motivation for helping. *Journal of Personality and Social Psychology,* 45, 706–18.

Batson, C. D., Sager, K., Garst, E., Kang, M., Rubchinsky, K., & Dawson, K. (1997). Is empathy-induced helping due to self-other merging? *Journal of Personality and Social Psychology,* 73, 495–509.

Baucom, D. H., Sayers, S. L., & Duhe, A. (1989). Attributional style and attributional patterns among married couples. *Journal of Personality and Social Psychology,* 56, 596–607.

Baumeister, R. F., & Campbell, W. K. (1999). Sadism, sensational thrills and threatened egotism. *Personality and Social Psychology Review,* 3, 210–21.

Baumrind, D. (1964). Some thoughts on the ethics of research after reading Milgram's 'Behavioral Study of Obedience'. *American Psychologist,* 19, 421–3.

Becker, J. A. (1994). Pragmatic socialization: Parental input to preschoolers. *Discourse Processes,* 17, 131–48.

Becker, M. H., & Maiman, L. A. (1975). Sociobehavioral determinants of compliance with health and medical care recommendations. *Medical Care,* 8, 10–24.

Bell, P. A. (1992). In defense of the negative affect escape model of heat and aggression. *Psychological Bulletin,* 111, 342–6.

Bellezza, F. S., & Bower, G. H. (1981). Person stereotypes and memory for people. *Journal of Personality and Social Psychology,* 41, 856–65.

Belli, R. F. (1989). Influences of misleading post-event information: Misinformation interference and acceptance. *Journal of Experimental Psychology: General,* 118, 72–85.

Bellis, M. A., & Baker, R. R. (1990). Do females promote sperm competition? Data for humans. *Animal Behaviour,* 40, 997–9.

Bem, D. J. (1965). An experimental analysis of self-persuasion. *Journal of Experimental Social Psychology,* 1, 199–218.

Bem, D. J. (1972). Self-perception theory. *Advances in Experimental Social Psychology,* 6, 1–62.

Bennett, M. (1985–6). Developmental changes in the attribution of dispositional features. *Current Psychological Research and Reviews,* 4, 323–9.

Bennett, M. (1993). Introduction. In M. Bennett (Ed.), *The child as psychologist. An introduction to the development of social cognition* (pp. 1–25). New York: Harvester Wheatsheaf.

Bennett, M., Yuill, N., Banerjee, R., & Thomson, S. (1998). Children's understanding of extended identity. *Developmental Psychology*, 34, 322–31.

Bentler, P. M., & Speckart, G. (1979). Models of attitude–behavior relations. *Psychological Review*, 86, 452–64.

Berger, J., Rosenholtz, S. J., & Zelditch, J. (1980). Status organizing processes. *Annual Review of Sociology*, 6, 479–508.

Berger, J., & Zelditch, J. (1993). *Theoretical research programs.* Stanford, CA: Stanford University Press.

Berkman, L. F., & Syme, S. L. (1979). Social networks, host resistance, and mortality: A nine-year follow-up study of Alameda County residents. *American Journal of Epidemiology*, 109, 186–204.

Berkowitz, L. (1962). *Aggression: A social psychological analysis.* New York: McGraw-Hill.

Berkowitz, L. (1964). Aggressive cues in aggressive behavior and hostility catharsis. *Psychological Review*, 71, 104–22.

Berkowitz, L. (1969). The frustration–aggression hypothesis revisited. In L. Berkowitz (Ed.), *Roots of aggression* (pp. 1–28). New York: Atherton Press.

Berkowitz, L. (1974). Some determinants of impulsive aggression: The role of mediated associations with reinforcements of aggression. *Psychological Review*, 81, 165–76.

Berkowitz, L. (1978). Decreased helpfulness with increased group size through lessening the effects of the needy individual's dependency. *Journal of Personality*, 46, 299–310.

Berkowitz, L. (1983). The experience of anger as a parallel process in the display of impulsive, 'angry' aggression. In R. G. Geen & E. I. Donnerstein (Eds.), *Aggression. Theoretical and empirical reviews* (Vol. 1). New York: Academic Press.

Berkowitz, L. (1989). The frustration–aggression hypothesis: An examination and reformulation. *Psychological Bulletin*, 106, 59–73.

Berkowitz, L. (1990). On the formation and regulation of anger and aggression – A cognitive-neoassociationistic analysis. *American Psychologist*, 45, 4, 494–503.

Berkowitz, L. (1993). *Aggression: Its causes, consequences, and control.* New York: McGraw-Hill.

Berkowitz, L. (1999). Evil is more than banal: Situationism and the concept of evil. *Personality and Social Psychology Review*, 3, 246–53.

Berkowitz, L., Cochran, S., & Embree, M. (1981). Physical pain and the goal of aversively stimulated aggression. *Journal of Personality and Social Psychology*, 40, 687–700.

Berkowitz, L., & Cottingham, D. R. (1960). The interest value and relevance of fear-arousing communications. *Journal of Abnormal and Social Psychology*, 60, 37–43.

Berkowitz, L., & Daniels, L. R. (1964). Affecting the salience of the social responsibility norm: Effects of past help on the response to dependency relationships. *Journal of Abnormal and Social Psychology*, 68, 275–81.

Berkowitz, L., & Heimer, K. (1989). On the construction of the anger experience: Aversive events and negative priming in the formation of feelings. In L. Berkowitz (Ed.), *Advances in experimental social psychology* (Vol. 22, pp. 1–37). San Diego, CA: Academic Press.

Berkowitz, L., & Knurek, D. A. (1969). Label-mediated hostility generalization. *Journal of Personality and Social Psychology*, 13, 200–6.

Berkowitz, L., & LePage, A. (1967). Weapons as aggression-eliciting stimuli. *Journal of Personality and Social Psychology*, 7, 202–7.

Berlin, L. J., & Cassidy, J. (1999). Relations among relationships: Contributions from attachment theory and research. In J. Cassidy & P. Shaver (Eds.), *Handbook of attachment: Theory, research, and clinical applications* (pp. 688–712). New York: Guilford Press.

Berscheid, E. (1985). Interpersonal attraction. In G. Lindzey & E. Aronson (Eds.), *Handbook of social psychology* (Vol. 2, pp. 413–84). New York: Random House.

Berscheid, E. (1991). The emotion-in-relationships model: Reflections and update. In A. Ortony, W. Kessen, & F. I. M. Craik (Eds.), *Memories, thoughts, and emotions: Essays in honor of George Mandler* (pp. 323–35). Hillsdale, NJ: Lawrence Erlbaum.

Berscheid, E. (1992). A glance back at a quarter century of social psychology. *Journal of Personality and Social Psychology*, 63, 525–33.

Berscheid, E., & Walster, E. (1974). A little bit about love. In T. Huston (Ed.), *Foundations of interpersonal attraction* (pp. 356–82). New York: Academic Press.

Bettencourt, B. A., Brewer, M. B., Croak, M. R., & Miller, N. (1992). Cooperation and the reduction of intergroup bias: The role of reward structure and social orientation. *Journal of Experimental Social Psychology*, 28, 301–9.

Betzig, L. (1992). Roman polygyny. *Ethology and Sociobiology*, 13, 309–49.

Bickman, L., & Henchy, T. (Eds.). (1972). *Beyond the laboratory: Field research in social psychology*. New York: McGraw-Hill.

Bierbrauer, G. (1979). Why did he do it? Attribution of obedience and the phenomenon of dispositional bias. *European Journal of Social Psychology*, 9, 67–84.

Bierhoff, H. W. (1994). On the interface between social support and prosocial behavior: Methodological and theoretical implications. In F. Nestmann & K. Hurrelmann (Eds.), *Social networks and social support in childhood and adolescence* (pp. 159–67). Berlin: De Gruyter.

Bierhoff, H. W. (in press). Skala der sozialen Verantwortung nach Berkowitz und Daniels. *Diagnostica*, 46.

Bierhoff, H. W., Buck, E., & Klein, R. (1986). Social context and perceived justice. In H. W. Bierhoff, R. L. Cohen, & J. Greenberg (Eds.), *Justice in social relations* (pp. 165–85). New York: Plenum Press.

Bierhoff, H. W., Klein, R., & Kramp, P. (1991). Evidence for the altruistic personality from data on accident research. *Journal of Personality*, 59, 263–80.

Bierhoff, H. W., Lensing, L., & Kloft, A. (1988). Hilfreiches Verhalten in Abhängigkeit von Vergehen und positiver Verstärkung. In H. W. Bierhoff & L. Montada (Eds.), *Altruismus* (pp. 154–78). Göttingen: Hogrefe.

Billig, M. (1976). *Social psychology and intergroup relations*. London: Academic Press.

Binet, A., & Henri, V. (1894). De la suggestibilité naturelle chez les enfants. *Revue Philosophique*, 38, 337–47.

Birns, B., & Hay, D. F. (Eds.). (1988). *The different faces of motherhood*. New York: Plenum Press.

Bischof-Köhler, D. (1994). Selbstobjektivierung und fremdbezogene Emotion. Identifikation des eigenen Spiegelbildes, Empathie und prosoziales Verhalten im 2. Lebensjahr. *Zeitschrift für Psychologie*, 202, 349–77.

Black, S. L., & Bevan, S. (1992). At the movies with Buss and Durkee: A natural experiment on film violence. *Aggressive Behavior*, 18, 37–45.

Blake, R. R., & Mouton, J. S. (1970). The fifth achievement. *Journal of Applied Behavioral Science*, 6, 413–26.

Blalock, S., DeVellis, R. F., Giorgino, K. B., Gold, D. T., Dooley, M. A., Anderson, J. J. B., & Smith, S. L. (1996). Osteoporosis prevention in premenopausal women: Using a stage model approach to examine the predictors of behavior. *Health Psychology*, 15, 84–93.

Blau, P. M. (1964). *Exchange and power in social life*. New York: Wiley.

Blaye, A., Light, P., Joiner, R., & Sheldon, S. (1991). Collaboration as a facilitator of planning and problem solving on a computer-based task. *British Journal of Developmental Psychology*, 9, 471–83.

Blaye, A., Light, P., & Rubtsov, V. (1992). Collaborative learning at the computer: How social processes 'interface' with human–computer interaction. *European Journal of Psychology of Education*, 7, 257–67.

Blazer, D. (1982). Social support and mortality in an elderly community population. *American Journal of Epidemiology*, 115, 684–94.

Bless, H., Bohner, G., Schwarz, N., & Strack, F. (1990). Mood and persuasion: A cognitive response analysis. *Personality and Social Psychology Bulletin*, 16, 331–45.

Bless, H., & Schwarz, N. (1998). Context effects in political judgment: Assimilation and contrast as a function of categorization processes. *European Journal of Social Psychology*, 28, 159–72.

Blumenthal, M., Kahn, R. L., Andrews, F. M., & Head, K. B. (1972). *Justifying violence: The attitudes of American men*. Ann Arbor, MI: Institute for Social Research.

Blumer, H. (1946). Collective behavior. In A. M. Lee (Ed.), *New outlines of the principles of sociology* (pp. 165–220). New York: Barnes & Noble.

Bodenhausen, G. V. (1990). Stereotypes as judgmental heuristics. Evidence of circadian variations in discrimination. *Psychological Science*, 1, 319–22.

Bodenhausen, G. V., & Lichtenstein, M. (1987). Social stereotypes and information-processing strategies: The impact of task complexity. *Journal of Personality and Social Psychology*, 48, 267–82.

Boer, H., & Seydel, E. R. (1996). Protection motivation theory. In M. Conner & P. Norman (Eds.), *Predicting health behaviour* (pp. 121–62). Buckingham: Open University Press.

Bohner, G., Moskowitz, G., & Chaiken, S. (1995). The interplay of heuristic and systematic processing of social information. *European Review of Social Psychology*, 6, 33–68.

Bohner, G., Rank, S., Reinhard, M.-A., Einwiller, S., & Erb, H.-P. (1998). Motivational determinants of systematic processing: Expectancy moderates effects of desired confidence on processing effort. *European Journal of Social Psychology*, 28, 185–206.

Bohner, G., Reinhard, M.-A., Rutz, S., Sturm, S., Kerschbaum, B., & Effler, D. (1998). Rape myths as neutralizing cognitions: Evidence for a causal impact of anti-victim attitudes on men's self-reported likelihood of raping. *European Journal of Social Psychology*, 28, 257–68.

Boiten, F. (1996). Autonomic response patterns during voluntary facial action. *Psychophysiology*, 33 (2), 123–31.

Bonanno, G. A., & Keltner, D. (1997). Facial expressions of emotion and the course of conjugal bereavement. *Journal of Abnormal Psychology*, 106 (1), 126–37.

Bond, C. F., & Titus, L. J. (1983). Social facilitation: A meta-analysis of 241 studies. *Psychological Bulletin*, 94, 265–92.

Bond, C. F., & Van Leeuwen, M. D. (1991). Can a part be greater than a whole? On the relationship between primary and meta-analytic evidence. *Basic and Applied Social Psychology*, 12, 33–40.

Bond, R., & Smith, P. B. (1996). Culture and conformity: A meta-analysis of studies using Asch's (1952b, 1956) line judgment task. *Psychological Bulletin*, 119, 111–37.

Bornstein, G. (1992). The free-rider problem in intergroup conflicts over step-level and continuous public goods. *Journal of Personality and Social Psychology*, 62, 597–606.

Boster, F. J., & Mongeau, P. (1984). Fear-arousing persuasive messages. In R. N. Bostrom (Ed.), *Communication yearbook* (Vol. 8, pp. 330–75). Beverly Hills, CA: Sage.

Bourhis, R. Y., Turner, J. C., & Gagnon, A. (1997). Interdependence, social identity and discrimination: Some empirical considerations. In R. Speers, P. J. Oakes, N. Ellemers, & S. A. Haslam (Eds.), *The social psychology of stereotyping and group life* (pp. 273–95). Oxford: Blackwell.

Bower, G. H. (1981). Emotional mood and memory. *American Psychologist*, 36, 129–48.

Bowlby, J. (1969). *Attachment and loss. Vol. 1. Attachment*. London: Hogarth.

Bowlby, J. (1988). *A secure base. Parent–child attachment and healthy human development*. New York: Basic Books.

Bradbury, T. N., Beach, S. R. H., Fincham, F. D., & Nelson, G. M. (1996). Attributions and behavior in functional and dysfunctional marriages. *Journal of Consulting and Clinical Psychology*, 64, 569–76.

Bradbury, T. N., & Fincham, F. D. (1990). Attributions in marriage: Review and critique. *Psychological Bulletin*, 107, 3–33.

Bradbury, T. N., & Fincham, F. D. (1992). Attributions and behavior in marital interaction. *Journal of Personality and Social Psychology*, 63, 613–28.

Brandstädter, J. (1990). Development as a personal and cultural construction. In G. R. Semin & K. J. Gergen (Eds.), *Everyday understanding: Social and scientific implications* (pp. 83–107). Newbury Park, CA: Sage.

Branthwaite, A., Doyle, S., & Lightbown, N. (1979). The balance between fairness and discrimination. *European Journal of Social Psychology*, 9, 149–63.

Brauer, M., & Judd, C. M. (1996). Group polarization and repeated attitude expressions: A new take on an old topic. In W. Stroebe & M. Hewstone (Eds.), *European review of social psychology* (Vol. 7, pp. 173–207). Chichester: Wiley.

Brauer, M., Judd, C. M., & Gliner, M. D. (1995). The effects of repeated attitude expressions on attitude polarization during group discussions. *Journal of Personality and Social Psychology, 68*, 1014–29.

Breckler, S. J. (1984). Empirical validation of affect, behavior, and cognition as distinct components of attitude. *Journal of Personality and Social Psychology, 47*, 1191–1205.

Breckler, S. J. (1993). Emotion and attitude change. In M. Lewis & J. M. Haviland (Eds.), *Handbook of emotions* (pp. 461–74). New York: Guilford Press.

Brehm, J. W. (1972). *Responses to loss of freedom: A theory of psychological reactance.* Morristown, NJ: General Learning Press.

Bremner, J. G. (1994). *Infancy* (2nd ed.). Oxford: Blackwell.

Breslow, L., & Enstrom, J. E. (1980). Persistence of health habits and their relationship to mortality. *Preventive Medicine, 9*, 469–83.

Bretherton, I. (1992). The origins of attachment theory: John Bowlby and Mary Ainsworth. *Developmental Psychology, 28*, 759–75.

Brewer, M. B. (1979). Ingroup bias in the minimal intergroup situation: A cognitive motivational analysis. *Psychological Bulletin, 86*, 307–24.

Brewer, M. B., & Kramer, R. M. (1986). Choice behavior in social dilemmas: Effects of social identity, group size, and decision framing. *Journal of Personality and Social Psychology, 50*, 543–9.

Brewer, M. B., & Miller, N. (1984). Beyond the contact hypothesis: Theoretical perspectives on desegregation. In N. Miller & M. B. Brewer (Eds.), *Groups in contact: The psychology of desegregation* (pp. 281–302). New York: Academic Press.

Brickner, M. A., Harkins, S. G., & Ostrom, T. M. (1986). Effects of personal involvement: Thought provoking implications for social loafing. *Journal of Personality and Social Psychology, 51*, 763–70.

Broadbent, D. E. (1958). *Perception and communication.* New York: Pergamon.

Brockner, J., & Wiesenfeld, B. M. (1995). An integrative framework for explaining re-actions to decisions: Interactive effects of outcomes and procedures. *Psychological Bulletin, 102*, 189–208.

Brown, J. D., & Dutton, K. A. (1995). The thrill of victory, the complexity of defeat: Self-esteem and people's emotional reactions to success and failure. *Journal of Personality and Social Psychology, 68* (4), 712–22.

Brown, R. (1965). *Social psychology.* New York: Macmillan.

Brown, R. (1973). *A first language.* Cambridge, MA: Harvard University Press.

Brown, R. (1980). The maintenance of conversation. In D. R. Olson (Ed.), *The social foundations of language and thought.* New York: Norton.

Brown, R., & Fish, D. (1983). The psychological causality implicit in language. *Cognition, 14*, 233–74.

Brown, R. C., & Tedeschi, J. T. (1976). Determinants of perceived aggression. *Journal of Social Psychology, 100*, 77–87.

Brown, R. J. (1978). Divided we fall: An analysis of relations between sections of a factory workforce. In H. Tajfel (Ed.), *Differentiation between social groups: Studies in the social psychology of intergroup relations.* London: Academic Press.

Brown, R. J. (1984a). The role of similarity in intergroup relations. In H. Tajfel (Ed.), *The social dimension* (Vol. 2, pp. 603–23). Cambridge: Cambridge University Press.

Brown, R. J. (Ed.). (1984b). Intergroup processes. *British Journal of Social Psychology, 23* (Whole no. 4).

Brown, R. J. (1995). *Prejudice: Its social psychology.* Oxford: Blackwell.

Brown, R. J. (2000). *Group processes: Dynamics within and between groups* (2nd ed.). Oxford: Blackwell.

Brown, R. J., Condor, S., Matthews, A., Wade, G., & Williams, J. A. (1986). Explaining intergroup differentiation in an industrial organization. *Journal of Occupational Psychology, 59*, 273–86.

Brown, R. J., & Deschamps, J.-C. (1980–1). Discrimination entre individus et entre groupes. *Bulletin de Psychologie, 34*, 185–95.

Brown, R., Hinkle, S., Ely, P. G., Fox-Cardamore, L., Maras, P., & Taylor, L. A. (1992). Recognising groups' diversity: Individualist–collectivist and autonomous–relational social orientations and their implications for intergroup processes. *British Journal of Social Psychology*, 31, 327–42.

Brown, R. J., & Ross, G. R. (1982). The battle for acceptance: An exploration into the dynamics of intergroup behaviour. In H. Tajfel (Ed.), *Social identity and intergroup relations* (pp. 155–78). Cambridge: Cambridge University Press.

Brown, R., & Smith, A. (1989). Perceptions of and by minority groups: The case of women in academia. *European Journal of Social Psychology*, 19, 61–75.

Brown, R. J., Tajfel, H., & Turner, J. C. (1980). Minimal group situations and inter-group discrimination: Comments on the paper by Aschenbrenner and Schaefer. *European Journal of Social Psychology*, 10, 399–414.

Brown, R. J., & Turner, J. C. (1979). The criss-cross categorization effect in intergroup discrimination. *British Journal of Social and Clinical Psychology*, 18, 371–83.

Brown, R. J., & Turner, J. C. (1981). Interpersonal and intergroup behaviour. In J. C. Turner & H. Giles (Eds.), *Intergroup behaviour* (pp. 33–65). Oxford: Blackwell.

Brown, R. J., Vivian, T., & Hewstone, M. (1999). Changing attitudes through intergroup contact: The effects of group membership salience. *European Journal of Social Psychology*.

Brown, R. J., & Wade, G. S. (1987). Superordinate goals and intergroup behaviour: The effects of role ambiguity and status on intergroup attitudes and task performance. *European Journal of Social Psychology*, 17, 131–42.

Brown, R. J., & Williams, J. A. (1984). Group identification: The same thing to all people? *Human Relations*, 37, 547–64.

Brown, R., & Wootton-Millward, L. (1993). Perceptions of group homogeneity during group formation and change. *Social Cognition*, 11, 126–49.

Bruner, J. S. (1957). On perceptual readiness. *Psychological Review*, 64, 123–52.

Bruner, J. S., & Goodman, C. D. (1947). Value and need as organizing factors in perception. *Journal of Abnormal and Social Psychology*, 42, 33–44.

Buchanan, G., & Seligman, M. E. P. (Eds.). (1995). *Explanatory style*. Hillsdale, NJ: Erlbaum.

Buck, R. (1985). Prime theory: An integrated view of motivation and emotion. *Psychological Review*, 92, 389–413.

Buehler, R., Griffin, D., & Ross, M. (1995). It's about time: Optimistic predictions in work and love. In W. Stroebe & M. Hewstone (Eds.), *European review of social psychology* (Vol. 6, pp. 1–32). Chichester: J. Wiley.

Burger, J. M. (1991). Changes in attributions over time: The ephemeral fundamental attribution error. *Social Cognition*, 9, 182–93.

Burnstein, E., Crandall, C., & Kitayama, S. (1994). Some neo-Darwinian decision rules for altruism: Weighing cues for inclusive fitness as a function of the biological importance of the decision. *Journal of Personality and Social Psychology*, 67, 773–89.

Burnstein, E., & McRae, A. V. (1962). Some effects of shared threat and prejudice in racially mixed groups. *Journal of Abnormal and Social Psychology*, 64, 257–63.

Bushman, B. J. (1998). Priming effects of media violence on the accessibility of aggressive constructs in memory. *Personality and Social Psychology Bulletin*, 24, 537–45.

Buss, A. H. (1961). *The psychology of aggression*. New York: Wiley.

Buss, A. H. (1971). Aggression pays. In J. L. Singer (Ed.), *The control of aggression and violence* (pp. 112–30). New York: Academic Press.

Buss, A. R. (Ed.). (1979). *Psychology in social context*. New York: Irvington.

Buss, D. M. (1988). The evolution of human intrasexual competition: Tactics of mate attraction. *Journal of Personality and Social Psychology*, 54, 616–28.

Buss, D. M. (1989). Sex differences in human mate preferences: Evolutionary hypotheses tested in 37 cultures. *Behavioral and Brain Sciences*, 12, 1–49.

Buss, D. M. (1994). *The evolution of desire: Strategies of human mating*. New York: Basic Books.

Buss, D. M. (1995). Evolutionary psychology: A new paradigm for psychological science. *Psychological Inquiry*, 6, 1–30.

Buss, D. M. (1996). The evolutionary psychology of human social strategies. In E. T. Higgins & A. W. Kruglanski (Eds.), *Social psychology: Handbook of basic principles* (pp. 3–38). New York: Guilford Press.

Buss, D. M., & Bedden, L. A. (1990). Derogation of competitors. *Journal of Social and Personal Relationships*, 7, 395–422.

Buss, D. M., & Kenrick, D. (1998). Evolutionary social psychology. In D. T. Gilbert, S. T. Fiske, & G. Lindzey (Eds.), *The handbook of social psychology* (4th ed., Vol. 2, pp. 982–1026). New York: McGraw-Hill.

Buss, D. M., Larsen, R. J., Westen, D., & Semmelroth, J. (1992). Sex differences in jealousy: Evolution, physiology, and psychology. *Psychological Science*, 3, 251–5.

Buss, D. M., & Schmitt, D. P. (1993). Sexual strategies theory: An evolutionary perspective of human mating. *Psychological Review*, 100, 204–32.

Butler, R., & Neumann, O. (1995). Effects of task and ego achievement goals on help-seeking behaviors and attitudes. *Journal of Educational Psychology*, 87, 261–71.

Button, S. B., Mathieu, J. E., & Zajac, D. M. (1996). Goal orientation in organizational research: A conceptual and empirical foundation. *Organizational Behavior and Human Decision Processes*, 67 (1), 26–48.

Buunk, B. P. (1987). Conditions that promote break-ups as a consequence of extradyadic involvements. *Journal of Social and Clinical Psychology*, 5, 237–50.

Buunk, B. P. (1994). Social comparison processes under stress: Towards an integration of classic and recent perspectives. In W. Stroebe & M. Hewstone (Eds.), *European review of social psychology* (Vol. 5, pp. 211–41). Chichester: Wiley.

Buunk, B. P. (1995). Comparison direction and comparison dimension among disabled individuals: Towards a refined conceptualization of social comparison under stress. *Personality and Social Psychology Bulletin*, 21, 316–30.

Buunk, B. P., Angleitner, A., Oubaid, V., & Buss, D. M. (1996). Sex differences in jealousy in evolutionary and cultural perspective. *Psychological Science*, 7, 359–63.

Buunk, B. P., & Bakker, A. B. (1997). Commitment to the relationship, extradyadic sex, and AIDS-preventive behavior. *Journal of Applied Social Psychology*, 27 (14), 1241–57.

Buunk, B. P., Collins, R., VanYperen, N. W., Taylor, S. E., & Dakoff, G. (1990). Upward and downward comparisons: Either direction has its ups and downs. *Journal of Personality and Social Psychology*, 59, 1238–49.

Buunk, B. P., & Prins, K. S. (1998). Loneliness, exchange orientation and reciprocity in friendships. *Personal Relationships*, 5, 1–14.

Buunk, B. P., & Schaufeli, W. B. (1999). Reciprocity in interpersonal relationships: An evolutionary perspective on its importance for health and well-being. In W. Stroebe & M. Hewstone (Eds.), *European Review of Social Psychology* (Vol. 10, pp. 259–91). Chichester: Wiley.

Buunk, B. P., & Van den Eijnden, R. J. J. M. (1997). Perceived prevalence, perceived superiority, and relationship satisfaction: Most relationships are good, but ours is the best. *Personality and Social Psychology Bulletin*, 23 (3), 219–28.

Buunk, B. P., & Van Driel, B. (1989). *Variant lifestyles and relationships*. Newbury Park, CA: Sage.

Buunk, B. P., & VanYperen, N. W. (1991). Referential comparisons, relational comparisons and exchange orientation: Their relation to marital satisfaction. *Personality and Social Psychology Bulletin*, 17, 710–18.

Byrne, D. (1971). *The attraction paradigm*. New York: Academic Press.

Byrne, D., Ervin, C. R., & Lambert, J. (1970). Continuity between the experimental study of attraction and real life computer dating. *Journal of Personality and Social Psychology*, 16, 157–65.

Byrne, D., London, O., & Griffit, W. (1968). The effect of topic importance and attitude similarity–dissimilarity on attraction in an intrastranger design. *Psychonomic Science*, 11, 303–304.

Byrne, D. G., Whyte, H. M., & Butler, K. L. (1981). Illness behavior and outcome following survived myocardial infarction: A prospective study. *Journal of Psychosomatic Research*, 25, 97–107.

Cacioppo, J. T., & Gardner, W. L. (1993). What underlies medical donor attitudes and behaviour? *Health Psychology*, 12, 269–71.

Cacioppo, J. T., Harkins, S. G., & Petty, R. E. (1981). The nature of attitudes and cognitive responses and their relationships to behavior. In R. E. Petty, T. M. Ostrom, & T. C. Brock (Eds.), *Cognitive responses in persuasion* (pp. 31–54). Hillsdale, NJ: Erlbaum.

Cacioppo, J. T., Klein, D. J., Berntson, G. C., & Hatfield, E. (1993). The psychophysiology of emotion. In M. Lewis & J. M. Haviland (Eds.), *Handbook of emotions* (pp. 119–42). New York: Guilford Press.

Cacioppo, J. T., & Petty, R. E. (1979). Effects of message repetition and position on cognitive response, recall, and persuasion. *Journal of Personality and Social Psychology*, 37, 97–109.

Cacioppo, J. T., & Petty, R. E. (1982). The need for cognition. *Journal of Personality and Social Psychology*, 42, 116–31.

Cacioppo, J. T., Petty, R. E., Feinstein, J. A., & Jarvis, W. B. G. (1996). Dispositional differences in cognitive motivation: The life and times of individuals varying in need for cognition. *Psychological Bulletin*, 119, 197–253.

Cacioppo, J. T., Petty, R. E., Kao, C. F., & Rodriguez, R. (1986). Central and peripheral routes to persuasion: An individual difference perspective. *Journal of Personality and Social Psychology*, 51, 1032–43.

Caddick, B. (1982). Perceived illegitimacy and intergroup relations. In H. Tajfel (Ed.), *Social identity and intergroup relations* (pp. 137–54). Cambridge: Cambridge University Press.

Campbell, A. (1995). A few good men: Evolutionary psychology and female adolescent aggression. *Ethology and Sociobiology*, 16, 99–123.

Campbell, D. T. (1950). The indirect assessment of attitudes. *Psychological Bulletin*, 47, 15–38.

Campbell, D. T., & McCandless, B. R. (1951). Ethnocentrism, xenophobia, and personality. *Human Relations*, 4, 185–92.

Cannon, W. B. (1929). *Bodily changes in pain, hunger, fear and rage* (2nd ed.). New York: Appleton.

Carey, M. (1978). Does civil inattention exist in pedestrian passing? *Journal of Personality and Social Psychology*, 36, 1185–93.

Carleton, R. A., Lasater, T. M., Assaf, A. R., Feldman, H. A., McKinlay, S., and the Pawtucket Heart Health Program Writing Group (1995). The Pawtucket Heart Health Program: Community changes in cardiovascular risk factors and projected disease risk. *American Journal of Public Health*, 85, 777–85.

Carlson, M., Charlin, V., & Miller, N. (1988). Positive mood and helping behavior: A test of six hypotheses. *Journal of Personality and Social Psychology*, 55, 211–29.

Carlson, M., Marcus-Newhall, A., & Miller, N. (1990). Effects of situational aggression cues: A quantitative review. *Journal of Personality and Social Psychology*, 58, 622–33.

Carlson, M., & Miller, N. (1987). Explanation of the relation between negative mood and helping. *Psychological Bulletin*, 102, 91–108.

Carnevale, P. J. (1986). Mediating disputes and decisions in organizations. In R. J. Lewicki, B. H. Sheppard, & M. H. Bazerman (Eds.), *Research on negotiation in organizations* (Vol. 1, pp. 251–70). Greenwich, CT: JAI Press.

Carnevale, P. J., & Pruitt, D. G. (1992). Negotiation and mediation. *Annual Review of Psychology*, 43, 531–82.

Carpenter, E. M., & Kirkpatrick, L. A. (1996). Attachment style and presence of a romantic partner as moderators of psychophysiological responses to a stressful laboratory situation. *Personal Relationships*, 3 (4), 351–67.

Carroll, J. M., & Russell, J. A. (1997). Facial expressions in Hollywood's portrayal of emotion. *Journal of Personality and Social Psychology*, 72 (1), 164–76.

Cartwright, D. (1979). Contemporary social psychology in social perspective. *Social Psychology Quarterly*, 42, 82–93.

Carver, C. S., Pozo, C., Harris, S. D., Noriega, V., Scheier, M. F., Robinson, D. S., Ketcham, A. S., Moffat, L., Jr., & Clark, K. C. (1993). How coping mediates the effects of optimism on distress: A study of women with early stages breast cancer. *Journal of Personality and Social Psychology*, 65, 375–90.

Cate, R. M., Lloyd, S. A., & Long, E. (1988). The role of rewards and fairness in developing premarital relationships. *Journal of Marriage and the Family*, 50, 443–52.

Chaiken, S., Giner-Sorolla, R., & Chen, S. (1996). Beyond accuracy: Defense and impression motives in heuristic and systematic information processing. In P. M. Gollwitzer & J. A. Bargh (Eds.), *The psychology of action: Linking motivation and cognition to behavior* (pp. 553–78). New York: Guilford Press.

Chaiken, S., Liberman, A., & Eagly, A. H. (1989). Heuristic and systematic information processing within and beyond the persuasion context. In J. S. Uleman & J. A. Bargh (Eds.), *Unintended thought* (pp. 212–52). New York: Guilford Press.

Chaiken, S., & Maheswaran, D. (1994). Heuristic processing can bias systematic processing: Effects of source credibility, argument ambiguity, and task importance on attitude judgment. *Journal of Personality and Social Psychology*, 66, 460–73.

Chaiken, S., Pomerantz, E. M., & Giner-Sorolla, R. (1995). Structural consistency and attitude strength. In R. E. Petty & J. A. Krosnick (Eds.), *Attitude strength: Antecedents and consequences* (pp. 387–412). Mahwah, NJ: Erlbaum.

Chaiken, S., & Stangor, C. (1987). Attitudes and attitude change. *Annual Review of Psychology*, 38, 575–630.

Chaiken, S., Wood, W., & Eagly, A. H. (1996). Principles of persuasion. In E. T. Higgins & A. W. Kruglanski (Eds.), *Social psychology: Handbook of basic principles* (pp. 702–42). New York: Guilford Press.

Chang, E. C. (1998). Dispositional optimism and primary and secondary appraisal of a stressor: Controlling for confounding influences and relations to coping and psychological adjustment. *Journal of Personality and Social Psychology*, 74, 1109–20.

Chen, S., & Chaiken, S. (1999). The heuristic-systematic model in its broader context. In S. Chaiken & Y. Trope (Eds.), *Dual-process theories in social psychology* (pp. 73–96). New York: Guilford Press.

Cheng, P. W. (1997). From covariation to causation: A causal power theory. *Psychological Review*, 104, 367–405.

Cheng, P. W., & Novick, L. R. (1992). Covariation in natural causal induction. *Psychological Review*, 99, 365–82.

Chevalier-Skolnikoff, S. (1973). Facial expression of emotion in nonhuman primates. In P. Ekman (Ed.), *Darwin and facial expression* (pp. 11–89). New York: Academic Press.

Chiva, M. (1985). *Le doux et l'amer: Sensation gustative, émotion et communication chez le jeune enfant*. Paris: PUF.

Choi, I., & Nisbett, R. E. (1998). Situational salience and cultural differences in the correspondence bias and actor–observer bias. *Personality and Social Psychology Bulletin*, 24, 49–60.

Choi, I., Nisbett, R. E., & Norenzayan, A. (1999). Causal attributions across cultures: Variation and universality. *Psychological Bulletin*, 125, 47–63.

Chomsky, N. (1959). Review of Skinner (1957). *Language*, 35, 26–58.

Chomsky, N. (1965). *Aspects of the theory of syntax*. Cambridge, MA: MIT Press.

Christie, R., & Jahoda, M. (Eds.). (1954). *Studies in the scope and method of the authoritarian personality*. New York: Free Press.

Cialdini, R. B., Borden, R. J., Thorne, A., Walker, M. R., Freeman, S., & Sloan, L. R. (1976). Basking in reflected glory: Three (football) field studies. *Journal of Personality and Social Psychology*, 34, 366–75.

Cialdini, R. B., Brown, S. L., Lewis, B. P., Luce, C., & Neuberg, S. L. (1997). Reinterpreting the empathy–altruism relationship: When one into one equals oneness. *Journal of Personality and Social Psychology*, 73, 481–94.

Cialdini, R. B., & Trost, M. R. (1998). Influence, social norms, conformity and compliance. In D. T. Gilbert, S. T. Fiske, & G. Lindzey (Eds.), *The handbook of social psychology* (4th ed., Vol. 2, pp. 151–92). New York: McGraw-Hill.

Cialdini, R. B., Trost, M. R., & Newsom, J. T. (1995). Preference for consistency: The development of a valid measure and the discovery of surprising behavioral implications. *Journal of Personality and Social Psychology*, 69, 318–28.

Clark, K. B., & Clark, M. P. (1947). Racial identification and preference in Negro children. In E. E. Maccoby, T. M. Newcomb, & E. L. Hartley (Eds.), *Readings in social psychology*. London: Methuen.

Clark, M. S. (1984). Record keeping in two types of relationships. *Journal of Personality and Social Psychology*, 47, 549–57.

Clark, M. S., & Mills, J. (1993). The difference between communal and exchange relationships: What it is and is not. *Personality and Social Psychology Bulletin*, 19, 684–91.

Clark, M. S., Mills, J., & Powell, M. C. (1986). Keeping track of needs in communal and exchange relationships. *Journal of Personality and Social Psychology*, 51, 233–8.

Clark, M. S., Ouellette, R., Powell, M. C., & Milberg, S. (1987). Recipient's mood, relationship type, and helping. *Journal of Personality and Social Psychology*, 53, 94–103.

Clark, R. D., III, & Hatfield, E. (1989). Gender differences in receptivity to sexual offers. *Journal of Psychology and Human Sexuality*, 2, 39–55.

Clary, E. G., & Snyder, M. (1991). A functional analysis of altruism and prosocial behavior: The case of volunteerism. In M. S. Clark (Ed.), *Prosocial behavior* (pp. 119–48). Newbury Park, CA: Sage.

Clayton, D. A. (1978). Socially facilitated behavior. *The Quarterly Review of Biology*, 53, 373–92.

Clore, G. L., Schwarz, N., & Conway, M. (1994). Cognitive causes and consequences of emotion. In R. S. Wyer & T. K. Srull (Eds.), *Handbook of social cognition* (2nd ed., pp. 323–417). Hillsdale, NJ: Erlbaum.

Cobb, S. (1976). Social support as a moderator of life stress. *Psychosomatic Medicine*, 38, 300–14.

Cochrane, R. (1988). Marriage, separation and divorce. In S. Fisher & J. Reason (Eds.), *Handbook of life stress, cognition and health* (pp. 137–60). Chichester: Wiley.

Codol, J. P. (1975). On the so-called 'superior conformity of the self' behaviour: Twenty ex-perimental investigations. *European Journal of Social Psychology*, 5, 457–501.

Cohen, D. (1996). Law, social policy and violence: The impact of regional cultures. *Journal of Personality and Social Psychology*, 70, 761–78.

Cohen, D., & Nisbett, R. E. (1994). Self-protection and the culture of honor: Explaining southern violence. *Personality and Social Psychology Bulletin*, 20, 551–67.

Cohen, S., Frank, E., Doyle, W. J., Skoner, D. P., Rabin, B. S., Gwaltney, J. M., Jr. (1998). Types of stressors that increase susceptibility to the common cold in healthy adults. *Health Psychology*, 17, 214–23.

Cohen, S., & Hoberman, H. M. (1983). Positive events and social supports as buffers of life change stress. *Journal of Applied Social Psychology*, 13 (2), 99–125.

Cohen, S., Kessler, R. C., & Gordon, L. U. (1995). Strategies for measuring stress in studies of psychiatric and physical disorders. In S. Cohen, R. C. Kessler, & L. U. Gordon (Eds.), *Measuring stress* (pp. 3–26). New York: Oxford University Press.

Cohen, S., Tyrell, D., & Smith, A. (1993). Negative life events, perceived stress, negative affect, and susceptibility to the common cold. *Journal of Personality and Social Psychology*, 64, 131–40.

Cohen, S., & Williamson, G. M. (1988). Perceived stress in a probability sample of the United States. In S. Spacapan & S. Oskamp (Eds.), *The social psychology of health* (pp. 17–67). Newbury Park, CA: Sage.

Cohen, S., & Wills, T. A. (1985). Stress, social support, and the buffering hypothesis. *Psychological Bulletin*, 98, 310–57.

Combs, B., & Slovic, P. (1979). Newspaper coverage of causes of death. *Public Opinion Quarterly*, 56, 837–43.

Comstock, G., & Paik, H. (1991). *Television and the American child*. San Diego, CA: Academic Press.

Comte, A. (1853). *The positive philosophy* (Vol. 1). London: Longmans, Green.

Conger, J. A. (1990). The dark side of leadership. *Organizational Dynamics*, 19, 44–55.

Converse, P. E. (1964). The nature of belief systems in mass publics. In D. E. Apter (Ed.), *Ideology and discontent* (pp. 206–61). New York: Free Press.

Cook, S. W. (1962). The systematic analysis of socially significant events. *Journal of Social Issues*, 18, 66–84.

Cook, T. D., & Campbell, D. T. (1979). *Quasi-experimentation: Design and analysis issues for field settings*. Chicago, IL: Rand McNally.

Cooper, H. (1990). Meta-analysis and the integrative research review. In C. Hendrick & M. S. Clark (Eds.), *Research methods in personality and social psychology* (*Review of Personality and Social Psychology*, Vol. 11, pp. 142–63). Newbury Park, CA: Sage.

Cooper, J., & Brehm, J. W. (1971). Prechoice awareness of relative deprivation as a determinant of cognitive dissonance. *Journal of Experimental Social Psychology*, 7, 571–81.

Cooper, J., & Fazio, R. H. (1984). A new look at dissonance theory. *Advances in Experimental Social Psychology*, 17, 229–66.

Corwin, R. G. (1969). Patterns of organizational conflict. *Administrative Science Quarterly*, 14, 507–20.

Cosmides, L. (1989). The logic of social exchange: Has natural selection shaped how humans reason? Studies with the Wason selection task. *Cognition*, 31, 187–276.

Cosmides, L., & Tooby, J. (1992). Cognitive adaptations for social exchange. In J. H. Barkow, L. Cosmides, & J. Tooby (Eds.), *The adapted mind* (pp. 163–228). New York & Oxford: Oxford University Press.

Costanza, R. S., Derlega, V. J., & Winstead, B. A. (1988). Positive and negative forms of social support: Effects of conversational topics on coping with stress among same sex friends. *Journal of Experimental Social Psychology*, 24, 182–93.

Cotton, J. L., & Baron, R. S. (1980). Anonymity, persuasive arguments and choice shifts. *Social Psychology Quarterly*, 43, 391–404.

Cottrell, N. B. (1968). Performance in the presence of other human beings: Mere presence, audience and affiliation effects. In E. C. Simmel, R. A. Hoppe, & G. A. Milton (Eds.), *Social facilitation and imitative behavior* (pp. 245–50). Boston: Allyn & Bacon.

Cottrell, N. B. (1972). Social facilitation. In C. G. McClintock (Ed.), *Experimental social psychology* (pp. 185–236). New York: Holt, Rinehart & Winston.

Coupland, N., & Coupland, J. (1995). Discourse, identity, and aging. In J. Nussbaum & J. Coupland (Eds.), *Handbook of communication and aging research* (pp. 79–103). Mahwah, NJ: Lawrence Erlbaum Associates.

Cowles, M., & Davis, C. (1987). The subject matter of psychology: Volunteers. *British Journal of Social Psychology*, 26, 289–94.

Cranny, C. J., Smith P. C., & Stone, E. F. (1992). *Job satisfaction: How people feel about their jobs and how it affects their performance*. New York: Lexington Books.

Crawford, C., & Krebs, D. L. (1998). *Handbook of evolutionary psychology*. Mahwah, NJ: Lawrence Erlbaum.

Crick, N. R., & Dodge, K. A. (1994). A review and reformulation of social information-processing mechanisms in children's adjustment. *Psychological Bulletin*, 115, 74–101.

Crocker, J., & Luhtanen, R. (1990). Collective self esteem and ingroup bias. *Journal of Personality and Social Psychology*, 58, 60–7.

Crocker, J., Thompson, L. J., McGraw, K. M., & Ingermann, C. (1987). Downward comparison, prejudice, and evaluations of others: Effects of self esteem and threat. *Journal of Personality and Social Psychology*, 52, 907–16.

Cromer, R. F. (1991). *Language and thought in normal and handicapped children*. Oxford: Blackwell.

Cronbach, L. J. (1951). Coefficient alpha and the internal structure of tests. *Psychometrika*, 16, 297–334.

Cronin, H. (1991). *The ant and the peacock*. Cambridge & New York: Cambridge University Press.

Cropanzano, R., & Folger, R. (1996). Procedural justice and worker motivation. In R. M. Steers, L. W. Porter, & G. A. Bigley (Eds.), *Motivation and leadership at work* (pp. 72–83). McGraw-Hill.

Crosby, F. (1976). A model of egotistical relative deprivation. *Psychological Review*, 83, 85–113.

Crutchfield, R. A. (1955). Conformity and character. *American Psychologist*, 10, 191–8.

Cunningham, J. D., & Kelley, H. H. (1975). Causal attributions for interpersonal events of varying magnitude. *Journal of Personality*, 43, 74–93.

Cunningham, M. R. (1986). Measuring the physical in physical attractiveness: Quasi experiments on the sociobiology of female facial beauty. *Journal of Personality and Social Psychology*, 50, 925–35.

Cunningham, M. R., Barbee, A. P., & Pike, C. L. (1990). What do women want? Facialmetric assessment of multiple motives in the perception of male physical attractiveness. *Journal of Personality and Social Psychology*, 59, 61–72.

Cunningham, M. R., Roberts, A. R., Barbee, A. P., Druen, P. B., & Wu, C. (1995). 'Their ideas of beauty are, on the whole, the same as ours': Consistency and variability in the cross-cultural perception of female physical attractiveness. *Journal of Personality and Social Psychology*, 68, 261–79.

Daly, M., Salmon, C., & Wilson, M. (1997). Kinship: The conceptual hole in psychological studies of social cognition and close relationships. In J. A. Simpson & D. T. Kenrick (Eds.), *Evolutionary social psychology* (pp. 265–96). Mahwah, NJ: Erlbaum.

Daly, M., & Wilson, M. (1982). Whom are newborn babies said to resemble? *Ethology and Sociobiology*, 3, 69–78.

Daly, M., & Wilson, M. (1985). Child abuse and other risks of not living with both parents. *Ethology and Sociobiology*, 6, 197–210.

Daly, M., & Wilson, M. (1988). *Homicide*. New York: Aldine de Gruyter.

Danis, A. (1997). Effects of familiar and unfamiliar objects on mother–infant interaction. *European Journal of Psychology of Education*, 12, 261–72.

Danziger, K. (1983). Origins and basic principles of Wundt's *Völkerpsychologie*. *British Journal of Social Psychology*, 22, 303–13.

Danziger, K. (1992). The project of an experimental social psychology: Historical perspectives. *Science in Context*, 5, 309–28.

Danziger, K. (1997). *Naming the mind: How psychology found its language*. London: Sage.

Darley, J. M. (1992). Social categorization for the production of evil. *Psychological Inquiry*, 3, 199–218.

Darley, J. M., & Batson, C. D. (1973). From Jerusalem to Jericho: A study of situational and dispositional variables in helping behavior. *Journal of Personality and Social Psychology*, 27, 100–8.

Darwin, C. (1871). *The descent of man, and selection in relation to sex*. London: John Murray.

Darwin, C. (1872/1965). *The expression of the emotions in man and animals*. London: John Murray/Chicago: University of Chicago Press.

Darwin, C. (1872/1998). *The expression of the emotions in man and animals* (3rd ed., Ed. P. Ekman). London: HarperCollins.

Davey, A. (1983). *Learning to be prejudiced*. London: Edward Arnold.

Davidson, A. R., & Jaccard, J. J. (1979). Variables that moderate the attitude–behavior relation: Results of a longitudinal survey. *Journal of Personality and Social Psychology*, 37, 1364–76.

Davies, J. C. (1969). The J-curve of rising and declining satisfactions as a cause of some great revolutions and a contained rebellion. In H. D. Graham & T. R. Gurr (Eds.), *The history of violence in America: Historical and comparative perspectives*. New York: Praeger.

Davis, J. H. (1969). *Group performance*. Reading, MA: Addison-Wesley.

Davis, J. H. (1973). Group decision and social interaction: A theory of social decision schemes. *Psychological Review*, 80, 97–125.

Davis, J. H. (1996). Group decision making and quantitative judgements: A consensus model. In E. Witte & J. H. Davis (Eds.), *Understanding group behavior: Consensual action by small groups* (Vol. 1, pp. 35–60). Mahwah, NJ: Lawrence Erlbaum.

Davis, M. H. (1983). Measuring individual differences in empathy: Evidence for a multidimensional approach. *Journal of Personality and Social Psychology*, 44, 113–26.

Davis, M. H. (1994). *Empathy: A social psychological approach*. Boulder, CO: Westview Press.

Davitz, J. R. (1964). *The communication of emotional meaning*. New York: McGraw-Hill.

Dawber, T. R. (1980). *The Framingham study.* Cambridge, MA: Harvard University Press.

Dawes, R. M. (1980). Social dilemmas. *Annual Review of Psychology*, 31, 169–93.

Dawes, R. M., McTavish, J., & Shaklee, H. (1977). Behavior, communication, and assumptions about other people's behavior in a common dilemma situation. *Journal of Personality and Social Psychology*, 35, 1–11.

Dawkins, R. (1976). *The selfish gene.* Oxford: Oxford University Press.

Dawkins, R. (1979). Twelve misunderstandings of kin selection. *Zeitschrift für Tierpsychologie*, 51, 184–200.

Dawkins, R. (1986). *The blind watchmaker.* London: Longman.

Dawkins, R. (1989). *The selfish gene* (2nd ed.). New York: Oxford University Press.

De Dreu, C. K. W. (1997). Productive conflict: The importance of conflict management and conflict issue. In C. K. W. De Dreu & E. Van de Vliert (Eds.), *Using conflict in organizations* (pp. 9–22). Thousand Oaks, CA: Sage.

De Dreu, C. K. W., & De Vries, N. K. (1993). Numerical support, information processing and attitude change. *European Journal of Social Psychology*, 23, 647–63.

De Dreu, C. K. W., Giebels, E., & Van de Vliert, E. (1998). Social motives and trust in integrative negotiation: The disruptive effects of punitive capability. *Journal of Applied Psychology*, 83, 408–22.

De Dreu, C. K. W., & McCusker, C. (1997). Gain–loss frames and cooperation in two-person social dilemmas: A transformational analysis. *Journal of Personality and Social Psychology*, 72, 1093–1106.

De Dreu, C. K. W., & Van Lange, P. A. M. (1995). The impact of social value orientation on negotiator behavior and cognition. *Personality and Social Psychology Bulletin*, 21, 1178–88.

De Dreu, C. K. W., Weingart, L. R., & Kwon, S. (in press). Social motives in integrative negotiation: A meta-analytic review and test of two theories. *Journal of Personality and Social Psychology*.

De Dreu, C. K. W., Yzerbyt, V. Y., & Leyens, J.-Ph. (1995). The dilution of stereotype-based cooperation in mixed-motive interdependence. *Journal of Experimental Social Psychology*, 21, 575–93.

De Gilder, D., & Wilke, H. A. M. (1994). Expectation states theory and the motivational determinants of social influence. In W. Stroebe & M. Hewstone (Eds.), *European review of social psychology* (Vol. 5, pp. 243–69). London: Wiley.

De Montmollin, G. (1977). *L'influence sociale. Phénomènes, facteurs et théories.* Paris: Presses Universitaires de France.

De Vries, N. K., De Dreu, C. K. W., Gordijn, E., & Schuurman, M. (1996). Majority and minority influence: A dual role interpretation. In W. Stroebe & M. Hewstone (Eds.), *European review of social psychology* (Vol. 7, pp. 145–72). Chichester: Wiley.

Deci, E. L. (1971). Effects of externally mediated rewards on intrinsic motivation. *Journal of Personality and Social Psychology*, 18, 105–15.

Delbecq, A. L., Van de Ven, A. H., & Gustafson, D. H. (1975). *Group technique from program planning.* Glenview, IL: Scott, Foresman.

Denmark, F. L. (1994). Engendering psychology. *American Psychologist*, 49, 329–34.

DePaulo, B. M., Brown, P. L., Ishii, S., & Fisher, J. D. (1981). Help that works: The effects of aid on subsequent task performance. *Journal of Personality and Social Psychology*, 41, 478–87.

DePaulo, B. M., & Friedman, H. S. (1998). Nonverbal communication. In D. T. Gilbert, S. T. Fiske, & G. Lindzey (Eds.), *The handbook of social psychology* (4th ed., Vol. 2, pp. 3–40). New York: McGraw-Hill.

DeRubeis, R. J., & Hollon, S. D. (1995). Explanatory style in the treatment of depression. In G. Buchanan & M. E. P. Seligman (Eds.), *Explanatory style* (pp. 99–112). Hillsdale, NJ: Erlbaum.

Deschamps, J.-C. (1977). Effect of crossing category memberships on quantitative judgements. *European Journal of Social Psychology*, 7, 517–21.

Deschamps, J.-C., & Brown, R. J. (1983). Superordinate goals and intergroup conflict. *British Journal of Social Psychology*, 22, 189–95.

Deschamps, J.-C., & Doise, W. (1978). Crossed category memberships in intergroup relations. In

H. Tajfel (Ed.), *Differentiation between social groups*. London: Academic Press.

Desforges, D. M., Lord, C. G., Ramsey, S. L., Mason, J. A., Van Leeuwen, M. D., West, S. C., & Lepper, M. R. (1991). Effects of structured cooperative contact on changing negative attitudes towards stigmatized groups. *Journal of Personality and Social Psychology*, 60, 531–44.

Deutsch, M. (1949a). An experimental study of the effect of cooperation and competition upon group process. *Human Relations*, 2, 199–231.

Deutsch, M. (1949b). A theory of cooperation and competition. *Human Relations*, 2, 129–52.

Deutsch, M. (1975). Equity, equality, and need: What determines which value will be used as the basis of distributive justice? *Journal of Social Issues*, 31, 137–49.

Deutsch, M., & Gerard, H. B. (1955). A study of normative and informational social influences upon individual judgement. *Journal of Abnormal and Social Psychology*, 51, 629–36.

Devine, P. G. (1989). Stereotypes and prejudice: Their automatic and controlled components. *Journal of Personality and Social Psychology*, 56, 5–18.

Devine, P. G. (1995). Prejudice and out-group perception. In A. Tesser (Ed.), *Advanced social psychology* (pp. 467–524). New York: McGraw-Hill.

Devos, T., Cornby, L., & Deschamps, J. C. (1996). Assymmetries in judgements of ingroup and outgroup variability. In W. Stroebe & M. Hewstone (Eds.), *European review of social psychology* (Vol. 7, pp. 95–144). Chichester: Wiley.

De Waal, F. (1983). *Chimpanzee politics: Power and sex among apes*. New York: Harper & Row.

De Waal, F. B. M. (1996). *Good natured: The origins of right and wrong in humans and other animals*. Cambridge, MA: Harvard University Press.

Di Vesta, F. J. (1959). Effects of confidence and motivation on susceptibility to informational social influence. *Journal of Abnormal and Social Psychology*, 59, 204–9.

Diamond, J. (1991). *The rise and fall of the third chimpanzee*. London: Radius Books.

Diehl, M. (1988). Social identity and minimal groups: The effects of interpersonal and intergroup attitudinal similarity on intergroup discrimination. *British Journal of Social Psychology*, 27, 289–300.

Diehl, M. (1989). Justice and discrimination in minimal groups: The limits of equity. *British Journal of Social Psychology*, 28, 227–38.

Diehl, M., & Stroebe, W. (1987). Productivity loss in brainstorming groups: Toward the solution of a riddle. *Journal of Personality and Social Psychology*, 53, 497–509.

Diener, E. (1980). Deindividuation: The absence of self-awareness and self-regulation in group members. In P. Paulus (Ed.), *The psychology of group influence* (pp. 209–42). Hillsdale, NJ: Erlbaum.

Dijkstra, A., De Vries, H., Roijackers, J., & Van Breukelen (1998). Tailored interventions to communicate stage-matched information to smokers in different motivational stages. *Journal of Consulting and Clinical Psychology*, 66, 549–57.

Dodge, K. A. (1980). Social cognition and children's aggressive behavior. *Child Development*, 54, 1386–99.

Dodge, K. A. (1986). A social information processing model of social competence in children. In M. Perlmutter (Ed.), *Eighteenth annual Minnesota symposium on child psychology* (pp. 77–125). Hillsdale, NJ: Erlbaum.

Dodge, K. A., & Somberg, D. R. (1987). Hostile attributional biases among aggressive boys are exacerbated under conditions of threat to the self. *Child Development*, 58, 213–24.

Doise, W. (1976). *L'articulation psychosociologique et les relations entre groupes*. Brussels: de Boeck. (Translated as *Groups and individuals: Explanations in social psychology*. Cambridge: Cambridge University Press, 1978.)

Doise, W. (1996). The origins of developmental social psychology: Baldwin, Cattaneo, Piaget and Vygotsky. *Swiss Journal of Psychology – Schweizerische Zeitschrift Für Psychologie – Revue Suisse de Psychologie*, 55, 139–49.

Doise, W., & Hanselmann, C. (1990). Interaction sociale et acquisition de la conservation du volume. *European Journal of Psychology of Education*, 5, 21–31.

Doise, W., & Mugny, G. (1984). *The social development of the intellect*. Oxford: Pergamon.

Doise, W., Mugny, G., & Perret-Clermont, A.-N. (1975). Social interaction and the development of cognitive operations. *European Journal of Social Psychology*, 5, 367–83.

Doise, W., & Palmonari, A. (1984). Introduction: The sociopsychological study of individual development. In W. Doise & A. Palmonari (Eds.), *Social Interaction in Individual Development* (pp. 1–16). Cambridge: Cambridge University Press.

Doise, W., Rijsman, J. B., Van Meel, J., Bressers, I., & Pinxten, L. (1981). Sociale markering en cognitieve ontwikkeling. *Pedagogische Studien*, 58, 241–8.

Doll, J., & Ajzen, I. (1992). Accessibility and stability of predictors in the theory of planned behavior. *Journal of Personality and Social Psychology*, 63, 754–65.

Dollard, J., Doob, L. W., Miller, N. E., Mowrer, O. H., & Sears, R. T. (1939). *Frustration and aggression*. New Haven, CT: Yale University Press.

Doms, M., & Van Avermaet, E. (1980). Majority influence, minority influence and conversion behaviour: A replication. *Journal of Experimental Social Psychology*, 16, 283–92.

Donnerstein, E., Donnerstein, M., Simons, S., & Dittrichs, R. (1972). Variables in interracial aggression. *Journal of Personality and Social Psychology*, 22, 236–45.

Donnerstein, E., & Wilson, D. W. (1976). The effects of noise and perceived control upon ongoing and subsequent aggressive behavior. *Journal of Personality and Social Psychology*, 34, 774–81.

Doob, L. W. (1947). The behavior of attitudes. *Psychological Review*, 54, 135–56.

Doty, R. M., Peterson, B. E. A., & Winter, D. G. (1991). Threat and authoritarianism in the United States, 1978–1987. *Journal of Personality and Social Psychology*, 61, 629–40.

Dovidio, J. F., Evans, N. E., & Tyler, R. B. (1986). Racial stereotypes: The contents of their cognitive representations. *Journal of Experimental Social Psychology*, 22, 22–37.

Dovidio, J. F., Gaertner, S. L., & Validzic, A. (1998). Intergroup bias: Status, differentiation and a common ingroup identity. *Journal of Personality and Social Psychology*, 75, 109–20.

Dovidio, J. F., Gaertner, S. L., Validzic, A., Matoka, K., Johnson, B., & Frazier, S. (1997). Extending the benefits of recategorization: Evaluations, self-disclosure and helping. *Journal of Experimental Social Psychology*, 33, 401–20.

Doyle, A.-B., Beaudet, J., & Aboud, F. (1988). Developmental patterns in the flexibility of children's ethnic attitudes. *Journal of Cross-Cultural Psychology*, 19, 3–18.

Dryer, D. C., & Horowitz, L. M. (1997). When do opposites attract? Interpersonal complementarity versus similarity. *Journal of Personality and Social Psychology*, 72 (3), 592–603.

Duck, S. (1998). *Human relationships* (3rd ed.). London: Sage.

Duda, J. L. (1992). Motivation in sport settings: A goal perspective approach. In G. C. Roberts (Ed.), *Motivation in sport and exercise* (pp. 57–91). Champaign, IL: Human Kinetic Books.

Dunkel-Schetter, C., Blasband, D. E., Feinstein, L. G., & Bennett, H. T. (1992). Elements of supportive interactions: When are attempts to help effective? In S. Spacapan & S. Oskamp (Eds.), *Helping and being helped. Naturalistic studies* (pp. 83–114). Newbury Park, CA: Sage.

Dunn, J. (1988). *The beginnings of social understanding*. Oxford: Blackwell.

Dunn, J. (1999). Mindreading and social relationships. In M. Bennett (Ed.), *Developmental psychology: Achievements and prospects* (pp. 55–71). London: Psychology Press.

Durkheim, E. (1898). Représentations individuelles et représentations collectives. *Revue de Métaphysique et de Morale*, 6, 273–302. (English trans. in E. Durkheim (1974), *Sociology and philosophy*, New York: Free Press.)

Durkin, K. (1995). *Developmental social psychology: From infancy to old age*. Oxford: Blackwell.

Dutton, D. G., & Aron, A. P. (1974). Some evidence for heightened sexual attraction under conditions of high anxiety. *Journal of Personality and Social Psychology*, 28, 510–17.

Dweck, C. S. (1975). The role of expectations and attributions in the alleviation of learned helplessness. *Journal of Personality and Social Psychology*, 36, 951–62.

Dweck, C. S., & Leggett, E. L. (1988). A social-cognitive approach to motivation and personality. *Psychological Review*, 95, 256–73.

Eagly, A. H. (1998). Attitudes and the processing of attitude-relevant information. In J. G. Adair & D. Belanger (Eds.), *Advances in psychological science. Vol. 1: Social, personal, and cultural aspects* (pp. 185–201). Hove: Psychology Press.

Eagly, A. H., & Chaiken, S. (1993). *The psychology of attitudes*. Fort Worth, TX: Harcourt Brace Jovanovich.

Eagly, A. H., & Chaiken, S. (1998). Attitude structure and function. In D. T. Gilbert, S. T. Fiske, & G. Lindzey (Eds.), *The handbook of social psychology* (4th ed., pp. 269–322). New York: McGraw-Hill.

Eagly, A. H., Chen, S., Chaiken, S., & Shaw-Barnes, K. (1999). The impact of attitudes on memory: An affair to remember. *Psychological Bulletin*, 125, 64–89.

Ebbesen, E. B., & Bowers, R. J. (1974). Proportion of risky to conservative arguments in a group discussion and choice shifts. *Journal of Personality and Social Psychology*, 29, 316–27.

Ebbesen, E. B., Kjos, G. L., & Konecni, V. J. (1976). Spatial ecology: Its effects on the choice of friends and enemies. *Journal of Experimental Social Psychology*, 12, 505–18.

Eckardt, G. (1971). Problemgeschichtliche Untersuchungen zur Völkerpsychologie der zweiten Hälfte des 19. Jahrhunderts. *Wissenschaftliche Zeitschrift der Friedrich-Schiller-Universität, Gesellschafts- und sprachwissenschaftliche Reihe*, 20 (4), 7–133.

Edwards, W. (1954). The theory of decision-making. *Psychological Bulletin*, 51, 380–417.

Eibl-Eibesfeldt, I. (1995). *Die Biologie des menschlichen Verhaltens: Grundriss der Humanethologie* [Biology of human behavior: Fundamentals of human ethology] (3rd ed.). Munich: Piper.

Eisenberg, N., & Fabes, R. A. (1990). Empathy: Conceptualization, assessment, and relation to prosocial behavior. *Motivation and Emotion*, 14, 131–49.

Eisenberg, N., & Fabes, R. A. (1991). Prosocial behavior and empathy: A multimethod developmental perspective. In M. S. Clark (Ed.), *Prosocial behavior* (pp. 34–61). Newbury Park, CA: Sage.

Eisenberg, N., Fabes, R. A., Carlo, G., Speer, A. L., Switzer, G., Karbon, M., & Troyer, D. (1993). The relations of empathy-related emotions and maternal practices to children's comforting behavior. *Journal of Experimental Child Psychology*, 55, 131–50.

Ekman, P. (1972). Universals and cultural differences in facial expression of emotion. In J. R. Cole (Ed.), *Nebraska symposium on motivation* (pp. 207–83). Lincoln, NE: University of Nebraska Press.

Ekman, P. (1979). About brows: Emotional and conversational signals. In M. V. Cranach, K. Foppa, W. Lepenies, & D. Ploog (Eds.), *Human ethology* (pp. 169–202). Cambridge: Cambridge University Press.

Ekman, P. (Ed.). (1982). *Emotion in the human face* (2nd ed.). Cambridge: Cambridge University Press.

Ekman, P. (1984). Expression and the nature of emotion. In K. R. Scherer & P. Ekman (Eds.), *Approaches to emotion* (pp. 319–44). Hillsdale, NJ: Erlbaum.

Ekman, P. (1989). The argument and evidence about universals in facial expressions of emotion. In A. Manstead & H. Wagner (Eds.), *Handbook of social psychophysiology* (pp. 143–64). Chichester: Wiley.

Ekman, P. (1992). An argument for basic emotions. *Cognition and Emotion*, 6, 169–200.

Ekman, P. (1998). Afterword, In C. Darwin, *The expression of emotions in man and animals* (3rd ed., Ed. P. Ekman). London: HarperCollins.

Ekman, P., & Friesen, W. V. (1969). The repertoire of nonverbal behaviour: Categories, origins, usage, and coding. *Semiotica*, 1, 49–98.

Ekman, P., & Friesen, W. V. (1975). *Unmasking the face: A guide to recognizing emotions from facial clues*. Englewood Cliffs, NJ: Prentice-Hall.

Ekman, P., & Friesen, W. V. (1986). A new pan-cultural facial expression of emotion. *Motivation and Emotion*, 10, 159–68.

Ekman, P., Levenson, R. W., & Friesen, W. (1983). Autonomic nervous system activity distinguishes among emotions. *Science*, 221, 1208–10.

Ekman, P., & Rosenberg, E. L. (Eds.). (1997). *What the face reveals: Basic and applied studies of spontaneous expression using the Facial Action Coding System (FACS)*. New York: Oxford University Press.

Ekman, P., Sorenson, E. R., & Friesen, W. V. (1969). Pan-cultural elements in facial displays of emotion. *Science*, 164, 86–8.

Elig, T. W., & Frieze, I. H. (1979). Measuring causal attributions for success and failure. *Journal of Personality and Social Psychology*, 37, 621–34.

Elkin, R. A., & Leippe, M. R. (1986). Physiological arousal, dissonance, and attitude change: Evidence for a dissonance arousal link and a 'don't remind me' effect. *Journal of Personality and Social Psychology*, 51, 55–65.

Ellemers, N., Van Knippenberg, A., de Vries, N., & Wilke, H. (1988). Social identification and permeability of group boundaries. *European Journal of Social Psychology*, 18, 497–513.

Ellemers, N., Wilke, H., & Van Knippenberg, A. (1993). Effects of the legitimacy of low group or individual status as individual and collective status-enhancement strategies. *Journal of Personality and Social Psychology*, 64, 766–78.

Ellis, H. C., & Ashbrook, P. W. (1988). Resource allocation model of the effects of depressed mood states on memory. In K. Fiedler & J. P. Forgas (Eds.), *Affect, cognition, and social behavior* (pp. 25–43). Toronto: Hogrefe.

Emlen, S. T. (1997). The evolutionary study of human family systems. *Social Science Information*, 36, 563–89.

Emler, N., & Reicher, S. (1995). *Adolescence and delinquency*. Oxford: Blackwell.

Emler, N., & Valiant, G. L. (1982). Social interaction and cognitive conflict in the development of spatial coordination skills. *British Journal of Psychology*, 73, 295–303.

Endler, N. (1965). The effects of verbal reinforcement on conformity and deviant behaviour. *Journal of Social Psychology*, 66, 147–54.

Epping-Jordan, J. E., Compas, B. E., & Howell, D. C. (1994). Predictors of cancer progression in young adult men and women: Avoidance, intrusive thoughts, and psychological symptoms. *Health Psychology*, 13, 539–47.

Epstein, S. (1966). Aggression toward outgroups as a function of authoritarianism and imitation of aggression models. *Journal of Personality and Social Psychology*, 3, 574–79.

Eron, L. D., & Huesmann, L. R. (1980). Adolescent aggression and television. *Annals of the New York Academy of Science*, 347, 319–31.

Eron, L. D., Huesmann, L. R., Lefkowitz, M. M., & Walder, L. O. (1972). Does television violence cause aggression? *American Psychologist*, 27, 253–63.

Eron, L. D., Walder, L. O., & Lefkowitz, M. M. (1971). *The learning of aggression in children*. Boston: Little, Brown.

Erwin, P. (1993). *Friendship and peer relations in children*. Chichester: Wiley.

Esser, J. K., & Lindoerfer, J. S. (1989). Groupthink and the space shuttle Challenger accident: Toward a quantitative case analysis. *Journal of Behavioral Decision Making*, 2, 167–77.

Estrada-Hollenbeck, M., & Heatherton, T. F. (1998). Avoiding and alleviating guilt through prosocial behavior. In J. Bybee (Ed.), *Guilt in children* (pp. 215–31). San Diego, CA: Academic Press.

Fabes, R. A., Eisenberg, N., Karbon, M., Troyer, D., & Switzer, G. (1994). The relations of children's emotion regulation to their vicarious emotional responses and comforting behaviors. *Child Development*, 65, 1678–93.

Farquhar, J. W., Fortman, S. P., Flora, J. A., Taylor, B., Haskell, W. L., Williams, P. T., Maccoby, N., & Woods, P. D. (1990). Effects of a community-wide education on cardiovascular disease risk factors: The Stanford Five-City project. *Journal of the American Medical Association*, 264, 359–65.

Farquhar, J. W., Maccoby, N., Wood, P. D., Alexander, J. K., Breitrose, H., Brown, B. W., Jr., Haskell, W. L., McAlister, A. L., Meyer, A. J., Nash, J. D., & Stern, M. P. (1977). Community education for cardiovascular health. *Lancet* (4 June), 1192–5.

Farr, J. L., Hofmann, D. A., & Ringenbach, K. L. (1993). Goal orientation and action control theory: Implications for industrial and organizational psychology. In C. L. Cooper & I. T. Robertson (Eds.), *International Review of Industrial and Organizational Psychology*, 8, 193–232.

Farr, R. M. (1980). On reading Darwin and discovering social psychology. In R. Gilmour & R. Duck (Eds.), *The development of social psychology* (pp. 111–36). London: Academic Press.

Farr, R. M. (1996). *The roots of modern social psychology 1872–1954.* Oxford: Blackwell.

Farrell, D., & Rusbult, C. E. (1981). Exchange variables as predictors of job satisfaction, job commitment, and turnover: The impact of rewards, costs, alternatives and investments. *Organizational Behavior and Human Performance*, 27, 78–95.

Farrington, D. P. (1994). Childhood, adolescent, and adult features of violent males. In L. R. Huesmann (Ed.), *Aggressive behavior: Current perspectives* (pp. 215–40). New York: Plenum Press.

Fazio, R. H. (1990). Multiple processes by which attitudes guide behavior: The MODE model as an integrative framework. In M. P. Zanna (Ed.), *Advances in experimental social psychology* (Vol. 23, pp. 75–109). New York: Academic Press.

Fazio, R. H. (1995). Attitudes as object-evaluation associations: Determinants, consequences, and correlates of attitude accessibility. In R. E. Petty & J. A. Krosnick (Eds.), *Attitude strength: Antecedents and consequences* (pp. 247–82). Mahwah, NJ: Erlbaum.

Fazio, R. H., Chen, J., McDonel, E. C., & Sherman, S. J. (1982). Attitude accessibility, attitude–behavior consistency, and the strength of the object-evaluation association. *Journal of Experimental Social Psychology*, 18, 339–57.

Fazio, R. H., & Williams, C. J. (1986). Attitude accessibility as a moderator of the attitude–perception and attitude–behavior relations: An investigation of the 1984 presidential election. *Journal of Personality and Social Psychology*, 51, 505–14.

Fazio, R. H., & Zanna, M. P. (1981). Direct experience and attitude–behavior consistency. *Advances in Experimental Social Psychology*, 14, 161–202.

Fazio, R. H., Zanna, M. P., & Cooper, J. (1977). Dissonance versus self-perception: An integrative view of each theory's proper domain of application. *Journal of Experimental Social Psychology*, 13, 464–79.

Feather, N. T. (Ed.). (1982). *Expectations and actions: Expectancy-value models in psychology.* Hillsdale, NJ: Erlbaum.

Feather, N. T. (1995). Values, valences, and choice: The influence of values on the perceived attractiveness and choice of alternatives. *Journal of Personality and Social Psychology*, 68, 1135–51.

Feeney, J. A. (1994). Attachment style, communication patterns, and satisfaction across the life cycle of marriage. *Personal Relationships*, 1, 333–48.

Feeney, J. A., Noller, P., & Patty, J. (1993). Adolescents' interactions with the opposite sex: Influence of attachment style and gender. *Journal of Adolescence*, 16, 169–89.

Feingold, A. (1992). Good-looking people are not what we think. *Psychological Bulletin*, 111, 304–41.

Feldman, R. S., & Rimé, B. (Eds.). (1991). *Fundamentals of nonverbal behaviour.* Cambridge: Cambridge University Press.

Felson, R. B. (1984). Patterns of aggressive interactions. In A. Mummendey (Ed.), *Social psychology of aggression: From individual behavior to social interaction.* New York: Springer.

Ferguson, T. J., & Rule, B. G. (1983). An attributional perspective on anger and aggression. In R. Geen & E. Donnerstein (Eds.), *Aggression: Theoretical and empirical reviews. Vol. I: Method and theory* (pp. 41–74). New York: Academic Press.

Fernald, A. (1989). Intonation and communicative intent in mothers' speech to infants: Is the melody the message? *Child Development*, 60, 1497–1510.

Festinger, L. (1950). Informal social communication. *Psychological Review*, 57, 271–82.

Festinger, L. (1954). A theory of social comparison processes. *Human Relations*, 7, 117–40.

Festinger, L. (1957). *A theory of cognitive dissonance.* Stanford, CA: Stanford University Press.

Festinger, L. (1964). *Conflict, decision, and dissonance.* Stanford, CA: Stanford University Press.

Festinger, L. (1980). Looking backward. In L. Festinger (Ed.), *Retrospection on Social Psychology* (pp. 236–54). New York: Oxford University Press.

Festinger, L., & Carlsmith, J. M. (1959). Cognitive consequences of forced compliance. *Journal of Abnormal and Social Psychology*, 58, 203–10.

Festinger, L., Riecken, H. W., & Schachter, S. (1956). *When prophecy fails*. Minneapolis, MN: University of Minnesota Press.

Festinger, L., Schachter, S., & Back, K. (1950). *Social pressures in informal groups: A study of human factors in housing*. New York: Harper.

Fhanér, G., & Hane, M. (1979). Seat belts: Opinion effects of law-induced use. *Journal of Applied Psychology*, 64, 205–12.

Fiedler, F. E. (1968). Personality and situational determinants of leadership effectiveness. In D. Cartwright & A. Zander (Eds.), *Group dynamics* (pp. 362–80). New York: Harper & Row.

Fiedler, K. (1982). Causal schemata: Review and criticism of research on a popular construct. *Journal of Personality and Social Psychology*, 42, 1001–13.

Fiedler, K. (1986). Person memory and person judgments based on categorically organized information. *Acta Psychologica*, 61, 117–35.

Fiedler, K. (1991). The tricky nature of skewed frequency tables: An information loss account of distinctiveness-based illusory correlations. *Journal of Personality and Social Psychology*, 60, 24–36.

Fiedler, K., Hemmeter, U., & Hofmann, C. (1984). On the origin of illusory correlations. *European Journal of Social Psychology*, 14, 191–201.

Fiedler, K., & Semin, G. R. (1988). On the causal information conveyed by different interpersonal verbs: The role of implicit sentence context. *Social Cognition*, 6, 12–39.

Fincham, F. D. (1983). Clinical applications of attribution theory: Problems and prospects. In M. Hewstone (Ed.), *Attribution theory: Social and functional extensions* (pp. 187–203). Oxford: Blackwell.

Fincham, F. D. (1985). Attributions in close relationships. In J. H. Harvey & G. Weary (Eds.), *Attribution: Basic issues and applications* (pp. 203–34). Orlando, FL: Academic Press.

Fincham, F. D. (1998). Child development and mental relations. *Child Development*, 69, 543–74.

Fincham, F. D., Beach, S. R. H., Arias, I., & Brody, G. (in press). Children's attributions in the family: The Children's Relationship Attribution Measure. *Journal of Family Psychology*.

Fincham, F. D., & Bradbury, T. N. (1987). The impact of attributions in marriage: A longitudinal analysis. *Journal of Personality and Social Psychology*, 53, 481–9.

Fincham, F. D., & Bradbury, T. N. (1988). The impact of attributions in marriage: An experimental analysis. *Journal of Social and Clinical Psychology*, 7, 147–62.

Fincham, F. D., & Bradbury, T. N. (1990). Social support in marriage: The role of social cognition. *Journal of Social and Clinical Psychology*, 9, 31–42.

Fincham, F. D., & Bradbury, T. N. (1991). Cognition in marriage: A program of research on attributions. In W. H. Jones & D. Perlman (Eds.), *Advances in personal relationships* (Vol. 2, pp. 159–204). London: Jessica Kingsley.

Fincham, F. D., & Bradbury, T. N. (1992). Assessing attributions in marriage: The Relationship Attribution Measure. *Journal of Personality and Social Psychology*, 62, 457–68.

Fincham, F. D., & Bradbury, T. N. (1993). Marital satisfaction, depression, and attributions: A longitudinal analysis. *Journal of Personality and Social Psychology*, 64, 442–52.

Fincham, F. D., Bradbury, T. N., Byrne, C. A., & Karney, B. R. (1997). Marital violence, marital distress and attributions. *Journal of Family Psychology*, 11, 367–72.

Fincham, F. D., & Jaspars, J. M. F. (1980). Attribution of responsibility from man the scientist to man as lawyer. In L. Berkowitz (Ed.), *Advances in experimental social psychology* (Vol. 13, pp. 82–139). London: Academic Press.

Fincham, F. D., & O'Leary, K. D. (1983). Causal inferences for spouse behavior in maritally distressed and nondistressed couples. *Journal of Social and Clinical Psychology*, 1, 42–57.

Fishbein, M. (1967a). A behavior theory approach to the relations between beliefs about an object and the attitude toward the object. In M. Fishbein (Ed.), *Readings in attitude theory and measurement* (pp. 389–400). New York: Wiley.

Fishbein, M. (1967b). A consideration of beliefs, and their role in attitude measurement. In M.

Fishbein (Ed.), *Readings in attitude theory and measurement* (pp. 257–66). New York: Wiley.

Fishbein, M., & Ajzen, I. (1974). Attitudes toward objects as predictors of single and multiple behavioral criteria. *Psychological Review*, 81, 59–74.

Fishbein, M., & Ajzen, I. (1975). *Belief, attitude, intention, and behavior: An introduction to theory and research*. Reading, MA: Addison-Wesley.

Fishbein, M., & Coombs, F. S. (1974). Basis for decision: An attitudinal analysis of voting behavior. *Journal of Applied Social Psychology*, 4, 95–124.

Fisher, J. D., DePaulo, M., & Nadler, A. (1981). Extending altruism beyond the altruistic act: The mixed effects of aid on the self-recipient. In J. P. Rushton & R. M. Sorrentino (Eds.), *Altruism and helping behavior* (pp. 367–422). Hillsdale, NJ: Lawrence Erlbaum.

Fiske, A. P., Kitayama, S., Markus, H. R., & Nisbett, R. E. (1998). The cultural matrix of social psychology. In D. T. Gilbert, S. T. Fiske, & G. Lindzey (Eds.), *The handbook of social psychology* (4th ed., Vol. 2, pp. 915–81). New York: McGraw-Hill.

Fiske, S. T. (1993). Controlling other people: The impact of power on stereotyping. *American Psychologist*, 48, 621–8.

Fiske, S. T., & Neuberg, S. L. (1990). A continuum of impression formation from category-based to individuating processing: Influences of information and motivation on attention and interpretation. In M. P. Zanna (Ed.), *Advances in experimental social psychology* (Vol. 23, pp. 1–74). Orlando, FL: Academic Press.

Fiske, S. T., & Taylor, S. E. (1991). *Social cognition* (2nd ed.). New York: McGraw-Hill.

Fitness, J. (1996). Emotion knowledge structures in close relationships. In G. J. O. Fletcher & J. Fitness (Eds.), *Knowledge structures in close relationships: A social psychological approach* (pp. 195–217). Mahwah, NJ: Lawrence Erlbaum.

Flavell, J. H. (1999). Cognitive development: Children's knowledge about the mind. *Annual Review of Psychology*, 50, 21–45.

Fletcher, G. J. O., Danilovics, P., Fernandez, G., Peterson, D., & Reeder, G. D. (1986). Attributional complexity: An individual differences

measure. *Journal of Personality and Social Psychology*, 51, 875–84.

Fletcher, G. J. O., & Fincham, F. D. (Eds.). (1991). *Cognition in close relationships*. Hillsdale, NJ: Erlbaum.

Flick, U. (Ed.). (1998). *The psychology of the social*. Cambridge: Cambridge University Press.

Flowers, M. L. (1977). A laboratory test of some implications of Janis's groupthink hypothesis. *Journal of Personality and Social Psychology*, 35, 888–96.

Folger, R., & Baron, R. A. (1996). Violence and hostility at work: A model of reactions to perceived injustice. In G. R. VandenBos & E. Q. Bulatao (Eds.), *Violence on the job: Identifying risks and developing solutions* (pp. 51–85). Washington, DC: American Psychological Association.

Folkman, S., & Lazarus, R. S. (1985). If it changes it must be a process: Study of emotion and coping during three stages of a college examination. *Journal of Personality and Social Psychology*, 48, 150–70.

Folkman, S., Lazarus, R. S., Dunkel-Schetter, C., DeLongis, A., & Gruen, R. (1986). The dynamics of a stressful encounter. *Journal of Personality and Social Psychology*, 50, 992–1003.

Forgas, J. P. (1991). *Emotion and social judgments*. Oxford: Pergamon Press.

Forgas, J. P. (1992). Affect in social judgments and decisions: A multiprocess model. In M. P. Zanna (Ed.), *Advances in experimental social psychology* (Vol. 25, pp. 227–75). San Diego, CA: Academic Press.

Forgas, J. (1998). On being happy and mistaken: Mood effects on the fundamental attribution error. *Journal of Personality and Social Psychology*, 75, 318–31.

Forgas, J. P., & Bower, G. H. (1987). Mood effects in person perception judgments. *Journal of Personality and Social Psychology*, 53, 53–60.

Försterling, F. (1988). *Attribution theory in clinical psychology*. Chichester: Wiley.

Försterling, F. (1989). Models of covariation and causal attribution: How do they relate to the analysis of variance? *Journal of Personality and Social Psychology*, 57, 615–25.

Försterling, F. (1995). The functional value of realistic attributions. In W. Stroebe & M. Hewstone (Eds.), *European review of social psychology* (Vol. 5, pp. 151–80). Chichester: Wiley.

Foster, C. A., Witcher, B. S., Campbell, W. K., & Green, J. D. (1998). Arousal and attraction: Evidence for automatic and controlled processes. *Journal of Personality and Social Psychology*, 74, 86–101.

Fox, J., & Guyer, M. (1977). Group size and others' strategy in an N-person game. *Journal of Conflict Resolution*, 21, 323–38.

Fox, S. (1980). Situational determinants in affiliation. *European Journal of Social Psychology*, 10, 303–7.

Frazier, P. A., Byer, A. L., Fischer, A. R., Wright, D. M., & DeBord, K. A. (1996). Adult attachment style and partner choice: Correlational and experimental findings. *Personal Relationships*, 3, 117–36.

Freeze, L., & Cohen, B. P. (1973). Eliminating status generalization. *Sociometry*, 36, 177–93.

French, J. R. P., & Raven, B. H. (1959). The bases of social power. In D. Cartwright (Ed.), *Studies in social power* (pp. 118–49). Ann Arbor: Institute of Social Research.

Freud, S. (1920). *A general introduction to psychoanalysis*. New York: Boni & Liveright.

Freud, S. (1933). *New introductory lectures in psychoanalysis*. New York: Norton.

Freud, S. (1953). *Group psychology and the analysis of the ego*. In J. Strachey (Ed.), *The standard edition of complete psychological works of Sigmund Freud* (Vol. 18). London: Hogarth.

Frey, D. (1986). Recent research on selective exposure to information. In L. Berkowitz (Ed.), *Advances in experimental social psychology* (Vol. 19, pp. 41–80). New York: Academic Press.

Frey, D., & Rosch, M. (1984). Information seeking after decisions: The roles of novelty of information and decision reversibility. *Personality and Social Psychology Bulletin*, 10, 91–8.

Frick, R. W. (1985). Communicating emotion: The role of prosodic features. *Psychological Bulletin*, 97, 412–29.

Fridlund, A. J. (1994). *Human facial expression: An evolutionary view*. San Diego, CA: Academic Press.

Frijda, N. H. (1986). *The emotions*. Cambridge and New York: Cambridge University Press.

Frijda, N. H. (1987). Emotion, cognitive structure, and action tendency. *Cognition and Emotion*, 1, 115–43.

Frijda, N. H., & Tcherkassoff, A. (1997). Facial expressions as modes of action readiness. In J. A. Russell & J. M. Fernandez-Dols (Eds.), *The psychology of facial expression. Studies in emotion and social interaction* (2nd series, pp. 78–102). New York: Cambridge University Press.

Fruin, D. J., Pratt, C., & Owen, N. (1991). Protection motivation theory and adolescents' perceptions of exercise. *Journal of Applied Social Psychology*, 22, 55–69.

Funder, D. C. (1982). On the accuracy of dispositional vs. situational attributions. *Social Cognition*, 1, 205–22.

Funder, D. C. (1987). Errors and mistakes: Evaluating the accuracy of social judgment. *Psychological Bulletin*, 101, 75–90.

Gaertner, S. L., Dovidio, J. F., Anastasio, P. A., Bachman, B. A., & Rust, M. C. (1993). The common ingroup identity model: Recategorization and the reduction of intergroup bias. In W. Stroebe & M. Hewstone (Eds.), *European review of social psychology* (Vol. 4, pp. 1–26). Chichester: Wiley.

Gaertner, S. L., & McLaughlin, J. P. (1983). Racial stereotypes: Associations and ascriptions of positive and negative characteristics. *Social Psychology Quarterly*, 46, 23–30.

Gaertner, S., Rust, M. C., Dovidio, J. F., Backman, B. A., & Anastasio, P. A. (1994). The contact hypothesis: The role of a common ingroup identity on reducing intergroup bias. *Small Group Research*, 25, 224–49.

Gaes, G. G., Kalle, R. J., & Tedeschi, J. T. (1978). Impression management in the forced compliance situation: Two studies using the bogus pipeline. *Journal of Experimental Social Psychology*, 14, 493–510.

Gaines, S. O., Reis, H. T., Summers, S., Rusbult, C. E., Cox, C. L., Wexler, M. O., Marelich, W. D., & Kurland, G. J. (1997). Impact of attachment style on reactions to accommodative dilemmas in close relationships. *Personal Relationships*, 4, 93–113.

Galati, D., Scherer, K. R., & Ricci-Bitti, P. (1997). Voluntary facial expression of emotion: Comparing congenitally blind to normal sighted encoders. *Journal of Personality and Social Psychology*, 73, 1363–80.

Gangestad, S. W., & Buss, D. (1993). Pathogen prevalence and human mate preferences. *Ethology and Sociobiology*, 14, 89–96.

Gangestad, S. W., & Thornhill, R. (1997a). Human sexual selection and developmental stability. In J. A. Simpson & D. T. Kenrick (Eds.), *Evolutionary social psychology* (pp. 169–95). Mahwah, NJ: Erlbaum.

Gangestad, S. W., & Thornhill, R. (1997b). The evolutionary psychology of extrapair sex: The role of fluctuating asymmetry. *Evolution and Human Behavior*, 18, 69–88.

Ganong, L. H., & Coleman, M. (1994). *Remarried family relationships*. Thousand Oaks, CA: Sage.

Garland, H., Hardy, A., & Stephenson, L. (1975). Information search as affected by attribution type and response category. *Personality and Social Psychology Bulletin*, 4, 612–15.

Geen, R. G. (1998). Aggression and antisocial behavior. In D. T. Gilbert, S. T. Fiske, & G. Lindzey (Eds.), *The handbook of social psychology* (4th ed., Vol. 2, pp. 317–56). New York: McGraw-Hill.

Geen, R. G., & Stonner, D. (1971). Effects of aggressiveness habit strength on behavior in the presence of aggression-related stimuli. *Journal of Personality and Social Psychology*, 17, 149–53.

Geen, R. G., & Thomas, S. L. (1986). The immediate effects of media violence on behavior. *Journal of Social Issues*, 42, 7–28.

Gelles, R. J. (1997). *Intimate violence in families*. Thousand Oaks, CA: Sage.

Gelles, R. J., & Straus, M. A. (1979). Determinants of violence in the family: Towards a theoretical integration. In W. Burr, R. Hill, F. I. Nye, & I. L. Reiss (Eds.), *Contemporary theories about the family* (Vol. 1, pp. 549–81). New York: Free Press.

Gerard, H. B. (1963). Emotional uncertainty and social comparison. *Journal of Abnormal and Social Psychology*, 66 (6), 568–73.

Gerard, H. B., & Mathewson, G. C. (1966). The effects of severity of initiation on liking for a group: A replication. *Journal of Experimental Social Psychology*, 2, 278–87.

Gerard, H. B., Wilhelmy, R. A., & Connolley, E. S. (1968). Conformity and group size. *Journal of Personality and Social Psychology*, 8, 79–82.

Gerbner, G., Cross, L., Morgan, M., & Signorelli, N. (1982). Charity and mainstream: Television contributions to political orientations. *Journal of Communication*, 32, 100–27.

Gergen, K. J. (1973). Social psychology as history. *Journal of Personality and Social Psychology*, 26, 309–20.

Gergen, K. J. (1978). Experimentation in social psychology: A reappraisal. *European Journal of Social Psychology*, 8, 507–27.

Gergen, K. J., & Gergen, M. M. (1983). The social construction of helping relationships. In J. D. Fisher, A. Nadler, & B. M. DePaulo (Eds.), *New directions in helping* (Vol. 1, pp. 143–63). New York: Academic Press.

Gibson, J. J. (1979). *The ecological approach to visual perception*. Boston: Houghton Mifflin.

Giddens, A. (1982). *Profiles and critiques in social theory*. London: Macmillan.

Gigerenzer, G., & Hug, K. (1991). Domain-specific reasoning: Social contracts, cheating, and perspective change. *Cognition*, 43, 127–71.

Gigone, D., & Hastie, R. (1993). The common knowledge effect: Information sharing and group judgement. *Journal of Personality and Social Psychology*, 65, 959–74.

Gigone, D., & Hastie, R. (1997). The impact of information on small group choice. *Journal of Personality and Social Psychology*, 72, 132–40.

Gilbert, D. T. (1995). Attribution and interpersonal perception. In A. Tesser (Ed.), *Advanced social psychology* (pp. 99–147). New York: McGraw-Hill.

Gilbert, D. T. (1998). Ordinary personology. In D. T. Gilbert, S. T. Fiske, & G. Lindzey (Eds.), *The handbook of social psychology* (4th ed., Vol. 2, pp. 89–150). New York: McGraw-Hill.

Gilbert, D. T., Fiske, S. T., & Lindzey, G. (Eds.). (1998). *The handbook of social psycho-logy* (4th ed., 2 vols.). New York: McGraw-Hill.

Gilbert, D. T., & Malone, P. S. (1995). The correspondence bias. *Psychological Bulletin*, 117, 21–38.

Gilbert, D. T., Pelham, B. W., & Krull, D. S. (1988). On cognitive business: When person perceivers meet persons perceived. *Journal of Personality and Social Psychology*, 54, 733–40.

Giles, H., & Coupland, N. (1991). *Language: Contexts and consequences*. Pacific Grove, CA: Brooks Cole.

Giles, H., & Powesland, P. (1975). *Speech style and social evaluation*. London: Academic Press.

Giles, H., & Robinson, W. P. (Eds.). (1990). *Handbook of language and social psychology*. Chichester: Wiley.

Gilmore, D. D. (1990). *Manhood in the making: Cultural concepts of masculinity*. New Haven, CT, & London: Yale University Press.

Gilovich, T. (1981). Seeing the past in the present: The effect of associations to familiar events on judgments and decisions. *Journal of Personality and Social Psychology*, 40, 797–808.

Gleicher, F., & Petty, R. E. (1992). Expectations of reassurance influence the nature of fear-stimulated attitude change. *Journal of Experimental Social Psychology*, 28, 86–100.

Goffman, E. (1959). *The presentation of self in everyday life*. Garden City, NY: Doubleday Anchor.

Goffman, E. (1963). *Behavior in public places*. New York: Free Press.

Goffman, E. (1971). *Relations in public: Micro-studies in the public order*. New York: Basic Books.

Goldstein, A. P. (1994). *The ecology of aggression*. New York: Plenum Press.

Golinkoff, R. M. (Ed.). (1983). *The transition from prelinguistic to linguistic communication*. Hillsdale, NJ: Erlbaum.

Gonzales, M. H., & Meyers, S. A. (1993). 'Your mother would like me': Self-presentation in the personal ads of heterosexual and homosexual men and women. *Personality and Social Psychology Bulletin*, 19, 131–42.

Gonzalez, R., & Brown, R. (1999). Reducing intergroup conflict by varying the salience of subgroup and superordinate group identifications. Paper presented to General Meeting of European Association of Experimental Social Psychology. Oxford, July 1999.

Gordon, R. M. (1987). *The structure of emotions: Investigations in cognitive philosophy*. New York: Cambridge University Press.

Gosselin, P., Kirouac, G., & Doré, F. Y. (1995). Components and recognition of facial expression in the communication of emotion by actors. *Journal of Personality and Social Psychology*, 68 (1), 83–96.

Gottman, J. M. (1993). Studying emotion in social interaction. In M. Lewis & J. M. Haviland (Eds.), *Handbook of emotions* (pp. 475–88). New York: Guilford Press.

Gouldner, A. W. (1960). The norm of reciprocity: A preliminary statement. *American Sociological Review*, 25, 161–78.

Grafen, A. (1982). How not to measure inclusive fitness. *Nature*, 298, 425–6.

Graham, S., & Folkes, V. (Eds.). (1990). *Attribution theory: Applications to achievement, mental health, and interpersonal conflict*. Hillsdale, NJ: Erlbaum.

Grant, P. R., & Brown, R. (1995). From ethnocentrism to collective protest: Responses to relative deprivation and threats to social identity. *Social Psychology Quarterly*, 58, 195–211.

Graumann, C. F. (1976). Modification by migration: Vicissitudes of cross-national communication. *Social Research*, 43, 367–85.

Graumann, C. F. (1986). The individualization of the social and the desocialization of the individual: Floyd H. Allport's contribution to social psychology. In C. F. Graumann & S. Moscovici (Eds.), *Changing conceptions of crowd mind and behavior* (pp. 97–116). New York: Springer Verlag.

Graumann, C. F. (1989). The origin of social psychology in German-speaking countries. In J. A. Keats, R. Taft, R. A. Heath, & S. H. Lovibond (Eds.), *Mathematical and theoretical systems* (pp. 333–43). Amsterdam: Elsevier.

Graumann, C. F. (1996). Psyche and her descendants. In C. F. Graumann & K. J. Gergen (Eds.), *Historical dimensions of psychological discourse* (pp. 83–100). New York: Cambridge University Press.

Graumann, C. F. (1999). Continuities, ruptures and options: Construing history of psychology in Germany. In W. Maiers, B. Baier, B. D. Esgalhado, R. Jorna, & E. Schraube (Eds.), *Challenges to theoretical psychology* (pp. 1–18). North York (Canada): Captus University Publications.

Graumann, C. F., & Moscovici, S. (Eds.). (1986a). *Changing conceptions of leadership.* New York: Springer Verlag.

Graumann, C. F., & Moscovici, S. (Eds.). (1986b). *Changing conceptions of crowd mind and behavior.* New York: Springer Verlag.

Graumann, C. F., & Moscovici, S. (Eds.). (1987). *Changing conceptions of conspiracy.* New York: Springer Verlag.

Graziano, W. G., & Eisenberg, N. (1997). Agreeableness: A dimension of personality. In R. Hogan, J. Johnson, & S. Briggs (Eds.), *Handbook of personality psychology* (pp. 795–824). San Diego, CA: Academic Press.

Greenberg, J. (1990). Employee theft as a reaction to underpayment inequity. The hidden costs of pay cuts. *Journal of Applied Psychology, 75,* 561–8.

Greenstein, T. N., & Knottnerus, J. D. (1980). The effects of differential evaluations on status generalization. *Social Psychology Quarterly, 43,* 147–54.

Greenwald, A. G. (1968). Cognitive learning, cognitive response to persuasion, and attitude change. In A. Greenwald, T. Brock, & T. Ostrom (Eds.), *Psychological foundations of attitudes* (pp. 148–70). New York: Academic Press.

Greenwald, A. G. (1975). On the inconclusiveness of 'crucial' tests of dissonance versus self-perception theories. *Journal of Experimental Social Psychology, 11,* 490–9.

Greenwald, A. G., & Banaji, M. R. (1995). Implicit social cognition: Attitudes, self-esteem, and stereotypes. *Psychological Bulletin, 102,* 4–27.

Greenwald, A. J. (1975). Does the Good Samaritan parable increase helping? A comment on Darley and Batson's no-effect conclusion. *Journal of Personality and Social Psychology, 32,* 578–83.

Grice, H. P. (1975). Logic in conversation. In P. Cole & J. L. Morgan (Eds.), *Syntax and semantics* (Vol. 3, pp. 41–58). New York: Academic Press.

Griesinger, D. W., & Livingston, J. W., Jr. (1973). Toward a model of interpersonal motivation in experimental games. *Behavioral Science, 18,* 173–88.

Griffit, W., & Veitch, R. (1974). Preacquaintance attitude similarity and attraction revisited: Ten days in a fall-out shelter. *Sociometry, 37,* 163–73.

Groebel, J., & Krebs, D. (1983). A study of the effects of television on anxiety. In C. D. Spielberger & R. Diaz-Guerrero (Eds.), *Cross cultural anxiety* (Vol. 2, pp. 89–98). Washington, DC: Hemisphere.

Gross, J. J. (1998). The emerging field of emotion regulation: An integrative review. *Review of General Psychology, 2* (3), 271–99.

Grossman, M., & Wood, W. (1993). Sex differences in intensity of emotional experience: A social role interpretation. *Journal of Personality and Social Psychology, 65* (5), 1010–22.

Gruder, C. L., Romer, D., & Korth, B. (1978). Dependency and fault as determinants of helping. *Journal of Experimental Social Psychology, 14,* 227–35.

Guerin, B. (1993). *Social facilitation.* Cambridge: Cambridge University Press.

Guimond, S., & Dubé-Simard, L. (1983). Relative deprivation theory and the Quebec nationalist movement: The cognition–emotion distinction and the personal–group deprivation issue. *Journal of Personality and Social Psychology, 44,* 526–35.

Gump, B. B., & Kulik, J. A. (1997). Stress, affiliation, and emotional contagion. *Journal of Personality and Social Psychology, 72,* 305–19.

Gunter, B. (1985). *Dimensions of television violence.* Aldershot: Gower.

Gunter, B. (1994). The question of media violence. In J. Bryant & D. Zillmann (Eds.), *Media effects: Advances in theory and research* (pp. 163–211). Hillsdale, NJ: Lawrence Erlbaum.

Gurr, T. R. (1970). *Why men rebel.* Princeton, NJ: Princeton University Press.

Gusella, J. L., Muir, D., & Tronick, E. Z. (1988). The effect of manipulating maternal behavior during an interaction on three- and six-month-olds' affect and attention. *Child Development, 59,* 1111–24.

Gustafson, R. (1986). Human physical aggression as a function of frustration: Role of aggression cues. *Psychological Reports*, 58, 103–10.

Gustafson, R. (1989). Frustration and successful vs. unsuccessful aggression: A test of Berkowitz' completion hypothesis. *Aggressive Behavior*, 15, 5–12.

Guzzo, R. A., & Dickson, M. W. (1996). Teams in organizations: Recent research on performance and effectiveness. *Annual Review of Psychology*, 47, 307–38.

Hackett, R. D. (1989). Work attitudes and employee absenteeism: A synthesis of the literature. *Journal of Occupational Psychology*, 62, 235–48.

Hackman, J. R. (1990). Work teams in organizations: An orienting framework. In J. R. Hackman (Ed.), *Groups that work (and those that don't): Creating conditions for effective teamwork* (pp. 1–14). San Francisco: Jossey-Bass.

Hackman, J. R., & Morris, C. G. (1975). Group tasks, group interaction process and group performance effectiveness: A review and proposed integration. In L. Berkowitz (Ed.), *Advances in experimental social psychology* (Vol. 8, pp. 47–99). New York: Academic Press.

Hagedoorn, M., VanYperen, N. W., Van de Vliert, E., & Buunk, B. P. (1999). Employees' reactions to problematic events: A circumplex structure of five categories of responses, and the role of job satisfaction. *Journal of Organizational Behavior*, 20, 309–21.

Hagendoorn, L., & Henke, R. (1991). The effect of multiple category membership on intergroup evaluations in a North-Indian context: Class, caste, and religion. *British Journal of Social Psychology*, 30, 247–60.

Haines, H., & Vaughan, G. M. (1979). Was 1898 a 'great date' in the history of experimental social psychology? *Journal of the History of the Behavioral Sciences*, 15, 323–32.

Hall, J. A. (1998). How big are nonverbal sex differences? The case of smiling and sensitivity to nonverbal cues. In D. J. Canary & K. Dindia (Eds.), *Sex differences and similarities in communication: Critical essays and empirical investigations of sex and gender in interaction* (pp. 155–77). Mahwah, NJ: Lawrence Erlbaum.

Hamilton, D. L. (1981). Illusory correlations as a basis for stereotyping. In D. L. Hamilton (Ed.), *Cognitive processes in stereotyping and intergroup behavior* (pp. 333–53). Hillsdale, NJ: Erlbaum.

Hamilton, D. L., & Gifford, R. K. (1976). Illusory correlation in interpersonal perception: A cognitive basis of stereotypic judgments. *Journal of Experimental Social Psychology*, 12, 392–407.

Hamilton, D. L., Katz, L. B., & Leirer, V. O. (1980). Cognitive representation of personality impressions: Organizational processes in the first impression formation. *Journal of Personality and Social Psychology*, 39, 1050–63.

Hamilton, D. L., & Rose, R. L. (1980). Illusory correlation and the maintenance of stereotypic beliefs. *Journal of Personality and Social Psychology*, 39, 832–45.

Hamilton, D. L., & Sherman, J. W. (1994). Stereotypes. In R. S. Wyer & T. K. Srull (Eds.), *Handbook of social cognition* (2nd ed., Vol. 1, pp. 1–68). Hillsdale, NJ: Erlbaum.

Hamilton, W. D. (1964). The genetical evolution of social behavior, I and II. *Journal of Theoretical Biology*, 7, 1–52.

Hamilton, W. D., & Zuk, M. (1982). Heritable true fitness and bright birds: A role for parasites. *Science*, 218, 384–7.

Hanson, D. J., & Blohm, E. R. (1974). Authoritarianism and attitudes towards mental patients. *International Behavioural Scientist*, 6, 57–60.

Hardin, C. D., & Higgins, E. T. (1996). Shared reality: How social verification makes the subjective objective. In R. M. Sorrentino & E. T. Higgins (Eds.), *Handbook of motivation and cognition. Vol. 3: The interpersonal context* (pp. 28–84). New York: Guilford Press.

Hardin, R. G. (1968). The tragedy of the commons. *Science*, 162, 1243–8.

Harkins, S. (1987). Social loafing and social facilitation. *Journal of Experimental Social Psychology*, 23, 1–18.

Harkins, S., & Jackson, J. (1985). The role of evaluation in eliminating social loafing. *Personality and Social Psychology Bulletin*, 11, 457–65.

Harkins, S., & Petty, R. E. (1982). Effects of task difficulty and task uniqueness on social loafing.

Journal of Personality and Social Psychology, 43, 1214–29.

Harkins, S., & Szymanski, K. (1989). Social loafing and group evaluation. *Journal of Personality and Social Psychology*, 56, 934–41.

Harkness, S., & Super, C. M. (1985). The cultural context of gender segregation in children's peer groups. *Child Development*, 56, 219–24.

Harper, N. L., & Askling, L. R. (1980). Group communication and quality of task solution in a media production organization. *Communication Monographs*, 47, 77–100.

Harré, R. M. (1986). *The social construction of emotions*. Oxford: Blackwell.

Harris, R. J. (1994). The impact of sexually explicit media. In J. Bryant & D. Zillmann (Eds.), *Media effects: Advances in theory and research* (pp. 247–72). Hillsdale, NJ: Lawrence Erlbaum.

Harrison, J. A., Mullen, P. D., & Green, L. W. (1992). A meta-analysis of studies of the health belief model with adults. *Health Education Research*, 7, 107–16.

Hart, C. H., Nelson, D. A., Robinson, C. C., Olsen, S. F., & McNeilly-Choque, M. K. (1998). Overt and relational aggression in Russian nursery-school-age children: Parenting style and marital linkages. *Developmental Psychology*, 34, 687–97.

Hartup, W. W. (1991). Social development and social psychology: Perspectives on interpersonal relationships. In J. H. Cantor, C. C. Spiker, & L. Lipsitt (Eds.), *Child behavior and development: Training for diversity* (pp. 1–33). Norwood, NJ: Ablex.

Hartup, W. W., & Stevens, N. (1997). Friendships and adaptation in the life course. *Psychological Bulletin*, 121 (3), 355–70.

Hastie, R. (1980). Memory for information that confirms or contradicts a general impression. In R. Hastie, T. M. Ostrom, E. B. Ebbesen, R. S. Wyer, D. L. Hamilton, & D. E. Carlston (Eds.), *Person memory: The cognitive basis of social perception* (pp. 155–77). Hillsdale, NJ: Erlbaum.

Hastie, R. (1986). Review essay: Experimental evidence on group accuracy. In G. Owen & B. Grofman (Eds.), *Information pooling and group decision making* (pp. 129–57). Westport, CT: JAI Press.

Hastie, R., & Park, B. (1986). The relationship between memory and judgment depends on whether the judgment task is memory-based or on-line. *Psychological Review*, 93, 258–68.

Hastie, R., Penrod, S. D., & Pennington, N. (1983). *Inside the jury*. Cambridge, MA: Harvard University Press.

Hatala, M. N., & Prehodka, J. (1996). Content analysis of gay male and lesbian personal advertisements. *Psychological Reports*, 78, 371–4.

Hatfield, E. (1988). Passionate and companionate love. In R. J. Sternberg & M. L. Barnes (Eds.), *The psychology of love* (pp. 191–217). New Haven, CT: Yale University Press.

Hatfield, E., Cacioppo, J. T., & Rapson, R. L. (1994). *Emotional contagion*. Cambridge and New York: Cambridge University Press.

Hatfield, E., & Sprecher, S. (1986). *Mirror, mirror . . . The importance of looks in everyday life*. New York: SUNY Press.

Haugtvedt, C. P., & Priester, J. R. (1997). Conceptual and methodological issues in advertising effectiveness: An attitude strength perspective. In W. D. Wells (Ed.), *Measuring advertising effectiveness. Advertising and consumer psychology* (pp. 79–93). Mahwah, NJ: Lawrence Erlbaum Associates.

Hay, D., Vespo, J. E., & Zahn-Waxler, C. (1998). Young children's quarrels with their siblings and mothers: Links with maternal depression and bipolar illness. *British Journal of Developmental Psychology*, 16, 519–38.

Hayden-Thompson, L., Rubin, K. H., & Hymel, S. (1987). Sex preferences in sociometric choices. *Developmental Psychology*, 23, 558–62.

Hays, R. B. (1988). Friendship. In S. Duck (Ed.), *Handbook of personal relationships* (pp. 391–408). Chichester: Wiley.

Hazan, C., & Shaver, P. (1987). Romantic love conceptualized as an attachment process. *Journal of Personality and Social Psychology*, 52, 511–24.

Hearold, S. (1986). A synthesis of 1043 effects of television on social behavior. In G. Comstock (Ed.), *Public communication and behavior* (Vol. 1, pp. 65–133). New York: Academic Press.

Hebb, D. O., & Thompson, W. R. (1979). The social significance of animal studies. In G. Lindzey & E. Aronson (Eds.), *Handbook of social psychology*

(2nd ed., pp. 729–74). Reading, MA: Addison-Wesley.

Heckhausen, H. (1989). *Motivation und Handeln*. Berlin: Springer.

Hedges, L. V., & Olkin, I. (1985). *Statistical methods for meta-analysis*. New York: Academic Press.

Heider, F. (1944). Social perception and phenomenal causality. *Psychological Review*, 51, 358–74.

Heider, F. (1946). Attitudes and cognitive organization. *Journal of Psychology*, 21, 107–12.

Heider, F. (1958). *The psychology of interpersonal relations*. New York: Wiley.

Heise, D. R., & O'Brien, J. (1993). Emotion expression in groups. In M. Lewis & J. M. Haviland (Eds.), *Handbook of emotions* (pp. 489–98). New York: Guilford Press.

Hellpach, W. (1933). *Elementares Lehrbuch der Sozialpsychologie*. Berlin: Springer.

Henchy, T., & Glass, D. C. (1968). Evaluation apprehension and the social facilitation of dominant and subordinate responses. *Journal of Personality and Social Psychology*, 10, 446–54.

Hensley, T. R., & Griffin, G. W. (1986). Victims of groupthink: The Kent State University Board of Trustees and the 1977 gymnasium controversy. *Journal of Conflict Resolution*, 30, 497–531.

Hepworth, J. T., & West, S. G. (1988). Lynchings and the economy: A time series analysis of Hovland and Sears (1940). *Journal of Personality and Social Psychology*, 55, 239–47.

Herbert, T. T., & Estes, R. W. (1977). Improving executive decisions by formalizing dissent: The corporate devil's advocate. *Academy of Management Review*, 2, 662–7.

Herr, P. M., Sherman, S. J., & Fazio, R. H. (1983). On the consequences of priming: Assimilation and contrast effects. *Journal of Experimental Social Psychology*, 19, 323–40.

Hersey, P., & Blanchard, K. (1982). *Management of organizational behavior*. New York: Prentice-Hall.

Herzog, T., Abrams, D. B., Emmons, K. M., Linnan, L., & Shadel, W. G. (1999). Do processes of change predict smoking stage movements? A prospective analysis of the transtheoretical model. *Health Psychology*, 18, 369–75.

Hewstone, M. (1989). *Causal attribution: From cognitive processes to collective beliefs*. Oxford & Cambridge, MA: Blackwell.

Hewstone, M. (1990). The 'ultimate attribution error': A review of the literature on intergroup causal attribution. *European Journal of Social Psychology*, 20, 311–35.

Hewstone, M., & Augoustinos, M. (1998). Social attributions and social representations. In U. Flick (Ed.), *The psychology of the social* (pp. 60–76). Cambridge: Cambridge University Press.

Hewstone, M., & Brown, R. J. (1986). Contact is not enough: An intergroup perspective on the contact hypothesis. In M. Hewstone & R. Brown (Eds.), *Contact and conflict in intergroup encounters* (pp. 1–44). Oxford: Blackwell.

Hewstone, M., Fincham, F., & Jaspars, J. (1981). Social categorization and similarity in intergroup behaviour: A replication with penalties. *European Journal of Social Psychology*, 11, 101–7.

Hewstone, M., Islam, M. R., & Judd, C. M. (1993). Models of crossed categorization and intergroup relations. *Journal of Personality and Social Psychology*, 64, 779–93.

Hewstone, M., & Jaspars, J. M. F. (1987). Covariation and causal attribution: A logical model of the intuitive analysis of variance. *Journal of Personality and Social Psychology*, 53, 663–72.

Hewstone, M., & Ward, C. (1985). Ethnocentrism and causal attribution in Southeast Asia. *Journal of Personality and Social Psychology*, 48, 614–23.

Higgins, E. T. (1996). Knowledge activation: Accessibility, applicability, and salience. In E. T. Higgins & A. W. Kruglanski (Eds.), *Social psychology: Handbook of basic principles* (pp. 133–68). New York: Guilford Press.

Higgins, E. T., Bargh, J. A., & Lombardi, W. (1985). The nature of priming effects on categorization. *Journal of Experimental Psychology: Learning, Memory, and Cognition*, 11, 59–69.

Higgins, E. T., King, G. A., & Mavin, G. H. (1982). Individual construct accessibility and subjective impressions and recall. *Journal of Personality and Social Psychology*, 43, 35–47.

Higgins, E. T., & Kruglanski, A. W. (Eds.). (1996). *Social psychology: Handbook of basic principles*. New York: Guilford Press.

Higgins, E. T., Rholes, W. S., & Jones, C. R. (1977). Category accessibility and impression formation. *Journal of Experimental Social Psychology*, 13, 141–54.

Hildum, D. C., & Brown, R. W. (1956). Verbal reinforcement and interviewer bias. *Journal of Abnormal and Social Psychology*, 53, 108–11.

Hilton, D. J. (1990). Conversational processes and causal explanation. *Psychological Bulletin*, 107, 65–81.

Hilton, D. J. (1991). A conversational model of causal attribution. In W. Stroebe & M. Hewstone (Eds.), *European review of social psychology* (Vol. 2, pp. 51–82). Chichester: Wiley.

Hilton, D. J., & Slugoski, B. R. (1986). Knowledge-based causal attribution: The Abnormal Conditions Focus model. *Psychological Review*, 93, 75–88.

Hilton, J. L., Fein, S., & Miller, D. T. (1993). Suspicion and dispositional inference. *Journal of Personality and Social Psychology*, 19, 961–78.

Himmelfarb, S. (1993). The measurement of attitudes. In A. H. Eagly & S. Chaiken (Eds.), *The psychology of attitudes* (pp. 23–87). Fort Worth, TX: Harcourt Brace Jovanovich.

Hinde, R. A. (1974). *Biological bases of human social behavior.* New York: McGraw-Hill.

Hinde, R. A., & Tamplin, A. (1983). Relations between mother–child interaction and behaviour in preschool. *British Journal of Developmental Psychology*, 1, 231–57.

Hinkle, S., & Brown, R. (1990). Intergroup comparisons and social identity: Some links and lacunae. In D. Abrams & M. Hogg (Eds.), *Social identity theory: Constructive and critical advances* (pp. 48–70). Hemel Hempstead: Harvester Wheatsheaf.

Hobbes, T. (1651/1968). *Leviathan* (Ed. C. B. MacPherson). Harmondsworth: Penguin.

Hochschild, A. R. (1983). *The managed heart: The commercialization of human feeling.* Berkeley, CA: University of California Press.

Hoeksema-VanOrden, C. Y. D., Gaillard, A. W. K., & Buunk, B. P. (1998). Social loafing under fatigue. *Journal of Personality and Social Psychology*, 75, 1179–90.

Hoffman, M. L. (1990). Empathy and justice motivation. *Motivation and Emotion*, 14, 151–72.

Hogg, M., & Abrams, D. (1990). Social motivation, self-esteem and social identity. In D. Abrams & M. Hogg (Eds.), *Social identity theory: Construc-*

tive and critical advances (pp. 28–47). Hemel Hempstead: Harvester Wheatsheaf.

Hogg, M. A., & Sunderland, J. (1991). Self esteem and intergroup discrimination in the minimal group paradigm. *British Journal of Social Psychology*, 30, 51–62.

Hogg, M. A., & Turner, C. (1987). Intergroup behaviour, self stereotyping and the salience of social categories. *British Journal of Social Psychology*, 26, 325–40.

Hogg, M. A., Turner, J. C., & Davidson, B. (1990). Polarized norms and social frames of reference: A test of the self-categorization theory of group polarization. *Basic and Applied Social Psychology*, 11, 77–100.

Hogg, M. A., & Vaughan, G. M. (1998). *Social psychology.* London: Prentice-Hall.

Hollon, S. D., Shelton, R. C., & Loosen, P. T. (1991). Cognitive therapy and pharmacotherapy for depression. *Journal of Consulting and Clinical Psychology*, 58, 88–99.

Holmes, J. G., & Rempel, J. K. (1989). Trust in close relationships. In C. Hendrick (Ed.), *Review of personality and social psychology* (Vol. 10, pp. 187–220). London: Sage.

Holmes, T. H., & Rahe, R. H. (1967). The social readjustment rating-scale. *Journal of Psychosomatic Research*, 11, 213–18.

Holtzworth-Munroe, A., & Jacobson, N. S. (1988). Toward a methodology for coding spontaneous causal attributions: Preliminary results with married couples. *Journal of Social and Clinical Psychology*, 7, 101–12.

Homans, G. C. (1961). *Social behavior: Its elementary forms.* New York: Harcourt Brace & World.

Hoover, R., & Fishbein, H. D. (1999). The development of prejudice and sex role stereotyping in white adolescents and white young adults. *Journal of Applied Developmental Psychology*, 20, 431–48.

Horneffer, K. J., & Fincham, F. D. (1995). The construct of attributional style in depression and marital distress. *Journal of Family Psychology*, 9, 186–95.

Horowitz, I. A. (1969). Effects of volunteering, fear, arousal, and number of communications on attitude change. *Journal of Personality and Social Psychology*, 11, 34–7.

Horwitz, M., & Rabbie, J. M. (1982). Individuality and membership in the intergroup system. In H. Tajfel (Ed.), *Social identity and intergroup relations* (pp. 241–74). Cambridge: Cambridge University Press.

House, J. S. (1981). *Work stress and social support*. Reading, MA: Addison- Wesley.

House, J. S., Landis, K. R., & Umberson, D. (1988). Social relationships and health. *Science*, 241, 540–5.

House, J. S., Robbins, C., & Metzner, H. L. (1982). The association of social relationships and activities with mortality: Prospective evidence from the Tecumseh Community Health Study. *American Journal of Epidemiology*, 116, 123–40.

Houston, D. A., & Fazio, R. H. (1989). Biased processing as a function of attitude accessibility: Making objective judgments subjectively. *Social Cognition*, 7, 51–66.

Hovland, C. I., Janis, I. L., & Kelley, H. H. (1953). *Communication and persuasion: Psychological studies of opinion change*. New Haven, CT: Yale University Press.

Hovland, C., & Sears, R. R. (1940). Minor studies in aggression: Correlation of lynchings with economic indices. *Journal of Psychology*, 9, 301–10.

Howard, D. J. (1997). Familiar phrases as peripheral persuasion cues. *Journal of Experimental Social Psychology*, 33, 231–43.

Howe, C. J., Rodgers, C., & Tolmie, A. (1990). Physics in the primary school: Peer interaction and the understanding of floating and sinking. *European Journal of Psychology of Education*, 5, 459–75.

Howe, C. J., Tolmie, A., & Rodgers, C. (1992). The acquisition of conceptual knowledge in science by primary school children: Group interaction and the understanding of motion down an incline. *British Journal of Developmental Psychology*, 10, 113–30.

Hraba, J., & Grant, G. (1970). Black is beautiful: A re-examination of racial preference and identification. *Journal of Personality and Social Psychology*, 16, 398–402.

Hrdy, S. B. (1979). Infanticide among animals: A review, classification and examination of the implications for reproductive strategies of females. *Ethology and Sociobiology*, 1, 3–40.

Huesmann, L. R., Lagerspetz, K., & Eron, L. D. (1984). Intervening variables in the TV violence–aggression relation: Evidence from two countries. *Developmental Psychology*, 20, 746–75.

Huesmann, L. R., & Miller, L. S. (1994). Long-term effects of repeated exposure to media violence in childhood. In L. R. Huesmann (Ed.), *Aggressive behavior: Current perspectives* (pp. 153–87). New York: Plenum Press.

Hulin, C. (1991). Adaptation, persistence, and commitment in organizations. In M. D. Dunette & L. M. Hough (Eds.), *Handbook of industrial and organizational psychology* (2nd ed., Vol. 2, pp. 445–505). Palo Alto, CA: Consulting Psychologists Press.

Hunt, M. (1990). *The compassionate beast. What science is discovering about the human side of humankind*. New York: William Morrow.

Iaffaldano, M. T., & Muchinsky, P. M. (1985). Job satisfaction and job performance: A meta-analysis. *Psychological Bulletin*, 97, 251–73.

Ickes, W., & Gonzalez, R. (1996). 'Social' cognition and *social* cognition. In J. L. Nye & A. M. Brown (Eds.), *What's social about social cognition?* (pp. 285–308). London: Sage.

Ingham, A. G., Levinger, G., Graves, J., & Peckham, V. (1974). The Ringelmann effect: Studies of group size and group performance. *Journal of Personality and Social Psychology*, 10, 371–84.

Insko, C. A., Schopler, J., Pemberton, M. B., Wieselquist, J., McIlraith, S. A., Currey, D. P., & Geartner, L. (1998). Long-term outcome maximization and the reduction of interindividual–intergroup discontinuity. *Journal of Personality and Social Psychology*, 75, 695–710.

Isen, A. M. (1993). Positive affect and decision making. In M. Lewis & J. M. Haviland (Eds.), *Handbook of emotions* (pp. 261–77). New York: Guilford Press.

Isen, A. M. (1994). Toward understanding the role of affect in cognition. In R. S. Wyer & T. K. Srull (Eds.), *Handbook of social cognition* (Vol. 3). Hillsdale, NJ: Erlbaum.

Isen, A. M., Clark, M., & Schwartz, M. F. (1976). Duration of the effect of good mood on helping: 'Footprints on the sands of time'. *Journal of Personality and Social Psychology*, 34, 385–93.

Isen, A. M., Daubman, K. A., & Nowicki, G. P. (1987). Positive affect facilitates creative problem solving. *Journal of Personality and Social Psychology*, 52, 1122–31.

Isen, A. M., Horn, N., & Rosenhan, D. L. (1973). Effects of success and failure on children's generosity. *Journal of Personality and Social Psychology*, 27, 384–8.

Isen, A. M., Johnson, M. M. S., Hertz, E., & Robinson, G. F. (1985). The effects of positive affect on the unusualness of word associations. *Journal of Personality and Social Psychology*, 48, 1413–14.

Isen, A. M., Means, B., Patrick, R., & Nowicki, G. P. (1982). Some factors influencing decision-making and risk taking. In M. S. Clark & S. T. Fiske (Eds.), *Affect and cognition* (pp. 243–61). Hillsdale, NJ: Erlbaum.

Isen, A. M., Shalkner, T. W., Clark, M., & Karp, L. (1978). Positive affect, accessibility of material in memory, and behavior: A cognitive loop? *Journal of Personality and Social Psychology*, 36, 1–12.

Isenberg, D. J. (1986). Group polarization: A critical review and meta-analysis. *Journal of Personality and Social Psychology*, 50, 1141–51.

Islam, M., & Hewstone, M. (1993a). Dimensions of contact as predictors of intergroup anxiety, perceived outgroup variability, and outgroup attitude: An interactive model. *Personality and Social Psychology Bulletin*, 19, 700–10.

Islam, M. R., & Hewstone, M. (1993b). Intergroup attributions and affective consequences in majority and minority groups. *Journal of Personality and Social Psychology*, 65, 936–50.

Israel, J., & Tajfel, H. (Eds.). (1972). *The context of social psychology: A critical assessment*. London: Academic Press.

Izard, C. E. (1971). *The face of emotion*. New York: Appleton-Century-Crofts.

Izard, C. E. (1990). Facial expression and the regulation of emotions. *Journal of Personality and Social Psychology*, 58, 487–98.

Izard, C. E. (1991). *The psychology of emotions*. New York: Plenum Press.

Izard, C. E. (1992). Basic emotions, relations among emotions, and emotion–cognition relations. *Psychological Review*, 99, 561–5.

Jackson, J. M., & Harkins, J. M. (1985). Equity in effort: An explanation of the social loafing effect. *Journal of Personality and Social Psychology*, 49, 1199–1206.

Jackson, J. M., & Williams, K. D. (1985). Social loafing on difficult tasks. *Journal of Personality and Social Psychology*, 49, 937–42.

Jacobs, K. C., & Campbell, D. T. (1961). The perpetuation of an arbitrary tradition through several generations of a laboratory microculture. *Journal of Abnormal and Social Psychology*, 62, 649–58.

Jaffe, P. G., Wolfe, D. A., & Wilson, S. K. (1990). *Children of battered women*. Newbury Park, CA: Sage.

Jaffe, Y., & Yinon, Y. (1983). Collective aggression: The group individual paradigm in the study of collective antisocial behavior. In H. H. Blumberg, A. P. Hare, V. Kent, & M. Davies (Eds.), *Small groups and social interaction* (Vol. 1). New York: Wiley.

James, W. (1884). What is an emotion? *Mind*, 9, 188–205. (Reprinted in M. B. Arnold (Ed.). (1968). *The nature of emotion: Selected readings* (pp. 17–36). Harmondsworth: Penguin.)

James, W. (1894). The physical basis of emotion. *Psychological Review*, 1, 516–29.

Janis, I. L. (1972). *Victims of groupthink*. Boston, MA: Houghton Mifflin.

Janis, I. L. (1982a). *Groupthink* (2nd ed.). Boston: Houghton Mifflin.

Janis, I. L. (1982b). *Victims of groupthink* (2nd ed.). Boston: Houghton Mifflin.

Janz, N., & Becker, M. H. (1984). The health belief model: A decade later. *Health Education Quarterly*, 11, 1–47.

Jaspars, J. (1983). The task of social psychology. *British Journal of Social Psychology*, 22, 277–88.

Jaspars, J. (1986). Forum and focus: A personal view of European social psychology. *European Journal of Social Psychology*, 16, 3–15.

Jellison, J. M., & Davis, D. (1973). Relationships between perceived ability and attitude extremity. *Journal of Personality and Social Psychology*, 27, 430–6.

Jenni, D. A. (1974). Evolution of polyandry in birds. *American Zoologist*, 14, 129–44.

Jepson, C., & Chaiken, S. (1990). Chronic issue-specific fear inhibits systematic processing of persuasive communications. *Journal of Social Behavior and Personality*, 5, 61–84.

Johns, G. (1997). Contemporary research on absence from work: Correlates, causes and consequences. In C. L. Cooper & I. T. Robertson (Eds.), *International review of industrial and organizational psychology* (Vol. 12, pp. 115–73). Chichester: Wiley.

Johnson, D. J., & Rusbult, C. E. (1989). Resisting temptation: Devaluation of alternative partners as a means of maintaining commitment. *Journal of Personality and Social Psychology*, 57, 967–80.

Johnson, E. J., & Tversky, A. (1983). Affect, generalization, and the perception of risk. *Journal of Personality and Social Psychology*, 45, 20–31.

Johnson, M. H., & Morton, J. (1991). *Biology and cognitive development: The case of face recognition.* Oxford: Blackwell.

Johnson, M. K., & Raye, C. L. (1981). Reality monitoring. *Psychological Review*, 88, 67–85.

Johnson, R. C. et al. (1989). Cross-cultural assessment of altruism and its correlates. *Personality and Individual Differences*, 10, 855–68.

Johnson, T. E., & Rule, B. G. (1986). Mitigating circumstances information, censure, and aggression. *Journal of Personality and Social Psychology*, 50, 537–42.

Johnson, W. G., Ross, J. M., & Mastria, M. A. (1977). Delusional behaviour: An attribution analysis of development and modification. *Journal of Abnormal Psychology*, 86, 421–6.

Johnston, J. J., Hendricks, S. A., & Fike, J. M. (1994). The effectiveness of behavioral safety belt interventions. *Accident Analysis and Prevention*, 26, 315–23.

Johnston, L., & Hewstone, M. (1992). Cognitive models of stereotype change (3): Subtyping and the perceived typicality of disconfirming group members. *Journal of Experimental Social Psychology*, 28, 360–86.

Johnstone, T., & Scherer, K. R. (2000). Vocal communication of emotion. In M. Lewis & J. Haviland-Jones (Eds.), *Handbook of emotions* (2nd ed., pp. 220–35). New York: Guilford Press.

Jonas, K. (1993). Expectancy-value models of health behaviour: An analysis by conjoint measurement. *European Journal of Social Psychology*, 31, 295–306.

Jones, E. E. (1985). Major developments in social psychology during the past four decades. In G. Lindzey & E. Aronson (Eds.), *The handbook of social psychology* (3rd ed., Vol. 1, pp. 47–107). New York: Random House.

Jones, E. E. (1990). *Interpersonal perception.* New York: Macmillan.

Jones, E. E., & Davis, K. E. (1965). From acts to dispositions: The attribution process in person perception. In L. Berkowitz (Ed.), *Advances in experimental social psychology* (Vol. 2, pp. 219–66). New York: Academic Press.

Jones, E. E., & Gerard, H. B. (1967). *Foundations of social psychology.* New York: Wiley.

Jones, E. E., & Harris, V. A. (1967). The attribution of attitudes. *Journal of Experimental Social Psychology*, 3, 1–24.

Jones, E. E., & Nisbett, R. E. (1972). The actor and the observer: Divergent perceptions of the causes of behaviour. In E. E. Jones, D. E. Kanouse, H. H. Kelley, R. E. Nisbett, S. Valins, & B. Weiner (Eds.), *Attribution: Perceiving the causes of behaviour* (pp. 79–94). Morristown, NJ: General Learning Press.

Jones, E. E., Wood, G. C., & Quattrone, G. A. (1981). Perceived variability of personal characteristics in ingroups and outgroups: The role of knowledge and evaluation. *Journal of Personality and Social Psychology*, 7, 523–8.

Jordan, N. (1953). Behavioral forces that are a function of attitudes and of cognitive organization. *Human Relations*, 6, 273–87.

Joule, R.-V., & Beauvois, J.-L. (1998). Cognitive dissonance theory: A radical view. *European Review of Social Psychology*, 8, 1–32.

Judd, C. M., & Kenny, D. A. (1981a). *Estimating the effects of social interventions.* New York: Cambridge University Press.

Judd, C. M., & Kenny, D. A. (1981b). Process analysis: Estimating mediation in treatment evaluations. *Evaluation Review*, 5, 602–19.

Judd, C. M., & Kulik, J. A. (1980). Schematic effects of social attitudes on information processing and recall. *Journal of Personality and Social Psychology*, 38, 569–78.

Kahneman, D., Slovic, P., & Tversky, A. (Eds.). (1982). *Judgment under uncertainty: Heuristics and biases*. Cambridge: Cambridge University Press.

Kahneman, D., & Tversky, A. (1972). A judgment of representativeness. *Cognitive Psychology*, 3, 430–54.

Kanazawa, S. (1992). Outcome or expectancy? Antecedent of spontaneous causal attribution. *Personality and Social Psychology Bulletin*, 18, 659–68.

Kanfer, R., & Ackerman, P. L. (1989). Motivation and cognitive abilities: An integrative/aptitude-treatment interaction approach to skill acquisition. *Journal of Applied Psychology*, 74, 657–90.

Kaplan, K. J. (1972). On the ambivalence-indifference problem in attitude theory and measurement: A suggested modification of the semantic differential technique. *Psychological Bulletin*, 77, 361–72.

Kaplan, M. F., & Miller, C. E. (1987). Group decision making and normative versus informational influence: Effects of type of issue and assigned decision rule. *Journal of Personality and Social Psychology*, 53 (2), 306–13.

Karambaya, R., & Brett, J. M. (1989). Managers handling disputes: Third-party roles and perceptions of fairness. *Academy of Management Journal*, 32, 687–704.

Karney, B. R., Bradbury, T. N., Fincham, F. D., & Sullivan, K. T. (1994). The role of negative affectivity in the association between attributions and marital satisfaction. *Journal of Personality and Social Psychology*, 66, 413–24.

Karpf, F. B. (1932). *American social psychology – its origins, development and European background*. New York: Macmillan.

Katz, D. (1960). The functional approach to the study of attitudes. *Public Opinion Quarterly*, 24, 163–204.

Katz, D. (1978). Social psychology in relation to the social sciences. *American Behavioral Scientist*, 5, 779–92.

Katz, D., Sarnoff, I., & McClintock, C. (1956). Ego-defence and attitude change. *Human Relations*, 9, 27–46.

Kaye, K. (1982). *The mental and social life of babies*. Chicago: Chicago University Press.

Kelley, H. H. (1967). Attribution theory in social psychology. In D. Levine (Ed.), *Nebraska symposium on motivation* (Vol. 15, pp. 192–238). Lincoln, NE: University of Nebraska Press.

Kelley, H. H. (1972). Causal schemata and the attribution process. In E. E. Jones, D. E. Kanouse, H. H. Kelley, R. E. Nisbett, S. Valins, & B. Weiner (Eds.), *Attribution: Perceiving the causes of behavior* (pp. 151–74). Morristown, NJ: General Learning Press.

Kelley, H. H. (1973). The processes of causal attribution. *American Psychologist*, 28, 107–28.

Kelley, H. H., & Grzelak, J. L. (1972). Conflict between individual and common interests in an n-person relationship. *Journal of Personality and Social Psychology*, 21, 190–7.

Kelley, H. H., & Stahelski, A. J. (1970). Social interaction basis of cooperators' and competitors' beliefs about others. *Journal of Personality and Social Psychology*, 16, 66–91.

Kelley, H. H., & Thibaut, J. W. (1978). *Interpersonal relations: A theory of interdependence*. New York: Wiley.

Kelly, C. (1989). Political identity and perceived intragroup homogeneity. *British Journal of Social Psychology*, 28, 239–50.

Kelly, C., & Breinlinger, S. (1995). Attitudes, intentions, and behavior: A study of women's participation in collective action. *Journal of Applied Social Psychology*, 25, 1430–45.

Kelly, C., & Breinlinger, S. (1996). *The social psychology of collective action: Identity, injustice, and gender*. London: Taylor & Francis.

Kelman, H. C., & Hamilton, V. L. (1989). *Crimes of obedience: Toward a social psychology of authority and responsibility*. New Haven, CT: Yale University Press.

Keltner, D., Ellsworth, P. C., & Edwards, K. (1993). Beyond simple pessimism: Effects of sadness and anger on social perception. *Journal of Personality and Social Psychology*, 64 (5), 740–52.

Kemper, S. (1996). Elderspeak: Speech accommodation to older adults. *Aging Neuropsychology and Cognition*, 1, 17–28.

Kemper, S., Ferrell, P., Harden, T., Finter-Urczyk, A., & Billington, C. (1998). Use of elderspeak by young and older adults to impaired and unimpaired listeners. *Aging Neuropsychology & Cognition*, 5, 43–55.

Kenny, D. A., Kashy, D. A., & Bolger, N. (1998). Data analysis in social psychology. In D. T. Gilbert, S. T. Fiske, & G. Lindzey (Eds.), *The handbook of social psychology* (4th ed., Vol. 1, pp. 233–65). New York: McGraw-Hill.

Kenrick, D. T., & Trost, M. R. (1989). A reproductive exchange model of heterosexual relationships: Putting proximate economics in ultimate perspective. In C. Hendrick (Ed.), *Review of personality and social psychology: Close relationships* (pp. 92–118). Newbury Park, CA: Sage.

Kerr, N. L. (1983). Motivation losses in small groups: A social dilemma analysis. *Journal of Personality and Social Psychology*, 45, 819–28.

Kerr, N. L. (1992). Issue importance and group decision making. In S. Worchel, W. Wood, & J. A. Simpson (Eds.), *Group process and productivity* (pp. 68–88). London: Sage.

Kerr, N. L. (1996). 'Does my contribution really matter?': Efficacy in social dilemmas. In W. Stroebe & M. Hewstone (Eds.), *European review of social psychology* (Vol. 7, pp. 209–40). Chichester: Wiley.

Kerr, N. L., & Bruun, S. E. (1981). Ringelmann revisited: Alternative explanations for the social loafing effect. *Personality and Social Psychology Bulletin*, 7, 224–31.

Kerr, N. L., & Bruun, S. E. (1983). Dispensability of member effort and group motivation losses: Free-rider effects. *Journal of Personality and Social Psychology*, 44, 78–94.

Kerr, S. (1995). On the folly of rewarding A, while hoping for B. *Academy of Management Executive*, 9 (1), 7–14.

Kessler, R. C. (1997). The effects of stressful life events on depression. *Annual Review of Psychology*, 48, 191–214.

Kinder, D. R., & Sears, D. O. (1985). Public opinion and political action. In G. Lindzey & E. Aronson (Eds.), *Handbook of social psychology* (3rd ed., Vol. 2, pp. 659–741). New York: Random House.

King, B. T., & Janis, I. L. (1956). Comparison of the effectiveness of improvised versus non-improvised role-playing in producing opinion change. *Human Relations*, 9, 177–86.

King, K. B., Reis, H. T., Porter, L. A., & Norsen, L. H. (1993). Social support and long-term recovery from coronary artery surgery: Effects on patients and spouses. *Health Psychology*, 12, 56–63.

Kingdon, J. W. (1967). Politicians' beliefs about voters. *The American Political Science Review*, 61, 137–45.

Kirchler, E., & Davis, J. H. (1986). The influence of member status differences and task type on group consensus and member position change. *Journal of Personality and Social Psychology*, 51, 83–91.

Kirkpatrick, S. A., & Locke, E. A. (1991). Leadership: Do traits matter? *Academy of Management Executive*, 5, 48–60.

Kirsh, S. J., & Cassidy, J. (1997). Preschoolers' attention to and memory for attachment-relevant information. *Child Development*, 68, 1143–53.

Kitson, G. C. (1982). Attachment to the spouse in divorce: A scale and its applications. *Journal of Marriage and the Family*, 44, 379–93.

Klauer, K. C., & Meiser, T. (in press). A source-monitoring analysis of illusory correlations. *Personality and Social Psychology Bulletin*.

Kleinginna, P. R., & Kleinginna, A. M. (1981). A categorized list of emotion definitions, with suggestions for a consensual definition. *Motivation and Emotion*, 5, 345–79.

Kleinke, C. L., Peterson, T. R., & Rutledge, T. R. (1998). Effects of self-generated facial expressions on mood. *Journal of Personality and Social Psychology*, 74 (1), 272–9.

Kleinot, M. C., & Rogers, R. W. (1982). Identifying effective components of alcohol misuse prevention programs. *Journal of Studies on Alcohol*, 43, 802–11.

Knight, J. A., & Vallacher, R. R. (1981). Interpersonal engagement in social perception: The consequences of getting into the action. *Journal of Personality and Social Psychology*, 40, 990–9.

Koch, S. (1985). Forward: Wundt's creature at age zero – and as centenarian. Some aspects of the institutionalization of the new 'psychology'. In S. Koch & D. E. Leary (Eds.), *A century of psychology as a science* (pp. 7–35). New York: McGraw-Hill.

Kochanska, G. (1997). Mutually responsive orientation between mothers and their young children: Implications for early socialization. *Child Development*, 68, 94–112.

Koffka, K. (1935). *The principles of Gestalt psychology*. New York: Harcourt Brace & World.

Kokkinaki, F., & Lunt, P. (1997). The relationship between involvement, attitude accessibility and attitude–behaviour consistency. *British Journal of Social Psychology*, 36, 497– 509.

Komorita, S. S., & Parks, C. D. (1995). Interpersonal relations: Mixed-motive interaction. *Annual Review of Psychology*, 46, 183–207.

Kramer, R. M., & Tyler, T. R. (1995). *Trust in organizations*. Thousand Oaks, CA: Sage.

Krantz, S. E., & Rude, S. (1984). Depressive attributions: Selection of different causes or assignment of different meanings? *Journal of Personality and Social Psychology*, 47, 193–203.

Kraus, S. (1995). Attitudes and the prediction of behavior: A meta-analysis of the empirical literature. *Personality and Social Psychology Bulletin*, 21, 58–75.

Krauss, R. M., & Fussell, S. R. (1996). Social psychological models of interpersonal communication. In E. T. Higgins & A. W. Kruglanski (Eds.), *Social psychology: Handbook of basic principles* (pp. 655–701). New York: Guilford Press.

Kraut, R. E., & Johnston, R. (1979). Social and emotional messages of smiling: An ethological approach. *Journal of Personality and Social Psychology*, 37, 1539–53.

Kravitz, D. A., & Martin, B. (1986). Ringelmann rediscovered: The original article. *Journal of Personality and Social Psychology*, 50, 936–41.

Krebs, D. (1975). Empathy and altruism. *Journal of Personality and Social Psychology*, 32, 1134–46.

Kring, A. M., & Gordon, A. H. (1998). Sex differences in emotion: Expression, experience, and physiology. *Journal of Personality and Social Psychology*, 74 (3), 686–703.

Krosnick, J. A., Boninger, D. S., Chuang, Y. C., Berent, M. K., & Carnot, C. G. (1993). Attitude strength: One construct or many related constructs? *Journal of Personality and Social Psychology*, 65, 1132–51.

Kruglanski, A. W. (1975). The endogenous–exogenous partition in attribution theory. *Psychological Review*, 82, 387–406.

Kruglanski, A. W. (1989). *Lay epistemics and human knowledge*. New York: Plenum Press.

Kruglanski, A. W., & Ajzen, I. (1983). Bias and error in human judgment. *European Journal of Social Psychology*, 13, 1–44.

Kruglanski, A. W., & Freund, T. (1983). The freezing and unfreezing of lay-inferences: Effects on impressional primacy, ethnic stereotyping, and numerical anchoring. *Journal of Experimental Social Psychology*, 19, 448–68.

Kruglanski, A. W., & Mackie, D. M. (1990). Majority and minority influence: A judgemental process analysis. In W. Stroebe & M. Hewstone (Eds.), *European review of social psychology* (Vol. 1, pp. 229–61). Chichester: Wiley.

Krull, D. S., & Erickson, D. J. (1995). On judging situations: The effortful process of taking dispositional information into account. *Social Cognition*, 13, 417–38.

Kuhlman, D. M., & Marshello, A. (1975). Individual differences in game motivation as moderators of preprogrammed strategic effects in prisoner's dilemma. *Journal of Personality and Social Psychology*, 32, 922–31.

Kuhn, M. H., & McPartland, T. S. (1954). An empirical investigation of self-attitudes. *American Sociological Review*, 19, 68–76.

Kulik, J. A. (1983). Confirmatory attribution and the perpetuation of social beliefs. *Journal of Personality and Social Psychology*, 44, 1171–81.

Kulik, J. A., & Mahler, H. I. M. (1989). Stress and affiliation in a hospital setting: Preoperative roommate preferences. *Personality and Social Psychology Bulletin*, 15, 183–93.

Kunda, Z., & Oleson, K. C. (1995). Maintaining stereotypes in the face of disconfirmation:

Constructing grounds for subtyping. *Journal of Personality and Social Psychology*, 68, 565–79.

Kunda, Z., & Oleson, K. C. (1997). When exceptions prove the rule: How extremity of deviance determines the impact of deviant examples on stereotypes. *Journal of Personality and Social Psychology*, 72, 965–79.

Kuppens, M., De Wit, J., & Stroebe, W. (1996). Angstaanjagendheid in gezondheidsvoorlichting: Een dual process analyse. (Fear arousal in health education: A dual-process analysis). *Gedrag en Gezondheid*, 24, 241–8.

La Freniere, P., Strayer, F. F., & Gauthier, R. (1984). The emergence of same-sex affiliative preferences among pre-school peers: A developmental/ethological perspective. *Child Develop-ment*, 505, 1958–65.

Laird, J. D. (1974). Self-attribution of emotion: The effect of expressive behaviour on the quality of emotional experience. *Journal of Personality and Social Psychology*, 29, 475–86.

Lalljee, M. (1981). Attribution theory and the analysis of explanations. In C. Antaki (Ed.), *The psychology of ordinary explanations of social behaviour* (pp. 119–38). London: Academic Press.

Lamb, M. E., & Nash, A. (1989). Infant–mother attachment, sociability, and peer competence. In T. J. Berndt & G. W. Ladd (Eds.), *Peer relationships in child development* (pp. 219–45). New York: Wiley.

Lamm, H., & Myers, D. G. (1978). Group-induced polarization of attitudes and behaviour. In L. Berkowitz (Ed.), *Advances in experimental social psychology* (Vol. 11, pp. 145–95). New York: Academic Press.

Lange, C. (1885). *Om Sinsbevaegelser: Et psykofysiologiske Studie*. Copenhagen: Rasmussen.

Lange, F. (1971). Frustration–aggression. A reconsideration. *European Journal of Social Psychology*, 1, 59–84.

Langer, E. J. (1978). Rethinking the role of thought in social interaction. In J. H. Harvey, W. J. Ickes, & R. F. Kidd (Eds.), *New directions in attribution research* (Vol. 2). Hillsdale, NJ: Erlbaum.

Lanzetta, J. T., Cartwright-Smith, J., & Kleck, R. E. (1976). Effects of nonverbal dissimulation on emotional experience and autonomic arousal. *Journal of Personality and Social Psychology*, 33, 354–70.

LaPiere, R. (1934). Attitudes versus actions. *Social Forces*, 13, 230–7.

Larson, J. R., Jr., Christensen, C., Abbott, A. S., & Franz, T. M. (1996). Diagnosing groups: Charting the flow of information in medical decision-making teams. *Journal of Personality and Social Psychology*, 71 (2), 315–30.

Larson, J. R., Jr., Foster-Fishman, P. G., & Keys, C. B. (1994). Discussion of shared and unshared information in decision-making groups. *Journal of Personality and Social Psychology*, 67 (3), 446–61.

Latané, B. (1981). The psychology of social impact. *American Psychologist*, 36, 343–56.

Latané, B. (1986). Responsibility and effort in organizations. In P. S. Goodman (Ed.), *Designing effective work groups* (pp. 277–304). San Francisco: Jossey-Bass.

Latané, B., & Darley, J. M. (1969). Bystander 'apathy'. *American Scientist*, 57, 244–68.

Latané, B., & Darley, J. M. (1970). *The unresponsive bystander: Why doesn't he help?* New York: Appleton-Century-Crofts.

Latané, B., & Darley, J. M. (1976). *Help in a crisis: Bystander response to an emergency*. Morristown, NJ: General Learning Press.

Latané, B., & Nida, S. (1981). Ten years of research on group size and helping. *Psychological Bulletin*, 89, 308–24.

Latané, B., & Rodin, J. (1969). A lady in distress: Inhibiting effects of friends and strangers on bystander intervention. *Journal of Experimental Social Psychology*, 5, 189–202.

Latané, B., & Wolf, S. (1981). The social impact of majorities and minorities. *Psychological Review*, 88, 438–53.

Latané, B., Williams, K., & Harkins, S. (1979). Many hands make light work: The causes and consequences of social loafing. *Journal of Personality and Social Psychology*, 37, 822–32.

Lau, R. R., & Russell, D. (1980). Attributions in the sports pages. *Journal of Personality and Social Psychology*, 39, 29–38.

Laughlin, P. R. (1980). Social combination processes of cooperative problem-solving groups on verbal intellective tasks. In M. Fishbein (Ed.), *Progress in social psychology* (Vol. 1). Hillsdale, NJ: Erlbaum.

Laughlin, P. R., & Ellis, A. L. (1986). Demonstrability and social combination processes on mathematical intellective tasks. *Journal of Experimental Social Psychology*, 22, 177–89.

Lazarus, J. (1990). The logic of mate desertion. *Animal Behaviour*, 39, 672–84.

Lazarus, R. S. (1966). *Psychological stress and the coping process*. New York: McGraw-Hill.

Lazarus, R. S. (1968). Emotions and adaptation: Conceptual and empirical relations. In W. J. Arnold (Ed.), *Nebraska symposium on motivation* (pp. 175–270). Lincoln, NE: University of Nebraska Press.

Lazarus, R. S. (1991). *Emotion and adaptation*. New York: Oxford University Press.

Lazarus, R. S., & Folkman, S. (1984). *Stress, appraisal, and coping*. New York: Springer.

Lazarus, R. S., Speisman, J. C., Mordkoff, A. M., & Davison, L. A. (1962). A laboratory study of psychological stress produced by a motion picture film. *Psychological Monographs: General and Applied*, 76, 1–35.

LeBon, G. (1895). *Psychologie des foules*. Paris: Alcan.

LeBon, G. (1960). *The crowd*. New York: Viking. (First published 1895 as *Psychologie des foules*.)

Leary, M. R., & Forsyth, D. R. (1987). Attributions of responsibility for collective endeavors. In C. Hendrick (Ed.), *Review of personality and social psychology: Group processes* (Vol. 8, pp. 167–88). Newbury Park, CA: Sage.

Leavitt, H. J. (1951). Some effects of certain communication patterns on group performance. *Journal of Abnormal and Social Psychology*, 46, 38–50.

Lee, M. T., & Ofshe, R. (1981). The impact of behavioral style and status characteristics on social influence: A test of two competing theories. *Social Psychology Quarterly*, 44, 73–82.

Legerstee, M. (1991). Changes in the quality of infant sounds as a function of social and non-social stimulation. *First Language*, 11, 327–43.

Lehman, D. R., Ellard, J. H., & Wortman, C. B. (1986). Social support for the bereaved:

Recipients' and providers' perspectives on what is helpful. *Journal of Consulting and Clinical Psychology*, 54, 438–46.

Lemaine, G. (1966). Inegalité, comparaison et incomparabilité: Esquisse d'une théorie de l'originalité sociale. *Bulletin de Psychologie*, 20, 1–9.

Lemyre, L., & Smith, P. M. (1985). Intergroup discrimination and self esteem in the minimal group paradigm. *Journal of Personality and Social Psychology*, 49, 660–70.

Lepper, M. R., & Greene, D. (1978). *The hidden cost of reward*. New York: Wiley.

Lepper, M. R., Greene, D., & Nisbett, R. E. (1973). Undermining children's intrinsic interest with extrinsic reward: A test of the 'overjustification' hypothesis. *Journal of Personality and Social Psychology*, 28, 129–37.

Lerner, M. J. (1980). *The belief in a just world: A fundamental delusion*. New York: Plenum Press.

Levenson, R. W., Ekman, P., & Friesen, W. V. (1990). Voluntary facial action generates emotion-specific autonomic nervous system activity. *Psychophysiology*, 27, 363–84.

Levenson, R. W., Ekman, P., Heider, K., & Friesen, W. V. (1992). Emotion and autonomic nervous system activity in the Minangkabau of West Sumatra. *Journal of Personality and Social Psychology*, 62, 972–88.

Levenson, R. W., & Ruef, A. M. (1997). Physiological aspects of emotional knowledge and rapport. In W. J. Ickes (Ed.), *Empathic accuracy* (pp. 44–72). New York: Guilford Press.

Leventhal, G. S. (1980). What should be done with equity theory? New approaches to the study of fairness in social relationships. In K. J. Gergen, M. S. Greenberg, & R. H. Willis (Eds.), *Social exchange: Advances in theory and research* (pp. 27–55). New York: Plenum Press.

Leventhal, H. (1970). Findings and theory in the study of fear communication. In L. Berkowitz (Ed.), *Advances in experimental social psychology* (Vol. 5, pp. 120–86). New York: Academic Press.

Leventhal, H., & Cleary, P. D. (1980). The smoking problem: A review of the research and theory in behavioral risk modification. *Psychological Bulletin*, 88, 370–405.

Levine, J. M., & Murphy, G. (1943). The learning and forgetting of controversial material. *Journal of Abnormal and Social Psychology*, 38, 507–17.

Levy, R. I. (1984). The emotions in comparative perspective. In K. R. Scherer & P. Ekman (Eds.), *Approaches to emotion* (pp. 397–410). Hillsdale, NJ: Erlbaum.

Lewicki, R. J., & Sheppard, B. H. (1985). Choosing how to intervene: Factors affecting the use of process and outcome control in third party dispute resolution. *Journal of Occupational Behavior*, 6, 49–64.

Lewin, K. (1948). *Resolving social conflicts: Selected papers on group dynamics*. New York: Harper & Row.

Lewin, K. (1951). *Field theory in social science*. New York: Harper.

Lewit, E. M., & Coate, D. (1982). The potential for using excise taxes to reduce smoking. *Journal of Health Economics*, 1, 121–45.

Leyens, J.-P., Yzerbyt, V., & Schadron, G. (Eds.). (1994). *Stereotypes and social cognition*. London: Sage.

Leymann, H. (1993). *Mobbing: Psychoterror am Arbeitsplatz und wie man sich dagegen wehren kann* [Psycho-terror in the workplace and what can be done against it]. Reinbeck: Rowohlt.

Liberman, A., & Chaiken, S. (1992). Defensive processing of personally relevant health messages. *Personality and Social Psychology Bulletin*, 18, 669–79.

Liebert, R. N., & Baron, R. A. (1972). Some immediate effects of televised violence on children's behavior. *Developmental Psychology*, 6, 469–78.

Liebkind, K., & McAlister, A. L. (1999). Extended contact through peer modelling to promote tolerance in Finland. Unpublished MS, University of Helsinki.

Liebrand, W. B. G., & Van Run, G. (1985). The effects of social motives across two cultures on behavior in social dilemmas. *Journal of Experimental Social Psychology*, 21, 86–102.

Light, P., Littleton, K., Messer, D., & Joiner, R. (1994). Social and communicative processes in computer-based problem solving. *European Journal of Psychology of Education*, 9, 93–109.

Lightfoot, D. (1998). *The development of language: Acquisition, change and evolution*. Oxford: Blackwell.

Likert, R. (1932). A technique for the measurement of attitudes. *Archives of Psychology*, 140, 5–53.

Lind, E. A., & Tyler, T. R. (1988). *The social psychology of procedural justice*. New York: Plenum Press.

Linder, D. E., Cooper, J., & Jones, E. E. (1967). Decision freedom as a determinant of the role of incentive magnitude in attitude change. *Journal of Personality and Social Psychology*, 6, 245–54.

Lindner, G. A. (1871). *Ideen zur Psychologie der Gesellschaft als Grundlage der Sozialwissenschaft*. Vienna: Gerold.

Linville, P. W., Fischer, F. W., & Salovey, P. (1989). Perceived distributions of characteristics of ingroup and outgroup members: Empirical evidence and a computer simulation. *Journal of Personality and Social Psychology*, 42, 193–211.

Linz, D., Donnerstein, E., & Adams, S. M. (1989). Physiological desensitization and judgments about female victims of violence. *Human Communication Research*, 15, 509–22.

Liu, J. L., & Steele, C. M. (1986). Attributional analysis as self-affirmation. *Journal of Personality and Social Psychology*, 51, 531–40.

Lloyd, P., Camaioni, L., & Ercolani, P. (1995). Assessing referential communication skills in the primary school years: A comparative study. *British Journal of Developmental Psychology*, 13, 13–29.

Lloyd, P., & Fernyhough, C. (Eds.). (1999). *Lev Vygotsky: Critical assessments. Vygotsky's theory, Vol. 1*. New York: Routledge.

Locke, E. A., & Latham, G. P. (1990). *A theory of goal setting and task performance*. Englewood Cliffs, NJ: Prentice-Hall.

Locksley, A., Ortiz, V., & Hepburn, C. (1980). Social categorization and discriminatory behaviour: Extinguishing the minimal intergroup discrimination effect. *Journal of Personality and Social Psychology*, 39, 773–83.

Loftus, E. F. (1979). *Eyewitness testimony*. Cambridge, MA: Harvard University Press.

Lombardi, W. J., Higgins, E. T., & Bargh, J. A. (1987). The role of consciousness in priming effects on categorization: Assimilation versus contrast as a function of awareness of the priming task. *Personality and Social Psychology Bulletin*, 13, 411–29.

Lord, C. G., Ross, L., & Lepper, M. R. (1979). Biased assimilation and attitude polarization: The effects of prior theories on subsequently considered evidence. *Journal of Personality and Social Psychology*, 37, 2098–2109.

Lorenz, K. (1963). *Das sogenannte Böse* [The so-called evil]. Vienna: Borotha-Schoeler.

Löschper, G., Mummendey, A., Linneweber, V., & Bornewasser, M. (1984). The judgement of behaviour as aggressive and sanctionable. *European Journal of Social Psychology*, 14, 391–404.

Lösel, F., Averbeck, M., & Bliesener, T. (1997). Gewalt zwischen Schülern der Sekundarstufe: Eine Untersuchung zur Prävalenz und Beziehung zu allgemeiner Aggressivität und Delinquenz [Violence between schoolchildren at the senior level: An analysis of its prevalence and relation to general aggressiveness and delinquency]. *Empirische Pädagogik*, 11, 327–49.

Luce, R. D., & Raiffa, H. (1957). *Games and decisions: Introduction and critical survey*. London: Wiley.

Lück, H. E. (1987). A historical perspective on social psychological theories. In G. Semin & B. Krahé (Eds.), *Issues in contemporary German social psychology* (pp. 16–35). London: Sage.

Luepker, R. V., Murray, D. M., Jacobs, D. R., Mittelmark, M. B., Bracht, N., Carlaw, R., Crow, R., Elmer, P., Finnegan, J., Folsom, A., Grimm, R., Hannan, P. J., Jeffrey, R., Lando, H., McGovern, P., Mullis, R., Perry, C. L., Pechacek, T., Pirie, P., Sprafka, M., Weibrod, R., & Blackburn, H. (1994). Community education for cardiovascular disease prevention: Risk factor changes in the Minnesota Heart Health Program. *American Journal of Public Health*, 84, 1383–93.

Lujansky, H., & Mikula, G. (1983). Can equity theory explain the quality and the stability of romantic relationships? *British Journal of Social Psychology*, 22, 101–12.

Lukes, S. (1973a). *Individualism*. Oxford: Blackwell.

Lukes, S. (1973b). *Emile Durkheim. His life and work. A historical and critical study*. London: Allen Lane.

Lutz, C., & White, G. M. L. (1986). The anthropology of emotions. *Annual Review of Anthropology*, 15, 405–36.

Maass, A., & Clark, R. D., III (1983). Internationalization versus compliance: Differential processes underlying minority influence and conformity. *European Journal of Social Psychology*, 13, 197–215.

Maass, A., & Clark, R. D., III (1984). Hidden impact of minorities: Fifteen years of minority influence research. *Psychological Bulletin*, 95, 428–50.

Maass, A., Corvino, P., & Arcuri, L. (1994). Linguistic intergroup bias and the mass media. *Revue de Psychologie Sociale*, 1, 31–43.

Maass, A., Salvi, D., Arcuri, L., & Semin, G. R. (1989). Language use in intergroup contexts: The linguistic intergroup bias. *Journal of Personality and Social Psychology*, 57, 981–93.

Maccoby, E., & Jacklin, C. (1987). Gender segregation in childhood. *Advances in Child Development and Behaviour*, 20, 239–87.

Machiavelli, N. (1513/1946). *The Prince*. New York: Hendricks House.

Mackenzie, K. D. (1976). *A theory of group structures*. New York: Gordon & Breach.

Mackie, D. M. (1987). Systematic and nonsystematic processing of majority and minority persuasive communication. *Journal of Personality and Social Psychology*, 53, 41–52.

Mackie, D. M., & Worth, L. T. (1989). Cognitive deficits and the mediation of positive affect in persuasion. *Journal of Personality and Social Psychology*, 57, 27–40.

Macrae, C. N., Hewstone, M., & Griffith, R. J. (1993). Processing load and memory for stereotype-based information. *European Journal of Social Psychology*, 23, 77–87.

Macrae, C. N., Milne, A. B., & Bodenhausen, G. V. (1994). Stereotypes as energy-saving devices: A peek inside the cognitive toolbox. *Journal of Personality and Social Psychology*, 66, 37–47.

Maddux, J. E., & Rogers, R. W. (1983). Protection motivation and self-efficacy: A revised theory of fear appeals and attitude change. *Journal of Experimental Social Psychology*, 19, 469–79.

Madsen, D. B. (1978). Issue importance and choice shifts: A persuasive arguments approach. *Journal of Personality and Social Psychology*, 36, 1118–27.

Maheswaran, D., & Chaiken, S. (1991). Promoting systematic processing in low motivation settings: The effect of incongruent information on processing and judgment. *Journal of Personality and Social Psychology*, 61, 13–25.

Manis, J. G., & Meltzer, B. N. (1980). *Symbolic interaction*. Boston: Allyn & Bacon.

Mann, L., Newton, J. W., & Innes, J. M. (1982). A test between deindividuation and emergent norm theories of crowd aggression. *Journal of Personality and Social Psychology*, 42, 260–72.

Mann, L., Samson, D., & Dow, D. (1998). A field experiment on the effects of benchmarking and goal setting on company sales performance. *Journal of Management*, 24, 73–96.

Manstead, A. S. (1991). Expressiveness as an individual difference. In R. S. Feldman & B. Rimé (Eds.), *Fundamentals of nonverbal behaviour* (pp. 285–328). Cambridge: Cambridge University Press.

Manstead, A. S. R., & Semin, G. R. (1980). Social facilitation effects: Mere enhancement of dominant responses? *British Journal of Social and Clinical Psychology*, 19, 119–36.

Mantell, D. M. (1971). The potential for violence in Germany. *Journal of Social Issues*, 27, 101–12.

Maras, P., & Brown, R. J. (1996). Effects of contact on children's attitudes to disability: A longitudinal study. *Journal of Applied Social Psychology*, 26, 2113–34.

Marcus-Newhall, A., Miller, N., Holtz, R., & Brewer, M. B. (1993). Cross-cutting category membership with role assignment: A means of reducing intergroup bias. *British Journal of Social Psychology*, 32, 125–46.

Markova, I. (1982). *Paradigm, thought, and language*. Chichester: Wiley.

Markova, I. (1983). The origin of the social psychology of language in German expressivism. *British Journal of Social Psychology*, 22, 315–25.

Markus, H. (1977). Self-schemata and processing information about the self. *Journal of Personality and Social Psychology*, 35, 63–78.

Markus, H. (1978). The effect of mere presence on social facilitation: An unobtrusive test. *Journal of Experimental Social Psychology*, 14, 389–97.

Markus, H. R., & Kitayama, S. (1994). The cultural construction of self and emotion: Implications for social behavior. In S. Kitayama & H. R. Markus (Eds.), *Emotion and culture: Empirical studies of mutual influence* (pp. 89–130). Washington, DC: American Psychological Association.

Marrow, A. J. (1968). *The practical theorist: The life and work of Kurt Lewin*. New York: Basic Books.

Martin, L. L., Ward, D. W., Achee, J. W., & Wyer, R. S., Jr. (1993). Mood as input: People have to interpret the motivational implications of their moods. *Journal of Personality and Social Psychology*, 64, 317–26.

Martin, M. W., & Sell, J. (1985). The effect of equating status characteristics on the generalization process. *Social Psychology Quarterly*, 48, 178–82.

Martin, R. (1998). Majority and minority influence using the after-image paradigm: A series of attempted replications. *Journal of Experimental Social Psychology*, 34, 1–26.

Marx, M. H., & Hillix, W. A. (1979). *Systems and theories in psychology* (3rd ed.). New York: McGraw-Hill.

Masataka, N. (1992). Pitch characteristics of Japanese maternal speech to infants. *Journal of Child Language*, 19, 213–23.

Maslach, C., & Jackson, S. E. (1981). The measurement of experienced burnout. *Journal of Occupational Behaviour*, 2, 99–113.

Maslow, A. H. (1954). *Motivation and personality*. New York: Harper & Row.

Matsumoto, D. (1989). Cultural influences on the perception of emotion. *Journal of Cross-cultural Psychology*, 20, 92–105.

Mausner, B. (1954). Prestige and social interaction. The effect of one partner's success in a relevant task on the interaction of observer pairs. *Journal of Abnormal and Social Psychology*, 49, 557–60.

Mayer, J. D., & Salovey, P. (1988). Personality moderates the interaction of mood and cognition. In K. Fiedler & J. P. Forgas (Eds.), *Affect, cognition, and social behavior* (pp. 87–99). Toronto: Hogrefe.

Maynard Smith, J. (1977). Parental investment: A prospective analysis. *Animal Behaviour*, 29, 1–9.

Mazur, A. (1983). Hormones, aggression, and dominance in humans. In B. Svare (Ed.), *Hormones and aggressive behavior* (pp. 563–76). New York: Plenum Press.

Mazur, A., Halpern, C., & Udry, J. R. (1994). Dominant looking male teenagers copulate earlier. *Ethology and Sociobiology*, 15, 87–94.

McArthur, L. A. (1972). The how and what of why: Some determinants and consequences of causal attributions. *Journal of Personality and Social Psychology*, 22, 171–93.

McArthur, L. Z. (1981). What grabs you? The role of attention in impression formation and causal attribution. In E. T. Higgins, C. P. Herman, & M. P. Zanna (Eds.), *Social cognition: The Ontario symposium* (Vol. 1, pp. 201–46). Hillsdale, NJ: Lawrence Erlbaum.

McArthur, L. Z., & Post, D. L. (1977). Figural emphasis and person perception. *Journal of Experimental Social Psychology*, 13, 520–35.

McCauley, C. (1989). The nature of social influence in groupthink: Compliance and internalization. *Journal of Personality and Social Psychology*, 57, 250–60.

McClelland, D. C. (1961). *The achieving society*. Princeton, NJ: Van Nostrand.

McClintock, C. G. (1972). Social motivation – a set of propositions. *Behavioral Science*, 17, 438–54.

McClintock, C. G., & Liebrand, W. B. G. (1988). The role of interdependence structure, individual value orientation and other's strategy in social decision making: A transformational analysis. *Journal of Personality and Social Psychology*, 55, 396–409.

McClure, J. L. (1998). Discounting causes of behaviour: Are two reasons better than one? *Journal of Personality and Social Psychology*, 74, 7–20.

McDougall, W. (1908). *Introduction to social psychology*. London: Methuen.

McDougall, W. (1920). *The group mind*. Cambridge: Cambridge University Press.

McFarland, D. J. (1993). *Animal behaviour* (2nd ed.). London: Pitman.

McGarty, C., & Penney, R. E. C. (1988). Categorization, accentuation and social judgement. *British Journal of Social Psychology*, 27, 147–57.

McGinnis, J. M., & Foege, W. H. (1993). Actual causes of death in the United States. *Journal of the American Medical Association*, 270, 2207–12.

McGrath, J. E. (1984). *Groups: Interaction and performance*. Englewood Cliffs, NJ: Prentice-Hall.

McGuire, W. J., & Papageorgis, D. (1962). Effectiveness of forewarning in developing resistance to persuasion. *Public Opinion Quarterly*, 26, 24–34.

McIntosh, D. N. (1996). Facial feedback hypotheses: Evidence, implications, and directions. *Motivation and Emotion*, 20 (2), 121–47.

McKeon, R. (Ed.). (1941). *The basic works of Aristotle*. New York: Random House.

McNeill, D. (1970). *The acquisition of language. The study of developmental psycholinguistics*. New York: Harper & Row.

McPhail, C. (1991). *The myth of the madding crowd*. New York: Aldine de Gruyter.

McTear, M. (1985). *Children's conversation*. Oxford: Blackwell.

Mead, G. H. (1934). *Mind, self and society from the standpoint of a social behaviorist*. Chicago: University of Chicago Press.

Mead, G. H. (1934/1977). *On social psychology* (Ed. A. Strauss). Chicago: University of Chicago Press.

Meeus, W. H. J., & Raaijmakers, Q. A. W. (1986). Administrative obedience: Carrying out orders to use psychological-administrative violence. *European Journal of Social Psychology*, 16, 311–24.

Meindl, J. R., Ehrlich, S. B., & Dukerich, J. M. (1985). The romance of leadership. *Administrative Science Quarterly*, 30, 78–102.

Meins, E. (1997). *Security of attachment and the social development of cognition*. Hove: Psychology Press/Erlbaum.

Meloen, J. D., Hagendoorn, L., Raaijmakers, Q., & Visser, L. (1988). Authoritarianism and the revival of political racism: Reassessments in the Netherlands of the reliability and validity of the concept of authoritarianism by Adorno et al. *Political Psychology*, 9, 413–29.

Mesquita, B., Frijda, N. H., & Scherer, K. R. (1997). Culture and emotion. In J. E. Berry, P. B. Dasen, & T. S. Saraswathi (Eds.), *Handbook of cross-cultural psychology. Vol. 2: Basic processes and developmental psychology* (pp. 255–97). Boston: Allyn & Bacon.

Messé, L. A., & Sivacek, J. M. (1979). Predictions of others' responses in a mixed-motive game: Self-justification or false consensus. *Journal of Personality and Social Psychology, 37,* 602–7.

Messer, D., & Collis, G. (1996). Early interaction and cognitive skills: Implications for the acquisition of culture. In A. Lock and C. R. Peters (Eds.), *Handbook of human symbolic evolution* (pp. 432–68). Oxford: Clarendon Press/Oxford University Press.

Messick, D., & Brewer, M. B. (1983). Solving social dilemmas: A review. In L. Wheeler & P. Shaver (Eds.), *Review of personality and social psychology* (Vol. 4, pp. 11–44). Beverly Hills, CA: Sage.

Messick, D. M., & Sentis, K. P. (1985). Estimating social and non-social utility functions from ordinal data. *European Journal of Social Psychology, 15,* 389–99.

Metalsky, G. I., Halberstadt, L. J., & Abramson, L. Y. (1987). Vulnerability to depressive mood reactions: Toward a more powerful test of the diathesis-stress and causal mediation components of the reformulated theory of depression. *Journal of Personality and Social Psychology, 52,* 386–93.

Meyer, J. P., & Allen, N. J. (1991). A three-component conceptualization of organizational commitment. *Human Resource Management Review, 1,* 61–98.

Miceli, M. P., & Near, J. P. (1992). *Blowing the whistle: The organizational and legal implications for companies and employees.* New York: Lexington Books.

Michotte, A. (1963). *The perception of causality.* New York: Basic Books.

Migdal, M. J., Hewstone, M., & Mullen, B. (1998). The effects of crossed categorization on intergroup evaluations: A meta-analysis. *British Journal of Social Psychology, 37,* 303–24.

Mikelson, K. D., Kessler, R. C., & Shaver, P. R. (1997). Adult attachment in a nationally representative sample. *Journal of Personality and Social Psychology, 73,* 1092–1106.

Mikula, G. (1994). Perspective-related differences in interpretation of injustice by victims and victimizers: A test with close relationships. In M. J. Lerner & G. Mikula (Eds.), *Injustice in close relationships: Entitlement and the affectional bond* (pp. 175–203). New York: Plenum Press.

Mikulincer, M., Florian, V., & Weller, A. (1993). Attachment styles, coping strategies, and posttraumatic psychological distress: The impact of the Gulf War in Israel. *Journal of Personality and Social Psychology, 64,* 817–26.

Milgram, S. (1963). Behavioral study of obedience. *Journal of Abnormal and Social Psychology, 67,* 371–8.

Milgram, S. (1965). Some conditions of obedience and disobedience to authority. *Human Relations, 18,* 57–76.

Milgram, S. (1974). *Obedience to authority.* New York: Harper & Row.

Milgram, S., & Toch, H. (1969). Collective behavior: Crowds and social movements. In G. Lindzey & E. Aronson (Eds.), *The handbook of social psychology* (2nd ed., Vol. 4, pp. 507–610). Reading, MA: Addison-Wesley.

Millar, M. G., & Tesser, A. (1986). Effects of affective and cognitive focus on the attitude–behavior relation. *Journal of Personality and Social Psychology, 51,* 270–6.

Miller, A. G., Collins, B. E., & Brief, D. E. (Eds.). (1995). Perspectives on obedience to authorities: The legacy of the Milgram experiments. *Journal of Social Issues, 51,* 1–20.

Miller, A. G., Gordon, A. K., & Buddie, A. M. (1999). Accounting for evil and cruelty: Is to explain to condone? *Personality and Social Psychology Review, 3,* 254–68.

Miller, D. T. (1977a). Altruism and threat to a belief in a just world. *Journal of Experimental Social Psychology, 13,* 113–24.

Miller, D. T. (1977b). Personal deserving versus justice for others: An exploration of the justice motive. *Journal of Experimental Social Psychology, 13,* 1–13.

Miller, D. T., & McFarland, C. (1991). When social comparison goes away: The case of pluralistic ignorance. In J. Suls & T. Wills (Eds.), *Social comparison: Contemporary theory and research* (pp. 287–313). Hillsdale, NJ: Lawrence Erlbaum.

Miller, D. T., Norman, S. A., & Wright, E. (1978). Distortion in person perception as a consequence of the need for effective control. *Journal of Personality and Social Psychology, 36,* 598–607.

Miller, D. T., & Porter, C. A. (1980). Effects of temporal perspective on the attribution process. *Journal of Personality and Social Psychology, 39,* 532–41.

Miller, D. T., & Ross, M. (1975). Self-serving biases in the attribution of causality: Fact or fiction? *Psychological Bulletin, 82,* 213–25.

Miller, F. D., Smith, E. R., & Uleman, J. (1981). Measurement and interpretation of situational and dispositional attributions. *Journal of Experimental Social Psychology, 17,* 80–95.

Miller, G. E., & Bradbury, T. N. (1995). Refining the association between attributions and behavior in marital interaction. *Journal of Family Psychology, 9,* 196–208.

Miller, J. G. (1984). Culture and the development of everyday social explanation. *Journal of Personality and Social Psychology, 46,* 961–78.

Miller, N., Brewer, M. B., & Edwards, K. (1985). Cooperative interaction in desegregated settings: A laboratory analogue. *Journal of Social Issues, 41,* 63–79.

Miller, N., & Carlson, M. (1990). Valid theory-testing meta-analyses further question the negative state relief model of helping. *Psychological Bulletin, 107,* 215–25.

Miller, N. E., & Bugelski, R. (1948). Minor studies in aggression: The influence of frustrations imposed by the ingroup on attitudes toward outgroups. *Journal of Psychology, 25,* 437–42.

Miller, N. E., Sears, R. R., Mowrer, O. H., Doob, L. W., & Dollard, I. (1941). The frustration–aggression hypothesis. *Psychological Review, 48,* 337–42.

Mills, J., & Clark, M. S. (1982). Communal and exchange relationships. In L. Wheeler (Ed.), *Review of Personality and Social Psychology* (Vol. 3, pp. 121–44). Beverly Hills, CA: Sage.

Milne, S., Sheeran, P., & Orbell, S. (2000). Prediction and intervention in health-related behavior: A meta-analytic review of protection motivation theory. *Journal of Applied Social Psychology, 30,* 106–43.

Mintzberg, H. (1973). *The nature of managerial work.* New York: Harper & Row.

Mitchell, P. (1997). *Introduction to theory of mind. Children, autism and apes.* London: Arnold.

Mobley, W. H., Griffeth, R. W., Hand, H. H., & Meglino, B. M. (1979). Review and conceptual analysis of the employee turnover process. *Psychological Bulletin, 86,* 493–522.

Mock, D. W., & Fujioka, M. (1990). Monogamy and long-term pair bonding in vertebrates. *Trends in Ecology and Evolution, 5,* 39–43.

Modigliani, A., & Rochat, F. (1995). The role of interaction sequences and the timing of resistance in shaping obedience and defiance to authority. *Journal of Social Issues, 51,* 107–23.

Moede, W. (1920). *Experimentelle Massenpsychologie.* Leipzig: Hirtzel.

Moerk, E. L. (1992). *A first language taught and learned.* Baltimore: Bookes.

Molleman, E., Pruyn, J., & Van Knippenberg, A. (1986). Social comparison processes among cancer patients. *British Journal of Social Psychology, 25,* 1–13.

Montada, L. (in press). Denial of responsibility. In A. E. Auhagen & H. W. Bierhoff (Eds.), *Responsibility: The many faces of a social phenomenon.* London: Routledge.

Montada, L., & Bierhoff, H. W. (1991). Studying prosocial behavior in social systems. In L. Montada and H. W. Bierhoff (Eds.), *Altruism in social systems* (pp. 1–26). Lewiston, NY: Hogrefe.

Montagner, H., Restoin, A., Ullmann, V., Rogriguez, D., Godard, D. & Viala, M. (1984). Development of early peer interaction. In W. Doise & A. Palmonari (Eds.), *Social interaction in individual development* (pp. 34–60). Cambridge: Cambridge University Press.

Moore, B. S., Sherrod, D. R., Liu, T. J., & Underwood, B. (1979). The dispositional shift in attribution over time. *Journal of Experimental Social Psychology, 15,* 553–69.

Moore, M. J. (1996). Death and tobacco taxes. *Rand Journal of Economics, 27,* 415–28.

Morgan, D. L. (1990). Combining the strengths of social networks, social support, and personal relationships. In S. Duck & R. C. Silver (Eds.), *Personal relationships and social support* (pp. 190–215). London: Sage.

Morris, D. (1977). *Manwatching: A field guide to human behavior.* New York: Harry N. Abrams.

Morris, J. A., & Feldman, D. C. (1996). The dimensions, antecedents, and consequences of emotional labor. *Academy of Management Review*, 21 (4), 986–1010.

Morris, M. W., & Larrick, R. P. (1995). When one cause casts doubt on another: A normative analysis of discounting in causal attribution. *Psychological Review*, 102, 331–55.

Morris, M. W., Nisbett, R. E., & Peng, K. (1995). Causal understanding across domains and cultures. In D. Sperber, D. Premack, & A. J. Premack (Eds.), *Causal cognition: A multidisciplinary debate* (pp. 577–612). Oxford: Oxford University Press.

Morris, M. W., & Peng, K. (1994). Culture and cause: American and Chinese attributions for social and physical events. *Journal of Personality and Social Psychology*, 67, 949–71.

Moscovici, S. (1972). Society and theory in social psychology. In J. Israel & H. Tajfel (Eds.), *The context of social psychology: A critical assessment* (pp. 17–68). London: Academic Press.

Moscovici, S. (1976). *Social influence and social change.* London: Academic Press.

Moscovici, S. (1980). Toward a theory of conversion behaviour. In L. Berkowitz (Ed.), *Advances in experimental social psychology* (Vol. 13, pp. 208–39). New York: Academic Press.

Moscovici, S. (1981a). *L' âge des foules.* Paris: Fayard.

Moscovici, S. (1981b). On social representations. In J. P. Forgas (Ed.), *Social cognition: Perspectives on everyday understanding.* London: Academic Press.

Moscovici, S. (Ed.). (1984). *Psychologie sociale.* Paris: Presses Universitaires de France.

Moscovici, S. (1985). Social influence and conformity. In G. Lindzey & E. Aronson (Eds.), *Handbook of social psychology* (3rd ed., Vol. 2, pp. 347–412). New York: Random House.

Moscovici, S., & Lage, E. (1976). Studies in social influence III: Majority versus minority influence in a group. *European Journal of Social Psychology*, 6, 149–74.

Moscovici, S., Lage, E., & Naffrechoux, M. (1969). Influence of a consistent minority on the responses of a majority in a color perception task. *Sociometry*, 32, 365–80.

Moscovici, S., & Personnaz, B. (1980). Studies in social influence V: Minority influence and conversion behaviour in a perceptual task. *Journal of Experimental Social Psychology*, 16, 270–82.

Moscovici, S., & Zavalloni, M. (1969). The group as a polarizer of attitudes. *Journal of Personality and Social Psychology*, 12, 125–35.

Mowday, R. T. (1996). Equity theory predictions of behavior in organizations. In R. M. Steers, L. W. Porter, & G. A. Bigley (Eds.), *Motivation and leadership at work* (pp. 53–71). McGraw-Hill.

Mowday, R. T., Steers, R. M., & Porter, L. W. (1979). The measurement of organizational commitment. *Journal of Vocational Behavior*, 14, 224–47.

Mugny, G. (1982). *The power of minorities.* New York: Academic Press.

Mugny, G., Levy, M., & Doise, W. (1978). Conflit sociocognitif et développement cognitif. *Revue Suisse de Psychologie Pure et Appliquée*, 37, 22–43.

Mulilis, J. P., & Lippa, R. (1990). Behavioral change in earthquake preparedness due to negative threat appeals: A test of protection motivation theory. *Journal of Applied Social Psychology*, 20, 619–38.

Mullen, B. (1986). Atrocity as a function of lynch mob composition: A self-attention perspective. *Personality and Social Psychology Bulletin*, 12, 187–97.

Mullen, B., & Johnson, C. (1990). Distinctiveness-based illusory correlations and stereotyping: A meta-analytic integration. *British Journal of Social Psychology*, 29, 11–28.

Mullen, B., Johnson, C., & Salas, E. (1991). Productivity loss in brainstorming groups: A meta-analytic integration. *Basic and Applied Social Psychology*, 12, 3–24.

Mummendey, A., Linneweber, V., & Löschper, G. (1984a). Actor or victim of aggression: Divergent perspectives – divergent evaluations. *European Journal of Social Psychology*, 14, 297–311.

Mummendey, A., Linneweber, V., & Löschper, G. (1984b). Aggression: From act to interaction. In A. Mummendey (Ed.), *Social psychology of aggression: From individual behavior to social interaction* (pp. 69–106). New York: Springer.

Mummendey, A., & Otten, S. (1989). Perspective specific differences in the segmentation and evaluation of aggressive interaction sequences. *European Journal of Social Psychology*, 19, 23–40.

Mummendey, A., & Otten, S. (1993). Aggression: Interaction between individuals and social groups. In R. B. Felson & J. T. Tedeschi (Eds.), *Aggression and violence. Social interactionist perspectives* (pp. 145–67). Washington, DC: American Psychological Association.

Mummendey, A., & Otten, S. (1998). Positive–negative assymetry in social discrimination. In W. Stroebe & M. Hewstone (Eds.), *European review of social psychology*. Chichester: Wiley.

Mummendey, A., Simon, B., Dietze, C., Grünert, M., Haeger, G., Kessler, S., Lettgen, S., & Schäferhoff, S. (1992). Categorization is not enough: Intergroup discrimination in negative outcome allocations. *Journal of Experimental Social Psychology*, 28, 125–44.

Murray, N., Surjan, H., Hirt, E. R., & Surjan, M. (1990). The influence of mood on categorization: A cognitive flexibility interpretation. *Journal of Personality and Social Psychology*, 59, 411–25.

Murray, S. L., & Holmes, J. G. (1997). A leap of faith? Positive illusions in romantic relationships. *Personality and Social Psychology*, 23, 586–604.

Murray, S. L., Holmes, J. G., & Griffin, D. W. (1996). The benefits of positive illusions: Idealization and the construction of satisfaction in close relationships. *Journal of Personality and Social Psychology*, 70 (1), 79–98.

Myers, D. G. (1978). Polarizing effects of social comparison. *Journal of Experimental Social Psychology*, 14, 554–63.

Myers, D. G. (1982). Polarizing effects of social interaction. In H. Brandstatter, J. H. Davis, & G. Stocker-Kreichgauer (Eds.), *Group decision making* (pp. 125–61). New York: Academic Press.

Myers, D. G., & Kaplan, M. F. (1976). Group-induced polarization in simulated juries. *Personality and Social Psychology Bulletin*, 2, 63–6.

Nadler, A. (1987). Determinants of help seeking behaviour: The effects of helper's similarity, task centrality and recipient's self esteem. *European Journal of Social Psychology*, 17, 57–67.

Nadler, A. (1991). Help-seeking behavior. Psychological costs and instrumental benefits. In M. S. Clark (Ed.), *Prosocial behavior* (pp. 290–311). Newbury Park, CA: Sage.

Nadler, A., & Fisher, J. D. (1986). The role of threat to self-esteem and perceived control in recipient reaction to help: Theory development and empirical validation. In L. Berkowitz (Ed.), *Advances in experimental social psychology* (Vol. 19, pp. 81–122). Orlando, FL: Academic Press.

Nemeth, C. (1977). Interactions between jurors as a function of majority versus unanimity decision rules. *Journal of Applied Social Psychology*, 7, 38–56.

Nemeth, C. (1982). Stability of fact position and influence. In H. Brandstatter, J. H. Davis, & G. Stocker-Kreichgauer (Eds.), *Group decision making* (pp. 185–200). New York: Academic Press.

Nemeth, C. (1986). Differential contributions of majority and minority influence. *Psychological Review*, 93, 23–32.

Nemeth, C. (1994). The value of minority dissent. In S. Moscovici, A. Mucchi-Faina, & A. Maass (Eds.), *Minority influence* (pp. 3–15). Chicago: Nelson-Hall.

Nemeth, C. (1995). Dissent as driving cognition, attitudes and judgments. *Social Cognition*, 13, 273–91.

Nemeth, C., & Kwan, J. (1987). Minority influence, divergent thinking, and the detection of correct solutions. *Journal of Applied Social Psychology*, 17, 788–99.

Nemeth, C. J., & Staw, B. M. (1989). The tradeoffs of social control and innovation in groups and organizations. In L. Berkowitz (Ed.), *Advances in experimental social psychology* (Vol. 22, pp. 175–210). New York: Academic Press.

Nemeth, C., Swedlund, M., & Kanki, G. (1974). Patterning of the minority's responses and their influence on the majority. *European Journal of Social Psychology*, 4, 53–64.

Nemeth, C., & Wachtler, J. (1983). Creative problem solving as a result of majority versus minority influence. *European Journal of Social Psychology*, 13, 45–55.

Nesdale, D. (in press). The development of prejudice in children. To appear in M. Augoustinos and K. Reynolds (Eds.), *The psychology of prejudice and racism*. Newbury Park, CA: Sage.

Neuberg, S. L., Cialdini, R. B., Brown, S. L., Luce, C., Sagarin, B. J., & Lewis, B. P. (1997). Does empathy lead to anything more than superficial helping? Comment on Batson et al. (1997). *Journal of Personality and Social Psychology*, 73, 510–16.

Neuberg, S. L., & Fiske, S. T. (1987). Motivational influences on impression formation: Outcome dependency, accuracy-driven attention, and individuating processes. *Journal of Personality and Social Psychology*, 53, 431–44.

Newcomb, T. M. (1961). *The acquaintance process.* New York: Holt, Rinehart, & Winston.

Newman, L. S. (1991). Why are traits inferred spontaneously? A developmental approach. *Social Cognition*, 9, 221–53.

Newman, R. S., & Goldin, L. (1990). Children's reluctance to seek help with schoolwork. *Journal of Educational Psychology*, 82, 92–100.

Newton, P., Reddy, V., & Bull, R. (2000). Children's everyday deception and performance on false-belief tasks. *British Journal of Developmental Psychology*, 18, 297–317.

Ng, S. H. (1980). *The social psychology of power.* London: Academic Press.

Ng, S. H., & Bradac, J. J. (1993). *Power in language.* Thousand Oaks, CA: Sage.

Niedl, K. (1995). *Mobbing/Bullying am Arbeitsplatz. Eine empirische Analyse zum Phänomen sowie zu personalwirtschaftlich relevanten Effekten von systematischen Feindseligkeiten* [Mobbing/bullying in the workplace. An empirical analysis of the phenomenon and the consequences of systematic hostility for personnel economy]. Munich: Hampp.

Nietzsche, F. (1968). *The will to power* (Ed. W. Kaufmann). New York: Vintage Books.

Ninio, A., & Snow, C. E. (1999). The development of pragmatics: Learning to use language appropriately. In W. C. Ritchie, William C. & T. K. Bhatia (Eds.), *Handbook of child language acquisition* (pp. 347–83). San Diego, CA: Academic Press.

Nisbett, R. E., Caputo, C., Legant, P., & Maracek, J. (1973). Behaviour as seen by the actor and as seen by the observer. *Journal of Personality and Social Psychology*, 27, 154–64.

Nisbett, R. E., & Cohen, D. (1996). *Culture of honor: The psychology of violence in the south.* Boulder, CO: Westview Press.

Nolen-Hoeksema, S., Girgus, J. S., & Seligman, M. E. P. (1992). Predictors and consequences of childhood depressive symptoms: Five-year longitudinal study. *Journal of Abnormal Psychology*, 101, 405–22.

Nolen-Hoeksema, S., & Larson, J. (1999). *Coping with loss.* Mahwah, NJ: Erlbaum.

Nolen-Hoeksema, S., McBride, A., & Larson, J. (1997). Rumination and psychological distress among bereaved partners. *Journal of Personality and Social Psychology*, 72, 855–62.

Noller, P., & Fitzpatrick, M. A. (1990). Marital communication in the eighties. *Journal of Marriage and the Family*, 52, 832–43.

Norman, R. (1975). Affective–cognitive consistency, attitudes, conformity, and behavior. *Journal of Personality and Social Psychology*, 32, 83–91.

Nuttin, J. M. (1985). Narcissism beyond Gestalt and awareness: The name letter effect. *European Journal of Social Psychology*, 15, 353–61.

Nye, J. L., & Brown, A. M. (Eds.). (1996). *What's social about social cognition?* London: Sage.

Nye, R. (1975). *The origins of crowd psychology.* London: Sage.

Oakes, P. J., & Turner, J. C. (1980). Social categorization and intergroup behaviour: Does minimal intergroup discrimination make social identity more positive? *European Journal of Social Psychology*, 10, 295–302.

Oatley, K. (1993). Social construction in emotions. In M. Lewis & J. M. Haviland (Eds.), *Handbook of emotions* (pp. 341–52). New York: Guilford Press.

Oatley, K., & Johnson-Laird, P. N. (1987). Towards a cognitive theory of emotions. *Cognition and Emotion*, 1, 29–50.

O'Connor, S. C., & Rosenblood, L. K. (1996). Affiliation motivation in everyday experience: A theoretical comparison. *Journal of Personality and Social Psychology*, 70, 513–22.

Ohbuchi, K., & Kambara, T. (1985). Attacker's intent and awareness of outcome, impression management and retaliation. *Journal of Experimental Social Psychology*, 21, 321–30.

Ohbuchi, K., Kameda, M., & Agarie, N. (1989). Apology as aggression control: Its role in mediating appraisal of and reponse to harm. *Journal of Personality and Social Psychology*, 56, 219–27.

Oliner, S. P., & Oliner, P. M. (1988). *The altruistic personality. Rescuers of Jews in Nazi Europe*. New York: Free Press.

Olweus, D. (1973). *Hackkycklingar och översittare. Forskning on skolmobbning*. Stockholm: Almqvist & Wicksell.

Olweus, D. (1994). Bullying at school: Long-term outcomes for the victims and an effective school-based intervention program. In L. R. Huesmann (Ed.), *Aggressive behavior. Current perspectives* (pp. 97–130). New York: Plenum Press.

Omoto, A. M., & Snyder, M. (1995). Sustained helping without obligation: Motivation, longevity of service, and perceived attitude change. *Journal of Personality and Social Psychology*, 68, 671–86.

Oppenheim, A. N. (1992). *Questionnaire design, interviewing and attitude measurement*. London: Pinter Publishers.

Orbell, J. M., Van der Kragt, A. J., & Dawes, R. M. (1988). Explaining discussion-induced cooperation. *Journal of Personality and Social Psychology*, 54, 811–19.

Organ, D. W., & Ryan, K. (1995). A meta-analytic review of attitudinal and dispositional predictors of organizational citizenship behavior. *Personnel Psychology*, 48, 775–802.

Orne, M. T. (1962). On the social psychology of the psychological experiment: With particular reference to demand characteristics and their implications. *American Psychologist*, 17, 776–83.

Orne, M. T. (1969). Demand characteristics and the concept of quasi-controls. In R. Rosenthal and R. L. Rosnow (Eds.), *Artifact in behavioral research* (pp. 143–79). New York: Academic Press.

Ortega y Gasset, J. (1932). *Revolt of the masses*. New York: Norton.

Osborn, A. F. (1957). *Applied imaginations*. New York: Scribner's.

Osgood, C. E., May, W. H., & Miron, M. S. (1975). *Cross-cultural universals of affective meaning*. Urbana, IL: University of Illinois Press.

Osgood, C. E., Suci, G. J., & Tannenbaum, P. H. (1957). *The measurement of meaning*. Urbana, IL: University of Illinois Press.

Ostrom, T. M. (1977). Between-theory and within-theory conflict in explaining contrast effects in impression formation. *Journal of Experimental Social Psychology*, 13, 492–503.

Otten, S., Mummendey, A., & Blanz, M. (1996). Intergroup discrimination in positive and negative outcome allocations: Impact of stimulus valence, relative group status and relative group size. *Personality and Social Psychology Bulletin*, 22, 568–81.

Ouellette, J. A., & Wood, W. (1998). Habit and intention in everyday life: The multiple processes by which past behavior predicts future behavior. *Psychological Review*, 124, 54–74.

Paicheler, G. (1985). *Psychologie des influences sociales*. Paris: Delachaux & Niestlé.

Papousek, M., & Papousek, H. (1989). Forms and function of vocal matching in interactions between mothers and their precanonical infants. *First Language*, 9, 137–58.

Park, B., Judd, C. M., & Ryan, C. S. (1991). Social categorization and the representation of variability information. In W. Stroebe & M. Hewstone (Eds.), *European review of social psychology* (Vol. 2, pp. 211–45). Chichester: Wiley.

Park, B., Ryan, C. S., & Judd, C. M. (1992). Role of meaningful subgroups in explaining differences in perceived variability for ingroups and outgroups. *Journal of Personality and Social Psychology*, 63, 533–67.

Park, R. E. (1972). *The crowd and the public*. Chicago: University of Chicago Press.

Parker, G. A. (1974). Courtship persistence and female-guarding as male time investment strategies. *Behaviour*, 48, 157–84.

Parkes, C. M., Benjamin, B., & Fitzgerald, R. G. (1969). Broken heart: A statistical study of increased mortality among widowers. *British Medical Journal*, 1, 740–3.

Parkinson, B. (1997). Untangling the appraisal–emotion connection. *Personality and Social Psychology Review*, 1, 62–79.

Parkinson, B., & Manstead, A. S. R. (1993). Making sense of emotions in stories and social life. *Cognition and Emotion*, 7, 295–323.

Passer, M. W., Kelley, H. H., & Michela, J. L. (1978). Multidimensional scaling of the causes for negative interpersonal behavior. *Journal of Personality and Social Psychology*, 36, 951–62.

Patnoe, S. (1988). *A narrative history of experimental social psychology – The Lewin tradition*. New York: Springer Verlag.

Patterson, G. R., Littman, R. A., & Bricker, W. (1967). Assertive behavior in children: A step toward a theory of aggression. *Monographs of the Society for Research in Child Development*, 32, 5 (Serial No. 113).

Pemberton, M. J., Insko, C. A., & Schopler, J. (1996). Memory for and experience of differential distrust of individuals and groups. *Journal of Personality and Social Psychology*, 71, 953–66.

Pennebaker, J. W. (1989). Confession, inhibition, and disease. In L. Berkowitz (Ed.), *Advances in experimental social psychology* (Vol. 22, pp. 211–44). New York: Academic Press.

Pennebaker, J. W., Colder, M., & Sharp, L. K. (1990). Accelerating the coping process. *Journal of Personality and Social Psychology*, 58, 528–37.

Pennebaker, J. W., Kiecolt-Glaser, J., & Glaser, R. (1988). Disclosure of traumas and immune function: Health implications for psychotherapy. *Journal of Consulting and Clinical Psychology*, 56, 239–45.

Penner, L. A., & Finkelstein, M. A. (1998). Dispositional and structural determinants of volunteerism. *Journal of Personality and Social Psychology*, 74, 525–37.

Penner, L. A., Fritzsche, B. A., Craiger, J. P., & Freifeld, T. S. (1995). Measuring the prosocial personality. In J. Butcher & C. D. Spielberger (Eds.), *Advances in personality assessment* (Vol. 10, pp. 147–63). Hillsdale, NJ: Lawrence Erlbaum.

Pepitone, A. (1981). Lessons from the history of social psychology. *American Psychologist*, 36, 972–85.

Perret-Clermont, A.-N. (1980). *Social interaction and cognitive development in children*. London: Academic Press.

Personnaz, B. (1981). Study in social influence using the spectrometer method: Dynamics of the phenomena of conversion and covertness in perceptual responses. *European Journal of Social Psychology*, 11, 431–8.

Pessin, J. (1933). The comparative effects of social and mechanical stimulation on memorizing. *American Journal of Psychology*, 45, 263–70.

Peterson, C. (1980). Memory and the 'dispositional shift'. *Social Psychology Quarterly*, 43, 372–80.

Peterson, C., Maier, S. F., & Seligman, M. E. P. (1993). *Learned helplessness: A theory for the age of personal control*. Oxford: Oxford University Press.

Pettigrew, T. F. (1958). Personality and sociocultural factors in intergroup attitudes: A cross-national comparison. *Journal of Conflict Resolution*, 2, 29–42.

Pettigrew, T. F. (1971). *Racially separate or together?* New York: McGraw-Hill.

Pettigrew, T. F. (1986). The intergroup contact hypothesis reconsidered. In M. Hewstone & R. Brown (Eds.), *Contact and conflict in intergroup encounters* (pp. 169–95). Oxford: Blackwell.

Petty, R. E., & Brock, T. C. (1981). Thought disruption and persuasion: Assessing the validity of attitude change experiments. In R. E. Petty, T. M. Ostrom, & T. C. Brock (Eds.), *Cognitive responses in persuasion* (pp. 55–79). Hillsdale, NJ: Erlbaum.

Petty, R. E., & Cacioppo, J. T. (1981). *Attitudes and persuasion: Classic and contemporary approaches*. Dubuque, IA: Brown.

Petty, R. E., & Cacioppo, J. T. (1986a). *Communication and persuasion: Central and peripheral routes to attitude change*. New York: Springer.

Petty, R. E., & Cacioppo, J. T. (1986b). The elaboration likelihood model of persuasion. In L. Berkowitz (Ed.), *Advances in experimental social psychology* (Vol. 19, pp. 123–205). New York: Academic Press.

Petty, R. E., Cacioppo, J. T., & Goldman, R. (1981). Personal involvement as a determinant of argument-based persuasion. *Journal of Personality and Social Psychology*, 41, 847–55.

Petty, R. E., Haugtvedt, C. P., & Smith, S. M. (1995). Elaboration as a determinant of attitude strength: Creating attitudes that are persistent, resistant, and predictive of behavior. In R. E. Petty & J. A. Krosnick (Eds.), *Attitude strength: Antecedents and consequences* (pp. 93–130). Mahwah, NJ: Erlbaum.

Petty, R. E., & Krosnick, J. A. (Eds.). (1995). *Attitude strength: Antecedents and consequences*. Mahwah, NJ: Erlbaum.

Petty, R. E., Ostrom, T. M., & Brock, T. C. (Eds.). (1981). *Cognitive responses in persuasion*. Hillsdale, NJ: Erlbaum.

Petty, R. E., Priester, J. R., & Wegener, D. T. (1994). Cognitive processes in attitude change. In R. S. Wyer, Jr., & T. K. Srull (Eds.), *Handbook of social cognition* (2nd ed., Vol. 2, pp. 69–142). Hillsdale NJ: Erlbaum.

Petty, R. E., & Wegener, D. T. (1998a). Attitude change: Multiple roles for persuasion variables. In D. T. Gilbert, S. T. Fiske, & G. Lindzey (Eds.), *The handbook of social psychology* (4th ed., Vol. 2, pp. 323–90). New York: McGraw-Hill.

Petty, R. E., & Wegener, D. T. (1998b). Matching versus mismatching attitude functions: Implications for scrutiny of persuasive messages. *Personality and Social Psychology Bulletin*, 24, 227–40.

Petty, R. E., & Wegener, D. T. (1999). The elaboration likelihood model: Current status and controversies. In S. Chaiken & Y. Trope (Eds.), *Dual process theories in social psychology* (pp. 41–72). New York: Guilford Press.

Petty, R. E., Wells, G. L., & Brock, T. C. (1976). Distraction can enhance or reduce yielding to propaganda: Thought disruption versus effort justification. *Journal of Personality and Social Psychology*, 34, 874–84.

Piaget, J. (1928). *Judgement and reasoning in the child*. London: Routledge & Kegan Paul.

Piaget, J. (1932a). *The moral judgment of the child*. Harmondsworth: Penguin.

Piaget, J. (1932b). *The origin of intelligence in children*. New York: International University Press.

Piaget, J. (1973). *Main trends in psychology*. London: George Allen & Unwin.

Piaget, J., & Weil, A. (1951). The development in children of the idea of the homeland and of relations with other countries. *International Social Science Bulletin*, 3, 561–76.

Pierce, G. R., Sarason, B. R., & Sarason, I. G. (1990). Integrating social support perspectives: Working models, personal relationships, and situational factors. In S. Duck & R. C. Silver (Eds.), *Personal relationships and social support* (pp. 173–89). London: Sage.

Piliavin, J. A., & Callero, P. (1991). *Giving blood: The development of an altruistic identity*. Baltimore: Johns Hopkins University Press.

Pinker, S. (1997). *How the mind works*. New York & London: Allen Lane.

Plutchik, P. (1980). *Emotion: A psychobioevolutionary synthesis*. New York: Harper & Row.

Postmes, T., & Spears, R. (1998). Deindividuation and anti-normative behavior: A meta-analysis. *Psychological Bulletin*, 123, 1–21.

Pratkanis, A. R. (1989). The cognitive representation of attitudes. In A. R. Pratkanis, S. J. Breckler, & A. G. Greenwald (Eds.), *Attitude structure and function* (pp. 71–98). Hillsdale, NJ: Erlbaum.

Prentice-Dunn, S., & Rogers, R. W. (1983). Deindividuation in aggression. In R. G. Geen & E. I. Donnerstein (Eds.), *Aggression: Theoretical and empirical reviews* (Vol. 2, pp. 155–71). New York: Academic Press.

Prentice-Dunn, S., & Rogers, R. W. (1989). Deindividuation and the self-regulation of behavior. In P. B. Paulus (Ed.), *Psychology of group influence* (2nd ed., pp. 87–109). New York: Academic Press.

Price-Bonham, S., Wright, D. W., & Pittman, J. F. (1983). A frequent 'alternative' in the 1970s. In E. Macklin & R. H. Rubin (Eds.), *Contemporary families and alternative lifestyles* (pp. 125–46). Beverly Hills, CA: Sage.

Prins, K. S., Buunk, A. P., & VanYperen, N. W. (1992). Equity, normative disapproval and extra-marital sex. *Journal of Social and Personal Relationships*, 10, 39–53.

Prislin, R. (1996). Attitude stability and attitude strength: One is enough to make it stable. *European Journal of Social Psychology*, 26, 447–77.

Prochaska, J. O., DiClemente, C. C., & Norcross, J. C. (1992). In search of how people change: Applications to addictive behaviors. *American Psychologist*, 47, 1102–14.

Prochaska, J. O., Velicer, W. F., Guidagnoli, E., Rossi, J. S., & DiClemente, C. C. (1991). Patterns of change: Dynamic typology applied to smoking cessation. *Multivariate Behavioral Research*, 26, 83–107.

Pruitt, D. G. (1981). *Negotiation behavior*. New York: Academic Press.

Pruitt, D. G., & Carnevale, P. J. (1993). *Negotiation in social conflict*. London: Open University Press.

Pruitt, D. G., & Kimmel, M. J. (1977). Twenty years of experimental gaming: Critique, synthesis, and suggestions for the future. *Annual Review of Psychology*, 28, 363–92.

Pruitt, D. G., & Rubin, J. Z. (1986). *Social conflict: Escalation, stalemate, and settlement*. New York: Random House.

Pugh, M. D., & Wahrman, R. (1983). Neutralizing sexism in mixed-sex groups: Do women have to be better than men? *American Journal of Sociology*, 88, 746–62.

Puska, P., Nissinen, A., Tuomilehto, J., Salonen, J. T., Koskela, K., McAlister, A., Kottke, T. E., Maccoby, N., & Farquhar, J. W. (1985). The community-based strategy to prevent coronary heart disease: Conclusions from ten years of the North Karelia Project. *Annual Review of Public Health* (Vol. 6, pp. 147–94). Palo Alto, CA: Annual Reviews.

Quattrone, G. A. (1982). Overattribution and unit formation: When behavior engulfs the person. *Journal of Personality and Social Psychology*, 42, 593–607.

Quattrone, G. A., & Jones, E. E. (1980). The perception of variability within ingroups and outgroups. *Journal of Personality and Social Psychology*, 38, 141–52.

Rabbie, J. M. (1963). Differential preference for companionship under threat. *Journal of Abnormal and Social Psychology*, 67, 643–8.

Rabbie, J. M. (1982). Are groups more aggressive than individuals? 'Henri Tajfel lecture' presented at the Annual Conference of the Social Psycho-logy Section of the British Psychological Society, 24–6 September 1982.

Rabbie, J. M., & Horwitz, M. (1969). Arousal of ingroup–outgroup bias by a chance win or loss. *Journal of Personality and Social Psychology*, 13, 269–77.

Rabbie, J. M., & Horwitz, M. (1982). Conflict and aggression between individuals and groups. In H. Hiebsch, H. Brandstätter, & H. H. Kelley (Eds.), *Social psychology*. Revisited and edited version of selected papers presented at the XXII International Congress of Psychology, Leipzig, No. 8.

Rabbie, J. M., & Horwitz, M. (1988). Categories versus groups as explanatory concepts in intergroup relations. *European Journal of Social Psychology*, 18, 117–23.

Rabbie, J. M., & Lodewijkx, H. (1983). Aggression toward groups and individuals. Paper presented to the East–West Meeting of the European Association of Experimental Social Psychology, Varna, Bulgaria, 17–20 May 1983.

Rabbie, J. M., Schot, J. C., & Visser, L. (1989). Social identity theory: A conceptual and empirical critique from the perspective of a behavioural interaction model. *European Journal of Social Psychology*, 19, 171–202.

Rafaeli, A., & Sutton, R. I. (1987). Expression of emotion as part of the work role. *Academy of Management Review*, 12 (1), 23–37.

Rahe, R. H. (1968). Life change measurement as a predictor of illness. *Proceedings of the Royal Society of Medicine*, 61 (1), 124–6.

Reber, R., Winkielman, P., & Schwarz, N. (1998). Effects of perceptual fluency on affective judgments. *Psychological Science*, 9, 45–8.

Redican, W. K. (1982). An evolutionary perspective on human facial displays. In P. Ekman (Eds.), *Emotion in the human face* (2nd ed., pp. 212–80). New York: Cambridge University Press.

Reeder, G., & Brewer, M. (1979). A schematic model of dispositional attribution in interpersonal perception. *Psychological Review*, 86, 61–79.

Regalski, J. M, & Gaulin, S. J. C. (1993). Whom are Mexican infants said to resemble? Monitoring and fostering paternal confidence in the Yucatan. *Ethology and Sociobiology*, 14, 97–113.

Regan, D. T., & Fazio, R. H. (1977). On the consistency between attitudes and behavior: Look to the method of attitude formation. *Journal of Experimental Social Psychology*, 13, 28–45.

Regan, D. T., Straus, E., & Fazio, R. (1974). Liking and the attribution process. *Journal of Experimental Social Psychology*, 10, 385–97.

Reicher, S. D., Spears, R., & Postmes, T. (1995). A social identity model of deindividuation phenomena. In W. Stroebe & M. Hewstone (Eds.), *European review of social psychology* (Vol. 6, pp. 161–98). Chichester: Wiley.

Reis, H. T., & Patrick, B. C. (1996). Attachment and intimacy: Component processes. In E. T. Higgins & A. W. Kruglanski (Eds.), *Social psychology: Handbook of basic principles* (pp. 523–63). New York: Guilford Press.

Reis, H. T., Senchak, M., & Solomon, B. (1985). Sex differences in the intimacy of social interaction: Further examination of potential explanations. *Journal of Social and Personality Psychology*, 48, 1204–17.

Reisenzein, R. (1983). The Schachter theory of emotion: Two decades later. *Psychological Bulletin*, 94, 239–64.

Reisenzein, R. & Hofmann, T. (1993). Discriminating emotions from appraisal-relevant situational information: Baseline data for structural models of cognitive appraisals. *Cognition and Emotion*, 7, 271–94.

Resnick, L. B., Levine, J. M., & Teasley, S. D. (Eds.). (1991). *Perspectives on socially shared cognition*. Washington, DC: American Psychological Association.

Reyes, R. M., Thompson, W. C., & Bower, G. H. (1980). Judgmental biases resulting from differing availabilities of arguments. *Journal of Personality and Social Psychology*, 39, 2–12.

Rhodes, S. R., & Steers, R. M. (1990). *Managing employee absenteeism*. Reading, MA: Addison-Wesley.

Rholes, W. S., & Pryor, J. B. (1982). Cognitive accessibility and causal attributions. *Personality and Social Psychology Bulletin*, 8, 719–27.

Ricci-Bitti, P., Brighetti, G., Garotti, P. L., & Boggi Cavallo, P. (1989). Is contempt expressed by pan-cultural facial movements? In J. P. Forgas

& J. M. Innes (Eds.), *Recent advances in social psychology: An international perspective* (pp. 329–39). Amsterdam: Elsevier.

Ridgeway, C. L. (1978). Conformity, group-oriented motivation, and status attainment in small groups. *Social Psychology*, 41, 175–88.

Ridley, M. (1994). *The red queen: Sex and the evolution of human nature*. Harmondsworth: Penguin.

Rijsman, J. B., Zoetebier, J. H. T., Ginther, A. J. F., & Doise, W. (1980). Sociocognitief conflict en cognitieve ontwikkeling. *Pedagogische Studien*, 57, 125–33.

Rijt-Plooj, H. H. C. van de, & Plooj, F. X. (1993). Distinct periods of mother–infant conflict in normal development: Sources of progress and germs of pathology. *Journal of Child Psychology and Psychiatry*, 34, 229–45.

Rimé, B., Finkenauer, C., Luminet, O., Zech, E., & Philippot, P. (1998). Social sharing of emotion: New evidence and new questions. In W. Stroebe and M. Hewstone (Eds.), *European Review of Social Psychology* (Vol. 9, pp. 145–89). Chichester: Wiley.

Rippetoe, P. A., & Rogers, R. W. (1987). Effects of components of protection-motivation theory on adaptive and maladaptive coping with a health threat. *Journal of Personality and Social Psychology*, 52, 596–604.

Robins, R. W., Spranca, M. D., & Mendelsohn, G. A. (1996). The actor–observer effect revisited: Effects of individual differences and repeated social interactions on actor and observer attributions. *Journal of Personality and Social Psychology*, 71, 375–89.

Robinson, E. J., & Whittaker, S. J. (1986). Learning about verbal referential communication in the early school years. In K. Durkin (Ed.), *Language development in the school years* (pp. 155–71). London: Croom Helm.

Robinson, J. P., Shaver, P. R., & Wrightsman, L. S. (Eds.). (1991). *Measures of personality and social psychological attitudes*. San Diego, CA: Academic Press.

Rochat, F., & Modigliani, A. (1995). The ordinary quality of resistance: From Milgram's laboratory to the village of Le Chambon. *Journal of Social Issues*, 51, 195–210.

Roethlisberger, F. J., & Dickson, J. (1939). *Management and the worker*. Cambridge, MA: Harvard University Press.

Rogers, R. W. (1975). A protection motivation theory of fear appeals and attitude change. *Journal of Psychology*, 91, 93–114.

Rogers, R. W. (1983). Cognitive and physiological processes in fear appeals and attitude change: A revised theory of protection motivation. In J. T. Cacioppo & R. E. Petty (Eds.), *Social psychophysiology: A source-book* (pp. 153–76). New York: Guilford Press.

Rogers, R. W. (1985). Attitude change and information integration in fear appeals. *Psychological Reports*, 56, 179–82.

Rogers, R. W., & Mewborn, C. R. (1976). Fear appeals and attitude change: Effects of a threat's noxiousness, probability of occurrence, and the efficacy of coping responses. *Journal of Personality and Social Psychology*, 34, 54–61.

Rogoff, B. (1990). *Apprenticeship in thinking: Cognitive development in a social context*. New York: Oxford University Press.

Rosch, E. (1978). Principles of categorization. In E. Rosch & B. B. Lloyd (Eds.), *Cognition and categorization* (pp. 27–48). Hillsdale, NJ: Erlbaum.

Roseman, I. J., Antoniou, A. A., & Jose, P. E. (1996). Appraisal determinants of emotions: Constructing a more accurate and comprehensive theory. *Cognition and Emotion*, 10, 241–77.

Roseman, I. J., Spindel, M. S., & Jose, P. E. (1990). Appraisals of emotion-eliciting events: Testing a theory of discrete emotions. *Journal of Personality and Social Psychology*, 59, 899–915.

Rosenbaum, M. E. (1986). The repulsion hypothesis: On the nondevelopment of relationships. *Journal of Personality and Social Psychology*, 51, 1156–66.

Rosenberg, M. J. (1960). An analysis of affective-cognitive consistency. In M. J. Rosenberg, C. I. Hovland, W. J. McGuire, R. P. Abelson, & J. W. Brehm (Eds.), *Attitude organization and change* (pp. 15–64). New Haven, CT: Yale University Press.

Rosenberg, M. J. (1968). Hedonism, inauthenticity, and other goads toward expansion of a consistency theory. In R. P. Abelson, E. Aronson, W. J. McGuire, T. M. Newcomb, M. J. Rosenberg, & P. H. Tannenbaum (Eds.), *Theories of cognitive consistency: A sourcebook* (pp. 73–111). Chicago: Rand McNally.

Rosenberg, M. J., & Hovland, C. I. (1960). Cognitive, affective, and behavioral components of attitudes. In M. J. Rosenberg, C. I. Hovland, W. J. McGuire, R. P. Abelson, & J. W. Brehm (Eds.), *Attitude organization and change* (pp. 1–14). New Haven, CT: Yale University Press.

Rosenberg, M., & Simmons, R. G. (1972). *Black and white self-esteem: The urban school child*. Washington, DC: American Sociological Association.

Rosenhan, D. L., Underwood, B., & Moore, B. (1974). Affect moderates self-gratification and altruism. *Journal of Personality and Social Psychology*, 30, 546–52.

Rosenstock, I. M., Strecher, V. J., & Becker, M. H. (1988). Social learning theory and the health belief model. *Health Education Quarterly*, 15, 175–83.

Rosenthal, R. (1966). *Experimenter effects in behavioral research*. New York: Appleton-Century-Crofts.

Rosenthal, R., & Rosnow, R. L. (1975). *The volunteer subject*. New York: Wiley.

Ross, E. A. (1908). *Social psychology*. New York: Macmillan.

Ross, L. (1977). The intuitive psychologist and his shortcomings: Distortions in the attribution process. In L. Berkowitz (Ed.), *Advances in experimental social psychology* (Vol. 10, pp. 173–220). New York: Academic Press.

Ross, L., Amabile, T. M., & Steinmetz, J. L. (1977). Social roles, social control and biases in social-perception processes. *Journal of Personality and Social Psychology*, 35, 485–94.

Ross, M., & Fletcher, G. J. O. (1985). Attribution and social perception. In G. Lindzey & E. Aronson (Eds.), *Handbook of social psychology* (3rd ed., Vol. 2, pp. 73–122). New York: Random House.

Rosse, J. G., & Miller, H. E. (1984). Relationship between absenteeism and other employee behaviors. In P. S. Goodman & R. S. Atkin (Eds.), *Absenteeism* (pp. 194–228). San Francisco: Jossey-Bass.

Roth, S., & Cohen, L. J. (1986). Approach, avoidance, and coping with stress. *American Psychologist*, 41, 813–19.

Rothbart, M., & Lewis, S. (1988). Inferring category attributes from exemplar attributes: Geometric shapes and social categories. *Journal of Personality and Social Psychology*, 55, 861–72.

Rothbart, M., & Park, B. (1986). On the confirmability and disconfirmability of trait concepts. *Journal of Personality and Social Psychology*, 50, 131–42.

Rotter, J. B. (1966). Generalized expectancies of internal versus external control of reinforcement. *Psychological Monographs*, 80, whole No. 609.

Ruberman, W., Weinblatt, E., Goldberg, J. D., & Chaudhary, B. S. (1984). Psychosocial influences on mortality after myocardial infarction. *New England Journal of Medicine*, 311, 552–9.

Rubin, M., & Hewstone, M. (1998). Social identity theory's self-esteem hypothesis: A review and suggestions for clarification. *Personality and Social Psychology Review*, 2, 40–62.

Ruble, D. N., Fleming, A. S., Hackel, L. S., Stangor, C. (1988). Changes in the marital relationship during the transition to first time motherhood: Effects of violated expectations concerning division of household labor. *Journal of Personality & Social Psychology*, 55, 78–87.

Rule, B. G., Dyck, R. J., & Nesdale, A. R. (1978). Arbitrariness of frustration: Inhibition or instigation effects in aggression. *European Journal of Social Psychology*, 8, 237–44.

Rule, B. G., & Ferguson, T. J. (1984). The relation among attribution, moral evaluation, anger, and aggression in children and adults. In A. Mummendey (Ed.), *Social psycho-logy of aggression: From individual behavior to social interaction* (pp. 143–55). New York: Springer.

Rule, B. G., & Nesdale, A. R. (1976). Emotional arousal and aggressive behavior. *Psychological Bulletin*, 83, 851–63.

Runciman, W. G. (1966). *Relative deprivation and social justice*. London: Routledge & Kegan Paul.

Rusbult, C. E. (1983). A longitudinal test of the investment model: The development (and deterioration) of satisfaction and commitment in heterosexual involvements. *Journal of Personality and Social Psychology*, 45, 101–17.

Rusbult, C. E., & Buunk, A. P. (1993). Commitment processes in close relationships: An interdependence analysis. *Journal of Social and Personal Relationships*, 10, 175–204.

Rusbult, C. E., & Farrell, D. (1983). A longitudinal test of the investment model: The impact on job satisfaction, job commitment, and turnover of variations in rewards, costs, alternatives, and investments. *Journal of Applied Psychology*, 68, 429–38.

Rusbult, C. E., & Martz, J. M. (1995). Remaining in an abusive relationship: An investment model analysis of nonvoluntary dependence. *Personality and Social Psychology Bulletin*, 21, 558–71.

Rusbult, C. E., & Van Lange, P. A. M. (1996). Interdependence processes. In E. T. Higgins & A. W. Kruglanski (Eds.), *Social psychology: Handbook of basic principles* (pp. 564–96). New York: Guilford Press.

Rusbult, C. E., Verrette, J., Whitney, G. A., Slovik, L. F., & Lipkus, I. (1991). Accommodation processes in close relationships: Theory and preliminary empirical evidence. *Journal of Personality and Social Psychology*, 60, 53–78.

Rushton, J. P. (1980). *Altruism, socialization, and society*. Englewood Cliffs, NJ: Prentice-Hall.

Russell, J. A. (1980). A circumplex model of affect. *Journal of Personality and Social Psychology*, 39, 1161–78.

Russell, J. A. (1983). Pancultural aspects of the human conceptual organization of emotions. *Journal of Personality and Social Psychology*, 45, 1281–8.

Rutland, A. (1999). The development of national prejudice, in-group favouritism and self-stereotypes in British children. *British Journal of Social Psychology*, 38, 55–70.

Ryan, A. M., Gheen, M. H., & Midgley, C. (1998). Why do some students avoid asking for help? *Journal of Educational Psychology*, 90, 528–35.

Ryan, A. M., & Pintrich, P. R. (1997). 'Should I ask for help?' The role of motivation and attitudes in adolescents' help seeking in math class. *Journal of Educational Psychology*, 89, 329–41.

Ryen, A. H., & Kahn, A. (1975). Effects of intergroup orientation on group attitudes and proxemic behaviour. *Journal of Personality and Social Psychology*, 31, 302–10.

Sachdev, I., & Bourhis, R. (1985). Social categorization and power differentials in group relations. *European Journal of Social Psychology*, 15, 415–34.

Sachdev, I., & Bourhis, R. (1987). Status differentials and intergroup behaviour. *European Journal of Social Psychology*, 17, 277–93.

Sadalla, E. K., Kenrick, D. T., & Vershure, B. (1987). Dominance and interpersonal attraction. *Journal of Personality and Social Psychology*, 52, 730–8.

Sadler, O., & Tesser, A. (1973). Some effects of salience and time upon interpersonal hostility and attraction during social isolation. *Sociometry*, 36, 99–112.

Saegert, S., Swap, W., & Zajonc, R. (1973). Exposure, context and interpersonal attraction. *Journal of Personality and Social Psychology*, 25, 234–42.

Salovey, P., & Mayer, J. D. (1990). Emotional intelligence. *Imagination, Cognition, and Personality*, 9, 185–211.

Salovey, P., Rothman, A. J., & Rodin, J. (1998). Health behavior. In D. T. Gilbert, S. T. Fiske, & G. Lindzey (Eds.), *The handbook of social psychology* (4th ed., Vol. 2, pp. 633–83). New York: McGraw-Hill.

Sampson, E. E. (1977). Psychology and the American ideal. *Journal of Personality and Social Psychology*, 35, 767–82.

Sampson, E. E. (1993). *Celebrating the other. A dialogic account of human nature*. New York: Harvester/Wheatsheaf.

Samuelson, C. D. (1993). A multiattribute evaluation approach to structural change in resource dilemmas. *Organizational Behavior and Human Decision Processes*, 55, 298–324.

Samuelson, C. D., Messick, D. M., Rutte, C. G., & Wilke, H. A. M. (1984). Individual and structural solutions to resource dilemmas in two countries. *Journal of Personality and Social Psychology*, 47, 94–104.

Sanders, G. S. (1981). Driven by distraction: An integrative review of social facilitation theory and research. *Journal of Experimental Social Psychology*, 13, 303–14.

Sanders, G. S., & Baron, R. S. (1977). Is social comparison irrelevant for producing choice shifts? *Journal of Experimental Social Psychology*, 13, 303–14.

Sanders, G. S., Baron, R. S., & Moore, D. L. (1978). Distraction and social comparison as mediators of social facilitation effects. *Journal of Experimental Social Psychology*, 14, 291–303.

Sanna, L. J. (1992). Self-efficacy theory: Implications for social facilitation and social loafing. *Journal of Personality and Social Psychology*, 62, 774–86.

Sanna, L. J., & Shotland, R. L. (1990). Valence of anticipated evaluation and social facilitation. *Journal of Experimental Social Psychology*, 26, 82–92.

Sarason, I. G., & Sarason, B. R. (1986). Experimentally provided social support. *Journal of Personality and Social Psychology*, 50, 1222–5.

Sasfy, J., & Okun, M. (1974). Form of evaluation and audience expertness as joint determinants of audience effects. *Journal of Experimental Social Psychology*, 10, 461–7.

Saxon, T. F. (1997). A longitudinal study of early mother–infant interaction and later language competence. *First Language*, 17, 271–81.

Schaap, C., Buunk, B., & Kerkstra, A. (1988). Marital conflict resolution. In P. Noller & M. A. Fitzpatrick (Eds.), *Perspectives on marital interaction* (pp. 203–44). Clevedon/Philadelphia: Multilingual Matters.

Schachter, S. (1951). Deviation, rejection and communication. *Journal of Abnormal and Social Psychology*, 46, 190–207.

Schachter, S. (1959). *The psychology of affiliation*. Palo Alto, CA: Stanford University Press.

Schachter, S. (1964). The interaction of cognitive and physiological determinants of emotional state. In L. Berkowitz (Ed.), *Advances in experimental social psychology* (Vol. 1). New York: Academic Press.

Schachter, S. (1970). The assumption of identity and peripheralist-centralist controversies in motivation and emotion. In M. B. Arnold (Ed.), *Feelings and emotions: The Loyola symposium* (pp. 111–21). New York: Academic Press.

Schachter, S., Nuttin, J., De Monchaux, C., Maucorps, P. H., Osmer, D., Duijker, H., Rommetveit, R., & Israel, J. (1954). Cross-cultural experiments on threat and rejection. *Human Relations*, 7, 403–39.

Schachter, S., & Singer, J. E. (1962). Cognitive, social and physiological determinants of emotional states. *Psychological Review*, 69, 379–99.

Schäfer, M. (1997). Verschiedenartige Perspektiven von Bullying [Different perspectives on bullying]. *Empirische Pädagogik*, 11, 369–83.

Schaffer, H. R. (1996). *Social development*. Oxford: Blackwell.

Schaller, M. (1992). In-group favoritism and statistical reasoning in social inference: Implications for formation and maintenance of group stereotypes. *Journal of Personality and Social Psychology*, 63, 61–74.

Scheier, M. F., & Carver, C. S. (1985). Optimism, coping, and health: Assessment and implications of generalized outcome expectancies. *Health Psychology*, 4, 219–47.

Scheier, M. F., Carver, C. S., & Bridges, M. W. (1994). Distinguishing optimism from neuroticism (and trait anxiety, self-mastery, and self-esteem): A reevaluation of the life orientation test. *Journal of Personality and Social Psychology*, 67, 1063–78.

Scheier, M. F., Matthews, K. A., Owens, J., Magovern, G. J., Sr., Lefebvre, R. C., Abbott, R. A., & Carver, C. S. (1989). Dispositional optimism and recovery from coronary artery bypass surgery: The beneficial effects on physical and psychological well-being. *Journal of Personality and Social Psychology*, 57, 1024–40.

Scheier, M. F., Weintraub, J. K., & Carver, C. S. (1986). Coping with stress: Divergent strategies of optimists and pessimists. *Journal of Personality and Social Psychology*, 51, 1257–64.

Schelling, T. C. (1960). *The strategy of conflict*. Cambridge, MA: Harvard University Press.

Scherer, K. R. (1984a). Emotion as a multicomponent process: A model and some cross-cultural data. In P. Shaver (Ed.), *Review of personality and social psychology* (Vol. 5, pp. 37–63). Beverly Hills, CA: Sage.

Scherer, K. R. (1984b). On the nature and function of emotion: A component process approach. In K. R. Scherer & P. Ekman (Eds.), *Approaches to emotion* (pp. 293–318). Hillsdale, NJ: Erlbaum.

Scherer, K. R. (1985). Vocal affect signalling: A comparative approach. In J. Rosenblatt, C. Beer, M. Busnel, & P. J. B. Slater (Eds.), *Advances in the study of behaviour* (pp. 189–244). New York: Academic Press.

Scherer, K. R. (1986). Vocal affect expression: A review and a model for future research. *Psychological Bulletin*, 99, 143–65.

Scherer, K. R. (1992a). Social psychology evolving. A progress report. In M. Dierkes & B. Bievert (Eds.), *European social science in transition. Assessment and outlook* (pp. 178–243). Frankfurt: Campus.

Scherer, K. R. (1992b). What does facial expression express? In K. Strongman (Ed.), *International review of studies on emotion* (Vol. 2, pp. 139–65). Chichester: Wiley.

Scherer, K. R. (1993a). Neuroscience projections to current debates in emotion psychology. *Cognition and Emotion*, 7, 1–41.

Scherer, K. R. (1993b). Studying the emotion-antecedent appraisal process: An expert system approach. *Cognition and Emotion*, 7, 325–55.

Scherer, K. R. (1993c). Two faces of social psychology: European and North-American perspectives. *Social Science Information*, 32, 515–52.

Scherer, K. R. (1994). Affect bursts. In S. van Goozen, N. E. van de Poll, & J. A. Sergeant (Eds.), *Emotions: Essays on emotion theory* (pp. 161–96). Hillsdale, NJ: Erlbaum.

Scherer, K. R. (1997a). Profiles of emotion-antecedent appraisal: Testing theoretical predictions across cultures. *Cognition and Emotion*, 11, 113–50.

Scherer, K. R. (1997b). The role of culture in emotion-antecedent appraisal. *Journal of Personality and Social Psychology*, 73, 902–22.

Scherer, K. R. (1999). Appraisal theories. In T. Dalgleish & M. Power (Eds.), *Handbook of cognition and emotion* (pp. 637–63). Chichester: Wiley.

Scherer, K. R., Banse, R., & Wallbott, H. G. (in press). Emotion inferences from vocal expression correlate across languages and cultures. *Journal of Cross-cultural Psychology*.

Scherer, K. R., & Ceschi, G. (1997). Lost luggage emotion: A field study of emotion-antecedent appraisal. *Motivation and Emotion*, 21, 211–35.

Scherer, K. R., Schorr, A., & Johnstone, I. T. (2000). *Appraisal processes in emotion: Theory, research, application*. New York: Oxford University Press.

Scherer, K. R., & Wallbott, H. G. (1994). Evidence for universality and cultural variation of differential emotion response patterning. *Journal of Personality and Social Psychology*, 66, 310–28.

Scherer, K. R., Wallbott, H. G., & Summerfield, A. B. (Eds.). (1986). *Experiencing emotion: A crosscultural study*. Cambridge and New York: Cambridge University Press.

Schlenker, B. R. (1974). Social psychology and science. *Journal of Personality and Social Psychology*, 29, 1–15.

Schlosberg, H. A. (1954). Three dimensions of emotion. *Psychological Review*, 61, 81–8.

Schopler, J., & Bateson, N. (1965). The power of dependence. *Journal of Personality and Social Psychology*, 2, 247–54.

Schopler, J., & Insko, C. A. (1992). The discontinuity effect in interpersonal and intergroup relations: Generality and mediation. In W. Stroebe & M. Hewstone (Eds.), *European review of social psychology* (Vol. 3, pp. 121–51). Chichester: Wiley.

Schreurs, K. S., & Buunk, B. P. (1996). Closeness, autonomy, equity, and relationship satisfaction in Dutch lesbian couples. *Psychology of Women Quarterly*, 20, 577–92.

Schuster, B. (1996). Rejection, exclusion, and harassment at work and in schools. *European Psychologist*, 1, 278–92.

Schuster, B., Rudolph, U., & Försterling, F. (1998). Attributions or covariation information: What determines behavioural reaction decisions? *Personality and Social Psychology Bulletin*, 24, 838–54.

Schwartz, S. H. (1977). Normative influences on altruism. In L. Berkowitz (Ed.), *Advances in experimental social psychology* (Vol. 10, pp. 221–79). New York: Academic Press.

Schwartz, S. H. (1992). Universals in the content and structure of values: Theoretical advances and empirical tests in 20 countries. In M. P. Zanna (Ed.), *Advances in experimental social psychology* (Vol. 25, pp. 1–65). San Diego, CA: Academic Press.

Schwartz, S. H. (1994). Are there universal aspects in the structure and contents of human values? *Journal of Social Issues*, 50 (4), 19–45.

Schwartz, S. H., & Gottlieb, A. (1976). Bystander reactions to a violent theft: Crime in Jerusalem. *Journal of Personality and Social Psychology*, 34, 1188–99.

Schwartz, S. H., & Howard, J. A. (1981). A normative decision-making model of altruism. In J. P. Rushton & R. M. Sorrentino (Eds.), *Altruism and helping behavior* (pp. 189–211). Hillsdale, NJ: Lawrence Erlbaum.

Schwarz, N. (1990a). Assessing frequency reports of mundane behaviors: Contributions of cognitive psychology to questionnaire construction. In C. Hendrick & M. S. Clark (Eds.), *Research methods in personality and social psychology* (*Review of Personality and Social Psychology*, Vol. 11, pp. 98–119). Newbury Park, CA: Sage.

Schwarz, N. (1990b). Feelings as information. Informational and motivational functions of affective states. In E. T. Higgins & R. M. Sorrentino (Eds.), *Handbook of motivation and cognition: Foundations of social behavior* (Vol. 2, pp. 527–61). New York: Guilford Press.

Schwarz, N., & Bless, H. (1992). Constructing reality and its alternatives: An inclusion-exclusion model of assimilation and contrast effects in social judgment. In L. L. Martin & A. Tesser (Eds.), *The construction of social judgment* (pp. 217–45). Hillsdale, NJ: Erlbaum.

Schwarz, N., Bless, H., & Bohner, G. (1991). Mood and persuasion: Affective states influence the processing of persuasive communications. In M. Zanna (Ed.), *Advances in experimental social psychology* (Vol. 24, pp. 161–97). New York: Academic Press.

Schwarz, N., Bless, H., Strack, F., Klumpp, G., Rittenauer-Schatka, H., & Simons, A. (1991). Ease of retrieval as information: Another look at the availability heuristic. *Journal of Personality and Social Psychology*, 61, 195–202.

Schwarz, N., & Bohner, G. (in press). The construction of attitudes. In A. Tesser & N. Schwarz (Eds.), *Blackwell handbook of social psychology: Intrapersonal processes* (pp. 489–512). Oxford: Blackwell.

Schwarz, N., & Clore, G. L. (1983). Mood, misattribution and judgments of well-being: Informative and directive functions of affective states. *Journal of Personality and Social Psychology*, 45, 513–23.

Schwarz, N., & Clore, G. L. (1988). How do I feel about it? The informative function of affective states. In K. Fiedler & J. P. Forgas (Eds.), *Affect, cognition, and social behavior* (pp. 44–62). Toronto: Hogrefe.

Schwarz, N., Groves, R. M., & Schuman, H. (1998). Survey methods. In D. T. Gilbert, S. T. Fiske, & G. Lindzey (Eds.), *The handbook of social psychology* (4th ed., Vol. 1, pp. 143–79). New York: McGraw-Hill.

Schwarzer, R. (1992). Self-efficacy in the adoption and maintenance of health behaviors: Theoretical approaches and a new model. In R. Schwarzer (Ed.), *Self-efficacy: Thought control of action* (pp. 217–42). Washington, DC: Hemisphere.

Schwarzer, R., & Leppin, A. (1989). Social support and health: A meta-analysis. *Psychology and Health*, 3, 1–15.

Schwarzer, R., & Leppin, A. (1992). Social support and mental health: A conceptual and empirical overview. In L. Montada, S. H. Filipp, & M. J. Lerner (Eds.), *Life crises and experiences of loss in adulthood* (pp. 435–58). Hillsdale, NJ: Lawrence Erlbaum.

Secord, P. F. (1959). Stereotyping and favorableness in the perception of Negro faces. *Journal of Abnormal and Social Psychology*, 59, 309–15.

Sedikides, C., & Ostrom, T. M. (1988). Are person categories used when organizing information about unfamiliar sets of persons? *Social Cognition*, 6, 252–67.

Self, C. A., & Rogers, R. W. (1990). Coping with threats to health. Effects of persuasive appeals on depressed, normal, and antisocial personalities. *Journal of Behavioral Medicine*, 13, 343–57.

Selye, H. (1956). *The stress of life*. New York: McGraw-Hill.

Semin, G. R. (1986). On the relationship between representations of theories in psychology and ordinary language. In W. Doise and S. Moscovici (Eds.), *Current issues in European social psychology* (Vol. 2, pp. 307–48). Cambridge: Cambridge University Press.

Semin, G. R., & Fiedler, K. (1988). The cognitive functions of linguistic categories in describing persons: Social cognition and language. *Journal of Personality and Social Psychology*, 54, 558–67.

Semin, G. R., & Fiedler, K. (1991). The linguistic category model, its bases, applications, and range. *European Review of Social Psychology*, 2, 1–30.

Semin, G. R., & Fiedler, K. (Eds.). (1992). *Language, interaction and social cognition*. Newbury Park, CA: Sage.

Semin, G. R., & Manstead, A. S. R. (1979). Social psychology: Social or psychological? *British Journal of Social and Clinical Psychology*, 18, 191–202.

Semin, G. R., & Manstead, A. S. R. (1983). *The accountability of conduct: A social psychological analysis*. London: Academic Press.

Semin, G. R., & Papadopoulou, K. (1990). The acquisition of reflexive social emotions: The transmission and reproduction of social control through joint action. In G. Duveen and B. Lloyd (Eds.), *Social representations and the development of knowledge* (pp. 107–25). Cambridge: Cambridge University Press.

Semin, G. R., & Strack, F. (1980). The plausibility of the implausible: A critique of Snyder and Swann (1978). *European Journal of Social Psychology*, 10, 379–88.

Senchak, M., & Leonard, K. E. (1993). The role of spouses' depression and anger in the attribution–marital satisfaction relation. *Cognitive Therapy and Research*, 17, 397–409.

Sergios, P., & Cody, J. (1985/86). Importance of physical attractiveness and social assertiveness skills in male homosexual dating behavior and partner selection. *Journal of Homsexuality*, 12, 71–84.

Shadish, W. R., & Fuller, S. (Eds.). (1994). *The social psychology of science*. New York: Guilford Press.

Shamir, B., House, R. J., & Arthur, M. B. (1993). The motivational effects of charismatic leadership: A self-concept based theory. *Organization Science*, 4, 577–94.

Shanab, M. E., & Yahya, K. A. (1978). A cross-cultural study of obedience. *Bulletin of the Psychonomic Society*, 11, 267–9.

Shaver, K. G. (1985). *The attribution of blame: Causality, responsibility, and blameworthiness*. New York: Springer Verlag.

Shaver, P., Hazan, C., & Bradshaw, D. (1988). Love as attachment: The integration of three behavioral systems. In R. J. Sternberg and M. Barnes (Eds.), *The anatomy of love* (pp. 68–99). New Haven, CT: Yale University Press.

Shaver, P., & Klinnert, M. (1982). Schachter's theories of affiliation and emotion: Implications of developmental research. In L. Wheeler (Ed.), *Review of personality and social psychology* (Vol. 3, pp. 37–72). Beverly Hills, CA: Sage.

Shaver, P., & Rubinstein, C. (1980). Childhood attachment experience and adult loneliness. *Review of Personality and Social Psychology*, 1, 42–73.

Shavitt, S. (1989). Operationalizing functional theories of attitude. In A. R. Pratkanis, S. J. Breckler, & A. G. Greenwald (Eds.), *Attitude structure and function* (pp. 311–37). Hillsdale, NJ: Erlbaum.

Shavitt, S., & Fazio, R. H. (1991). Effects of attribute salience on the consistency between attitudes and behavior predictions. *Personality and Social Psychology Bulletin*, 17, 507–16.

Shaw, M. E. (1964). Communication networks. In L. Berkowitz (Ed.), *Advances in experimental social psychology* (Vol. 1, pp. 111–47). New York: Academic Press.

Sheeran, P., & Abraham, C. (1996). The health belief model. In M. Conner & P. Norman (Eds.), *Predicting health behaviour* (pp. 23–61). Buckingham: Open University Press.

Sheeran, P., Abraham, C., & Orbell, S. (1999). Psychosocial correlates of heterosexual condom use: A meta-analysis. *Psychological Bulletin*, 125, 90–132.

Sheppard, B. H. (1984). Third party conflict intervention: A procedural framework. In B. Staw and L. Cummings (Eds.), *Research in organizational behavior* (Vol. 6, pp. 141–90). Greenwich, CT: JAI Press.

Sheppard, B. H., Hartwick, J., & Warshaw, P. R. (1988). The theory of reasoned action: A meta-analysis of past research with recommendations for modifications and future research. *Journal of Consumer Research*, 15, 325–43.

Sherif, M. (1935). A study of some social factors in perception. *Archives of Psychology*, No. 187.

Sherif, M. (1936). *The psychology of social norms*. New York: Harper.

Sherif, M. (1948). *An outline of social psychology*. New York: Harper & Brothers.

Sherif, M. (1966). *Group conflict and co-operation: Their social psychology*. London: Routledge & Kegan Paul.

Sherif, M., Harvey, O. J., White, B. J., Hood, W. R., & Sherif, C. W. (1961). *Intergroup conflict and cooperation: The robber's cave experiment*. Norman, OK: University of Oklahoma Press.

Sherif, M., & Hovland, C. I. (1961). *Assimilation and contrast effects in communication and attitude change*. New Haven, CT: Yale University Press.

Sherif, M., & Sherif, C. W. (1953). *Groups in harmony and tension: An integration of studies on intergroup relations*. New York: Octagon.

Sherif, M., White, B. J., & Harvey, O. J. (1955). Status in experimentally produced groups. *American Journal of Sociology*, 60, 370–9.

Sherrod, D. (1989). The influence of gender on same-sex friendships. In C. Hendrick (Ed.), *Review of personality and social psychology: Close relationships* (pp. 164–86). Newbury Park, CA: Sage.

Shiffrin, R. M., & Schneider, W. (1977). Controlled and automatic human information processing. II: Perceptual learning, automatic attending, and a general theory. *Psychological Review*, 84, 127–90.

Shiffrin, R. M., & Schneider, W. (1984). Automatic and controlled processing revisited. *Psychological Review*, 91, 269–76.

Shornstein, S. L. (1997). *Domestic violence and health care*. Thousand Oaks, CA: Sage.

Shultz, T. R., & Schleifer, M. (1983). Towards a refinement of attribution concepts. In J. Jaspars, F. D. Fincham, & M. Hewstone (Eds.), *Attribution theory and research: Conceptual, development, and social dimensions* (pp. 37–62). New York: Academic Press.

Shweder, R. A. (1975). How relevant is an individual difference theory of personality? *Journal of Personality*, 43, 455–84.

Shweder, R. A. (1993). The cultural psychology of the emotions. In M. Lewis & J. M. Haviland (Eds.), *Handbook of emotions* (pp. 417–31). New York: Guilford Press.

Siegel, A. E., & Siegel, S. (1957). Reference groups, membership groups, and attitude change. *Journal of Abnormal and Social Psychology*, 55, 360–4.

Sighele, S. (1891). *La folla delinquente*. Torino: Fratelli Bocca.

Silverberg, S. B., Vazsonyi, A. T., Schlegel, A. E., & Schmidt, S. (1998). Adolescent apprentices in Germany: Adult attachment, job expectations, and delinquency attitudes. *Journal of Adolescent Research*, 13, 254–71.

Simmel, G. (1908). *Soziologie – Untersuchungen über die Formen der Vergesellschaftung*. Leipzig: Duncker & Humblot.

Simon, B. (1992a). The perception of ingroup and outgroup homogeneity: Re-introducing the intergroup context. In W. Stroebe & M. Hewstone (Eds.), *European review of social psychology* (Vol. 3, pp. 1–30). Chichester: Wiley.

Simon, B. (1992b). Intragroup differentiation in terms of ingroup and outgroup attributes. *European Journal of Social Psychology*, 22, 407–13.

Simon, B., & Brown, R. J. (1987). Perceived intragroup homogeneity in minority–majority contexts. *Journal of Personality and Social Psychology*, 53, 703–11.

Simpson, J. A., & Kenrick, D. T. (Eds.). (1997). *Evolutionary social psychology*. Mahwah, NJ: Erlbaum.

Simpson, J. A., Rholes, W. S., & Nelligan, J. S. (1992). Support seeking and support giving within couples in an anxiety-provoking situation: The role of attachment styles. *Journal of Personality and Social Psychology*, 62, 434–46.

Sinclair, R. C., & Mark, M. M. (1992). The influence of mood state on judgment and action: Effects on persuasion, categorization, social justice, person perception, and judgmental accuracy. In L. L. Martin & A. Tesser (Eds.), *The construc-*

tion of social judgments (pp. 165–93). Hillsdale, NJ: Erlbaum.

Sinclair-de-Zwart, H. (1967). *Acquisition du lagage et développement de la pensée*. Paris: Dunod.

Singh, D. (1993). Adaptive significance of female physical attractiveness: Role of waist-to-hip ratio. *Journal of Personality and Social Psychology*, 65, 293–307.

Singh, D. (1995). Female judgements of male attractiveness and desirability for relationships: Role of waist-to-hip ratio and financial status. *Journal of Personality and Social Psychology*, 69, 1089–1101.

Singh, D., & Bronstad, P. M. (1997). Sex differences in the anatomical locations of human body scarification and tattooing as a function of pathogen prevalence. *Evolution and Human Behavior*, 18, 403–16.

Singh, D., & Luis, S. (1995). Ethnic and gender consensus for the effect of waist-to-hip ratio on judgement of women's attractiveness. *Human Nature*, 6, 51–65.

Sinha, R. R., & Hassan, M. K. (1975). Some personality correlates of social prejudice. *Journal of Social and Economic Studies*, 3, 225–31.

Skinner, B. F. (1938). *The behavior of organisms*. New York: Appleton-Century-Crofts.

Skinner, B. F. (1957). *Verbal behavior*. New York: Appleton-Century-Crofts.

Skowronski, N. J., & Carlston, D. E. (1989). Negativity and extremity biases in impression formation: A review of explanations. *Psychological Bulletin*, 105, 131–42.

Slavin, R. E. (1983). *Cooperative learning*. New York: Longman.

Smedslund, J. (1985). Necessarily true cultural psychologies. In K. J. Gergen and K. E. Davis (Eds.), *The social construction of the person* (pp. 73–88). New York: Springer.

Smith, B. L., Lasswell, H. D., & Casey, R. D. (1946). *Propaganda, communication, and public opinion*. Princeton, NJ: Princeton University Press.

Smith, C. A. (1989). Dimensions of appraisal and physiological response in emotion. *Journal of Personality and Social Psychology*, 56, 339–53.

Smith, C. A., & Ellsworth, P. C. (1985). Patterns of cognitive appraisal in emotion. *Journal of Personality and Social Psychology*, 48, 813–38.

Smith, C. A., & Ellsworth, P. C. (1987). Patterns of appraisal and emotion related to taking an exam. *Journal of Personality and Social Psychology*, 52, 475–88.

Smith, C. A., & Lazarus, R. S. (1993). Appraisal components, core relational themes, and the emotions. *Cognition and Emotion*, 7, 233–69.

Smith, C. A., & Scott, H. S. (1997). A componential approach to the meaning of facial expressions. In J. A. Russell & J. M. Fernández-Dols (Eds.), *The psychology of facial expression* (pp. 229–54). New York: Cambridge University Press.

Smith, E. R. (1991). Illusory correlation in a simulated exemplar-based memory. *Journal of Experimental Social Psychology*, 27, 107–23.

Smith, E. R. (1994). Social cognition contributions to attribution theory and research. In P. G. Devine, D. L. Hamilton, & T. M. Ostrom (Eds.), *Social cognition: Contributions to classic issues in social psychology* (pp. 77–108). New York: Springer Verlag.

Smith, E. R., & Miller, F. D. (1983). Mediation among attributional inferences and comprehension processes: Initial findings and a general method. *Journal of Personality and Social Psychology*, 44, 492–505.

Smith, E. R., Murphy, J., & Coates, S. (1999). Attachment to groups: Theory and management. *Journal of Personality and Social Psychology*, 77, 94–110.

Smith, E. R., & Zaraté, M. A. (1992). Exemplar-based model of social judgment. *Psychological Review*, 99, 3–21.

Smith, J. (1996). Planning about life: Toward a social-interactive perspective. In P. B. Baltes and U. M. Staudinger (Eds.), *Interactive minds: Life-span perspectives on the social foundation of cognition* (pp. 242–75). New York: Cambridge University Press.

Smith, M. B., Bruner, J. S., & White, R. W. (1956). *Opinions and personality*. New York: Wiley.

Smith, P. K., & Sharp, S. (Eds.). (1994). *School bullying. Insights and perspectives*. London: Routledge.

Smithson, M., Amato, P. R., & Pearce, P. (1983). *Dimensions of helping behaviour*. Oxford: Pergamon Press.

Snow, C. E. (1986). Conversations with children. In P. Fletcher and M. Garman (Eds.), *Language acquisition* (2nd ed., pp. 69–89). Cambridge: Cambridge University Press.

Snow, C. E. (1999). Social perspectives on the emergence of language. In B. MacWhinney (Ed.), *The emergence of language* (pp. 257–76). Mahwah, NJ: Lawrence Erlbaum Associates.

Snyder, C. R., & Forsyth, D. (1991). In C. R. Snyder & D. Forsyth (Eds.), *Handbook of social and clinical psychology* (pp. 3–17). New York: Pergamon Press.

Snyder, C. R., Lassegard, M. A., & Ford, C. E. (1986). Distancing after group success and failure: Basking in reflected glory and cutting off reflected failure. *Journal of Personality and Social Psychology*, 51, 382–8.

Snyder, M. (1974). Self-monitoring of expressive behavior. *Journal of Personality and Social Psychology*, 30, 526–37.

Snyder, M. (1984). When belief creates reality. In L. Berkowitz (Ed.), *Advances in experimental social psychology* (Vol. 18, pp. 247–305). New York: Academic Press.

Snyder, M., & DeBono, K. G. (1987). A functional approach to attitudes and persuasion. In M. P. Zanna, J. M. Olson, & C. P. Herman (Eds.), *Social influence: The Ontario symposium* (Vol. 5, pp. 107–25). Hillsdale, NJ: Erlbaum.

Snyder, M., & Kendzierski, D. (1982). Acting on one's attitudes: Procedures for linking attitude and behavior. *Journal of Experimental Social Psychology*, 18, 165–83.

Snyder, M., & Swann, W. B. (1976). When actions reflect attitudes: The politics of impression management. *Journal of Personality and Social Psychology*, 34, 1034–42.

Snyder, M., & Swann, W. B., Jr. (1978). Hypothesis-testing processes in social interaction. *Journal of Personality and Social Psychology*, 36, 1202–12.

Snyder, M., Tanke, E. D., & Berscheid, E. (1977). Social perception and interpersonal behavior: On the self-fulfilling nature of the social stereotype.

Journal of Personality and Social Psychology, 35, 656–66.

Snyder, M., & Uranowitz, S. W. (1978). Reconstructing the past: Some cognitive consequences of person perception. *Journal of Personality and Social Psychology*, 36, 941–50.

Sorensen, G., Emmons, K., Hunt, M. K., & Johnston, D. (1998). Implications of the results of community intervention trials. *Annual Review of Public Health*, 19, 379–416.

Sorrentino, R. M., King, G., & Leo, G. (1980). The influence of the minority on perception: A note on a possible alternative explanation. *Journal of Experimental Social Psychology*, 16, 293–301.

Spence, K. W. (1956). *Behavior theory and conditioning*. New Haven, CT: Yale University Press.

Spivey, E. B., & Prentice-Dunn, S. (1990). Assessing the directionality of deindividuated behavior: Effects of deindividuation, modeling, and private self-consciousness on aggressive and prosocial responses. *Basic and Applied Science Psychology*, 11, 387–403.

Sprecher, S., & Schwartz, P. (1994). Equity and balance in the exchange of contributions in close relationships. In M. J. Lerner, G. Mikula, et al. (Eds.), *Entitlement and the affectional bond: Justice in close relationships. Critical issues in social justice* (pp. 11–41). New York: Plenum Press.

Srull, T. K. (1981). Person memory: Some tests of associative storage and retrieval models. *Journal of Experimental Psychology: Human Learning and Memory*, 7, 440–63.

Srull, T. K., & Wyer, R. S. (1980). Category accessibility and social perception: Some implications for the study of person memory and interpersonal judgments. *Journal of Personality and Social Psychology*, 38, 841–56.

Staats, A. W., & Staats, C. K. (1958). Attitudes established by classical conditioning. *Journal of Abnormal and Social Psychology*, 57, 37–40.

Stagner, R., & Congdon, C. S. (1955). Another failure to demonstrate displacement of aggression. *Journal of Abnormal and Social Psychology*, 51, 695–66.

Stangor, C., & McMillan, D. (1992). Memory for expectancy-congruent and expectancy-incongruent information: A review of the social and social developmental literatures. *Psychological Bulletin*, 111, 42–61.

Stasser, G., Kerr, N. L., & Davis, J. H. (1989). Influence processes and consensus models in decision-making groups. In P. B. Paulus (Ed.), *Psychology of group influence* (2nd ed., pp. 279–326). Hillsdale, NJ: Erlbaum.

Stasser, G., & Stewart, D. (1992). Discovery of hidden profiles by decision-making groups: Solving a problem versus making a judgement. *Journal of Personality and Social Psychology*, 63, 426–34.

Stasser, G., Stewart, D. D., & Wittenbaum, G. M. (1995). Expert roles and information exchange during discussion: The importance of knowing who knows what. *Journal of Experimental Social Psychology*, 31, 244–65.

Stasser, G., Taylor, L. A., & Hanna, C. (1989). Information sampling in structured and unstructured discussions of three- and six-person groups. *Journal of Personality and Social Psychology*, 57, 67–78.

Stasser, G., & Titus, W. (1985). Pooling of unshared information in group decision making: Biased information sampling during group discussion. *Journal of Personality and Social Psychology*, 48, 1467–78.

Stasser, G., & Titus, W. (1987). Effects of information load and percentage of shared information on the dissemination of unshared information during group discussion. *Journal of Personality and Social Psychology*, 53, 81–93.

Staub, E. (1974). Helping a distressed person: Social, personality, and stimulus determinants. In L. Berkowitz (Ed.), *Advances in experimental social psychology* (Vol. 7, pp. 293–341). New York: Academic Press.

Staub, E. (1989). *The roots of evil. The origins of genocide and other group violence*. Cambridge: Cambridge University Press.

Staw, B. M. (1986). Organizational psychology and the pursuit of the happy/productive worker. *California Management Review*, 28, 40–53.

Staw, B. M., Sutton, R. I., & Pelled, L. H. (1994). Employee positive emotion and favorable outcomes at the workplace. *Organisation Science*, 5 (1), 51–71.

Steers, R. M., Porter L. W., & Bigley, G. A. (1996). *Motivation and leadership at work*. McGraw-Hill.

Steiner, I. D. (1972). *Group processes and productivity*. New York: Academic Press.

Steiner, I. D. (1976). Task-performing groups. In J. W. Thibaut, J. T. Spence, & R. C. Carson (Eds.), *Contemporary topics in social psychology*. Morristown, NJ: General Learning Press.

Steiner, J. E. (1979). Human facial expressions in response to taste and smell stimulation. In L. P. Lipsitt & H. W. Reese (Eds.), *Advances in child development and behaviour* (Vol. 13, pp. 257–95). New York: Academic Press.

Stemmler, G., Heldmann, M., Pauls, C. A., & Scherer, Th. (in press). Constraints for emotion specificity in fear and anger: The context counts. *Psychophysiology*.

Stephan, C. W., & Stephan, W. G. (1990). *Two social psychologies* (2nd ed.). Belmont, CA: Wadsworth.

Stephan, C. W., Stephan, W. G., & Pettigrew, T. F. (Eds.). (1991). *The future of social psychology: Defining the relationship between sociology and psychology*. New York: Springer Verlag.

Stephan, W. G., & Stephan, C. W. (1985). Intergroup anxiety. *Journal of Social Issues*, 41, 157–75.

Stephenson, G. M. (1978). Interparty and interpersonal exchange in negotiation groups. In H. Brandstätter, J. H. Davis, & H. Schuler (Eds.), *Dynamics of group decisions* (pp. 207–28). London: Sage.

Stern, D. N. (1985). *The interpersonal world of the infant. A view from psychoanalysis and developmental psychology*. New York: Basic Books.

Stern, L. D., Marrs, S., Millar, M. G., & Cole, E. (1984). Processing time and the recall of inconsistent and consistent behaviors of individuals and groups. *Journal of Personality and Social Psychology*, 47, 253–62.

Stewart, D., & Stasser, G. (1995). Expert role assignment and information sampling during collective recall and decision making. *Journal of Personality and Social Psychology*, 69, 619–28.

Stewart, D., & Stasser, G. (1998). The sampling of critical, unshared information in decision-making groups: The role of an informed minority. *European Journal of Social Psychology*, 28, 95–113.

Stogdill, R. M. (1948). Personal factors associated with leadership: A survey of the literature. *Journal of Psychology*, 25, 35–71.

Storms, M. D. (1973). Videotape and the attribution process: Reversing actors' and observers' points of view. *Journal of Personality and Social Psychology*, 27, 165–75.

Stoms, M. D., & Nisbett, R. E. (1970). Insomnia and the attribution process. *Journal of Personality and Social Psychology*, 16, 319–28.

Strack, F., & Mussweiler, T. (1997). Explaining the enigmatic anchoring effect: Mechanisms of selective accessibility. *Journal of Personality and Social Psychology*, 73, 437–46.

Strack, F., Schwarz, N., Bless, H., Kübler, A., & Wänke, M. (1993). Awareness of the influence as a determinant of assimilation vs. contrast. *European Journal of Social Psychology*, 23, 53–62.

Strack, F., Schwarz, N., & Gschneidinger, E. (1985). Happiness and reminiscing: The role of time perspective, mood, and mode of thinking. *Journal of Personality and Social Psychology*, 49, 1460–9.

Strack, F., Stepper, L. L., & Martin, S. (1988). Inhibiting and facilitating conditions of the human smile: A non-obtrusive test of the facial-feedback hypothesis. *Journal of Personality and Social Psychology*, 54, 768–77.

Strathman, A., Gleicher, F., Boninger, D. S., & Edwards, C. S. (1994). The consideration of future consequences: Weighing immediate and distant outcomes of behavior. *Journal of Personality and Social Psychology*, 66, 742–52.

Stratton, P., Heard, D., Hanks, H. G. I., Munton, A. G., Brewin, C. R., & Davidson, C. (1986). Coding causal beliefs in natural discourse. *British Journal of Social Psychology*, 25, 299–31.

Straus, M. A. (1993). Physical assaults by wives: A major social problem. In R. J. Gelles & D. R. Loeske (Eds.), *Current controversies on family violence* (pp. 67–87). Newbury Park, CA: Sage.

Stroebe, M., Schut, H., & Stroebe, W. (1998). Trauma and grief: A comparative analysis. In J. H. Harvey (Ed.), *Perspectives on loss: A sourcebook. Death, dying, and bereavement* (pp. 81–96). Philadelphia, PA: Brunner/Mazel.

Stroebe, W. (2000). *Social psychology and health* (2nd ed.). Buckingham: Open University Press.

Stroebe, W., & Diehl, M. (1994). Why groups are less effective than their members: On productivity loss in idea-generating groups. In W. Stroebe & M. Hewstone (Eds.), *European review of social psychology* (Vol. 5, pp. 271–304). London: Wiley.

Stroebe, W., Diehl, M., & Abakoumkin, G. (1992). The illusion of group effectivity. *Personality and Social Psychology Bulletin*, 18, 643–50.

Stroebe, W., & Frey, B. S. (1982). Self-interest and collective action: The economics and psychology of public goods. *British Journal of Social Psychology*, 21, 121–37.

Stroebe, W., Insko, C. A., Thompson, V. D., & Layton, B. D. (1971). Effects of physical attractiveness, attitude similarity, and sex on various aspects of interpersonal attraction. *Journal of Personality and Social Psychology*, 18, 79–91.

Stroebe, W., & Stroebe, M. S. (1986). Beyond marriage: The impact of partner loss on health. In R. Gilmour & S. Duck (Eds.), *The emerging field of personal relationships* (pp. 203–24). Hillsdale, NJ: Erlbaum.

Stroebe, W., & Stroebe, M. (1987). *Bereavement and health: The psychological and physical consequences of partner loss*. Cambridge: Cambridge University Press.

Stroebe, W., & Stroebe, M. S. (1997). The social psychology of social support. In E. T. Higgins & A. W. Kruglanski (Eds.), *Social psychology: Handbook of basic principles* (pp. 622–54). New York, NY: Guilford Press.

Stroebe, W., Stroebe, M., Abakoumin, G., & Schut, H. (1996). The role of loneliness and social support in adjustment to loss: A test of attachment versus stress theory. *Journal of Personality and Social Psychology*, 70, 1241–9.

Stroebe, W., Stroebe, M. S., & Domittner, G. (1988). Individual and situational differences in recovery from bereavement: A risk group identified. *Journal of Social Issues*, 44, 143–58.

Struch, N., & Schwartz, S. H. (1989). Intergroup aggression: Its predictors and distinctness from in-group bias. *Journal of Personality and Social Psychology*, 56, 364–73.

Stryker, S. (1995). Symbolic interactionism. In A. S. R. Mansfield & M. Hewstone (Eds.), *The*

Blackwell encyclopedia of social psychology (pp. 647–51). Oxford: Blackwell.

Stults, D. M., Messé, L. A., & Kerr, N. L. (1984). Belief-discrepant behavior and the bogus pipeline: Impression management or arousal attribution. *Journal of Experimental Social Psychology*, 20, 47–54.

Suess, G. J., Grossmann, K. E., & Sroufe, L. A. (1992). Effects of attachment to mother and father on quality of adaptation in preschool: From dyadic to individual organisation of self. *International Journal of Behavioral Development*, 15, 43–65.

Super, C. M., & Harkness, S. (1999). The environment as culture in developmental research. In S. L. Friedman and T. D. Wachs (Eds.), *Measuring environment across the life span: Emerging methods and concepts* (pp. 279–323). Washington, DC: American Psychological Association.

Sutton, S. (1998). Predicting and explaining intentions and behavior: How well are we doing? *Journal of Applied Social Psychology*, 28, 1317–38.

Swann, W. B., de la Ronde, C., & Hixon, J. G. (1994). Authenticity and positivity strivings in marriage and courtship. *Journal of Personality and Social Psychology*, 66, 857–69.

Swann, W. B., Giuliano, T., & Wegner, D. M. (1982). Where leading questions can lead: The power of conjecture in social interaction. *Journal of Personality and Social Psychology*, 42, 1025–35.

Sweeney, P. D., Anderson, K., & Bailey, S. (1986). Attributional style in depression: A meta-analytic review. *Journal of Personality and Social Psychology*, 50, 974–91.

Symons, D. (1979). *The evolution of human sexuality*. New York: Oxford University Press.

Symons, D. (1992). On the use and misuse of Darwinism in the study of human behavior. In J. H. Barkow, L. Cosmides, & J. Tooby (Eds.), *The adapted mind* (pp. 137–59). New York & Oxford: Oxford University Press.

Symons, D. (1995). Beauty is in the adaptations of the beholder: The evolutionary psychology of female sexual attractiveness. In P. R. Abramson & S. D. Pinkerton (Eds.), *Sexual nature, sexual culture* (pp. 80–118). Chicago & London: University of Chicago Press.

Symons, D., & Ellis, B. (1989). Human male–female differences in sexual desire. In A. S. Rasa, C. Vogel, & E. Voland (Eds.), *The sociobiology of sexual and reproductive strategies* (pp. 131–46). London: Chapman & Hall.

Symons, D. K., & Clark, S. E. (2000). A longitudinal study of mother–child relationships and theory of mind in the preschool period. *Social Development*, 9, 3–23.

't Hart, P. (1990). *Groupthink in government: A study of small groups and policy failure*. Amsterdam: Swets & Zeitlinger.

Tajfel, H. (1969). Cognitive aspects of prejudice. *Journal of Social Issues*, 225, 79–97.

Tajfel, H. (Ed.). (1978). *Differentiation between social groups: Studies in the social psycho-logy of intergroup relations*. London: Academic Press.

Tajfel, H. (1981). *Human groups and social categories: Studies in social psychology*. Cambridge: Cambridge University Press.

Tajfel, H. (1982). Social psychology of intergroup relations. *Annual Review of Psychology*, 33, 1–30.

Tajfel, H. (Ed.). (1984). *The social dimension: European developments in social psychology* (2 vols.). Cambridge: Cambridge University Press.

Tajfel, H., Flament, C., Billig, M. G., & Bundy, R. P. (1971). Social categorization and intergroup behaviour. *European Journal of Social Psychology*, 1, 149–78.

Tajfel, H., & Jahoda, G. (1966). Development in children of concepts and attitudes about their own and other nations: A cross-national study. *Proceedings of the XVIIIth International Congress of Psychology*, 36, 17–33.

Tajfel, H., Nemeth, C., Jahoda, G., Campbell, J. D., & Johnson, N. B. (1970). The development of children's preference for their own country: A cross-national study. *International Journal of Psychology*, 6, 245–53.

Tajfel, H., & Turner, J. (1986). The social identity theory of intergroup behaviour. In S. Worchel & W. G. Austin (Eds.), *Psychology of intergroup relations* (pp. 7–24). Chicago: Nelson.

Tajfel, H., & Wilkes, A. L. (1963). Classification and quantitative judgment. *British Journal of Psychology*, 54, 101–14.

Tanford, S., & Penrod, S. (1984). Social influence model: A formal integration of research on majority and minority influence processes. *Psychological Bulletin*, 95, 189–225.

Tannenbaum, P. H., & Zillmann, D. (1975). Emotional arousal in the facilitation of aggression through communication. In L. Berkowitz (Ed.), *Advances in experimental social psychology* (Vol. 8). New York: Academic Press.

Tarde, G. (1901). *L'opinion et la foule*. Paris: Alcan.

Tavecchio, L. W. C., & Thomeer, M. A. E. (1999). Attachment, social network, and homelessness in young people. *Social Behavior and Personality*, 27, 247–62.

Taylor, S. E., Crocker, J., Fiske, S. T., Sprinzen, M., & Winkler, J. D. (1979). The generalizability of salience effects. *Journal of Personality and Social Psychology*, 37, 357–68.

Taylor, S. E., & Fiske, S. T. (1981). Getting inside the head: Methodologies for process analysis in attribution and social cognition. In J. H. Harvey, W. J. Ickes, & R. F. Kidd (Eds.), *New directions in attribution research* (Vol. 3, pp. 459–524). Hillsdale, NJ: Erlbaum.

Taylor, S. E., & Koivumaki, J. H. (1976). The perception of self and others: Acquaintanceship, affect and actor–observer differences. *Journal of Personality and Social Psychology*, 33, 403–8.

Tedeschi, J. T. (Ed.). (1974). *Perspectives on social power*. Chicago: Aldine.

Tedeschi, J. T. (1981). *Impression management*. New York: Academic Press.

Tedeschi, J. T., & Felson, R. B. (1994). *Aggression and coercive actions: A social inter-actionist perspective*. Washington, DC: American Psychological Association.

Tedeschi, J. T., Lindskold, S., & Rosenfeld, P. (1985). *Introduction to social psychology* St Paul, MN: West.

Terry, D. J., & Hynes, G. J. (1998). Adjustment to a low-control situation: Reexamining the role of coping responses. *Journal of Personality and Social Psychology*, 74, 1078–92.

Tesser, A. (1978). Self-generated attitude change. In L. Berkowitz (Ed.), *Advances in experimental social psychology* (Vol. 11, pp. 289–338). New York: Academic Press.

Tesser, A., & Martin, L. L. (1996). The psychology of evaluation. In E. T. Higgins & A. W. Kruglanski (Eds.), *Social psychology: Handbook of basic principles* (pp. 400–32). New York: Guilford Press.

Tesser, A., & Shaffer, D. R. (1990). Attitudes and attitude change. In M. R. Rosenzweig & L. W. Porter (Eds.), *Annual review of psychology* (Vol. 41, pp. 479–523). Palo Alto, CA: Annual Reviews.

Tetlock, P. E., & Levi, A. (1982). Attribution bias: On the inconclusiveness of the cognition-motivation debate. *Journal of Experimental Social Psychology*, 18, 68–88.

Tetlock, P. E., & Manstead, A. S. R. (1985). Impression management versus intrapsychic explanations in social psychology: A useful dichotomy? *Psychological Review*, 92, 59–77.

Tett, R. P., & Meyer, J. P. (1993). Job satisfaction, organizational commitment, turnover: Path analyses based on meta-analytic findings. *Personnel Psychology*, 46, 252–93.

Thibaut, J., & Faucheux, C. (1965). The development of contractual norms in a bargaining situation under two types of stress. *Journal of Experimental Social Psychology*, 1, 89–102.

Thibaut, J. W., & Kelley, H. H. (1959). *The social psychology of groups*. New York: Wiley.

Thibaut, J. W., & Strickland, L. H. (1956). Psychological set and social conformity. *Journal of Personality*, 25, 115–29.

Thibaut, J. W., & Walker, L. (1975). *Procedural justice: A psychological analysis*. New York: Wiley.

Thomas, E. J., & Fink, C. F. (1961). Models of group problem solving. *Journal of Abnormal and Social Psychology*, 63, 53–63.

Thompson, M. M., Zanna, M. P., & Griffin, D. W. (1995). Let's not be indifferent about (attitudinal) ambivalence. In R. E. Petty & J. A. Krosnick (Eds.), *Attitude strength: Antecedents and consequences* (pp. 361–86). Mahwah, NJ: Erlbaum.

Thompson, P. R. (1980). And who is my neighbour? An answer from evolutionary genetics. *Social Science Information*, 19, 341–84.

Thompson, S. C., & Kelley, H. H. (1981). Judgments of responsibility in close relationships. *Journal of Personality and Social Psychology*, 41, 469–77.

Thornhill, R., Gangestad, S. W., & Comer, R. (1995). Human female orgasm and mate fluctuating asymmetry. *Animal Behaviour*, 50, 1601–15.

Thurstone, L. L. (1928). Attitudes can be measured. *American Journal of Sociology*, 33, 529–54.

Toi, M., & Batson, C. D. (1982). More evidence that empathy is a source of altruistic motivation. *Journal of Personality and Social Psychology*, 43, 281–93.

Tomasello, M. (1992). The social bases of language acquisition. *Social Development*, 1, 67–87.

Tomkins, S. S. (1984). Affect theory. In K. R. Scherer & P. Ekman (Eds.), *Approaches to emotion* (pp. 163–96). Hillsdale, NJ: Erlbaum.

Torestad, B. (1990). What is anger provoking? A psychophysical study of perceived causes of anger. *Aggressive Behavior*, 16, 9–26.

Torrance, E. P. (1954). The behavior of small groups under the stress of conditions of survival. *American Sociological Review*, 19, 751–5.

Travis, L. E. (1925). The effect of a small audience upon eye–hand coordination. *Journal of Abnormal and Social Psychology*, 20, 142–6.

Trevarthen, C. (1982). The primary motives for cooperative understanding. In G. Butterworth and P. Light (Eds.), *Social cognition. Studies of the development of understanding* (pp. 201–23). Chicago: University of Chicago Press.

Triandis, H. C. (1994). *Culture and social behavior*. New York: McGraw-Hill.

Triandis, K., Bontempo, R., Villareal, M. J., Asai, M., & Lucca, N. (1988). Individualism and collectivism: Cross cultural perspectives on self–ingroup relationships. *Journal of Personality and Social Psychology*, 54, 323–38.

Triplett, N. D. (1898). The dynamogenic factor in pacemaking and competition. *American Journal of Psychology*, 9, 507–33.

Trivers, R. L. (1971). The evolution of reciprocal altruism. *Quarterly Review of Biology*, 46, 35–57.

Trivers, R. (1972). Parental investment and sexual selection. In B. B. Campbell (Ed.), *Sexual selection and the descent of man* (pp. 136–79). Chicago: Aldine.

Trope, Y. (1986). Identification and inferential processes in dispositional attribution. *Psychological Review*, 93, 239–57.

Tschan, F. (1995). Communication enhances small group performance if it conforms to task requirements: The concept of ideal communication cycles. *Basic and Applied Social Psychology*, 17, 371–93.

Tudge, J. R. H. (1999). Processes and consequences of peer collaboration: A Vygotskian analysis. In P. Lloyd & C. Fernyhough (Eds.), *Lev Vygotsky: Critical assessments. The zone of proximal development* (Vol. 3, pp. 195–221). New York: Routledge.

Tulving, E., & Thomson, D. M. (1973). Encoding specificity and retrieval processes in episodic memory. *Psychological Review*, 80, 352–73.

Turnbull, W., & Slugoski, B. (1988). Conversational and linguistic processes in causal attribution. In D. Hilton (Ed.), *Contemporary science and natural explanation: Commonsense conceptions of causality* (pp. 66–93). Brighton: Harvester Press.

Turner, J., & Wheaton, B. (1995). Checklist measurement of stressful life events. In S. Cohen, R. C. Kessler, & L. U. Gordon (Eds.), *Measuring stress* (pp. 29–58). New York: Oxford University Press.

Turner, J. C. (1980). Fairness or discrimination in intergroup behaviour? A reply to Braithwaite, Doyle and Lightbown. *European Journal of Social Psychology*, 10, 131–47.

Turner, J. C. (1981). The experimental social psychology of intergroup behaviour. In J. C. Turner & H. Giles (Eds.), *Intergroup behaviour* (pp. 66–101). Oxford: Blackwell.

Turner, J. C. (1982). Towards a cognitive redefinition of the social group. In H. Tajfel (Ed.), *Social identity and intergroup relations* (pp. 15–40). Cambridge: Cambridge University Press.

Turner, J. C. (1991). *Social influence*. Buckingham: Open University Press.

Turner, J. C., Hogg, M. A., Oakes, P. J., Reicher, S. D., & Wetherell, M. S. (Eds.). (1987). *Rediscovering the social group. A self-categorization theory*. Oxford: Blackwell.

Turner, P. J. (1993). Attachment to mother and behaviour with adults in preschool. *British Journal of Developmental Psychology*, 11, 75–89.

Turner, R. H., & Killian, L. M. (1972). *Collective behavior* (2nd ed.). Englewood Cliffs, NJ: Prentice-Hall.

Tversky, A., & Kahneman, D. (1973). Availability: A heuristic for judging frequency and probability. *Cognitive Psychology*, 5, 207–32.

Tversky, A., & Kahneman, D. (1974). Judgment under uncertainty: Heuristics and biases. *Science*, 185, 1124–31.

Tversky, B., & Tuchin, M. (1989). A reconciliation of the evidence on eyewitness testimony: Comments on McCloskey and Zaragoza. *Journal of Experimental Psychology: General*, 118, 86–91.

Uchino, B. N., Cacioppo, J. T., & Kiecolt-Glaser, J. K. (1996). The relationship between social support and physiological processes: A review with emphasis on underlying mechanisms and implication for health. *Psychological Bulletin*, 119, 488–531.

Uleman, J. S., Newman, L. S., & Moskowitz, G. B. (1996). People as flexible interpreters: Evidence and issues from spontaneous trait inference. In M. P. Zanna (Ed.), *Advances in experimental social psychology* (Vol. 29, pp. 211–79). San Diego, CA: Academic Press.

Underwood, B., Froming, W. J., & Moore, B. S. (1977). Mood, attention, and altruism: A search for mediating variables. *Developmental Psychology*, 13, 541–2.

Urban, L. M., & Miller, N. (1998). A theoretical analysis of crossed categorization effects: A meta-analysis. *Journal of Personality and Social Psychology*, 74, 894–908.

Utman, C. H. (1997). Performance effects of motivational state: A meta-analysis. *Personality and Social Psychology Review*, 1, 170–82.

Valachich, J. S., Dennis, A. R., & Connolly, T. (1994). Idea generation in computer-based groups: A new ending to an old story. *Organizational Behavior and Human Decision Processes*, 57, 448–76.

Valiant, G., Glachan, M., & Emler, N. (1982). The stimulation of cognitive development through co-operative task performance. *British Journal of Educational Psychology*, 52, 281–8.

Valsiner, J., & Lawrence, J. A. (1997). Human development in culture across the life span. In J. W. Berry & P. R. Dasen (Eds.), *Handbook of cross-cultural psychology. Vol. 2. Basic processes and* human development (2nd ed., pp. 69–106). Boston: Allyn & Bacon.

Van de Ven, A. H., & Delbecq, A. L. (1974). The effectiveness of nominal, delphi and interacting group decision-making processes. *Academy of Management Journal*, 17, 605–21.

Van de Vliert, E. (1992). Questions about the strategic choice model of negotiation. *Negotiation Journal*, 8, 379–86.

Van de Vliert, E. (1996). Interventions in conflicts. In M. J. Schabracq, J. A. M. Winnubst, & C. L. Cooper (Eds.), *Handbook of work and health psychology* (pp. 405–25). Chichester: Wiley.

Van de Vliert, E. (1997a). *Complex interpersonal conflict behaviour: Theoretical frontiers.* Hove: Psychology Press.

Van de Vliert, E. (1997b). Enhancing performance by conflict-stimulating intervention. In C. K. W. De Dreu & E. Van de Vliert (Eds.), *Using conflict in organizations* (pp. 208–22). Thousand Oaks, CA: Sage.

Van de Vliert, E., Nauta, A., Giebels, E., & Janssen, O. (1999). Constructive conflict at work. *Journal of Organizational Behavior*, 20, 475–91.

Van den Bos, K., Lind, E. A., Vermunt, R., & Wilke, H. A. M. (1997). How do I judge my outcome when I do not know the outcome of others? The psychology of the fair process effect. *Journal of Personality and Social Psychology*, 72, 1034–46.

Van der Velde, F. W., & van der Pligt, J. (1991). AIDS-related health behavior: Coping, protection motivation, and previous behavior. *Journal of Behavioral Medicine*, 14, 429–51.

Van Dyne, L., Cummings, L. L., & McLean Parks, J. (1995). Extra-role behaviors: In pursuit of construct and definitional clarity (A bridge over muddied waters). In L. L. Cummings & B. M. Staw (Eds.), *Research in Organizational Behavior*, 17, 215–85.

Van Ginneken, J. (1992). *Crowds, psychology, and politics 1871–1899.* New York: Cambridge University Press.

Van Hooff, J. A. (1972). A comparative approach to the phylogeny of laughter and smiling. In R. Hinde (Eds.), *Non-verbal communication* (pp. 209–41). Cambridge: Cambridge University Press.

Van IJzendoorn, M. H. (1990). Developments in cross-cultural research on attachment: Some methodological notes. *Human Development*, 33, 3–9.

Van Lange, P. A. M. (1999). The pursuit of joint outcomes and equality in outcomes: An integrative model of social value orientation. *Journal of Personality and Social Psychology*, 77, 337–49.

Van Lange, P. A. M., Agnew, C. R., Harinck, F., & Steemers, G. E. M. (1997). From game theory to real life: How social value orientation affects willingness to sacrifice in ongoing close relationships. *Journal of Personality and Social Psychology*, 73, 1330–44.

Van Lange, P. A. M., & Kuhlman, D. M. (1994). Social value orientations and impressions of honesty and intelligence: A test of the might versus morality effect. *Journal of Personality and Social Psychology*, 67, 126–41.

Van Lange, P. A. M., Otten, W., De Bruin, E. M. N., & Joireman, J. A. (1997). Development of prosocial, individualistic, and competitive orientations: Theory and preliminary evidence. *Journal of Personality and Social Psychology*, 73, 733–46.

Van Lange, P. A. M., Rusbult, C. E., Drigotas, S. M., Arriaga, X. B., Witcher, B. S., & Cox, C. L. (1997). Willingness to sacrifice in close relationships. *Journal of Personality and Social Psychology*, 72, 1373–95.

Van Lange, P. A. M., & Visser, K. (1999). Locomotion in social dilemmas: How people adapt to cooperative, tit-for-tat, and noncooperative partners. *Journal of Personality and Social Psychology*, 77, 762–73.

Van Oudenhouven, J. P., Groenewond, J. T., & Hewstone, M. (1996). Co-operation, ethnic salience and generalization of interethnic attitudes. *European Journal of Social Psychology*, 26, 649–62.

Van Overvalle, F. (1998). Causal explanation as constraint satisfaction: A critique and a feed-forward connectionist alternative. *Journal of Personality and Social Psychology*, 74, 312–28.

Van Reekum, C. M., & Scherer, K. R. (1997). Levels of processing for emotion-antecedent appraisal. In G. Matthews (Ed.), *Cognitive science perspectives on personality and emotion* (pp. 259–300). Amsterdam: Elsevier Science.

Van Strien, P. J. (1997). The American 'colonization' of Northwest European social psychology after World War II. *Journal of the History of the Behavioral Sciences*, 33, 349–63.

Van Vugt, M., Van Lange, P. A. M., & Meertens, R. M., & Joireman, J. A. (1996). How a structural solution to a real-world social dilemma failed: A field experiment on the first carpool lane in Europe. *Social Psychology Quarterly*, 59, 364–74.

Vanbeselaere, N. (1991). The different effects of simple and crossed categorizations: A result of the category differentiation process or differential category salience. In W. Stroebe & M. Hewstone (Eds.), *European review of social psychology* (Vol. 2, pp. 247–78). Chichester: Wiley.

Vanneman, R. D., & Pettigrew, T. F. (1972). Race and relative deprivation in the urban United States. *Race*, 13, 461–86.

VanYperen, N. W. (1996). Communal orientation and the burnout syndrome among nurses: A replication and extension. *Journal of Applied Social Psychology*, 26, 338–54.

VanYperen, N. W. (1998a). Predicting stay/leave behavior among volleyball referees. *The Sport Psychologist*, 12, 427–39.

VanYperen, N. W. (1998b). Informational support, equity, and burnout: The moderating effect of self-efficacy. *Journal of Occupational and Organizational Psychology*, 71, 29–33.

VanYperen, N. W., & Buunk, A. P. (1990). A longitudinal study of equity in intimate relationships. *European Journal of Social Psychology*, 20, 287–309.

VanYperen, N. W., & Buunk, B. P. (1991). Sex-role attitudes, social comparison, and satisfaction with relationships. *Social Psychology Quarterly*, 54 (2), 169–80.

VanYperen, N. W., Buunk, B. P., & Schaufeli, W. B. (1992). Communal orientation and the burnout syndrome among nurses. *Journal of Applied Social Psychology*, 22, 173–89.

VanYperen, N. W., & Duda, J. L. (1999). Goal orientations, beliefs about success, and performance improvement among young elite Dutch soccer players. *Scandinavian Journal of Medicine and Science in Sports*, 9, 358–64.

VanYperen, N. W., Hagedoorn, M., & Geurts, S. A. (1996). Intent to leave and absenteeism as reactions to perceived inequity: The role of psychological and social constraints. *Journal of Occupational and Organizational Psychology*, 69, 367–72.

VanYperen, N. W., & Snijders, T. A. B. (2000). A multilevel analysis of the demands-control model: Is stress at work determined by factors at the group level or the individual level? *Journal of Occupational Health Psychology*, 5, 182–90.

VanYperen, N. W., Van den Berg, A. E., & Willering M. C. (1999). Toward a better understanding of the link between participation in decision-making and organizational citizenship behavior: A multilevel analysis. *Journal of Occupational and Organizational Psychology*, 72, 377–92.

Vaughan, G. M. (1978). Social change and intergroup preferences in New Zealand. *European Journal of Social Psychology*, 8, 297–314.

Verplanken, B., & Aarts, H. (1999). Habit, attitude, planned behavior: Is habit an empty construct or an interesting case of goal directed automaticity? In W. Stroebe & M. Hewstone (Eds.), *European review of social psychology* (Vol. 10, pp. 100–34). Chichester: Wiley.

Vinokur, A., & Burnstein, E. (1978). Novel argumentation and attitude change: The case of polarization following group discussion. *European Journal of Social Psychology*, 8, 335–48.

Voland, E. (1993). *Grundriss der Soziobiologie*. Stuttgart: Fischer.

Von Winterfeldt, D., & Edwards, W. (1986). *Decision analysis and behavioral research*. Cambridge: Cambridge University Press.

Vroom, V. H. (1964). *Work and motivation*. New York: Wiley.

Vygotsky, L. S. (1962). *Thought and language*. Cambridge, MA: MIT Press.

Vygotsky, L. S. (1978). *Mind in society. The development of higher psychological processes*. Cambridge, MA: Harvard University Press.

Wänke, M., Bohner, G., & Jurkowitsch, A. (1997). There are many reasons to drive a BMW: Does imagined ease of argument generation influence attitudes? *Journal of Consumer Research*, 24, 170–7.

Wagner, M., Schütze, Y., & Lang, F. R. (1999). Social relationships in old age. In P. B. Baltes and K. U. Mayer (Eds.), *The Berlin Aging Study. Aging from 70 to 100* (pp. 282–303). Cambridge: Cambridge University Press.

Walker, I., & Mann, L. (1987). Unemployment, relative deprivation and social protest. *Personality and Social Psychology Bulletin*, 13, 275–83.

Walker, I., & Pettigrew, T. F. (1984). Relative deprivation theory: An overview and conceptual critique. *British Journal of Social Psychology*, 23, 301–10.

Walker, K. (1995). 'Always there for me': Friendship patterns and expectations among middle- and working-class men and women. *Sociological Forum*, 10, 273–96.

Walker, L. E. (1999). Psychology and domestic violence around the world. *American Psychologist*, 54, 21–9.

Walker, W. D., Rowe, R. C., & Quinsey, V. L. (1993). Authoritarianism and sexual aggression. *Journal of Personality and Social Psychology*, 65, 1036–45.

Wallbott, H. G., & Ricci-Bitti, P. (1993). Decoders' processing of emotional facial expression: A top-down or bottom-up mechanism? *European Journal of Social Psychology*, 23 (4), 427–43.

Wallbott, H. G., & Scherer, K. R. (1986). Cues and channels in emotion recognition. *Journal of Personality and Social Psychology*, 51, 690–9.

Wallbott, H. G., & Scherer, K. R. (1995). Cultural determinants in experiencing shame and guilt. In J. P. Tangney & K. W. Fischer (Eds.), *Self-conscious emotions: The psycho-logy of shame, guilt, embarrassment, and pride* (pp. 465–87). New York: Guilford Press.

Walster, E., Aronson, V., Abrahams, D., & Rottman, L. (1966). The importance of physical attractiveness in dating behavior. *Journal of Personality and Social Psychology*, 4, 508–16.

Walster, E., Berscheid, E., & Walster, G. W. (1973). New directions in equity research. *Journal of Personality and Social Psychology*, 25, 151–76.

Walster, E., Walster, G. W., & Berscheid, E. (1978). *Equity: Theory and research*. Boston: Allyn & Bacon.

Walters, R. H., & Brown, M. (1963). Studies of reinforcement of aggression: III. Transfer of responses to an interpersonal situation. *Child Development*, 34, 536–71.

Walton, R. E. (1969). *Interpersonal peacemaking: Confrontations and third party consultation*. Reading, MA: Addison-Wesley.

Wason, P. C. (1966). Reasoning. In B. Foss (Ed.), *New horizons in psychology* (pp. 135–51). London: Penguin.

Watson, D. (1982). The actor and the observer: How are their perceptions of causality divergent? *Psychological Bulletin*, 92, 682–700.

Watson, D., & Pennebaker, J. W. (1989). Health complaints, stress, and distress: Exploring the central role of negative affectivity. *Psychological Review*, 96, 234–54.

Watson, J. B. (1928). *Psychological care of infant and child*. New York: Norton.

Weary, G. (1980). Examination of affect and egotism as mediators of bias in causal attributions. *Journal of Personality and Social Psychology*, 38, 348–57.

Weary, G., Harvey, J. H., Schwieger, P., Olson, C. T., Perloff, R., & Pritchard, S. (1982). Self-presentation and the moderation of self-serving attributional biases. *Social Cognition*, 1, 140–59.

Webb, E. J., Campbell, D. T., Schwartz, R. F., Sechrest, L., & Grove, J. B. (1981). *Nonreactive measures in the social sciences*. Boston: Houghton Mifflin.

Weber, R., & Crocker, J. (1983). Cognitive processes in the revision of stereotypic beliefs. *Journal of Personality and Social Psychology*, 45, 961–77.

Webster, D. M. (1993). Motivated augmentation and reduction of the overattribution bias. *Journal of Personality and Social Psychology*, 65, 261–71.

Wegner, D. M., Wenzlaff, R., Kerker, R. M., & Beattie, A. E. (1981). Incrimination through innuendo: Can media questions become public answers? *Journal of Personality and Social Psychology*, 40, 822–32.

Weick, K. E. (1985). Systematic observational methods. In G. Lindzey and E. Aronson (Eds.),

Handbook of social psychology (3rd ed., Vol. 1, pp. 567–634). New York: Random House.

Weigel, R. H., & Newman, L. S. (1976). Increasing attitude–behavior correspondence by broadening the scope of the behavioral measure. *Journal of Personality and Social Psychology*, 33, 793–802.

Weiner, B. (1979). A theory of motivation for some classroom experiences. *Journal of Educational Psychology*, 71, 3–25.

Weiner, B. (1985). 'Spontaneous' causal thinking. *Psychological Bulletin*, 97, 74–84.

Weiner, B. (1986). *An attributional theory of motivation and emotion*. New York: Springer Verlag.

Weiner, B. (1990). Searching for the roots of applied attribution theory. In S. Graham & V. Folkes (Eds.), *Attribution theory: Applications to achievement, mental health, and interpersonal conflict* (pp. 1–13). Hillsdale, NJ: Erlbaum.

Weiner, B. (1995). *Judgments of responsibility: A foundation for a theory of social conduct*. New York & London: Guilford Press.

Weiner, B., & Kukla, A. (1970). An attributional analysis of achievement motivation. *Journal of Personality and Social Psychology*, 15, 1–20.

Weinstein, N. D., & Sandman, P. M. (1992). A model of the precaution adoption process: Evidence from home radon testing. *Health Psychology*, 10, 25–33.

Weiss, R. S. (1975). *Marital separation*. New York: Basic Books.

Werner, C., & Parmelee, P. (1979). Similarity of activity preferences among friends: Those who play together stay together. *Social Psychology Quarterly*, 42, 62–6.

Wertheimer, M. (1945). *Productive thinking* (1st ed.). New York: Harper & Row.

Wertsch, J. V., & Tulviste, P. (1992). L. S. Vygotsky and contemporary developmental psychology. *Developmental Psychology*, 28, 548–57.

Wetherell, M. (1982). Cross-cultural studies of minimal groups: Implications for the social identity theory of intergroup relations. In H. Tajfel (Ed.), *Social identity and intergroup relations* (pp. 207–40). Cambridge: Cambridge University Press.

Wetherell, M. (1987). Social identity and group polarization. In J. C. Turner, M. A. Hogg, P. J.

Oakes, S. D. Reicher, & M. S. Wetherell (Eds.), *Rediscovering the social group. A self-categorization theory* (pp. 142–70). Oxford: Blackwell.

Wethington, E., Brown, G. W., & Kessler, R. C. (1995). Interview measures of stressful life events. In S. Cohen, R. C. Kessler, & L. U. Gordon (Eds.), *Measuring stress* (pp. 59–79). New York: Oxford University Press.

Wheeler, L., & Janis, I. L. (1980). *A practical guide for making decisions*. New York: Free Press.

White, G. L., Fishbein, S., & Rutstein, J. (1981). Passionate love and the misattribution of arousal. *Journal of Personality and Social Psychology*, 41, 56–62.

Wicker, A. W. (1969). Attitude versus action: The relationship of verbal and overt behavioral responses to attitude objects. *Journal of Social Issues*, 25 (4), 41–78.

Wigboldus, D. H. J., Semin, G. R., & Spears, R. (2000). How do we communicate stereotypes? Linguistic bases and inferential consequences. *Journal of Personality and Social Psychology*, 78, 5–18.

Wilder, D. A. (1977). Perceptions of groups, size of opposition, and influence. *Journal of Experimental Social Psychology*, 13, 253–68.

Wilder, D. A. (1984). Intergroup contact: The typical member and the exception to the rule. *Journal of Experimental Social Psychology*, 20, 177–94.

Wilke, H. A. M. (1991). Greed, efficiency, and fairness in resource management situations. In W. Stroebe & M. Hewstone (Eds.), *European review of social psychology* (Vol. 2, pp. 165–87). London: Wiley.

Wilkinson, G. S. (1988). Reciprocal altruism in bats and other animals. *Ethology and Sociobiology*, 9, 85–100.

Williams, J. K. (1966). *Adaptation and natural selection*. Chicago, IL: Aldine-Atherton.

Williams, K. D., Harkins, S. G., & Latané, B. (1981). Identifiability as a deterrent to social loafing: Two cheering experiments. *Journal of Personality and Social Psychology*, 40, 303–11.

Williams, K. D., Karau, S. J., & Bourgeois, M. (1993). Working on collective tasks: Social loafing and social compensation. In M. A. Hogg &

D. M. Abrams (Eds.), *Group motivation: Social psychological perspectives* (pp. 130–48). London: Harvester Wheatsheaf.

Williams, R. B., Jr., Haney, T. L., Lee, K. L., Kong, Y., Blumenthal, J., & Whalen, R. (1980). Type A behavior, hostility, and coronary atherosclerosis. *Psychosomatic Medicine*, 42, 539–49.

Wills, T. A. (1991). Social support and interpersonal relationships. In M. S. Clark (Ed.), *Prosocial behavior* (pp. 265–89). Newbury Park, CA: Sage.

Wills, T. A. (1992). The helping process in the context of personal relationships. In S. Spacapan & S. Oskamp (Eds.), *Helping and being helped. Naturalistic studies* (pp. 17–48). Newbury Park, CA: Sage.

Wilson, D. W., & Schafer, R. B. (1978). Is social psychology interdisciplinary? *Personality and Social Psychology Bulletin*, 4, 548–52.

Wilson, E. O. (1975). *Sociobiology: The new synthesis*. Cambridge, MA: Harvard University Press.

Wilson, M., & Daly, M. (1992). The man who mistook his wife for a chattel. In J. H. Barkow, L. Cosmides, & J. Tooby (Eds.), *The adapted mind* (pp. 289–321). New York & Oxford: Oxford University Press.

Wilson, T. D., Dunn, D. S., Kraft, D., & Lisle, D. J. (1989). Introspection, attitude change, and attitude–behavior consistency: The disruptive effects of explaining why we feel the way we do. *Advances in Experimental Social Psychology*, 22, 287–343.

Wilson, T. D., & Hodges, S. D. (1992). Attitudes as temporary constructions. In L. L. Martin & A. Tesser (Eds.), *The construction of social judgments* (pp. 37–65). Hillsdale, NJ: Erlbaum.

Wilson, T. D., Laser, P. S., & Stone, J. I. (1982). Judging the predictors of one's own mood: Accuracy and the use of shared theories. *Journal of Experimental Social Psychology*, 18, 537–56.

Wilson, T. D., & Schooler, J. W. (1991). Thinking too much: Introspection can reduce the quality of preferences and decisions. *Journal of Personality and Social Psychology*, 60, 181–92.

Winter, L., Uleman, J. S., & Cunniff, C. (1985). How automatic are social judgments? *Journal of Personality and Social Psychology*, 49, 904–17.

Winters, D., & Latham, G. (1996). The effects of learning versus outcome goals on a simple versus a complex task. *Group & Organization Management*, 21, 236–50.

Wood, W., Lundgren, S., Ouellette, J. A., Busceme, S., & Blackstone, T. (1994). Minority influence: A meta-analytic review of social influence processes. *Psychological Bulletin*, 115, 323–45.

Wood, W., Wong, F. Y., & Cachere, J. G. (1991). Effects of media violence on viewers' aggression in unconstrained social situations: Effects of an aggressive model on the behavior of college student and prisoner observers. *Psychonomic Science*, 24, 193–4.

Worchel, S., Andreoli, V. A., & Folger, R. (1977). Intergroup cooperation and intergroup attraction: The effect of previous interaction and outcome of combined effort. *Journal of Experimental Social Psychology*, 13, 131–40.

Wortman, C. B., & Conway, T. L. (1985). The role of social support in adaptation and recovery from physical illness. In S. Cohen & S. L. Syme (Eds.), *Social support and health* (pp. 281–302). Orlando, FL: Academic Press.

Wright, J. C., Giammarino, M., & Parad, H. W. (1986). Social status in small groups: Individual–group similarity and the social 'misfit'. *Journal of Personality and Social Psychology*, 50, 523–36.

Wright, R. (1994). *The moral animal: Evolutionary psychology and everyday life*. New York: Pantheon.

Wright, S. (1922). Coefficients of inbreeding and relationship. *American Naturalist*, 56, 330–8.

Wright, S. C., Aron, A., McLaughlin-Volpe, T., & Ropp, S. A. (1997). The extended contact effect: Knowledge of cross-group friendships and prejudice. *Journal of Personality and Social Psychology*, 73, 73–90.

Wright, S. C., Taylor, D. M., & Moghaddam, F. M. (1990). Responding to membership in a disadvantaged group: From acceptance to collective protest. *Journal of Personality and Social Psychology*, 58, 994–1003.

Wundt, W. (1874). *Grundzüge der physiologischen Psychologie*. Leipzig: Engelmann.

Wundt, W. (1900–20). *Völkerpsychologie. Eine Untersuchung der Entwicklungsgesetze von Sprache,*

Mythos und Sitte (10 vols.). *Band I. Die Sprache* (1900). [Psychology of cultures: A study of the developmental laws of language, myth and customs. Vol. 1. Language]. Leipzig: Kröner.

Wurtele, S. K. (1988). Increasing women's calcium intake: The role of health beliefs, intentions, and health value. *Journal of Applied Social Psychology*, 18, 627–39.

Wurtele, S. K., & Maddux, J. E. (1987). Relative contributions of protection motivation theory components in predicting exercise intentions and behavior. *Health Psychology*, 6, 453–66.

Wurtele, S. K., Roberts, M. C., & Leeper, J. D. (1982). Health beliefs and intentions: Predictors of return compliance in a tuberculosis detection drive. *Journal of Applied Social Psychology*, 12, 128–36.

Wyer, R. S., & Gordon, S. E. (1982). The recall of information about persons and groups. *Journal of Experimental Social Psychology*, 18, 128–64.

Wyer, R. S., Jr., & Srull, T. K. (Eds.). (1993). *Perspectives on anger and emotion*. Hillsdale, NJ: Lawrence Erlbaum.

Wyer, R. S., & Srull, T. K. (Eds.). (1994). *Handbook of social cognition* (2nd ed., 2 vols.). Hillsdale, NJ: Erlbaum.

Xiang, P., Lee, A. M., & Solmon, M. A. (1997). Achievement goals and their correlates among American and Chinese students in physical education: A cross-cultural analysis. *Journal of Cross-cultural Psychology*, 28, 645–60.

Yamagishi, T. (1986). The provision of a sanctioning system as a public good. *Journal of Personality and Social Psychology*, 51, 110–16.

Yamagishi, T. (1988). The provision of a sanctioning system in the United States and Japan. *Social Psychology Quarterly*, 51, 264–70.

Yee, M. D., & Brown, R. (1994). The development of gender differentiation in young children. *British Journal of Social Psychology*, 33, 183–96.

Yinon, Y., Goldenberg, J., & Neeman, R. (1977). On the relationship between structure of residence and formation of friendships. *Psychological Reports*, 40, 761–2.

Youngblade, L. M., & Belsky, J. (1992). Parent–child antecedents of 5-year-olds' close friendships: A longitudinal study. *Developmental Psychology*, 28, 700–13.

Yuill, N. (1992). Children's production and comprehension of trait terms. *British Journal of Developmental Psychology*, 10, 131–42.

Yuill, N. (1993). Understanding of personality and dispositions. In M. Bennett (Ed.), *The child as psychologist. An introduction to the development of social cognition* (pp. 87–110). New York: Harvester Wheatsheaf.

Yukl, G. (1994). *Leadership in organizations* (3rd ed.). Englewood Cliffs, NJ: Prentice-Hall.

Zacarro, S. J. (1984). Social loafing: The role of task attractiveness. *Personality and Social Psychology Bulletin*, 10, 99–106.

Zahn-Waxler, C., Radke-Yarrow, M., Wagner, E., & Chapman, M. (1992). Development of concern for others. *Developmental Psychology*, 28, 126–36.

Zahn-Waxler, C., & Smith, K. D. (1992). The development of prosocial behavior. In V. B. Van Hasselt & M. Hersen (Eds.), *Handbook of social development: A lifespan perspective* (pp. 229–56). New York: Plenum Press.

Zajonc, R. B. (1965). Social facilitation. *Science*, 149, 269–74.

Zajonc, R. B. (1968). Cognitive theories in social psychology. In G. Lindzey & E. Aronson (Eds.), *Handbook of social psychology* (2nd ed., Vol. 1, pp. 320–411). Reading, MA: Addison-Wesley.

Zajonc, R. B. (1980). Compresence. In P. B. Paulus (Ed.), *Psychology of group influence* (pp. 35–60). Hillsdale, NJ: Erlbaum.

Zajonc, R. B., & Burnstein, E. (1965). The learning of balanced and unbalanced social structures. *Journal of Personality*, 33, 153–63.

Zajonc, R. B., Heingartner, A., & Herman, E. M. (1969). Social enhancement and impairment of performance in the cockroach. *Journal of Personality and Social Psychology*, 13, 83–92.

Zanna, M. P., & Cooper, J. (1974). Dissonance and the pill: An attribution approach to studying the arousal properties of dissonance. *Journal of Personality and Social Psychology*, 29, 703–9.

Zanna, M. P., & Fazio, R. H. (1982). The attitude–behavior relation: Moving toward a third generation of research. In M. P. Zanna, E. T. Higgins,

& C. P. Herman (Eds.), *Consistency in social behavior: The Ontario symposium* (Vol. 2, pp. 283–301). Hillsdale, NJ: Erlbaum.

Zapf, D. (1999). Mobbing in Organisationen – Überblick zum Stand der Forschung [Mobbing in organizations: A survey on the current state of research]. *Zeitschrift für Organisationspsychologie, 43*, 1–15.

Zebrowitz McArthur, L., & Baron, R. M. (1983). Toward an ecological theory of social perception. *Psychological Review, 90*, 215–38.

Zillmann, D. (1971). Excitation transfer in communication-mediated aggressive behavior. *Journal of Experimental Social Psychology, 7*, 419–34.

Zillmann, D. (1979). *Hostility and aggression.* Hillsdale, NJ: Erlbaum.

Zillmann, D. (1988). Cognitive-excitation interdependencies in aggressive behavior. *Aggressive Behavior, 14*, 51–64.

Zillmann, D., Johnson, R. C., & Day, K. D. (1974). Attribution of apparent arousal and proficiency of recovery from sympathetic activation affecting excitation transfer to aggressive behavior. *Journal of Experimental Social Psychology, 10*, 503–15.

Zillmann, D., Katcher, A. H., & Milavsky, B. (1972). Excitation transfer from physical exercise to subsequent aggressive behavior. *Journal of Experimental Social Psychology, 8*, 247–59.

Zimbardo, P. G. (1969). The human choice. Individuation, reason, and order versus deindividuation, impulse, and chaos. In D. Levine (Ed.), *Nebraska symposium on motivation* (pp. 237–307). Lincoln, NE: University of Nebraska Press.

Zuckerman, M. (1979). Attribution of success and failure revisited, or: The motivational bias is alive and well in attribution theory. *Journal of Personality, 47*, 245–87.

Zuckerman, M., Koestner, R., Colella, M. J., & Alton, A. O. (1984). Anchoring in the detection of deception and leakage. *Journal of Personality and Social Psychology, 47*, 301–11.

Zumkley, H. (1981). Der Einfluß unterschiedlicher Absichtsattributionen auf das Aggressionsverhalten und die Aktivierung [The impact of the attribution of intentionality on aggressive behaviour and its activation]. *Psychologische Beiträge, 23*, 115–28.

Subject Index

Author Index